L I K E   A   F A M I L Y

THE FRED W. MORRISON SERIES

IN SOUTHERN STUDIES

Like a Family
The Making of a Southern
Cotton Mill World

Jacquelyn Dowd Hall, James Leloudis
Robert Korstad, Mary Murphy
Lu Ann Jones, Christopher B. Daly

The University of North Carolina Press

Chapel Hill and London

©1987 The University of North Carolina Press

All rights reserved

Manufactured in the United States of America

The paper in this book meets the guidelines

for permanence and durability of

the Committee on Production Guidelines for

Book Longevity of the Council on Library Resources

91 90 89 88 87   5 4 3 2 1

Library of Congress Cataloging-in-Publication Data

Like a family.

(The Fred W. Morrison series in Southern studies)

Bibliography: p.

Includes index.

1. Cotton trade—Southern States—History.

2. Cotton trade—Southern States—Employees—History.

3. Southern States—Social conditions. 4. Textile

factories—Southern States—History. I. Hall,

Jacquelyn Dowd. II. Series.

HD9077.A13L55   1987   305'.9677   87-40135

ISBN 0-8078-1754-6

ISBN 0-8078-4196-X (pbk.)

The rising generation, Augusta, Georgia, 1909. Detail from a photograph by Lewis Hine.
(Courtesy of the Photography Collections, Albin O. Kuhn Library and Gallery, University of
Maryland at Baltimore County)

To Our Families

in Every Sense of the Word

and to DC, AG, and DL

CONTENTS

MAPS AND ILLUSTRATIONS

Maps

Illustrations

---

*I guess there were two hundred houses on this village, and I knew
practically all of them from a kid up. It was kind of a cliché: You grew up
here and you knew everybody. It had its bad points; we didn't make too
much money, I know my father didn't. But like I said, it was kind of one
big family, and we all hung together and survived. It was a two-hundred-
headed family. Everybody on this hill, we looked after one another.*

Hoyle McCorkle

*You don't have to be famous for your
life to be history.*

Nell Sigmon

TEXTILE MILLS built the New South. Beginning in the 1880s, as
the South emerged from the wreckage of the Civil War, business and
professional men tied their hopes for prosperity to the whirring of
spindles and the beating of looms. Agriculture continued to dominate
the southern economy until well into the twentieth century. But in the
Piedmont, a region of gentle hills and rushing rivers that stretches
from southern Virginia through the central Carolinas and into northern Georgia and Alabama, a new society rapidly took shape. By the
mid-1920s this land of farms and farmers had been crisscrossed by
railroad tracks and dotted with mill villages, and the Piedmont had
eclipsed New England as the world's leading producer of yarn and
cloth. World War I marked a turning point in this regional transformation, setting the stage for two decades of modernization and rebellion
that culminated in the General Textile Strike of 1934. In the aftermath of that conflict, manufacturers began to abandon the mill village
system, and a distinctive form of working-class community gradually
disappeared. Through the words of Piedmont millhands like Hoyle
McCorkle and Nell Sigmon, *Like a Family* tells the story of the making
and unmaking of this cotton mill world.

Like a Family had its genesis in a project undertaken in the late

1970s by the Southern Oral History Program at the University of North Carolina at Chapel Hill. We saw in the timing of Piedmont industrialization a rare and fleeting opportunity, a chance to learn by listening to men and women whose roots lay in an agrarian past and whose lives and identities had been transformed by factory labor. With a grant from the National Endowment for the Humanities, the Program staff set out to conduct life history interviews that could serve as firsthand sources for a new chapter in American labor history: the incorporation of the South's common folk—former slaves and yeoman whites—into an industrial capitalist economy.[1]

This project also aimed to pick up the threads of a tradition of regional sociology and documentary studies that had flourished in the South during the 1930s. At Chapel Hill, the Institute for Research in Social Science and the University of North Carolina Press had sheltered scholars, writers, and activists whose work suggested a model of collaborative research in which individual projects could become part of a larger mosaic. We traced the lineage of oral history back to the Slave Narratives and the Southern Life Histories collected by the Federal Writers' Project during the Great Depression, but we brought to our venture the questions and tools of our own academic generation.[2]

Fieldworkers traveled to seven core interviewing sites in North Carolina, South Carolina, and Tennessee. Each community represented a distinctive pattern of industrialization. In North Carolina, Bynum offered an example of a small, rural mill village built in the 1870s. Burlington's industrial ancestry reached back to the antebellum era; by the 1930s the town had become the capital of the state's new hosiery industry and the headquarters of Burlington Mills, which eventually mushroomed into the largest textile corporation in the world. Charlotte followed yet another course. Beginning as a farmers' market, it burgeoned first into a mill town and then into the financial and transportation hub of the Carolinas. We chose Durham because its tobacco factories employed a sizable black work force. To the west, Catawba County's diversified economy gave us access to furniture, hosiery, and glove workers. Elizabethton, Tennessee, located just across the Blue Ridge Mountains, industrialized only in the mid-1920s with the arrival of German-owned rayon plants. Finally, there was Greenville, South Carolina—the self-styled "Textile Capital of the World." This city, like Charlotte, offered a preeminent example of an industrial setting made up of unincorporated mill villages and marked by tensions between mill and town.

Partly by design and partly by good fortune, we found the very people we were looking for—that distinctive group of southerners whose labor fueled the South's industrial revolution. Researchers outlined each community's history, then proportioned their interviews to reflect the area's occupational structure in the 1920s. We adopted a strategy of network interviewing. That is, we contacted retired workers through senior citizens' centers, door knocking, and other means; introductions to friends and neighbors allowed us to follow one network until it melded into another. By definition we interviewed survivors and, for the most part, lifetime workers. Those who left early or died young escaped our net. Interview guidelines suggested topics to be covered; our reading of the existing literature and our individual research interests informed the questions we pursued. But our goal was to allow people to narrate their own lives, emphasizing what seemed most meaningful and important to them. Our efforts were rewarded, for the stories we heard—funny and shrewd, diverse and self-assured—forced us to reformulate questions and leave received wisdom behind. Eventually, the Oral History Program staff interviewed more than 360 men and women who had worked in the region's major industries before World War II. These tapes and transcripts—rich with information for students of labor history, southern history, women's history, and Afro-American history—were deposited in the university's Southern Historical Collection and are now available to the public.

In the spring of 1982, the six of us decided to write this book. Four choices, made early on, have continued to anchor our work. First, we decided to narrow our attention to textile mills, which clustered in the Carolinas, served as the opening wedge for industrialization, and continue to shape the Piedmont's economy. Second, we agreed that a full-scale study of management lay beyond our scope; we would investigate managerial and technological change but keep a tight focus on the workers' world. Third, we planned to write a gender-conscious history appropriate to an industry that depended heavily on women's labor. Finally, we committed ourselves to presenting our arguments in a storytelling style; by allowing millhands' voices to drive the narrative, we hoped to reach an audience that makes history but seldom reads it.

Like a Family is based on more than 200 interviews with textile workers, equally divided between men and women. Because blacks were employed in tobacco—and, to a lesser extent, furniture—but excluded from most textile jobs, all but a handful of these former millhands were white. Our narrators fell mainly into three age groups: 26 percent were born between 1891 and 1900, 41 percent between 1901 and 1910, and 25 percent between 1911 and 1920. Twenty-four percent began work before the age of fourteen, and more than one-third of that number held their first cotton mill job before they were ten years old. Roughly half of these men and women were the first in their families to enter factory work, while the other half were born to mill parents. Generally speaking, most of our interviewees' children abandoned the mills for other manufacturing and service jobs in the years after World War II. We also drew on conversations with owners, managers, and a supporting cast of townspeople. But in the main, our interviews offered a collective biography of those who lived in the mill villages and tended the spindles and looms.[3]

As we pored over the interviews, we were struck time and again—as we had been in our personal encounters—by the grace and authenticity of these seldom-heard voices. We knew that memory does not provide a direct window on the past, but we had learned from experience to trust the interpretive authority of ordinary people. We also assumed the moral and intellectual value of listening to those who lacked access to power and, thus, the means of influencing historical debate.[4]

Our point of departure was the stories themselves. But we were also mindful of the limitations of oral sources. Seeking common patterns in unique lives, we turned to written records, balancing memory against immediacy, recollections against observations made at the time. Mill workers described a village life that turned on sharing and mutuality; for a fuller understanding of the poverty that made sharing necessary, we went to government reports on family budgets, diet, and disease. Millhands remembered working conditions that "just kept getting worse and worse"; for the economic pressures and human choices behind the modernization campaign of the 1920s, we read the trade press, particularly the *Southern Textile Bulletin*, which spoke for businessmen on the cutting edge of managerial and technological innovation. Interviews indicated constant movement from mill to mill, so we shifted from the community focus of the original oral history project to a broader regional view. Once alerted to the existence of a regionwide workers' community, we became more sensitive to emerging forms of commercialized culture, especially to the impact of radio and to the country music that became one of the nation's great popular sounds.

In one case at least—the 1934 General Strike—silence, not memory, propelled our search for archival sources. With some notable exceptions, our interviewees said little about that wrenching event. In part, that silence reflected our interviewing strategy: we had not searched systematically for the activists of 1934, nor had we looked outside the networks of retired mill workers for those who had been fired and blacklisted or who had left of their own free will. But also at work was a kind of social amnesia, born of defeat and of the failure of trade unionism to take root in a living tradition. Pressed to tell us about a strike during which she was fired and evicted and some of her friends were killed, Rosa Holland, a Marion, North Carolina, mill worker explained. "You see, after we come back and got out of the union and got back to work, why that was a thing of the past. You don't think about such things. If I'd been in the union right along, you see, I'd have it all in my mind. You forget about things in the past, 'cause you don't think about them, you don't talk about them, and that leaves your mind. I worked in the mill, and Lord, I wouldn't have mentioned the union in there for nothing, because if I had I'd have been fired again." Looking for the repressed and forgotten, we discovered the stunning, and inexplicably neglected, letters that southern workers had written to Franklin D. Roosevelt and the National Recovery Administration during the 1930s. In a sense, we had come full circle: beginning with an oral history project that tried to let working people speak for themselves, we discovered that they had done so—quite eloquently—fifty years before.[5]

Workers' testimonies, in combination with other sources, revealed a broad process of cultural, technological, and managerial change. The textile industry, like all institutions, was shaped by struggle—sometimes bloody and dramatic, sometimes quiet and nearly imperceptible. Neither millhands nor employers fully achieved their goals; for each, industrialization had mixed and unexpected effects. The effort to capture this story, in all its historical contingency and human detail, took us on an intellectual journey more circuitous—and more compelling—than any we could have imagined in 1982.

"The mill village is a curious institution," wrote historian Frank Tannenbaum in 1923. "It has no life of its own. Its destinies are spun by the mill." To Tannenbaum's eye, the authority of mill owners appeared to shape every aspect of village life, reducing mill folk "to a state of childish impotence." "They *are* like children," he insisted, "but rather strange, lost-looking, and bereaved. Their faces seem stripped, denuded, and empty . . . and their eyes drawn and stupid. They give the impression of being beyond the realm of things daily lived and experienced by other people . . . they are men and women who have been lost to the world and have forgotten its existence."[6]

Tannenbaum's picture of the southern mill village had an ironic genealogy. It originated in turn-of-the-century uneasiness about the creation of a dependent, wage-earning white working class. When the cotton mill building campaign began in the 1880s, it was touted as a positive good, a boon to sturdy yeomen down on their luck, and a way of lifting the South from a Civil War legacy of poverty and defeat. But as the factory population expanded and mill villages increasingly clustered on the outskirts of towns, a less sanguine view emerged. The proudly independent men and women who had left the small farms of the Piedmont or the hollows and hillsides of southern Appalachia came to be seen as desperate refugees from a virtually uninhabitable land. As a town-based commercial class created and refined its own standards of decorum, domesticity, and accumulation, the working poor of the mill districts appeared increasingly alien and in need of reform. Later chroniclers of a benighted South debunked the notion of benevolent paternalism but did little to alter the idea that the mill village was a "spiritual cemetery." Where apologists had seen a school of civilization, critics found a closed society that robbed its residents of dignity and ambition.[7]

This mix of boosterism and muckraking has cast a long shadow over the historiography of the twentieth-century South. Two classics illustrate the point. Broadus Mitchell's *The Rise of Cotton Mills in the South*, published in 1921, portrayed the nineteenth-century founders of the textile industry as selfless aristocrats and the mill communities as white families unruffled by class conflict. Twenty years later, Wilbur J. Cash's *The Mind of the South* added an influential gloss to Mitchell's interpretation. Without questioning Mitchell's account of the pioneers' intentions, Cash drew a savage portrait of the results: stunted by poverty and isolation, the southern mill worker had become a pitiable "social type." Regional sociologists—most notably Harriet L. Herring, Jennings J. Rhyne, Liston Pope, and John Kenneth Morland—provided a more nuanced view. But in the late 1970s, when our oral history project began, few had pushed beyond the work of this earlier generation. Discussion seemed stalled, circling around questions of southern distinctiveness: Were southern mill owners uniquely paternalistic? Were southern millhands docile or individualistic, or some special blend of the two? Why was there no unionism in the South? By providing new evidence and asking fresh questions, we tried to shift the focus from *whether* to *how*. How were attitudes toward authority reflected in everyday life? How did labor-management relations change over time? How did millhands see themselves and their world?[8]

Our own preoccupations, of course, were rooted in place and time. Six scholars coming of age in the 1960s and 1970s could not help but be affected by the political and intellectual turbulence of those years. Movements for social change and the scholarship they inspired taught us to look for connections between the personal and the political and alerted us to the extraordinary significance of ordinary lives.

Like a Family paints a fine-grained picture of the Piedmont South, not to emphasize the peculiarity of southern industrialization but to reveal a history richer and denser than broad strokes could convey. Although we have not tried to synchronize our story with other sagas of the working poor, students of capitalist development elsewhere will find familiar voices here. *Like a Family* bridges the customary divide between the nineteenth and twentieth centuries and contributes to the steady stream of working-class histories in which women, children, and community life play major roles.

Again and again in our interviews, people chose a family metaphor to describe mill village life. Historians have usually interpreted that metaphor as evidence of a paternalistic management style that provided for workers' needs while depriving them of independence and responsibility. But as we pondered mill workers' stories, we realized that they were not using this imagery to describe their dependence on a fatherly employer so much as they were explaining their relationships to one another. Family, as an image and as an institution, winds its way through this book, multilayered and deeply felt. When people recalled past solidarities, they did so from the perspective of a fragmented and sometimes lonely present. Yet mixed with yearnings for a world they had lost were memories that pointed toward an understanding of family and community as arenas of conflict as well as reciprocity, able to exclude and repress as well as sustain.

Like a Family is divided into two parts, with World War I as the pivot on which the story turns. Part 1 provides a thematic description of the cotton mill world that evolved between 1880 and 1920. Many features of early mill village life persisted through World War I and beyond. But after 1920 the textile industry entered a period of quickened change. Accordingly, Part 2 adopts a chronological organization, highlighting the new in the midst of the old. Regional politics, although only alluded to here, form the backdrop for Part 1. In the second half of the book, which runs roughly from 1920 to 1935, national policies and cultural trends play a more palpable role.

The book opens with a look at the commercialization of agriculture that set the stage for industrialization. Chapter 1 explores the rural heritage that farmers-turned-millhands brought to their encounter with the machine and introduces the pioneer mill builders. Against the assumption that simple destitution drove people off the land, we suggest a variety of motivations, a host of pushes and pulls. We document change but stress continuity—in the culture that small landowners and tenants shared and in the ties between farm and mill.

The clashing agendas of owners and workers fashioned life on the factory floor. Chapter 2 describes the physical environment manufacturers created to produce yarn and cloth and the social world that evolved as men, women, and children brought their own expectations to a workplace dominated by boss men and machines. For some, the factory regimen was a torment. For others, the mill was an exciting place. Whatever their initial response, millhands managed to carve opportunities for sociability, pride, and achievement from the hard rock of factory labor.

In Chapter 3 we turn to the world outside the mill, emphasizing the resilience of rural people faced with the new demands of an industrial order. Although company-owned villages dictated the contours of everyday existence, workers managed to forge their own forms of expression and create a way of life beyond their employers' grasp. Kinship and a common culture knit hundreds of individual mill communities into an elaborate regional fabric that provided workers with a shared identity and a hedge against poverty and management control. At the same time, tensions between men and women, parents and children, rough and respectable villagers, stirred beneath the surface of community life.

In sum, Part 1 portrays factories and villages that were marked by sharp inequalities of power. The manufacturers' authority, however, was neither limitless nor monolithic; management styles changed over time in response to specific problems and opportunities. On the factory floor, the boss's control was restrained by high rates of labor mobility, technological problems, and family ties between low-level managers and workers. In the village, the intrusive presence of the mill owner gave way first to welfare work and then to disengagement, paving the way for the more bureaucratic forms of supervision that were developed in the 1920s.

Part 2 begins with the First World War, which drove wages up, encouraged overexpansion, and set in motion a fateful modernization campaign. Chapter 4 centers on the "stretch-out," workers' evocative term for the physical process and psychological costs of rationalization. In the 1920s the personal negotiations of earlier times gave way to public protest, as a series of violent rebellions against the stretch-out swept from eastern Tennessee through the Carolinas. These strikes pitted manufacturers committed to shoring up profits in an ailing industry against workers emboldened by rising expectations but pinched by the disadvantages of a glutted labor market. Drawing on the values of mill village life, on an intensifying group consciousness, and on the democratic implications of the wartime rhetoric of Americanism, mill workers simultaneously defended cherished aspects of the past and struck out for their own place in a changing world.

In Chapter 5 the critical developments of the 1920s and early 1930s are examined in detail through a close look at a mill community in Burlington, North Carolina. The focus here is on three extraordinary individuals: J. Spencer Love, the driving force behind the company that became the worldwide empire known as Burlington Industries; Icy Norman, a single woman who spent a lifetime working for Burlington Mills; and Preacher George Washington Swinney, an evangelical minister who took to the road and the radio, using modern means to traditional religious ends. In the 1920s Burlington was a place of ferment, and this chapter describes the tensions that arose as the textile industry diversified, the work force matured, and a younger generation of workers created new forms of sociability attuned to the radio, the automobile, and the motion picture show.

In 1929 the South plunged along with the rest of the nation into the Great Depression. After four years of suffering, the passage of the National Industrial Recovery Act seemed to promise workers a New Deal. Southern textile workers saw in Franklin Delano Roosevelt and the National Recovery Administration more than a chance for higher wages and shorter hours. They also thought they saw allies willing to help shift the balance of power in the mills. When the NRA failed to deliver on its promises, southern millhands led a nationwide walkout that paralyzed the textile industry. Chapter 6 ends with the General Textile Strike of 1934 and points toward the gradual unraveling of a cotton mill world.

Like a Family is more than the sum of its parts. Although each of us took on specific research and writing tasks, the book's argument and style were shaped collectively. Collaborative writing required collaborative thinking, which in turn demanded a generosity that was at times difficult to achieve. We learned to share ideas in their embryonic form, to think hard and creatively about each others' work, and to overcome defensiveness for the common good. Insights and discoveries sometimes took place in the privacy of an individual mind but more often occurred in the midst of intellectual give-and-take. As creatures of a society built more on hierarchy and competition than on mutuality and sharing, we inevitably had our ups and downs. But working together honed our skills and affirmed our values. By pooling our very different talents and passions, we glimpsed a past more multifaceted than any one of us, searching alone, could have seen.

We are grateful to each other, but above all, we are grateful to the people whose stories we have tried to tell. In the pages that follow, we speak as historians, taking responsibility for our own analysis while at the same time sharing authorship with hundreds of working people who speak for themselves. Our hope is that readers will be touched, as we have been, by these voices, in all their dignity, humor, and pain.

ACKNOWLEDGMENTS

THE FOUNDATION for this book was laid in 1978 when the Southern Oral History Program received a grant from the National Endowment for the Humanities to collect life histories of Piedmont working people. Mary Frederickson, Brent Glass, Jacquelyn Hall, and Allen Tullos launched the project. All four conducted interviews, as did Hugh Brinton, Douglas DeNatale, Patty Dilley, Scott Ellsworth, Sara Evans, Rosemarie Hester, Glenn Hinson, Dolores Janiewski, Beverly Jones, Lu Ann Jones, Cliff Kuhn, James Leloudis, Mary Murphy, Valerie Quinney, Lanier Rand, and Carol Shaw.

Neither the oral history project nor the research and writing of this book would have been possible without the administrative skills of the Southern Oral History Program's office staff. Della Coulter did a masterful job of coordinating the transcribing and cataloging of the interviews, as well as managing the paper trail left by over a dozen interviewers. Her preparation of the interviews for deposit in the Southern Historical Collection has guaranteed their accessibility. Pam Upton and Mary Anne McDonald put the finishing touches on that process. Amy Glass drew on an array of talents to help locate photographs and choreograph the work of six authors scattered across the continent. Her good cheer has been our constant companion. Jovita Flynn helped pull together loose ends in the book's final stages.

The Oral History Program has been blessed with an able group of researchers, transcribers, work-study students, and volunteers. Patricia Raub and Cathy Abernathy contributed their superb research skills. In Elizabethton, Bob Moreland and Mildred Kozsuch gave invaluable aid. With her fine ear for the cadences of southern speech, Jean Houston turned tapes into transcripts that are a model of their kind. Alisa Blackman, El Marie Erwin, Melody Ivins, and Michelle Penley were painstaking and enthusiastic about tasks both great and small. Jesse Alred, Wayne Durrill, Lynn Haessly, Lynn Hudson, Christopher Latta, Dale Martin, Liz Martin, James Cooper, Carl Dashman, and Richard McGuire helped move the research along.

Our work was also made easier by reference librarians and archivists. Preparation of the interviews for deposit would have been a fruitless effort had they not been welcomed by the Southern Historical Collection. Tim West, Becky McCoy, and Laura O'Keefe demonstrated their belief in the value of this material by their careful accessioning of tapes and transcripts. Once research for this book began, Dick Shrader guided us through the J. Spencer Love Papers; H. G. Jones, Alice Cotten, Jerry Cotten, Bob Anthony, Harry McGowan, and Jeff Hicks of the North Carolina Collection helped us track down elusive printed sources and photographs; Jerry Hess at the National Archives steered us through the vast collections of the National Recovery Administration; and Claire Sheridan at the Museum of American Textile History brought the Barnes Textile Reports to our attention. Members of the Folklife Section of the North Carolina Arts Council also helped in the photographic research and shared their knowledge of country music.

The book could not have been completed without additional financial assistance and fellowships from the William F. Sullivan Fund of the Museum of American Textile History, the University Research Council of the University of North Carolina at Chapel Hill, the Woodrow Wilson International Center for Scholars, the National Museum of American History at the Smithsonian Institution, and the Duke University–University of North Carolina Women's Studies Research Center.

The wisdom and suggestions of many colleagues have contributed to our understanding of southern cotton mill people. Sydney Nathans read the entire manuscript. At two critical junctures, he gave us the benefit of his fine, critical mind. Susan Porter Benson, David Carlton, Brent Glass, and Steven Hahn also gave our work a thorough reading; their knowledge of southern and labor history broadened our thinking and saved us from many errors of fact. Other scholars read individual chapters or essays drawn from the larger study. Especially helpful were the comments of James Barrett, Harry Bauld, Lawrence Boyette, Craig Calhoun, Peter Coclanis, Pete Daniel, Wayne Durrill, Leon Fink, Steven Fraser, Alice Kessler-Harris, William Leuchtenburg, Susan Levine, Cathy McHugh, Michael Perman, Anastatia Sims, Andor Skotnes, Christine Stansell, Tom Terrill, and Gavin Wright. We are also grateful for the patience and encouragement of Iris Hill, David Perry, and Ron Maner at the University of North Carolina Press.

Several sections of this book have appeared previously as journal articles. Major themes were outlined in the *American Historical Review*. Portions of the Preface and Chapter 3 were published in the *Interna-

tional Journal of Oral History, and parts of Chapter 4 appeared in the *Journal of American History*. Our work has benefited from the thoughtful comments offered by referees for those journals. To editors David Ransel and David Thelen we owe special debts.

Family and friends sustained this effort in many ways. Chris Daly thanks his wife, Anne K. Fishel, for her loving help and steady enthusiasm. Jacquelyn Hall is indebted to her grandfather Roy Branham for the stories that linked her life to the history *Like a Family* tells. Lu Ann Jones is grateful to her parents for lessons about the rewards of rural neighborliness and hard work and to Gary Dorsey for his love, support, and friendship during the long haul of this project. Robert Korstad thanks Karl and Frances for their commitment to the South and their support over the years. James Leloudis is grateful to Dianne, who has always shared his passion for this book, and to his parents, who taught respect for ordinary lives. Mary Murphy gives special thanks to Dale Martin and Mindy Quivik, who heard many more words about this book than are in it.

NOTE ON SOURCES

A DESIRE to present the past in direct, everyday speech guided our treatment of sources. We edited the interviews with special care, seeking to preserve the flavor of individual voices and to make the material accessible to readers. The words are those of the people we interviewed, although we sometimes rearranged phrases and omitted the digressions that are a normal part of conversation. We avoided the intrusive use of ellipses but provided transcript page numbers so that researchers could follow our tracks. Quotations from written sources are rendered in their original form, with no attempt to regularize spelling or punctuation.

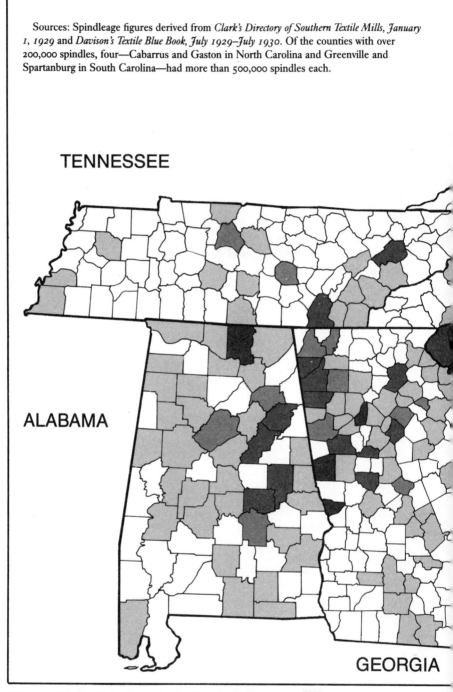

Sources: Spindleage figures derived from *Clark's Directory of Southern Textile Mills, January 1, 1929* and *Davison's Textile Blue Book, July 1929–July 1930*. Of the counties with over 200,000 spindles, four—Cabarrus and Gaston in North Carolina and Greenville and Spartanburg in South Carolina—had more than 500,000 spindles each.

TENNESSEE

ALABAMA

GEORGIA

MAP 1. *Textile Spindleage in the Southeast, 1929*

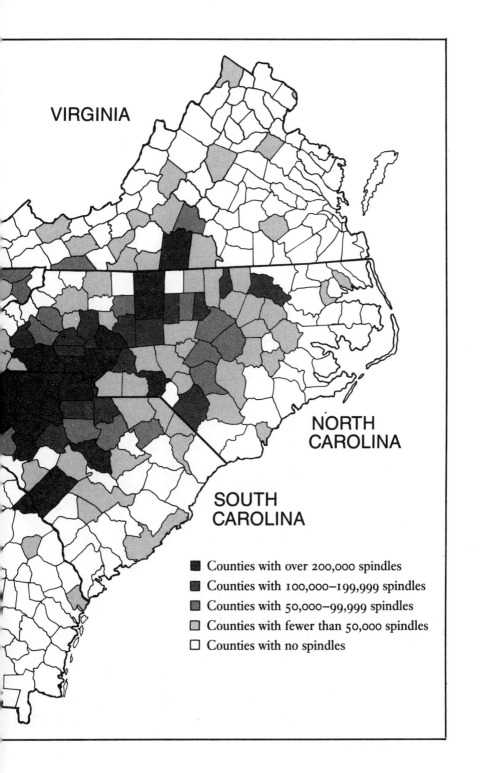

VIRGINIA

NORTH
CAROLINA

SOUTH
CAROLINA

■ Counties with over 200,000 spindles
■ Counties with 100,000–199,999 spindles
■ Counties with 50,000–99,999 spindles
□ Counties with fewer than 50,000 spindles
□ Counties with no spindles

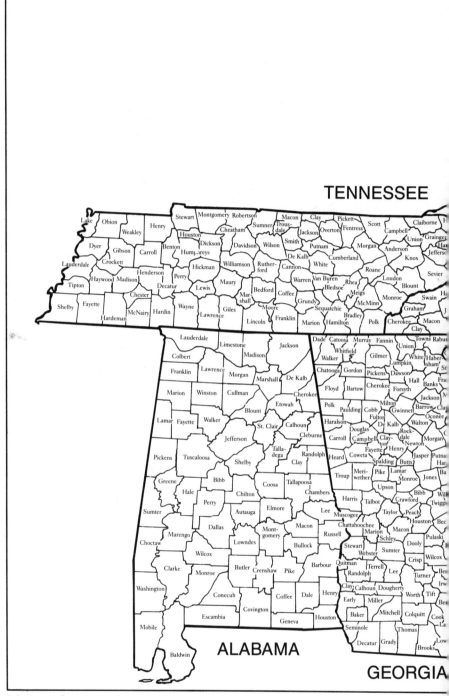

MAP 2. *Counties of the Southeast, 1929*

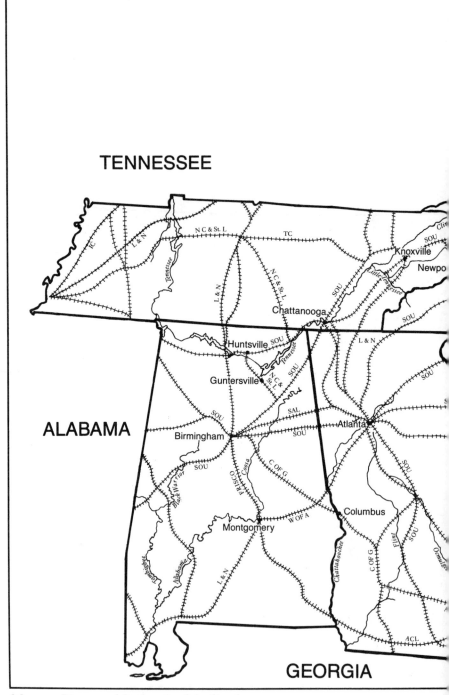

MAP 3. *Rivers and Railroads of the Southeast, 1930*

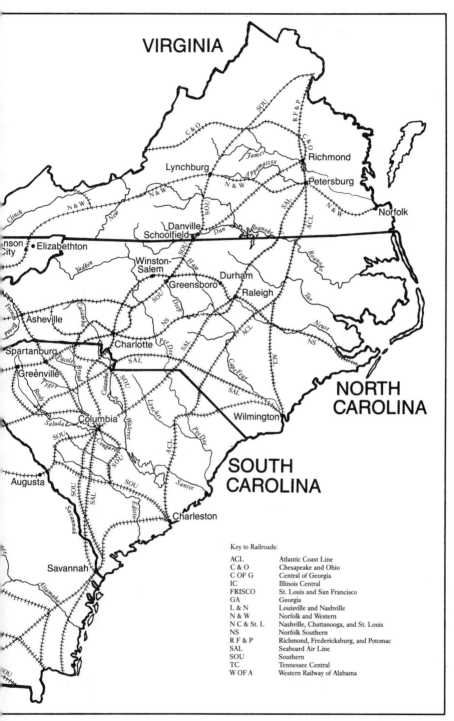

VIRGINIA

Richmond
Petersburg
Norfolk
Lynchburg
Danville
Schoolfield
Elizabethton
nson City
Winston-Salem
Durham
Greensboro
Raleigh
Asheville
Spartanburg
Charlotte
Greenville
Columbia
Wilmington
Augusta
Savannah
Charleston

NORTH CAROLINA

SOUTH CAROLINA

Key to Railroads:

ACL	Atlantic Coast Line
C & O	Chesapeake and Ohio
C OF G	Central of Georgia
IC	Illinois Central
FRISCO	St. Louis and San Francisco
GA	Georgia
L & N	Louisville and Nashville
N & W	Norfolk and Western
N C & St. L	Nashville, Chattanooga, and St. Louis
NS	Norfolk Southern
R F & P	Richmond, Fredericksburg, and Potomac
SAL	Seaboard Air Line
SOU	Southern
TC	Tennessee Central
W OF A	Western Railway of Alabama

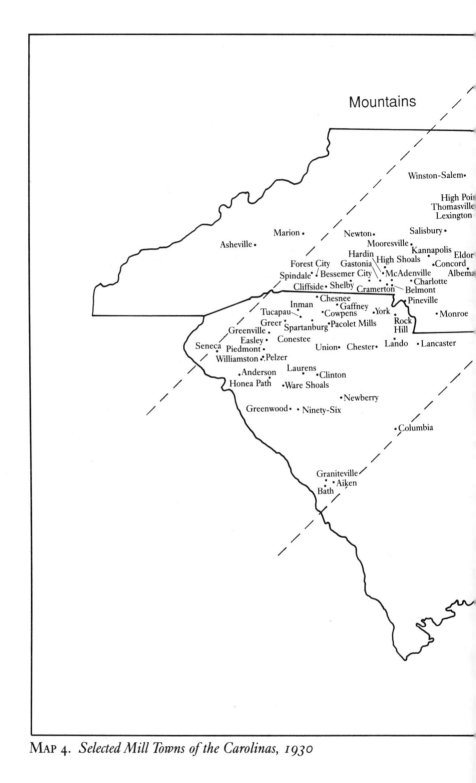

Mountains

Winston-Salem•

High Poi
Thomasville
Lexington

Marion •   Newton•   Salisbury •

                  Mooresville•
            Hardin   High Shoals Kannapolis Eldor
Asheville •   •Concord
    Forest City   Gastonia   •McAdenville   Albema
  Spindale• • Bessemer City \\ •McAdenville   •Charlotte
      Cliffside• Shelby Cramerton~ Belmont
              •Chesnee   •Pineville
        Inman   •Gaffney
    Tucapau~.   •Cowpens   •York
      Greer .   Rock
  Greenville . Spartanburg•Pacolet Mills Hill   •Monroe
    Easley • Conestee
Seneca. Piedmont •   Union• Chester• Lando •Lancaster
  Williamston •.Pelzer
    •Anderson   Laurens
  Honea Path • •Clinton
        •Ware Shoals
                      •Newberry
  Greenwood • • Ninety-Six

                      •Columbia

              Graniteville⁄
                •Aiken
            Bath

MAP 4. *Selected Mill Towns of the Carolinas, 1930*

Piedmont   Coastal Plain

• Draper   • Roanoke Rapids
y Leaksville   • Roxboro
    • Reidsville   • Henderson
  Altamahaw
coe   Burlington
  Elon •   • Haw River
Graham   • Hillsborough
ensboro Swepsonville • Durham • Rolesville   • Rocky Mount
 Saxapahaw   • Chapel Hill
    Bynum • Carrboro   • Raleigh
•
Franklinville

                 • Erwin

            • Fayetteville
• Rockingham

                    NORTH
                    CAROLINA

      SOUTH
      CAROLINA

ers, most of whom were small farmers, balked at the idea and thwarted their efforts. Realizing that the levy would fall most heavily on those least able to pay, opponents took their grievances to the General Assembly in a petition that accused a "sect of bissy boddys" of "taking the peoples Libertyes away by law power." This conflict foreshadowed divisions that would fragment southern society in the postbellum years.[4]

The Civil War altered more than relations between former masters and slaves. It also set in motion a transformation of the Piedmont economy that assured merchants a central role. In the plantation districts the abolition of slavery brought about a major reorganization of agriculture. The result was the notorious system of sharecropping. Planters still owned most of the land, but it was now divided into small plots, tended by individual black families who were paid with a share of the crop. Undergirding this system was a new mode of agricultural credit known as the crop lien and a new linchpin in the agricultural economy, the furnishing merchant. Lien laws were originally part of the compromise between freedmen in need of land and credit and planters who needed labor and demanded collateral to ensure loans. But the lien also gave new power to merchants. Through contacts with northern bankers and wholesalers, merchants provided credit and supplies in exchange for liens, or claims, on their customers' harvests. To ensure repayment—at high interest rates—merchants demanded that farmers plant crops such as cotton and tobacco, which could be sold for cash, instead of the customary food crops. The crop lien system soon ensnared freedmen and yeoman farmers alike.[5]

Many backcountry farmers came under a merchant's sway as they tried to get back on their feet after a war that left farms in disrepair, herds of livestock depleted, and networks of neighborhood trade disrupted. Desperate for credit, farmers started growing more cotton and tobacco, which commanded high prices in the late 1860s. This strategy of devoting more acreage to cash crops in order to repay debts was not completely new. Before the war small-scale farmers had often planted more cotton as a means of paying off the debt on newly acquired land. But the credit structure in the postwar South ambushed those farmers who intended to make a quick foray into commercial agriculture and then retreat to general farming.[6]

The crop lien was not the only means by which farmers were brought into the cash-crop economy and the merchants' orbit. Two other key developments were higher taxes and fence laws. These measures found support among a new group of Democrats who came to power at state and county levels at the end of Reconstruction in 1877 committed to economic development. To foot the bill for railway construction and the improvement of county roads, local governments levied new taxes and collected them vigilantly. Farmers found themselves between a rock and a hard place: they could either refuse to grow cash crops and risk losing their land because they could not pay the new taxes, or they could enter the treacherous commercial farm economy. Changes in fence laws, enacted township by township and county by county, also made it harder to make ends meet. Proponents of new laws that required livestock to be fenced in argued that enclosure would enable farmers to raise purebred stock and protect crops against roaming animals. Ending the open range, however, limited many farmers' access to the resources necessary for a semisubsistence way of life.[7]

Crop mix and land tenure patterns quickly reflected the transformation caused by these trends. In late nineteenth-century North Carolina, for example, cotton and tobacco production soared: the 145,000 bales of cotton raised in 1860 swelled to 460,000 in 1900. During the same period the tobacco crop increased nearly fourfold, from 33 million to 128 million pounds. Tenancy rates offer one way to gauge the impact of these developments on farm families. Although highest in the areas with a legacy of plantation agriculture, tenancy also increased in backcountry counties being absorbed into the ways of commerce. In the Piedmont counties from which most mill workers came, a third more farmers tended someone else's land in 1900 than in 1880. Counties surrounding major trading centers registered particularly dramatic increases; by 1900, for instance, more than half the farmers in the counties around Charlotte were tenants.[8]

Taken together, the crop lien, fence laws, and higher taxes added up to a virtual assault on Piedmont yeoman society and eroded its agricultural self-sufficiency. Farmers who were once participants in a system of direct exchange of goods and services among producers increasingly became participants in a rural economy dominated by merchants and cash exchange. This new vulnerability to market conditions came home to farmers when crop prices fell in the 1870s, languished in the 1880s, and nosedived in the 1890s. By 1894 a pound of cotton sold for about five cents, half the price that a farmer needed simply to break even. Similarly, bright leaf tobacco brought seven cents a pound in 1897, returning a mere fourteen-dollar profit per acre for more than

400 hours of labor invested. As conditions deteriorated, yeomen and tenants limped along from year to year, burdened by debt and pressed by merchants.[9]

To a child like Fred Yoder, who grew up in Catawba County during the late nineteenth century, hard times meant a lean Christmas stocking. "I remember in the early 'nineties, when it came Christmas one year, the only thing that we received as children was two sticks of peppermint candy. The country stores used to sell a little box of peppermint candy in sticks about six inches long. And we'd hung up our stockings by the chimney. We got up the next morning, and all we found was the two sticks of candy." Hard times had more serious consequences for Yoder's father. "I remember one time he was talking to my mother, and he said that he had to pay his taxes and he didn't have any money to pay the taxes with. So he sacked up some wheat, and he sacked up some corn, and he sacked up some potatoes and maybe loaded a ham or two—half a dozen different products—and went to the town of Newton. Just sat there in his wagon on the street trying to sell these products; he tried the merchants and so on. When he returned home, he had sold some things, but not all of these things. I might say that my father was maybe the most prosperous man in the immediate neighborhood in which we were living. So everybody had this problem of getting even enough money to pay their taxes."[10]

The Yoders had a lot of company. When the North Carolina Bureau of Labor Statistics asked farmers how they were faring in the 1880s and 1890s, it heard a chorus of laments. From Stanly County came a report that because of "droughts, overflows, chintz-bug, high taxes . . . the common landless laborer is down and very low in humility, and for the last five years very much depressed in spirits. . . . Putting all these things together, the aggregate is, that depression, to a great extent, is universal in this and adjoining counties." From Mecklenburg County came the assessment that farmers were "poorer than they were fifteen years ago" and that the "credit system in which the farmer pays from 40 to 75 per cent. for six or seven months' credit is enough within itself to keep him down to the bottom." From Durham County came this word: "Very few farmers are in good condition. Even the landlords are in a bad fix, and tenants worse." A Chatham County farmer observed that "there is quite a depressed condition seen and felt on every hand among farmers on account of short crops and low prices. There is much unrest and dissatisfaction. . . . Farmers are moving to the towns, leaving very good farms to grow up untenanted. I do not see the boom that the newspapers say exists in this State. It must be in the towns. It is not in the country."[11]

Financial distress brought worry and pain. Being trapped in a cycle of debt was more than some men could bear. One upcountry farmer was so mired in debt that he fled to Alabama, leaving his wife behind to settle the account. When the price brought by the farmer's cotton failed to cover what he owed, the merchant sued and had the farmer captured and returned to face charges. The farmer had a simple explanation for his actions. "I just got tired of working for the other fellow. I worked and toiled from year to year and all the fruits of my labor went to the man that never struck a lick."[12]

Desperation and resentment over a new economic order in the countryside that rewarded manipulators of credit more than cultivators of the land led other farmers to spark an agrarian revolt. Thousands fought back through the Southern Farmers' Alliance, organized in Texas in 1886 and transplanted by means of local chapters throughout the Southeast. As members of separate organizations within the Farmers' Alliance, black and white farmers worked toward common goals. The Alliance advocated the creation of cooperatives that would give farmers more control over the purchase of supplies and the sale of commodities. In many ways, the Alliance tried to codify and defend familiar features of rural life. The ideal of cooperation recognized that independence and interdependence were crucially linked. Acknowledging that farming was a family enterprise, the organization officially encouraged women to join. Entire families piled into wagons to make the pilgrimage to local Alliance rallies, where members addressed one another as "brothers" and "sisters," using a family metaphor to express their solidarity.[13]

By the 1890s many Alliance members who hoped for political solutions to their problems turned to the People's Party. In the spring of 1892 Alice Mull of Catawba County reported to the *Progressive Farmer*, the official voice of the North Carolina State Alliance, that "sentiment here is now strong for the People's Party. . . . All the laboring classes are anxious for a complete change and rejoice that they now have that in their power by uniting and putting their demands in the ballot box. . . . We believe there is a better time coming for the laboring classes, but they must not only pray now but work too. Our cause is a just one and if God be for us, who can be against us." Mull proved an astute political observer. Catawba County, once a Democratic stronghold, soon moved squarely into the Populist column. As a child, Fred Yoder had to suffer the ridicule that his father's switch of political loyalties provoked. "In the schools the children of Democratic Party parents would say, 'Oh, you're nothing but a little old Pop. You're nothing but a little old Pop.'" The flurry of Populist successes, however, could not be sustained. Party leaders vacillated and compromised. Democrats mounted bitter campaigns based on virulent racism that by 1898 brought a weakened agrarian revolt to its knees. New laws, which restricted the right to vote, effectively eliminated political participation by blacks and poorer whites in the early twentieth century.[14]

As Piedmont farmers battled and lost, a different set of circumstances—but one that yielded similar results—was at work in the southern Appalachian mountains. Until the late nineteenth century, mountain farmers had few links with the larger economic world. Early settlers monopolized the best land, relegating later arrivals to the hills and hollows. Still, a rough equality prevailed, and most families made an ample living by hunting and fishing, cultivating grain on small farms, and grazing livestock in pastures and woodlands that custom held open to all. Barter was a major means of exchange. Farmers hauled logs, distilled corn into whiskey, or drove herds of swine into town, trading with local merchants for what they could not produce at home. Scattered settlement patterns contributed to the perception of mountaineers as notorious individualists. Yet the notion of individualism is misleading, for these "individuals" were tightly bound to immediate families and wider tracings of kin.

In the 1870s Appalachia's timber and mineral resources attracted the attention of capitalists elsewhere in the United States and abroad, and an era of railroad building and land speculation began. Construction gangs started hacking their way through the mountain passes of West Virginia, Virginia, Kentucky, Tennessee, and North Carolina. The timber and coal companies soon followed the railroads, which they could use for shipping raw materials to the industrializing cities of the North and South. As absentee owners, in collaboration with large landowners and merchants, gained control of vast tracts of land and profits flowed into corporate coffers, the old agricultural economy was irrevocably changed. Timber barons stripped away the forests, leaving hillsides stark and vulnerable to erosion. Although most families still owned their own land, the size of farms fell precipitously. In 1880 the average Appalachian farm was 187 acres; fifty years later mountain farmers made do on 76 acres. Moreover, the unimproved woodlands where farmers had grazed their hogs steadily declined. Game, driven beyond reach in the mountains, no longer served as a dependable source of supplemental food. The railroad construction boom and then the coal mines drew farm men into seasonal wage labor, tying them to the vicissitudes of a national market economy. Then, by the turn of the century, labor recruiters were scouring the hills in search of workers for Piedmont textile mills.[15]

For Piedmont farmers, the turn of the century brought a rebounding of crop prices as demand for cotton and tobacco rose. Although prices climbed one year only to plummet the next, the first two decades of the twentieth century proved to be fairly flush times. But the economic revival cut two ways. Higher earnings slowed the growth of tenancy and diminished the threat of foreclosure; but increased property values made it harder for younger farmers to buy land of their own and move out of the ranks of tenantry. In addition, the size of farms declined steadily as the many children borne by the mothers of the South pressed against the available land. Even the boll weevil turned out to have mixed effects: the pest ruined farmers as it moved eastward, yet, by reducing the supply of cotton, the weevil helped boost prices.[16]

In any case, farmers remained vulnerable to the whims of a market over which they had no control. A few good years proved only a prelude to agricultural depression. In the fall of 1920 cotton that had commanded thirty-five cents a pound the year before brought only fifteen cents or less; tobacco prices fell from thirty-nine to twenty-one cents a pound. Throughout the southern countryside conditions went from bad to worse over the next decade. The poverty documented by photographers and writers during the Great Depression captured the cumulative effect of economic changes begun half a century before.[17]

Profound as they were, the effects of economic change on rural culture should not be exaggerated. Neither the reorganization of agriculture along capitalist lines nor the exploitation of mountain resources was accomplished overnight. Both proceeded in ever-building waves, only gradually eroding rural roots. Many white farmers in the Piedmont and the mountains, as well as a smaller group of blacks, managed to hold on to their land. Even as they accommodated to a market economy, tenants and smallholders alike continued to draw sustenance from time-honored patterns of cultivation, family labor, and neighborhood exchange.

A North Carolina mountain farm in the early twentieth century. This family grew tobacco for cash and dried fruit for consumption and to trade with neighbors.
(Courtesy of the North Carolina Collection, University of North Carolina at Chapel Hill)

To be sure, standards of living varied up and down the agricultural ladder. Large farmers often bought up more and more land, took advantage of the people who worked it, and prospered. Families who owned modest farms exercised more control over their operations and lived better than sharecroppers. Renters who could provide their own draft animals and implements and pay cash in exchange for land to cultivate usually fell somewhere in between. But sociologist Margaret Jarman Hagood, a sensitive student of Piedmont rural life, concluded that both small owners and tenants faced "the common plight of those engaged in agricultural labor—inadequate returns for productive work." Many families who owned small farms were still hard pressed to sustain the kind of life they believed they deserved. George Dyer, whose father owned 150 acres of land, declared that "unless you's a big rich farmer, unless he had good equipment and everything, he couldn't make a living. We had plenty of food to eat, but our clothes wasn't too much. We got by, but it wasn't like people ought to have."[18]

The complex social relations that bound tenant and landlord together could also blur social distinctions. An example from Chatham County illustrates the point. A 1922 study revealed that half of the fifty-one white tenants in two townships rented and cultivated a relative's land. These sons, sons-in-law, and nephews shared "in small or large measure in the properties and products of tribal farming," as tenant and landlord ate each other's food, used each other's work stock, and traded favors. Tenants who worked land not owned by their kin were at a disadvantage when it came to negotiating rental agreements, but both groups of tenants were part of the same social world as owners. All occupied the same pews in church on Sunday mornings, applauded each other's children at school commencements, exchanged visits, and hunted and fished together.[19]

Sharecroppers fared worst of all tenants, yet their dependence upon landlords and merchants for housing and supplies did not necessarily translate into servility. The amount of control exercised over tenants varied from landlord to landlord and fell most heavily upon blacks. In the 1930s a black cropper assessed his past two decades on the land. "The men I've had crops with has always talked to me kind and treated me like I was a man. Except Mr. Leroy Collins; he was rough, naggin' and cussin' me like I was a dog. It ain't my landlords I'm complainin' about, for they been as good as any I reckon, maybe better'n most. It's sharecroppin' that's wrong." A white sharecropper, on the other hand, maintained, "Our landlord never bothers us. We ain't never asked him for anything, and he seems just satisfied to leave us alone." Looking back on twenty years working for the same merchant-landlord, a white sharecropper in the 1930s declared that "he never give me a slack word but one time, and then in twenty minutes he come back to apologize for it. I ain't never heard a grumble out o' him, and he out o' me. . . . I hear 'em talkin' 'bout landowners that's mean and hard to get along with, but I've never had no experience durin' my fifty-two years with sech as that. . . . Mr. Davison lets me farm jus' like 'twas my own land; he hardly ever comes down here, for he says I'm a good farmer and know [as] much how to tend a crop as he does and so I run it like I please." In sum, labor relations between landlords and tenants were personal, the cash nexus still had a human face, and tenants retained some autonomy. Some landlords were cruel and harsh, but they could not impose total control. When tenants felt unduly cheated or abused, they often packed up and searched for greener pastures down the road.[20]

Most portraits of the rural South between 1880 and the 1930s have emphasized poverty and suffering. Indeed, the crop lien and cash-crop farming as practiced in the region produced great hardship. Many people did not have enough of the right kinds of food to eat; many lived in houses where, as the saying went, it was "possible to study astronomy through the holes in the roof and geology through the cracks in the floor." But even as they fell under the harsh logic of the marketplace, most farm families were able to sustain much of an older rural culture that stressed mutuality and the ideal of self-sufficiency. The persistence of familiar ways of doing things helped rural folk cope with change.[21]

One way of coping was simply to work harder, to exploit the one factor over which farm families had the most control—their own labor. Another strategy was to try to meet as many of their own needs as possible in an effort to avoid absolute dependence on merchants and to have money to spend on amenities rather than necessities. In the early twentieth century, Wesley Snipes's descendants still slaughtered their own beef, made their own hominy and lye soap, stuffed pillows with down plucked from their own geese, and swapped wool and cowhides for cloth and tanned leather. On the mountain farm in western North Carolina where Vesta Finley grew up, "You just raised the food you ate; and they had cattle and sheep. Back in those days, you know, we had our own meats. We raised sheep to have our own wool, and my mother and grandmother made blankets and socks, and our toboggans and our gloves and all that." Alice Hardin, whose family raised cotton and wheat on rented land in South Carolina until the 1920s, captured the outlook of people accustomed to doing for themselves when she commented, "Oh yes, we grew our bread."[22]

Traditional beliefs held steadfast. Many rural people still looked to the moon and planets for guidance as they prepared to plant and butcher. Good Friday was the best time to plant gardens; hogs slaughtered when the moon was waning released their fat more easily. Nor did modern medicine supplant faith in folk remedies. Wesley Snipes's great-grandson, John Wesley Snipes, believed the tea that a neighboring black "grannie midwife" steeped from sheep manure hastened the onset and completion of a case of measles. Sarah Andrews's mother swore by the curative powers of peach leaf tea. Indeed, gifted healers were considered valuable assets in rural communities, where doctors and the money to pay them were in short supply.[23]

Farming continued to be a family effort, and all members were partners—albeit unequal ones—in production. Men saw to the field work, the care of draft animals, and farm maintenance. They also claimed the right to make decisions and assign chores. Men's work varied according to the season and the needs of the cash crop. For tobacco farmers, there was something to do almost all the time: cutting wood for the curing barns in winter; setting out plant beds in January; breaking the land and transplanting the seedlings in late spring; plowing, chopping, suckering, worming, and topping the crop throughout the early summer; harvesting for six weeks in the late summer; and grading the leaves and hauling the tobacco to market in the fall. Cotton, on the other hand, required a more sporadic work routine. Farmers plowed and planted in the spring and chopped out weeds during the summer. By midsummer the crop could be laid by until pickers entered the fields in the fall. After they picked and ginned the cotton, farmers suspended field work until the next spring.[24]

Rural men also plied trades that brought in extra cash. Lee Workman's father, owner of a modest Catawba County farm, shod his neighbors' horses, repaired their wagons and plows, and fashioned the cradles they used to harvest grain. Workman and his father also supplemented the family diet and pocketbook by catching possums in the winter. With the help of a trusted hunting dog, they returned home about daybreak with as many as eight live possums squirming in a sack. The elder Workman "had a big box, and he'd put them in that, and he'd feed them cornbread and milk. Fatten them up. And when he'd get them fattened up, he'd kill them and eat the meat and send the hides off and get money." Other men cut and sold railroad crossties, joined railroad construction crews, or, like George Dyer's father, cut lumber during the winter. "That's how he made some money," Dyer explained, "and then in the summer, he'd raise crops."[25]

Farm women faced a cupboard full of chores that took them from kitchen to barnyard. Household and family maintenance kept them busy cooking, cleaning, washing, and sewing. Often arduous and monotonous, domestic work also required women to master a host of skills that could be sources of pride and satisfaction. Sarah Andrews admired her mother's ability to manufacture soap, brew Easter-egg dye from boiled cedar branches and broomstraw, and rob bees of their honey without suffering a sting. Her mother's talent for subduing a feisty cow drew special praise. "We had an old cow; she was mean. I was scared to death of her. Nobody couldn't milk that cow but my mother. And when she had to go off and get somebody to milk that cow, they had to put on her dress. When [that cow] made a lunge at her, she just met her in the forehead or the face with a fist. And that cow learned her; she knew better than to tackle my ma." Besides milking cows and churning butter, women also cultivated gardens, preserved vegetables and fruits, fed chickens, and gathered eggs. The products of women's labor often served as the readiest coin of exchange; their eggs and butter were easily swapped for merchandise at country stores.[26]

Otherwise, chances for rural women to earn money were limited. One option was to become a sharecropper like Glenn Hollar's mother, who grew cotton on rented land. "She'd get a third of whatever it brung," Hollar remembered. "That's how we'd buy our clothes and things to go to school." More commonly, women washed other people's clothes or picked and hoed other people's crops, their earnings usually a meager twenty-five or fifty cents a day and their field work valued at about one-half that of men's. Many women also took in boarders. When a gold mine opened near Sarah Andrews's home in Montgomery County, North Carolina, her mother provided food and lodging for eight men who slept in the house in two shifts. She packed dinners, which Sarah and her younger sister delivered to the miners.[27]

Central to farm women's work was bearing and rearing the children who would grow into the family's labor force. Although the average birthrate for American women was declining during the late nineteenth and early twentieth centuries, southern farm women bore the largest families in the country. It was not at all unusual for a woman to have a baby every two years. John Wesley Snipes was the fourth child his mother had borne in six years. "The babies come so fast," he remarked, "that they was all the same size." Vesta Finley, one of ten children, remembered that her mother "was mostly tied up with tending the babies, having babies, and taking care of the home." Frequent pregnancies, coupled with regular duties, took a toll on women's health and energy, and ambivalence toward motherhood was commonplace. Women's pride in having borne and nurtured large families was usually tempered by a hope that no more pregnancies would follow.[28]

While children increased a mother's responsibilities, youngsters were also expected to shoulder their share of farm and household chores. By the time they were five or six years old, boys and girls performed a variety of tasks. "Before we went to school in the morning," recalled Vesta Finley, "we had to carry in stove wood, and feed the chickens, and carry in enough water from the springs to do Mother during the day. And then we had to walk about a mile and a half to school."

Older daughters in particular were indispensable mother's helpers. Betty Davidson, born in 1913 in a "little four-room house in the country," was the fourth child, and the oldest girl, in a family of twelve children. Her workload increased as she grew older and the family grew larger: she made bread three times a day, built fires in the cookstove, milked and churned, helped to wash and iron, and took care of younger siblings. "My mother had so much to do," Betty explained, "I had to take the children, and take care of them while she cooked and prepared the meals." In fact, there was so much to do that Betty learned to perform two jobs at once. As each new brother and sister came along, she carried the baby propped on one hip while she used her free arm to cook and clean. Carrying those children on her hip during "a growing stage," she believed, made one side of her body lower than the other.[29]

Girls and boys alike worked in the fields. Catawba County sisters Blanche Bolick and Kathryn Killian recalled their gradual initiation to field labor. Under the watchful eye of older siblings they helped to weed row middles at the age of five or six. Within a few years, when they could distinguish between blades of grass and corn or between weeds and cotton, Bolick and Killian assumed responsibility for hoeing entire rows. Frank Webster was pressed into service on his family's farm when he was too small to reach the plow handles. "I had to reach a crossbar on the plow," he recalled. "I was around twelve or thirteen then. I was doing almost a man's work by that time."[30]

Fathers routinely counted on their daughters and wives to work in the fields, but mothers rarely expected their older sons and husbands to help with indoor work. The amount and the kinds of field work that women performed varied according to the family's economic status and the number of grown sons. A fairly strict sexual division of labor could be honored on the relatively prosperous tobacco farm that Mary Harrington's father owned near Danville, Virginia. During the early years of her marriage, Harrington's mother worked in the fields until she produced enough children to take her place there. With four

brothers, Mary and her sisters helped only during critical planting and harvesting periods: the girls performed lighter, tedious tasks such as dropping seeds and pulling suckers off plants, while their brothers plowed. "We were very fortunate," Harrington concluded. "A lot of women did things that we didn't. It was just because I had four brothers, and all of them worked real hard. They wasn't lazy. That took off us. In fact, we really didn't have a lot to do. We had our chores; we couldn't just sit around and do anything. But we were really treated like women." Nonetheless, when necessary, Harrington's father could command his daughters' presence in the fields and tobacco barns, although her mother could never command her sons' help in the kitchen. "I had the kind of brothers," Harrington explained, "that were really men. They didn't do anything around the house. Their work was strictly on the farm."[31]

The fewer males there were in a family, the more field work was required from girls and women. Eunice Austin was the oldest of four daughters, and her parents supplemented the eleven acres they owned with rented land. As a result, Austin recalled, "I had to be boy and girl. I had to do work that a boy would ordinarily do, because my daddy didn't have any other help to do that. I hauled hay and shocked wheat and just anything [there] was to do. I didn't do much plowing. He never did think that was a woman's place. But I would always help plant the crop and do a lot of hoeing. Daddy just depended on me. I knew it had to be done, and we just didn't have money to buy things with, and we just had to cooperate and do the best we could." Austin's mother joined in too. "She could do about anything a man could. She plowed, and she'd help haul hay and all them kind of chores that we had to do."[32]

Women's increasing participation in field work was one sign of how the reorganization of the farm economy forced changes in the household economy. Indeed, these changes worked a particular hardship on women and children. For even as women turned their attention to the cash crops in the fields, they also tried to maintain many of the traditional subsistence activities such as growing and preserving food. A sharecropper's wife described her summer routine to a visitor. "This season o' year men folks get a little breathin' spell, with the crops laid by, but it's a woman's hardest time, standin' over the hot stove cannin' and picklin' and preservin'. . . . Besides the cannin' I try to get the house and yard cleaned up before the cotton opens and calls me to the field, for there won't be no more fixin' till Christmas. Then there's the sewin', mendin', choppin' down weeds in the garden, washin' and ironin'. . . . [T]he women down this way go to the field 'bout as reg'lar as the men. Cotton will be openin' now in four weeks, and that'll be the last of the house except for cookin' and washin' and ironin' till it's all picked."[33]

Although many women preferred field work to household duties and took pleasure in their ability to "work like men," others acknowledged the burden that all their duties could impose. On her parents' 200-acre farm Ila Rice's responsibilities ranged from cooking to plowing. "We done all kinds of work," she recalled. "We done men's work. We done women's work. You name it and we done it." Another woman related this image of her mother: "Bless her heart, she would pick cotton and pull a kid on the cotton sack, and be pregnant. And she never complained; she was always willing."[34]

Children also testified to the demands on their time. "We stayed occupied," observed Myrtle Gentry, who grew up on an East Tennessee farm. "We was glad to get to play a little bit. On Sunday afternoon, after we went to church, is the only time we ever got to play." George Dyer agreed. The nine children in his family "all had to work when we got big enough to work. We couldn't lay around and play off like something was wrong with us. [Daddy] made us work. That's the way people was brought up years ago. They had no idle time to get into anything. You had off from Saturday afternoon on to Sunday."[35]

Commercial agriculture also tipped the household balance of power in favor of men, who linked the family to the marketplace. It was men who negotiated rental agreements and arranged for credit and supplies in the spring; in the fall it was men who hauled crops to market, settled accounts, and pocketed any proceeds. And it was men who determined how the family's labor would be divided. Male authority and prerogatives could sometimes spark resentment. Eula Durham remembered an occasion when her father insisted that his daughters help a neighbor pick cotton. "We picked cotton all day long that day for that old man. Thought, well, I was going to have me some money. I got through picking that evening late, started home, and [the man] said, 'Well, I don't know. I reckon you're worth a dime.' And he give me a dime for picking cotton all day. I went home and I cried, I was so mad. Papa said, 'If you don't sit down and hush I'm going to tear you all to pieces. That's all that old man had.' I said, 'Well, he ought to have told me that before I picked that cotton. I wouldn't have picked it.' He said, 'Well, you're going back tomorrow and you're going to pick cotton if he don't give you but a nickel.' I went back, but I didn't pick much cotton. Yes sir, give me a dime for picking cotton all day long. Couldn't buy nothing with that dime. I thought I was going to have some money."[36]

Married women, it seemed, could exercise little control over their husbands' decisions and behavior. Nannie Pharis, born on a Virginia farm in 1892, remembered that her maternal grandmother disapproved of her husband's moonshining operation, which kept him away from home and at his still on a stream. "She didn't like it at all," Pharis observed, "but she didn't argue about it. She just let him have his way." Sarah Andrews believed her mother's workload would have been much lighter if her father had consented to sell some of the timber on his farm. And Mary Harrington felt that had her father not indulged in harvesttime drinking sprees, her family of thirteen could have lived more comfortably. "Then, farmers only got money once a year," she explained. "After [my daddy] was honest, and those debts were paid, the rest was spent. My mother once said that our daddy lost a small fortune because of his drinking. You know, to raise that many children, it almost took a fortune. She said we could have been rich. He didn't have anything to say."[37]

Widows gained more autonomy but paid for it dearly. After seventeen-year-old Dolly Moser married in 1903, her husband "done the bossing" on their Catawba County farm. Twelve years later, Mr. Moser died, leaving her the sole support of four stepchildren and seven children. One of those children, Gladys Moser Hollar, was five years old at the time. "We just had to work that much harder," she recalled. "I wasn't hardly big enough to work. I carried a hoe ever since I was big enough to carry one, though. But [Daddy] had just bought some land the year before he died, and he was supposed to pay for it the next year. And I can remember that Mama said that she didn't know if she would lose it or not, but said the next year the cotton crop and everything was so good, had such a good year, and they paid off the land." The whole family pitched in, but Hollar acknowledged that her mother "worked the hardest"—preserving large quantities of fruits and vegetables, cooking meals, and sharing field duties with her children. Worry about her family's welfare accompanied Mrs. Moser's widowhood. "I know Mama said a lot of times she'd go to bed of a night, and she wouldn't know where the food was going to come from for the next day." Some of the emotional and economic strain, however, was relieved by Hollar's maternal grandparents, who lived just four miles away. Her grandmother would come "with a big basket of food on her arm; I can see her come down the road yet."[38]

Like Gladys Moser Hollar's family, other farm people looked to their kin and neighbors for help. A study of white tenants and farm owners in Wake County conducted in the 1920s revealed that trading extra food was a common practice, especially among poorer families. "If one family has more of one product than it can consume," the researchers found, "it gives this supply to a neighboring or related family. As a result it is believed that considerable food is passed from family to family and is therefore a saving for the family."[39]

Rural social life revolved around visiting. The frequency of visits might drop when the demands of planting and harvesting kept people busiest, then pick up again as the workload declined. "Most of the time people visited you was Sundays," recalled Frank Webster, "maybe come home from church. Wasn't too much visiting through the week." In some neighborhoods visiting followed a set pattern. Icy Norman, who grew up on a North Carolina mountain farm, described how visits were exchanged. "The neighbors there lived a half a mile, maybe a mile apart. Some of them two miles. Some would always come to my house. We'd take a circle and we'd visit everybody; they'd take a circle until they'd visited everybody."[40] In this way social debts were accrued and repaid, and neighbors traded information about the welfare of community members.

Churchgoing accomplished social as well as spiritual ends. Asa Spaulding, the son of black farm owners, admitted that as much visiting as praying went on at his childhood church. "People would gather around the churchyard and talk. That's where you had your social life, you know. And I'm not saying it was as much religious fervor as it was you got a chance to meet the people in the community, to socialize. See, if you're working six days a week, and right on the farm, you're glad to see Sunday come, to see somebody. And when the people would meet there after church was out, they'd stand out there in the churchyard for at least thirty minutes. Speaking to different ones, you know, and exchanging views, just kind of bringing them up to what's happening in the community." The overlap between church and community life was equally apparent when Pauline Griffith remembered how her family piled into a wagon to ride across the mountain to attend church services conducted by an uncle. "That was a big day," she recalled. "We had a good, happy life. Our community in which we lived, the people were thoughtful of each other. We had good fellowship among our neighbors." Church provided respite from work, spiritual solace, and a fellowship from which help flowed.[41]

A common pattern among rural churchgoers broadened the reach of fellowship from one congregation to the next and diminished denominational differences. Because there were too few preachers to keep every rural pulpit filled each Sunday, people attended the church of their own faith only when the preacher was present. In his absence they joined other congregations whose ministers were delivering sermons. According to one farmer, "We'd all belong to one and the same church if it wasn't for the preachers."[42]

Church could also be a place where differences in wealth were dramatized and values came into conflict. Sarah Andrews remembered that the local storekeeper's wife, Mrs. Thare, thought "she was better than anybody else" and took every opportunity to display what her money could buy. "She'd come into church and have on silk, and she just rattled as she walked, just rattling. And she just had better than anybody else. She had a rug on the floor. She claimed to be a good Christian, but she didn't have nothing to do with nobody. And she didn't want her children to play with nobody else 'cause she thought she was the cock of the walk. That's not Christianity; that's not the right kind of heart to have." But Andrews's mother had taught herself to nurse and heal—skills that provided leverage over the haughty Thares. "You let one of [her children] get sick, and boy, she was glad for my mammy to come down there and us to go with her."[43]

Indeed, interdependence in the countryside came into sharp relief in times of crisis. If illness struck one family, its predicament became the concern of many. Jesse Brooks, who grew up on a farm in Alamance County, North Carolina, remembered that if a farmer "got sick in a neighborhood and couldn't tend his crops," other farmers worked his fields for him. Lillie Price noted the same practice among mountain farmers. "When we lived in the country, everybody helped everybody if they needed help. You know, if a man got sick, they'd come in and tend his farm for him. You know, people helped; they was neighbors." But mutual aid did not wait for a calamity. "It was just a neighborhood thing," explained Asa Spaulding, "that people would come together and enjoy themselves helping each other. They were accommodating. They didn't look for pay. A farm life in a way was a hard life, and yet there were many things in it. It was not exactly communal living, but certainly the matter of the spirit of sharing."[44]

Rooted in necessity, the spirit of sharing became particularly tangible when one family had work to do that it could not accomplish alone. At harvesttime neighbors gathered for cornshuckings, carefully orchestrated events that blended work, recreation, and celebration. "About the time of the frost," remembered John Wesley Snipes, "they'd get up the corn in big piles and have a big dinner and have a neighborhood cornshucking. That was a common custom. They don't do it any more 'cause they've got these combines and pickers and all to pick it in the field and shuck it in the field. But that was a big occasion, those big old cornshuckings." The actual shucking was predominantly the province of men, their work hastened by competition for a jug of whiskey hidden at the bottom of a corn pile or a promise that the shucker who discovered a red ear of corn among the yellow could kiss a pretty girl. While the men shucked, their wives and daughters made quilts or kept an eye on the food to be served at suppertime. As the shucking ended and drinking began, specially invited musicians tuned their fiddles and banjos for the square dancing that lasted into the night. This pattern was repeated until each family's obligation to the others had been repaid. "People would come in and help shuck your corn," Icy Norman explained. "Maybe the next neighbor would have his ready and we'd all go to his house. That's the way they done until everybody got their corn shucked."[45]

Performed within a group, work was a means to many ends. There was room for individual achievement: the women gathered for a quilting bee displayed their prowess with needle and fabric, much as men at cornshuckings exhibited personal speed and dexterity. At the same time, the sponsoring family benefited from this collective work, for corn was a staple of their diet and quilts kept them warm. And cooperative work established networks of reciprocity among participants, all of whom reaped rewards as each repaid the others' labor and hospitality.

Work bound families and neighbors together, and so did the music that often accompanied these gatherings. Musically inclined families made up bands of their own and used their talents to leaven their labor and entertain friends. While Alice Hardin played the organ and her father played the violin, the entire family sang hymns after they left the fields for the noon dinner hour. In northwestern North Carolina, where Roy Ham was raised, "the mountain people had their instruments—banjos and fiddles—everywhere there was a gathering. People would bring their musical instrument in and play hillbilly music.

Men gathered for wheat threshing on a Chatham County, North Carolina, farm in 1912. Wheat threshing, like corn shucking, required cooperation among neighbors.
(Courtesy of the North Carolina Collection, University of North Carolina at Chapel Hill)

That's the way the songs were handed down from family to family for years, from generation to generation."[46]

Family, kin, and neighbors defined the boundaries of the social world in the countryside. As they grew older, rural children courted in parlors and on front porches, within earshot of parents. Or they met future spouses while attending church or candy-making parties, where adult supervision was difficult to elude. Many people went a lifetime without stepping beyond their own communities. Claude Thomas's childhood memories demonstrate vividly how limited was his contact with the outside world. Thomas and his five brothers and sisters helped his parents farm in Union County, where he was born in 1895. As a reward for their hard work one year, Claude's father promised the children a trip to the fair in Monroe, the county seat, just eighteen miles away. It was the longest trip Thomas had ever taken, and he remembered it as if it had happened only yesterday. "I didn't miss anything between our home and Monroe. Every pig path I re-corded in my memory. And when we got to Monroe, I made this statement: I said, 'There just couldn't possibly be as much on the other side of Monroe as we've already seen on this side, between here and home. But if there should be,' I said, 'it's a whoppin' big old world.' "[47]

The rise of industrial capitalism in the postbellum South went hand in hand with the transformation of agriculture. The same conditions that crippled farmers feathered the nests of many merchants and breathed life into the small towns where they made their homes. By the 1880s merchants with money to invest were backing mill construction. This accumulation of capital coincided with a new southern ethos that equated progress with industrialization. Small-town elites fell captive to a dream of individual gain and community prosperity. Towns vied for the railroad lines and mills that promised to quicken the pulse of commerce, and newspaper editors spun visions of a "New South" inhabited by ambitious entrepreneurs. A Durham newspaper declared in 1886: "Nothing stands still. There is very little loafing in Durham. A man who stands on the street corner and gazes at the sky is apt to be run over. Everybody works. Everybody is busy. The word 'Durham' is synonymous with 'Business.' "[48]

Mill men received help from a supporting cast of middle-class professionals composed of bankers, lawyers, doctors, preachers, and teachers. Many lent financial backing for mill building. Perhaps more important, they sanctioned an aggressive, enterprising spirit and fueled the "cotton mill campaign" that took on the fervor of a social movement in the 1880s. Mill building became synonymous with town building and served as an index to community prosperity. Local governments granted tax concessions, and from their pulpits ministers granted the approval of religious authority. Presiding over the dedication of a mill in Cabarrus County, North Carolina, in 1882, a local preacher celebrated the "roar of the machinery" as "work's anthem to the Lord" and blessed the smoke from the chimney as a "daily incense to God." The economic and cultural foundations for a mill-building boom were laid.[49]

The expansion of railroads after the Civil War was handmaiden to the spread of commercial agriculture, the growth of towns, and the rise of cotton mills. Financed with northern investments and stock purchased by local entrepreneurs, railroad track mileage increased substantially. By 1880, for example, some 1,500 miles of track laced North Carolina; twenty years later, track mileage had grown more

than two-and-one-half times. Snaking into the Piedmont, railroads brought in the fertilizers and supplies essential for cotton and tobacco culture and hauled farmers' crops to market. Merchants, the heart of the system, were the chief beneficiaries, along with the Piedmont towns where they did business.[50]

The rise of upcountry towns caused significant shifts of population, tipping the balance of social and economic power in the Carolinas away from the East and to the Piedmont. In 1870 the coastal town of Wilmington was the only North Carolina city boasting a population of more than 10,000. By the turn of the century five other towns, all in the Piedmont or mountains, had moved into this category. The populations of Greensboro and Winston each skyrocketed from fewer than 500 residents in 1870 to more than 10,000 in 1900, and Charlotte added nearly 14,000 people during the same period. The number of towns with 5,000 to 10,000 inhabitants rose from two to six: Durham, for instance, did not even appear in the 1870 census but registered nearly 7,000 residents by century's end. Even more spectacular was the growth in the number of small towns with populations of 1,000 to 5,000: from fourteen in 1870 to fifty-two in 1900. The interior of South Carolina witnessed a similar explosion in the growth of towns. Greenville, a sleepy courthouse town before the Civil War, became a booming cotton market and saw its population quadruple to 6,000 between 1860 and 1880 and surpass 10,000 by 1900. Along rail lines, older towns burgeoned and newer towns sprang up to serve farmers and then become centers for mill building.[51]

Although New England held undisputed sway over the American textile industry before the Civil War, while southerners usually channeled capital into land and slaves, a handful of mills had been established in the South. Most were small mills that spun yarn for sale in local markets, serving as adjuncts to an agricultural society, much as gristmills did. Still, antebellum mills demonstrated that processing cotton could be profitable, and they served as training grounds for future owners and managers. Some survived the Civil War and flourished, providing a thread of continuity between textile manufacturing in the Old South and the New.[52]

An example is the Alamance Mill, built by Edwin Michael Holt in 1837 on the banks of Cane Creek, a stream that feeds into the powerful Haw River. Holt's mill contained 528 spindles producing undyed yarn that was sold to country peddlars or hauled to nearby villages for hand-knitting and weaving. In 1845 Holt installed looms, and in 1853 an itinerant French dyer, passing through Alamance County, showed one of Holt's sons the fundamentals of mixing dyes. The result was a cloth woven with colored stripes. According to a textile manufacturer whose father was a contemporary of Holt, the mill was "a tremendous operation in the South for this period in history. The Alamance Mill was known for the Alamance Plaids, and they sold a lot of these plaids from covered wagons. They'd drive them all over North and South Carolina and into Tennessee, selling the cloth known as Alamance plaid. It was a sturdy cloth that people could use on farms and for working." The cloth also made the Holt family's fortune.

After the Civil War, Holt turned the factory over to his sons, and the family proceeded to build an industrial dynasty. Between 1865 and 1879 Edwin Holt and his sons and sons-in-law built or bought numerous mills located along the Haw River or Alamance Creek. By the early twentieth century they controlled twenty-four of the twenty-nine cotton mills in Alamance County. Among them was the Plaid Mill built in 1883 in the town of Company Shops, where the engines of the North Carolina Railroad were repaired. Company Shops would later be renamed Burlington and become the home of Burlington Industries.[53]

As the success of the Holt family suggests, the 1880s marked a turning point for the southern textile industry. Construction of mills accelerated: in North Carolina six new mills, on average, were built each year between 1880 and 1900. By 1900 there were 177 mills, 90 percent of them located in the Piedmont. Rather than rely on individual financing, businessmen turned to stock subscription campaigns that pooled investments. Loans from textile machinery and commission firms located in the North supplemented capital raised by native entrepreneurs. Not only were there more mills; there were also bigger mills. Spindleage increased, and there was a new emphasis on weaving. Finally, postbellum mill building was accompanied by an unprecedented public zeal that turned factories into potent symbols of regional regeneration, yardsticks of a town's progress, and badges of civic pride.[54]

A combination of factors helped account for the takeoff of southern industrialization in the late nineteenth century. Nationally, a six-year financial depression ended in 1879, creating a climate more hospitable for business. Closer to home, merchants and large landowners—

Advertisement for Altamahaw Plaids from the turn of the century. The Altamahaw mill, a Holt family concern, was one plant manufacturing the plaid material that made the family's fortune.

(Courtesy of Robert Horne, Burlington, N.C.)

often one and the same—were profiting from commercial agriculture. When crop prices started to sag, capitalists looked for investments that promised steadier, more reliable returns. Cotton mills, as well as banks and railroads, fit the bill. The way this process worked itself out is captured in the story of R. R. Haynes, a Rutherford County, North Carolina, planter, merchant, and entrepreneur. After the Civil War, Haynes grew cotton and ran a store. The commissions he received as tax collector for his township allowed him to buy more land, and he rented much of it for cash or shares of the crop. He also operated a sawmill, cotton gins, and wheat threshers, and he bought and sold cotton. In 1884 Haynes purchased land and water rights on Second Broad Creek and formed a joint-stock company to finance construction of Henrietta Mills. Other mill ventures followed, and by 1913 Haynes was one of the South's leading manufacturers of ging-ham. Eventually, Haynes had his fingers in many pies, including a branch railroad, several banks, a lumber business, and a line of general stores.[55]

One of Haynes's partners, Simpson Bobo Tanner, also followed the store-to-mill route. Tanner's father worked at an iron furnace in the South Carolina Piedmont, and was able to survive the native iron industry's collapse after the Civil War when other men "broke under the strain of that savage crisis." The elder Tanner bounced back as a railroad contractor, and his son started clerking in a store in 1870 at the age of eighteen. Bobo Tanner began honing his skills as a salesman, saved his money, and according to his biographer, "gambled everything he had on the theory that his brain was superior to his brawn." The young man, who could claim only three months of formal education, packed off for a winter of study at a Baltimore business school.

Returning to the Piedmont, Tanner became a traveling salesman for a Charlotte merchant. The job provided an ideal vantage point from which to chart changes in the region and take advantage of them. "He saw villages that were picking up and growing into towns," noted his biographer. "He knew where the really good farm land lay and when a desirable property came on the market; and he was, of course, a specialist on the credit rating of everybody in a hundred communities. So he was able now and then to turn a neat profit in real estate and to pick up something by discounting notes."[56]

Despite his growing prosperity, Tanner was not satisfied. By the 1880s he wanted more. He wanted "to be an important man, as well as a rich man." He wanted the "satisfaction of building, of creating, of erecting a great structure where nothing was before." For a salesman familiar with the cotton trade like Tanner the logical next step was cotton manufacturing. But Tanner needed the capital that business connections could supply, and such connections came his way when he landed a job in a Charlotte bank. Tanner further cemented his financial ties when in 1888 he married the boss's daughter.

Teaming up with R. R. Haynes in 1887, Tanner took the plunge into textiles. He quickly raised enough money to build Henrietta Mills. The firm "made money practially from the day the wheels first began to turn; within three years it was making big money; within seven years its return was terrific." Within two decades Bobo Tanner owned several other mills and was president of the American Cotton Manufacturers Association.[57]

In Durham, mill men first made their fortunes in tobacco manufacturing and then channeled surplus capital into cotton mills. After helping his family build a tobacco empire, Brodie Duke founded the Pearl Cotton Mill in 1893. That same year his brothers and father established the Erwin Cotton Manufacturing Company, named for William A. Erwin, who was hired as its superintendent. Related by marriage to the Holt family of Alamance County, Erwin had been a merchant between 1878 and 1882 and then served as treasurer and general manager of the E. M. Holt Plaid Mill until moving to Durham.[58]

Another tobacco manufacturer turned cotton mill entrepreneur was Julian Shakespeare Carr. Born in 1845, the son of a well-to-do Chapel Hill merchant, Carr attended the University of North Carolina and served in the Confederate army. In 1870, the elder Carr established his son in business when he bought a one-third interest in a Durham tobacco company. Eventually, Julian Carr, "an abstemious Methodist to whom work was all important," became sole owner.[59]

By the 1880s Durham ministers and editors were clamoring for cotton mills "for the town's sake, for the poor people's sake, for the South's sake, literally for God's sake." Carr answered the call in 1884 when he founded the Durham Cotton Manufacturing Company in East Durham. On a sweltering July day, Carr presided over the laying of the mill cornerstone. Ministers gave their blessings, a church choir sang a hymn, and the editor of the local weekly counted it a "joyous day for Durham citizens."

Both "moral responsibility" and "fiscal possibilities" figured in Carr's decision to start a cotton mill. Weighing his prospects, he knew that raw cotton and poor farm families willing to process it for meager wages were readily available. While Carr "prided himself on being an ideal 'bossman'—benevolent, protective, and always accessible—" a recent biographer concluded that "he saw nothing amiss in making large profits from cheap labor, nor was he alone in his viewpoint."[60] Like his tobacco factory, Carr's mill proved a lucrative venture. He soon multiplied his investments to include a bank, a newspaper, an electric lighting company, and stock in four railroads. His growing wealth also earned Carr a reputation as a philanthropist who endowed churches, schools, and charities. And Carr's money allowed him to set his four sons up in business and build a palatial home.

That home, Somerset Villa, was a showplace. The three-story Queen Anne structure featured a huge reception hall dominated by a mantel that cost $1,800, two parlors, a banquet-size dining room, billiard and smoking rooms, servants' quarters, and five bedrooms with adjoining dressing rooms and baths. Expensive decorating details added to the extravagance. When Carr's daughters looked at their bedroom ceiling, they saw a painting of clouds and life-size cupids. Of the $125,000 spent on construction, $5,000 went for chandeliers, $40,000 for carpets and furniture, and $6,000 for stained glass windows. Landscaping by French and Dutch gardeners added the finishing touches.[61]

Carr the mill owner was also Carr the family patriarch. His wife taught his sons about "Character, Duty and Right living," and Carr taught them how to succeed in business. Before leaving for the University of North Carolina, Carr's eldest son and namesake imposed upon himself a set of strict resolutions. Julian, Jr., vowed privately never to go to bed before praying and reading the Bible; nor would he drink, smoke, gamble, or have sex. Eventually, all of Carr's sons followed him through the university and into the Durham Hosiery Mill that he started in 1898. In 1910 Carr retired, and five years later he rejoiced that his "four dear good boys" were in business together. "Don't separate," he advised them. "In unity there is strength. Carry the Golden Rule into your business, and especially in your relations with each other. . . . Let the interest of one be the interest of all." Other maxims followed: "DON'T GO INTO DEBT"; "DON'T EN-DORSE PAPER for anyone, not even for each other"; "DON'T SCAT-TER YOUR INVESTMENTS"; and "go to Church at LEAST ONCE each Sunday." Julian, Marvin, Claiborn, and Austin continued to build the family's fortunes.[62]

Only after local entrepreneurs like Carr had gotten the textile industry off the ground did southern mills attract northern capital, usually channeled through machinery manufacturers and commission houses. This was how Ceasar and Moses Cone, sons of a Baltimore wholesale grocer, eventually became southern mill men. "I guess we sorta got into [the textile business] by the back door," explained Ceasar Cone's son, Ben. "I understand that a lot of my grandfather's customers were cotton mill commissary stores operated by various southern cotton mills for the benefit of their employees, and he got to know the mill management. When money was tight, he wasn't able to collect cash for his groceries; he would frequently have to take yarn or cloth in trade for his coffee, sugar, and his tobacco products. Through that connection he got to know a good many of the early textile pioneers in the South." After the family grocery business closed in 1890, Moses and Ceasar founded the Cone Export and Commission Company the next year. With headquarters in New York, the company served as the selling, financing, billing, and collection agent for many southern mills. Later in the decade the brothers opened the first of several large cotton mills in Greensboro. Another of Ceasar Cone's sons, his namesake, explained how other mills were brought under the corporate umbrella: "A good many of the mills that Cone Export and Commission Company sold for were financed by Cone Export and Commission Company. It acquired some of the stock and it made some loans, and some of the mills went bust, and the Cone Export and Commission Company took them over."[63]

Whatever their origins, mill builders and their supporters thought they offered salvation even as they helped create a new economic and cultural order based on acquisitiveness and individual accumulation. Fusing the profit motive and a philanthropic impulse, mill promoters often cast themselves as public benefactors who were creating jobs for the growing number of rural poor. Textile work, reserved almost exclusively for whites, was supposed to free white farmers from poverty and teach them the virtues of thrift, regularity, and industrial discipline.[64] Such reasoning obscured the fact that mills rested on a paradox: the same conditions that made life on the land precarious contributed to the accumulation of capital by merchants and other professionals. Amid stalks of cotton and tobacco in the Piedmont and on worn-out mountains in the Appalachians grew the pool of cheap labor that southern industrialists counted as one of the region's chief assets. Under these conditions, farm families were confronted by a powerful push off the land and an increasingly attractive pull into the mills.

There were many paths leading from southern farms to Piedmont cotton mills. Any number of considerations might prompt the decision to move, but in one way or another the journey from field to factory had its origins in the transformation of the countryside that was making it more and more difficult to earn an adequate living from the land.

The move might come when a widow suddenly found herself the head of a large family of young children. Or a small farm owner, lacking the resources to compete successfully in the market-based economy, might calculate that prospects for his maturing children were brighter in the mills, which offered ready cash and steady em-

*Officers and superintendents of the Cone family's Proximity and White Oak plants
in Greensboro, North Carolina, 1909. Ceasar Cone is seated at the center.*
(Courtesy of the National Archives and Records Service)

ployment. The move could come when a labor recruiter visited the
farm and persuaded families to pack up and head for the mills or when
neighbors and kin who already held mill jobs sent back word that farm
folks "could make more money" in the factory. Some moves occurred
when a father decided that his daughters could better contribute to
the family economy by earning mill wages than by working in the fields
or when a son or daughter figured that a farm future would add up to
unrewarded hard work and prolonged dependence on parents. Others
occurred when poor crop prices or bothersome pests turned the gam-

ble on farming into a forfeit. Opportunities on the land, the availability of jobs in the mills, the age and sex of family members—all were weighed when deciding whether to tend the land or tend machines.

For many families, however, the choice was not between farm or factory. Rather, the question was how to combine the two, how to incorporate one into the other. Some people worked in the mills seasonally, after crops were harvested. Other families divided their labor between the land and the mills year round. Furthermore, the reaction to industrial life varied: some regretted their departure from the farm and soon returned, while others preferred their new way of life.

From the diversity of human experience, patterns of migration do emerge. During the latter part of the nineteenth century there were two broad waves of movement off the land and into the mills. Some people, naturally, felt the repercussions of changes in the countryside harder and sooner than others. Among the first to feel the pinch were female-headed tenant households. Landlords were reluctant to bargain with women unless they had several older sons who could perform the physically demanding work of cotton and tobacco cultivation. Farm laborers became another hard-pressed group, as more and more families fell back on their own resources rather than hiring help. Within families the labor of daughters was often deemed most expendable. Thus, widows, female-headed households, single women, and laborers—those with least access to the land, labor, and capital necessary for survival in the emerging market-based economy—predominated among the first wave of migrants to Piedmont factories during the 1870s and early 1880s.[65] In 1880, for example, widows headed nine of the fourteen households in the Bynum mill village. In both female- and male-headed households there was a preponderance of girls and women: the households headed by widows had only eight males out of a total of fifty-seven members, and there were only ten males out of the thirty-six members of the households headed by men. All seven of the boarders in the village were women.[66]

By the late 1880s and the 1890s—as merchants tightened credit, cash-crop farming took firmer hold, and prices collapsed—push came to shove for an increasing number of families headed by men. Landowning and tenant farm families alike turned to the mills. A man with limited acreage and poor soil could offer little help for maturing sons who wanted to establish farms of their own. Rather than continue to grow cotton and risk becoming so indebted that he would lose his farm while watching his children drift away, he could sell out, relocate in a mill village, and keep his family intact.[67]

Flossie Moore Durham and Albert Sanders each saw how impersonal economic forces intersected with personal circumstances to shape their families' decisions to move. Flossie's parents rented land in Chatham County until 1893, when her father died. Her mother was suddenly responsible for eight children whose ages ranged from infancy to nineteen. Mr. Moore's death, Flossie recalled, "left us, left my mother in a bad shape. Along in them days there wasn't any money coming in much. We lived; we never went hungry, we never went cold. But I've often wondered how she kept us all a-going." After harvesting that year's crops and seeking the neighbors' advice, the Moores moved to Bynum. "There were several of the men that come out and met first," Flossie remembered, "trying to decide what to do because there was a big family of us, and all of it like it was, didn't know hardly what to do. They knew about Bynum, and it was a good little place to live. It's always been a real quiet, nice place to live, almost just in the country. And of course the cotton mill was running here then." The village was already familiar, for Flossie's father had carted corn to be ground and cotton to be ginned at the Bynum family's gristmill and gin. Now his children sold their labor to the Bynums' cotton mill. At the age of ten, Flossie Moore Durham stopped picking cotton and started spinning it.[68]

An untimely death and unfavorable crop prices brought both sides of Albert Sanders's family together in Union, South Carolina. His mother's parents, the Ledbetters, hailed from the North Carolina mountains, where they ran a saw- and gristmill and did a little farming. When Mr. Ledbetter died in the early 1890s, his wife brought her eight girls and baby boy to the new Union Buffalo Mills, where several of her daughters got jobs. About the same time, the farm depression was setting in motion a move to the mill by Sanders's paternal grandparents. After suffering a sunstroke in the 1880s, Albert's grandfather, Joe Sanders, was unable to farm, so he opened a country store and became a small-time furnishing merchant. According to the family story, "Mr. Sanders was a good man, he just gave everybody credit. And wouldn't foreclose on anybody. Anyway, they just go along and the cotton prices go down, down, down. And then you get to that bumper year of 'ninety-two, when my daddy said [they] had cotton growing on stumps in the fields. Just perfect season, wonderful crop, that sold for about five cents [a pound]. Now, 'course, it cost about

The Gaffney Manufacturing Company, Gaffney, South Carolina, ca. 1915. Many of the families who brought their cotton to the mills eventually came to sell their labor.

(*Reproduced from the* Southern Textile Bulletin, *November 25, 1915*)

eight cents to make it, so there wasn't much money in that. And as a result of the spring panic of 'ninety-three (you see, it ties all together) my grandfather lost his store and lost his farm. And then he packs up his family and comes to the mill. So, evidently the mill was recruiting both through the Piedmont countryside and in the mountains, to get enough labor to open this new mill. This is the Union Buffalo Mills, which is a pretty big operation. Big village.

"My grandfather, from red hills, Tyger River, Piedmont Carolina, brought his family to this mill village, about the same time that my grandmother, a Clear Creek, Henderson County mountaineer, brought her family to the mill. So the two streams come together." While his sons worked in the mill, Joe Sanders operated a store on the edge of the village. Mrs. Ledbetter, "a very timid, shy woman," unaccustomed to living so close to so many people, returned to the mountains with two of her daughters. Albert's father later married one of the Ledbetter daughters who stayed behind, and he opened a grocery store that catered to "the city trade."[69]

In the early twentieth century another pattern of migration emerged, as more favorable crop prices weakened the push off the land and a second mill-building boom created more jobs than there were workers to fill them. Between 1890 and 1908 the number of spindles in southern cotton mills increased more than sixfold. To bolster the pull into the mills, owners resorted to recruiting labor from the countryside. One tactic was to inundate a town with fliers touting the benefits of mill work when a circus or celebration had attracted farm families there. Often, the labor agent was the head of a family who had been successful in the mill and was hired to return to his rural neighborhood, testify to the advantages of mill work, and lure back old friends. One labor agent made a direct appeal to Nannie Pharis's father, persuading him to abandon the family's rented farm and bring his ten children to town. "[The agents] would come to our home, because there was so many of us. They needed help, hands in the mill. That's how we started. They got our father to move into town and we all went to work." When the Rhode Island Mill opened in Spray, North Carolina, in 1905, Nannie, aged nine, "run the first spinning machine that ever started up."[70]

To satisfy their need for labor, mill owners also began eyeing the Appalachian mountains as a source of workers, and sent recruiters there to sing the praises of factory work. In 1905 labor agents arrived in Newport, Tennessee, and persuaded Jessie Lee Carter's father, grandfather, and uncles to move to the Brandon Mill in Greenville. "It must have been some big boss man," Carter remarked, "and he was going around the country getting people to come to work because they had just made the mill." The Carters packed the horse-drawn wagons supplied by the mill and, with a milk cow in tow, made the week-long trip. "My daddy and my grandfather and my uncles begin to work in the mill as quick as they brought us down here," Carter recalled. "They brought us to the house right over there at Brandon now, number fourteen. We moved in that house, and [my daddy] lived there forty years and worked in the mill." In 1907 J. M. Robinette's family began a similar journey from the North Carolina mountains to Charlotte when a former neighbor returned to solicit workers. "The man that owned the plant that we went to hired him to go out and hire help for him," Robinette explained. "So he just went up there in the mountains and picked up help, families that didn't know nothing about working, and took them and trained them."[71]

Mountain farmers could barely scrape a living out of the land, so it was small wonder that mill work appeared attractive. Martin Lowe's story captured the dynamics of economic change in eastern Tennessee that first drew him, like other men, into wage labor and the logic that led him to a Greenville cotton mill. Born in 1889, Lowe left his family's Sevier County farm as a teenager to work as a cook in a railroad camp that served logging crews. "It was mostly steep, hilly land," Lowe explained, and by the time "I was up about grown, why, about all of it that was of any account was cleared up and worn out, and you couldn't hardly make a living on it." When he married at age seventeen, Lowe moved in with his wife's family and helped his widowed mother-in-law farm. To make ends meet, Lowe figured that he would have to supplement the farm income by returning to wage labor with logging or railroad crews. Such an arrangement, however, would have kept him away from his family for days at a time. Cotton mill work, on the other hand, would allow the family to live and work together. Lowe explained his reasoning. "I said, 'Well, if I had to go to public works, why not move to them [mills] where it would be in my family?' And I told my father, 'I believe I can find a place where I can make a better living,' and I come to the mill. 'Well,' he said, 'you won't be there long. You'll be writing for money to come back.' 'Well,' I said, 'nobody here ain't got the money.' Well, they didn't. Now times was hard back there; it was the dickens. I'd seen some people that were working in a mill and went back, and then they was always wishing that they'd stayed at the mill when they went back in the mountains. It was rough up there." Lowe and his wife—along with her mother, brothers, and sisters—packed up and moved to Poe Mill. After forty-five years of factory work, Lowe concluded, "I've never begrudged it a day that I come to the mill at all."[72]

As Lowe's experience and that of others makes clear, knowing a friend or relative who had already gone to the mills was often an important factor in the decision to abandon the land. Grover Hardin's mother tried to run their eastern Tennessee farm after her husband died in 1913, leaving her with three children, the youngest just four months old. "She just couldn't make it," Hardin observed. "She'd have to hoe corn two or three days for somebody to get them to plow for her one. She just couldn't make it. She'd do washing over in the mountains and work all day for maybe twenty-five or thirty cents. She just couldn't make the going." The Hardins left for Greenville when a friend "wrote and told my mother that if she'd come down she could get a job, you know, and make a living for us." Grover cared for the younger children while his mother worked. When he was eleven, he got a job as a sweeper in the mill.[73]

One of Pauline Griffith's aunts eased her family's transition from their mountain farm to the Greenville mills. Although Griffith's parents would have preferred to remain on the land, by 1915 their farm could barely sustain the family. Griffith, who was seven years old at the time, remembered conditions leading up to the move. "The crops were kind of failing and [my parents] thought that it would be better to move. It was a necessity to move and get a job, rather than depend on the farm. That's why we came. You've heard of famines in the Bible. It was kind of like that." Through contacts with bosses, Griffith's aunt found jobs for Pauline's father and two older sisters, and she shared her house with them when they came to Greenville.[74]

Ernest Hickum's father was losing ground to big timber companies when a relative who worked at a Greenville mill offered a way out of his dilemma. The Hickums owned a 110-acre farm in the mountains of western North Carolina, where they grew tobacco, corn, and wheat and raised most of what they ate in a good garden. Like many mountain farmers, Mr. Hickum also cut and hauled lumber to make extra money. But that source of income dwindled when the elder Hickum's mule-drawn wagon had to start competing with the logging companies' chain-driven trucks. A man with a truck "couldn't haul very little more than my daddy could haul on that wagon," Ernest Hickum explained, "but he could make two trips a day and my daddy couldn't make but one. Now it wasn't but a year or two that they got to bringing them other kinds of trucks in there and just cut the poor farmers plumb out of the sawmill, hauling lumber." Denied that economic cushion, the Hickums' independence was threatened.

At about the same time, Hickum's brother began prodding him to come to Greenville's Woodside Mill. "He kept wanting my daddy to come down," Ernest recalled with irony, "bring all us kids, and start working in the cotton mill. We'd get rich." In the 1920s, the family packed its belongings—including a supply of home-canned vegetables and fruits and home-cured ham—into an old Dodge truck. Upon arrival, the elder Hickum did not like what he found. "He just studied and grieved about selling everything he had and coming down here.

He got around that machinery and he never seen nothing like it. You know what a racket machinery makes. I think the machinery scared him too much to try to run a job. He'd never seen nothing like that. He'd been around old sawmills and stuff, outside, but a lot of difference in that. Now when all [the food we had brought with us] was gone, we had to start going to the store and living out of a tin can. That's what hurt. My daddy didn't like that. He couldn't work in no cotton mill, so he went back to the mountains." So legion were pie-in-the-sky promises about mill work that songwriting worker Dave McCarns must have had people like Ernest Hickum's father in mind when he wrote the satiric "Cotton Mill Colic No. 3":

> Lots of people with a good free will
> Sold their homes and moved to the mill.
> We'll have lots of money they said,
> But everyone got hell instead.
> It was fun in the mountains rolling logs,
> But now when the whistle blows we run like dogs.[75]

Some farm families answered the factory whistle's call with the express hope that mill work would be temporary because the wages would make possible a return to the land. Dovie Lawson Gambrell's father was one farmer who saw that vision come true. Because he could neither read nor write, Mr. Lawson turned his savings from his mill job over to Dovie for deposit in her name. "When he got so many dollars saved up," she explained, "he sent me to the bank and I drawed it out. He went to Tennessee and bought a farm." Dovie and her sister, however, remained in Greenville with their older brother, and eventually each married a mill worker.[76]

Other families combined farm and factory work, making the transition from rural to industrial life in a piecemeal fashion as they improvised a complex deployment of labor. Betty Davidson's parents shared a set of looms in the Dan River Cotton Mill. "My father would run the looms in the wintertime," Davidson remembered, "and go to and from work by horseback. And in the summertime when he was farming, my mother run the looms and she stayed in town because she couldn't ride the horse. Then on the weekends, she would come home. They'd go get her in the wagon." A variation on this theme runs through Emma Whitesell's story. Her father and two of her sisters worked in a Haw River mill while her brother ran their nearby farm. Although

Emma's father preferred working outdoors to fixing a mill's looms, he "had to do it to raise us children." Yet another common division of labor occurred in Blanche Bolick and Kathryn Killian's family when their father, apparently convinced that his oldest daughters could make a more valuable contribution to the family by earning mill wages than by wielding a hoe, found them jobs at a nearby factory. On the farm, Killian explained, there was no money. "We just scratched out our living, that's all. We felt [that working in the factory] was what we wanted to do, to get out so we'd have a little more income then. After we went to work, we bought the [youngest] kids clothes, and this and that."[77] By combining farming and factory work, a family could forestall total dependence on either one.

As Lee Workman's experience demonstrated, access to land provided mill workers with leverage when dealing with bosses. In 1918 the superintendent of the Newton Cotton Mill came to the Workmans' Catawba County farm in search of hands to help him supply the demand for cloth during World War I. The elder Workman sold his mules and cows but, contrary to the superintendent's advice, held on to his land. Each spring he returned to craft the farm implements that his neighbors needed. "He'd tell Mr. Stamey, the superintendent, 'You can just get somebody else to run these frames, because I'm going back to make cradles for my friends.' [He'd] come back in the wintertime and work in the mill." Such independence did not sit well with the mill superintendent, but Lee's father had the upper hand: "Well, he told them, 'If you don't want to do that, I'll move back to the country and take the family.'" When the war ended, he did just that.[78]

Sharecroppers—who farmed with borrowed animals, tools, and supplies—could move even more easily from farm to mill and back again. "A lot of people leaned toward farming," explained Mack Duncan. "But when they'd harvest their crops—say, their cotton in the fall—they had plenty of time during the winter, so they'd go to the mill and see if they could get them a job and work during the winter, and then they'd move back, as tenant farmers, to the farms in the springtime and plant another crop."[79]

No matter how much someone wanted to remain on the land, the choice between mill and farm could become no choice at all. Unpredictable prices, unfavorable weather, and unstoppable pests could sabotage a season's work nearly overnight. Then, a family's dependence on a single crop for cash was thrown into stark relief. Claude

Thomas, Alice Hardin, John Wesley Snipes, and Josephine Glenn all knew this.

Claude Thomas gave up farming only after a hard fight. In early 1913 he left his family's Union County farm for the Highland Park Mill in Charlotte. Within a few weeks he had met, courted, and married a spinner, and the newlyweds headed back to the farm. "As hard as I knew it would be, I taken a chance. My wife has made this statement: I've heard her say that it's easy enough to get a man out of the country, but it's hard to get the country out of the man. I hadn't worked at public work long enough to have mastered a trade and demand what would have been a reasonable wage. And everything that I did do, it was starting at the bottom for a very meager amount of pay." The decision to gamble on farming did not pay off either. "My story is going to sound like I was in the middle of a bad fix and everything, but in 1914, which was the first and only year my wife and I farmed, we sold our cotton for five and a half cents. We didn't make enough to pay the fertilizer bill and eat. I went under and failed to make enough to pay my bills. I figured it like this: wherever I would go, whatever I did, I couldn't make it any worse than this. Just working like convicts and not making a living." The Thomases headed back to town.[80]

For Alice Hardin's family, a tornado compounded the vulnerability of tenantry in the 1920s. "We moved down on Guilty Creek and was living here, and the tornado come. It tore up everything we had, blowed away everything we had, half of our house and everything. Then we moved to another place and we lived there for about two or three years, and then we moved to the Woodside cotton mill. Daddy had about five or six hands to go to work in the mill at one time. Things had got tough in the country the way they started doing, so he just went and asked for a job, and they give us a job and a house. Farming, where you rented, was getting difficult to make a living. That's the reason we moved to the mill." The children adjusted to the abrupt change more easily than their father did. "Us children liked the mill work better," Hardin recalled, "because when we worked our hours, we was off. We thought it was easier. We had more time to do what we wanted. I don't think my father liked it at all, because he had rather be on the farm."[81]

John Wesley Snipes and his wife rented land from his father, and they rode the cotton market roller coaster until low prices and the boll weevil derailed them. Many years later Snipes retraced the course. "Cotton jumped up high right after World War I. It was thirty or forty cents. We'd never heard tell of cotton being like that in our lives. Well, a five-hundred-pound bale of cotton at forty cents'd bring you a couple of hundred dollars. Well, we thought we was rich." In the 1920s prices collapsed, and the boll weevil, with its voracious appetite for cotton, appeared in Chatham County. "The last year I raised four bales of cotton, and I carried a five-hundred-pound bale of cotton to Chapel Hill and it brought me twenty-five dollars: five cents a pound. The boll weevil hit. And I had four or five bales at four and five cents. And I told my wife, I said, 'Never will I work on the farm and spend maybe seventy-five or a hundred dollars for fertilizer, and it'd take every bit of cotton I make to pay that fertilizer and not have a dime for the whole year for my work.' So I quit." On Thanksgiving Day 1929 the Snipeses moved to Bynum "without prospect of a job." The next night Snipes started working in the mill, and within a few days his wife joined him there, just as she had joined him in the fields.[82]

Josephine Glenn and her husband tried to support their four children by farming on shares until the mid-1930s. "As soon as the Depression came on," Glenn remarked, "there just wasn't anything on the farm, especially for sharecroppers, and we didn't have our own home. We started working in the mill part-time, have a little crop and work in the mill, too, but we eventually sold all our farming equipment and just worked in textiles." Although Glenn liked farming, taking a mill job "wasn't a matter of choice," she concluded with a laugh. "I had four little reasons."[83]

The Depression also prompted Eva Hopkins's husband to leave a South Carolina farm for Charlotte textile mills. "He was 'country comes to town,'" Hopkins recalled. "He wanted to come to town and make some money. He got tired of walking behind a plow, I suspect. He wanted to make some money that he could jingle in his pockets. Farmers, they didn't have much money back then. He came and went to work in the mill down there and learned to work."[84]

Short of being in dire straits, some people found that staying on the farm could simply be a dead end. This seemed particularly apparent to young women, whose labor was considered superfluous in some cases and a source of exploitation in others. Because Mary Harrington's brothers handled most of the field work on their parents' farm, she and her sisters "just ventured out because we didn't have a lot to do down in the country." Harrington credited her oldest sister with setting the daring example that the other girls followed, much to their mother's chagrin. "My oldest sister," Harrington believed, "was very brave. Now you wouldn't count it as that, but then you would, for somebody out of the country to say, 'Well, we'll go and see if we can find a job.' I really don't know why she did it. But anyway, had she not, we would have all been right in the country. We probably wouldn't have wound up in the city. I guess my sister was a little different from the rest of us. Now, I just don't see how I did it. I guess at that time it was something so new to me, being from the country. I still can't recall my feelings, except I must have just thought it would be exciting."[85]

If Mary Harrington's going to Burlington took on an air of excitement, Ila Rice's departure from her parents' Catawba County farm represented an escape from years of doing "men's work" on top of "women's work" for little reward. The blast of factory whistles in Hickory reached her family's fields. "On a cold, clear morning," she recalled, "you could hear them whistles so plain." Finally, at the age of seventeen, Rice answered their call when she ran away with the hired hand "to keep from plowing." In a similar fashion, Sarah Andrews, witness to her mother's hard work, married at age sixteen and left Montgomery County to get "out of that hole up there. You couldn't never get nowhere up there. There just wasn't nothing to do." Chances of realizing her dream of becoming a nurse seemed slim "'cause we was just penned up there at that little old wide place in the road."[86]

From 1880 through the Great Depression, then, thousands of farmers traded fields for factories, or moved gingerly between the two. Throughout the period, rural people found themselves at a crossroads, contemplating which path to take as they surveyed prospects on the land, prospects in the mills, and familial and personal resources. As they made their decisions and embarked on their journeys, they did not go empty-handed. Along with the belongings piled in a horse-drawn wagon in the 1880s or a Dodge truck in the 1920s, they carried the cultural baggage of the countryside. Rural values and ways of life helped farmers-turned-millhands create a new industrial world in the Piedmont South.

Public Work

WHEN SOUTHERN FARMERS left the land and took a cotton mill job, they called it "public work." The phrase gained currency during the Great Depression as government programs put thousands of the unemployed on federal payrolls, but for at least two generations southern millhands had used it to describe their encounter with factory labor. Men and women who had once tilled the soil left their plows and mules and set out to earn an hourly cash wage—most for the first time in their lives. Despite a long history of small-scale textile manufacturing in the South that left in place scattered survivors from the antebellum years, most mill owners and workers were novices in a new industrial world. Both groups had much to learn, about machines and about each other.[1]

The principal investors in early mills—successful merchants, planters, and professionals—had little knowledge of the manufacturing techniques necessary to operate their factories. Their business skills were essential to the financial health of the companies, but profitable manufacturing also required technical know-how and the ability to organize a work force. The successful manufacturer soon learned that it paid to know the business in all its details. Added to the pressures of buying cheap and selling dear was the need to employ capital and labor efficiently. Only slowly, through trial and error, did industrialists succeed in combining self-confidence and business acumen with the skillful management of people and machines.[2]

Their command of capital gave manufacturers a free hand in designing the physical environment of the mill, but they never held full sway over the shop floor. Millhands themselves helped fashion the social world of work in a way that blunted the shock of their encounter with bosses and machines. Workers who migrated from nearby farms

found themselves in unfamiliar circumstances. Instead of feeding and
clothing their families directly through their own efforts, they offered
their labor for wages to buy the things they needed. But the value of
labor could not be measured by cash alone. Millhands also expected
work to provide a measure of self-esteem and a feeling of accomplishment. While they toiled mightily to create one of life's necessities—
clothing—workers also sought to wrest from the mills some of life's
rewards. Even the most routine jobs required initiative, creativity, and
dexterity—traits that were transmitted from worker to worker and
added some dignity to mere toil. Millhands also learned to maneuver
in an arena that offered no formal means for redressing their grievances; they used personal negotiation, frequent quitting, and occasional walkouts to check mill owners' authority. Thus emerged an
informal compromise between labor and management in which the
social fabric of the workplace was often stretched tightly and sometimes tore apart.

For hundreds of years, the production of yarn and cloth had been
carried out by women, at home, to meet family needs. But in the
eighteenth century, the growth of European cities and the spread of
the British Empire increased the demand for cotton goods, and farmers in northern England began producing textiles in their cottages to
supplement earnings from the land. Under the "putting out" system, a
merchant provided raw materials to weavers, who employed carders
and spinners—often the women and children in their own families—
to prepare the yarn, which they in turn wove into cloth and returned to
the merchant. This reorganization of production increased output
dramatically, yet supply still lagged behind demand. Over time, the
search for increased productivity sparked a cycle of mechanical innovation that laid the foundation for the Industrial Revolution. First,
John Kay's flying shuttle allowed weavers to produce cloth more
quickly, upsetting the balance between spinning and weaving. Then
began the search for a more efficient method of spinning, culmi-
nating with James Hargreaves's spinning jenny, Richard Arkwright's
water frame, and Samuel Crompton's "mule." Spinning operations
expanded in the workshop and eventually found a home in the cotton
mill. But spinning in turn outpaced weaving, compelling manufacturers to develop a mechanical loom. The adoption of the power loom
doomed the outwork system, limiting and then destroying the independence of handloom weavers.[3]

England tried to monopolize the Industrial Revolution by prohibiting the export of textile machinery and skilled workers. But, by hook or by crook, secrets crossed the Atlantic, and in the late eighteenth century the United States began to establish its own industry. The spiral of technological innovation continued with two key advances: ring spinning and the automatic loom. Seeking to reduce their reliance on a scarce and sometimes rebellious supply of skilled male mule spinners, American manufacturers first perfected the ring spinning frame. The ring frame increased the speed of yarn production and required little physical strength to operate, thus enabling mill men to employ large numbers of women and children. The final product of this cycle of improvements was the Northrop loom. Power looms, which had changed relatively little since the early 1800s, stopped when the shuttle ran out of yarn (about once every eight minutes in 1900), requiring the weaver to insert a new bobbin and restart the loom. Although costly, the Northrop loom came with a rotating battery of bobbins that automatically fed into the shuttle, drastically reducing the number of machine stops and cutting labor costs in half. With these two machines, the ring spinning frame and the Northrop loom, the industry reached a plateau. Not until the 1920s would entrepreneurs launch another round of mechanical and organizational change.[4]

When southern businessmen set out to become manufacturers, the textile industry was already one of the most technologically advanced in the world—the embodiment in steel of precision and power, ingenuity and occasional mayhem. The timing of their entry into the industry had important benefits. They did not have to wrest craft control from handloom weavers or mule spinners. Because they were not burdened by investments in outmoded machines, they could take full advantage of the latest technological advances. By the 1880s a textile machine making industry was firmly established in New England, and competing companies were seeking buyers for ever more precise and automated systems of production. With sufficient capital, Piedmont mill men could acquire the most up-to-date equipment and begin making cloth with a work force unschooled in the craft tradition.[5]

Nevertheless, roaring mill cities did not spring up in the South overnight. It took time to accumulate the social and technical experience and construct the links to markets needed to support large-scale textile manufacturing. As had been the case in England and New

England, the availability of cheap waterpower was a primary consideration in the location of early factories. When southern manufacturers set to work in the 1880s, they had the option of using steam engines. But until the southern Appalachian coal fields opened in the 1890s and railroads reached small communities a decade later, the coal necessary to fuel steam engines was expensive and hard to get. Instead, aspiring manufacturers looked to the Piedmont's rapidly falling streams. "At the falls of the Roanoke," the North Carolina Department of Agriculture boasted, "on the Tar river, on the rapid declivities of Haw and Deep rivers, on ever-falling streams in Cumberland and Richmond counties, on the enormous forces of the two Catawbas, and perhaps elsewhere, a second thought would never be given to the application of any other power than that so exhaustlessly provided by nature and so easily and economically controlled." The story was much the same in other southern states. The Pacolet, Enoree, Reedy, and Saluda rivers powered many of South Carolina's most important mills, and the mighty Dan River helped establish Danville as the center of Virginia's textile industry.[6]

At a water-powered mill, a dam accompanied by a canal known as a millrace transferred nature's power to the machinery. In 1860, for example, local merchants built a dam across the Haw River at Bynum to provide power for a cotton gin and a gristmill; in 1872 it served a newly built cotton mill as well. Constructed of wood, the dam reached 475 feet across the river at a height of three feet. It formed a ten-acre pond that raised the stream and increased the fall to sixteen feet. The pond also served as a reservoir in the summer when rainfall was scarce. Slightly upstream from the dam, the millrace channeled water down to the mill. The Bynum millrace ran parallel to the river for 600 yards before returning to the river below the factory. At the head of the race a sluice controlled the water's flow, and a turbine housed beneath the mill captured the energy of the water as it surged through the wheelhouse. That energy turned a vertical shaft, which transferred power through a series of gears, belts, and pulleys to the line shafts on the floors above. Other belts and pulleys provided power to individual machines.[7]

Waterpower was a boon to early manufacturers, but, as Alamance mill owner Thomas Holt observed, it was "a poor man's blessing and a rich man's curse." Cheap energy from a river made it possible for men with limited capital to enter the business, but it also hampered production and restricted growth. Few streams could provide enough water in times of drought to keep a mill running all day. When the water got too low, the mill stopped. The natural force of the water's fall also set a limit on the number of machines a given mill could run, while the river itself formed a boundary that prevented the expansion of mill buildings.[8]

These limitations caused most manufacturers to favor steam when it was available. Being more dependable, steam freed the mills from the vagaries of nature and allowed them to locate near urban areas. Steam also made it easier to build large, integrated spinning and weaving operations able to compete on an equal footing with northern firms. As mining companies exploited the rich coal deposits of the southern mountains and railroads reached most urban centers, coal competed successfully with water as a source of energy for Piedmont mills. Small water-powered mills could be found in operation as late as 1930—and many, though unused, still stand today. But by the turn of the century steam had become the power of choice.[9]

The application of electricity gave manufacturers an even cheaper, steadier, and more flexible source of power. In 1893 the Columbia Mills Company in Columbia, South Carolina, became the first textile mill in the United States to run on electricity, drawing power for its generator from the nearby Congaree River. Although a few other mills followed suit, it was not until the Southern Power Company (later Duke Power) began harnessing and distributing hydroelectric power from the Catawba River in 1905 that Piedmont mills had easy access to cheap electricity. By 1910 approximately half of the mills in urban areas like Charlotte and Greenville used electric power. But city mills remained the exception. In the Carolina Piedmont as a whole, three-quarters of all textile factories still ran on water or steam.[10]

Mill design was part function, part fancy. Small, rural mills like the one at Bynum were built of wood and resembled the gristmills with which they shared space on the riverbanks. But after 1880 Piedmont manufacturers increasingly copied northern architectural styles. The Arista Mill in Salem, North Carolina, for example, was erected in 1880 "on the most approved plans of the successful New England cotton mills." Still, mill design had to conform to local conditions. Long and narrow buildings fit the rugged river terrain, and multiple stories allowed for the most efficient transfer of power by means of belts and pulleys. Wood-frame brick-veneer buildings took advantage of a plentiful lumber supply and could easily house light machines, which ran at slow speeds with little vibration.[11]

The mill at Glencoe, North Carolina, still stands as a representative type. The main building of three stories was fifty feet wide and extended 200 feet along the millrace. The mill was simplicity itself, but the ornamental features of the facade spoke of grander aspirations. The stair tower, corbeled cornice, and stuccoed quoins and lintels stood in sharp contrast to the plain form of the Glencoe village and heralded the prosperous world mill owners hoped to create. Such architectural embellishments reflected mill owners' commitment to the ornate styles that adorned their own homes and reinforced their sense of social importance and power.[12]

Whether run by water, steam, or electricity, an integrated mill was designed to move cotton through a precise series of production processes that separated, straightened, and twisted cotton fibers, combined them into yarn, and then wove the yarn into cloth. Manufacturing began in the opening room, where workers removed the ties and bagging from bales of raw cotton. Because of the dust and dirt and the ever-present danger of fire, this room was often located in an adjacent warehouse or in the basement of the mill. The opening machine tore apart the compressed cotton, removing dirt and short fibers. As the cotton was fluffed, a vacuum system carried it through a giant tube to the picker room, where pickers—or lappers as they were also known—continued to clean the cotton and organized it into continuous, even sheets. Card hands then fed these sheets into carding machines, where sharp metal teeth again tore apart the cotton, removed any remaining twigs or dirt, and converted the mass into a continuous sliver, or loosely compacted rope, that coiled into cans.[13]

The fibers in the sliver were almost parallel, but because the cotton tended to twist and curl, it needed more processing. Workers directed four or more slivers through a series of rollers in the head of a drawing frame, where they were combined into a single strand. Since each set of rollers ran at increasing speeds, the drawing frame straightened—or drew out—the sliver and made it thinner. To ensure the permanent union of the fibers, the yarn was then subjected to roving, where it was slightly twisted, and to spinning, where the fibers were wound still more tightly around one other. As bobbins on the spinning frames filled with thread, doffers replaced them with empty ones. The spinner's job was to move quickly up and down a row of machines repairing breaks and snags. "What the spinners have to do," recalled a Bynum worker, "is put the ends up—we call it putting up ends—put this thread up that breaks and falls. You take the end of that thread and you stick it up to where that's coming out between these rollers. It'll twist it and then run on down and keep going."[14]

Spoolers ran machines that combined the thread from ten to fifteen bobbins. Operating a spooling frame was relatively simple, but problems resulted when the threads broke. At this stage broken ends could be repaired only by tying them with a knot rather than simply twisting them together. If a stronger or larger yarn was desired, single threads were twisted together to produce multi-ply yarn. A final step, winding, prepared the yarn for its various uses. It could be wound into balls for sale, put into cops for the weaver to use in the shuttle of a loom, or wound on cones, tubes, cheeses, or reels for later processes in the mill.

The production of cloth began in the weave room. Yarn that ran lengthwise, called warp, was interlaced with yarn running crosswise, called filling or weft. The first step was the preparation of the warp, as workers mounted yarn from the winder on a large frame called a creel. They directed threads from each cone through individual parallel wires onto a rotating beam. The yarn from several beams was combined, dipped into a bath of hot starch and oil, dried over steam-heated drums, and wound onto a giant spool known as a loom beam.

Before weavers placed the beam on a loom, draw-in hands laced each warp thread through individual metal eyes in the harness. The harness raised and lowered threads in the warp, separating them to allow for the introduction of the weft. Mary Thompson, a draw-in hand, explained the operation. "They'd be finer than your hair. We went by a draft or pattern, and the way we drawed it is the way the cloth come out. Back then, there was lots of woven material. There'd be from one thousand ends in the whole pattern to, maybe, I have drawn twenty thousand. Every thread had to be counted. After they got all the looms filled with patterns, they'd tie [additional warps] behind the looms and just keep running the same patterns 'til they changed styles, and then they'd have to be drawn again."[15]

Once "drawing-in" was completed, weavers put the beam and harness on the loom, which could be very simple or very elaborate depending on the type of cloth desired. A simple loom had two harnesses, one that raised a section of the warp and another that lowered a section. The shuttle, which contained the weft, passed between the openings in the warp, and the union of warp and weft was completed as the reed beat the filling back against the previously woven cloth. The harnesses then changed position, and the process continued until the desired length of cloth was produced. This type of loom made simple cloth like sheeting, but more complicated looms produced fabric with an almost infinite variety of patterns and designs.

The level of technological development contrasted sharply with management and labor resources in the region. The antebellum economy's dependence on King Cotton and chattel slavery had retarded the development of industry and discouraged the immigration of experienced workers from Europe, with the result that few southerners had ever seen a factory, much less worked in one. To make up for this lack of skilled labor, nineteenth-century mill owners concentrated on producing coarse yarn and simple weaves. Southern mill men left the production of fine yarn to northern manufacturers, installed Northrop looms more rapidly than their competitors above the Mason-Dixon line, and quickly cornered the growing market in coarse goods.[16]

While technological innovation enabled southern manufacturers to employ less-skilled and less-expensive labor, it also imposed new responsibilities on management. Until the turn of the century, technical training could be acquired only at northern schools or in northern mills. A few southern textile men made the journey north themselves, but most larger mills found it easier at first to recruit experienced technicians and managers from outside the region. Partly as a result, the supervisory structure in southern mills reflected Yankee traditions. Management was in the hands of a superintendent or agent. Overseers coordinated production in each department but relied on "second hands" to discipline workers and on "section men" to repair the machinery. Outsiders, of course, could not fill all the management positions in southern mills; native southerners had to be trained quickly and placed in positions of authority. By the twentieth century the majority of frontline supervisors had risen through the ranks.[17]

The opportunity to buy modern equipment, combined with the scarcity of skilled male workers and the availability of women and children, encouraged southern mill men to adopt a system of labor that harkened back to the industry's early days. In the beginning of the nineteenth century northern manufacturers had developed two very different strategies for building mills and securing a labor force. In southern New England entrepreneurs organized small spinning mills according to the Rhode Island or family labor system. Relying exclusively on waterpower, employing large numbers of children, and concentrating on the spinning of yarn, these mills coexisted with domestic cloth making. Farther north, a consortium of Boston merchants built their own version of the power loom and integrated the spinning and weaving processes into a single operation. These mills relied on the famous Lowell or boardinghouse system to attract a work force made up of farmers' daughters from the surrounding countryside.[18]

Despite scattered experiments with boardinghouses for single girls, southern mill owners quickly settled on the family labor system. Rather than hiring individual workers, owners purchased family labor as a package, paying adult workers less than a living wage and offering employment to children. A "dodger" distributed in the North Carolina mountains in the early twentieth century contained a typical appeal.

> The Pacolet Manufacturing Company, of Pacolet, S.C., can furnish steady employment for over 300 days in the year for boys and girls over 12 years old, men and women at average wages, as follows:
>
> > Experienced 12 to 16-year old boys and girls from $.50 to $1.25.
> > Experienced boys and girls over 16, and men and women, $.75 to $1.50
> > Old men, 60 to 70 years old, $.75 to $1.
>
> We want whole families with at least three workers for the mill in each family.[19]

In this way, mills attracted a core of mature workers at low cost along with younger, and even cheaper, laborers who could perform simple tasks and move in and out of the mills in response to market fluctuations. The sad state of southern agriculture pushed whole families into the labor market just at the time when the ring spinning frame and other technological advancements were creating a demand for unskilled labor and making its use very profitable.[20]

With a work force in place, manufacturers had assembled the human and technical resources needed to manufacture yarn and cloth. Yet each component of this industrial enterprise presented problems. The river might be too high or too low to power the mill; the cotton fibers might be too short for spinning; badly adjusted looms might produce too many "seconds." But no ingredient was more challenging than the human element. In a business sense, workers were like any other factor of production—a commodity to be purchased as cheaply and used as efficiently as possible. But experience proved that mill-hands could not be "driven." Owners depended on workers to master their jobs and labor cooperatively with supervisors and with one another. Otherwise, goods could not be produced, profits could not be realized, and wages could not be paid. Manufacturers held the upper hand, but both sides had to acknowledge the other's needs in shaping life on the shop floor.

First-generation workers in southern mills had more to learn than just the mechanics of a new job. On the farm they had chosen and ordered their tasks according to their needs and the demands of their crops. Now they drove themselves to the continuous pace of a machine. Whereas most men, women, and children had once worked together and enjoyed the fruits of their own labor, now they were "hands," working under a boss's orders and for someone else's profit. Farm work, to be sure, had been hard, but mill work took a different toll. Millhands rose early in the morning, still tired from the day before. For ten, eleven, or twelve hours they walked, stretched, leaned, and pulled at their machines. Noise, heat, and humidity engulfed them. The lint that settled on their hair and skin marked them as mill workers, and the cotton dust that silently entered their lungs could eventually cripple or kill them. At best, mill work was a wrenching change.

Chester Copeland came from a long line of farmers and carpenters in rural Orange County, North Carolina, and he remained a devoted farmer except for brief, and unhappy, sojourns in the mills. To him, mill work was "nothing but a robot life. Robot-ing is my word for it—in the mill you do the same thing over and over again—just like on a treadmill. There's no challenge to it—just drudgery. The more you do, the more they want done. But in farming you do work real close to nature. There's always something exciting and changing in nature. It's never a boring job. There's some dirty jobs in farming, but there's nothing you get more pleasure out of than planting, growing, and then harvesting. In other words, you get the four seasons just like there are in a person's life—the fall and winter and spring and summer."[21]

Despite this loss of control, most workers stayed with the factory because it provided a steady income and the work seemed easier than farming, at least to some. Forrest Lacock found farming "a very

Workers at the Franklinville Manufacturing Company, Franklinville, North Carolina, 1892. Photograph by George Russell, mill superintendent.
(Courtesy of Mac Whatley, Franklinville, N.C.)

satisfactory job—you've got no boss man." "But," he continued, "the trouble with what we call one-horse farming, you can't have an income sufficient to take care of all your bills. A public job is more interesting because you can meet your bills." Dewey Helms's father had another reason for coming to the mill. "He wasn't worried about the income he made on the farm; he made as much as he cared about. He wanted to get rid of the harder work. Working in the cotton mill was not as hard work as running one of them mountain farms." Mill work was not for everybody, but the majority of those who came to the factories "never did want to live on the farm no more. They learned how to work in the mill."[22]

Reliance on the family labor system meant that the southern textile industry's growth was based to a large extent on the labor of children. Between 1880 and 1910 manufacturers reported that about one-quarter of their work force was under sixteen years of age, and many more child workers went unreported. Indeed, in the industry's early years, youngsters of seven or eight commonly doffed, spun, and did all sorts of casual labor. Originally the official definition of "children" applied to youngsters up to age eight but later rose to age twelve, then fourteen, and finally sixteen; nevertheless, young people remained crucial, both to the industry's profit margins and to their own families' survival.[23]

Child labor was by no means unique to the South. The textile industry, wherever established, tended to rely on the labor of women and children. But the technical breakthroughs that enabled the South to enter and eventually capture the market in cotton goods also encouraged a particularly intense exploitation of the young. Women and children led the first wave of migrants to the region's mills, and manufacturers matched them with the low-skill jobs created by the advent of ring spinning. A study of women and children laborers conducted by the U.S. Bureau of Labor in 1907–8 found that half the spinners were under fourteen and 90 percent were under twenty-one. As Naomi Trammel put it, "That's where they put the children. You could run a frame where you couldn't run anything else."[24]

Technology made child labor practical, but not necessary. The practice spread primarily as a solution to problems of labor recruitment and as a system of socializing and controlling a prospective labor force. South Carolina industrialist William Gregg, founder of Graniteville, the Old South's premier cotton mill, had hoped to attract the daughters of impoverished farmers. Young single women failed to

Doffers at the Bibb Mill No. 1, Macon, Georgia, 1909.
Photograph by Lewis Hine.
(Courtesy of the National Archives and Records Service)

show up in large numbers, but Gregg continued to believe that the "large class of miserable poor white people among us . . . might be induced to place their children in a situation in which they would be educated and reared in industrious habits." His words captured the industry rationale: children made up a large portion of the surplus labor in the countryside; the lure of wages for everyone in the family could induce hard-pressed farmers to cast their lot with the mills; and children who went to work at an early age would eventually grow into efficient, tractable, long-term workers.[25]

Critics of child labor were not hard to find. In the 1880s and 1890s the opposition was led by the Knights of Labor and the National Union of Textile Workers (NUTW), who complained that the low wages paid to children held down the earnings of adults. But after the turn of the century a new group of middle-class social reformers took up the banner of the child labor crusade. Educational and religious leaders such as Alabama's Edgar Gardner Murphy and North Carolina's Alexander J. McKelway organized opposition at the state level and then helped form the National Child Labor Committee (NCLC).

These reformers worried that the mills' unlettered children would one day become a blight on the body politic. "In a democracy," Mc-Kelway argued, "the people all rule. Also, the people are ruled. And when it comes to the people's ruling us by their votes, electing our governors and presidents, initiating and vetoing legislation, taxing our incomes, we grow mightily concerned over the intelligence and independence of the electorate. We do not like to trust our interests now and the lives and fortunes of our children to a mass of voters who have been deprived of all opportunity for an education . . . who have been embittered by the robbery of their childhood, who are the material for the agitator, and the prey of the demagogue."[26]

Mill men themselves were divided on the issue of child labor. Some firmly believed that hard work, commencing at a young age, was the best education available. Others championed the practice as a necessary evil in the natural progress of society. Daniel Augustus Tompkins traced the problem to the poverty caused by the Civil War, particularly to the resultant lack of educational opportunities. "In the absence of schools, the discipline of the mill and its training down to twelve years of age is much better for children than idleness and no discipline or training. . . . It would be far better to have ample school facilities and compel all children to go to school ten months in the year, and give them the other two months for vacations and recreation. But in the absence of such facilities, the discipline and training of the mill is best for the children of working people." Whatever the personal feelings of mill men, their duties to their stockholders demanded that they oppose restrictions on the employment of children. The fact of the matter, as the president of the American Cotton Manufacturers Association admitted to McKelway, was that without the labor of boys and girls under the age of fourteen, Piedmont mills simply could not operate.[27]

Bit by bit, reformers chipped away at the opposition. By 1913 North Carolina, South Carolina, Alabama, and Georgia had laws that prohibited the employment of children under twelve and restricted the hours of labor for those below fourteen. Exemptions and lack of enforcement, however, enfeebled state regulations. The 1907–8 Bureau of Labor study found that an astounding 92 percent of the mills in South Carolina and 75 percent of those in North Carolina ignored child labor regulations. Flora McKinney's boss was one of those who paid little attention to the law. Her family moved to Lando, South Carolina, when she was nine or ten, and she soon followed her father into the mill. "When I got old enough, well, I really weren't old enough, but they'd take children to work then. We were supposed to be twelve years old before we could go to work, but I've hid from inspectors a lots of times. They'd come through and the section in front of us would send word to hide the kids, and we'd run to the water house. Then we'd all cram in there 'til they left."[28]

Given the inadequacy of state legislation, members of the NCLC felt the need for federal action. To mobilize public opinion against child labor, the NCLC devised a highly effective propaganda campaign. Key to this effort were the photographs of Lewis Hine, which poignantly revealed the youthfulness of southern workers. Hines's images—of little girls dressed in long skirts and aprons and little boys wearing their workingmen's caps and suspenders, all swallowed up in rows of towering machines—became the crusade's symbols of the worst evils of industrialization. The NCLC convinced the public and members of Congress that the employment of children had to be stopped. In 1916 President Woodrow Wilson signed the Keating-Owen Child Labor bill to achieve that end.[29]

Adamantly opposed to federal intervention, which might open the way to other protective laws and undermine their competitive advantage over the North, southern industrialists fought back. When federal child labor legislation was first suggested, David Clark, editor of the *Southern Textile Bulletin*, organized mill owner opposition. The son of Walter Clark, who was chief justice of the North Carolina Supreme Court and one of the South's most liberal jurists, David Clark seemed an unlikely opponent of progressive reform. But as a young man, Clark embarked on a course quite different from his father's. After earning degrees in civil and mechanical engineering from the North Carolina College of Agriculture and Mechanic Arts and Cornell University in the late 1890s, David entered the textile business, first as a mill designer and later as an investor. When his own mill failed in 1907, he turned to textile journalism. As founder and editor of the *Southern Textile Bulletin*, Clark gained a reputation as "a volunteer spokesman for an ultra-conservative philosophy in business and education matters" and "a stirrer-upper of no mean proportions." Shortly after passage of the Keating-Owen bill, he arranged to test the constitutionality of the law. At Clark's behest, a Charlotte mill worker—perhaps fearful of losing his job, his children's earnings, or a combination of the two—petitioned the courts to restrain a local mill from discharging his two underage sons. A federal judge agreed that the law violated the rights of the worker, and a year later the Supreme Court concurred. The child labor law was dead.[30]

Despite this setback, child labor gradually did decline, largely in response to changes in the industry and the growing supply of adult workers. The trend toward finer yarns, the integration of yarn spinning with cloth-weaving operations that required more strength and skill, and the technological advances of the 1920s all worked against the practice. By World War I the number of children under sixteen employed in the Carolinas had decreased to 6 percent of the total work force, almost the level in the leading New England textile states. Yet until 1938, when the federal Fair Labor Standards Act outlawed employment of children under sixteen, many southern industrialists skirted the law so as to make use of the mill village's young, and captive, work force.[31]

Child labor involved more, however, than the exploitation of youth. There were stories behind the expressions captured on film by Lewis Hine, stories that fit neither the rationalizations of mill owners nor the fears of reformers. Mill work was a source of pride as well as pain, of fun as much as suffering; and children made choices, however hedged about by their parents' authority and their bosses' power.

For mill children, life was paced from the outset by the ringing of the factory bell. Working women, who often had to return to their jobs within a few weeks of childbirth, adapted their nursing schedule to breaks in the workday. "People used to go out," recalled Ada Mae Wilson. "They didn't have bottle babies like they do now. They nursed the breast. A lot healthier children. You'd come out at nine o'clock, and then at twelve you'd come home for lunch. And then at three they'd let you come back, and then you'd be off at six." If labor was scarce, a woman who had neither relatives nor older children at home might take her baby to the mill. Jessie Lee Carter had a neighbor with a nursing baby who would "take a quilt and lay that baby in her roping box while she worked. And she'd bring her baby down and keep it in the mill all day long."[32]

As children got older, the mill was like a magnet, attracting their youthful curiosity and, all too soon, their labor. Until the 1920s no barbed wire fences, locked gates, or bricked-in windows separated the factory from the village. Children could easily wander in and out of the mill, and their first "work" might be indistinguishable from play. After school and in the summers, Emma Williams accompanied her mother to the mill. "I'm sure I didn't work for the money. I just wanted to work, I reckon. Oodles of kids. All of us used to do it together. [We] didn't do much, and it was real fun. I guess maybe one reason that it was fun was because that was the only time we got with other children. When we stayed home, well, we stayed home."[33]

Most children first learned about factory labor when they tagged along with a parent or sibling, carried hot meals to the mill at dinnertime, or stopped by after school. But this casual contact had serious consequences, for on such visits relatives began teaching children the skills they would need when they were old enough for jobs of their own. Ethel Faucette carried lunch to her sister. "While she was eating," Faucette explained, "I learned how to work her job. I was already learned when I went to work." Geddes Dodson's father gave him specific chores during his daily visits. "When I was a little fellow, my daddy was a-working in the Poinsett Mill. He was a loom fixer. He'd run the weavers' looms through the dinner hour so they could go eat their dinner. We lived about a mile and a quarter from the mill, and I'd carry his lunch every day. He'd tell me to come on in the mill, and he made me fill his batteries while he run the weavers' looms—and I was just a little fellow. See, I knew a whole lot about the mill before I ever went in one."[34]

"Helping," then, was a family affair, a form of apprenticeship by which basic skills and habits were transmitted to each new generation. But helping was also a vital part of the family economy and the mill labor system. A child's help could increase a parent's or older sibling's piecework earnings or simply relieve the strain of keeping up production. An Englishman who reported on the American textile industry visited a mill in South Carolina where weavers who had their sons or little brothers helping could take on two additional looms. Besides, with parents working twelve-hour days in the mills, children often had no place else to go. Owners profited from such family needs. Early child labor legislation in the Carolinas only prohibited "employing" children under certain ages, so owners could stay within the letter of the law by "permitting" or "suffering" underage children to "help." A story related by a federal investigator in Georgia illustrated the system's coercive potential. "A woman reported that her little daughter ten years old worked every day helping her sisters. The child quit for a while, but the overseer said to the mother, 'Bring her in; the two girls cannot tend those machines without her.' The mother asked that the child be given work by herself, but the overseer replied that the law would not permit it."[35]

Given the laxity of enforcement, mill owners could essentially set their own policies according to individual conscience or the bottom line of profit and loss. Allie Smith provided a child's-eye view of the confusion that often resulted. Shortly after Allie's birth, her family moved to Saxapahaw, a community in Alamance County on the Haw River. By the time they left for Carrboro, in neighboring Orange County, when Allie was eleven, she knew how to spin from having helped an older sister. But Julian Shakespeare Carr, owner of the Carrboro mill, believed that mill men should voluntarily avoid child labor in order to stave off government interference. "When we moved to Carrboro," Allie recalled, "I thought I could go in and help her, and I did. But Mr. Carr owned this cotton mill, and I hadn't been over here long when he came over and said I couldn't come in and help. I would have to be on the payroll, so they put me on the payroll. And I worked there, I don't know how long—several months—and they said I couldn't work unless my father signed me up for being twelve years old. Well, he wouldn't do it. He said he didn't want me to work. They put me out and wouldn't let me work. And then when I got to be twelve, I went in and went to work."[36]

Playing and helping could thus shade into full-time work. But getting that first official, full-time job was a major turning point. Managers, parents, and children themselves influenced the decision. Occasionally, mills openly dictated the age at which a child had to begin work. In 1904 the owners of a South Carolina mill mandated that "all children, members of a family above twelve years of age, shall work in the mill and shall not be excused from service therein without the consent of the superintendent for good cause." More often, pressure came from supervisors, who were personally responsible for keeping a quota of workers on hand. Jessie Lee Carter was four in 1905 when her family left their Tennessee farm for the Brandon Mill in Greenville. Six of her older brothers and sisters went to work right away; eight years later Jessie joined them. "When I got twelve years old, my uncle [who was a second hand in the spinning room] come to my daddy, and daddy let me quit school and go to work." During slack times children like Jessie Lee could be sent back to school, then called in again when the need arose.[37]

For a large family with many mouths to feed, outside pressure was often unnecessary. Lela Ranier's parents took her out of school when she was twelve and sent her to the mill. "Ma thought it was time. They thought maybe it would help 'em out, you know. They was making such a little bit. And they thought the little bit I made would help." Lacy Wright's father asked him to quit school when he reached twelve because his two oldest sisters had married and Lacy's father could not support the family on $1.25 a day. Other children realized the importance of their labor to the family's well-being and took it upon themselves to get a job. This was particularly true in families where the father was dead or disabled. Grover Hardin, for example, dropped out of school after the second grade. "I started out in the mill—the main reason—to help my mother. She wanted me to go to school until I got in the fifth grade. I told her, 'You need the help worse than I need the education, because I can get it later on, or I can do without it.' And so I went to work as quick as I possibly could. I started in as a sweeper."[38]

Many parents wanted their children to stay in school, but youngsters often had their own plans. Ila Dodson insisted on quitting school when she was fourteen. "I wanted to make my own money. I done had two sisters go to work, and I seen how they was having money, and so I couldn't stand it no longer. My parents wanted me to go on to school, but I couldn't see that. Back then, didn't too many children go on to high school. It was just a common thing that when they'd get old enough, let them go to work. I like to worried them to death." Finally, Ila's parents relented and agreed to sign her worker's permit, required at that time in South Carolina for children under sixteen. But, she recalled, "Mama wouldn't even take me to town to get it, and my daddy wouldn't go with me. I said, 'Well, give me the Bible and give me a dime and I'll go get it.' A nickel streetcar fare up there and a nickel back, and I [took] the Bible because I had to prove my age."[39]

Alice Evitt and Curtis Enlow also preferred mill work to schoolwork. "They'd let you go in there seven, eight years old," Alice recalled. "I'd go in there and mess around with my sisters; they'd be spinning. I liked to put up the ends and spin a little bit, so when I got twelve years old, I wanted to quit school. So I just quit and went to work, and I was twelve years old!" Both of Curtis's parents and two of his sisters worked in the card room at a Greenville mill. During summer vacation Curtis joined them there. "I was about thirteen years old, and I decided I would go to work. Well, I went to work, and my dad says if I quit when school started, he'd let me work. I went back to school, but I wasn't learning nothing—I didn't think I was. So I went and told him, and he says, 'All right, you ain't learning nothing. Well, you can go back to the mill.'"[40]

Mamie Shue's parents had better luck keeping her in school. Although North Carolina's compulsory education law at the time required attendance only until age fourteen, Mamie's folks used it to frighten her into staying in school until she was sixteen. "I hated school all my life. But my parents told me if I didn't go to school, they'd put my daddy in jail. And I loved my daddy to death. So I went to school 'til I was sixteen." She did, however, start working after school in the spooling room. "I was fifteen when I started doing that. So when I was sixteen years old, they just give me a job, 'cause I could spool as good as the rest of them."[41]

Learning to "spool as good as the rest of them" was often a by-product of helping in the mills, but for those who had not started out as helpers—and even for some who had—learning constituted a memorable initiation into shop floor life. Few mills had a formal training program. Instead, "they would put you with someone to train you," or "your parents would take you in and train you theirself." Parents and surrogate parents took time out from their own work, which sometimes cost money out of their pockets, to help the young learn a trade. "That's the way the whole generation in Lando learned what they knowed," remembered John Guinn, "by the older generation." From the evidence of our interviews, adults did so willingly and well.[42]

Mill managers expected children to master their jobs within a set length of time, usually about six weeks. During that period children worked for free or for a token wage. "I don't think they paid us anything to learn. But after we learnt, we got a job, a machine of our own." Some mills used this probationary period to take advantage of young people who were eager to work in the mill. Mary Thompson saw this happen in Greenville. "When I first went to work at Slater, they had boys to put up the warps on the back of the frames because they was heavy. They'd go out there in the country and get them boys and hire them and tell them they'd have to work six weeks without money. Well, that just tickled them to death, that they'd get a chance to work in a mill. And they'd work them six weeks, and they'd find something wrong with them and lay them off, and get other boys. And they run it a long time like that."[43]

Almost all workers recalled proudly their ability to learn their jobs despite their youth. Naomi Trammell was an orphan when she went to work in the Victor Mill at Greer, South Carolina. "Well, I didn't know hardly about mill work, but I just went in and had to learn it. Really, I had to crawl up on the frame, because I wasn't tall enough. I was a

Learning to spin, ca. 1910. Photograph by Lewis Hine.
(Courtesy of the Archives of Labor and Urban Affairs, Wayne State University)

little old spindly thing. I wasn't the only one, there's a whole place like
that. And they had mothers and daddies [but they] wasn't no better off
than I was. They had to learn us, but it didn't take me long to learn.
They'd put us with one of the spinners and they'd show us how. It was
easy to learn—all we had to do was just put that bobbin in there and
put it up." Children learned quickly because most entry-level jobs
required more dexterity than technical know-how. It took a while to be
proficient, but most children could learn the rudiments of spinning,
spooling, or doffing in a few weeks.[44]

To an outsider, any job in a cotton mill might seem much like any
other—dirty, tedious, and tiring—but there were a few highly prized
positions to which workers could aspire. While job promotions meant
little in terms of status outside the mill, even small improvements were
important in the largely self-contained world of the factory. When mill
workers reached their late teens, they began giving some thought to
the future, calculating their chances to "get ahead and get a better
job." No written rules dictated who could seek a promotion or how to
go about it. But family connections clearly influenced the prospects

for advancement; an overseer or second hand was more likely to give a chance to a son, daughter, niece, or nephew than to someone who was unrelated. The tendency was to keep workers in the department in which they began, so the location of a worker's first job was also crucial. A millhand who started out in a spinning room, for example, had little opportunity to become a weaver. The state of the economy also had its effects, for with boom times came the possibility of moving up by moving to a new mill. Above all, though, race and gender determined the paths of advancement.[45]

The most striking feature of the labor system in southern mills was the exclusion of blacks from "production jobs." Slaves had worked in the spinning and weaving rooms of antebellum factories. But when slave prices rose during the cotton boom of the 1850s, manufacturers turned to poor white farmers for cheaper labor. After the Civil War textiles became a white domain. The promotion of the mills as the salvation of poor whites, the taboo against bringing black men into association with white women, the desire to tie blacks to agricultural labor, the substitution of whites for blacks in a range of skilled and semiskilled jobs, the deepening of segregation in every walk of life— all these factors conspired to limit black opportunities in the textile industry.[46]

By and large, occupational segregation was accomplished informally. But South Carolina wrote custom into law. The Segregation Act of 1915, making it illegal for anyone "engaged in the business of cotton textile manufacturing . . . to allow. . . operatives . . . of different races to labor and work together within the same room," stayed on the books until 1960. The law, however, had a second clause that excluded a whole range of non-machine-tending jobs. This left owners a good deal of leeway, and long before employment barriers fell in the 1960s, manufacturers were paying blacks rock-bottom wages to perform essential tasks in the mills.[47]

In many mills, the dirtiest and heaviest work went to black men. They labored in the "yard," moving bales of cotton and loading boxcars and wagons with finished goods. They also worked in the opening and picker rooms. Noise Crockett spent many years in the mill at Lando. He remembered there "wasn't nothing in the picker room but the colored. The onliest white man in there was the boss man." T. B. Fitzgerald, president of Riverside Mills in Danville, summed up his company's policy. "As regards colored people, we only employ them as sweepers, scourers, truck drivers, and in the dye house and picker rooms: we do not have them in the mills proper, except in the above-mentioned menial capacities." Opportunities for black women were even more limited. In many places they simply "were not allowed to work in the mill." When they did find employment, Jessie Lee Carter remembered, "they cleaned out the bathroom and the moppings on the floor."[48]

While black women were shut out altogether, white women were welcomed with open arms. Spinning operations claimed most of the mills' early recruits, so the preponderance of women and children in the initial migration dovetailed nicely with manufacturers' need for cheap, unskilled labor. Weavers required more training, but even in the weave room young women were in demand. "Whenever I see a strong, robust country girl," admitted Samuel Patterson, a young mill superintendent who would go on to become one of North Carolina's leading industrialists, "I am almost on my knees in my effort to try to get her to go to the mill to learn to weave." This preference for young women had tangled roots, but foremost among them was the profit motive: women's wages were about 60 percent of men's.[49]

On the shop floor, women found themselves channeled into sex-typed jobs. According to Mack Duncan, "There's some jobs that women could run, some that's always been classed for men. Loom fixers in the weave room has always been men. And usually the weavers were either man or woman. It's always been that way with weaving. But now spinners in the spinning room, they were all women. No man wanted to spin. Men weren't going to spin; that was it." A worker from Bynum remembered that a similar division prevailed there. "Winding and spinning, that was mostly the women's jobs. Now once in a while when they would be real short of help, they would have some of the men spinning. But there's not too many men that like to spin. I guess because they thought it was a woman's job." In comparison to more prestigious, better-paying occupations, textiles treated men and women with a relatively even hand. Still, distinctions were made and rigidly observed. Men and women's work lives were separate but overlapping—like the warp and weft itself.[50]

The sexual division of labor in southern mills was grounded in the family labor system. Having purchased women's labor as part of the family package, owners designed a system of job assignments based on hierarchies of sex and age that were familiar both on the farm and in many cotton mills elsewhere. Behind these job assignments were assumptions embedded in the culture that laborers and owners

Men opening bales of cotton at the White Oak Mill in Greensboro, North Carolina, 1907. This was one of the few cotton mill jobs available to blacks.
(Courtesy of Robert Vogel, National Museum of American History)

shared. Children of both sexes were at the bottom of the pyramid, charged with the lowest-paying, most routine tasks. Women's age-old responsibilities for child care and domestic tasks fed the notion that they were patient, neat, careful workers; their deft, nimble fingers seemed self-evidently suited to fast-moving repetitive machines. Men, accustomed to doing field work and heading farms, were supposed to be strong and authoritative; jobs that were "heavy" or involved authority over others belonged to them. Moreover, men were expected to be long-term workers, so a lengthy training period for them would pay the mill back in skilled work over the years. This system allowed male workers to maintain their privileged positions. It also helped owners match a heterogeneous work force to a variety of jobs and hold the line on men's wages.[51]

Once established, this pattern became accepted wisdom and persisted even as the family labor system faded away. Before World War I the typical female laborer was either a widow working until her children could take her place in the mill or a young woman earning an income until she could marry and start a family of her own. Under such circumstances, treating women as "unskilled workers" not only fit popular custom, it also had the appearance of good economic sense. With the decline of child labor, however, adult women returned to the mills to stay. In 1920 the majority of women workers were between the ages of fifteen and twenty-four; in 1940 they were between twenty-five and forty-four. Women became committed, lifetime workers, but they were still denied opportunities by a labor system created generations before.[52]

Except for the presence of doffer boys, the spinning room remained, as it began, a female realm. By contrast, entry-level jobs in the card room were reserved for boys. It was hardly a privilege to sweep and clean amid the dust and dangerous machines, but these jobs served as apprenticeships for the carding room's better-paying positions. For that reason, and because of the skill and physical strength required, carding became a "man's job." As the cotton moved through the drawing and roving processes, the tasks required less training but still demanded a degree of physical strength. Stronger women, usually ones who had experience in the spinning room, could be found alongside men in these operations, but not in large numbers.

Weaving was the one job in the mill where men and women worked together under more or less equal conditions. The weaver had to possess a quick, deft touch in tying broken warp threads and an ability to keep watch over a number of machines. Because adult workers were a scarce commodity in the early mills, it would have been difficult to reserve the weave room for either men or women exclusively. Custom maintained this relative equality, and over the years the ratio of men to women in the weave room generally reflected that of the mill as a whole. In one respect men had an advantage. Pauline Griffith remembered that it helped to be tall, because rather than having to "climb up on the loom to draw an end in," a tall weaver "could reach over and get it real quick." Mack Duncan also believed that size was an advantage. "Years ago, the short man had to walk around the loom, maybe go two or three looms to get to the back of the loom to repair

Card room hands at the Franklinville Manufacturing Company, Franklinville,
North Carolina, 1916. Photograph by George Russell, mill superintendent.
(Courtesy of Mac Whatley, Franklinville, N.C.)

the damage that had been done to the thread. A tall man could reach
through and maybe tie it without making the steps around the machine." But other attributes also counted—skill, motivation, and will.
"There was a lot of people that couldn't weave," Mack Duncan continued. "They couldn't make a go of it. It seemed like they couldn't
use their hands as well. And a lot of people said it was just too hard
work." What made a good weaver was a combination of speed, dexterity, and size, along with the determination to stick with the job—
attributes found in both men and women.[53]

The greatest barrier women faced in the mill was the male monopoly on machine-fixing and supervisory jobs. Boys aspired to be
fixers because of the curiosity, self-confidence, and manual skill they
presumably acquired as a "natural" part of growing up and because it
was the best-paying job. In turn, adult fixers expected boys, not girls,
to be mechanically inclined and gave them the training that led to that

*Men and women weaving at the White Oak Mill in
Greensboro, North Carolina, 1909.*
(Courtesy of Robert Vogel, National Museum of American History)

coveted role. Such self-perpetuating expectations effectively barred women from formal machine-fixing jobs. But mechanically inclined or not, women who spent years in the mill (and whose piecework earnings depended on a machine's good repair) could build up a significant fund of informal knowledge. Late in her career Eula Durham had a run-in with a young supervisor. One of her spinning frames was broken, and she told the supervisor what she thought was wrong. He disagreed and did not do anything about it. "After he went home," she remembered, "I stopped the frame off and went in the basement and got me a chain and come back and put it on. Started the frame up and it run just as pretty as you ever seen. I told them I've been down there forty-five years; I know when anything was running right and when it weren't. Cause weren't a frame in that mill I hadn't tore down and put back together. I know exactly what's the matter with them."[54]

Similarly, women who taught younger workers the ropes of a new job called on informal managing skills. But the taboo against giving women supervisory power over men was even stronger than the association between men and mastery of the machine. Indeed, fixing was men's work in part because fixers often had supervisory responsibilities and because the job could serve as a springboard to being a second hand or overseer. There is no evidence that owners ever considered giving female workers authority over men; nor is there evidence that women asked for such promotions. Blan Kilpatrick of Kannapolis, North Carolina, explained why: "Back then, if we had demanded to be supervisors or anything like that, we would have been laughed right out of there."[55]

The effects of this division of labor shaped the course of a working life. When young people first entered the mills, girls had the advantage. Because spooling, winding, and spinning required more skill than doffing and sweeping, girls usually made more money than boys. That edge, however, was short-lived. If a boy stayed in the mill past his mid-teens, he began moving up to positions held by his father or older brothers. From the outset most girls worked alongside women, and they remained on those jobs as long as they stayed in the mill.[56]

Such disparities in opportunity affected the attitudes men and women brought to their work. The impact of technology was to reduce the skill and autonomy of most jobs. But textile workers of all stripes had more in common with their craft-conscious ancestors than meets the eye. To be sure, they did not own their own tools, they could not control access to their occupations, and they were less likely than their predecessors to take an artisan's pride in the fruits of their labor. But that did not prevent them from identifying with their work and making the most of the possibilities it offered. Men often found pride in acquiring new skills and in taking small steps up the job ladder. Women deepened the skills they learned early on, took advantage of small openings for advancement, and wrung satisfaction from their friendships at work and from their role in their families' survival.[57]

Paul Cline started out sweeping floors in the weave rooms at the Slater Mill in Greenville, but he wasn't content. "I was always looking to try and get ahead and get a better job. I was just young, kept my eyes and ears open. Doffing cloth paid a nickel more an hour, so I got a job a-doffing cloth. Then I hauled filling a while. When I caught up—the jobs wasn't stretched out like they are now—I kept watching people [to see] how to start up looms. I always tried to learn something more. I got to wanting to learn how to weave. I'd run these women's looms while they was going to eat their lunch, or go to the bathrooms. [The supervisors] got to watching me [and] I went to weaving."[58]

An uncle got Baxter Holman his first job at the Hanes mill outside Winston-Salem. Since he was black, his prospects for promotion were limited, but he made the most of available opportunities. "I started off working with a woman scrubbing in the mill, scrubbing floors and different things. I was pretty swift, so the yard foreman wanted me out there unloading cotton. I stayed on the yard for ten years and finally a job of running a machine came open in the opening room. After a number of years I got a chance to move up to the picker room."[59]

Because he was white, Baxter Merritt could combine a "habit of not staying in one place too long" with a gradual move up the ladder in the card room. After starting out as a sweeper in the spinning room, he got transferred. "I started to running drawing in the card room. Then I moved up to the slubbers. See, back then you could learn up on one job as you worked on your job. Then [I went] from the slubbers to the intermediates. I kept moving up; didn't stay on a job too long. Then intermediates to speeders. After I done all that, I started to fixing— running sections in the card room, and that's what I ended up doing as long as I worked."[60]

Geddes Dodson's experience filling batteries for his father was the beginning of his advancement in the weave room. After a period of odd jobs in the spinning room, he was assigned to sweeping in the weave room. His father, a loom fixer, made him a reed hook out of a coffee spoon and taught him to draw in broken threads. Then he learned to tie a weaver's knot. "Nobody didn't teach me how to weave. I just watched the weavers." When the second hand found out he could weave, Geddes got a set of looms a couple hours a day. Soon they became his own. The movement from weaver to loom fixer proved more difficult, but Geddes kept on "watching people." "There was some old loom fixers down there, and I picked it up from them. I'd ask them questions and help them do things and run their job. After I got learned, them old men would come to me and ask me questions." In addition to on-the-job training, the mill where Geddes worked held classes at night for prospective loom fixers. "We didn't get paid to learn to fix looms like they do now, these young folks. We was a-working ten hours a day, and we'd go back down there at night and work."[61]

With few exceptions, the men we interviewed recounted proudly the skills they had acquired in the mill. This was understandable in the case of fixers and supervisors, but even workers who never advanced beyond machine-tending jobs had a detailed knowledge of the technical operations of their machines and the part their work played in the complete production process. Martin Lowe said he "always did like to work with machinery. I'd just get behind them when they were running and study them, see what effect one part took on the other. That's the reason I learned so quick."[62]

In the weave room, where women's opportunities most closely approximated men's, a few women had a chance to enjoy this sense of skill. Indeed, the weave room brought women as well as men a rare independence. Mary Thompson started spooling and creeling during the summers when she was fourteen. Two years later she married, quit school, and "went to the draw-in room and learned to draw in. My sister drawed in, and she was the one that taught me. Drawing-in was piecework; they paid you so much for a warp. Now anyone that come in there and didn't have nobody to teach them, had to pay somebody to teach them. They wouldn't hire you unless you could hire someone to teach you, because it was expensive to teach anyone. It'd take more skill. And the bosses couldn't teach you that, because they didn't know it theirself. He could see how it was supposed to be done and all like that, but he couldn't have sat down and done it hisself. [This] was fancy work. They have got plain work, but it wasn't too hard to teach people plain work, because that was just drawing straight threads through. They paid you so much for a warp, so I got pay from the start. Of course, I was slow and I didn't make very much. When your speed picks up, you make more and more.

"I loved drawing-in. I enjoyed it more than anything I've done. I tell you, lots of people would complain about the work, but honest to goodness, I'd rather draw in than eat when I was hungry. I liked piecework the best. That gives you more incentive to get more interested in your work, to see how much you can do. I was always up to working late, getting in all the work I could. It was all piecework, and if I drawed in fast, I made more money. Somebody else fool around and go to the bathroom or sit around and talk and such as that. Why, they just lost their money. But I was out for getting all the money I could

Women drawing in at the White Oak Mill in Greensboro, North Carolina, 1909.
(Courtesy of Robert Vogel, National Museum of American History)

get. I really loved it. The only thing I ever done in my life that I really loved."[63]

Mary Thompson's attitude was certainly not representative of the views of the majority of women mill workers, but then neither was her job. Skilled draw-in hands were much in demand throughout the Piedmont because mills needed their services every time they changed patterns. This gave women like Mary Thompson, whose husband left her shortly after their marriage, unusual autonomy. "If a place wanted draw-in hands, they'd call a company that had draw-in hands and ask them if they'd have one to come. One company would call another, that's the way it went. I had a little girl, but she stayed at my mother's most of the time, so I was free to go. I could make more money like that. I worked for several companies in Virginia, North Carolina, South Carolina, and Tennessee. Most of them was wanting fancy, because it didn't pay them to learn a bunch of people. It took special drawing-in hands for the fancy, on account of it's harder to do. It was cheaper to pay our way—they'd pay our way there and our expenses and then pay us a salary—than it was to teach a draw-in hand."[64]

Other women, particularly those who worked in the spinning and winding departments, had few opportunities to learn the more technical jobs, and they tailored their aspirations accordingly. Mary Auton saw no sense in wasting her energy on learning how to run different machines since there was no extra money involved. "Winding—I never done anything else in my life. That's the only thing I wanted to do, because I didn't know how to do nothing else and I didn't want to learn. If you learn to do different things, they'll change you around. I wanted to know what I had to do when I went in in the morning." Mamie McCorkle worked as a spinner from the time she was eight or nine until she retired at sixty-five. Nevertheless, she gained a measure of satisfaction from being able to take on more machines. "I never did work myself up no better. [But] I got to where I could run more sides. I got up to eight sides and that was pretty good. You make more money that way." For Icy Norman, a job well done was its own reward. "After I got used to being in there," she remembered, "I really loved my work. I enjoyed working on my job. I got pleasure out of it, and it made me happy to do my job. When I come out of that mill, I know that I done the very best I could. Somewhere along the way I felt a peaceable mind. It's wonderful to feel that way." Icy's attitude toward her job reflected her own sense of self-worth and a commitment to her fellow workers and the company. "I believe in doing your job and not laying down on it, not slacking back waiting on somebody else. They don't expect you to lay back and let it be in a mess when the next man come in on that job. I can always say that my job, when I left it, was straightened out. The next one that come in on my job didn't have any problems."[65]

Even when the work itself was unsatisfying, there could be rewards. Alice Copeland found tying weaver's knots "tedious work," and the noise in the mill contributed to her deafness, but she stuck with it and had no regrets. "There never was a time that I wasn't proud of my job, because I knew that instead of my children having to stop school and go to work, that by me and their daddy both working they could go to school. I was proud when I worked six days a week, and I don't regret any days that I worked in the mill."[66]

For some people, of course, mill work was just a job. They did just enough to earn a living and to keep from being fired but refused to apply themselves wholeheartedly. John Wesley Snipes, for one, shared Chester Copeland's contempt for the "robot life." "I never had no use for a cotton mill. Look at it run twelve hours a day, and the same old thing in the morning, and the same old thing next morning. I didn't like it at all, but I had to do it. I had to make bread and butter."[67]

Wherever they labored, and however they felt about their jobs, all mill workers endured the long hours and low wages that characterized the industry. Six twelve-hour days represented a normal work week in the late nineteenth century. The shift started at 6:00 A.M., with quitting time around 6:00 P.M. The piercing sound of the steam whistle replaced the rooster as the herald of the new day. In summer, winter, spring, and fall, in hot weather or in cold, rain, sleet, or snow, "they'd blow their whistle to wake everybody up and then about fifteen minutes later they'd blow it again to make sure that you was up." At Bynum the notice came from a bell, but the message was the same: "time to go to work."[68]

From the early days of the industry, millhands complained about the long hours. "Twelve hours a day is too long for any one to work in a mill," wrote a worker from Gaston County to the North Carolina Bureau of Labor Statistics. Beginning in the 1880s, the Knights of Labor and the National Union of Textile Workers agitated for change. By 1903 North Carolina, South Carolina, and Georgia had laws limiting the work week to sixty-six hours. South Carolina, a pacesetter among southern states on labor legislation, went further, mandating a sixty-hour week in 1907 and a fifty-five-hour week in 1922. But passing laws was one thing; enforcing them was another. Without vigilant inspection or serious penalties, these regulations meant little. Mills continued, by and large, to set their own schedules. When John Wesley Snipes began work at Bynum in 1929, the workday was still twelve hours, with a half-day on Saturday. Southern textile workers did not enjoy the eight-hour day until 1933, when the federal government began regulating hours under the National Industrial Recovery Act.[69]

When millhands "got their time" every other Saturday, the wages they drew were meager compensation for the long hours they worked.

The prospect of "cash wages" had lured thousands of people to the mills, and even though money could not be "picked off trees," the "little bit they made" was enough to keep most from returning to the farm. But, of course, nobody got rich working in a cotton mill.

The hierarchy of mill wages reflected cultural assumptions about men, women, and children and the value of their labor. Jobs performed by adult white men received the highest compensation, followed by those assigned to white women. Blacks earned slightly more than children. Wage rates were important to workers because even small changes in either hourly or piece rates affected their standard of living. But wages also provided some indication of a person's status or worth as a millhand. Manufacturers were keenly interested in the amount of money paid to their employees. Next to cotton, labor was the most costly ingredient in the production of yarn and cloth.[70] (See Table 1 for the average weekly wage rates at seven North Carolina mills in 1904.)

In the spinning room, workers' wages were based on the number of machines they tended, so until children became fairly proficient, their pay was low. Until the early 1900s spinners commonly received ten to twelve-and-one-half cents a day per side. Flossie Moore Durham earned twenty-five cents for her first day in the mill in 1893. And in case the point remained unclear, she reiterated, "That was *a day*; that weren't an hour. That was a day." Seventeen years later, Alice Evitt, at age twelve, took her first job for the same wage. "The first day I went to work, I run two sides, twelve and a half cents a side, twenty-five cents a day, from six 'til six. That's a long time for twenty-five cents a day and just got paid off every two weeks." Wages increased as workers got older. With more experience and greater physical maturity, they could tend more machines and earn more money. As Alice Evitt said, "You just had to build yourself up." By the time she married in 1915, she could run twelve sides and earned $1.44 a day.[71]

Male workers in the card room, on the other hand, usually received an hourly or daily wage rather than piece rates, and they increased their earnings by taking on more-demanding tasks. Martin Lowe began at Greenville's Poe Mill at the age of twenty-one in 1912. "A dollar a day, ten cents an hour. Sixty hours and six dollars, that's what we made." After a few months he moved to nearby American Spinning and got a set of cards that paid $1.25 a day. Within a few years he was grinding cards, for which he received $2.25. These patterns might

TABLE I.

Average Weekly Wages Paid in Seven North Carolina Mills, 1904

Occupation	Rate per Week
Picker Room	
Opener	$ 4.50
Picker hand	5.10
Card hand	4.50
Boss carder	12.00
Spinning Room	
Drawing frame	4.50
Slubber hands	5.40
Intermediate hands	5.40
Speeder hands	4.50
Spinners	3.00[a]
Head doffer	3.60
Doffers	2.40
Spoolers	4.00
Twisters	4.80
Warpers	7.50
Overseer of spinning	10.50
Section hand	7.00
Overseer of twisting	7.00
Band boys	2.50
Sweepers	3.60
Oiler and bander	3.60
Weaving Room	
Filler	3.90
Creelers	4.00
Beam warper	4.50
Slash tender	6.00
Drawing-in girls	6.00
Weavers	5.40[b]
Finishing Room	
Calendar ⎫	⎧6.00
Folder ⎬ 2 men	⎨
Baler ⎭	⎩4.50
Weave boss	15.00
Section bosses	8.40

Table 1. *continued*

Occupation	Rate per Week
Engineer	8.25[c]
Firemen	6.00

Source: Holland Thompson, *From Cotton Field to Cotton Mill*, p. 284.

    a. Ranges from $1.20 to $6.00; due to variations in the number and skill of these operatives, the exact average wage is seldom the same for two consecutive weeks.

    b. Ranges from $2.50 to $9.00; due to variations in the number and skill of these operatives, the exact average wage is seldom the same for two consecutive weeks.

    c. Ranges from $7.50 to $9.00

continue until a worker was in his thirties, at which time his ability to earn top wages would begin to decline.[72]

A weaver's wages depended on the amount of cloth produced. "They paid by the cut," Pauline Griffith recalled, "so many yards to the cut. It was according to how much work you turned out, to how much you got paid. You worked at your own speed, and it's according to how your looms run." The rates varied considerably because the types of looms, widths of cloth, and complexity of patterns all differed. Most mills made an effort to adjust the rates so that weavers with equal skills made equivalent wages.[73]

Wage rates for southern workers did increase over time, particularly when labor was scarce, but compared to northern textile workers, southern millhands were grossly underpaid. Indeed, cheap labor was the foundation of the southern textile industry. Between the 1880s and the imposition of a national minimum wage in the 1930s, southern workers could expect to receive roughly 60 percent of the wage paid for the same job in the North. Manufacturers advanced a number of justifications for this differential. Above all, they cited the lower cost of living in the Piedmont—cheaper food, fuel, and housing—which supposedly made real wages comparable to those in the North. Although there was some truth to the argument, studies done in the 1910s and 1920s showed only a slightly lower cost of living in the South—nowhere near enough to justify the wage differential. The other rationale rested on the fact that the South produced coarser goods than the North, with a lower "value added" in manufacturing; therefore, it was said, the southern mills could not afford to pay wages as high as those in the North. While this argument, too, had some validity, southern manufacturers also paid a smaller percentage of their value added to workers, thus retaining for themselves a greater share of the profits.[74]

Southern manufacturers could pay less because they purchased labor in a regional market where the general level of economic development kept wages low. Lower labor costs, in turn, made southern products more competitive in national and international markets, and mill owners, rather than workers, reaped the rewards. From the outset, textile entrepreneurs realized generous returns on their investments. "It was not unusual for mills in [the early] years," according to historian Broadus Mitchell, "to make 30 per cent to 75 per cent profit."[75] Earnings leveled off after the initial boom, but until the textile depression of the 1920s mill stocks continued to pay substantial dividends.

Workers' health was another casualty of the drive for profits in a region that placed no restrictions on capital and offered workers no protection. Without unions, and without the legal and administrative apparatus that now provides a basic level of industrial health and safety, millhands were at the mercy of dangerous machinery. The threat to a worker's health could be as sudden and violent as the snapping of a bone or as insidious as the relentless clouding of a lung.

Cotton dust was a killer in the card room. "Some of that dust was terrible," Carl Durham remembered. "Whew! That dust would accumulate and you had to strip them cards out every three hours, get all that stuff out. It would get to where it wouldn't do its work, it would be so full of particles and dust. When I was coming along, and for a long time, that was all in the air. It's a wonder I can breathe, but somehow or another it didn't affect me like it did some folks. It just killed some folks." Durham's observations echoed the findings of medical researchers on both sides of the Atlantic. Cotton dust caused a number of health problems, sometimes resulting in death, but it did not affect everyone in the same way. It is now well understood that byssinosis, or brown lung, is a disease that results from prolonged exposure to cotton dust. Although the British government recognized the existence of byssinosis and began compensating victims in 1940, lack of research and resistance by the textile industry delayed any action on the disease in the United States until the 1970s.[76]

Anyone who worked in the card room knew that the dust caused problems, but, like Grover Hardin, they "didn't pay much attention to it. See, there was a continuous fog of dust in the carding department at all times. When you hit the mill on Monday morning, you'd have a tough time. You'd cough and sneeze and fill your mouth full of tobacco and anything else to keep this dust from strangling you." This "Monday morning sickness" was the first stage of byssinosis, caused by irritation of the air passages. There would be little recurrence of the problem during the rest of the week as workers adjusted to the dust. But the coughing returned every Monday because a day or two away from the mill increased "susceptibility." After a period of ten years or more, the coughing became more persistent. Grover Hardin "got to noticing it bothering me. I took these coughs and I couldn't get over them, and I'd go home and cough and cough and cough." Rather than pay doctor's fees, he asked the advice of other workers who had the same problem—"the ones that was able to go to the doctor, I'll put it like that." Most told him they had "a little touch of asthma," so Grover took "home remedies" for asthma. "As time passed on, it'd get worse. On Mondays, I'd go in and it'd sure enough be worse by the night. Tuesday, Wednesday, it'd get a little better. I guess I'd get my lungs plugged up good. Over the weekend you'd clear your lungs up pretty good, then Monday morning, it'd be the same thing."

Like many workers with byssinosis, Hardin gradually began having difficulty running his job and started missing work. "Nothing I could take for asthma would do this breathing any good. I couldn't get no air in my lungs, and I slowed up. It got to where I had to push on the job to stay up in the mill. And when I'd get a spare minute I'd go over and lay in the windows and get all the air I could." Finally, he had to quit.[77]

Dust was only one hazard in the card room. Accidents around the machinery mangled hands and arms; one worker called carding the "dangerousest job in the mill." In the early days, belts connected the machines to drive shafts high above, and carders had to pay careful attention as they cleaned and adjusted their equipment. "It was pretty dangerous," explained Carl Thompson. "You'd have to watch yourself. There were so many things that you could do. Even cleaning up, if maybe your brush would get caught in a belt or a pulley, it's going to jerk your hand. I've seen them jerked in the cards thataway and maybe get their whole arm and all broke and the skin pulled off, maybe slam through the bone."[78]

The card room at the White Oak Mill in Greensboro, North Carolina, 1909.
Fast-moving belts and powerful machines made carding
a particularly dangerous job.
(Courtesy of Robert Vogel, National Museum of American History)

One incident in particular accounted for Thompson's fears. "I'd seen so many get hurt on them, get their arms broke. That was when they had overhead pulleys, had the pulleys at the top of the mill. There was one man, his shirt or something or other got caught in that belt, and that belt throwed him to the top of the mill and busted his brains out. He just hit the ceiling of the mill. They had big beams up there, and he hit them, right at the back of his head. It killed him."[79]

Working conditions were even more disagreeable in the weave room. The environment was dominated by the constant noise of banging looms and the eerie mist that descended from overhead sprinklers. "It was a loud, noisy place, and awful dusty and linty," remembered Edna Hargett. The moisture was particularly troublesome. "The weave room was always wet," explained Mack Duncan. "Back then, you had to have a lot of water in the weave room. The air wasn't conditioned like it is now, scientifically; there was just water being sprayed out. It was atomized and sprayed out to make the weaving run. It was wet in that back alley. There was a loom fixer taking a loom down one time, and he slipped and grabbed at the beam on the rail, and the beam probably weighed two hundred and fifty pounds, maybe more. It was above him, and it fell on him and killed him."[80]

Less dramatic than occasional accidents, but no less threatening, were the complications that resulted from breathing warm, moist air filled with lint. Naomi Trammell was one of the fortunate ones; she had a doctor who recognized the problem. "I went to the weave room one time, and I like to took galloping TB. It'd be just wet all over, so hot, you know. And that just give 'em TB. That doctor told me when he doctored me about two weeks, 'Now, young lady, you can go back to the cloth room and live, or you can go back to the weave room and die, whichever you want to do.' So I went back to the cloth room."[81]

Spinning had its own peculiar hazards. "Oh, it was awful hot," Alice Evitt remembered. "All that machinery a-runnin' makin' heat. It was bad. Terrible hot out here. You'd come out of there, your clothes was plumb wet." Mozelle Riddle described conditions in the Bynum mill. "It used to be so hot before they put air-conditioning in there. You could walk into the frames and burn your legs, that's how hot the heat was. Them motors'd burn you, when you'd walk around them. But we just got used to it. Didn't think nothing about it. It'd be eighty, oh shoot, it'd be ninety degrees in there in that spinning room. Work and sweat, yes sir." Eva Hopkins recalled the heat, too. "They didn't have air-conditioning in the mills and it was terribly hot. They wouldn't let you raise the windows very high: air would come in; it would make the ends come down. Sometimes they'd let you prop a bobbin under them. I'd put the window up at the end of my frame, then here'd come the section man along and take it down. When he'd leave and go off, I'd raise it again. I couldn't stand the heat."[82]

The threat of serious injuries was all around. Most of the fast-moving machine parts were exposed, and any slip-up could have disastrous consequences. Alice Evitt remembered getting her "apron tore off two or three times a week" while running speeder frames. "Back then, they didn't wear pants. Them big flyers flyin' around, they'd grab you and just wind your apron plumb up. I was just lucky I managed to stop 'em and didn't get my arms in them. Them flyers would break your bones. I know one lady—I didn't see her get it done—but she said she wore wigs [because] she'd got her hair caught and it pulled her whole scalp out—every bit of her hair. Them speeders was bad to catch you." Evitt and her co-workers often joked about such things. "Sometimes they'd get under the frames and reach and get a-hold of somebody's dress and jerk 'em. Make 'em think the machine had 'em. Try to scare them."[83]

When accidents did occur, there was little relief for those who suffered. "Back before now," Mack Duncan recalled, "if you got hurt on the job, you just was hurt. If you couldn't work, you had to go home; you lost your pay. Back before World War II you didn't get much help." James Pharis remained bitter about the way he was treated when he had an accident in the mill. "I was about nine or ten years old when I got that hand hurt. I was riding on an elevator rope in the mill. My hand got caught under the wheel. That thing was mashed into jelly; all of it was just smashed to pieces. They took me down to the company store—the drug store was in the front end of the company store—never even notified my people or nothing. There were only two doctors in town at that time, and both of them was out of town on country calls. I sat there until about four o'clock. Nobody done nothing in the world for me. My people was never notified. Nothing said about it. You tear yourself all to pieces then, nothing said about getting anything out of it. Poor people like us, no use in suing. Poor people didn't stand a chance. If you done anything the company didn't like, they'd just fire you and tell the rest of [the owners] not to hire you. So there'd you be. People who lived under them circumstances, back in them days, was nothing they could do. So they didn't try to do nothing."[84]

Lloyd Davidson summed up the situation. "The only insurance back then they had was to protect the company. They looked out for the company interest, but you didn't have any benefit. There was no retirement, no hospitalization, no benefits whatsoever, as far as for helping you. They carried insurance to protect the company. [People] probably have [sued], but it's a losing cause when you do. They have their own lawyers and they always have the upper hand, you might say. Kind of like David and Goliath. I reckon you could put it that way."[85]

Despite the pace and the pressures, life in the early mills was not all drudgery. Southerners traditionally took time off in the middle of the day for their big meal, and mill workers as a rule kept up that custom. But each company had its own policy. Grover Hardin explained. "Usually, they would stop a full hour for dinner. Everything'd close down at dinner. Then I have known them to run right on through dinner. You'd either double up [or] all the spare hands that was off that day, they'd come in and work from eleven until one. They'd start letting them out at eleven o'clock for dinner, as many as they could, and everybody'd pitch in and run their job until they got back." Those who worked at night were less fortunate; they normally got only fifteen minutes to eat. The reason, according to one manager, was that if workers were given a longer time to rest, they would fall asleep.[86]

Those who went home had a chance to be with family, eat, and perhaps lie down for a few minutes. Young people often used the time for other pursuits. Pauline Griffith remembered how she spent some of her lunch breaks. "When they used to run ten hours a day, they gave you an hour for lunch, and you could eat and you could lie down and rest. But during that time Paul and I were courting, and I'd hurry back, and he did too. That's the way we spent our lunch hour. And Mama, she would say, 'Now, Pauline, you ought to rest some.' But she didn't know I had to get back to talk to Paul."[87]

Even though there were no other scheduled breaks during the day, workers still found time to get away from their machines. Before the 1920s, existing production technology limited manufacturers' ability to impose strict time discipline. Millhands recalled that the work ran slowly and "everybody just had small jobs." Frank Durham described how easy it was to take a few minutes off. "I don't care what they was running, they got good enough at it that they could catch up. They'd get a little catch-up time. One of them would watch one another's work, and they'd go out to smoke or go to the bathroom or go anywhere." "Just as long as you kept your work up," Viola Pitts recalled, "you could sit in the windows, or you could go outside and sit in the grass. We knew about what time we had to be back. If they'd see too many ends down, they'd whistle for us." Things ran so well in the weave room at Highland Park Mill in North Charlotte that Howard Mosely sometimes took the whole afternoon off to go to a baseball

Girls enjoying a break from work, outside a Georgia cotton mill, 1909.
Photograph by Lewis Hine.
(Courtesy of the Photography Collections, Albin O. Kuhn Library and Gallery, University of Maryland
at Baltimore County)

issues large and small. What, for example, constituted a "good day's work"? What was a "fair day's pay"? How could workers' desires for fresh air, an occasional day off, time to chat with their neighbors, or a say-so in how they did their jobs be reconciled with the supervisors' goal of high productivity and the manufacturers' pursuit of profits? In their daily activities on the shop floor, workers tried to carve out room for personal dignity and control. Management's response to that effort differed from place to place and changed markedly over the years.

Manufacturers used various methods to ensure that workers put forth their maximum effort. Authority ultimately resided with stockholders, but in practice a single individual—usually a president or secretary-treasurer who was also a majority stockholder—ran the mill. This "master of the mill" was something of a folk legend in the South, earning the undying admiration of some and the unending animosity of others. These New South industrialists may have displayed some of the flair of their plantation ancestors, but there was nothing particularly southern about their behavior. They acted like nascent capitalists and small businessmen everywhere, seeking to motivate their employees and create a bond of loyalty through individual contact. They exercised their authority in direct, personal terms; they could be benefactors and autocrats at the same time.[99]

Most millhands remembered having personal contact with the men for whom they worked. But each manufacturer was different. In a small mill, the officers might be directly involved with production decisions and with workers. Everett Padgett remembered that when he went to work at Union Bleachery in Greenville, "I was not a number on the payroll; I was Everett Padgett." Three brothers—Nelson, John, and Richard Arrington—ran the company. They had offices in the mill and maintained daily contact with their employees. "Richard—Dick, they called him—was president. He was well thought of. All of them were, but Dick was much more friendlier. He would walk through that plant and he'd stop and talk to you. I mean he'd do it regular, too. And if they hired anybody, the employment application was on his desk the next morning, who was hired and where they was from. So when he come through and met you, why, he wasn't exactly meeting a stranger."[100]

Benjamin D. Heath, on the other hand, who had an interest in a number of mills in the Carolinas, displayed some of the style of the paternal mill owner but little of the substance. From his office in Charlotte, Heath made regular trips to the Manetta Mills, forty miles away in Lando, South Carolina. Lela Rainer remembered his visits. "He come in on the dummy and go thro' the mill lookin'. I wouldn't think he would know most of the people that worked in the mill cause he wasn't here long enough to learn 'em. They'd come around in the spinnin' room and tell us, 'We got to get it cleaned up now. Mr. Heath's a-comin.' And everybody'd get to cleaning and everything'd be just shining and Mr. Heath'd come through the spinnin' room lookin'. Then after he left, everything got back to normal."[101]

Despite these visits, owners such as Heath rarely concerned themselves with daily operations in the mill. They were primarily businessmen who directed the financial affairs of the company and delegated responsibility for organizing work and disciplining the help to a small coterie of supervisors. In most places operations were in the hands of a superintendent. Before World War I many superintendents "rose from the ranks" and combined an intimate knowledge of the "practical side" of production with an ability to "manage the help." The three-piece suit and gold watch chain that signified the superintendent's authority could easily be replaced by a pair of overalls if a troublesome machine needed repair.[102]

Under the superintendent were overseers for each room and every shift. Commonly known as the "card room boss" or "boss weaver," these men had the technical ability to adjust machines and coordinate the flow of materials through their departments. Direct supervision of workers, however, fell to the second hands. The way Harry Rogers saw it, "The second hand was the man who did all the work. He helped directly with the help, and was the man that was responsible for production and quality." A second hand in a pre–World War I mill described what was expected of him. "You had the cotton, the machinery, and the people—and you were supposed to get out the production. How you did it was pretty much up to you; it was production management was interested in and not how you got it." Before the 1920s, then, supervision was a highly personal affair; there were as many approaches to the problem as there were superintendents, overseers, and second hands. As one observer explained, "There was nothing that could be identified as a general pattern of supervisory practice." In a sense, each part of the mill was an independent domain, and the individual in charge had to find his own means of disciplining and encouraging "his" workers.[103]

Supervision proved most challenging in the rooms filled with children. Overseers in the spinning room, "generally known as the children's department," had "more trouble in contending with help than any of the rest of the overseers in a mill." One observer noted that "as their chief indoor sport [children] claimed the privilege of hanging onto the shafting belts as the machinery slowly started and riding towards the twenty-foot ceiling. To them what was a good calling down, or more severe discipline in comparison with the dare-devil thrill of the journey up or the admiration gained from an acrobatic drop. A game of catch, with a ball improvised from yarn was [also] a very natural way in which to wish to spend one's time while waiting for the machines to fill, not to mention the American boy's love of just plain 'scuffling,' or making life miserable for the girls and women." All in all, children showed a greater interest in playing—"just like kids would"—than in paying careful attention to their machines.[104]

Often the contest between children and supervisors became a game itself. A favorite pastime among boys was spitting tobacco juice out of mill windows onto the heads of unwary boss men below. Children also

played cat and mouse with supervisors who sometimes found it difficult to keep them in the mill. Eula Durham remembered how much
fun such a game could be. "One time we went fishing, down there
behind the mill. We made a fishing hook out of a pin, and got us a
stick. And we kept putting threads together to make it strong enough.
There was about seven or eight of us setting back there behind the
mill on the riverbank fishing. John Durham was boss man back then.
We was setting there just a-fishing up a storm, and heard the weeds a-
cracking. We looked up and there he was. He said, 'I want every one of
you'—we weren't nothing but young'uns, none of us—'I want every
one of you back in the mill right now!' He marched us back in the mill.
Well then, they had an old elevator, that you pulled ropes and would
carry you up. We studied after we seen his feet go up. One of the boys
got up on the platform and motioned that he'd gone upstairs. And we
took off again. Tom Hearne [an older man in the winding room] said,
'I'll tell you right now, you kids are about to worry me to death. Can't
keep you in here to save your life. That man's coming back there
getting ready to kill every one of you.' "[105]

Supervisors, of course, could not countenance such behavior, and
at times their discipline could be harsh, erratic, and arbitrary. In some
cases they tried to frighten children into obedience. James Pharis
remembered that "you used to work for the supervisor because you
were scared. I seen a time when I'd walk across the road to keep from
meeting my supervisor. They was the hat-stomping kind. If you done
anything, they'd throw their hat on the floor and stomp it and raise
hell." Icy Norman worked for similar men. "Old man Smith, now he
was a fair old scratch. Him and old man Spivey. I've seen them get
mad. They'd pull their old hat off, throw it down and spit on it and
jump on that hat and stomp it."[106]

When hat stomping failed, some supervisors might resort to the
rod. Eva Hopkins's mother told her how it was in those days. "She said
the overseers could whip the children back then. If they didn't stay on
the job and do the job, they could spank them or whip them, or send
for their parents to come get them." Paul Cline related another tactic
used to discipline children. "Some second hands in the mills, back
years ago, used to take little old kids by their heels and stick them out
the window and say, 'I'm going to drop you if you don't behave
yourself.' That's the way they done."[107]

Even supervisors, writing in the *Southern Textile Bulletin*, admitted
that "some overseers, second hands and section men have a disposi-

tion to abuse the help. Whoop, holler, curse and jerk the children around." Frank Durham heard that in the early years in Bynum the overseers "was mighty rough to the folks." Looking back, Durham, who became a supervisor himself, felt there was some justification for the overseers' behavior. "They had a lot of children to deal with. A whole lot of children worked in the mill, and they were aggravating. You couldn't get much out of them; you couldn't do much with them. About the only way you could do it was fear, I reckon. Some of the young'uns would have half-killed them if they could, I reckon. I've heard it said, you know, that they'd send away for their daddy or send the person home, about like a schoolteacher. If they couldn't get nothing out of him, they'd send him home. Then his daddy was liable to whip him and send him back."[108]

The policy of calling on fathers to enforce good behavior may have become more common after 1905, as increasing numbers of adult men entered the work force. When Paul Cline was growing up, mill fathers often insisted on the right to discipline their own children. "That's one thing about those people back then, they didn't let nobody else whip their children. You don't go around whipping other people's children. You go and tell their daddy if they done something wrong." Fathers might administer a whipping, or they might deliver a lecture like the one Letha Ann Sloan Osteen remembered. "My daddy told us before we ever went to work in the mill that you must respect age. People that's older than you and telling you things to do, you must respect 'em and do that. Because they wouldn't be telling you if it wasn't for your good."[109]

The threat of punishment by parents and supervisors helped keep children under control because youngsters had little choice but to obey. Grover Hardin explained the vulnerability of a child who could not strike out on his own and whose labor was needed to support the family. "You done what you was told to do, or else you didn't have a job. That's what would make it hard on the younger people. They couldn't say, 'Well, I quit; I'll go somewheres else.' Besides under the company's jurisdiction, you was under your parents'. You was obligated to obey them. And they just wouldn't listen. They hardly couldn't afford to. It worked in their livelihood. It was either you do, or that's it. And you couldn't do nothing but go ahead and do it."[110]

Wrangling between adult workers and bosses was a more complicated matter. The pressures of keeping up production in rooms crowded with people and machines put workers and supervisors on edge. Long days of hard work and low pay made flare-ups a normal part of every shift. The room might be too hot or too cold. One week there was too much work, and the next, not enough. Sometimes the cotton was "running good"; other times ends broke as fast as they could be put up. Day-to-day tensions provoked constant complaints and sometimes led to altercations that focused on real or perceived abuses of management authority. Although millhands acknowledged the relations of power in the mill, they did not simply accept them. They were quick to assert their own preferences about the organization and pace of work and their relations to supervisors.

Superintendents and overseers managed the mills, but they could not manage them exactly as they pleased. For one thing, authority on the shop floor was complicated by family ties. Edgar Moore, superintendent of the Bynum mill from 1904 to 1955, was carefully groomed for his job. Edgar's sister, Flossie, recalled how he attained his position. "They told my brother, 'Now if you'll come down there and work through the mill, start at the first, just learn the machinery, when you get through with it, I'll put you overseer.'" Moore worked through the mill and eventually got promoted to superintendent. As time went on, he became known for his threats to fire workers at the least provocation, although he seldom acted on his words. He was involved both inside and outside the mill in relationships other than that of manager to worker. His brothers and sisters, nieces and nephews, had married established Bynum residents or newcomers from other mills. Moore also took advantage of his position to further his family's interests, promoting his brother-in-law and three of his nephews to supervisory positions. These kinship ties gave him access to details of workers' private lives, but they also meant that blatant injustice on his part might have repercussions on his own family. Even after Moore had been superintendent for sixteen years, he was forced to leave Bynum when "he got into trouble one time with a woman." Frank Durham recalled that "the help wouldn't have worked for him no more. They were planning to come out and strike. Planning to walk out." Moore returned to Bynum only after the woman's "family died out and left."[111]

The contradictions of authority bore most heavily on overseers and second hands, who were most deeply enmeshed in the social life of the close-knit communities where the mills were located. In order to "get production" and satisfy the demands of owners and superintendents, these men had to maintain good relations with workers who were often friends, relatives, and neighbors. As a result, lower-level managers were sometimes as loyal to the hands as to the company. Eva Hopkins's father, an overseer in the Mercury Mill in Charlotte, "worked with the help. He didn't work against them. He didn't work just for the company, he worked with the people." When a superintendent issued an unpopular order, such an overseer might pass the order along but yield to pressures from below not to enforce it. Mildred Edmonds remembered when second hands in the Piedmont Heights mill in Burlington were told to ban talking among workers. "They made a rule up there one time. They said you couldn't talk to the other one on the other side of you. Well, the boss man went around and he told all of them. He got down to me and he said, 'Mil, I'll have to tell you but I know it won't do no good. You're not supposed to talk to each other.' I said, 'God gave me a tongue and I'm going to use it.' It didn't last long. He didn't want to do it. But you see, the man above him put that on him."[112]

Supervision was further complicated by owners' visits to their factories. Although most manufacturers relinquished day-to-day authority to underlings, they were ever-present figures, touring the mill to chat with workers and check up on all their help. These visits were intended to inspire hard work and company loyalty, but an owner's presence also divided power in the mill. Workers had direct access to their employer and sometimes came to view him as a mediator between themselves and supervisors, a "force that could bring an arbitrary and unreasonable overseer back into line." Mack Duncan of Greenville felt that in the early years "most all the owners seemed like they had a little milk of human kindness about them, but some of the people they hired didn't. Some of the managers didn't have that. They were bad to exploit people."[113]

Under these circumstances, the commands of an overseer were subject to review by the owner or his superintendent. Workers felt free to complain about unjust treatment, and owners or superintendents, eager to keep up production, sometimes reversed their lieutenants' orders. At Bynum a worker would first take his complaint to "the one that's ahead of him. If he thought his boss man wasn't doing like he ought to, he'd go over him. Go to the head man, and see what he'd do about it." Writing in 1910, federal investigators saw such individual negotiations as the norm. "When an employee is dissatisfied about mill conditions he may obtain a hearing from the chief officer of the mill . . . and present his side of the case. Not infrequently when complaints are thus made, the overseer is overruled and the operative upheld."[114]

Harry Rogers recalled the power of workers at the Plaid Mill in Burlington to rein in an unpopular supervisor. "We had a dispute in the weave room one time, we had this fellow here that they had imported from South Carolina. His personality, and the way he approached you about something, just made you mad before he had hardly gotten started. He was more of a dictator type. Well, the weave room made up their mind that they weren't going to put up with him, so they signed a petition to run him off. They elected me to take the petition to the superintendent, Walt Williams. I took it out there and told him what it was, and why I was there. He said, 'Well, Harry, you didn't have to bring that thing to me. You could have come to me and talked to me about it. I don't need the petition. I don't want to see it. I don't intend to read it. All you had to do was just come and tell me.' He didn't fire the fellow, but the fellow straightened up."[115]

Mildred Edmonds related a similar story from the Piedmont Heights mill. "We got a boss man up there, Daddy Smith. He wanted us all to wear uniforms. And of all things, white uniforms. We had to order them. He had his niece come in there. She measured us all up. She modeled them on herself and walked up and down through the mill. Didn't none of them like it. Anyway, we bought them. Two and a half dollars for some of them. You'd get awful dirty in them. You'd get grease all over you. They wouldn't clean. You'd have to change them uniforms every day. Kept you busy washing. We went in one morning, and oh me, I was always the leader. We went in and I didn't wear no uniform. He said he was going to send me back home. I didn't do a thing but just walk on down through the mill to the superintendent's office—Mert Odell was superintendent at the time. They came trotting along behind me. We went on down there and I said, 'Mr. Odell, do we have to wear them old white uniforms?' He said, 'No, Ma'am. If you don't want to, you don't have to. And they can't take your job away from you.' From that it got out, and every one of them began to shed them off."[116]

Such compromises, of course, were tenuous at best. Management rarely conceded the prerogative of power. Although complaints sometimes resulted in a change of company policy, there were limits on the millhands' ability to control the conditions of their labor. When negotiations failed, workers could swallow their pride and go back to the job or directly challenge their boss's decision.

Men sometimes took matters into their own hands. Workers confided to sociologist Glenn Gilman that some people "wouldn't recognize any authority but a pair of fists" and "seemed to go around with a chip on their shoulder all the time. It was a word and a blow with them." Lloyd Davidson knew "people to have fights. Oh yeah, they had fights sometimes, disagreements over something." Although such anger was often present, not everyone could afford to act on it. "You get mad enough just any time. But when your job depends on it and you might not be able to get another one, why you have to grin and bear it."[117]

Geddes Dodson recounted a story of a run-in his father had with a worker who was quick to pull a knife. "My daddy was overseer at a little old mill, and when he took the job, the fellows come to him and said, 'You see that fellow over yonder? He's the bully around here. He'll run you off.' My daddy said, 'He won't run me. I ain't the running kind.' This fellow come in the mill after payday about half drunk. He told my daddy, 'I want my time. I've quit.' My daddy said, 'You know the rules of the company. You have to work out two weeks' notice to get your time.' The fellow run his hand in his pocket to get his knife and says, 'You'll give me my time.' Before he got his hand out of his pocket, he was lying on the floor. My daddy was standing over him when he got up, and he knocked him down the second time. When he got up, he knocked him plumb out the door and pulled it to and locked it. On payday daddy went to town and carried my oldest brother with him. He was back in the meat market in the back of the store. This fellow seen him, and come in after him with his knife open. My daddy had a pair of knucks [brass knuckles] in his pocket and he put them on. This fellow went to cutting at him, and he'd bust him with those knucks and then jump out of the way of the knife. My daddy dropped them knucks, and when he done that he reached back and got that old thirty-eight. He hit him and was afraid he'd killed him. He laid out in the woods all night, thought the law'd be a-hunting him. They found he hadn't killed him, and they fined him five dollars for shooting him, and the mill paid that. I worked with that fellow down here at Dunean, and at Monaghan, too. One of the best friends I ever had. He'd talk to me about how rough he used to be and all that stuff, and said it didn't pay. But he never mentioned that, and I never let on like I knew it."[118]

Workers usually vented their anger in these individual ways, but the frustrations of the shop floor could also provoke a group response.

The spontaneous strike occupied a prominent place in the lore of the early mills. Virtually every chronicler of the period noted the phenomenon, yet the details of such actions remain sketchy. Local newspapers rarely mentioned short-term walkouts, and owners tried to downplay them. Lacy Wright recalled the efforts he and other speeder hands went to during World War I to prevent Cone Mills from lowering their piece rates. "Everybody got worked up about it. They said, 'We're going to shut it down. We're going to get old man Tom Gardner down here and talk to us, and if he don't raise the price of the hank, we ain't running no speeders.' So he come on down there and talked to us. He said, 'No, absolutely not. We're not going to do one thing. You can take it or you can leave it.'

"Some of the fellows cursed pretty badly, and they said, 'Well, by God, we're going to leave.' And they walked out and I walked out with them. There wasn't no organization, it was each man making up his mind what he was going to do. We stood around and talked a little bit and all of them said: 'Well, by God, let them fire us. We'll just go somewhere else and get us a job.'" A few hours after the speeder hands walked out, the whole plant shut down. Lacy and his father set out to find other jobs. The first group of mills they tried had no openings—Lacy figured that Cone officials had already alerted neighboring mills not to hire striking workers. But finally Lacy found employment at a small mill in Randolph County. When he returned to Greensboro to get his belongings, the company decided to offer the strikers more money and they all returned to work.[119]

Personal strategies of resistance and accommodation defined the fabric of everyday life in the mills. But it would be wrong to conclude that mill folk were peculiarly individualistic or untouched by the uprisings of laboring people across America in the late nineteenth century. Millhands' first attempts to develop a lasting organization came in the 1880s. The stimulus was a national depression that threatened workers' already meager standard of living; the vehicle was the Knights of Labor. The Noble and Holy Order of the Knights of Labor was a loose coalition of America's "producing classes"—predominately farmers, laborers, craftsmen, and small businessmen—that captured the imagination of thousands of workers in the 1880s. The Knights concentrated their efforts on politics and the formation of producer cooperatives but in many locales also served as a labor union for newly industrialized workers. The Knights' criticism of the increasing concentration of political and economic power by a financial and industrial elite resonated with the experiences of southern workers. By the end of 1885 hundreds of millhands had joined skilled urban laborers to establish local assemblies of the Knights throughout the textile heartland.[120]

In the South, however, the Knights were poorly situated to battle the emerging industrial order. Manufacturers took immediate steps to "nip in the bud" the spread of labor organization. Mill owners in South Carolina reportedly conspired to "crush the Knights beyond resurrection" by discharging any operatives who joined. A weak national organization could provide little help in such cases, and local government—despite some electoral success by Knights of Labor candidates—could not, or would not, intervene on workers' behalf. Equally decisive was the youthfulness—in terms of age and industrial experience—of the southern work force. Millhands who had just arrived in town were unlikely candidates to lead a revolt against an increasingly powerful manufacturing class. Nevertheless, several years of agitation—highlighted by a three-month strike by thousands of textile workers in Augusta, Georgia, in 1886—served notice that millhands' discontents were not to be taken lightly.[121]

If the Knights were the trailblazers of organized protest in the South, the National Union of Textile Workers brought the ideals of permanent trade unionism into the region. The NUTW originated in 1890 among craft workers in northern mills, but quickly welcomed skilled and unskilled alike into the organization. Internal conflicts led to the election in 1897 of a weaver from Columbus, Georgia, as president of the union, and the headquarters subsequently moved south. With the financial support of American Federation of Labor (AFL) president Samuel Gompers and the experience of organizers from southern craft unions, the NUTW mounted a sustained organizing drive among southern millhands. Between 1898 and 1900 organizational meetings were held in every important textile center in the Piedmont. Workers responded enthusiastically, and the union reported the formation of ninety-five different locals by late 1900. The NUTW's strength lay in urban manufacturing areas such as Columbus and Atlanta, Georgia; Horse Creek Valley and Columbia, South Carolina; and Danville, Virginia. But there were also locals in the small mill villages of North Carolina.[122]

Although the NUTW passed quickly across the horizon of southern history—by 1902 there was only a scattering of active locals—this brief insurgency revealed much about the consciousness of southern mill folk in the late nineteenth century. The ideals and discontents that stirred hundreds to join the union stemmed from a combination of immediate concerns and long-standing resentments. Low wages, long hours, and child labor were the leading complaints. W. W. Oakes, president of the local at Altamahaw, in northern Alamance County, denounced wages that were "too low for the average man, woman and child who are toiling day by day for their daily bread," and long hours that were turning women to "skin and bones" and the children to "dwarfs." "We need better wages," wrote another union leader, "shorter hours, better schools, and above all we need a child labor law and a compulsory school law."[123]

Also embedded in the protests of Piedmont millhands was lingering resentment of the forces that had driven them from the land. To be sure, farm life had been hard and many textile workers had experienced a partial erosion of their independence in the countryside before entering the mills; still, the land had been their birthright and many continued to mourn its loss. T. A. Allen, a member of the NUTW in Durham, described the concerns that brought many workers into the ranks of organized labor. "The people who furnish the supply of labor for the factories are taken directly from the country and are unskilled laborers. They go to the towns and enter the factories fresh from the country, sound in body and mind. They have been accustomed to freedom and liberty, which are the characteristics of North Carolinians. When they enter the factories they are no longer free men and free women, but are considered part of the machinery which they operate. The operatives, becoming aware of their appalling condition, desire to organize."[124]

In the countryside, networks of kin and habits of mutuality had helped farmers survive the hardships and deprivations of life. Some workers saw the NUTW as an extension of those rural ways. Faced with the "appalling condition" of life in the mill, they organized for "mutual benefit" and out of "a burning desire to help their fellow-man in time of need." "There is no other way by which the conditions of the working people can be improved," wrote one worker, "save and except in the banding of ourselves together and all putting their shoulders to the wheel and pushing one way."[125]

Having lost the land, tools, and animals that had safeguarded their freedom and liberty as farmers, millhands sought to ensure their independence as workers by demanding a just price for the one commodity they had left to sell—their labor. "People who earn their living in the sweat of their faces sell their labor for money," declared another NUTW member, "and they have as much right to put a price upon it as any manufacturer has to place a value upon his products. The purpose of organizing the laboring people of any industry is simply to protect the wage-earner from any unfairness that his employer may force upon him. It seeks to do this by placing labor where it naturally belongs, as a power independent within itself in the business world. . . . In order that . . . employees may be independent, so far as the price to be secured for their labor is concerned, all thoughtful and really intelligent people see the pressing need for organization."[126]

Textile unionists, like agrarian protesters of the 1890s, especially feared the increasing power of trusts and monopolies. "I think that as the manufacturers are organized," wrote W. W. Oakes, "or in an association or combination to protect their interests, it is equally necessary for the operatives to organize or come together in some way to protect their interests." The manufacturers' organization Oakes referred to was the Southern Cotton Spinners Association; although the group had been in existence for only three years, many mills had joined. The *Charlotte Observer* reported that members of the association were already meeting with Philadelphia yarn dealers to set prices. Collusion on wages, unionists feared, might be next.[127]

The threat of monopoly was particularly apparent to workers in Alamance County. The descendants of textile pioneer Edwin M. Holt controlled the majority of that county's mills, and it was at one of those mills that an intense conflict flared up in September 1900. The trouble began when an overseer dismissed Anna Whitesell, a weaver at the Thomas M. Holt Manufacturing Company in Haw River, for making unnecessary trips to get filling for her looms. Whitesell "flew into a passion, denying his charges and scorning his threat," telling him that she "would go when she pleased, where she pleased." The overseer then made some "rough statements about the union" and gave Whitesell's looms to an orphan girl. After hearing of the circumstances of Whitesell's dismissal, the girl refused the assignment and asked to speak to one of the union leaders.[128]

Union members gathered that evening and selected a committee to meet with management, believing that Whitesell "had been unjustly and rudely treated." Their only demand was that the boss weaver be dismissed. The owners, however, would have no part of a meeting. B. S. Robertson, treasurer of the mill, replied, "We do not hire help through committees but individually, and we certainly will not treat them in any other way than as individuals." The union met again and the weavers decided not to work until the offending boss weaver was fired. The next Tuesday morning everyone reported to work, but the weavers shut down their machines. The superintendent told them to start work or leave the mill. When the workers refused, the officers quickly closed the Holt mill, along with the nearby Cora and Granite mills, which they also managed. Approximately 300 union members and 900 nonunion workers were affected.

Two days later, Alamance County textile manufacturers met in Burlington to plot strategy. The vice-president of the Holt Mill explained the group's position. "We did not ourselves want union labor because of the character of people of whom the union is composed. There are many good men and women in it, but they are in the minority. All the worst element among the operatives were quick to join, and children compose a large per cent of its membership. The idea of turning the management of our property over to such hands is absurd. . . . We are determined to run with non-union labor or not run at all." Alamance owners sent notice that they intended to reopen the mills on October 15 with nonunion labor and requested that workers either renounce the NUTW or vacate their company-owned houses by that date. When the deadline arrived, only a handful of workers reported for work. Approximately 3,000 millhands, both union and nonunion, stayed home in solidarity with the Haw River strikers.

The owners' decision to ban union labor from their mills confirmed workers' worst fears about the emerging social order. "The privilege of all free men of belonging to anything . . . that's honorable and lawful" was not to be extended to millhands. This action raised serious questions about the meaning of democracy and citizenship in the New South. "Is it right," asked a union committee, "that mill owners shall organize, meet together, fix prices on their yarns, their loom product, and regulate wages, and then say to the laborer: 'You take what we give you, do what we tell you, and say nothing.'" T. A. Allen concluded that the attacks on the NUTW showed "that freedom of thought and action is not allowed among the common people. When a body of citizens are denied the right and privilege to unite for the common good into a lawful organization, we may then say our liberty is no longer our own, but is to be utilized for the benefit of some one who controls the purse strings of hundreds of men and women."[129]

Despite widespread support, the NUTW lacked the power to force the owners to accept union labor. At most of the mills a small contingent of nonunion workers kept up minimum production. In any case, manufacturers seemed in no hurry to return to normal. Autumn was the "dull season" in textiles; and they were happy to await a return of higher prices. Once evictions began, workers who had declared earlier that the strike would go on "until we win out or are starved out" began to realize that their only choice was to quit the union and go back to work or to leave; there was no hope that they could work in the Alamance mills as union men and women. Some renounced the union and went back to work. But "the great majority," reported the *Alamance Gleaner*, "remain firm and are moving away."[130]

The NUTW's campaign dovetailed with the efforts of the Southern Farmers' Alliance and the Populist Party to shape the contours of the new social order. This broad movement, which embraced blacks and whites, farmers and factory workers, crested at the turn of the century with the victory of "fusion" parties—parties that linked black Republicans with white Populists in attempts to wrest control from the Democratic Party. Between 1895 and 1902 southern Democrats turned to race baiting, fraud, intimidation, and violence to destroy this challenge to their power. The passage of state constitutional amendments disfranchised blacks, and the accompanying flurry of Jim Crow laws guaranteed that they would have little to say about the political contours of the New South. Politicians wooed the support of white workers and farmers for black disfranchisement with promises of prosperity and protection against black competition. But they quickly turned the weapon of disfranchisement on whites themselves. Literacy tests, short voter registration periods, and high residency requirements kept large numbers of millhands from the polls. The result was a one-party South in which political opposition was stifled.[131]

As prospects for collective protest diminished, Piedmont millhands opted for a personal strategy as old as the industry itself—relocation. In Alamance County alone, hundreds of union stalwarts left after the 1900 strike to find jobs in South Carolina and Georgia. "Among them," reported the *Alamance Gleaner*, "are a great many excellent people who prefer to go elsewhere rather than surrender rights and privileges which they as citizens deem their own and should enjoy." Striking workers in Augusta, Georgia, voiced a similar response when they were unable to force concessions from local manufacturers. "The only way we can whip the master now," explained one man, "is by lighting out for other districts. They don't mind having their mills closed . . . because with cotton so dear they can't make much money anyhow just now—and that's our bad luck—but they don't like to see the skilled help going away." In choosing to leave in search of better conditions, these workers set a pattern for the next two decades. Until the end of World War I quitting was textile workers' most effective alternative to public protest or acquiescence. According to one student of the southern textile industry, a millhand's "ability to move at a moment's notice was his Magna Carta, Declaration of Independence, and Communist Manifesto."[132]

The movement from job to job could be touched off by any number of factors—curtailed production, a promise of higher wages elsewhere, or a simple desire to move on—but it could also be a response to a perceived abuse of authority, and thus a means of voicing discontent. "A lot of people in textile mills come and go," Josephine Glenn of Burlington remembered. "They're more or less on a cycle. They're not like that as a whole, but a lot of them are. They're dissatisfied, you might say, restless. They just go somewhere and work for a while, and, if everything don't go just like they think it should, why, they walk out. They'd just [say], 'I've had it,' and that was it." Alice Hardin explained the millhands' predicament. "Some of the overseers wasn't real good to people. [But] there wasn't anything [workers] could do about it. They could quit or work, because they didn't have any union to go to. If they were mistreated, they just had to work or quit." Under such circumstances, many people chose to follow George Dyer's advice. "I think if you can run your job, ain't no use to be scared of it—ain't no use to be scared of the boss either. Sometimes some boss don't like you, gets it in for you. It's best then just to quit. Don't work under conditions like that. I don't want to work for a man that don't respect me."[133]

The decision to move was usually made by men, and it could be hard on women and children. Although Edna Hargett worked in the mill, she was evicted from her house every time her husband quit his job. "He was bad about getting mad and quitting. He was just hot-tempered and didn't like it when they wanted to take him off his job and put him on another job. When you work in the card room, you have to know how to run every piece of machinery in there. He liked to be a slubber, and they wanted to put him on drawing or something else. Well, he didn't like to do that." Edna understood her husband's motives but finally left him to settle down and rear her children on her own.[134]

Restlessness among southern workers was a continual concern for mill men. But in the nineteenth century high labor turnover did not pose a serious threat to the industry's prosperity. Workers might come and go at will or be spirited away by competing firms, but a general labor surplus meant that there were always others, eager to take their place. After the turn of the century, however, manufacturers began complaining that machines were standing idle for lack of hands.

Mill owners had unwittingly contributed to their problems by taking part in a rapid expansion of the industry that dramatically increased the demand for labor. The early success of cotton mills in the South boosted the confidence of old and new investors alike. The result was a sudden increase in looms and spindles. From 1900 to 1902 thirty-four mills were built in North Carolina alone. Workers, of course, were needed to tend these new machines and thousands responded to the call of the steam whistle. In the same two years approximately 8,000 additional workers obtained jobs in North Carolina mills. But such rapid expansion quickly depleted the supply of "native help" and, when combined with the effects of high turnover, created an overall labor shortage. As jobs became more plentiful, millhands were free to move even more frequently. Workers remembered that "it wasn't no job at all to get a job then." By 1907 the annual labor turnover rate in the southern textile industry had reached 176 percent, and various mill owners estimated that anywhere from 20 to 40 percent of their employees belonged to the "floating" population.[135]

The inability to maintain a full complement of help posed serious problems for mill earnings in the first two decades of the twentieth century. The *American Textile Manufacturer* reminded readers that because "the big profits in cotton manufacturing are made in the extra thousands of pounds we get above a certain production," it was easy for "the losses of prosperity" to exceed "the losses of . . . adversity." A mill suffered more when it could not meet the demand for its goods because of lack of labor than it did when times were hard. But more threatening than the failure to take advantage of short-term price inflation was the slowing of development caused by the shortage of labor. Journalist August Kohn observed in 1907 that "there is plenty of capital, energy, enthusiasm, business ability, water power and cotton for South Carolina to have many more spindles than she now has. The one difficulty is that of securing additional labor."[136]

Millhands began to use their newfound power in the labor market to challenge management on the shop floor. "The labor conditions are getting very bad," reported one mill owner; "the hands fly up and leave on the slightest pretext, knowing there is a good job awaiting them at every mill in the county." Zelma Murray remembered the time a foreman separated her from a friend and caused her to quit. "A friend of mine and I worked in the same alley. They got me to swap with another party for so long, and then they would give me my regular sides back. [Once] when the time come for me to go back on my regular job, this boss man, he wouldn't give it back to me. He give it to somebody else. He took me the whole length of the mill, over on the back alley. And I had to walk the whole length of the mill. I was young then and that walking didn't bother me, but it was just the principle of the thing. And I quit and I never would go back to the spinning room no more." Alice Hardin also quit when a second hand insisted that she do more than her job entailed. She objected to the way he spoke to her, not so much the extra work. "He didn't do it right," she remembered. "He was kind of overbearing with it. So I just walked out."[137]

In urban areas where there were many mills, and at times when jobs were plentiful, workers could afford impulsive reactions to differences with their bosses. Although Alice Evitt was quite young when the following incident occurred, she, like thousands of others, voted her displeasure with her feet. "Right after I went to work spinning at the Highland Park Mill I worked at night a little bit. They had a parade here the twentieth of May. Of course young people was going to see that parade. I did, and I didn't get to sleep none that day much. That night I went to work, and I asked 'em to let me off. They wouldn't do it, and I got so sleepy in the night, I couldn't hold my eyes open. They wouldn't let me off, and I just quit and went home, and we moved. I wouldn't have missed that parade for nothing."[138]

Millhands' ability to move in search of more satisfying employment made it difficult for supervisors to maintain discipline in the mill. South Carolina mill owner Thomas Parker understood how this freedom affected operations in his own factories. "These people, even when extremely poor, are very independent in their attitude towards an employer, often too much so for their own good. Being familiar with mill and farm conditions they do not hesitate when dissatisfied to move from mill to mill or back to farm work. This has been done frequently from mere restlessness, and is very annoying to the mills, but the ability to do so at any time is a wholesome check on mill managements and has been of great benefit to the operative." Blaine Wofford, a Charlotte millhand, explained. "The drawback on the mill was that a whole family would get mad and quit; if one would get mad, all would quit. There'd be all those jobs and nobody on them. That kind of put the mill behind the eight ball. I guess back then the overseers had to walk lightly with them." After a tour of North and South Carolina mills in 1906, a superintendent vented his frustrations in the pages of the *Southern and Western Textile Excelsior*. "Unfortunately," he lamented, "the help have come to think that they and not the mill owners control the situation."[139]

In an effort to counter what one observer characterized as millhands' "consciousness of their own industrial importance," recruiters began to cast a wider net. Shortly after the turn of the century, labor agents ventured into the mountains of North Carolina and Tennessee in search of workers. "The mountain people would be benefitted," encouraged the *Gastonia News*, "by being induced to come out from the dales and coves and go in some of the mills and come in contact with the world and make something." Thousands of people responded to the call, although they were drawn more by the money than by the "civilizing" influence of the mills. But even with these new recruits, shortages continued.[140]

In the eyes of many, the only solution to the problem of labor scarcity lay in attracting European immigrants to the South. "The predominant topic throughout the whole Central South," declared the *Manufacturers' Record* in 1907, "is the need of immigration. Men who could largely increase their business interests find all of their efforts hampered by their inability to secure labor and so there has suddenly sprung up among those who a few years ago thought but little about the subject an earnest desire for a great influx of foreign immigration." Various southern states set up immigration commissions to recruit European workers. In 1906 the South Carolina Cotton Manufacturers' Association financed the immigration of more than 500 Belgians. These unskilled workers—"able-bodied and industrious men and women were desired rather than skilled operatives"—scattered across the cotton mills of Piedmont South Carolina. Although some stayed and integrated themselves into the local mill community, within a year the majority went looking for greener pastures to the west. But more problematic than the restlessness of immigrants was southern workers' hostility toward foreign labor. Having just escaped the economic competition of blacks on the land, they had no desire to see their jobs given to men and women from across the sea. When the Riverside Mills in Danville hired twelve German workers from New York, native workers went on strike and the Germans had to leave town.[141]

Attempts to recruit immigrant workers represented a rare moment of cooperation on the labor issue. More often than not, manufacturers' solution to labor scarcity was to compete with one another. In hopes of attracting and keeping reliable workers, many mill men raised wages. Between 1902 and 1907 the earnings of male weavers in South Carolina rose by 58 percent, those of female weavers by 65 percent, and those of spinners by 138 percent, while the cost of living increased by only 9 percent. Manufacturers reasoned that higher wages would tame workers' roving disposition because "well paid help would know that they can't do any better by changing." But if owners sought stability and regularity, they did not achieve it with wage competition. In fact, in many cases pay hikes appear to have had the opposite effect. "High wages and short hours do not seem to content the help in most cases," complained an Alabama manufacturer. "The more the help can earn the less they work, that is the prices paid at present have gotten to be so high that an average family, or individual, can make in four days what it once took a full week to earn, and the result is in most instances, such help work only about four-sixths of their time. The average mill hand is inclined to care only for enough to live on and when they have made that, they rest the balance of the week. Therefore to further increase wages would only tend to decrease the labor supply."[142]

A more drastic response to the competition for workers was labor pirating. The desire for skilled workers and large families had always tempted managers to steal workers away from neighboring mills. By 1905 mills throughout the Piedmont hired recruiters to circulate through other villages and induce workers to leave their jobs. Alice Evitt's family responded to recruiters' enticements on more than one occasion. "They used to pay our moving bill to get us from mill to mill here in Charlotte. They'd come in and talk, say they liked our work and all, they'd love for us to come back. They'd move us from Highland Park and pay our moving bill and everything. They needed help bad." Many manufacturers pressured their superintendents to use any means necessary to find more workers. The situation reportedly got so bad that "the mill operative could scarcely sleep for the rapping of the labor agent upon his door. Nothing was stopped at and even murder was done in the desperate efforts to get labor."[143]

As with wage increases, such practices only exacerbated the problems they were intended to solve. "It is a fact," complained one superintendent, "that the help are kept in a constant state of unrest by agents from different mills slipping in at night and also in the daytime and holding out promises which no mill could live up to and prosper. These inducements are as varied as the imaginations of the labor agents. The agent agrees to pay the transportation of the family and to pay up any debts they may have and to give them a little better and easier job than they have ever had at a little higher wages than they have ever gotten." But that was only the beginning. For soon another mill offered even more money, "and so the game goes on and maybe there are enough operatives on the trains all the time going from place to place to operate nearly all the idle spindles in the South."[144]

If manufacturers needed to be reminded of the pernicious effects of labor pirating, they had only to recall an incident at Hardin, North Carolina. Alice Evitt, who once lived in the Hardin village, remembered the night when the mill owner's son shot Frank Wilson, superintendent of a nearby mill, for stealing his father's workers. "Mr. Carpenter owned that whole place, the mill and everything there. He had a son, Earl Carpenter. There was a feller up there at High Shoals. He'd slip up there and hire their hands, and they'd slip up there and hire his. This Earl caught him one evening down there in a buggy beside the road and shot him—killed him. He accused him of coming to hire hands. His daddy sent him off. They never did try him. Nobody didn't know where he was at, so they never did try him."[145]

Even before the Hardin murder, many mill owners had begun to realize that the solution to their problems lay not in fighting among themselves but in rethinking their relationship to one another and the nature of mill management. In 1907 mill men supported an antipirating law in North Carolina that imposed penalties on agents soliciting help from another mill, and Georgia manufacturers banded together in the North Georgia Mutual Association to "break up the methods by which the mills have been securing their help from each other."[146]

An even more significant development came in 1908 with the formation of the Southern Textile Association (STA), an organization that was headed initially in a much different direction. In the summer of that year a group of overseers in Spray, North Carolina, began meeting to discuss common problems. Some of those who attended hoped to expand the Spray Textile Overseers Association into a regional overseers union and called a meeting for the fall in Charlotte. David Clark, at that time editor of the *American Textile Manufacturer*, and G. S. Escott, editor of the *Mill News*, went to the meeting and argued that the men's interests would not be served by unionization. E. E. Bowen, a leader of the group, agreed and advised his friends to see themselves as "mediators between labor and capital," not as owners' antagonists. In that role they could "do more toward establishing the much desired mutual feeling between the two than anybody else concerned." Convinced by what they heard, the overseers organized the STA and invited all superintendents, overseers, master mechanics, electricians, engineers, editors of textile publications, and instructors at textile schools to become members. Among the various objects of the association were to encourage experimentation in "scientific methods of cotton and textile manufacturing; to gather and promulgate information concerning cotton spinning; to promote social intercourse among superintendents and overseers of different departments of cotton mills, or allied pursuits; to bring men in charge of operation of the mills into closer relationship with their employers and employees, and to advance their knowledge in the manufacture of textiles and the more economical operation of the mills." Over the years, the association played a major role in the industry's development, serving as a conduit for the introduction of new technologies and theories of industrial relations.[147]

Cooperation between manufacturers and their shop floor lieutenants represented growing concern over the "labor problem." Although its efforts fell terribly short, the NUTW had crystallized workers' discontents. In day-to-day life millhands accepted what they could not change, but tensions persisted, however subterranean. Choices made by hundreds of individual men and women constrained employers' ability to maintain and discipline a work force. Through quitting, absenteeism, defiance, and the occasional walkout, textile workers defended a conception of labor that entailed more than a concern for productivity and profit. The result was a situation in which owners as well as operatives had to accommodate themselves to a work environment not entirely of their own choosing. Neither millhands nor employers fully achieved their goals; for each, industrialization had mixed and unexpected results. For a fuller sense of why that was so, we must look beyond the factory to the villages where workers made their homes.

From the Cradle
to the Grave

AT THE turn of the century 92 percent of southern textile families lived in villages owned by the men who gave them work. For these people, perhaps more than for any other industrial work force, the company town established the contours of everyday existence. It was not only a place to work and earn a living; it was also the setting in which men and women fell in love, married, reared their children, and retired in old age. Within the village, millhands created a new way of life by adapting their rural heritage to the unfamiliar realities of industrial labor.[1]

Piedmont mill villages were born of necessity and intent. Since most early mills were built in the countryside along the banks of swift-flowing streams, manufacturers had little choice but to provide housing where none existed before. A typical village consisted of a superintendent's residence, a cluster of single-family dwellings, one or more frame churches, a modest schoolhouse, and a company store. These facilities were essential to securing a labor force and carrying on the business of the mill, yet manufacturers also saw in them the means of exercising control over their employees. It seemed to federal investigators in 1907–8 that "all the affairs of the village and the conditions of living of all of the people are regulated entirely by the mill company. Practically speaking, the company owns everything and controls everything, and to a large extent controls everybody in the mill village."[2]

But millhands proved less pliant than the cotton they fashioned into yarn and cloth. When country people moved to the village, they did not leave behind old habits and customs. Instead, they tried to live "just like we did on the farm." They brought their hogs, chickens, and cows with them, recreating many of the patterns of rural life alongside the mechanical rhythms of the factory. In the words of one observer, "Pastures and piggeries and chicken coops took their place in the manufacture of cotton cloth." Mill villages thus evolved out of the different, sometimes conflicting, needs of workers and owners.[3]

The resulting compromise revealed itself most readily in the physical layout of the village. When mill men began building factory housing in the 1880s, they did not look for models in the industrial cities of England and New England. They turned instead to the familiar architecture of the nearby countryside. In 1898 Tom Lloyd commissioned rural carpenters to build the village surrounding his Alberta Cotton Mill in Carrboro. The carpenters worked according to traditional designs rather than blueprints, and they relied on building methods that had long served farmers' need for housing that was inexpensive and easily erected with neighbors' help. Chester Copeland's grandfather participated in both the original construction and later expansion of the Alberta village. The story of his work was handed down through the family. "Lloyd would send word that he needed another mill house, and my grandfather would cut it out of the woods—cut the logs, cut the lumber, build the whole thing and take it to town and put it up for him. Then Mr. Lloyd [would] pay him for it, and that allowed another family to move in and to work at the mill."[4]

Glencoe, one of the best examples of late nineteenth-century mill village architecture, still stands along the banks of the Haw River in rural Alamance County. Although the mill is now used as a warehouse and most of the houses are abandoned, time has done little to change the physical character of the village. James and William Holt, descendants of antebellum textile entrepreneur Edwin M. Holt, built Glencoe between 1880 and 1882. Their reliance on vernacular forms is obvious. All the dwellings are built of clapboard, set on brick piers, and arranged in two parallel rows opposite the factory. Roughly half are two-story, four-room I-houses, some with their original detached kitchens still standing. The remaining structures are one-and-one-half story versions of the traditional hall-and-parlor style. These houses consist of two rooms separated by a central hall downstairs, a sleeping loft upstairs, and a kitchen ell attached to the rear. Both house designs had long been common in the Piedmont countryside, and they gave the village the appearance of a rural hamlet more than a manufacturing settlement. If work in the mill seemed alien to men and women fresh off the farm, at least the village offered the comfort of familiar surroundings.[5]

At the turn of the century Daniel Augustus Tompkins codified the vernacular forms that characterized Glencoe and other early textile communities, ensuring them a permanent place in southern mill village design. Tompkins had been born into an aristocratic South Carolina family, but he left his father's plantation to earn an engineering degree from Rensselaer Polytechnic Institute in 1873. He moved to Charlotte ten years later and quickly established himself as a leading textile manufacturer and mill engineer. In 1899 he published a handbook titled *Cotton Mill, Commercial Features*, which became a standard text for mill officials and later for students at the South's textile colleges. Tompkins included a section on "Operatives' Homes" in which he provided detailed drawings of standard three- and four-room "factory cottages." Most mill housing built after 1900 reflected Tompkins's recommendations. The mill village, begun as a spontaneous settlement, had become by the twentieth century an institution of conscious design.[6]

After 1900, as more mills clustered on the outskirts of small towns and cities, Piedmont industrialists might have followed the lead of their northern counterparts and turned the housing of their employees over to real estate investors and local landlords. But they clung instead to proven forms. As a result, places such as Charlotte, Greenville, and Burlington developed less as real cities than as loose collections of unincorporated mill villages joined by central business districts. Moreover, the suburban villages retained a distinctively rural appearance. With help from engineering firms like the E. S. Draper Company of Charlotte, manufacturers sought to preserve the features of Glencoe and other riverside communities. Architects often tried to de-emphasize a village's practical purpose by arranging the houses along an irregular network of streets and screening them from the factory with trees and shrubs. Their designs also provided for large open spaces and numerous variations on traditional house styles, both intended to counter critics who claimed that mill towns gave an impression of "monotonous ugliness."[7]

Manufacturers' fondness for the nineteenth-century mill village derived in part from self-interest. In 1854 William Gregg, builder of the Piedmont's first mill village at Graniteville, South Carolina, warned other manufacturers that allowing operatives to live "beyond

The superintendent's house at the Franklinville Manufacturing Company,
Franklinville, North Carolina, ca. 1910.
(Courtesy of Mac Whatley, Franklinville, N.C.)

the control of the proprietors" would make them "unsteady and not reliable help." Nearly fifty years later, Daniel Tompkins echoed this advice, suggesting that in a rural or suburban location industrialists could avoid city taxes and at the same time isolate their employees from lawyers who promoted "law suits . . . for operatives that may be hurt in the mill in any accidental way." Another "important advantage" of locating beyond the city limits, he concluded, "is that employees go to bed at a reasonable hour and are therefore in better condition to work in day time."[8]

But the mill villages' survival also owed much to the men and women who lived in them. Tompkins emphasized this point in his discussion of village design. "The whole matter of providing . . . habitations for cotton mill operatives in the South," he instructed manufacturers, "may be summarized in the statement that they are essentially a rural people. They have been accustomed to farm life, where there is plenty of room. While their condition is in most cases decidedly bettered by going to the factory, old instincts cling to them. The ideal arrangement is to preserve the general conditions of rural life." Tompkins's advice was partly an attempt to rationalize the village's continued existence, but it also addressed the problem of at-

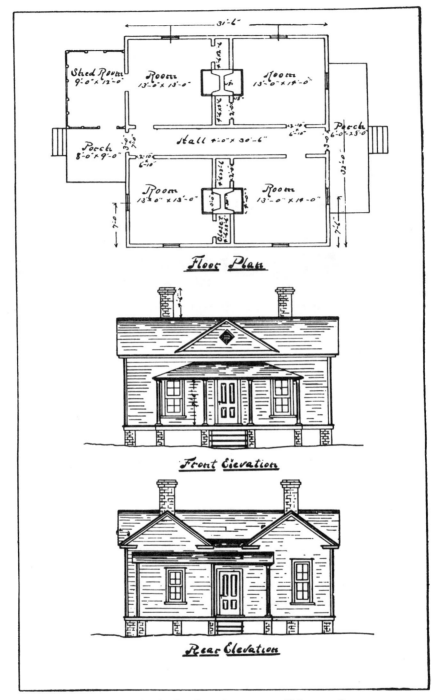

D. A. Tompkins's plan for a four-room mill house, 1899.
(*Reproduced from* Cotton Mill, Commercial Features)

tracting and keeping workers who remained wedded to a way of life at odds with industrial labor.[9]

Piedmont farmers who moved to the mill village found much of what they had come for—regular pay, easier work, and familiar sur-roundings—yet at a cost they could not have foreseen. At first, "it was heaven to them to work in the mills and draw a payday, however small." But drawing a payday did not always lead to a better life, partly because of conditions in the factory villages. Federal investigators who toured the South in 1907–8 reported that "the smaller mill villages and those in the country are often primitive in the extreme. The streets are mere wagon roads and there are no sidewalks. Frequently the yards are not fenced off, and chickens, pigs, and cows run at large." Larger villages, particularly those located in urban areas and owned by sizable corporations, boasted of graded roads, cinder paths, and pens and stalls for livestock. But these communities were the exceptions, not the rule. Even in the mid-1920s one observer con-cluded that in a majority of cases the "villages are dirty and the streets unkept, and the very sight of the village is a horror." During winter months many village streets were "excessively muddy, impassable ex-cept at crossings and in a number of cases impassable there." In summer, when the mud dried, dust blew into the houses and settled on the millhands' food, clothes, and furniture.[10]

Workers enjoyed few household conveniences. In 1907–8 kerosene lamps lit most mill houses and open fireplaces provided heat. Families drew their water from common wells or hydrants, and less than 7 percent of villages had sewage systems that amounted to more than rows of outdoor privies. Mack Duncan recalled that in Greenville "the villages had pumps on the street, maybe one or two pumps to a street, and the people would go to these pumps to get the daily water. It was a chore of the children to go keep the water supply up, and they'd gang to the pumps and play." At Marion, North Carolina, four or five families shared a well, and the entire neighborhood used "johnny houses back out in the field." These conditions started to change during the 1910s as more mills switched to electricity and began wiring operatives' homes. A federal study of company-owned housing revealed that by 1916 nearly half of all mill families benefited from electric lighting. But improvements in sanitation came more slowly. Only 24 percent of village households had running water, and 78 percent still used wooden pit or surface privies located at the back of their lots. Even those houses with indoor flush toilets were seldom connected to centralized disposal systems of the type becoming common in most towns. Instead, the toilets emptied into vaults that required regular cleaning by mill employees who carted waste away on a truck known as the "honey wagon." During hot weather, the vaults, and especially the privies, generated a stench that permeated the neighborhood and attracted swarms of flies that invaded workers' homes and spread disease. Mill houses "sounded like a beehive," and "typhoid fever just flourished."[11]

Millhands dealt with the harshness of village life as best they could. After all, mud, flies, and disease had not been uncommon on the farm. More difficult to accept, however, was the loss of independence that accompanied the move to a factory town. Most villages, including those in urban areas, sat beyond the boundaries of incorporated municipalities and thus suffered "a distinct absence of self-government." Mill officials rather than town councils established the rules of public life. "The people are not allowed any participation whatever in the political affairs of the village," reported investigators from the Women's Bureau of the U.S. Department of Labor. "They must sacrifice some of their individual rights or leave the place. The president, agent, or superintendent is the mill official usually vested with dictatorial power. His will is supreme in the village; his decisions final, so long as they do not conflict with the laws of the State."[12]

Millhands were not completely shut out of politics. They occasionally elected a sympathetic legislator or local official, especially in South Carolina, where factional divisions made the Democratic Party less cohesive than in North Carolina. But such triumphs were always hard won and difficult to sustain. South Carolina workers' most notable victory came in 1910, when they helped send Coleman L. Blease to the governor's mansion. Blease is best remembered as a racist demagogue, but his election also exposed bitter class feelings that had been festering in the state's factory towns since the turn of the century. When Blease warned millhands that manufacturers aimed to place them "on the same basis as a free negro," he captured white workers' fears of lost independence with one of the most potent images available in a society obsessed with the privileges of color. Blease's indictment of mill owners brought unprecedented numbers of textile workers to the polls; nevertheless, he failed to transform momentary passions into a lasting political organization. Haunted by the legacies of the earlier battle for black disfranchisement, the governor and his supporters could not imagine—much less build—the kind of biracial, working-class coalition that might have secured their hold on political power. Blease lost his bid for a seat in the U.S. Senate in 1914 and saw most of his associates swept from office by middle-class Democrats who had built their party on the exclusion of blacks but now denounced Bleasites as racial extremists.[13]

Stunned by defeat, Blease lived up to his critics' charges. He abandoned his attack on manufacturers and tried to broaden his constituency by turning almost exclusively to race baiting. But appeals to white supremacy alone would not suffice. By the 1930s mill folk and struggling white farmers had forsaken Blease's brand of demagoguery for the more tempered rhetoric and New Deal liberalism of a "millboy-attorney" named Olin D. Johnston. Born in 1896 to tenant farming parents who soon left the land for cotton mill work, Johnston put himself through school and began his political career as a state representative from the mill districts of Anderson and Spartanburg counties. In 1934 he defeated Blease in a bid for the governor's office. Johnston was not above using race to forward his career—few southern politicians were—but his pursuit of class issues branded him a maverick. As governor, Johnston supported labor reform on the national level and fought for state laws mandating a forty-hour workweek and improved conditions in the state's factories.[14]

Such limited victories, however, should not obscure the very real limits on political expression in the one-party South. In North Carolina, the Democratic Party remained firmly in the hands of an "aggressive aristocracy" of lawyers, bankers, and manufacturers. And even in South Carolina the absence of local self-government in the mill villages meant that politics never took on the immediacy it held for immigrant workers in the industrial Northeast. Millhands who could pass a literacy test and pay their poll tax used the vote as best they could, but until the ratification of woman suffrage in 1920 even that restricted opportunity was reserved for men in an industry dominated by women and children. Under such circumstances, most mill folk had little choice but to confront the new industrial order where they felt its effects most profoundly—on the shop floor and in the routines of mill village life.[15]

Particularly in the years before World War I, when many mills were relatively small enterprises, workers experienced their employers' authority in direct, personal terms. Few mill men lived in or near their villages, but most sought to create a bond of loyalty between themselves and the help. That effort often entailed little more than a monthly tour of the village, dispensing encouragement "in habits of thrift, morality, and temperance." Only rarely did owners take an active interest in workers' personal troubles; but when they did, the result could be lasting gratitude. Everett Padgett had fond memories of the time Dick Arrington, president of the Union Bleachery in Greenville, rescued him from a financial jam. "I hadn't been married long, and my wife had appendicitis and they had to operate on her. Well, we had a little old thing we called sick benefits; you put a dime a week into it. You could go up [to the mill office] and borrow from the sick benefit as much as a hundred dollars. So I went up there to borrow the money to pay that hospital bill and doctor bill. The hospital bill wasn't [but] two dollars and a half a day for a room, but Dr. Parker—he was the company doctor—charged one hundred and fifty dollars for operating on her. I told [Dick Arrington], 'Now I've got to borrow a hundred and fifty dollars to pay Dr. Parker.' And he said, 'You can't borrow but a hundred dollars. How come you owe him that much?' I said, 'Well, that's his charge for operating on my wife.' 'Just wait a minute.' He picked up the phone, and he called Dr. Parker. He said, 'Now look here, this boy and girl just started out. They've just been married, just started housekeeping. I mean they can't stand no kind of bill like that. Couldn't you do something about it?' I don't know what Dr. Parker told him. Anyway, Dick said, 'Well, that'd be fine, that'd be all right. I'll make a check out to you and him then.' And he made out a check to me and Dr. Parker for fifty dollars. Now that's the kind of people they were."[16]

However effective, the personal touch in mill village affairs did not imply the social familiarity that is sometimes depicted as the hallmark of southern labor relations. A superintendent at the Alamance Mill, which was owned by the Holt family and located near Glencoe, kept a diary during the 1870s and 1880s that made the point. On July 8, 1878, J. Y. Holt, the grandson of textile magnate Edwin M. Holt, left home "with Jin Ashworth to get married." Jin's father was a skilled and respected mechanic who worked for the Holts installing machinery and supervising the start-up of new factories. But the two families moved in different circles, and J. Y.'s relatives considered the marriage an affront to their social standing. After several failed attempts to heal the breach, the young couple left Alamance for good in 1880. They were never mentioned again in seven years of entries in the superintendent's diary.[17]

Verna Stackhouse's experiences as a mill manager forty years later confirmed the persistence of strict class distinctions. As manager of the King Cotton Mill in Burlington, she served as a surrogate for the mill president, who lived far away in Richmond. She kept the company books, supervised the purchase of raw cotton and the sale of finished yarn, and involved herself in mill village life. "We had, I think, about a hundred houses for employees. And of course we were in close contact with them to see that everything was running all right. I went in their homes and had a very close contact with the children. At Christmastime I'd have me a Christmas tree for the children of the village. They would write a letter to Santa Claus and send it to the mill, and then I would go to Greensboro and buy presents for them. Sometimes, if there was a family and one child was so much brighter and needed something in particular, I'd spend more money on him." Verna felt that she shared a "close feeling" with her employees but admitted that "you didn't exactly associate with them. They didn't go to the places that I went; we didn't have any social contact." Charity aside, the lives of workers moved on a different plane from those of mill men and their agents.[18]

Millhands welcomed kindness whenever it was forthcoming, but they also realized that generosity and intrusiveness frequently went hand in hand. Workers in Bynum encountered an authority more invasive than anything country folk—even debt-bound sharecroppers —had experienced before. John Wesley Snipes remembered hearing that in the early days "if you stubbed your toe, they'd fire you. They'd fire them here for not putting out the lights late at night. Old Mr. Bynum used to go around over the hill at nine o'clock and see who was up. And if you were up, he'd knock on the door and tell you to cut the lights out and get into bed." Luther Bynum also kept close tabs on his employees' private lives. "Anybody a-fussing, or maybe drinking or something like that," explained Louise Jones, "he'd go out and see into it. And of course, I won't say they didn't do wrong, but they had to be pretty good to keep their jobs in the mill. The best that I can figure it out, if they didn't live kind of like they ought to, I think he would just move them out."[19]

As mills grew larger and their villages more populous, owners turned matters of surveillance over to superintendents and village policemen. By the time Carl Thompson went to work in 1917, many factory towns had their own lawmen paid by the company and deputized by the county sheriff. These men turned a watchful eye on village morals. The superintendent at the mill in Rolesville, North Carolina, sometimes chided women who smoked on their porches, but he was hardest on men who drank. According to one worker, "You don't have no private life at all. I used to pull a high lonesome once in a while, and I go back in Monday morning; first thing boss would say: 'You drunk Friday, Saturday, and Sunday.' "[20]

Mill officials usually talked directly to offenders and gave them a chance to change their "way of doing," but sometimes "they just fired them and made them move." Sociologist Marjorie Potwin thought that such harsh discipline was not particularly "constructive social work, but at least it prevents the contamination of a whole barrel of apples by one bad one." Millhands Paul Cline and Blaine Wofford saw things differently. "It was almost like slavery," said Cline. "They tried to run your life—tell you what to do outside the mill. They thought they owned you." Wofford agreed. "They could really browbeat the people, no doubt about that. They had them over a barrel. They would threaten you with [taking away] your house. They pretty well had the upper hand over you all the time."[21]

Dismissal and eviction were radical measures, and most mill men sought to avoid them whenever possible. They much preferred the way of the church, which encouraged operatives to lead orderly, hard-working lives as an outward emblem of righteousness. When several Bynum workers left their jobs and went to the river to drink and fix a chicken stew, superintendent Edgar Moore "sentenced them to go to church for so many Sundays. They wasn't churchgoers, but the mill told them that they had to go." Moore had good reason to believe that the punishment would be effective, for, as in most villages, the Bynum church preached a conservative faith. Even when they themselves belonged to other denominations, many manufacturers encouraged only Baptist and Methodist clergymen to become active in "their" villages. As sociologist Harriet Herring explained, these ministers tended to "believe and preach doctrines which would be acceptable in the main to a capitalistic employer—a gospel of work, of gratitude for present blessings, and of patience with economic and social malad-justment as temporal and outside the sphere of religious concern—if indeed they mention such things at all in the course of their evangelical appeals and their descriptions of the glories to come." Mill worker Mary Thompson was unfamiliar with the fine points of theology, but she understood what the mill churches taught. "It's just in the Bible that people is supposed to make their living by the sweat of their brow. They preached that."[22]

But mill owners relied on more than biblical authority to work their influence. They also played an active role in village congregations, sometimes as Sunday school teachers and almost always as benefactors. "You was asking about if the companies supported the churches," Mack Duncan said. "They did; they owned the buildings." After sharing a sanctuary with a Methodist congregation for years, Duncan's Baptist neighbors at the Chiquola Mill in Honea Path, South Carolina, decided to build their own church. "They called it the Chiquola Baptist Church, after the mill. The mill gave them the land, and it furnished part of the money for the building. And the pastor was on the company's payroll. Every month, the church got a check to help pay the preacher, in case the congregation couldn't raise the money." Just as the mills built housing for the workers, so they contributed to the churches and often supplied them with coal and lights, and with water as well. The details were different in each case, but churchgoers in every community remembered that village ministers enjoyed the mills' support.[23]

Naturally, this support shaped the message from the pulpit. Most ministers simply accepted their position. Whatever misgivings they may have had, they kept their feelings to themselves. As a correspondent for the Raleigh *News and Observer* noted in 1929, "Pastors are very human. . . . They cannot bite the hand that feeds them." But some were not so easily controlled. Mack Duncan described the case of a minister at the Poe Mill in Greenville who apparently insisted on voicing criticism of the factory's management. "Preacher Anderson was preaching here at Poe Baptist, and some of the officials of the company didn't like some of the things he preached. They ordered him out of the church, [but] he didn't go too freely. So the church was locked up by the company. He couldn't get in to preach to the congregation, so he stood on his porch—the house was furnished by the company—and preached to the congregation standing out in the yard." When Preacher Anderson again refused to end his ministry, the company evicted him from the village and found a new pastor.[24]

All in all, mill pastors seem to have served manufacturers well. Mill owners supported the churches, and most ministers returned the favor. The lesson was not lost on workers, but what they made of it differed from person to person. Luther Riley sketched one reading of the situation. "The truth of it is, if you went to church, it had some influence on your job whether you knew it or not. Now, if you didn't go to church, and there was an opening available for someone to better himself, usually the church member got the job—because, for some reason or other, a little bit more was expected from a man who went to church. And if a man didn't go to church, they didn't expect quite so much from him, because he wasn't doing for himself. They took the attitude that if you weren't willing to do for yourself, they didn't expect you to do very much for them."[25]

Other millhands had less sympathy for the owners' point of view. Regardless of the consequences, they simply stayed away from the village churches. Mill owners and village ministers complained constantly that workers "either would not or could not be interested" in church attendance. What those complaints meant, however, is not at all clear. The vast majority of the people we interviewed claimed to have been regular churchgoers. It is certainly possible that people exaggerated their religious devotion or that we interviewed an inordinate number of the faithful. But a more likely explanation is that many of the millhands who were considered irreligious by owners actually chose to worship outside the village. In Bynum, for instance, a number of workers shunned the village's Methodist chapel and attended services in nearby rural churches. And in Carrboro, Baptists and Methodists alike refused to use the sanctuary provided by the mill, preferring instead to worship in their own churches elsewhere in town. The appeal of nonmill churches became particularly powerful during the 1910s and 1920s as factories began clustering around the outskirts of growing urban centers. Churches in the new towns and cities tended to take on distinct class identities, dividing neatly between those that served working people and those that catered to the "uptown folks." Moreover, an urban environment gave millhands easy access by foot or streetcar to a variety of places of worship. On Sunday, at least, they could escape their employers' scrutiny and share their pews with men and women who understood their values and concerns.[26]

Manufacturers, however, depended on the village to do more than simply police workers' behavior and beliefs. Its other purpose, as millhand Blaine Wofford explained, was "to get and to keep help." Mill owners rented houses to their employees at relatively cheap rates. In 1908 millhands living in factory-owned housing paid an average monthly rent of $3.57, which accounted for 6 percent of their total monthly expenditures. By comparison, workers renting privately owned dwellings paid almost twice as much. Mill men used low-cost, single-family housing both to entice and to coerce: only by providing shelter could owners attract workers to their factories, but once installed in a company-owned home, families found that they could stay only so long as they supplied the firm with a quota of hands. According to federal investigators, "The general rule in the South [was] that families occupying company-owned houses . . . must furnish one employee for each room occupied." Those who failed to meet this quota usually had no choice but to accept a smaller house or simply leave.[27]

Such regulations not only helped enforce the family labor system; they also had important consequences for the way millhands lived. Southern textile workers occupied crowded quarters as compared to their New England counterparts. In 1907–8 the average southern mill family of seven lived in a four-room house, whereas in New England a family of the same size typically occupied six rooms. Southern mill families used all their rooms except the kitchen for sleeping, while New England workers had one and sometimes two rooms left solely for other purposes. Bessie Buchanan remembered what these statistics meant to her. She grew up in a four-room mill house with eight brothers and sisters. "The boys slept in one room, and the girls slept in another. And Mother and Daddy had a room. And the kitchen. We never knew what it was to have a dining room. We didn't have a living room or a den or nothing like that; we wasn't used to it." While the design of middle-class homes in town increasingly emphasized privacy and the separation of public and private spaces, the interior of mill homes remained shared and relatively undifferentiated.[28]

Mill children's educational opportunities also differed significantly from those of their town-dwelling peers. With few exceptions, mill schools were established and administered separately from existing town and county systems. In some cases, mill companies subsidized the schools in lieu of paying local taxes for education. They often provided the buildings and carried the teachers on the factory payroll. Other schools received their funds from county boards of education but were administered by mill officials appointed by the boards as local trustees. In either case, village schools operated more as extensions of the factory than as independent institutions.[29]

A particularly candid mill owner acknowledged that "the school is a part of our business." Evidence of that view proved easy to find. In 1907–8, before the passage of compulsory attendance laws, federal observers noted that "the school work of the child from 12 to 16 years

Children six to eight years old in the school at the Lynchburg Cotton Mills,
Lynchburg, Virginia, 1911. There was no school for older children, who, according
to the teacher, "were just waiting . . . to go into the mill."
Photograph by Lewis Hine.
(Courtesy of the Photography Collections, Albin O. Kuhn Library and Gallery,
University of Maryland at Baltimore County)

of age is frequently interrupted by a hurry call from the mill superintendent. . . . It was the custom for the overseers in the mill to
send to the schoolhouse at any time of day for workers. The mill came
first always, the school after." Owners had little to gain by enforcing school attendance, since children who became ensnared by the
factory at an early age were less likely to seek employment elsewhere
as adults. These conditions improved only in the mid-1910s after
schooling was made mandatory for all children under twelve years of
age. By 1925 North Carolina's mill schools enrolled on average 79
percent of all eligible thirteen-year-olds, as compared to 83 percent
for rural schools and 88 percent for city schools.[30]

Even then, mill schools continued to shape children's opportunities
in a way that encouraged them to follow their parents into the factory.
The course of study in North Carolina during the 1920s included
seven years of elementary education and four years of high school, yet
in a large majority of the state's mill villages, schools provided only the
first seven grades free of charge. State law required that children in
these communities enroll in a town or county high school and pay
tuition if they wished to continue their education. Mill schools were

considered separate institutions for purposes of taxation; therefore, students who attended them were not entitled to a high school education at public expense. George Shue was typical of many mill village students. "I finished the sixth grade and that's as far as it went. I wanted to finish seventh grade, but you had to go to Charlotte High School and you had to pay. Well, my daddy couldn't afford to do that making fifteen dollars a week."[31]

Other factors also influenced the decision to leave school, including family needs and children's own desires to assume adult responsibilities, but, at least by the mid-1920s, the availability of free secondary education was an equally important consideration. In villages that had high schools, as many as 13 percent of the students continued their education beyond the seventh grade. But only 3 percent of the students from seven-grade mill schools went on to high school, as compared to 10 percent for rural schools and 21 percent for city schools. Many mill children, then, were far less likely than even rural students to acquire the credentials that might have taken them out of the factory. As a result, the cotton mill labor force became largely self-reproducing. A 1927 study of four Gaston County textile communities found that only 18 percent of married millhands had mill-working parents, but that 71 percent of unmarried millhands above the age of fourteen had been born in a mill village. Thus, over the course of two generations the percentage of persons "occupied permanently in cotton mill work" had nearly quadrupled.[32]

Company housing and mill schools gave manufacturers access to every able-bodied family member and helped create a self-perpetuating labor force, but they did little to tame millhands' "moving habit." For that, owners turned first to company stores and then to experiments in welfare capitalism. Like much else in the village, company stores had their origins in necessity. When factories were built in remote country locations, the stores served the needs of workers who otherwise would have had to travel several miles to shop. Many early mills were also undercapitalized, and company stores helped protect their cash reserves by keeping the workers' wages flowing back to the company. Daniel Tompkins advised prospective manufacturers that "a mill . . . can operate its own store and thereby get back in mercantile profit much of the money paid for wages." But above all, mill men relied on their stores to maintain a stable work force by keeping operatives constantly in debt. "Their theory," explained a federal report, "is that if operatives can be kept in debt to the company store they will . . . be more apt to remain at work at the mill instead of moving elsewhere."[33]

Employers used several methods to achieve this end. Some spread paydays far apart. Federal investigators reported that "if employees are not paid oftener than once in two weeks, only those who are most provident will keep money enough on hand to buy needed supplies during the fortnight." When their earnings had been spent, most families had no choice but to go to the company store because they found it difficult to obtain credit elsewhere. Other mills paid their workers in scrip or trade checks that were negotiable only at the village store. "If hands trade their checks to any other firm and they present them for cash," explained a worker to the North Carolina Bureau of Labor Statistics, "this firm demands a discount. . . . The best trade check used in this county is not worth over 75 per cent. Some of the checks . . . are almost worthless."[34]

Most manufacturers simply deducted employees' bills from their weekly earnings, ensuring a cycle of indebtedness very much like the plight of sharecroppers. Don Faucette often heard his daddy talking about it. "Said if you worked at the mill, they'd just take your wages and put it in the company store and you didn't get nothing. For years and years they didn't get no money; they just worked for the house they lived in and what they got at the company store. They just kept them in the hole all the time." Alice Evitt worked at the mill in Hardin, where workers who could not meet their debts received an empty pay envelope marked "balance due." "People said that [on payday] frogs sat on the river and hollered, 'Balance due, balance due.' They'd tell that around 'cause so many people didn't draw a thing. Some of them people, they wouldn't have nothing."[35]

More than one-third of all southern mills operated company stores at the turn of the century, but by 1920 only a handful of stores remained in business. Some simply fell victim to the industry's growth and maturation. Workers in urban areas had easy access to a variety of merchants and were less easily bound to a single company store. Operatives at North Charlotte's four mills, for instance, supported what one millhand characterized as a "little town" of their own, complete with barber shops, dry goods stores, and pool halls. In addition, the larger mills of the 1910s enjoyed more financial security than their predecessors and so had less need for company stores to recycle their capital. But many manufacturers closed their stores in response to millhands' complaints. They conceded that debt, like eviction, was a heavy-handed and often counterproductive instrument of control that left workers feeling "as if they are enslaved." During the decade before World War I, a growing number of mill men turned to other means of securing "faithful and regular workers."[36]

Manufacturers' most ambitious undertaking was the implementation of company-sponsored "welfare work." Taking their cue from the National Civic Federation and major northern corporations, southern mill men embarked on a campaign to beautify their villages and provide new social services for their employees. They built community centers, landscaped their factory grounds, sponsored YMCAs, and organized a variety of recreational and educational activities. In one sense, there was nothing particularly novel about such projects. As we have seen, cotton manufacturers had always used small acts of kindness to reward dependable service and encourage company loyalty. But welfare work systematized those efforts and substituted the expertise of professional intermediaries—social workers, nurses, and teachers—for the personal authority of the employer. Welfare work was expensive and therefore gained only a limited following among small-scale manufacturers. Large firms, however, embraced the new approach to mill village relations with enthusiasm. Between 1905 and 1915 eight Piedmont mills ranked among the nation's leading practitioners of company-sponsored welfare work.[37]

Owners may have been sincere in their efforts to better workers' living conditions, yet as they and their spokesmen were quick to admit, welfare work was essentially "a matter of self-defense." Lena Rivers Smyth, a reporter for the *Charlotte Observer*, acknowledged that had millhands' high rates of mobility not aggravated the turn-of-the-century labor shortage, "there would possibly have been no welfare work." "The mills are doing more, infinitely more, than any other industry," she continued, "but . . . the average cotton mill man is no better and no worse than the average man engaged in other business." Manufacturers' first objective was to foster "permanency of residence and regularity of work" among the operatives who turned raw cotton into cloth and profit. The *Southern Textile Bulletin* warned managers that they had no more right to consider philanthropy "as an end in designing or operating a mill" than they had to use "mill money to make a personal subscription to foreign missions or settlement work. Any one of these may be worthy and it may be of personal gratification to assist in good work but it is not a proper means of employing mill money." Welfare work was to be viewed less as a "humanitarian" venture than as a "cold blooded business proposition."[38]

Mill men also considered welfare work a way "to keep down public criticism." During the early years of mill building, few observers had questioned the claim that cotton factories would uplift poor white farmers and solve the New South's persistent problems of poverty and illiteracy. But by the turn of the century enthusiasm gave way to nagging doubt among the town-dwelling middle class. The mill building boom of the late 1890s fed their fears by greatly expanding the factory population, but perhaps even more important was the growing number of urban mills that brought townspeople and factory operatives into close daily contact. As townsfolk created and refined their own standards of decorum, domesticity, and accumulation, they found themselves surrounded by workers whose way of life seemed increasingly alien and in need of reform. Millhands were a "nomadic population," ill fed and ill clad. Worst of all, their children began work at a tender age and were denied the education that townspeople considered necessary for responsible citizenship. Acting on these concerns, reformers organized missions to the mill villages and rallied behind the effort to abolish child labor.[39]

Welfare advocates hoped to ward off such meddling by outsiders. They acknowledged the industry's faults but insisted that mill owners were blamed unfairly for the workers' plight. "It was natural," explained the South Carolina commissioner of agriculture, commerce, and immigration, "that when great manufacturing plants were springing up one after another like mushrooms, drawing their labor from the farms, crude labor that had to be trained . . . that there should have been shortcomings." To prove the point, the *Textile Manufacturer* encouraged townsfolk to conjure up familiar images of the "environment of those who came to the mills." A superintendent from South Carolina explained that millhands had once lived in "floorless cabins with perhaps only one or two rooms, only one or two small openings in the walls for windows, and a large open fireplace for heating and cooking. . . . Their bath room for the morning toilet was the nearby branch. . . . They had no books or newspapers in the home. The sound of music [was] almost unheard except for a home-made cat skin banjo." In such a home "there was little . . . to foster the higher traits of human character—such as modesty, culture and a desire for social development. There was scarcely a dream of living a life of usefulness and helpfulness among the fairest of the maidens and the bravest of the youths. They were content to live, breed and die no step in advance of their sires." The men and women who came to the mills were "new arrivals from primitive districts" who had "everything to learn." Their poverty and ignorance were not the fault of mill men but rather vestiges of their own uncivilized past.[40]

Supporters of welfare work promised a "metamorphosis," insisting that they could reshape the individual millhand "as the lump of clay is taken and moulded into brick." "Suppose a family of folks who are slovenly, unclean in their habits, 'don't care,' enter a mill village that has comfortable houses and well-kept grounds," advised the *Southern and Western Textile Excelsior*. "Straightaway those same people will brace up and begin to take some pride in their work and will begin to have some respect for themselves." Through welfare work the cotton mill would fulfill its promise as a social as well as economic enterprise, "not only converting raw cotton into a fine finished product, but of vastly greater importance . . . discovering and converting raw, crude human material . . . into a prosperous, happy, industrious citizenship." As proof of that claim, the *Southern Textile Bulletin* published special "Health and Happiness" issues, complete with photographs of manicured villages and well-scrubbed children. The notions of citizenship embodied in these words and pictures, however, bore little resemblance to the ideals of workers who recalled rural traditions of independence and sharing. Promoters of welfare work aimed to create worker-citizens who would adopt "regular habits," accept their employers' authority, and believe that in the mills there was "nothing to be lost and everything to gain."[41]

Welfare work was a bold experiment in social engineering. But how were such mundane activities as sewing clubs, flower shows, and organized recreation to achieve a wholesale transformation of village residents? First of all, welfare programs encouraged workers to view their houses as homes rather than items in a company inventory. Mills often distributed flower seeds and shrubs in the spring and then held contests in late summer to select the most beautiful yard and the most skilled gardener. The purpose of such activities was "to secure an attachment for the village to decrease the migratory tendency." By inspiring millhands to take pride in their surroundings, employers hoped to produce "permanent citizens" who would not roam from job to job but would "find a good mill . . . and become identified with the same."[42]

Welfare programs also attempted to heighten workers' dependence on the company by extending its influence into the ways they entertained and sustained themselves. At larger mills professional social workers played a pivotal role in that effort. Ceasar Cone, who pioneered the use of welfare agents at Greensboro's Proximity Mills in 1903, explained that "these young ladies establish themselves in the heart of the village. A club house, a mill tenement, a room over the company's store, or other convenient quarters are given over to them and becomes the nucleus of their work. . . . They organize social clubs, give parties and entertainments . . . picnics and ice cream suppers. . . . They visit every family in the village and form close, personal friendships. . . . They make the new families in the village feel at home; visit the sick, and look after the poor."[43] In short, welfare agents set themselves up as the arbiters of village life.

Welfare agents sometimes provided useful services but not without intruding deeply into workers' personal lives. The Spray Cotton Mill established a day nursery for young children after "the shocking discovery one day of the half-charred body of a little child" near an open fireplace. The child's death bespoke the difficulties faced by mothers who had to leave their children to work in the mills. Factory nurseries helped diminish the danger and eased parental fears, but they also established a company claim to the child. As Thomas Parker, one of the leading proponents of welfare work, explained, children were "valuable assets, to be used wisely and not wastefully, and to be saved and developed for the future as well as to be profitably employed for the present." To that end, many firms organized mothers' clubs to train women in the latest methods of child care and held "better baby" contests to judge the quality of the women's work. The properly reared mill child belonged not only to the family that gave it life but also to the mill that would one day profit from its labor. Icy Norman's mother confronted that lesson every morning when she delivered her children to the company nursery at the Dan River Mills in Schoolfield, Virginia. Icy was too young to remember much about the experience, but she did recall that "when you went in that nursery, they changed your clothes—they put their clothes on you." Each child was "checked" for health and cleanliness and then dressed in a tiny company uniform.[44]

Nurseries were but one example of mill owners' efforts to integrate the lives and leisure time of workers with the functioning of the firm. Many manufacturers took the work further by establishing "domestic

Welfare worker conducting a domestic science class at the Proximity Mills,
Greensboro, North Carolina, 1909.
(Courtesy of Robert Vogel, National Museum of American History)

science" classes in which young women learned the arts of house-keeping and cooking from a home economist rather than their mothers and grandmothers. Other employers financed brass bands or built YMCAs to structure workingmen's leisure and combat the habit of "hang[ing] round the store." Mills also financed workers' baseball teams and organized factory leagues in an effort to transform sandlot games into a sport sponsored by and identified with the company. A winning team was often vital to that effort. The superintendent at the Highland Park Mill in Charlotte frequently hired men better known for their batting averages than their work records. According to Hoyle McCorkle, "He'd give them ragtag jobs—they didn't have to do much—and we got a good ball club." Through each of these activities, mill men strove to create a relationship of "mutual friendliness" that would persuade workers to remain in the mills "for longer periods of service."45

Above all, welfare work aimed to change the way millhands thought about the meaning of human labor. Advocates of welfare programs reminded mill men that "labor is a commodity to be purchased much as coal, machinery and cotton—with the exception that the guiding

The mill baseball team at Bynum, North Carolina, ca. 1910. The man in a suit is mill superintendent Edgar Moore.

(*Courtesy of Sallie Mae Fowler, Bynum, N.C.*)

element in man—his spirit—cannot be bought." The human soul had, instead, to be courted and cultivated. "The trouble with labor," warned the *Southern Textile Bulletin*, was that working people possessed a "spirit of self-expression" that was out of place amid the "whirr of the spindles and the rattle of the looms." When thwarted by cotton mill discipline, that spirit gave rise first to "careless neglect; then 'withholding efficiency'; then Sabotage; then open strife; then destruction." To combat this cycle of dissatisfaction, welfare work offered millhands the "recreation, exercise, [and] entertainment" that would enable them "to look on the bright side of things and withstand the physical discomforts of standing for long hours by one machine and doing the same thing over and over." Brass bands, baseball teams, and YMCAs could thus become instruments of accommodation to factory life. If profits were to be maintained, the cotton mill could afford only limited concessions to individual pride and creativity; manufacturers' best hope for a contented work force was to adjust human nature to the demands of industrial labor.[46]

Organized recreation seemed particularly well suited to that task.

A. S. Winslow, superintendent of the Clinton Cotton Mills in South Carolina, noted that as farm youths, most millhands had learned little of "real child play life." They had seldom engaged in organized sports, and their games rarely made a clear distinction between winners and losers. Such forms of play perhaps suited children to country life, but they left young men and women unprepared for the "fixed hours of labor . . . the necessary discipline and the close attention to details of manufacturing." To correct that inadequacy, employers built playgrounds where mill folk—young and old—might enjoy "play of the right sort, systematized . . . and truly directed." Structured recreation, whether a men's game of baseball or a children's game of kickball, could "be so planned that lessons in our social, civil and business contracts can be taught and right deductions made." Through the proper kind of play, children would learn obedience to abstract authority in the form of written rules, the importance of striving for good performance, and the necessity of maintaining "self (and playmate) control." When carried to the shop floor, such lessons held the power to transform "a whole body of raw recruits . . . into a trained and disciplined army of . . . wealth producers."[47]

Those who were to produce wealth, however, had first to learn the true value of labor and the uses of money. As we have already seen, millhands sought more from their work than monetary rewards and did not always share their employers' conviction that "keeping everlastingly at it brings success." The results could include high rates of absenteeism and what manufacturers perceived to be "loafing." One contributor to the *Southern Textile Bulletin* estimated that for "each employee absent from work for any cause . . . not less than $3,000 of protective investment in machinery is idle, eating into dividends." Welfare work promised to safeguard stockholders' earnings by imbuing operatives with the complementary virtues of consumerism and thrift. Here the domestic science and mothers' clubs served double duty, schooling their members in a middle-class vision of domestic life. Home economists taught young women and girls to make fashionable clothes, cook fancy meals, and keep neat homes furnished with stylish upholstered couches and chairs. But before mill families could enjoy these luxuries, they would have to "learn the all important idea" of working for future needs rather than "present gratification." To help them on, employers encouraged investments in local dime savings banks or awarded prizes for garden shows and baby contests "in the form of a bank book with a dollar deposit." The *Southern and*

Children participating in organized recreation at the Franklinville Manufacturing Company, Franklinville, North Carolina, ca. 1915. Manufacturers expected such recreation to build strong bodies and disciplined minds.
(Courtesy of Mac Whatley, Franklinville, N.C.)

Western Textile Excelsior voiced owners' confidence that if these measures did not change the present generation of mill workers, they would at least influence their children. "Their needs must be increased to equal the rise in wages to get them to work steadily," one mill president explained. "The people are not sufficiently ambitious to care to work all the time, but as we are throwing about them elevating influences their needs are growing greater and the next generation will be all right."[48]

Despite assurances that it would promote industrial harmony and tame millhands' "moving habit," welfare work actually produced disappointing results. Many workers recognized the purpose of welfare activities and refused to participate. Mack Duncan believed that "the textile plants liked to keep something for the people to do"; their philosophy was "keep a man happy and don't let him think too much, and he won't bother you too much." Another millhand, writing to the Charlotte *Labor Herald*, claimed that mill men had substituted "cunning" for authoritarianism in their dealings with employees. "How this could best be done, was a question of much speculation, and has caused no little experimenting," he explained. "Said some, 'We will build nurseries for the babies . . . kindergartens for the tots, and Y.M.C.A.'s for the adults. . . . Thus from the cradle to the grave, we will mould their minds and formulate their convictions. . . .' To accomplish this, they learned that a good staff of social workers was as necessary as the tusks in the mouth of a vicious wild beast."[49]

Other workers acted less self-consciously, often turning welfare work to their own advantage rather than denouncing it. Roy Auton and his friends enjoyed playing "cow pasture ball" and cared little for "go[ing] by the rules, like umpires and things." Nevertheless, they were eager to join a mill team and participate in a factory league. Scheduled games guaranteed team members time away from work, provided neighbors regular opportunities to visit, and gave young folks a place to court. At the Cone mills in Greensboro, programs aimed at young mothers reinforced workers' belief that certain services were owed them as rights rather than privileges. Like their counterparts in other communities, the women shunned child care classes and steered clear of social workers who tried to offer them "help for beginners." But when winter weather brought a rash of colds and flu, they lined up at company-sponsored baby clinics to demand free medicine and nursing care. In other places, efforts to spur workers' desires for more of the good things in life only served to highlight the limitations of their wages. Many recipients of welfare services, reported one observer, "in place of showing appreciation, were severely critical, some suggesting that they would prefer an addition to their pay envelope." Such responses discouraged manufacturers who had hoped to win millhands' gratitude and redirect their loyalties. As an economic depression settled over the textile industry in the years after World War I, many mill owners concluded that welfare work's results did not justify the expense. Only a handful of mills initiated new programs after 1920, while many others abandoned their welfare activities altogether.[50]

Welfare work fell short of owners' expectations because millhands did not arrive at the factory gates empty-handed. Rather than embrace the world of manufacturers and townspeople, they struggled to forge their own forms of expression and limit their dependence on the mill. Workers fashioned customary ways of thinking and acting into a distinctively new way of life suited to their changed circumstances and needs. This adaptation occurred at no single moment in time; rather, it evolved, shaped and reshaped by successive waves of migration off the farm and by the constant movement of families from village to village. Nor did it produce a self-conscious culture of rebellion. The men and women who labored in the mills simply tried to accommodate the new order, while preserving as best they could familiar values and habits. Yet, the gradual accumulation of shared experience and group identity was not without political implications. Mill village culture provided comfort and reassurance in an often hostile world. It also offered a potential alternative to a society based on individualism and self-interest. And it could, under certain circumstances, sustain resistance to management authority.

The village's inner life was rooted in family ties. Kinship guided migration to the mills and continued to play a powerful unifying role. Indeed, intermarriage was the cement of village society. This is not to reinforce the stigma of "inbreeding" that has dogged observations of the mill worker as a "social type." Rather, the children of the first generation off the land married newcomers of the second and third. A recent study of Bynum concluded that by the 1920s the community "could make a reasonable claim to being 'one big family,' simply by virtue of marriage relationships." Through a careful reconstitution of more than three generations of genealogical information, it became clear that most village residents had "some connection to each other, however distant, by marriage."[51]

There is no reason to think that Bynum was unique. Opportunities for courtship took place most commonly in the village and the factory. Even after the passage of effective child labor laws in the 1910s, most children entered the mill by their mid-teens. Inevitably, they met their spouses on the job and courted there as well. Like many couples, Grover and Alice Hardin fell in love in the mill. "My wife worked in the spinning room," Grover recalled. "We met, and it must have been love at first sight because it wasn't very long after we met that we married. She was a spinning room person, and I would go, when I could, up to the spinning room, and we'd lay in the window and court a little bit. We decided then just to get married." For others, marriage evolved out of the friendships formed while growing up in the mill village. As one married worker recalled, "We knowed each other from childhood. Just raised up, you might say, together. All lived here on the hill, you see. That's how we met."[52]

Under such circumstances, mill parents found it difficult to impose on their children the strict rules that had governed their own youth.

On the farm, where children's labor was valuable and marriage could be a means of acquiring or consolidating land, parents did their best to control the timing of marriage and the choice of a spouse. Child labor remained important in the mill village and often conflicted with young folks' plans. When Bessie Hensley announced that she had decided to marry, her mother objected. "She wanted to keep me and all the rest. Mama needed the money we older ones was bringing in." But land ownership was no longer an issue among mill families, and young men did not have to acquire or inherit land before starting households of their own. While the age of marriage remained unchanged for women, it declined for mill-working men, so that by 1900 they were about twice as likely as other white males to marry before the age of twenty-four.[53]

Nevertheless, courtship generally remained a sponsored activity, closely supervised by adults. James Pharis explained that dating in the mill village followed a regular pattern. "The way they dated back in those days—and everybody done practically the same thing because it was a habit with all of them—they'd date Wednesday night, Saturday night, and Sunday evening." On Wednesdays, young men visited in their girlfriends' homes, often in the company of brothers and sisters who also were of courting age. Eula Durham remembered that "most [families] had a little front room, and they'd go in there and court" until the girl's father called bedtime. But some boys were mischievous and not easily sent away. One of Eula's sisters had a boyfriend named Wessie Eubanks, who called her father's bluff. "There was a bunch of us in the parlor one night, and Papa said, 'All right. It's bed time in there. If it ain't, come in here and I'll fix you a bed and you can go to bed if you're going to stay all night.' When he told us that, Wessie said, 'All right, Mr. Cooper, fix my bed. Now where am I going to sleep?' Wessie was so bad!"[54]

Saturday was a special day. Work ended at noon, and in the evening parents organized house parties. Some families gained a reputation for "really enjoy[ing] having young folks" around—perhaps they had several children of marrying age. In any case, young men and women "knew where to go to be well liked, and not be disturbed too much." House parties provided an occasion for playing out the individual dramas of romance. "Boys and girls would get together at different homes and play games," Mary Thompson recalled, "spinning the bottle, things like that. We'd have times where they'd all come to one house, and some of them had pianos. We'd play and sing and then sit

around and talk. Like all boys and girls, we loved to talk. We'd talk
about music and church, and then we just liked to talk to one another.
Boys and girls then fell in love and fell out, just like now."[55]

On Sunday, courting centered around church activities. Young couples worshiped with their parents in the morning and enjoyed the walk
home together afterward. On spring and summer afternoons they
attended box suppers on the church lawn. Naomi Trammel met her
husband that way. "The families would have the thing. They'd fix the
boxes and sell them. And these boys would buy them, and then they'd
go and get the girl they wanted to eat them with." But the suppers
could provide occasions for sabotaging romances as well as arranging
them. Eula Durham remembered how she and a friend spoiled the
plans of a rival. "This gal, the preacher's daughter, she thought she
was really tops. She thought her box was so pretty, and Silas Hatley,
she kind of went wild over him. Well, Silas bought her box, and, Lord,
it just tickled her to death. She bragged, 'I'll get to eat with Silas.' And
I thinked to myself, 'No you won't neither.' I said, 'I'm going to get that
box.' And this gal I ran around with, she says, 'Well, get it. We'll go
somewhere and eat the thing.' I got the box, and that was the best fried
chicken I ever eat in my life." In the evening, after a box supper or
some other church activity, people gathered again for prayer meeting.
For many young folks, however, prayer was a mere pretext. "On
Sunday evenings everybody would meet and go over to prayer meeting. And didn't half of them go in the church. They'd sit outside and
court!"[56]

Sometimes, of course, young couples managed to escape parental supervision altogether. In Bynum, Eula Durham and her friends
would often "all gang up together and cook a chicken stew and have a
sing-out down on the river." But even when they eluded their parents'
watchful eyes, young men and women were seldom alone. Wherever
they went "there'd be a group. It was just a rule. You wasn't allowed to
go just maybe two of you, there would be no way." As Kathryn Killian
explained, "It was so different, because we didn't date alone. With the
man I married, I'll bet I didn't date with him alone over a dozen
times. We were always with someone else. We never thought of dating
alone."[57]

Beginning in the 1920s, courtship in the mill village took on new
twists as automobiles provided couples greater privacy and the means
of traveling farther away from home. It became commonplace for
couples in North Carolina mill villages to run away to York and

Chester, South Carolina, where they could get married without parental consent. Ralph Austin, a carder at the Highland Park Mill in North Charlotte, took a fancy to a young woman in the spinning room. "A time or two I went to see her, and after I'd been there fifteen minutes, the old man called bedtime on me." One Sunday the couple took matters into their own hands. They drove down Highway 49 to York in a borrowed Model T Ford and were married the same day with no questions asked. They came back home, told their parents what they had done, and returned to work Monday morning.[58]

George and Mamie Shue were married the same way, although they ran into a bit more difficulty. The couple met at a baseball game and courted furtively for nearly a year. Their parents opposed their plans to marry, but George was persistent. "He worked in the slasher room and I worked in the quill room," Mamie recalled, "and he'd pass by and he'd holler and say, 'Will you?' And I shook my head. He done that, oh, I don't know how long he went on with that. And one day, I done the wrong thing; I said, 'Yes.'" George and Mamie kept their plans a secret and enlisted the help of other workers in a plot to sneak out of the mill and make their way to York. "This lady, Mrs. Newcombe, she was working that afternoon," Mamie explained, "and she said she'd send after me, that she'd have to have help. So I dressed and all, and she sent after me and I just went on to work. I went through the mill, out the back, down the railroad, and met him. And we lit out." But they failed in their first attempt because Mamie was only seventeen, and—at eighty-five pounds—looked even younger. The justice of the peace in York scolded George for "robbing the cradle" and sent the couple home. On a second try several weeks later, they found a magistrate in Chester willing to marry them.[59]

Couples like the Shues and the Austins defied their parents' authority, but the claims of the neighborhood were less easily ignored. Few mill couples could afford the private honeymoons that came to characterize middle-class marriages in the late nineteenth century. Instead, they found themselves "celebrated" in traditional fashion. "Back then, when anybody got married," explained Edna Hargett, "we'd celebrate them, beat on tin cans and things like that, give them a serenade. They didn't go off on honeymoons back then, you know. They went on back to work right after they were married. So we'd go down there and we'd take cans and beat them together and holler. They'd raise the window and come out and speak to us, and then we'd come home. We had a good time celebrating them." The serenade reminded even rebellious couples that marriage involved more than an individual commitment. Newlyweds might escape parental authority, but they remained firmly bound within the web of neighborly relations.[60]

Concern for those relations also found expression in the way villagers treated new families and single workers who moved into the community. A study completed in the late 1920s revealed that 41 percent of mill families had moved fewer than three times in ten years. Most of these settled households appear to have been headed by middle-aged men and women who had "just kept the road hot" until finding a job and a village they liked. Letha Ann Osteen and her husband, George, began married life as "scat-abouts" in search of greener pastures. "All the new married people done that. Be here today and gone tomorrow. It was rough, but people didn't know no better. They had to live and learn. But after a year or two we found out that you had to take advantage of things. If you got a good thing, hold to it as long as it lasted." Once they settled down, couples like the Osteens joined a relatively stable core of residents who made movement possible for others by providing the contacts through which news of job opportunities spread. Established residents also preserved ways of life that mitigated the ill effects of transiency and made it easy for newcomers to feel at home.[61]

In these ways the entire Piedmont became what journalist Arthur W. Page described in 1907 as "one long mill village." Through kinship, shared work experiences, and a common culture, individual communities were woven together into an elaborate regional fabric. According to Lacy Wright, who worked at Greensboro's White Oak Mill, "We had a pretty fair picture, generally speaking, of what you might say a two-hundred-mile radius of Greensboro. News traveled by word of mouth faster than any other way in those days, because that's the only way we had. In other words, if something would happen at White Oak this week, you could go over to Danville by the weekend and they'd done heard about it. It looked like it always worked out that there would be somebody or another that would carry that information all around." Rooted as they were in a regional mill village culture, workers like Wright took the entire Piedmont as their frame of reference. Millhands' ramblings did not so much undermine as reinforce a shared regional identity and sense of belonging.[62]

Single workers also found themselves quickly absorbed into established patterns of community life. Widows and older couples often ran boardinghouses that helped them earn needed income and drew unattached men and women into stable households. "You took someone you liked, a nice person," recalled Louise Jones of Bynum, "and they lived just the same as your family." There simply were no strangers in the village—at least not for long. Mary Thompson, whose skills as a drawing-in hand took her to towns across the Piedmont, explained that boardinghouses gave single workers a sense of connection to the community. "Boardinghouses were kind of familylike. Most every boardinghouse I lived in was real nice. Usually someone real nice ran it, and it's kind of like living in a family. You'd get acquainted with everyone after you stayed there awhile. And you'd just hate to see them leave, or you'd hate to leave yourself, because you'd made lots of friends and enjoyed yourself. It was almost like leaving home. There ain't no place like home, but I guess that's the nearest place like home there is, a boardinghouse."[63]

Together, these customs of incorporation created in each locality a broad network of obligation, responsibility, and concern. In times of need family relations might be extended to include the village as a whole. Ethel Faucette remembered that "it wasn't nothing unusual" for mill families to adopt orphaned children, even in the absence of blood ties. Her own parents adopted a five-year-old girl named Kate whose mother died unexpectedly. Ethel's mother and Kate's mother "were good friends. They weren't a bit of kin in the world; they were just good friends." When Kate's mother fell ill, Ethel's parents stayed with her until she died. "And Kate went out on the porch and told Daddy—she always called him Uncle Man—she says, 'Uncle Man, I ain't got nobody, Mama's gone. I want to come and stay with you.' Daddy said, 'I got eight of my own, but one more won't make no difference, just come on when you get ready.'" When men from the children's home in the nearby town of Elon, North Carolina, came to claim Kate, the Faucettes refused to give her up. "Mama told them, 'I got eight of my own, but I'm going to keep her. I dare every one of you to touch her; if you do, I'll kill you. I got the gun right here.' That's just what she told 'em. So she sent to the mill after Daddy." When Ethel's father got home, he challenged the men to take him to jail and defied their order to surrender the girl. "He just got rid of them. And him and mother went to [the courthouse in] Graham and had it fixed so that they could keep her."[64]

By the same token, the community could serve as a substitute for the responsibilities and rewards of family life. Icy Norman never married and never had a family of her own. Instead, she devoted herself to friends and neighbors. "For me, the greatest joy is if I can do you a favor. I get more joy out of that and more happiness. If somebody's sick that I know, I can go to them and help them—any hour, day or night. I said I didn't have no family. But in the other sense of the word, I've got a big family, because I try to go in fellowship and do for other people." Although married, Mary Harrington also made up for her lack of children by helping others. "I like to see other people's need, and to do something about it. I have tried to live for other people more than for myself. I had this friend to say, 'Well, you're not really being fair to yourself. You shouldn't always go when there's somebody in need or sick.' Well, I look at it in a different way. Everybody has their reasons for things. A lot of times, you have a need yourself when you reach out so much. You really satisfy yourself, as well as fulfilling a need of that other person."[65]

Hoyle McCorkle captured the essence of mill village life when he described the Highland Park community in North Charlotte as a single household bound together by relations of real and fictive kin. "I guess there were two hundred houses on this village, and I knew practically all of them from a kid up. It was kind of a cliché: You grew up here and you knew everybody. It had its bad points; we didn't make too much money, I know my father didn't. But like I said, it was kind of one big family, and we all hung together and survived. It was a two-hundred-headed family. Everybody on this hill, we looked after one another."[66] That commitment to support each other bound workers together and provided a hedge against misfortune in an uncertain world.

A close-knit community was only one of many sources of independence transferred from the countryside and then modified to meet mill village demands. Even as they labored in the factories, millhands tried to maintain their ties to the land. Most village houses had a garden plot and perhaps a chicken coop, while outlying areas owned by the mill served as communal pastures and hog lots. Children rose early in the morning to take the family cow to pasture and returned in the evening to bring her home for milking. Those too young to work in the mill during the day helped their mothers bake bread, gather eggs, and churn butter. Men gardened and tended hogs. Curtis Enlow's father continued small-scale farming within sight of the Poe Mill in Greenville, cultivating "every patch he could get." "He'd grow corn

and potatoes mostly. We had a cow might nigh all the time, and my dad always kept two of them old Berkshire hogs—one for meat and one for lard." Edna Hargett's father also planted a large garden, but could not afford a mule to help till the land. He made do by putting "a harness around himself" and having his children "stand behind and guide the plow."[67]

Just as farmers had tried to bypass the furnishing merchant, mill-hands adapted familiar strategies to avoid getting into debt at the company store. Gardening and husbandry skills helped mill families survive on meager wages. "You didn't make but four and five dollars a week," explained Ethel Faucette, and it took "a whole lot for a family of twelve." In Bynum, Louise Jones's family managed to produce most of their own food. Her parents "had a big garden and a corn patch and a few chickens around the yard. We'd have maybe six or eight hens, and we'd let the hens set on the eggs and hatch chickens, and have frying-size chickens, raise our own fryers." During the winter, her family ate "homemade meat" along with fish from the Haw River and the vegetables her mother had either canned or dried. Much of what the Joneses and other families could not produce for themselves they bought or bartered from neighbors, just as farm families had done in the countryside. Edna Hargett's father supplied his community with honey; Mary Thompson's mother sold surplus milk and butter. "We didn't have nothing to buy but sugar and flour and coffee and something like that," recalled Jessie Lee Carter of Greenville. "We had plenty of other stuff."[68]

While mill families tried to meet many of their own needs, this goal was difficult to achieve when every member of the household was working a ten- or twelve-hour day. For most millhands life was hard. "Back in the earlier days," explained Herman Truitt, "there probably was more class distinction among people than there is today because a man doing ordinary work in a cotton mill, making less than eleven dollars a week, had probably enough to pay rent, buy him a little something to eat, a few clothes, and that was about all." There was sel-dom enough money even for necessities. On many occasions Emma Whitesell's family "didn't know where the next meal was coming from," and Grover Hardin's family had "very little furniture, just a couple of beds. Just enough to get by on is about all we had." Parents also found it difficult to clothe all of their children, and the youngest in most families wore hand-me-downs. Eula Durham "didn't know what a new dress was, or a pair of shoes," until she was old enough to go to

Raising chickens in the mill village, ca. 1910. Chickens provided mill families with eggs and fresh meat. Photograph by Hugh Parks, Jr.
(Courtesy of Mac Whatley, Franklinville, N.C.)

work in the mill and contribute to the family income. "There was twelve of us, and whenever one would outgrow anything, Mama would take that thing and cut it down and fix it so the younger ones could wear it. And when they got where they couldn't wear it and they hadn't wore it out, she'd patch that thing and fix it up and the one down below you got it."[69]

At Christmas, mill families could not afford to lavish on their children the kinds of presents purchased by townspeople. Instead, they filled their youngsters' stockings with a few pieces of candy and fruit and sought to protect them from realizing their poverty. "Papa and Mama didn't teach us no Santa Claus," recalled Emma Thomas of Lando. "They'd say it wasn't no Santa Claus. Papa would. But Mama would hide the things and make us go to bed [after] we hung up our stockings. We always got a stick of candy and an apple and an orange, that was about it. There wasn't no money back in them days."

For most children, however, the shared poverty of the mill village offered protection from feelings of deprivation. "We was all happy," remembered Nannie Pharis. "We didn't have anything, so we didn't know what to wish for and long for."[70]

What gifts children did receive, they learned to guard and cherish. Eula Durham took her first job in the Bynum spinning mill at the age of thirteen, earning five dollars a week. "My daddy give me twenty-five cents out of my pay," she remembered, "and I thought I was rich." Eula used her money to buy treats at a nearby store. "This old man lived up above us and ran a little old store. When I'd get my quarter on Saturday morning, I'd run up there and I'd get me some Oh Boy chewing gum and some Mary Janes. They was a penny. Boy, when you got a big piece of candy then, or chewing gum, you was really sitting pretty. Well, we lived in this old house and you could walk up under it—it weren't underpinned or nothing. It had rafters up under there. Well, I took my candy and chewing gum, put it in a little sack, went under the house and hid it up under there in one of them rafters. And the next day I went out there to get a piece of my candy and chewing gum. Got my sack down and it was just loaded with ants. The ants had found it. I said, 'Lord-a-mercy, what am I going to do? They've got my candy and my chewing gum.' Well, this here old friend of mine, she said, 'Well, I'll tell you what we'll do. We'll take it down to the branch and wash them ants off.' We took it down to the branch and washed the candy, and I said, 'You eat a piece first.' She said, 'No, you eat a piece.' We finally throwed it away. We nary one could get nerve enough to eat that candy. And I never did put any more of my candy under the house. I won't never forget that thing as long as I live."

On another occasion, Eula received a doll as a gift from her parents. This time she did not hide her treasure away, but enjoyed it. The results were the same. "Got an old doll, one Christmas—the only thing I remember in my life getting as a kid. Along then they didn't make them out of rubber; made them out of some old stuff like pasteboard and painted them. We had a big branch down there in front of the house, and Saturday after dinner we was going to have a baptizing. We carried our dolls down there and banked up some water, baptized the dolls and laid them out. Well, come up a cloud and we run up to the house and forgot our dolls and left them down there. After the cloud was over and some sun come out bright, I went down there and that doll looked like it was ninety years old; it was just cracked all to pieces. I said, 'Lord, I have ruint the doll!' And this girl had one, had some hair. And every bit of her hair come off. We never did bring our dolls to no more baptizing."[71]

If childhood stories reveal something of the emotional burdens of a life lived close to the bone, the mill village diet makes clear its physical effects. Even with their gardens, few families could sustain a varied diet beyond summer and fall. Herman Truitt's father owned a store in Burlington, and the younger Truitt grew up observing differences between the lives of millhands and townspeople. "Workers in the mill," he recalled, "on weekdays—on working days—would eat dried beans cook[ed] with a piece of fatback meat. Pinto beans, pink beans, white beans, black-eyed peas would be the main ones. And, of course, they'd eat potatoes and sweet potatoes and onions along with these." A typical weekday meal also included cornbread, which mothers or daughters made two or three times a day. "Then came the weekend— back in those early days the weekend meant Saturday noon to Monday morning." Workers celebrated this break in the work routine with a big meal and, perhaps, meat. "Chicken was probably the most popular meat, but they would get pork chops or some beef of some kind, and have that for Sunday dinner. And then for Sunday they'd probably have a cake or a pie, too, which they didn't eat much of during the week."[72]

Such a diet was monotonous and often unhealthy. In 1916 investigators from the U.S. Public Health Service discovered that pellagra was a chronic problem in Piedmont mill villages, affecting 16 percent of the households studied. Pellagra resulted from a protein deficiency generally associated with inadequate amounts of milk, cheese, and fresh meat in the diet. Characterized by scaly, red blotches on the skin, the disease usually sapped its victims with debilitating diarrhea and profound lethargy, but in advanced stages it could also result in nervous disorders, insanity, and death. Pellagra struck hardest at children and at women of child-rearing age. Youngsters between two and fifteen suffered two-thirds of all cases. Another 24 percent occurred among women aged twenty to fifty, who were ten times more likely than their male counterparts to fall ill. This pattern of sickness arose primarily from the hierarchal relations that governed family life. The dietary diaries millhands kept as part of the federal pellagra study suggested that when protein-rich foods were in short supply, men received "more favorable consideration at the . . . table," while their wives and children warded off hunger with bread, potatoes, and molasses.[73]

Outbreaks of pellagra followed a seasonal pattern, first appearing in the spring and then declining rapidly in late summer. By spring, most families had depleted their supplies of lean meat laid away in the fall, and the family cow was likely to be nursing a newborn calf, reducing the supply of fresh milk and butter. The beans that mill women canned and dried provided a good source of protein, but they proved inadequate when supplemented only with cornmeal and inexpensive cuts of salt pork containing little or no lean. The result for families without the resources to buy milk or fresh meat was an annual cycle of malnutrition, sickness, and want.[74]

Under these conditions, tradition and necessity dictated a turn to rural practices of mutual aid. In the spring, millhands tilled their gardens and planted summer crops. Although each family claimed a small plot of land, villagers shared what they grew. As one worker explained to a labor organizer in the 1920s, "We live in common like, us six families here. Each one's got a little patch. Wages being what they is, we couldn't get along without. One raises beans and peas, another, yams and potatoes. And me, I raise corn. When meal time comes, we just go and help ourselves." In the late summer and early fall, families gathered for the rituals of harvesting and hog killing. Paul and Don Faucette remembered how it was done in Glencoe. "We'd kill our hogs this time, and a month later we'd kill yours. Well, you can give us some and we can give you some. They'd have women get together down in the church basement. They'd have a quilting bee and they'd go down and they'd all quilt. One of them would have a good crop of cabbage, [and] they'd get together and all make kraut. And up there at the [mill company's] barn they'd have a cornshucking." Villagers helped one another, not with an expectation of immediate return but with the assurance of community support in meeting their individual needs. "They'd just visit around and work voluntarily. They all done it, and nobody owed nobody nothing."[75]

Cooperation ensured group and individual survival at a time when state welfare services were limited and industrialists often refused to assume responsibility for job-related sickness and injury. The "safety net" for most cotton mill people was the village community itself: "When trouble hits any family, you know that you're going to have friends that'll stand by you. They'll really fall in and help out." If someone in the village was ill, neighbors were quick to give the stricken family a "pounding." "They'd all get together and help. They'd cook food and carry it to them, all kinds of food—fruits, vegetables, canned goods." Villagers also helped sick neighbors by taking up a "love offering" in the mill. Edna Hargett was in charge of such collections in the weave room at Charlotte's Chadwick-Hoskins Mill. "When the neighbors got paid," she recalled, "they'd come and pay us, and we'd take their money and give it to [the sick weaver's family], and they'd be so proud of it, because they didn't have any wage coming in. The mill community was a close bunch of people. We were just like one big family. We just all loved one another."[76]

During economic hard times, simple sharing was not enough, and villagers sometimes pooled their resources for common use. At one point, families in Glencoe staved off hunger by cooking in a communal pot. "You take during the Depression years," Don Faucette remembered, "everybody had a few beans. Well, they had a great big old pot, five or six of the neighbors had a big old pot out there. Put all the beans in one pot and made a big pot which would go around to all the families instead of just feeding one." In Glencoe, as in other villages, people lived by a simple rule: "If you need it, [and] we got it, it's yours."[77]

Embodied in everyday behavior, communal values made poverty survivable and distanced millhands from the possessive individualism that characterized the world of factory owners and middle-class townsfolk. To be sure, workers understood the value and power of money. They struggled against dependency and claimed an economic competence as their due. But they did so less as a means of striving for wealth or status than as an attempt to shelter themselves from economic hardships. As one sociologist observed in the 1920s, millhands had "their own deeply entrenched ideas about what constitute[d] the 'good life.'" A commitment to cooperation rather than competition remained an abiding feature of mill village culture.[78]

To argue that sharing and neighborliness gave substance to the family metaphor is not to suggest that the mill village conformed to an idealized image of family life. Families are institutions to which people look for support regardless of their achievements as individuals or their ability to contribute to the group. But families are also based on power relationships; they are arenas of conflict as well as reciprocity. In the mill village much of that conflict took place along gender lines.

The move to the mill accelerated the redefinition of sex roles already underway on the farm. Although husbands and wives often labored side by side in the mill, they experienced factory life differently. While men's identities became increasingly centered on work, women's roles tended to cut across divisions separating the workplace, the family, and the neighborhood.

The first generation of men to come off the land in the 1880s and 1890s found it particularly difficult to adapt to the regimen of factory labor. On the farm they had exercised authority over the family and held responsibility for planting, harvesting, and selling crops. They had also been able to look at accomplished tasks with a sense of pride and satisfaction. In becoming millhands, they lost much of their freedom and compromised their roles as producers. The patriarch of a rural family had to accept subordination to owners and supervisors; and in the repetitive tasks of machine tending, the satisfaction of accomplishment—a good crop harvested, a perfect row plowed—could at first be hard to find. For some men, the strictures of factory life were a torment. A fellow worker once told Grover Hardin, " 'I'm going back to the farm. I don't like this. I work all day and I look back and I can't see a thing I've done.' At that time he was laying up roping [in the card room], and they'd take it down as fast as he'd lay it up. He didn't like that. In about a couple of weeks he was gone, sure enough."[79]

Other men sought a balance between the mill and the farm. When James Pharis's parents moved to Spray in the late 1890s, his father managed to save his most valued possession: his team of horses. While the children worked at factory jobs, the elder Pharis raised vegetables on a rented plot of ground and "done hauling around for people." James's wife, Nannie, told a similar story. Her father tried to work in the Rhode Island Mill in Spray, but "he just didn't like it at all." He soon moved his family back to the country. Twice a week he drove his wagon into the mill village to sell "vegetables and fryers and eggs and butter and milk and pork," while his wife and children walked five miles each day to work in the factory.[80]

Mill owners and townspeople scorned such men as "cotton mill drones," parasites who preferred to live off the labor of innocent children rather than do an honest day's work. According to one manufacturer, "drones" spent their days "loitering around the premises, fishing, hunting, or otherwise wasting their time in idleness." He and others advocated public flogging or a stint on the chain gang as appropriate punishments for the father who would "put his poor little uneducated children in the cotton mill to earn a livelihood while he plays gentleman." But most fathers who farmed, hunted, and fished were not, as outsiders imagined, exploiting their wives and children. They were trying instead to support their families in long-familiar ways. The combination of odd jobs, farming, and wage labor seemed an appropriate survival strategy to men who believed that mill work would prove to be a temporary condition. It also represented a desperate attempt to hold on to the forms of independence that in the countryside had provided men with a sense of dignity and self-respect.[81]

Nevertheless, most mill-working men had to give up their traditional sources of identity. That loss contributed to the hostility with which some husbands greeted the idea of their wives taking a factory job. Married men sometimes sought to impose on their wives a sexual division of labor more stringent than anything women had known on the farm. Perhaps they embraced the vision of family life that had taken shape among the town-dwelling middle class, a vision that emphasized men's role as providers and women's role as guardians of the home. More likely, mill husbands simply tried to maintain the prerogatives they had always enjoyed. Few farm women had ever performed public work, and as wage labor became increasingly important to family survival, men claimed it as a sign of their authority. Icy Norman recalled a particularly heated exchange between her parents. After the birth of a second child, her father insisted that her mother's place was in the home. "One morning there my daddy told her, 'I didn't marry you to work. You got all the work you need at home with your children. It's not a wife's place to work. Your place is at home, and that's where you're going to be. If a man can't make a living for his wife and children, he ain't no business marrying. Now if you're going to work, I'll quit and come home and tend to our children.' So Mama [went] in and worked her notice and come home."[82]

A strict division of labor sometimes worked for early mill families, but it proved impractical for their children and for later arrivals from the farm. Between 1907 and 1922 the percentage of southern textile families with wives and mothers in the mills nearly tripled, rising from 17 to 46 percent. The change came largely as a result of child labor laws, which deprived parents of their children's earnings and forced increasing numbers of married women into the labor force. Carrie Yelton's mother "just liked to be at home, a housewife," but Yelton herself "had to work and wanted to work." Some husbands also took on domestic chores they would have seldom performed on the farm. Carrie and William Gerringer managed to keep their jobs and rear their children by working opposite shifts. "He worked the third shift sometimes and me the first, and sometimes I'd work the second and he'd work the first, and that's the way it would go. He would tend the young'uns when they came home [from school]. Yes, Lord, he was a better housekeeper than me. He was a good cook, too. He could do about anything. He wouldn't wash dishes; that was the one thing you couldn't get him to do. And bake bread, now, he didn't like that. But outside of that, he could just cook anything." Such arrangements marked an important change in family life and stood as an example of working-class pragmatism. Yet domestic chores remained "women's work"; when men pitched in, they were only "helping."[83]

Regardless of when they arrived at the mill village, most married women were eventually drawn into public work—at least temporarily—by economic necessity. Typically, they moved in and out of the labor market according to changes in family and personal needs. Women tried to limit full-time work to the years before childbirth and after their children were grown. "Usually my dad just worked," Mack Duncan remembered. "Mama didn't work much in my lifetime while I was home. She worked after all of us children got grown, but when we were small, she was home mostly with us. Sometimes they'd have a shortage and they'd want her to work a while, and she'd work. She might work a year, and she might not work that long, 'til all the family got out from under. And then she got a job and worked all the time. She must have been in her forties when she went to work regularly. Then she retired when she was sixty-two."[84]

Few women, however, managed to strike such a neat balance between work and family life. Some, in fact, never attempted to do so. For them, working in the mill provided an opportunity to escape the routine of housework and child care. "I'd rather be at work than be at the house anytime," explained Carrie Gerringer. "I've thought about it lots of times; if I hadn't had no children, I wonder if I'd have wanted to work. You know, sometimes you can't understand what your reasoning was. But when [the children] was little and growing up, I'd rather be at the mill, somehow or another." More often, though, mothers with young children entered the mill in response to a family crisis or the need for additional income. Myrtle Cleveland's mother had to get a mill job after Myrtle's father died in an accident. "My mother worked, I imagine, until maybe the first child was born, and then she stayed home. She didn't work any more until my father got killed in 1932, and after that she went back to the mill." The likelihood of a woman's returning to the mill also increased as her family grew. A husband could support one or two children alone, but the arrival of more than two often required the supplemental income a wife could earn. As Mamie McCorkle explained, "You hardly didn't make enough if the husband and wife both didn't work." Like many women, Gertrude Shuping quit work when her first child was born, but the arrival of a third forced her back into the mill to relieve the strain on the family budget. Although Shuping enjoyed her job, the combination of caring for children and making the money that kept them fed and clothed left her bone tired: "I always felt like I was taking one step towards home and two back toward the mill."[85]

Women also performed a great deal of work outside the mill that made the difference between comfort and deprivation in good times and was absolutely crucial to family survival in bad. Lewis Durham's mother contributed to the family income by taking in sewing and selling household goods for a mail-order house. She used the money she earned to "buy pieces of furniture—trunks for the boys and such things as that." Other women supplemented the family income by taking in boarders. Edna Hargett's mother worked all day in the mill and then came home to cook for the single men who rented her rooms. "It was pretty hectic, because we had to get in there and clean up behind the boarders, wash the dishes and all like that, and get everything fixed up for the next morning and take a bath and get ready to go back to work the next day. It was just routine work; there weren't no pleasure about it. It was just, as you might say, hard work."[86]

This combination of wage and domestic labor imposed a double burden on mill village women. Edna Hargett testified to the difficulty of working in the mill and managing a household. "It was a job. I'd get up at five o'clock in the mornings, because you had to be at work at six. I got up in the morning and I'd make up the dough and have biscuits for my children, so whenever they got up they'd put it in the oil stove oven and cook them. Then we'd come home and do a washing, and had to wash on a board outdoors and boil your clothes and make your own lye soap. It was just a day of drudgery, but with God's help, I got it done." Esther Jenks remembered that the washing could often trail long into the night, as women huddled around their kettle fires for warmth. "It wasn't nothing to see those women work all day, and you would see a wash pot out in the yard, you know, with the fire around it, after dark sometimes."[87]

Mothers with young children sometimes hired black domestics to help with daily chores. At larger mills black families often lived on the outskirts of the white village. The Hanes mill near Winston-Salem, for example, maintained housing for nine black families along a street behind the plant known as "colored row." The men worked as janitors, boiler stokers, openers, and yardmen, while their wives, excluded from most mill jobs, labored as housekeepers. Like many of those women, Billie Douglas began to "go and babysit in mill workers' houses" when she was only fourteen years old. "See, that was all that you knew, I mean that was what you did. We didn't have any other choices." Other black women found themselves forced by the state to enter domestic service. Mary Thompson remembered that the women who worked for her in Greenville did so as a condition for receiving county welfare assistance. "There was always plenty of help in Greenville because there was lots of colored people and lots of them were on welfare. I went to the welfare office lots of times and asked for somebody to do the housework and keep my child. They'd tell them that they'd have to work or they'd be took off the welfare."[88]

The mill workers we interviewed never questioned such arrangements, but black women were quick to point out the injustice. Although Billie Douglas was fond of the white children she cared for, she grew bitter at having to leave her own children at home alone. "We'd fall in love with those kids and they would love you. You'd raise those children, and sometimes they'd cry to come home with you. But when my children were born, I would try to do for my child because it seemed like I would be away from mine all day taking care of somebody else's." Douglas also resented working so hard for very little money. For her and other black women even a low-wage mill job would have opened the way to a better life. Billie often walked by the mill thinking that her family's problems would be solved "if I was in there, if I could bring a check like that home. You know, they would probably pay us for a week with what they made in a day, and sometimes less, and of course we resented it. But that was what we was used to and we did what we had to do."[89]

Despite black domestics' meager wages, hiring servants remained a luxury. Most village women ran their households single-handedly, aided only by children and neighbors. They suffered constant exhaustion and were often sick or absent from work. A federal survey of female millhands conducted in 1922 found that women in southern mills missed 27 percent of their possible workdays. The highest proportion of absences occurred among women of childbearing age—between twenty and forty years old—who shouldered "the home burden as well as the industrial responsibility." These women missed nearly a third more time than older or younger women. The leading causes of absenteeism were personal and family illness and "home duties," which accounted for 53 percent of all lost time. But the figure for illness alone is perhaps the most revealing. Among female millhands poor health was responsible for 23 percent of all missed days, the highest rate of absenteeism due to sickness for any industrial work force in the nation. Mill women were also sick more often than their nonmill neighbors. A study of seven South Carolina mill villages in 1916 reported that the rate of disabling illness among mill-working women was 45 per thousand as compared to 39 per thousand for nonmill women. When the poorest households in both categories were compared, the figures grew even more striking. Mill women in households earning sixteen dollars or less a month suffered disabling illnesses at a rate of 68 per thousand, while the rate for their nonmill counterparts stood at 50 per thousand.[90]

Under such circumstances, the ambivalent attitudes rural women held toward marriage and motherhood persisted, if indeed they did not grow stronger. Like many women, Fannie Marcom disliked working long hours in the mill, but she recalled, "I didn't marry no job until I got married." She thought about leaving both situations, but financial necessity kept her in the mill, and her conscience kept her married: "You know, you take those vows 'til death do us part." Childbirth, too, was a fact of life over which women often felt they had little control. Carrie Gerringer remembered that she was ignorant of sex when she married. "I didn't know no more than a two-year-old young'un. I was dumb as an ox." Aliene Walser had similar memories. "The first time I ever started my period I was going to the spring to get a bucket of water. I was living with my brother and his wife then. All at once I looked and blood was going down my leg, and it scared me to death. I didn't know what to do. I ran in the house and told my brother's wife and she told me what to do. And that was all that was ever said to me about it. She told me that it would happen again. I said, 'What for?' She never did explain nothing like that to me. Didn't nobody." Walser neared the end of her first pregnancy before she understood the mechanics of childbirth. "When I was pregnant for the first time, I was sitting there sewing with my mother-in-law one night and I said, 'I wouldn't mind having this baby if I didn't have to have my stomach cut open.' She looked at me and said, 'Honey, you mean that you don't know no better than that and fixin' to have a baby?' I said, 'What do you mean?' And when she told me, I said, 'Ain't no way I'm going to go through that!' That like to have scared me to death. See, I didn't understand anything about my body."[91]

Of course, young mothers soon learned about their bodies and about various methods of birth control, too. After the arrival of a third or fourth child, couples began to use condoms, or they were just "kind of careful." On rare occasions older women in the neighborhood shared instructions for self-induced abortions. But attitudes toward sex and family life inhibited careful planning. "All our children was born accidentally," recalled Mack Duncan. "We didn't plan our family at all." Many parents felt that in marrying they had made the decision to have children and were obliged to abide by it. To do otherwise was to oppose God's will. "You know that a man's sperm," explained Fannie Marcom, "better that it be wasted in the belly of a whore than spilled on the earth. The Bible says 'Be fruitful and multiply.' "[92]

Nevertheless, motherhood remained a bittersweet experience. Kathryn Killian thought pregnancy was "awful"; Carrie Gerringer remembered that she "like to died with every one" of her six children; and Gertrude Shuping, although she loved her children dearly, felt relieved when she had to have a hysterectomy. Rearing large numbers of children to face an uncertain future brought "terrific responsibility," often accompanied by guilt at not having met one's parental obligations. "Not that I don't love my children," explained Carrie Gerringer, "but so many! I think it's better to have one or two that you can keep going and do the best you can by them." Having lived through these experiences, many older women, even if they considered their own marriages happy, tended to view weddings as tragic rather than joyful occasions. "I never did like to go to a wedding," declared Louise Jones. "I don't know; it was always sad to me, and I don't like to go. I've heard several people speak that way about it; said it was sad. It was more like a funeral to them than anything else."[93]

Just as the move to industrial life imposed new hardships on women, it also reshaped the lives of children. Most youngsters entered the factory willingly, feeling obliged to help support their parents and siblings. But this commitment to family often required sacrifices that children remembered for the rest of their lives. Edna Hargett was born in 1907 in a mill village near Rock Hill, South Carolina. She explained that the difference between factory children and their peers was that "a mill child had to go in the mill and the others didn't. We knew that was the way of life we was brought up to, and that would be the way of life we had to expect."[94]

Like their mothers, village children also shouldered a double burden of household and factory labor. "We didn't get to play like children do nowadays," Hargett remembered. "You'd come home and you had cows to stake out and hogs to feed and gardens to work. We didn't get to play." As a child, Mary Thompson combined a half day of school with work in the mill and a regular round of household chores. "When I went to school, we had to do all of the washing and hang it out before we went to work in the morning, and come home and do all the ironing. Mama had a houseful of children, and we were made to work. I had to milk the cow every morning. I've got under a cow many a time when it was snowing and raining in the milk."[95]

When children did get a chance to play, they fished in nearby streams, explored the woods, and played games in their neighbors' yards or on a company playground. Roy Auton spent his summer days swimming in a creek near his uncle's house. "We'd go out to our creek and cut grapevines to make swings where we could swing out across the creek and back. And when we'd run out of grapevines, we'd take a rope and make one. Some of them couldn't get across, but I never did end up in the water." Play offered children a refuge from the demands of family life and an arena for creativity. Nannie Pharis remembered that there "wasn't any games then like there are now"; children "invented homemade games" from materials close at hand. "Taggy" was a favorite in Roy Auton's neighborhood. "You just cut a stick and you taper it off on one end, kind of sharp. And you have a stake in the ground, so you lay that thing up on it with the tapered end sticking out. Then you have a straight stick that you use for a bat. You walk up there and you hit this thing, and it'd fly up there maybe four or five feet high, spinning. Then you take a swing at it and knock it as far as you can. And if you get a good lick on it, you might knock it a hundred yards. I forget just how the rules was, but somebody else runs and gets it for you, and then if he can throw it back and hit the stick that you batted it with, it's his turn. We'd spend a lot of hours like that."[96]

But the small delights of childhood were frequently punctuated with adult responsibilities. Both of Harry Rogers's parents worked in

Caring for livestock, one of children's most important responsibilities. These children lived at the Wylie mill village in Chester, South Carolina, 1908. Photograph by Lewis Hine.
(Courtesy of the Photography Collections, Albin O. Kuhn Library and Gallery, University of Maryland at Baltimore County)

the mill, and while they were away, he was "the mother" in the family. "That meant that I had to do the cooking, and the scrubbing the floors, and making the beds, and so forth," he recalled. "Usually when I got home from school my job was to clean the house and cook supper. When I was small, I had a stool that I'd have to stand up on to make the cornbread. I made my own bread, and cooked pinto beans and fatback. Anything that had to be cooked, I'd cook it, just about, when I was knee-high to a grasshopper. My sister was four years younger than me, and my brother was two years younger, so I really was the mother." Some young folks resented their duties and rebelled in quiet, personal ways. Lora Wright's sister disliked caring for her younger brothers and sisters, "so she'd pinch 'em and make 'em cry." Most children, however, simply endured. "I can look back now and say we wouldn't gripe about what we had to do," said Mary Thompson, "we was raised not to. And anyway, there wasn't no use in griping." In either case, mill children often grew up feeling that they had been denied their youth. "Childhood," said Ralph Austin, "I didn't have much."[97]

Factory labor also generated new conflicts between parents and children over the nature of work and its rewards. Children's work on the farm had been part of the daily routine of family life, but wage labor in the mill introduced a new element of possessiveness. When children worked in the fields, their labor blended with that of other family members, and the harvest was truly a return on the efforts of all. In the factory, a child performed a job and received a cash wage in return, even if it was paid to a parent. Wage earning defined a new condition of owning one's labor and provoked new feelings of independence that stood in opposition to the demands of a cooperative family economy. Charles Foster quit his mill job when he was nineteen and traveled from Swepsonville to nearby Greensboro to find work with the railroad that would enable him to live on his own. "I come back home and told Dad about it, and he said, 'You ain't going to take that. You're too young, you belong to me.' I said, 'Yes, that's right, but I can make my own money, Daddy.' He said, 'Well, you ain't going to make none, because I'll forbid them paying you if you go.' So that knocked that in the head."[98]

Parents considered their children's earnings a family resource, not individual income. Even into their late teens, most mill children gave up their wages. A federal report estimated that in 1907–8 girls over the age of fifteen surrendered 89 percent of their earnings to the family while boys of the same age turned over 73 percent. Mack Duncan remembered, "I weren't any different than anybody else. When I went to work, my daddy always got all my pay. Any money I made went to him automatically." Some parents gave their children part of their wages as an allowance or bought them small presents, but that did not prevent many children from harboring a secret feeling of unfair treatment. Carrie Gerringer began working in the Glen Raven Mill when she was fourteen years old. "We worked five days and a half, ten hours [a day]," she recalled, "and just made five dollars and a half a week. Mama would take it all but fifty cents. We felt like it wasn't right, but we didn't say nothing; we knowed better. She had three young'uns to raise."[99]

Such quiet resentment often shaped workers' memories of parental discipline. Walter Vaughn was typical in remembering that his father "made you walk the chalk line. He whipped my brother when he was nineteen years old. Took a strap and tore him up. You done what he said do. You talk back to him, you were tore all to pieces." In the mill village, as in the countryside, this kind of discipline was important to family survival. A family's fate depended on cooperation, and it was essential that children learn at an early age to subordinate their individual desires to the larger interests of the group. But under the new conditions of life and labor, such discipline could leave memories of harsh treatment and deprivation.[100]

Once they entered their teens, many children looked to marriage to solve their problems. In a society where work was an accepted part of childhood, getting married—rather than getting a job—marked the passage into adulthood and independence. "I didn't consider myself as grown 'til I married," recalled Edna Hargett. "I was a grown person, and I was my own boss then. I knowed Daddy couldn't fuss with me and scold me like he used to." But young newlyweds soon discovered that marriage and parenthood were more confining than anything they had experienced as children. "I just think you just more or less get trapped," observed Eva Hopkins. "My husband and I got married, and we started having babies, and you just have to go on from there. You're just more or less trapped in the job you're in, because when you have children you can't quit and go looking for something else." As a child, she had dreamed that marriage would set her free, but the realities of mill work left her with only the hope that her children might have a better life. "I daydreamed when I was young. Before I was married, I would daydream about who I was going to marry. I was going to marry somebody that was rich so that I wouldn't have to work; I could have a nice home and beautiful clothes. Then, after I married, I still had daydreams. And after I had my children, I still had daydreams. I dreamed of wanting a better life for them. It's been a good life, but I'd like for them not to have to work in the mills, to live in better sections of town, to have nicer homes, more conveniences, nicer cars, nicer everything than we had. Dreams like that."[101]

Married life sometimes brought disappointment to men as well. They viewed themselves as masters of the household; yet other men directed their families' labor, and only the earnings of their wives and children made the difference between comfort and want. Many fathers reacted by withdrawing from their families, becoming sullen and aloof. "I don't remember our daddy telling us nothing, only just giving us orders," recalled Ila Dodson. "But our mama would talk to us." Emma Williams's father removed himself physically and emotionally. "He never took up any time with his children, of any description. I knew my father very well, [but] I never cared too much for him. I think we bored him. He was home to sleep. He was always there at mealtime." Mavis Pearce's father was a good provider but never considered children his responsibility. He stayed home with Mavis and her brothers while their mother worked, but "he weren't much of a person to tend to children. He never was the type of person to take up no time over children."[102]

Mill fathers often escaped the difficulties of work and family life in the company of other men. In rural mill villages, the local store rather than a saloon served as their refuge. Hanging out at the store offered a chance to swap stories, share a drink, and find comfort among friends. The store that Herman Truitt's father ran in Burlington was a gathering place for mill workers. "Father would stay open until nine o'clock on Saturday nights. At that time they had a bunch of pretty regular customers who would maybe celebrate a little bit by smelling the bottle, or tasting a little when they'd come by. Sometimes there was a Jew's harp, and a violin, which he'd call a fiddle. They'd sit around and eat pigs' feet and crackers and sausage and snack like a person drinking likes to do sometimes." Older men might test themselves in a game of checkers, while those of lesser years sought a more vigorous challenge in a footrace. Charles Foster remembered that the young men in Swepsonville often raced to the movie house in Graham, five miles away. "When I was a young fellow and we wanted to go up to the show, why, after the mill stopped we'd eat supper, and there'd be seven or eight of us meet down at the store. Somebody'd say, 'Let's run up to Graham and see the show.' Well, the fellow that didn't trot all the way to Graham, he had to pay the whole fare. We'd trot all the way to Graham."[103]

There was a fine line between hanging out at the store and what mill villagers called the "rough life." Every community had its group of high-spirited individuals known for drinking and fighting. Often, they were young men sowing their wild oats before settling down to family responsibilities. But the "rough element" included older residents as well, people who enjoyed Saturday night sprees as a respite from the grind of steadiness and sobriety demanded by factory labor. Alcohol also unleashed feelings of defiance and hostility usually hidden or repressed in everyday life. In Bynum these "folks'd mix up white lightning and beer together" on payday "and go crazy and fight." In other communities they won their villages nicknames such as "Little

Chicago," as well as a reputation among outsiders for drunkenness and violence. George Shue claimed with a touch of pride that North Charlotte "was known all over the United States. Said that was the meanest place there was—they thought that was like a western town down there, they carried guns on each side. There often would be a fight every day. But still, they respected women when they come there, and children. But you come out hunting trouble, you'd get trouble right quick."[104]

Strong drink helped men forget their worries. Ruth Elliot's husband, Jesse, spent most of his life in a tragic cycle of binges and sobriety. "He got so he was a periodic alcoholic. He would stay sober about three weeks, and in those three weeks he was the best thing; he was the soberest man in town with a vest on. He was a good worker when he was sober. Jesse was so utterly good when he was sober. I reckon that's the only reason I tolerated him at all. But about once a month he pulled a week's drunk, and he'd drink 'til he couldn't hold any more. And then he'd be sick two or three days. It kind of made me bitter. I couldn't count on Jesse for anything. So I just lived from day to day. I didn't have decent clothes to wear, and the kids, [their] clothes were just used—donated. Well, that's no way to live."

Ruth often wished that she could jerk her husband into line, yet she understood that Jesse drank to "escape" the disappointments of work and the burden of becoming a father at a young age. She accepted his behavior with a blend of resignation and compassion. "I've often wished I was a man, because I thought I could change the situation a little bit, and maybe sometimes when Jesse would make me good and mad I'd wish I was a man like him just so I could beat the tar out of him. But I think it's entirely stupid to keep butting your head against a stone wall. I don't care how much I'd want to be a man; there's nothing I can do about it; I'm not a man. I said it's like a woman getting pregnant; it didn't care whether she wanted to have that baby or not, there wasn't much choice about it. She was going to have the baby.

"But I can look back now, and I can see why he would drink, because when we were married we wasn't anything but kids. We had three babies, one right after the other, and somebody had to settle down. And it had to be me. Jesse never did settle down. It was too much of a load on him. If he had stayed single and hadn't saddled himself with a wife and kids, he would have sowed his wild oats and got over it. Instead of that, he planted a permanent garden, and it was disastrous. I know that now. But that didn't help me out a bit then. Jesse and I ended up with nothing in the world in common but a bed pillow, and so that wasn't even in common."[105]

Sarah Andrews told a similar story marked by the same blend of anger and compassion. Sarah met her husband, Gene, while he was a boarder in her mother's home in the gold-mining town of Eldorado, North Carolina. The couple courted for two years and finally decided to marry in 1916. Sarah was deeply in love with her husband, but their marriage soon began to sour. Her father had left her 150 acres of prime timberland, which Gene sold, over her objections. Sarah was only sixteen, so she had no legal claim on the property. "He sold it for mighty near nothing," she explained. "I was underage and I didn't know he'd been put in as my guardian, but he had. My mother turned [the land] over to him when we got married. I didn't have no say-so in it. I told him we ought not to get rid of that. We had about two children, I believe, we had a family started. I said, 'We'll need that one day.' And he got mad at me, and that's the first time he ever hit me. He kicked me. And then he said he didn't know what made him do that. I didn't like it, but I took it."

Over the next thirteen years Gene moved his family from mill to mill in search of a job that would provide a living wage and a sense of accomplishment. As his search grew more and more futile, Gene became increasingly jealous and violent. He refused to allow Sarah out of the house to shop for groceries and guarded her from other men by buying clothes that made her unattractive. "When these children was coming up, when we first married, if I had to have a dress, he had to pick it out. And when he did get one, it was just an old straight thing with a band on each side you tied behind. He didn't want me to look like nothing. He thought I was pretty, and he thought everybody else thought it. And I didn't look like nothing. He was a jealous-hearted person."

Gene also began to suffer fits of anger in which he beat Sarah and their children for no apparent reason. "We had a laundry heater in the kitchen, and one of the [boys] got up and went between [Gene] and the heater. [Gene] knocked him across that heater, and I grabbed him and I told him, 'You ought not to never do a thing like that.' He had a razor strap hanging on the wall in there, and he jumped up and got that to hit me with. And his mama stood up and says, 'Don't you hit her. If you want to hit anybody, you hit me.' Just because he walked between him and the heater. Lord, what I went through!" On other occasions Gene would "pick at the children and make them sass, and then he'd whip them. He'd just pick at them to make them sass him back and tease them and get them mad. They was little and just talked back. And if I said anything, he'd whip them to spite me. I had to keep my mouth shut when he would be beating on them."

Sarah tried "to live as the underdog to keep the peace," but late in her marriage her patience snapped and she finally confronted Gene. One evening she angered him by cooking dinner before he had finished listening to the radio news. "I'd fried out some meat; the grease was deep. I heard him a-coming, and I looked out and he was going through that hall door out in the porch, and he had his fist balled up. He had started in there; he was going to hit me for cooking when I did. And that pan had a long handle, and I picked up that grease, and he stopped and looked at me and said, 'What are you going to do?' I said, 'You hit me and I'll show you. I've took my last lick off of you. I've seen these children beat, and I've took my last lick off of you. And if you hit me, I'll pour this all over you.' He said, 'I believe you meant that.' I said, 'I did, and if you ever hit me again, I'll get you if I have to pour it on you in the bed when you're asleep; I'm going to get you.' And you know, he never did offer to hit me no more after that." Sarah put an end to her husband's abuse, but she also realized that they no longer shared the love that had brought them together. "I don't know why I married him. I didn't have to marry him. I knowed that, and he did too. But I just thought a lot of him. Whatever I did have with him, though, he killed it. And that's the dead level."

Still, Sarah did not denounce Gene as an evil person. Instead, she saw that he suffered from failed ambition and the inability to provide for his family as he thought he should. "When them spells weren't on him, there weren't a better-hearted person that ever lived in the world. But I'll just tell you, he wanted to be a bigger person than he really was; that was it. It was just pride, and pitiful with it. And I think another thing was just having one young'un after another. I think that got on his nerves. You know, a parent like that's got responsibility on them. And some people can't take it. That family was a big responsibility, and you see their future ahead of them and try to want to get them started off in something, and it's a lot to think about. And it got on his nerves. Have you ever been nervous? Well, you know nothing don't seem right, does it? He'd just look like he'd just get full and just wanted to do something. He just wanted to fight it out. And when he'd empty out, he was all right."[106]

Whether they indulged in the rough life or simply withdrew, mill fathers commonly left their wives to manage family affairs. Harvey Ellington and Sam Pridgen remembered that the musical tastes of second-generation millhands reflected the character of parental roles. "Most of the people liked those mother's songs, like 'M Is for the Million Things She Gave You.' There was a lot of those mother's songs. Mama always stands out. Papa don't stand out too well. Papa bears the brunt, but Mama's the one that gets the credit."[107]

In some cases, men's withdrawal from family life was a source of both embarrassment and economic hardship. Jesse Elliot's drinking left his wife and children humiliated in the eyes of the community. Ruth had to take a night shift job in order to make ends meet. Work left her so exhausted in the morning that she sometimes fell asleep before she could get her children fed and dressed. Often the children would sneak away to a neighbor's house for a hot meal. "I got so mad at one of my neighbors one time. I went to a little old store up there on the mill village, and it was cram-packed with people. And one of the neighbors up there, I detested—I still do, and I detested him before, and by then it was even worse—he made a loud, blaring announcement. He said, 'Well, here's that woman that sleeps all day while I tend her kids every morning.' Oh, I felt like killing him in front of everybody." In an attempt to recover her dignity, Ruth shot back sarcastically that perhaps she had been wrong in looking to God for help with her troubles. "I said, 'Well, thank you, Cliff. Here I am been thinking about having to wait to die to thank God, and now I can just get it off my mind and thank old Cliff Johnson.' I was so mad at him I could have shot him, mainly because he told the truth. Mrs. Johnson got up early, and [the children] would go down there and sit behind the stove and scream 'til they'd feed them hot biscuits and butter."[108]

The Elliots, however, seem to have been an exception to the rule. Mary Thompson's family was more typical of the households in which second-generation millhands grew up. Her mother took responsibility for sustaining the family, from disciplining the children to managing the budget. Mary's father often bought his children presents and took them on family outings, but he had neither the energy nor the inclination to form close personal relations or deal with household affairs. "I had a real good daddy; I was lucky. But he was one of these 'live today and let tomorrow take care of itself' [types]. And if it had been left up to him, we'd have starved to death. My mother could manage real good, and she managed enough to pay for the things that we needed. I have knowed my daddy to want a Coca-Cola, and she'd fuss that that was throwing money away. She wasn't mean that she wouldn't let you have what you wanted, but there wasn't too much money to spend for things like that—not with seven children to raise. If she was like my daddy, I don't know what would have become of us, because he was one of these that didn't try to make us do much. That wasn't none of his job; it was Mama's job."[109]

Married women also linked their families into the networks of exchange and reciprocity that lay at the heart of village life. Husbands and wives had shared that responsibility more equally on the farm, but in the mill village many traditionally male forms of cooperation and sharing lost their place. Men no longer gathered to raise houses and barns; with only small gardens to tend, they shared the work of clearing land and harvesting less often; and because mill companies often provided fuel, men no longer joined in the springtime ritual of cutting firewood. But they did continue to hunt and fish. Like most of the men in Swepsonville, Charles Foster's father fished in the Haw River with a hook and line. "Haw River was a fisher's paradise at that time. You could just catch them anyplace." When the fishing was particularly good, neighbors might gather for a fish fry. "If he'd catch enough for the neighbors, why, he'd call them out. We'd have a fish fry out in the open doors."[110] Unlike their wives, though, men became distanced from the day-to-day issues of survival and making-do that gave substance to the idea of community. When asked what held their neighborhoods together, men and women alike pointed to predominantly female activities. With the exception of occasional hunting and fishing stories and references to store culture and the rough life, there was in our interviews a pervasive and startling silence concerning the social lives of men.

Women's acts of sharing and mutual aid nourished the bonds that held mill communities together. From birth to death, women attended one another through crises, both grand and small, and performed rituals that reaffirmed the cohesiveness of the neighborhood. When a child was born, women showered the mother with gifts and boxes of second-hand clothes. In the face of illness, they organized the poundings that ensured family survival and "sat up all night, tak[ing] a turn about," to administer medicine and comfort. And in times of death, women washed the body and prepared it for burial.[111]

Women also shared the mundane duties of child rearing. Children belonged to the community as well as the family. Female relatives and close neighbors cared for infants and toddlers while their mothers worked in the mill. When children were old enough to venture away from home and play with friends, more distant neighbors joined in the responsibilities of discipline. James Pharis learned how effective such informal cooperation could be when he and a friend decided to skip school. "Me and another boy was going to school one morning and we passed the Methodist church. We got even with the church and one of us suggested to the other one, 'Let's play hooky'—go up in that bell tower until after school started, then we'd come down and go off somewhere. Some women across the street seen us go up in there and they come over and took the ladder down. So we were sitting up there in that dark bell tower and had to stay up there from nine o'clock in the morning until two o'clock in the evening before they ever come over and put the ladder back. That taught us a lesson."[112]

Cooperation grew out of the close personal relationships women created and maintained through a porch culture of visiting and gossip. The proximity of mill houses made it easy for women to get together. Frances Latta's mother developed a daily ritual of social calls with other women who had left work to stay at home with their children. "As soon as my mother finished [lunch], the ladies next door and around would come and sit on the porch. Every afternoon they visited one another. And they sat there and talked until five o'clock. Then they would go in, prepare [supper], serve it, wash their dishes, and be back on the porch again." By contrast, women who had to work did most of their visiting at night. Edna Hargett and her friends in East Charlotte "always went to see every new baby. And if we got a new recipe or made a cake or something and it was good, we'd divide it with the others. We'd go and stay awhile with them, and all of us understood we couldn't stay long because we had to get up for work and all."[113]

As in the country, Sunday remained the most important visiting day. Women opened their homes to friends and relatives, many of whom stopped by unannounced. "Sunday evening is mostly when we did our visiting with people. When you'd go spend a day with people, they'd fix you up a nice meal. On Sundays the whole family would go and spend a day with neighbors, and maybe two or three Sundays later they'd come and spend a day with us." Such reciprocity was expected, and few families waited for an invitation. According to Nannie Pharis, "A lot of people would come in unexpected, and they'd be welcome to sit down and eat with us. That was the way they done in those days.

They didn't give you warning they were coming. But we had enough to divide with them."[114]

Women used these visits to keep up with events in the village. Gossip was the currency of community life, and through it women learned of others' needs. As Don Faucette explained, "If one of the neighbors was sick, didn't nobody have to go tell the neighbors you're sick and need help or anything. Somehow or another they just sensed it and they'd go in. They'd all come in and pitch in to it." Through talk, women "looked after one another" and regulated the flow of goods and services in the mill community.[115]

Women's warding and watching, however, could easily shade into policing; it could repress as well as sustain. Older women kept a close eye on village romances and matters of sexual propriety. A young man who came to court knew that his behavior would be carefully observed. "Sometimes the boys'd stay until nine-thirty on Saturday night, being the end of the week. Nine o'clock, nine-thirty, was late bedtime. I've heard remarks made of neighbors, 'You know, that boy stayed up there last night to see that girl until nearly ten o'clock.' That was awful, that was just terrible." In a close-knit community too many lingering visits could make a couple the talk of the village. But the most disapproving words were spoken when a child was born out of wedlock. Single women were vulnerable to the advances of a demanding boss man and to visions of romance that linked sex to the promise of security and a home independent of parents. These circumstances could lead to illegitimacy and sometimes to community censure. Edna Hargett remembered that "there wasn't many of them; there was very few that had babies. But people didn't associate with them like they used to, because they'd been disgraced. Parents didn't want you to speak to them or nothing."[116]

Efforts at self-policing could also intertwine with company prerogatives. This was particularly true of "respectable" villagers' attempts to control the rough element and maintain an honorable reputation for their neighborhood. A community's first choice was to police itself. In Glencoe "the strongest man in the community was sort of the head; he'd take care of any uproar or disturbance." But when that failed, village residents called on the disciplinary power of the mill. At the Erwin Mills in Durham company officials always seemed to know when a worker got drunk. "They knew! I don't know how they knew, but somebody at the company would know all about it," one worker said. For those who became disorderly the penalty was "an automatic discharge, that was a company rule." A similar rule governed mill life in Charlotte. "If anybody'd done anything wrong and you reported them, they had to move."[117]

Some villagers praised company-imposed discipline for making their communities "a good place to live." Paul and Pauline Griffith of Greenville recalled that "the mill had a good standard that the people had to live by. There were no roughnecks allowed in the village. They were choice people. They just simply wouldn't have anybody that wasn't the best type people. And it was a good thing. Because without some kind of standard, people's lives deteriorate, and it affects communities in the ways they don't want to be affected."[118]

Millhands who acknowledged the owners' authority to police their behavior forfeited some of their rights as citizens and accepted a measure of dependency. Perhaps, for many women, the bargain seemed worth the cost. As long as they were primarily responsible for the care of children and could not earn enough to support themselves outside the family, their interests lay in using every means available to make men settled, dependable breadwinners. But the moral force of the community did not weigh on men alone. Collaboration with mill officials to weed out undesirable elements could lead to the rejection of anyone who was somehow "different." In using the owners' authority to advance the community's goals, millhands reinforced some of the repressive aspects of village life. A Bynum proverb best sums up this double-edged quality: "If you went along, your neighbors would tend to your business and theirs, too. And the old saying here, you know, 'Bynum's red mud, if you stick to Bynum, it'll stick to you when it rains.'" The community provided comfort and security, but it also proved intrusive and difficult to evade.[119]

Given the tensions within mill village life, we were struck by how fondly most workers recalled their communities. Recollections of factory work were something else again, but the village—red mud and all—was generally described with affection. The reasons are not hard to find. Group solidarity served as a buffer against poverty and, above all, represented a realistic appraisal of working people's prospects. Only after World War II, with the expansion of service industries and skilled trades, did the Piedmont offer alternatives to low-wage factory work for more than a lucky few. Until then, casting one's lot with family and friends offered more promise and certainly more security than the slim hope of individual gain.

This is not to say that mill village culture destroyed individuality. On the contrary, it conferred forms of status that the workplace did not always provide. Although millways encouraged group welfare at the expense of personal ambition, they did support individual accomplishment of a different sort. The practice of medicine provides one example, music another.

Folk medicine formed an important part of millhands' "live-at-home" culture. Until well into the twentieth century, workers viewed doctors with distrust and fear. As Lewis Durham explained, "The doctors in those days didn't know much about it, just countrified doctors. They'd make a stab at it, and that was it. Nothing they could do for you." Moreover, millhands could not afford medical fees. In emergencies the village turned to specialists within. Among the earliest of these in Bynum was Louise Jones's mother, Medlena Riggsbee. "She was what you'd say was a midwife. She could hold up under anything. Unless they were bound and compelled to have the doctor, they'd usually get her."[120]

In the 1920s and 1930s the Bynum mill retained the services of a doctor, paid for with funds withheld from workers' wages. But in the eyes of the villagers he served as a partner—indeed as a junior partner—to Medlena Riggsbee's successor, Ida Jane Smith. As a healer and a midwife, Smith was one of the most respected figures in the community. "Lord, she was a good old woman," Carrie Gerringer recalled, "she knowed more about young'uns than any doctor. She sure was good. One of my daughters, the third one, she had the measles and pneumonia. The doctor checked her and said she wouldn't live through the night. But me and Mrs. Ida Smith sat there all night long and put on tar jackets with Vicks pneumonia salve and everything. We just kept putting them on and putting them on and keeping her warm. And doggone if she didn't come out of there. He said she wouldn't live through the night, but she's still here. She's forty-nine years old, be fifty in September."[121]

In Burlington Dr. Carroll Lupton also had to acknowledge the skill and prestige of the local "granny woman." "We had a midwife; her name was Granny Lewis. And lots of women thought that there's no way in God's world that they could have a baby if Granny wasn't there." When he began practicing medicine, Lupton had no experience with midwives and viewed them with suspicion. He soon learned better. "Some of the doctors would see Granny and run her off. But she knew how to boil water, and I quickly found out that she knew how to handle a family. She could help you along in managing [a] poor little girl's emotional approach to delivery." Granny Lewis could also teach a "good lesson in obstetrics." "When the woman was just a little tired and the baby was right ready to be delivered and just needed a mighty push, Granny would say, 'Doctor, it's time to quill her.' I had never heard the term. But I knew her well enough to know that she never suggested anything that was really going to hurt anybody. And I'd say, 'Well, Granny, go ahead and do it.' Granny would get her something like a drinking straw and put a little snuff in it. And she'd get that little old girl, about the time she needed to have her pain, and blow that snuff in her nose. She'd have the awfullest sneeze you ever saw, and the baby would be 'Wah! Wah! Wah!' And that's Granny Lewis's quill job. The doctor's thing is what we call forceps, slip a little forceps on the baby's head and give that little extra traction and slip it out. But a good big sneeze does exactly the same thing, and it cuts down on the incidence of infection. I learned that one from her. Maybe some of the old-time remedies were not too bad."[122]

If the midwife was the most prestigious member of the female community, the musician held that place among men. Stringbands had been the mainstay of country gatherings, and they multiplied in the mill villages, where musicians lived closer together and had more occasions to play. Mastery of an instrument brought a man fame as the local "banjo king" or expert guitar picker. But, above all, music provided an opportunity to enjoy the company of friends and neighbors. Musicians sometimes played simply for their own enjoyment. Paul Faucette and a small group of friends and kinfolk used "to get together on the porch on Saturday night and just have a big time." On other occasions they performed for house dances and community celebrations. Harvey Ellington remembered that on Saturday nights "you'd have a dance in somebody's house—they'd take the beds and all out, and then we'd just play." The dance might end before midnight, but the musicians' performance often continued into the morning. "We'd be going home and decide we didn't want to go to bed. So we'd take the fiddle and the guitar and the banjo and stop at the corner and harmonize—do what they call serenade. The people would raise the windows and listen. That's the best-sounding music, wake up at night and hear somebody playing."[123]

Often, musicians won a following in nearby villages and the surrounding countryside as well as among homefolks. After a long day in the mill, they might pack their instruments and travel several miles to perform in another community. Fiddler Homer Sherrill remembered what it was like playing the "kerosene circuit" of rural and mill village schoolhouses. "Back in those days you just rode and rode and played and played. It didn't matter how small the buildings were, you played 'em anyway, and just put on the full show. And you got up there and picked your heart out—with no p.a. system, sweat running off your elbows, you couldn't hardly feel the strings on the fiddle. Man, that was rough days then. We played many a place that had no electricity. They'd have an old gas lantern, setting on each side of the stage; that's all the light you had. The windows would be setting full of people, and you just had 'em crowded around the walls. You couldn't even get your breath hardly." With the advent of radio and inexpensive sound recordings in the 1920s, a few village musicians used their popularity to launch careers that enabled them to leave the mill behind. But most continued to play for sheer enjoyment rather than fame and fortune. "The real thing," recalled Avril Hogan, "was that we loved the music."[124]

Musicians and healers earned a permanent place in their neighbors' memories. But most mill villagers never achieved such distinction. They lived instead in quiet anonymity, often guided and strengthened by religious faith. Churchgoing millhands were predominantly evangelical Protestants, most of them Baptists and Methodists, whose trust in Jesus was not reserved for Sunday-morning worship but pervaded everyday life. Pauline Griffith prayed while running looms in the mill. "Even though I had to work to make a living, I really enjoyed it. And my looms, they just run good. I'd pray a lot while I was working, and I felt like the Lord helped my looms to run." Ruth Williams remembered calling on God during a drought. "One time we needed rain so bad. I was just a little girl, but they were praying for rain. Before we got home, we was all wet. And I kind of believe in that. The Lord's good to us. He's better to us than we are to Him." For her Bynum neighbor, Mozelle Riddle, the Lord was a constant companion. "If I hadn't had the faith in God, I'd have never got by. I feel like if I hadn't, I wouldn't be here today. 'Cause He's really stood by me in hard times and rough times. I've been really down and out. But with God, somehow, someway, something come along. Made a way."[125]

The cornerstones of evangelical faith were the Bible and prayer. Some people belonged to tiny, independent churches, while others were part of major worldwide movements, but they all maintained a strong belief in the Scriptures as the true word of God. Not all mill workers could read, but many made the effort just so they could share the Word, and anyone could listen to Bible readings—from a parent, a neighbor, a preacher, or a Sunday school teacher. Mary Thompson told a familiar story. "We always had religious teaching in my home. We were taught what to do and what not to do, and we was taught what the Bible said. My mother would get some of us around. My daddy was a good man, but he left everything, even the teaching, up to Mama, and he done the work. She taught us what the Bible said we should do. What's taught a child stands in their mind the rest of their life."[126]

The other great arena for moral teaching and Bible study was the church itself. Churches sustained the faithful throughout the week with evening prayer meetings, choir practice, Bible classes, missionary societies, and youth groups. But before all of these came the observance of the Sabbath. Sunday was literally a day of rest from the labors of home and factory; by foot, wagon, or car the faithful found their way to a pew. "Yes, we went to church," Nannie Pharis recalled, "we'd go with our mother. She was a Primitive Baptist. I remember sitting there. The preacher would preach three or four hours; the seats would be hard, and I'd hurt. That Primitive Baptist, it commenced about ten o'clock and lasted until about four. And the benches was homemade—they made them out of logs. You can imagine how hard they was."[127]

Likewise, George Shue learned to keep the Sabbath under the watchful eye of his father. "Daddy went to church every Sunday and took us with him. We'd better go there, too, and stay for preaching. I remember one time I slipped off from preaching. I decided I wanted to go somewhere else, do something else—like any kid does. I thought he'd forget about it. But he didn't. He come in there at night when I went to bed and said, 'Boy, why'd you slip off from church?' And I couldn't say nothing. Wasn't no way to plead out of it. Took off his belt and, boy, wore it out on me. I never did do it no more."[128]

Doctrinal concerns played only a minor role in millhands' decisions about where to worship. Trust in the Lord was what mattered. "It don't make any difference in what denomination you belong," explained Ralph Simmons, "as long as it proclaims Christ and His crucifixion and works on that ground, solid and sound." In that spirit, Baptists and Methodists often agreed to share a "union" church when one congregation lacked the wherewithal to build its own building. On

Sundays, some people just stayed all day and attended two or three different services, one after another.[129]

Social ties also tended to mute the importance of denominational differences. Lora Wright and her sisters and brother were brought up in the Baptist church. "We joined the Baptist church after we were saved. [But] one of my sisters, Shirley, she married a boy that was a Methodist and she goes with him to the Methodist. Mary, the one younger than Shirley, her husband's people were Presbyterians, and she joined the Presbyterian church with him. Then Thelma, she married a boy that was a Baptist, but they had some friends that were Presbyterian and so they went to the Presbyterian church. And my brother Alton, he and his wife, they were both Baptists and they had some friends that were Episcopalians, and they joined the Episcopalian church. So that's their faiths."[130]

George Dyer's family followed a similar pattern, representing a small ecumenical movement of their own. When asked what church he belonged to, Dyer began by explaining that his parents had been Primitive Baptists. "That religion, they just believe in what's to be, what's going to happen to you, that's the way God intended, and that's the way it's going to be. I don't believe that way, so I joined the Missionary Baptist when I was a grown man. Then I married my wife here, and I converted to the Methodist church." At that point, Dyer's wife, Tessie, added her view. "When we were married, he joined the Methodists because I was a Methodist, and both my sons, they belonged to the Methodist. One of them married a Presbyterian, and the other married a Catholic. So we're Methodist, Baptist, Catholic, and Presbyterian, all in my family. All of them's good. They worship the same God."[131] Like the Dyers, millhands throughout the Piedmont worshiped with relatives and friends. Each congregation formed a self-selected gathering within the larger village community, a voluntary assemblage of people who cared for one another and professed a common faith.

What the faithful took from their religion was as complex and varied as their choice of places to worship. On one level, evangelical churches proved positively helpful, maybe even essential, to the mills. Like their counterparts in other industrializing areas, they inculcated the moral and social discipline that made an industrial way of life possible. This discipline was enforced from the top down by preachers who exhorted their followers to shun alcohol, idleness, and other forms of wickedness as an outward sign of their inner righteousness. The churches also fostered a kind of lateral discipline, as members policed one another and tried to help their neighbors follow the straight and narrow path. Finally, and most important, villagers disciplined themselves by accepting their ministers' preaching about sobriety, thrift, and duty. But there was also another side to evangelical religion, one that made the weak strong and brought them close to God.

Religion, like music and the practice of traditional medicine, combined individual distinction with a powerful sense of community. That fact became most apparent during revival season, a time of special exhortation and spiritual effort that supplemented the normal run of preaching and Bible study. Most often, revivals involved preachers from outside the community, many of whom made a living by traveling from town to town. Alice Evitt never forgot the first revival she attended as a young girl. "The preacher'd come and they'd have tent meeting. He just traveled with his tent from place to place. I remember going to tent meeting and seeing my mother shout. I was small, and I didn't know what shouting was. I remember seeing my mother praying and going on, and it scared me. I didn't know what it was. After we left, she told me she was shouting. She felt the Lord, she said, and she was shouting."[132]

The emotional fervor of a revival might frighten a child, but for adults it signified a blending of private exaltation and communal solidarity. As George Dyer explained to his younger brother, there was "nothing to be scared of." During a revival, faith turned to ecstasy; people "got happy and they shouted. They'd sing and hug each other and all that stuff—men and women both." The Holy Spirit moved individuals to public confessions of sin and testimonials of God's saving grace. As one of their number felt the Spirit's call, the entire body of worshippers joined in praise and thanksgiving. Revivals provided outlets for individual expression, while that expression, in turn, enriched and sustained the group.[133]

Revivals also dramatized the social and psychological distance between mill owners and many of their employees. As workers sang the Lord's praise, they celebrated the bonds of mutual respect and obligation that linked them to one another in everyday life. Whether they worshiped in a mill church or in a church of their own, the millhands' faith was not that of the owners. That distinction usually remained unspoken, but it broke to the surface when workers joined sects such as the Church of God and the Pentecostal Holiness, Free-Will Baptist, and Wesleyan Methodist churches. Sociologist Liston Pope considered the rise of these maverick denominations one of the most significant aspects of Piedmont religious history. He found that in Gastonia, North Carolina, the sects drew their entire membership from among mill workers. Between 1910 and 1939 they established twenty-six new congregations, while the older denominations abandoned twelve. Commonly known as "Holy Rollers," the sect churches institutionalized the passion and the participatory freedom of revivals, "fulfilling a need for self-expression and for identification of one's self with a greater power."[134]

Mill owners recognized religion's capacity for conferring a sense of liberation and autonomy, particularly through revivals and sect churches. Some manufacturers sought to win sect congregations over, or at least ensure a state of peaceful coexistence, by offering them the same kind of support provided to mainline denominations. So long as they became "stabilizing influences" and did not "cut up and make themselves objectionable," they were welcomed in many villages. Other mill owners, however, actively banned itinerant revivalists and sect ministers from their communities. According to one industrialist, the Holy Rollers "just tear up a village and a community, keep folks at the meetings till all hours of the night so that they are not fit to work the next day, and they keep such meetings going for two months with shouting and carrying on. Here they are the sorriest sort of folks and not desirable in the community on general principles." Manufacturers also worried that workers' fellowship might drive a wedge between themselves and their "loyal" employees. A mill president from Gaston County explained that his operatives were "over 99 per cent pure Anglo-Saxon; they are intelligent, smart, educated. There is no use letting them get all stirred up emotionally. I'm a Methodist, but I don't like the old type of revivals. . . . We don't care what road a man travels to get to heaven . . . but why should we let emotional sects get our people stirred up?"[135]

Sect churches reminded manufacturers that they were not the unquestioned masters of the world they had created. Viewed from the outside, mill villages seemed to deny workers the most basic forms of self-expression. But in muddy streets and cramped cottages cotton mill people managed to shape a way of life beyond their employers' grasp. Millhands' habits and beliefs were more than remnants of a rural past; they were instruments of power and protection, survival and self-respect, molded into a distinctive mill village culture. Sometimes that culture simply defended workers against condescension and economic hardship. At other times, it bred a spirit of independence that threatened the village's purpose as an institution of labor control. In either case, it offered assurance that mill folk were "fine, honest, hard-working people." "Back in them days," explained George Shue, "the cotton mill people was about the lowest class of people there were. They called them linthead. That's right, that's what you'd hear—linthead. Well, cotton mill people didn't worry about it; they were the best people in the world. They're about that way all the way around. They love people. They love to do things for people. And they don't take nothing off of people. People come and want to give them a dirty deal, they don't take it. They just fight for theirself."[136]

Air and Promises

Hard Rules

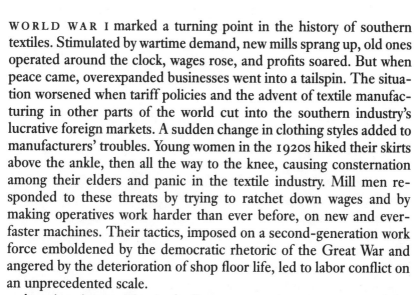

WORLD WAR I marked a turning point in the history of southern textiles. Stimulated by wartime demand, new mills sprang up, old ones operated around the clock, wages rose, and profits soared. But when peace came, overexpanded businesses went into a tailspin. The situation worsened when tariff policies and the advent of textile manufacturing in other parts of the world cut into the southern industry's lucrative foreign markets. A sudden change in clothing styles added to manufacturers' troubles. Young women in the 1920s hiked their skirts above the ankle, then all the way to the knee, causing consternation among their elders and panic in the textile industry. Mill men responded to these threats by trying to ratchet down wages and by making operatives work harder than ever before, on new and ever-faster machines. Their tactics, imposed on a second-generation work force emboldened by the democratic rhetoric of the Great War and angered by the deterioration of shop floor life, led to labor conflict on an unprecedented scale.

American intervention in the European war in 1917 aggravated the long-standing shortage of mill labor and drove wages up. Military recruitment and the construction of new army camps in the Piedmont robbed the mills of hundreds of men. Textile factories also lost workers when young women—and sometimes whole families—were called back to the farm to replace male relatives who had gone to war. Mills in diversified industrial centers such as Durham and Winston-Salem were particularly hard hit when black tobacco workers abandoned their jobs "to go to the automobile manufacturing centers, to the mines and munitions factories." Faced with the largest black exodus since Reconstruction, southern firms that had relied on black labor began competing for white workers. As a result of all these developments, cotton mills confronted "the most serious labor shortage in their history."[1]

Eager to cash in on lucrative military contracts at home and abroad, mill owners actively bid against one another for labor, as had long been the practice in the region. Manufacturers tried "every possible scheme to get the employees away from neighboring mills." *Southern Textile Bulletin* editor David Clark explained that "the first advances were made for the purpose of adjusting the pay envelope to meet the increased cost of living," but by 1918 wages had "gone so far beyond that point" that he believed they could "be classed only as an extravagance." In the context of such fierce competition, workers found that their old strategy of moving in search of better conditions was more effective than ever. Often, just the threat of moving was enough to secure a raise. The *Bulletin* complained that "the operatives have 'got on to the game' and go to the superintendent and 'report' that they have been offered advances by other mills when no such offers have been made."[2]

But even higher wages failed to solve the problem. Many millhands adjusted the length of their workweek to meet their immediate needs. They might take full advantage of better pay and work more regularly when children needed clothes or the family wanted an organ or an automobile. Once those needs had passed, workers might choose to take a day or more off. To combat such behavior and keep up with wartime demand, owners offered bonuses to employees who worked an entire week with no absences; but, as with wage increases, the bonus system soon spiraled out of control. According to David Clark, "A beginning was made with a 5 or 10 per cent bonus to secure full time work and then a neighboring mill made it 15 per cent and the first came back with a 25 per cent bonus. The effort to outbid each other has continued until the 100 per cent bonus has been reached." Once millhands could earn as much in one week as they had previously earned in two, some began to "lay off a full week at a time instead of the old policy of laying off one or two days." In a desperate attempt to control absenteeism, some mill owners accommodated workers' desire for a shorter workweek. Others simply incorporated the bonus into the daily wage.[3]

David Clark warned that the industry was "laying up trouble for the future." Manufacturers who were "noted for their level heads" seemed "to be losing all control of themselves." In their pursuit of wartime profits, mill men made unprecedented concessions to workers without gaining any significant improvements in productivity. "If the cotton mills expected to be in business for only a few months, the present system might be all right," Clark admonished his readers, "but there is a 'tomorrow' to be considered when business will be bad and the pressure of adversity felt." Clark promised that those who did not heed his warning would soon pay the price. "When the day of readjustment comes and the task is hard because of the wild deeds of today, those who brought about this state of affairs will be loudest with their whines and whimpers."[4]

Clark's prediction came true within a few months of the Armistice of November 11, 1918. By the following spring, southern mill men were suffering the consequences of peace. "The lot of the cotton manufacturer is not a happy one at this immediate time," reported the *Southern Textile Bulletin*. "He has upon his books many high priced orders that have been cancelled, either by the Government or private interests and he has been left with the high priced cotton which he had purchased for the orders that have since been cancelled." Most manufacturers adopted a wait-and-see attitude, but a few called for "immediate curtailment and retrenchment." In any case, mill owners agreed that readjustment to a peacetime economy would not come easily.[5]

Businessmen's pessimism contrasted sharply with the optimism of workers, who hungered for an expansion of wartime gains. The experience of the war years seemed to promise better times ahead—not only in rising prosperity but also in the growing power of ordinary people. Concerned that labor strife not disrupt production in war-related industries, President Woodrow Wilson had established the National War Labor Board (NWLB) in 1918 to mediate between manufacturers and their employees. In a series of rulings handed down across the nation, board members affirmed workers' right to organize, granted numerous demands for the eight-hour day, and generally endorsed requests for higher wages. Frank Walsh, who chaired the board along with former president William Howard Taft, explained that the political democracy America was defending abroad would prove to be a "delusion unless built upon and guaranteed by a free and virile industrial democracy."[6]

Walsh and his colleagues applied that principle in an important ruling concerning southern textile workers. In August 1918 millhands at the Swift Spinning Mills in Columbus, Georgia—most of whom were women—went on strike after the company discharged members of a recently formed local of the United Textile Workers of America

(UTW). The NWLB quickly intervened, forcing the company to rehire union workers, establish shop committees to hear employees' grievances, and abolish "yellow dog" contracts, which required millhands to forfeit their right to union membership as a condition of employment. These actions applied only to the Swift Spinning Mills, but they stirred new interest in the union and brought labor organizers their greatest success since the defeat of the National Union of Textile Workers in 1900. In his Labor Day message shortly after the strike, Frank Walsh encouraged southern millhands and workers nationwide to "organize your unions, strong and liberal, fearless and far-seeking." With "aggressive assistance" from unionized labor, he promised, reform would continue "until there will remain not one wage earner in the country deprived of full voice in determining the conditions of his job and consequently of his life." The NWLB failed to deliver the kind of sweeping change Walsh's rhetoric promised. Nevertheless, in each dispute brought before the board, workers gained greater leverage than they had possessed before the war.[7]

The Wilson administration also sought to rally popular support for the war effort through an aggressive patriotic campaign. The Committee on Public Information flooded the country with handbills, pamphlets, and newspaper advertisements that depicted the war as a crusade for freedom and democracy. Lecturers known as Four-Minute Men, 200 of them in South Carolina alone, exhorted audiences of farmers and laborers to secure an American victory by growing more food and producing more goods. Appeals to patriotism often led to the outright repression of dissent, igniting nativist attacks on immigrants and the suspension of civil liberties. But "100 percent Americanism" also contained a potentially radical message. The new patriotism held up the ideals of American life—justice, equality, and political liberty—as models for relations among individuals as well as nations. Workers who had helped win the war abroad hoped they might savor the fruits of victory in their own communities.[8]

The American Federation of Labor rushed to take advantage of the opportunities presented by the government's wartime policies. Rallying workers with demands for democracy on the shop floor and recognition of the eight-hour day, the AFL increased its membership to over 5 million by 1920. The United Textile Workers shared in that growth. Formed in 1901, the UTW began as a small, conservative craft union made up mostly of skilled male workers in New England mills. But that profile changed between 1914 and 1920 with the addition of nearly 70,000 new members nationwide. Most of the recruits were less-skilled women and young men who pushed for a more aggressive stance toward employers. Similar developments occurred in other unions as well. Samuel Gompers, president of the AFL, urged caution and insisted that the strike be reserved as a weapon of last resort, but his constituents were more optimistic and combative. In 1919 alone, nearly a quarter of all American workers waged strikes in an "unprecedented revolt of the rank and file."9

Southern millhands were no exception. In a series of walkouts between 1919 and 1921, they fought to secure and extend concessions won during the war. The offensive began in Columbus and in the Horse Creek Valley region of South Carolina, where hopes ran highest and the UTW had established a beachhead. Organized around the national union's demand for a forty-eight-hour week, workers in selected mills left their jobs after manufacturers refused to recognize their organization or meet their demands. Labor leaders echoed America's war aims and substituted "mill barons" for the Kaiser in their efforts to win public support for the workers' cause. "And we prate about democracy! We boast we have crushed autocracy," exclaimed a union editorialist. "We have done so on the other side of the Atlantic Ocean and thousands of our boys from the textile mills . . . helped to do it, many of them making the supreme sacrifice. But we have an industrial autocracy right here at home." Just three months after the Armistice, a war for freedom in Europe had become a war for "industrial emancipation" in the mills.10

The conflict spread into the heart of the textile region on February 25, 1919, when Charlotte's Highland Park Mill eliminated the 35 percent wartime bonus and cut operations to four days a week. At the Number 3 plant, 150 workers from the card and weave rooms walked off the job, claiming that the company had more than halved their weekly earnings. "Just to show you how the reduction works," one millhand said, "the order cuts my income from about $27 per week to $12 per week. . . . I'll live on bread and water before I'll work for that amount." Aided by a local attorney, the striking workers sought assistance from the UTW. The next week, employees at the Number 1 plant joined the walkout, and a majority signed union cards. Highland Park's management promptly closed both operations rather than negotiate with union labor. As news spread to outlying towns, millhands from nearby Belmont, Concord, and Kannapolis took up the UTW banner. These workers made no demands on their employers, but they, too, were met with a lockout. Mill owners, whose warehouses were filled with surplus inventories, decided to shut down and wait out what they assumed would be a temporary disturbance.[11]

As the conflict wore on, the *Charlotte Observer* editorialized against "the mill trouble." Calling for a return to "cordial relations" between millhands and employers, the paper denounced the strike as a rash and unwarranted act. But workers ignored the paper's advice. Mill-hands in North Charlotte—men and women alike—organized them-selves into armed patrols, intent on defending their community and their union. George and Mamie Shue remembered that "they had guns out there and they'd stack them guns up just like back in the old Civil War." One of their neighbors, Mrs. Sizemore, "was a great big old woman. She'd get her a gun and start out there to the mill. We knew she was going to kill somebody."[12]

On May 27, three months into the strike, Highland Park manage-ment ordered union families out of their houses. Anticipating trouble, the mill managers summoned "special policemen" into the village for the "protection of their property," but Mrs. Sizemore and her compa-triots attacked the "scab deputies" and forced them to leave. When Charles W. Johnston, president of the Highland Park mills, ventured into the area to talk with the strikers, he, too, was "threatened with rough treatment" and sent on his way. But, according to George Shue, the most serious confrontation occurred when millhands "got the boss weaver out there up in his loft, going to get him." The *Charlotte News* reported that "there were many firearms in the crowd, shotguns and other weapons. There was intermittent firing but apparently this was not intended to work any damage. The sheriff's office was called on to come to the relief of the overseer, and the officers went out in auto-mobiles and managed to get [him] out of the building." When asked to explain their actions, the strikers answered that "they did not propose to be put out of their homes without trouble."[13]

Fearful that the situation was spinning out of control, the mayor of Charlotte requested help from Thomas W. Bickett, North Carolina's reform-minded governor who had earned a reputation as an "advo-cate of the oppressed and disadvantaged." Bickett began his career as a lawyer in eastern North Carolina and had only loose ties to the cotton manufacturers of the Piedmont. A racial moderate, he devoted much of his political life to upgrading the state's prisons, establishing hospitals for the mentally ill, and improving the lot of sharecroppers and tenant farmers. The governor also defended workers' right to organize. "I don't care what is his color, what is his race, or what is his religion, every free born American citizen in North Carolina is entitled to the equal protection of the law," the governor declared, "and by the Eternal, during my administration, he shall have it. . . . The manufacturer has the right to say what he will sell his product for. The laboring man has something to sell also. He sells his brawn, he sells his blood; he sells his brain, and he sells the cunning of his hand. The Lord God in heaven knows that it is an outrage upon any free born American citizen to say that he has no right to club with his co-workers and say what his blood, brawn and brain work are worth."[14]

Bickett threatened to send the state militia to maintain order in Charlotte if owners and operatives could not settle the dispute. "The law must be upheld," he exclaimed. "Neither side to the controversy will be permitted to assert its contentions by a resort to violence." But the governor reserved his harshest words for the mill owners, denouncing their decision to impose a lockout as the real source of trouble. "This position on the part of the owners," Bickett exclaimed, "is unwise, unjust and cannot be maintained." Like workers, he, too, drew lessons from the recent war, identifying the right to join a union as a cornerstone of democracy. "Labor has just as much right to organize as capital. This right—the right to collective bargaining on the part of labor—is recognized by every civilized government in the world, this right is guaranteed to labor everywhere by the world treaty of peace that has just been framed in Paris." Pressured by state authorities and eager to take advantage of a momentary upturn in the market for cotton goods, Charlotte mill men agreed to a settlement under which they would observe a fifty-five-hour week and pay wages calculated on the former sixty-hour rate. Highland Park president Charles W. Johnston also promised that the mills would operate as open shops and not "discriminate against any person on account of organization affiliation." Within a few weeks, similar agreements were worked out in Belmont, Concord, and Kannapolis.[15]

The *Southern Textile Bulletin* greeted the settlements with "intense sadness." "The South has entered into a new era," lamented David Clark, "which will contain but memories of those days wherein the mill operative and the mill owners worked together in harmony and good feeling. . . . The open shop today means the closed shop tomorrow and with both there goes continual and never ending disputes and labor troubles." Although Clark ignored past tensions and exaggerated union strength, he correctly identified the workers' victory as a watershed in southern labor relations. Manufacturers insisted that their actions should not be "construed as recognition by the mills of collective bargaining," yet they had retreated, at least temporarily, from the staunch antiunionism of the past.[16]

In the view of most workers, the strike's outcome signaled the beginning of more equitable relations in the mills rather than the demise of industrial harmony. Charlotte workers celebrated the occasion in high style. Over the course of a week, they gathered at community suppers to affirm a "spirit of fellowship among the mill people." One millhand described the meal in his village as "the best feed we ever ate." The festivities ended with "a big get-together meeting and barbeque" in North Charlotte. Union members "invited all the mill owners, to show, as they stated, that there is no hard feeling and that the owners may depend upon them to deliver the goods in their mills." They also called on workers from outlying mill towns to join in the feast to promote the regional solidarity of newly formed locals and spread the union gospel.[17]

Union fever was contagious in the summer of 1919. Organizers who fanned out across the Piedmont received enthusiastic welcomes in one community after another. By autumn, forty-three locals had been chartered in North Carolina alone, and disputes over union recognition and wages had spread to Albemarle, McAdenville, Mooresville, Salisbury, Raleigh, and Gastonia in that state, as well as Rock Hill in South Carolina. The UTW estimated that as many as 40,000 North Carolina workers were "paid-up" members, with another 5,000 in South Carolina. These figures were no doubt "rounded on the favorable side," yet they reflected a profound shift in the political terrain. Despite their failure to win collective bargaining agreements, workers' success in matters of wages and hours taught important lessons in power. For the first time since the late nineteenth century, effective organization seemed within their grasp.[18]

But hopes that soared in 1919 began to tumble by 1921. The full force of the textile depression hit the South in the fall of 1920. Once again, mills cut wages, and many went on "short time." Others simply closed. The Chadwick-Hoskins Mill in Charlotte sat idle from November 17, 1920, to January 10, 1921, and when it reopened wages were reduced as much as 35 percent. E. L. Chapman, secretary of the UTW local, explained that at first workers accepted this wage reduction because the cost of living was also falling due to a general postwar deflation. But after another shutdown and wage cut in March, workers complained that they "did not receive sufficient pay on which to live properly and decently." Similar conditions existed at other Piedmont mills, and local unionists began pressuring the UTW to call a regionwide strike. Union officials were convinced that a victory was unlikely in the midst of an industrywide depression and encouraged workers to "bide their time" and try to negotiate with their employers. The UTW was also strapped for funds; recent strikes in New England had depleted the treasury, and the union could not afford the six dollars a week promised as a strike benefit to each member by its constitution. Piedmont millhands, however, were adamant. Recalling their success in 1919, they had the confidence to press their demands, arguing that "if the union won't fight, why pay dues?" Faced with the possible defection of southern loyalists, Thomas McMahon, vice-president of the UTW, reluctantly called a strike on June 1, 1921, at the Chadwick-Hoskins and Highland Park mills in Charlotte and at Cannon Mills in Concord and Kannapolis. Approximately 9,000 workers were involved.[19]

Union leaders chose these particular mills because they were "out after the big fellows." "We are not worrying about the smaller isolated mills," one official confided. "We can settle with them afterward. We are tackling some of the strongest mills in the country but we are fighting where we are strongest. We knew these Charlotte and Concord boys had been through this thing before and we knew they would stick to the fight once they were out." Indeed, the strike at first seemed to be a resumption of the 1919 action. But conditions had changed by 1921. Journalist Gerald Johnson reported that "the mill owners are in a particularly strong position; in the first place, the years 1919 and 1920 were much the most prosperous years ever known in the cotton manufacturing business, and in the second place, this season is one of the worst. Some of them maintain that the strike was a godsend, enabling them to avoid operating all summer at a loss."[20]

On the surface, workers' decision to go on strike in the midst of a severe business downturn seemed foolish. Many townspeople believed that manufacturers were doing workers a favor by keeping their plants open. The millhands' lack of gratitude could only be attributed to "the insidious influences" of northern labor organizers, editorialized the *Charlotte Observer*. "These native workers have been made the victims, in truth, of 'an organized system of alien penetration or infiltration,' the object of which is not to benefit the worker but to open the way for invasion into this former paradise of content." The paper admitted that townsfolk felt sympathy for the millhands, "but it is sympathy for the plight in which they have found themselves. . . . There is none for their cause, for they have no cause."[21]

The editorial angered E. L. Chapman, who wrote to set the record straight. From "a mill worker's side," he explained, the causes of the strike lay much closer to home. After detailing the numerous wage cuts of the past nine months, Chapman asked how workers could be expected to live and support a family on such meager earnings. "There is not much difference," he declared, "between starving while out of work and starving while working. If we can't get enough wages to live while we are working in the mills we certainly ought not to be criticized when quitting, as we can live on much less when we are not working." Particularly through the summer, Chapman and his neighbors would need little money and could survive on produce from their gardens.[22]

The *Southern Textile Bulletin* found such defiance bewildering. "We have often boasted, in sincere pride," wrote David Clark, "that the cotton mill operatives of the South were of pure Anglo-Saxon blood and that they were far superior in character to the 'scum of Europe' which operates the mills of New England. We have thought in years past that we understood the mill employees of the South but events during the past two years has made us wonder at the traits of character that have been shown." The problem, wrote Mrs. Ellington, a millhand from Charlotte, was that Clark had *never* understood the men and women who labored in the mills. "You call us ignorant to demand a living wage from the mill owners, and we know you must be absolutely ignorant when you make the assertions you have about us. . . . Now, Mr. Clark, please look upon us as we really are, a God-loving, God-fearing community of people that wish to stand and abide by truth and honest right, which will wrong no one. I don't think you could picture us so bad if you would pay a visit to any of our humble homes and see for yourself our conditions."[23]

For years Mrs. Ellington and her neighbors had struggled in quiet, personal ways to achieve better working conditions and a higher standard of living. But in the aftermath of World War I those longings seemed more attainable, and millhands felt spurred to public action. As in 1919, many Charlotte millhands saw the union effort as an extension of the battles they had fought overseas. James Barrett, president of the North Carolina State Federation of Labor, reported that veterans were the "leading spirit" in the 1921 strike. "It was the returned soldiers, the boys who were taken out of the mills into the United States Army and Navy, who went to Flanders Field to establish democracy for the whole world." These men were not stirred to action by "Northern agitators"; rather, they harbored a deep "feeling of resentment" at having risked their lives for ideals that were denied them at home. "They came back to North Carolina and returned to their jobs in the mills," Barrett said, "and here is the expression they put to me: 'We fought like the devil for democracy over yonder, and we want a pound or two of it in this little old North Carolina state.' "[24]

Wartime experiences were equally profound for those who stayed behind. The patriotic rhetoric used to rally support for the war effort reinvigorated a political language that had found little public expression since the collapse of Populism and the defeat of the National Union of Textile Workers two decades earlier. Union activists in the early 1920s consistently defended their cause in the name of citizenship, turning the mill owners' appeals to Americanism to their own advantage. Monroe Montgomery, a mill worker since the age of ten, explained why he and others were "not satisfied" with their lot. "True, our exploiters have surrounded some of us with pretty things to play with, but they have blotted that grand word 'Liberty' from our dialect. . . . And that is the very thing that we are fighting for, that is the very thing that we are determined to have—'Liberty.' . . . For we, the sons of the Musketeers that drove the British tories into the sea, still have the spirit and blood of our illustrious forefathers."[25] When workers struck against wage reductions, they wanted more than material comfort. "How can a hungry man be satisfied only by being fed," asked one man. "The workers . . . *are* hungry for more and better food, but they are also hungry for freedom, for independence, for a voice in their own lives."[26]

The principles of citizenship resonated with other values that shaped workers' daily lives, particularly the sense of justice they sometimes took from their religious faith. Again, Mrs. Ellington spoke for friends and neighbors, demanding that David Clark publish a "plain and truthful" account of the Charlotte strike. "Explain why the present conditions are our faults, instead of the mill grafters who probably pay you to make false statements about us when they will not pay the employes a sufficient amount to buy wholesome, decent food. . . . [Y]ou and I know that the truth will stand when this world is being destroyed by fire, and the Clarks and mill owners will have passed beyond to face the Divine Creator of us all. . . . You can only say you stood by and helped others to do what a higher power than we has commanded not to be done, that is to oppress the hearts of the poor."[27]

Despite workers' convictions, hunger ultimately took its toll. The 1921 strikes in Charlotte and Concord had begun with remarkable solidarity; careful observers estimated that the affected mills were 85 to 90 percent organized. Even in late July, two months after the initial walkout, workers rejected an offer to reopen the mills at old wages. Residents of the Chadwick-Hoskins and Highland Park communities filled the union hall in North Charlotte and voted unanimously to "stand firm . . . and carry the strike to a finish." But few families could stay out indefinitely. A correspondent for the *Greensboro Daily News* reported that millhands were most concerned over "the question of food." At the outset of the strike, workers had waived their right to union benefits; nevertheless, the UTW attempted to provide minimal support by distributing supplies through mill village commissaries. Strikers complained, however, that the commissaries had "chiefly flour, meal, bread, pork and such staples." The union could provide no milk, and as the summer growing season neared an end, millhands' supply of fresh vegetables would soon be depleted. Among many in North Charlotte there was "fear of pellagra," and by early August rumblings of "discontent" and "desperat[ion]" began to shake the union ranks.[28]

A back-to-work movement began on August 11 at the Locke Mills in Concord, which had gone on strike three months before the official call. As soon as the mill reopened, "strike sympathizers" from nearby communities gathered to "jeer and hoot" at returning workers. But "the backbone" of the strike was broken on August 15 when the state militia arrived in Concord and the remaining mills "resumed operations behind a hedge of bayonets." In contrast to the situation in 1919, in 1921 workers could not look to the governor as a potential ally. Cameron Morrison, a conservative with close family and professional ties to the Piedmont business elite, had won the office in 1920. The governor entered public life as a protégé of Furnifold Simmons, the architect of white supremacy, and learned his first lessons in political intimidation as a leader of the Red Shirts—Democratic vigilantes who terrorized Populists and black Republicans in the 1890s. Unlike his predecessor, Governor Bickett, Morrison refused to meet with striking workers, but he was quick to comply when mill owner Charles Cannon and the mayor of Concord requested troops "to preserve law

and order." The presence of the military overwhelmed the union. "The great purpose of the strike . . . was lost from the day the Concord company of the national guard mobilized," the *Greensboro Daily News* reported. "There only remain the treaties of peace . . . and these will be written . . . according to the desire of each mill owner."[29]

Most observers considered the strike an utter failure. Journalist Gerald Johnson reported that "the overwhelming nature of the mill owners' victory can hardly be overstated. Quietly, efficiently, ruthlessly, the union has been blotted out. There never was a hint at compromise, never even a suggestion of negotiation. The mill owners simply waited until the strikers' resources were exhausted, and then called on the governor for troops to prevent any resort to violence." Even so, workers' inability to win back wage reductions or force recognition of their union did not mean that all was lost. Small locals of "fire-tested" unionists survived in a dozen or so Carolina towns. Undaunted, they resolved to "rededicate our energies and our lives to the task of building our organization to the point that we . . . can declare our independence and assert our rights as citizens of a great state." More important, the strikes of 1919 and 1921 effectively checked deeper wage cuts, even though business conditions worsened. Edgar Smith, a member of the North Charlotte local, explained that "the biggest thing we gained . . . was the warding off of a still further reduction in wages, not only in the mills that came out on strike but in all the mills throughout that entire section. Further reductions were all figured out: that is a positive fact, in some of the mills." Although southern millhands ranked among the lowest-paid industrial workers in the nation, their real wages remained significantly above prewar levels throughout the 1920s. Millhands lost their battle on the picket line, but they made their message clear: manufacturers would not be able to shore up profits simply by cutting wages.[30]

The impasse created in 1921 by hard times and workers' protests marked the end of four decades of relatively steady growth and prosperity for the southern textile industry. Mills made money when the price for their finished goods exceeded the cost of raw cotton. The measure of that difference was known as the "mill margin." But the margin was not all profit. Out of it had to come wages, taxes, and overhead costs. What was left after those expenses represented a company's profit, some of which was reinvested, while the rest was paid out as dividends to stockholders. Prior to 1919 wages claimed a more or less stable portion of mill margins. Even during the war, when wages shot up, labor costs were offset by significant price increases for cotton goods. But that pattern was broken when prices collapsed and workers refused to surrender cherished improvements in their standard of living.[31]

Anxious to maintain profitability and satisfy investors, manufacturers grasped for a quick fix that would keep their businesses in the black. At first, owners believed that shrewd cotton buying was their best defense against insolvency, but the voracious appetite of the boll weevil undermined that strategy. The bug consumed 30 percent of the cotton crop in 1921 and caused uneven harvests well into the 1930s. Cotton prices fluctuated wildly, heightening competitive pressures and making textile operations as much a gamble as a business. When cotton was in short supply, wholesalers drove up the price of finished goods by doubling their cloth orders in anticipation of more shortages ahead. Manufacturers responded by scrambling to buy whatever cotton was available and running their mills at full capacity. But panic buying did not reflect a true increase in the demand for cloth, and overproduction soon began to force prices down again. If a burst of overproduction coincided with an improvement in the cotton supply, the consequences could be devastating. When cotton prices fell, wholesalers demanded a correspondingly lower price for cloth, leaving mill warehouses filled with stock that had to be sold at a loss or carried as surplus inventory. Throughout much of the decade, then, manufacturers rode a roller coaster of price advances and declines over which individual firms had little or no control.[32]

The mills that suffered most were those that had scurried to take advantage of flush wartime markets. They financed a rapid expansion of productive capacity by borrowing from commercial banks, floating bonds, and issuing new stock in lieu of paying dividends. During the war, such practices paid handsomely; but as earnings fell, mill officials were hard pressed to meet obligations to stockholders and creditors. By the mid-1920s, many firms faced bankruptcy. Some went under, but most were absorbed by competitors. Companies from New England were particularly keen to buy out Piedmont firms, even those that remained solvent and prosperous. During the war, New England mills had joined in courting workers with higher wages and shorter hours, but they were even less successful than their southern competitors in taking back wartime concessions. A bitter strike in 1922 crippled New England mills for nearly a year and forced employers to preserve wartime pay scales. Many manufacturers in Rhode Island and New Hampshire also surrendered to a forty-eight-hour week, which had been mandated by law in Massachusetts since 1919. These developments, along with growing southern competition in the production of fancy goods, undermined New England's textile industry. "The higher wages are a distinct disadvantage," one analyst explained, "but if it was only a question of wages . . . New England could probably hold its own. . . . It is the shorter hours that are the worst feature. . . . Our investment in plant and machinery is busy only 48 hours of every week. In the South your plant and machinery are busy 55 hours per week. The earning power of a plant full of machinery running seven hours more per week may equal the difference between a profit and a loss."[33]

Under these circumstances, northern firms looked to move their investments by buying out mills that had been in southern hands since the turn of the century. In 1923, for example, Boston's Lockwood, Green and Company acquired Pelzer Mills, long the showpiece of South Carolina's textile industry. Even at $8 million, the purchase proved more economical than the construction of a new factory, which would have cost sixty dollars a spindle as compared to the forty-three dollars paid by Lockwood, Green. Other companies chose to relocate their plants as well as their capital. By 1929 fifty-one mills with a total of 1.3 million spindles abandoned the Northeast for the better business climate of the Piedmont. Commenting on the northern industry's rapid decline, one observer compared reports of the "liquidation and abandonment" of mills to "wartime casualty lists." Between 1923 and 1933, 40 percent of New England's textile factories closed, and almost 100,000 of the 190,000 workers once employed there lost their jobs. At the same time, the Piedmont's share of the total number of textile workers rose from 46 to 68 percent. The center of American textile manufacturing had moved permanently southward.[34]

The shakeout of the textile industry coincided with the rise of a new generation of college-educated mill men, many of whom had formal business training. During the 1920s, the industry's founders gave way to younger relatives who abandoned the pioneers' intuitive methods and tried to operate on a more "scientific" basis. Bernard Cone became an increasingly important figure in his family's Greensboro mills during the war, and after the death of his older brother, Ceasar, in 1921, he assumed the presidency. The younger Cone held a degree from The Johns Hopkins University and "prided himself on introducing a new element of brains into the great cotton concern." Winston-Salem's P. Huber Hanes earned degrees from Trinity College (now Duke University) in Durham and the Eastman Business College in Poughkeepsie, New York. He took control of his family's cotton and knitting mills during the mid-1920s and developed the idea of a "suggested retail price" so that the firm's goods could be advertised nationally. But perhaps the most outstanding figure of this generation was J. Spencer Love. After a brief stint at Harvard Business School, he moved to North Carolina and transformed his family's failing mill holdings into one of the world's largest textile corporations.[35]

These self-styled "progressive mill men" led the search for new solutions to the problems of profitability and labor control. Increasing productivity was hardly a new concern for southern manufacturers. From the beginning, they had been conscious of the need to improve the efficiency of their work force and had ranked among the most enthusiastic users of labor-saving equipment such as the Northrop automatic loom. Nevertheless, measures to increase productivity had been piecemeal in the industry's early years. Low wages, combined with a strong demand for cotton goods, had kept earnings high and offered little incentive for aggressive technological innovation. But by the mid-1920s, "sticky" wages and growing competition convinced manufacturers that radical changes on the shop floor were essential to their survival.[36]

A ballooning labor supply aided mill owners in their efforts to restructure the workplace. As an agricultural depression settled over the countryside, farmers again came to the mills—in "droves," recalled John Wesley Snipes, "all of them hunting jobs." A story that made the rounds in mill villages summed up the situation. In Snipes's version, the supervisor of the Bynum mill told a desperate applicant, "No, we ain't got no job for you, not unless somebody dies." As the man walked away, "this fellow fell out of the window and got killed." So he ran back and said, "How about that man; can I have his job?" " 'No,' " replied the superintendent, " 'the man [who] pushed him out gets his [job].' They told that as a joke," Snipes concluded, "but it was rough, I'm telling you."[37]

For the first time since 1900, owners could press forward with innovations, unhindered by the power of workers to disrupt production by picking up and moving to another mill. Workers still moved, but for different reasons and with different results. As mills continued to curtail production in response to market declines, "running from wage cuts and short time [became] as common as running to increases had been." Companies kept long lists of "spare hands" who were desperate for work. According to one superintendent, "[We have] more than we want, but folks come from the farm and beg to be taken on, and if they can find a place in the village to live we give them a chance." These "extras" were available at a moment's notice to fill the job of any employee who dared complain, effectively undermining millhands' bargaining power on the shop floor. Thus, a personal strategy that had worked well in a time of labor shortage failed in a time of labor surplus. As one mill executive explained, the presence of spare hands rendered familiar forms of resistance useless and put workers in a position where "they would have to take it."[38]

Union workers in the Charlotte area understood the consequences of the "over-supply of labor" and tried to find a practical solution. In 1924 delegates to the Joint Council of Textile Workers of the Two Carolinas, a body representing surviving UTW locals, considered sending "missionaries" into "the great mountain regions of the Carolinas, and across the plains of the low-lands," encouraging farmers to stay at home. Unionists realized that rural folk were often enticed by "rosy pictures" of mill life that bore little resemblance to actual conditions. But after a "rude awakening" in the mill village, few families had "sufficient funds to leave and return to their former abode and resume their old occupations." To stem this flow of new recruits into an "already over-crowded industry," union members planned to tap into the same community networks used by mill recruiters. They proposed going door to door to collect the names and addresses of villagers' relatives and friends who were still on the farm. "With this to work from," the delegates concluded, "families who would likely come to the mills can be reached, and the actual truth given them about prevailing conditions, and this would put an end to the constant stream of people entering the textile industry. Of course, the benefits to those already in the industry can be seen at a glance." Imaginative as it was, such a scheme was beyond the joint council's reach and, in any case, could hardly have countered the forces driving farm families from the land and undermining millhands' leverage in the labor market.[39]

Manufacturers began their quest for improved productivity with simple cost-cutting measures. One approach was to run the mills around the clock. Owners had long realized the advantages of continuous production—night work spread overhead costs over a greater volume of goods, and the faster old machinery could be used up and paid for, the sooner new, efficient designs could be introduced. Before the 1920s, however, labor scarcity had often made the addition of a second shift unprofitable or even impossible. Mills paid a premium for night work, but rarely was it enough to attract experienced adults. As a result, manufacturers had to rely on children and "green hands," a practice that was seldom worth the cost. Children were "always falling asleep," and inexperienced workers produced goods that were of "inferior quality and less profitable." Once labor was abundant, these barriers to night work fell. By the mid-1920s more than half of all southern mills worked an evening shift as a "defensive measure designed to lower production costs and so stave off the threatened losses from the downward movement of cloth prices."[40]

A second strategy involved tightening operations throughout the mill. "In these days of closer competition, and higher prices for labor and raw materials," observed the *Southern Textile Bulletin*, "many of our leading mills are taking measures to prevent unnecessary wastes. . . . Every process must be chiselled and carved into economic shape. The man who can prevent the most losses, and manufacture in the most economical manner, will be sure to outsell his less expert competitor, and bag a big share of the game." Manufacturers worried about the inefficient use of light, heat, and power, but first on their list of concerns was the "waste of time." A "well known superintendent" explained that "there are many ways of wasting time. . . . too much talking, too much going after drinking water, and too much loitering around sink rooms. . . . Time is money and the waste of time is the waste of cash. . . . Margins of profit are now so close that waste of all kinds must be carefully guarded against. Leaks cost money which . . . must, of necessity, come out of the profits which would otherwise have been paid out to the owners."[41]

Millhands sometimes cooperated with their employers to "prevent leaks in mill operation." At a meeting of Carolina union locals in 1924, workers from one plant reported that they were "doing all in their power to save every little thing and moment about the mills, in an effort to reduce to the very minimum any loss that might be incurred." But most often, workers themselves were the objects of cost-cutting measures. Faced with declining profits, manufacturers sometimes attempted to extract more value from millhands' labor by extending the working day. Employees at Chadwick-Hoskins complained that the company was "gouging them" by requiring that they "start their work up ten minutes before regular time" and refusing them "payment for the extra ten minutes each day." Short time and curtailments, the workers insisted, had left many families so far in debt that they were "forced to take any old thing the bosses want to put upon them."[42]

Manufacturers also began questioning their long-standing commitment to the family labor system. In the past it had guaranteed the mills a full complement of laborers, but in the context of hard times it seemed to produce only featherbedding and waste. Gordon Johnstone, superintendent of Atlanta's Fulton Bag and Cotton Mill, complained to the *Southern Textile Bulletin* in 1923 that "instead of taking a worker connected with a family, and training him to be a productive employee, we have tried to make jobs for heads of families and children along the lines of least effort, and as a result, there are a great many jobs in cotton mills that are jobs in name only." Four years later, Johnstone moved to the Loray Mill in Gastonia—one of the region's largest operations—and was given an opportunity to act on his concerns. Founded with local capital at the turn of the century, Loray was purchased in 1919 by the Jenckes Spinning Company of Pawtucket, Rhode Island (later part of the Manville-Jenckes Company) and converted from the manufacture of cloth to the production of tire fabrics. Soon after Johnstone's arrival, a study of the weave room concluded that the department was "very much over-manned," and the company ordered an immediate reduction in the number of sweepers, oilers, cleaners, and inspectors. Within four months Johnstone had dismissed 68 of 107 weave room employees.[43]

Pruning the work force and plugging "leaks" were, at best, stopgap measures. Major increases in productivity required more fundamental changes. Mill owners decided that faster-running, labor-saving machinery had to be installed throughout the mill; jobs had to be reorganized; and new supervisory practices had to be put in place. In 1924 the *Southern Textile Bulletin* announced a "Better Equipment Campaign" designed to "show the great advantage of modern machinery and methods over old style or primitive forms of machinery." Over the next fifteen weeks the *Bulletin* described the most up-to-date machinery for every part of the mill. Among the contributors to the series was B. A. Peterson, an engineer for the Barber-Colman Company, who explained the relationship between high wages and mill owners' enthusiasm for better equipment. "Previous to the war wages were so low . . . that the savings to be obtained from the use of labor-saving machinery were not of sufficient importance to attract much attention.

In these times of high wages, however, the opportunity to make a material reduction in costs ... is attracting considerable attention among progressive and up-to-date mill men."[44]

Through the early 1930s, equipment manufacturers flooded the *Bulletin* and other trade journals with advertisements praising the cost-effectiveness of their machines. The Barber-Colman Company, for instance, lauded the ability of its new line of spoolers and warpers to remove the "human equation" from production. These machines were designed "to run at high speeds and perform mechanically much of the manual labor formerly required," thereby allowing the mills to employ "nine operatives where it used to take nineteen." But savings were not limited to the spooling and warping departments; they could be realized throughout the mill. Field trials demonstrated that warps prepared by Barber-Colman equipment contained fewer "kinks" and bad knots, which reduced loom stoppages by as much as 25 percent. As a result, weavers could "run more looms with less effort," and fewer weavers were needed to maintain production.[45]

New spooling and warping machinery rewarded mill men with their single largest increase in productivity, but such achievements cost workers dearly. Millhands who were lucky enough to keep their jobs found it a "strain" to operate the machines. Greenville's Lora Wright remembered that "we didn't have to work as hard on the old spoolers as we did on the Barber-Colman spoolers because it just didn't require it. Sometimes I would get all of my ends put up and I could rest two or three minutes—I could get me a drink of water." But Barber-Colman spoolers "were speeded up and you had to work pretty fast. Two spoolers done what thirty-six spoolers used to do on the old one. You'd be tired to death." The new equipment also diminished the importance of individual skill. Workers who had once taken pride in their ability to repair broken ends with an expertly tied weaver's knot now tended machines that did the job for them. "As the knots ... are all tied mechanically," boasted the Barber-Colman Company, "the human element is eliminated and all the knots are good uniform weaver's knots."[46]

General Electric and Westinghouse encouraged manufacturers to adopt "The Motor Way to Greater Production." Mills attached electric motors to each machine and abandoned less reliable belt-driven systems. Between 1926 and 1928, for instance, Bernard Cone undertook a $4 million "rehabilitation" of the family's White Oak and Proximity mills in Greensboro. As part of an effort to make the

LOST - 9 Men
But They'll Never Be Missed!

Thanks to Alemite and
Saco - Lowell, 4 Men
Replace the 13 Who Were
Formerly Needed to Keep
the Pickers Humming

*Advertisement for labor-saving machinery, 1927. Improvements in machine design
reduced the demand for labor throughout the mill. This advertisement suggests the
human cost of new "efficiencies" in the opening room.*
(*Reproduced from the* Southern Textile Bulletin, *March 14, 1927*)

factories into "models of modernness and efficiency," old machinery
was scrapped and "all old belting and shafting was removed and
individual motors . . . installed." With motor drives, the failure of any
one machine no longer stopped work in other parts of the mill. Equipment also ran at more uniform speeds, reducing mechanical break-
downs and damage to the goods. At the Dan River Mills, such improvements resulted in a 20 percent drop in the unit cost of production in weaving alone.[47]

The use of electric motors also gave superintendents a new means
of monitoring activities throughout the mill. Managers had always
found it difficult to maintain high rates of production because they
could never watch over every department and every employee at once.
With the introduction of electric drives, that problem was partially
resolved. W. S. Lee, president of the Southern Power Company,
explained that through the use of recording load meters, managers

could determine "whether the separate departments of the mill are started on time or stopped before closing time, and if the full load is kept on the machines during all work hours." Load meters, however, could not provide an accurate record of production on individual machines. For that, manufacturers turned to mechanical counting devices known as pick counters and hank clocks. Advertisements urged owners to "use Veeder-Root 'watch-dogs of the weave room' to detect looms that steal time, operatives that waste time; loom fixers that lose time for both." These monitors would serve as the supervisor's "all-seeing eye," putting "the screws on operating costs" by forcing every worker to "face the facts of his job." Operatives might "fool the foreman," but they would never "deceive the 'silent little superintendent' on the end of the frame."[48]

Technological innovation alone could not solve all of the mill men's problems. Equally important was the introduction of "practical scientific management." Building on the theories of Frederick W. Taylor, mill owners, with the help of industrial engineers, sought to reorganize and standardize workers' jobs. In the 1880s Taylor had begun advocating the rationalization of factory labor through a minutely calibrated system of instruction and enticement. In order to prevent laborers from establishing their own work patterns and setting ceilings on production, Taylor used time-and-motion studies to acquire the practical, detailed knowledge that once resided only "under the worker's cap." The first step in reform, said Taylor, was the "deliberate gathering in on the part of those on management's side of all of the great mass of traditional knowledge, which in the past has been in the heads of the workmen, and in the physical skill and knack of the workman, which he acquired through years of experience." Once "gathered in," this information could be used to prescribe detailed times and methods—"the one best way"—for the completion of each task. In place of the hourly wages demanded by skilled workers and the piecework rates that employers preferred, Taylor proposed elaborate scales of incentive pay that forced operatives to surpass production quotas before they began to earn more than a minimum wage. Under the old factory system, owners depended on individual foremen to spur workers to greater exertion; with scientific management, labor control would be embedded in impersonal rules and regulations.[49]

Although few mills adopted such practices across the board—they were too complicated and cumbersome for most employers' tastes—

Advertisement for Veeder-Root pick counters, 1929.
(Reproduced from the Southern Textile Bulletin, July 11, 1929)

scientific management represented the vanguard of manufacturers' quest for control over the production process. During the 1920s industrial engineering firms expanded their services to encompass the social as well as the physical relations of production. Not only the design of mill buildings, power plants, and villages but the organization of the entire manufacturing process became their domain. Piedmont mills increasingly employed consultants, such as the J. E. Sirrine Company of Greenville or Barnes Textile Service of Boston, to recommend efficiencies in every aspect of production from bookkeeping methods to machine loads and pay scales. Manufacturers hoped to make their mills operate as single, well-oiled machines, churning out better goods and higher profits. But while mill men sang the praises of this "scientific" approach to cloth making, workers called it the "pick pocket system"—a constellation of reforms that intensified their labor and robbed them of their rightful earnings.[50]

In mills all across the Piedmont, the weave room was the main target of reform. The Northrop loom, eagerly adopted by southern mills after the turn of the century, automated many tasks. Yet in an industry that had relentlessly stripped most jobs of initiative and skill, weavers remained more independent and better paid than most other textile workers. When Sam Finley started out as a weaver in 1916, he not only tended a set of twenty-six looms, he also cleaned them and kept them in good condition, maintained his own supply of materials, and removed his own finished cloth. This variety of tasks, along with high wages, made weaving a coveted position in the mill. In 1928 male weavers in North Carolina averaged thirty-seven cents an hour, compared to the twenty-seven cents earned by a card tender. Such differentials explained, in part, why weaving accounted for as much as 25 percent of total manufacturing costs.[51]

Mill men turned to the "multiple-loom" system to reduce expenses and undermine the weavers' privileged position. Under this system, tasks such as cleaning looms, filling batteries, and doffing cloth were performed by less-skilled workers at low pay. The weavers' only duty was to repair broken warps when a loom "went down"—and this they did according to a "standard patrol." Weavers were forbidden to "back track" even when they saw a nearby loom stop running. Instead, they fixed the machine only when they came to it in the course of their regular rounds. This culling of tasks and routinization of labor rendered weaving a less-skilled trade, requiring dexterity rather than craft knowledge and sound judgment. It also diminished the sociability of the weave room. Yoked to their work stations, weavers no longer moved about the mill and had fewer opportunities for conversation and companionship.[52]

The new division of labor also made loom tending more strenuous, since weavers were assigned an increasing number of machines. Geddes Dodson remembered that "all that improvement just made the weavers run more looms. They put more on them, they just got to overloading them." The logic of labor extension seemed to know no bounds, as Mack Duncan pointed out in an apocryphal story that was surely a weave room favorite. Duncan once met a man who claimed to run 200 looms. "And I asked him, 'Well, did you ever get them all running at one time?' He said, 'I don't really know. I couldn't see them all. I never did know when they was running, there was so many. There was about two or three acres of them I had to watch.' If he ever got them running, he didn't know it, because he was way behind all the time."[53]

But the multiple-loom system took its greatest toll on the hundreds of weavers who lost their jobs or were demoted to less-skilled and lower-paid positions. A millhand from Laurens, South Carolina, ex-

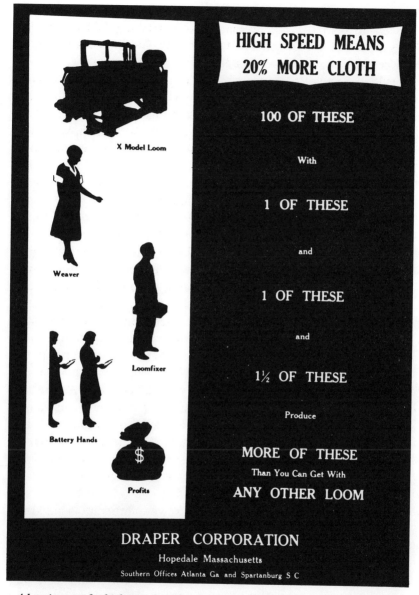

Advertisement for high-speed machinery, 1933. High-speed machines combined with the multiple-loom system to intensify labor and increase productivity. (Reproduced from the Southern Textile Bulletin, February 23, 1933)

plained in a letter to federal authorities the devastating effects of the process in his mill. The average weave room was laid off in eight alleys, each of which contained approximately ninety-six looms. "A few years ago . . . a weaver run 24 of these looms or four weavers too the alley. That was 32 weavers to a weave room." After the arrival of industrial engineers, this arrangement changed dramatically. "The boss brings in an unskilled worker . . . and his or her duty is put the bobbins of filling in the looms hopper. . . . now we take three weavers out of each alley [and] we give the whole alley too one weaver and a battery hand or 96 looms to one skilled and one unskilled worker thus laying off three skilled workers to each alley. . . . You will have 24 skilled workers out of work." The millhands who lost their jobs at Laurens and in plants throughout the Piedmont went "roving." A few found weaving jobs, but most had to settle for something less.[54]

Manufacturers tried to win weavers' acceptance of the new regime by promising that wages would rise with increases in productivity. Bernard Cone explained his conception of the multiple-loom system to students in the University of North Carolina's School of Commerce. "First you replace inadequate, uneconomical machines with modern and usually automatic and faster-running equipment. Second, you arrange the employees' work so that the skilled laborer may occupy his time more largely with skilled work, and the ordinary functions . . . are delegated to ordinary, unskilled labor. As the new machinery was more automatic . . . you give the operative more machines to run. Last and not least, you increase his pay." Apparently this remark raised eyebrows, but Cone insisted: "Yes, I am telling you, his pay is increased. And when you consider the overhead and additional expense of the change, the laborer gets a bigger share of the saving than the owner."[55]

Some workers did earn more, but most were fortunate to hold their own. Once the multiple-loom system was in place, industrial engineers set out to maximize each millhand's output by tying wage rates to production quotas that only the most diligent could achieve. Sam Finley remembered how it was done. "They got a stopwatch, and they followed them around. They figured out exactly how long it took you to tie that thread and start the loom up. They figured it right down to the tick of that stopwatch. Then they expected you to stretch it out a little bit, to do a little more. You couldn't please them. The more you done, the more they wanted done." To Finley, the multiple-loom system was simplicity itself: "Give you more work for no more pay."[56]

Similar efficiencies were achieved in other departments as well. At Gastonia's Loray Mill, for instance, superintendent Gordon Johnstone and consultants from the Barnes Textile Service found work routines in the spinning room to be a major impediment in their efficiency campaign. "It has been our chief function," Barnes engineers explained, "to make careful time studies, make definite recommendations for the extension of jobs . . . and encourage the management to make the changes necessary to secure maximum production and minimum costs." Among the problems they diagnosed were "very high labor cost due to low speed and small number of spindles per operative." The spinners' workload was limited by the fact that they spent 23 to 62 percent of their time cleaning around the frames rather than putting up ends. Barnes engineers recommended that cleaning be added to the responsibilities of other spinning room workers and that the number of spinners be reduced from 121 to 66 by giving each woman about twice as many sides to tend. When management made comparable reductions in other departments, the work force at Loray shrank from 3,500 to 2,200 millhands, producing a first-year savings to the company of $621,193.[57]

Little wonder, then, that "efficiency experts" were among the most hated men in the industry. Workers viewed time-and-motion studies and the stopwatch as instruments of exploitation. As work was speeded up and machine loads were increased, millhands found it more difficult to help one another or to take the short breaks they were accustomed to. Even worse, efficiency experts tried to harness workers' bodily needs to the company ledger. One man complained that engineers timed workers "in all their movements even to the Toiliets and to get a drink of water." The quickened pace also robbed millhands of their dinner hour, the only formal time they had to escape the noise, heat, and dust of the mill. Ada Mae Wilson remembered that in the past, "they'd come out for lunch and they'd all come out and sit in the grass and eat." But beginning in the late 1920s millhands had to eat as they worked. "Sometimes you'd start up several looms, then you'd eat a little," Lloyd Davidson recalled. "After you'd started two or three, then you'd eat a little more. You couldn't take any time to amount to anything for eating. You just had to work your eating in with your work." Mills encouraged that habit by operating "dope carts" that sold cold drinks and sandwiches. "They had what they called dope wagons," Mack Duncan explained. "People used to call Coca-Colas 'dope.' Dope wagons would come through the departments and people would go to the dope wagon when it came to where they were working. And if it came in the door at the far end from where you were, you weren't permitted to leave your job and go meet the dope wagon; he had to meet you." These changes rankled, and workers sometimes took matters into their own hands. Twice, when a time study man showed up at Erwin Mills in Durham, workers insisted that "they did not want to be studied" and pushed him out a window.[58]

Along with new technologies and the reorganization of work came an assault on the idiosyncratic relations of the shop floor. Larger mills began replacing supervisors who had come up through the ranks with young, college-trained men. No longer could a loom fixer like Sam Finley count on promotion. In the old days, he explained, "when it came a time when they needed a supervisor, you'd get that job." But during the 1920s such positions went increasingly to men whose textile degrees were a substitute for firsthand experience. "They didn't know a thing in the world about weaving. They'd bring them down there and in two or three weeks they'd have a supervisor out of him." Those who still managed to rise from production jobs did so by taking night school or correspondence courses in industrial psychology and practical math. James Pharis told how it was done at Carolina Cotton Mills in Spray. "They had what they called the Carolina Council, which was composed of all supervisors from management down to prospective supervisors. They'd have a meeting once a month and talk over business in the plant. And they paid for courses in supervising and mill calculations. They'd teach you how to get along with people and how to make a success as a supervisor."[59]

The turn to formally trained managers was dictated, in part, by the fact that "modern methods demand[ed] modern men." Writing in the *Southern Textile Bulletin*, W. M. McLaurine explained that "the day of the old time . . . overseers is fast passing. . . . We still hear occasionally the words 'Boss Weaver' and 'Boss Carder' . . . but these words have been outgrown. . . . [A]n overseer who only oversees won't be in an executive position long." In the weave room, for instance, efforts at "narrowing the work of the weaver from the management of his looms" to the repair of broken warps placed new responsibilities on supervisors, whose once "simple duties" had become "highly complex and technical." Rather than driving individual workers to maximum effort, the new breed of mill managers kept up production by maintaining careful records on the flow of materials and coordinating the performance of numerous interdependent tasks. By the 1920s, an overseer's job demanded more than the ability to solve "concrete problems"; it also required the "intellectual foresight" necessary to plan production. Whereas the "old time" overseer "worked by rule of thumb," his successor drew on "a scientific background."[60]

Manufacturers also expected "modern men" to resolve the contradictions of shop floor authority. Owners were no longer satisfied to employ men who were sometimes as loyal to the help as to the company. Lora Wright's father had to give up his job as a weave room overseer because "he didn't want to work his people like slaves. The children of Israel, why they were slaves to the Egyptians, and Papa didn't want that said of him, that he was making slaves out of the men and women that was working for him." Mill men demanded adherence to a strict chain of command in which their lieutenants would enforce orders from above "as if they owned the mills themselves." By the same token, owners and superintendents no longer made themselves available as mediators between overseers and disgruntled workers. To Grover Hardin it was "like taking orders in the armed forces. You was kind of under a fear, see, because there was nobody you could take your troubles to. You couldn't carry it high because [an overseer's] word went above yours regardless. If he's over you, he's over you. It was pretty well all the way down the line. You had to take it or lose your job." With his usual candor, Sam Finley explained how things had changed. "What they wanted was somebody when they whistled they'd jump. And make the others jump. And that's the difference."[61]

Even under this system, second hands, who were in most direct contact with workers, sometimes attempted to soften the effects of executive orders. Naomi Trammel remembered how a second hand tried to help her. " 'Now, Mrs. Trammel, you're the best battery hand I've got,' " he said. " 'I want to put you on extra batteries. You don't have to work a bit harder than you're working right now. Just take your time.' I took my time. I['d] just poke along. And he wouldn't fuss. He knew I couldn't run all them batteries." But that situation "didn't go on too long," because Trammel could not keep up production and was forced to quit her job.[62]

Looking back over the 1920s, southern millhands remembered conditions that "just kept getting worse and worse." The "stretch-out" was their term for the cumulative changes that set them tending machines "by the acre," filled every pore in the working day, and robbed them of control over the pace and method of production. Work became a constant struggle to meet ever-increasing production quotas. "It looked like every time you got where you could keep a job up," recalled Josephine Glenn, "they'd just add a little bit more to it. And you was always in a hole, trying to catch up. You'll think, 'Now I'll do this, and I'll be caught up; now I'll do this, and I'll be caught up; now I know I'm going to be caught up in just a minute.' But at the end you're just as far behind as you were to start with." When workers went home, the effects of the stretch-out followed them. Lloyd and Betty Davidson became so accustomed to eating on the run that they could never break the habit, not even in retirement. "If you'd ever eat lunch with us, you'd probably understand it better, because if we sit down to eat, we just eat like we don't have but about a minute. And it's real embarrassing because you don't get out of the habit. When we go out and eat with people, we're embarrassed still at the way we eat. We're through and sitting there waiting and the other people are just getting into the meal. I reckon you just get in that routine. It's hard to get out of it." The stretch-out preyed on Edna Hargett even in her sleep. "There's many a times I dreamt about it," she recalled. "Sometimes you'd be up on your job, and other times you'd be behind. So I just sweated it out in my dreams like I did when I was on the job, wanting to quit, and I knew I couldn't afford to."[63]

In 1929 this private anguish gave way to public conflict on an unprecedented scale. The issue in almost every case was rationalization and technological change. Faced with management attempts to turn back the clock on wartime wage gains and the breakdown of a tacit social contract that permitted workers a measure of dignity and autonomy in the village and on the shop floor, a rising generation of southern millhands rediscovered and sharpened the weapons of collective resistance forged a decade before.

A walkout in the summer of 1927 at the Harriet Mill in Henderson, North Carolina, signaled the turbulence to come. The protest was sparked by two changes in company policy. The first was the withdrawal of a bonus offered during the boom years. The second was a tightening of security at the plant gate, a move that symbolized the increasingly prisonlike atmosphere of factory work and threatened the traditional continuity between village and mill. "We are not a class of people to be locked in," the strikers proclaimed. At the behest of a company lawyer, the sheriff deputized the mill foremen and the National Guard soon arrived. The threat of evictions brought the conflict to an end, but not before 800 workers had signed UTW membership cards.[64]

The strike wave began in earnest on March 12, 1929, in Elizabethton, a small town nestled in the Blue Ridge Mountains of eastern Tennessee.[65] Initiated by young women recently recruited from hardscrabble farms, the walkout involved the entire work force of the German-owned Bemberg and Glanzstoff rayon spinning plants, more than 3,000 people in all. Paid by the piece, workers complained of low wages, rising production quotas, and "hard rules." The county court immediately issued an injunction forbidding all picketing near the mill, National Guardsmen mounted machine guns on the plant roofs, and soldiers escorted strikebreakers into town. The strike made national headlines when businessmen-vigilantes kidnapped union organizers and drove them out of the state. No one was prosecuted for this crime. Instead, these same men, sworn in as "special policemen," crisscrossed the county at night, stopping and searching cars and "driving the riff-raff off the road." In response, a strike leader arrested for violating the injunction denounced the "latter day industrialism" that presumed to "dictate the walks and ways of the native sons of Carter County" and promised that he and his compatriots would "fight to the last ditch [for] the right to remain in the land of [our] nativity and still be free."[66]

Fight they did, for three months, in a battle that owed its character as much to local circumstances as to larger trends. The contest in Elizabethton was an unequal one, but it was not so unequal in contemporary eyes as hindsight would have it. Many of the rayon workers commuted to the mills from their hillside farms, and they could count on help not only from their families but from the small country merchants who relied on those families for their trade. The nearby valley of Stoney Creek, for instance, was a hotbed of strike support. Stoney Creek's own J. M. Moreland was county sheriff, and he openly took the union side. A strike leader in the twisting room ran a country store and had often driven his working neighbors into town. "That's why he was pretty well accepted as their leader," said a fellow worker. "Some of them were cousins and other relations. Some of them traded at his store. Some of them rode in his taxi. All intertwined."[67]

Such backing helped the strikers hold out, and it may have prevented the drastic antiunion violence that marked other conflicts, but in the end the company prevailed. Sheriff Moreland was forced out of office, and his worker-farmer constituency had to bow before a multinational corporation in league with development-minded townspeople and backed by the armed force of the state. An industrial espionage agent cataloged the forces arrayed against the union: "800 state police, 700 business and professional men ... the United States government, the thirteen southeastern states, and the main state official in Tennessee and 'the main city official in Elizabethton." Also working against the strikers was the desperation of farmers farther back in the hills. While strikers patrolled the picket line, highlanders from Buladeen, the poorest and most remote hamlet on Stoney Creek, took their jobs in the mills. Still, it was UTW officials and federal mediators, not local unionists, who decided to give up the fight. On May 26, six weeks after the strike began, negotiators agreed on a settlement that made no mention of workers' demands. The company's only concession was a promise not to discriminate against union members, a promise on which it promptly reneged. Not surprisingly, "it took nine speeches and a lot of question answering lasting two and a half hours to get the strikers to accept the terms."[68]

Before the Elizabethton strike ended, the spirit of protest had jumped the Blue Ridge and spread through the Carolinas. Strikes against the stretch-out swept South Carolina, involving thousands of workers in thirteen different mills. Millhands in North Carolina quickly followed suit, with walkouts in Pineville, Forest City, Lexington, Bessemer City, Draper, and Charlotte. The role of the Communist-sponsored National Textile Workers Union (NTWU) and the shooting deaths, first of the police chief and then of Ella May Wiggins, the strikers' balladeer, brought the Loray Mill in Gastonia a special notoriety. But the carnage was even worse in Marion, where the strike was locally initiated and cautiously led by the adamantly anti-Communist UTW.[69]

Gaston County epitomized the phenomenal wartime growth of the southern textile industry, as well as its postwar instablity. Caldwell Ragan, whose father had helped to found the county's earliest mills, remembered "how wild things were in 1918, 1919, 1920." Local promoters "just kept organizing and building new mills. Some of the mills that were organized, before they even laid a brick, the stock went from a hundred dollars a share to two hundred dollars a share." By 1929, Gaston was the leading textile county in the region, third in the nation. Gastonia, the county seat, called itself "the South's City of Spindles," and Loray accounted for almost one fifth of those spindles. During the war the UTW had established a toehold in the mammoth mill; in 1928 the weavers walked out in response to draconian cost-cutting measures. The weavers' demand for "simple justice" was ignored, but their protests continued. A few months later, a group of Loray workers paraded down main street, carrying an effigy of the superintendent, Gordon Johnstone, in a coffin. At intervals, the effigy would sit up and shout, "How many men are carrying this thing?" The marchers would reply, "Eight," to which the effigy would answer, "Lay off two; six can do the work." When news came that Johnstone would be moved, the workers staged a modern-day charivari. They marched through Gastonia to the superintendent's home in an "exclusive" residential section, "shouting, laughing, singing, blowing horns, beating tin pans, [and] shooting fire crackers."[70]

The superintendent's departure did not stop the trouble. On April 1, 1929, a few weeks after NTWU organizer Fred Beal arrived in Gastonia, Loray workers walked out, demanding a minimum wage of twenty dollars a week, equal pay for women and children, abolition of the stretch-out, and union recognition. The strike spread to nearby Bessemer City and to other mills in Gaston County. The Gastonia *Gazette* warned of atheism, race mixing, free love, and revolution; the city outlawed picketing; and Governor O. Max Gardner sent in the state militia. On May 7 the company evicted sixty-two families, who promptly set up a tent colony complete with school, police, and recreation. A month later, during an attack on the colony, Gastonia Police Chief D. A. Aderholt was killed. The prosecution of the sixteen unionists charged with the killing ended in a mistrial, and a mob led by a motorcycle policeman roamed through the county, destroying union property and terrorizing union members. On September 14, armed men forced a truck full of Bessemer City unionists off the road. Shots rang out as the truck's occupants scattered through the fields. Ella May Wiggins, the union's most effective local organizer, died on the spot, with a bullet through her chest. Although the murder occurred in broad daylight with dozens of witnesses, it took the governor's intervention to bring the case to trial. With Ella May's death, the acquittal of her alleged killers, and the conviction of seven unionists in the second Aderholt murder trial, the Gastonia rebellion collapsed.[71]

In Marion, the strike at the Baldwin and Clinchfield mills fit a now-familiar pattern. Sam Finley, Lawrence Hogan, and a group of their friends, frustrated by a stretch-out that "just kept tightening down on people," asked the UTW for help in starting an organizing drive. Their efforts tapped a well of grievance against a gouging company store, an absentee owner, a factory that workers saw as "just a sweatshop, slave place," and mill village facilities that were among the worst of their type. At first, the fledgling local held "open-air service[s]," then switched to "sneaky meetings" for security's sake. When the company "found out where we was going to meet, they'd have somebody posted there," Sam Finley recalled. "Then when they found out [who] was going to these meetings, they fired them." With almost 90 percent of the millhands signed up, a union committee took their complaints to "the big man," R. W. Baldwin, who responded with ridicule. As Sam Finley remembered it, "He said, 'Well, I'll give you ten dollars apiece if you'll strike my mill.' And he laughed at them. He didn't think we could do it." The committee walked out of Baldwin's office, signaling to second-shift workers lying in the grass around the mill, who moved at once toward the gate; simultaneously, workers on the inside "started knocking off the machines and coming out. They stopped that thing down, whoosh, just like that. They had it organized and in ten minutes after he said that, it was dead."[72]

The Marion manufacturers secured an injunction, but strikers picketed the mill anyway. When Baldwin tried to go through the gate, someone hit him on the head with a walking stick. Families slated for eviction refused to leave their homes. According to Sam Finley, "They'd give them orders to move out of the house. Well, if they didn't move, the sheriff would get a bunch of deputies and tear every piece of furniture out, just cart it out in the street. A lot of times, that night the house would catch fire and burn down."[73]

One such incident, deliberately provoked by management, provided the occasion for summoning the National Guard. Perry Hicks, a nonunion worker who was "sworn to secrecy" and "let in the inside of what was going to happen," remembered the sequence of events. Troops had already been stationed at the courthouse, two miles from the mill village, but because no violence had erupted Governor Gardner refused to send them to the mill. On August 28, company men evicted a striking family and installed a "rough man" from South Carolina in the house. That night, unionists dumped the interloper's furniture on the street. Company spokesmen called the incident a "reign of terror"; National Guardsmen surrounded the mill; and 148 workers were indicted for various crimes, including "insurrection against the state of North Carolina."[74]

"The mill owners," commented the *Asheville Advocate*, "are hoping to crush the campaign to organize the South," and they could count on widespread public support. As Sam Finley told it, the "town fathers" of Marion owned stock in the mills. "All the store owners they opposed it. Whatever the company said, that's what they were for, you know. [County officials] were against it. The whole thing. Everything was against organized labor. There wasn't a law on the books in North Carolina to protect them in any way at all." Against such opponents, guerrilla tactics could go only so far. In the end, military force "turned the trick," and by September 1, 1929, nonunion millhands began straggling back to work.[75]

The UTW did win a few concessions, but as in Elizabethton, the settlement soon went by the board. A second walkout was set for the morning of October 2, two and a half months after the conflict began. When the pickets arrived, they found the law lying in wait. According to Finley, "The McDowell County sheriff got him a bunch of deputies; couldn't get anybody but a bunch of cutthroats. And they drunk a five-gallon keg of liquor. They had it in the boiler room and they drunk it that night, according to one of their own bunch. The next morning, they were ready, you see. When the crowd gathered up there in the street, the sheriff pulled tear gas and threw it in their face. When they turned to run, these other deputies shot them in the back. Three to five hundred yards, running down the road, shot and killed them right in the road. The morning that it happened I was at home. [My wife, Vesta] was sick and I couldn't get out. My name was on the list. One of these deputies told it: every man that got killed was marked. They had told them who to kill, the leaders." When the melee ended, twenty-five people lay wounded; six others eventually died. The killings were a "shock," "heartbreaking," the people were "tore up and scattered," and the organizing drive came to an end.[76]

For almost a year, the winds of rebellion appeared to subside. Then in September 1930 the Dan River and Riverside Cotton Mills Company in Danville, the largest textile firm in the South and a flagship of welfare capitalism, was engulfed in a protracted struggle. There, the issues were the stretch-out and wage cuts—both imposed over the objections of an employees' organization called "Industrial Democracy" that had been established by the company during World War I. In 1932 hosiery workers in High Point, North Carolina, also walked out rather than accept a wage cut; within a few days, more than 15,000 furniture, cotton, and hosiery workers had followed their example.[77]

The United Textile Workers union was ill-prepared to respond to these grass-roots uprisings. By the late 1920s the "new unionism" that had promised so much a decade before had almost collapsed under the combined weight of a nationwide probusiness climate and an aggressive corporate antiunion drive that had the backing of successive Republican administrations. During this critical decade, the courts served as handmaidens to business, crippling unions through injunctions and the enforcement of yellow-dog contracts. There were few restraints on company-sponsored unions or industrial espionage, and private police were legal everywhere. The AFL's constituent unions lost more than one million members, and the UTW suffered more than most. A series of costly strikes drained the UTW's treasury, and the flight of the textile industry southward eroded its New England base. Fighting for survival in a world made safe for business, the UTW counseled accommodation. Union officials argued that wages should be tied to productivity and that unions should cooperate with rationalization schemes. Higher wages and an improved standard of living, the UTW advised, depended on "an increase in industrial efficiency and the elimination of waste."[78]

The only spark of life in the UTW came from an autonomous affiliate, the American Federation of Hosiery Workers and, in particular, from Alfred Hoffmann, the hosiery workers' most impressive southern organizer. Trained at A. J. Muste's Brookwood Labor College in Katonah, New York, Hoffmann belonged to a generation whose radicalism was fashioned more from American democratic ideals than from Old World ideologies.[79] "Tiny" Hoffmann tipped the scale at 300 pounds. He was "a big fleshy fellow" who was "all fire in making speeches." Courageous, plainspoken, and sensitive to workers' culture, he blended easily into the local scene. Appearing first in Henderson, Hoffmann moved on to Durham, where he helped set in motion one of the strongest local labor movements in the region. He founded the Piedmont Organizing Council in 1928, then popped up in virtually every North Carolina trouble spot until he was tried for insurrection in Marion and sentenced to thirty days in jail.[80]

Yet even Hoffmann was less an instigator than a troubleshooter who usually arrived after the fact, and a number of the lesser-known but more successful walkouts ran their course with no official union involvement at all. During the 1929 strike wave, South Carolina workers formed their own relief committees, held mass meetings, and negotiated modifications in the stretch-out—all without assistance from the UTW.[81] Similarly, in the 1932 High Point walkout, hosiery workers used automobile caravans to spread their protest to neighboring towns, won a partial victory, and went on to establish an independent, citywide Industrial Workers Association for whites, paralleled by a similar organization for blacks.[82]

In South Carolina and in High Point some local strikers spurned UTW help, but for the most part it was the UTW's shortcomings—along with employers' intransigence—that kept the national union out. To most UTW officials, the South was a foreign land; they paid attention to southern workers only sporadically and then primarily as a low-wage threat to the union's strongholds in the Northeast. Although women made up a large percentage of the textile work force, the union sent few female organizers to the region, framed its strategy around the demand for a "family wage"—that is, a wage that would enable a man to keep his wife and children at home—and made no attempt to address working women's needs.[83] In Elizabethton, for instance, almost 40 percent of the rayon workers were women, and it was they who initiated the strike and were among the local's most enthusiastic members. But instead of capitalizing on women's contributions, UTW organizers yielded to middle-class fears of sexual misbehavior; at the height of the strike, they sent a quarter of the picketers back to their hillside homes, "chiefly young single girls whom we want to keep off the streets." "Criminal sluggishness" was Socialist leader Norman Thomas's term for the UTW's performance during the southern labor revolt. More charitably, the UTW was too poor, too beleaguered, too parochial, and too fainthearted to take on the daunting challenge of cracking the nonunion South.[84]

The Danville strike in 1930 was a partial exception, coming as it did on the heels of a dramatic 1929 convention in which the AFL resolved to seize the moment by launching a southern organizing drive. Counting on AFL support, the UTW poured its slender resources into Danville and sent its energetic vice-president, Francis Gorman, and a southern representative of the National Women's Trade Union League named Matilda Lindsay to the town. But the southern organizing campaign was fatally undermined by opposition from craft unionists within the AFL, and the Danville strike faltered in part because the AFL failed to provide strike relief.[85]

Under such circumstances, workers fell back on their own resources, and in village after village they turned habits of mutuality and self-help to novel ends. Marion villagers who "had a good garden" would "divide their gardens with people that didn't have any." Reluctant neighbors sometimes found themselves donating anyway. Sam

Finley remembered frying chickens for a picnic on the picket line—supplied by a boy who could "get a chicken off the roost and leave the feathers." Baseball games, string music, and singing buoyed spirits and fostered solidarity. In Gastonia men who had played on a mill-sponsored team renovated their old uniforms by covering "Loray" with "NTWU." Ella May Wiggins, with her "fine, ringing voice," had a special gift for putting new words to familiar tunes. But she was not alone. Daisy McDonald, who supported a sick husband and seven children on $12.90 a week, transformed the "Wreck of the Old 97" into a stirring union song. A spare hand named Odel Corley set "Up in Old Loray" to the tune of "On Top of Old Smoky," replacing the false-hearted lover with a crooked boss and the betrayed woman with a spirited striker.[86]

In some cases strikers gained a critical edge through their ties to the countryside and relations with small merchants in the towns. This was especially so in Elizabethton, where many workers still lived on family farms; in South Carolina, where the strikers enjoyed substantial local support; and in Danville, where the town's storekeepers depended heavily on the patronage of the huge Dan River Mill work force. Asked how farmers responded to the Marion strike, Sam Finley replied, "People with farms out in the country, they'd donate a lot of vegetables. We'd take our cars and trucks all around the county, and they'd load us up with beans, potatoes, corn, and cabbage. That's how they felt about it."[87]

By and large, mill village ministers opposed collective action. But independent and holiness churches, to which mill workers flocked in the 1920s and 1930s, sometimes sheltered the disaffected, and evangelicalism remained a resource upon which strikers could draw. Henderson workers put a popular Sunday school teacher on their negotiating committee, and a Pentecostal congregation endorsed the Gastonia strike. Gathering in an interdenominational tabernacle built for revivals, Elizabethton workers listened to a country preacher warn that "the hand of oppression is growing on our people. . . . You women work for practically nothing. You must come together and say that such things must cease to be." Each night, another crowd "came forward" to take the union oath. Like slaves in the Old South, Piedmont textile workers turned to Old Testament images of bondage, transcendence, and release. At Greenville's Brandon Mill strikers drew an analogy between "the cotton mill people" and the "children of Israel [who] were forced to work for the Egyptians. They made bricks for them and each day the Egyptians would beat them and want them to make more. The cotton mills are not as different . . . as people think." Such uses of sacred symbols were not lost on the mill owners and their allies in the towns, who often viewed workers' religion with mingled fear and scorn. "It is doubtless the sons and daughters of the 'Holy Roller' enthusiasts," asserted the *Southern Textile Bulletin*, "who followed the Communists into [the Gastonia] strike."[88]

The tangled role of the church in the Marion strike illuminates the lines of cleavage in village life and the complexity of mill village religious culture. Marion activists held "open-air services," sang hymns on the picket line, and invited strikebreakers to join the union and be "saved." Other workers, however, took to heart the Pentecostal preacher's warning that "you was taking the mark of the beast"— entering a compact with the devil—by joining the union. Vesta Finley, who was both a devout member of the sect and a committed unionist, mourned the "broken fellowship" that could result. "It brought discord to the churches," she remembered, "and that was a sad thing."[89]

Broken fellowship was a high price to pay for the union's promise of a new form of secular solidarity. But in Marion strike opponents were a decided minority among the millhands; the main fault lines in the churches ran between ordinary workers and the supervisors who shared their pews. Mill officials worshiped in town, but superintendents and overseers were prominent members of the village churches. The minister of the Methodist church, where the mill superintendent doubled as superintendent of the Sunday school, was among the strikers' worst enemies. The Baptist church, on the other hand, was divided. There, a millhand named Dan Elliott, who was the strike's chief orator, served as chairman of the board of deacons. The Baptist minister was careful not to take sides, but when Elliott left town to study at Brookwood Labor College, an overseer took his place on the board and led a move to dismiss twelve union members for "unchristian conduct." "They even turned them out of the Baptist church here for joining that union," Sam Finley recalled. "Church members. Kicked them out! That's how serious it was." From one quarter, however, came unequivocal support. The largest church in the village was an independent congregation formed by a splinter group of Baptist workers. Its pastor was a mill worker himself and the only local minister to participate in the funerals of the men killed in the Marion strike.[90]

In all these ways mill folk fashioned tools of resistance from established cultural forms. But the argument for continuity should not be pushed too far. The young people who led the protests of the 1920s had come of age in a society very different from the one their parents had known. Most had grown up in the mill villages or moved as children from the countryside. They did not see themselves as temporary sojourners, ready to beat a retreat to the land, or as destitute farmers for whom "it was heaven to draw a payday, however small." Their identities had been formed in the mill village; they had cast their fate with the mills.[91]

There were exceptions, to be sure. The Elizabethton strikers were recent migrants from the hills. But the chemical process that produced rayon yarn, together with the distant, authoritarian style of foreign-born managers, created a factory environment that was a far cry from the small, water-powered spinning mills that had characterized the industry in its early years. There were new arrivals from the countryside among Piedmont activists as well, but they too differed from those who had come before. For one thing, a deepening agricultural depression made it difficult for them to move back and forth between farm and mill. For another, they took up cotton mill work at a turning point in the industry, when surplus labor gave management a freer hand on the shop floor.

Whether greenhorns or seasoned workers, men and women who considered themselves "cotton mill people" lived in an increasingly stratified world. In urban centers changes in residential and employment patterns widened the gap between mill and town. Places such as Greenville and Charlotte acquired large populations of clerks, service workers, and professionals who defined their status in opposition to the millhands on the outskirts of town. Ada Mae Wilson, who lived in the Highland Park village in North Charlotte, remembered that "there was different classes of people that lived in different directions." The "real highfalutin people" lived in the fashionable suburbs of Dilworth and Myers Park. "But we was trash out here; we was poor white trash because we worked in the mill. We didn't have white-collar jobs, as they called them, like working in a bank or the stores and things like that. 'Poor white trash' they called us. They thought we ought to wear brogan shoes to church."[92]

Townspeople seldom ventured into the mill districts, but millhands went to town. Hoyle McCorkle remembered the hurt that could result. "The other children would kind of look down on you. You'd go to school and they'd call you a linthead and all that stuff. You was kind of from the wrong side of the tracks." Sam Finley had similar memories, from an adult point of view. Marion merchants "were glad to get your paycheck, glad for you to come up there and leave it with them, but to uptown people you were still cotton mill trash." According to McCorkle, the condescension ran so deep that it sometimes turned the racial hierarchy upside down. "Even the blacks looked down on us, yes they did. Called us white trash."[93]

Tensions between mill and town could give the most personal relationships a painful twist. Hoyle McCorkle, who grew up in North Charlotte, took music lessons in school and developed "quite a talent as a musician." But talent meant little or nothing compared to his parents' station in life. He began playing the guitar with a friend who lived in the middle-class district of Midwood. "His daddy was one of the editors of the *Charlotte News*. So I got to socializing with him, playing and sitting in with one another. One night we went over to his parents'—he'd been coming here—and he says, 'Don't tell them your parents works in a mill.' Now, I never did play with him anymore."[94]

As more mills sprang up in urban areas, town boys began to date village girls. But such cross-class liaisons could have unfortunate results. According to Clara Thrift, who grew up in Thomasville, North Carolina, "Uptown boys would go out with mill workers' girls, but they really didn't think these mill girls were good enough for them. That's what happened to me. I met this guy in church and I thought he really loved me. I think deep down inside he really did, but because I was from the mill section he didn't think I was good enough for him. He was the son of the Methodist minister, and he is the father of my first daughter. . . . I guess I trusted him because he was a minister's son, and I thought he was special. He thought he was pretty special too. When I told him I was pregnant, he just said that he had to finish getting his education and that he'd see me around. In other words, he didn't care what I planned to do. . . . This was typical, though. When I look back, a whole lot of girls I grew up with got pregnant by boys outside the mill village. The girl was usually so scared she let the boy off scot free."[95]

In the village as in the town, men dominated the streets and other public spaces, and they devised their own ways of drawing boundaries, excluding interlopers, and asserting masculine pride. While girls had new opportunities to date and even marry outsiders, boys found themselves locked more tightly than ever into the mills. Between 1880 and 1920 the proportion of the mill labor force made up of men between the ages of sixteen and twenty-four rose from 17 to 25 percent, reflecting in part the increasing difficulty of returning to the farm or otherwise escaping mill employment. Such circumstances could breed resentment against girls who dated outside the neighborhood and against the men who courted them. Almost every village came to have its band of rowdies known for patrolling neighborhood boundaries. They defended their turf against all comers, but they were especially adept at chasing away uptown suitors. In the Highland Park village in High Point, they were known as the "dirty-dozen," and their usual tactic was to stand on the railroad trestle above the road into the community, dropping rocks on intruders. Young men in the small town of Haw River employed similar strategies. "Haw River was pretty rough, and if any out-of-towners went to see any of the girls down there, they'd get rocked when they left. And they'd slip around and let the air out of their tires on cars. They'd be parked out in front of the girl's house, and they'd sneak around and let the air out of the tires."[96]

In North Charlotte, George Shue and his friends took a more direct approach. "These boys here, they'd fight for their own. They didn't allow people from other parts of town to come out here. They'd run them off. You'd catch some boy from the other side of town—you wouldn't bother him [at first]—but after he gets in here and settles down and thinks he's all right, then one'd get on one side of the door and one on the other, and they'd get up there and knock. Find out his name, say, 'I want to see so-and-so. Is he here?' He'd come to the door, they'd grab him and pull him out of there and the other two would take him on home and make him leave his overcoat and everything. They'd run him out." George found the story amusing, but his wife, Mamie, did not. "They thought we belonged to them," she explained. On one level, the protection of young women from outsiders was a game of male posturing and bravado. But it also revealed how the forces of class could shape the most intimate aspects of young people's lives. Romance became an arena of conflict between mill and town, with women as the prize.[97]

In the schools, the shops, and the streets, such confrontations affected different people in different ways. John Wesley Snipes "felt all the time just like the scum of the earth. It was a low-grade work and I weren't happy with it none of the time." Edna Hargett suffered what she termed an "inferiority complex." "We worked in the mill, and we didn't have the conveniences that other people had. We were very conscious of that." Others deflected insults with stubborn pride. One man explained why his neighbors went downtown straight from work with lint in their hair. "It seems like sometimes they were just stiff-necked about such things, like they were telling people, 'If you ain't willing to put up with me the way I come off the shift on Saturday morning, why to the devil with you.' "[98]

Alice Evitt, a Charlotte millhand who sat through the trial of the Gastonia workers charged with killing Police Chief Aderholt, watched the proceedings across a class divide. "I went up there to hear that trial. I wanted to know how the union worked. They was cotton mill people like I was, and I wanted to hear it. [The prosecuting attorney] called them old 'lintheads.' Everywhere you go you'll find people that way. 'Cause you work in a cotton mill they don't think much of you. I don't believe I could have took it if I had been tried and they had called certain things about me that way in court. I believe I would have met them out somewhere and got them told. I'd have told them I'd druther be a linthead than be like they are."[99]

It would be a mistake, however, to assume that insults and defensive strategies tell the whole story; the activists of the 1920s shared a generational experience in more positive ways as well. Most were between the ages of eighteen and thirty-five; they had entered the mills or started their families during the boom years of World War I, when rising wages and opportunities for promotion gave them reason to hope for better times ahead. Sam Finley, for instance, was twenty-eight in 1929 when the Marion strike broke out. At seventeen he had gone to work in the Marion mill, where Irene Hogan (whose brother Lawrence played a major role in the labor uprisings of the 1920s and 1930s) taught him how to weave. After a year as a spare hand, he got his own set of twelve looms. Until he married Vesta, Sam sang with a traveling quartet and moved from mill to mill whenever he "took a notion." But that did not keep him from circling back to Marion and working his way steadily up the ranks. By 1926 Sam was a loom fixer, the most autonomous and prestigious position in the mill—and one that provided a platform from which he might have bid for an over-seer's job. But by then times had changed. Along with the shutdown of opportunity came the stretch-out: "More work for the same pay" was not just a hardship; it was an insult to a man of Finley's diligent, but independent, disposition.[100]

The more highly skilled and better-paid workers, many of whom were adult men, were the chief targets of cost-cutting measures. But the stretch-out affected spinners as well as weavers, men and women alike. Whether or not they worked for wages, women bore responsibility for nurturing the work force, managing family income, and finding ways to make ends meet. For all these reasons, strikes, like mill work itself, were family affairs, and women—in their roles as workers and as nurturers—brought to them their own hopes, complaints, and contributions. "The women done as much, if not more, as the men," said Lillie Price. "They always do in everything."[101]

Ella May Wiggins was one example—and perhaps the best known —of the militant women who graced the 1929 strikes. Wiggins compelled attention in part because she expressed the needs of women who combined bread winning with child rearing under conditions that "just kept getting worse and worse." Born to an itinerant logging family in the mountains in 1900, Ella May had married a charming ne'er-do-well and followed a labor recruiter to the Piedmont in the 1920s. By 1929, when the Gastonia strike began, she had given birth to nine children—four of whom had died—her husband had deserted her, and she was supporting her family by working in the American Mill at Bessemer City for nine dollars a week. In speeches and ballads Ella May drew on her own experience, appealing directly to other women in their roles as mothers or potential mothers and attacking the mill for depriving women of the means to carry out their responsibility for nurturing human life. At rallies throughout Gaston County and beyond, workers called especially for "Mill Mother's Lament," her most powerful and best-loved song.[102]

> We leave our home in the morning,
> We kiss our children goodbye,
> While we slave for the bosses
> Our children scream and cry.
>
> And when we draw our money
> Our grocery bills to pay,
> Not a cent to spend for clothing,
> Not a cent to lay away.
>
> And on that very evening,
> Our little son will say:
> "I need some shoes, dear mother,
> And so does sister May."

How it grieves the heart of a mother,
You every one must know.
But we can't buy for our children,
Our wages are too low.

It is for our little children
That seems to us so dear,
But for us nor them, dear workers,
The bosses do not care.

But understand, all workers,
Our union they do fear,
Let's stand together, workers,
And have a union here.[103]

By expressing the exploitation of labor by capital as a violation of mothers' rights, Wiggins touched a chord of sentiment that was widely held and deeply felt. Yet Wiggins's mill mother was a far cry from the dominant culture's domestic ideal. She was a woman alone, embedded in a culture of wage-earning work. It was *she* who must buy for her children; it was *her* wages that were too low.

Wiggins was a fascinating, many-sided figure who reworked the material of her life to enhance its political appeal. She did lose four children to poverty; the youngest died of pellagra, the classic disease of mill village malnutrition. But her children had not, as her speeches would have it, "died with whooping cough, all at once." Portrayed by the union as a pious widow, she was in fact an independent woman who took back her maiden name and had a child by her cousin Charlie Shope after her husband disappeared. She saw in the union a chance to develop her talents and to escape the confines of the workaday world. Able to write and figure with ease, she served as secretary for the union and joined a delegation sent to Washington to lobby for the workers' cause. She lived in a black neighborhood outside the mill village and, alone among local unionists, tried to persuade black workers to sign union cards.[104]

Like her life, Ella May's music said more than it seemed to say. "Mill Mother's Lament" was set to the tune of "Little Mary Phagan," a ballad composed by mill worker Fiddlin' John Carson in commemoration of the thirteen-year-old factory girl whose murder resulted in the lynching of her boss, Leo Frank, in Atlanta in 1915. A Jew and a

Ella May Wiggins and a friend, probably Charlie Shope, 1929.
(Courtesy of UPI/Bettmann Newsphotos)

northerner, Frank was accused not only of murder but of perversion, and "Little Mary Phagan" was cast in the mold of traditional songs based on the tragedy of a young girl's sexually motivated slaying. Yellow journalism whipped up the hysteria surrounding the case, and prominent citizens led the lynch mob. But Leo Frank also became a magnet for the fears and resentments stirring in Atlanta's Fulton Bag and Cotton Mill community in the wake of a bitter strike.[105]

The owner of the American Mill in Bessemer City, where Ella May worked, was also Jewish and a northerner. But in contrast to Carson's original ballad, Ella May's gloss contains no hint of anti-Semitism; nor does it cast capitalism as a sexual threat. The "bosses" were the villains of "Mill Mother's Lament"; Ella May needed no larger-than-life outsider to blame for the injuries of class. Couching his song in the third person singular, Fiddlin' John Carson told a story of innocence victimized.

> She left her home at 'leven
> When she kissed her mother good bye;
> Not one time did the poor child think
> She was going there to die.[106]

Ella May replaced Carson's narrative with an account of the daily hardships of a woman's life and rewrote his song in the first person plural. "Mill Mother's Lament" did not abandon the familiar sentimental themes; suffering children and grieving mothers account in part for the ballad's appeal. But in Ella May's version, women are no longer victims; they are political actors, turning tradition to subversive use.[107]

In the Elizabethton strike, the feisty mill girl, not the child victim or the mill mother, took center stage. "Hundreds of girls" rode down main street "in buses and taxis, shouting and laughing at people who watched them from windows and doorsteps." When the National Guard began bringing strikebreakers into town, women blocked the roads and railroad tracks. Defying an injunction that forbade picketing at the plant, they marched down the highway "draped in the American flag and carrying the colors"—thereby forcing the guardsmen to present arms each time they passed.[108]

Among the most colorful of these "rebel girls" were Trixie Perry and her sidekick "Texas Bill." These two friends were ringleaders on the picket line. Both were charged with violating the injunction against demonstrating at the rayon plant, and both were brought to trial. Trixie Perry took the stand in a dress sewn from red, white, and blue bunting and a cap made of a small American flag. The prosecuting attorney began his cross-examination:

> "You have a United States flag as a cap on your head?"
> "Yes."
> "Wear it all the time?"
> "Whenever I take a notion."
> "You are dressed in a United States flag, and the colors?"
> "I guess so, I was born under it, guess I have a right to."

The main charge was that Perry and her friend had drawn a line across the road and dared the National Guardsmen to cross it. The defense attorney did not deny the charges. Instead, he used the women to mock the government's case. Had Trixie Perry threatened a lieutenant? "He rammed a gun in my face and I told him to take it out or I would knock it out." Had she blocked the road? "A little thing like me block a big road?" What had she said to the threat of a tear gas bomb? "That little old fire cracker of a thing, it won't go off."[109]

Texas Bill was an even bigger hit with the courtroom crowd. The defense attorney called her the "Wild Man from Borneo." A soldier said she was "the wildest human being I've ever seen." Texas Bill both affirmed and subverted her reputation. Her nickname came from her habit of wearing "cowboy" clothes. But when it was her turn to testify, she "strutted on the stand" in a fashionable black coat and a black hat. Besides her other transgressions, she was accused of grabbing a soldier's gun and aiming it at him. What was she doing on the road so early in the morning? "I take a walk every morning before breakfast for my health," Texas Bill replied with what a reporter described as "an assumed ladylike dignity."[110]

Witnesses for the prosecution took pains to contradict Texas Bill's "assumed ladylike dignity." A guardsman complained that she called him a " 'God damned yellow son-of-a-bitch' and then branched out from that." Texas Bill offered no defense: "When that soldier stuck his gun in my face, that did make me mad and I did cuss a little bit and don't deny it." Far from discrediting the strikers, the soldiers' testimony added to their own embarrassment and the audience's delight. In tune with the crowd, the defense attorney "enjoyed making the guards admit they had been 'assaulted' . . . by 16 and 18-year-old girls."[111]

Mock gentility, impertinent laughter, male egos on the line—the mix made for wonderful theater and proved effective in court as well. The judge reserved maximum sentences for three especially aggressive men; all the women and most of the men were found not guilty or were lightly fined. In the end, even those convictions were overturned by the state court of appeals.[112]

Trixie Perry and Texas Bill walked a fine line between ladyhood and lewdness, between good girls and bad. Using words that, for women, were ordinarily taboo, they refused to pay deference and signaled disrespect. They invaded public space usually reserved for men. They combined flirtation with fierceness on the picket line and adopted a provocative courtroom style. And yet, with the language of dress—a cap made of an American flag, an elegant wide-brimmed hat—they claimed their rights as citizens and as participants in the material promise of American life.

The activists of Elizabethton were well placed to play a powerful symbolic role. Their assaults against persons and property constituted an effective witness against injustice precisely because of assumptions about female passivity: only extraordinary circumstances could call forth such aggression. At the same time, since women were considered less rational and taken less seriously than men, they met less resistance and were punished less severely for their crimes.[113]

In one sense the Elizabethton strikers were acting on tradition, for they came from a backcountry society that had little use for gentility or abstract standards of femininity. But their behavior on the witness stand presupposed a certain sophistication: a passing familiarity allowed them to parody ladyhood and thumb a nose at the genteel standards of the town. Combining fragments from the local past with the garments of an expanding consumer culture, the women of Elizabethton assembled their own version of a brash, irreverent Jazz Age style.

This cultural creativity—which embraced continuity and discontinuity, self-expression and family values, native and borrowed elements—characterized the young activists of the 1920s, whether they had recently left the mountains or had grown up in the mill villages.[114] Firmly based in the world their parents had made, they expected more than their parents had received. The increase of literacy due to the

Flossie Cole Grindstaff, one of Elizabethton's striking flappers, 1927.
(*Courtesy of Flossie Cole Grindstaff, Elizabethton, Tenn.*)

decline of child labor and the spread of compulsory education, the advent of movies and radios bringing news of an affluent larger world, access to automobiles—all these raised expectations, broke down isolation, and fostered group identity.

Model T's were the chief means by which the spirit of revolt flashed across the Piedmont. When the Marion mills installed a stretch-out, Sam Finley and Lawrence Hogan drove across the Blue Ridge Mountains to Elizabethton, "hunting somebody to organize them as a union." They brought back Alfred Hoffmann, and soon twenty-five-year-old Lawrence Hogan became his right-hand man. Educating himself, as the *Greensboro Daily News* put it, for the "responsibilities of class leadership," Hogan became a full-time organizer. From his base in Marion, Hogan published *The Shuttle*, a newsletter designed to "carry the message to and fro." Hogan favored the "whirlwind system of distribution. Making about 40 [miles per hour] through a town I toss a bundle of *Shuttles* into the air, the wind whips them away, scatters them, and the mill workers, who have learned to expect them, run out and pick them up." When Hogan died—after a car wreck in 1935—he was mourned as "one of the clearest-eyed leaders of federated workingmen in this section."[115]

Creative tactics, indigenous leaders, lessons in "the power of group action"—these were among the legacies of the 1920s. Even in Elizabethton, Gastonia, and Marion, where the strikes were checked at every turn, there were tangible benefits and seeds of resistance took hold. In Elizabethton, an autocratic manager was recalled, wages went up, and hours went down. In Marion and Gastonia, the workweek was shortened, and conditions in the Marion mill village improved. For some individuals, the strikes brought a strengthened sense of self, a belief that they had made history and that later generations would benefit from what they had done. Bessie Edens, for one, had no regrets even though she was blacklisted after the Elizabethton strike. "I knew I wasn't going to get to go back. I wrote them a letter and told them I didn't care whether they took me back or not. I didn't! If I'd starved I wouldn't of cared, because I knew what I was a'doing when I helped to pull it. And I've never regretted it in any way. It did help the people, and it's helped the town and the country." Among unionists who held on to their jobs, a committed remnant kept the local alive. When the National Labor Relations Act went into effect in 1935, the Elizabethton plants were among the first to join the new Congress of Industrial Organizations (CIO). Even Marion and Gastonia, where the

Lawrence Hogan, 1931.
(Reproduced from Labor Age, *February 1931)*

strike had been so violently repressed, would be drawn back into the vortex of conflict by the General Textile Strike of 1934.[116]

The strikes of the 1920s riveted national, and even international, attention on the plight of southern workers and brought the textile industry into increasing disrepute. Fictionalized by proletarian novelists and covered in detail by the liberal and the radical press, the Gastonia conflict in particular came to symbolize the horrors of southern capitalism. The U.S. Senate held hearings on working conditions in the region. A committee of the South Carolina House of Representatives, spearheaded by Olin D. Johnston, called the strikes the workers' "final weapons of defense" and placed the blame on mill officials who put "more work on the employees than they can do." North Carolina workers had no comparable spokesman in the legislature, but even the *Southern Textile Bulletin* confessed that some strikes could be traced to "overdoing of the multiple loom or stretch-out system," and Governor O. Max Gardner, himself a textile manufacturer, admitted that all was not well with the industry and called for self-reform.[117]

North Carolina reformers, working chiefly through women's organizations, renewed their campaigns for protective legislation for women and children. They got unexpected help from the Cotton Textile Institute (CTI), a trade association formed in 1926 that sought to solve the industry's problems by substituting cooperation for cutthroat competition. The CTI rallied its members behind the elimination of night work for women. For the CTI, however, the purpose was profit: by cutting out night shifts, industry leaders hoped to curtail production and raise prices. In the legislative session of 1931, lobbyists pushed through laws that reduced the working hours of women, restricted night work, and prohibited the employment of children under fourteen. This was a considerable accomplishment in a state that was infamous for its role in defeating federal child labor legislation. But coming at a time when the the availability of adult men had already reduced the mills' reliance on the cheaper labor of women and children, such measures did little to ease the workers' lot.[118]

By the late 1920s and early 1930s, harsh criticism of the southern textile industry was not hard to find. But, by and large, reformers accepted the premises of the industrial engineers. They assumed that technological change was inevitable and value free. They advocated modernization, deplored the old-style mill village, and worried about the emergence in the mill village of a troubling "social type."[119]

The UTW, too, had conceded the deeper sources of workers' discontent. While millhands suffered the costs of rationalization, union leaders counseled cooperation in "scientific management" plans. But even a stronger and more aggressive union would have had difficulty making headway in the region. Southern mill owners stood united in their refusal to tolerate even the mildest form of unionism and were strengthened in their resolve by hard times. The stock market crash of 1929 would bring massive layoffs, further wage cuts, and efforts to recoup profits by "stretch[ing] out the stretch-out." The result was an atmosphere of simmering antagonism. Lawrence Hogan desribed Piedmont mills as "volcano-like. . . . Everywhere you go, they are ready to explode."[120]

CHAPTER FIVE

Turn Your Radio On

THE INTERWAR YEARS brought southern mill workers a mix of hope and desperation. New technologies threatened established patterns of work. At the same time, new channels of communication foreshadowed the end of cultural isolation. A bare flicker on the horizon in the early 1920s, by the end of the decade radio òffered millions of listeners a rich array of music, news, and drama. Automobiles, movies, and mass circulation magazines also worked their magic in the mill villages. But the lines of influence ran two ways. Mill workers were initiated into mass culture, but mass culture was also shaped by them. Searching for new audiences in the early 1920s, record companies discovered hillbilly music—the music of choice for farmers-turned-millhands—and began transforming ballad singing, fiddle playing, and banjo picking into one of America's great popular sounds. Radio helped turn local musicians into country music stars; the result was an explosion of cultural creativity and, for millhands who heard their own music over the air waves, an intensified sense of group identity. Workers' perpetual movement from mill to mill had already knit local communities into a regional fabric; as a younger generation crisscrossed the Piedmont in their Model T's, not only looking for jobs but also driving to dances, picnics, and revivals, they discovered shared grievances, loyalties, and aspirations. Not everyone approved of the razzmatazz of this cultural revolution. Older workers in particular often rallied around the familiar verities of village life. But no one could escape the currents of change entirely.

In an effort to survive the postwar slump, many mill owners also broadened their horizons and ventured into new areas of production. Manufacturers added dyeing and finishing plants to their operations and expanded their product lines to include woolens, knits, tire fabrics, and gloves. In 1925 some began experimenting with rayon, giving birth to the synthetic textile industry. Others turned to hosiery. Mills in which yarn was knit into socks and stockings rather than woven into cloth had appeared in the South in the late nineteenth century. But the demand for full-fashioned hose—the seamed stockings women wore with shorter skirts—gave southern manufacturers a golden opportunity to expand this branch of the industry. By 1929 North Carolina alone claimed nearly 20 percent of the nation's hosiery mills.[1]

The cultural and technological crosscurrents of the 1920s and 1930s can be traced in fine detail in one community: the Piedmont Heights mill village on the outskirts of Burlington in Alamance County. Some of the South's first cotton mills were located in the county, and by the turn of the century Burlington had become one of the Piedmont's textile centers. But in the years immediately after World War I Alamance textiles foundered. The ginghams, plaids, and chambrays that had once been the source of the county's prosperity were out of fashion. Mills were closing, and the skilled weavers of "Alamance Plaid" were idle. The early generations of textile men who had brought the mills to Alamance had died or retired, and the rising generation was proving neither as astute nor as energetic as its predecessors. The pioneering Holt dynasty, in particular, seemed to be in decline, unable to cope with postwar challenges. Alamance's textile industry needed a tonic, and it found one in J. Spencer Love and Burlington Mills. "It was the Holts and Williamsons who had run the old plain cotton mills," recalled Reid Maynard, owner of the Tower Hosiery Mill, "and they let 'em go down. They was at a low ebb, a lot of 'em closed, some of 'em bankrupt. The others just took their money out and quit. That was the day Spencer Love came to town."[2]

In 1924 J. Spencer Love built the Piedmont Heights mill village and the Pioneer Plant of Burlington Mills, the first in a chain of factories that within fifty years would become the largest textile manufacturing firm in the world. Love's founding of the mill and village brought together a cast of characters that embodied the central theme of the 1920s, a struggle to reconcile the traditions of mill workers' lives and work with postwar technology and cultural innovation. Spencer Love typified the "new mill man," seeking his fortune through experimentation with new yarns, modern machinery, and novel management methods. He was aided during the early years of his career by James Copland, Sr., a plant supervisor of great technical skill and ceaseless energy and ambition. Across the street from the Pioneer

The Piedmont Heights mill complex and village, early 1930s. The Pioneer Plant and the Glen Hope Baptist Church are on the right.

(*James Spencer Love Papers, Southern Historical Collection,*
University of North Carolina at Chapel Hill)

Plant stood the main institution of the mill village, the Glen Hope Baptist Church. There Preacher George Washington Swinney held the pulpit for forty years, ministering to his congregation and accumulating souls as Love accumulated mills. Swinney preached the values of old-time religion, but he, too, used new technologies, broadcasting services over the radio and driving thousands of miles through the Piedmont to appear at revivals. Icy Norman, raised on a North Carolina farm, worked at the Pioneer Plant for forty-seven years and prayed at Glen Hope even longer. Finally, there was Dr. Carroll Lupton, a skilled physician and a keen witness to mill village life, whose observations, tempered by the memories of Piedmont Heights villagers, provide a penetrating view of how one community dealt with the upheavals of the postwar years.

James Spencer Love, the son of James Lee and Julia Spencer Love, was born on July 6, 1896, in Cambridge, Massachusetts, where his father taught mathematics at Harvard College. The Love family, however, had deep roots in Gaston County, North Carolina. Spencer's great-grandfather, Andrew Love, was a wealthy slaveholder. Robert Calvin Grier Love, Spencer's grandfather—who married the eldest

daughter of Moses H. Rhyne, a pioneer of the Carolina textile industry—survived the Civil War with his plantation intact, and then broadened his interests to include cotton manufacturing. In 1887 he built
the Gastonia Manufacturing Company, one of the county's first textile
factories, which eventually became known as the "Old Mill."

Grier Love was an ardent proponent of southern industrialization
and did everything in his power to encourage the rise of cotton mills in
Gaston County. Convinced that prohibition was a prerequisite to the
establishment of a productive labor force, he was influential in steer-
ing through the state legislature a law that forbade the operation of
distilleries and saloons within two miles of a church or school. To
ensure the demise of liquor establishments, he then personally subsidized the construction of churches and schools within a two-mile
radius of existing saloons and distilleries, forcing them to close. Once
launched as a textile manufacturer, Grier Love pursued his new career zealously. Between 1887 and 1902 Love, three of his sons—
Edgar, Robert, and John—and other partners invested in the ventures
that built the Avon Mills, Ozark Mills, Lincoln Mills, and Gastonia's
Loray Mill.

Those years were flush times for the Love family, but their investment in the Loray Mill had disastrous consequences. The outbreak of
the Boxer Rebellion in China in 1900 destroyed the market for Loray's specialized narrow cotton cloth. The Loves could not afford to
await the rebellion's outcome and reequipped for alternate production. The cost of new machinery absorbed all profits and drained the
family's resources. By 1907 the Loves retained only the Old Mill and
Avon Mills. That same year Grier Love died of a heart attack. Robert
Love, Spencer's uncle, became manager of the Old Mill and its
majority shareholder, but he lacked his father's business acumen.
Although World War I helped the ailing mill, the postwar depression
was crippling.[3]

Such was the situation facing J. Spencer Love when he returned
from the war eager to embark on a business career. Love was twenty-
one when he joined the army after graduation from Harvard College
in the spring of 1918. Sent to France in October, he served as divi-
sional adjutant, excelling at the administrative duties that the position
entailed. The war was a proving ground for Love. He never participated in combat, but in the final month before the Armistice he
witnessed all of the horrors of the battlefield: bombs, mines, mustard
gas, the killing and maiming of fellow soldiers. When he returned

James Spencer Love, ca. 1918.
(James Spencer Love Papers, Southern Historical Collection,
University of North Carolina at Chapel Hill)

home, he was haunted by memories of the war, which he pushed "to the more remote portions of the mind where bad dreams find their resting." But he also realized that he would "never have missed it, with all its chances and horrors and thrills for the world." The war whetted his appetite for challenge, and in the months after his discharge he longed to continue testing his abilities.[4]

Military service focused Love's career interests. Combat did not stir his blood, but administration did. Love's rapid advancement from lieutenant to major reflected his organizational abilities and his mastery of the American Expeditionary Force's administrative procedures. Once the war was over, he was impatient to test his new skills. In a letter to his mother he boasted of "the cleverest and most daring thing I ever put through"—his own early discharge from the army. At twenty-two, six months seemed like a long time, and that is what Love calculated he saved by drawing on his "knowledge of how things are done, combined with nerve and a desire to get out of the army and get on to some real work."[5]

Love, like many of the "new mill men" of the 1920s, blended the Victorian code of manly virtue with twentieth-century organizational principles learned from military experience. Unlike his Harvard classmate John Dos Passos and other members of the literary "lost generation," Love was not disillusioned by his experience in Europe. Instead, the war gave him confidence in his abilities and affirmed his values. Unsentimental about the past, Love entered the 1920s with his energies turned to the future.[6]

Once discharged from the army, Love pondered a course of action. There was no question that he would pursue a career in business, but which business in particular? In March 1919 he decided to take a job under his uncle Robert, as paymaster at the Old Mill, in order to learn the textile business. By the end of the summer, Love and his father agreed that in order for the Old Mill to get back on a firm footing, and for Spencer to be properly launched in his career, a change had to be made. So Spencer and his father bought out Robert Love, and J. Spencer Love became sole manager of the mill. It was a rapid rise, even in a family business. Within eight months, Spencer had advanced from a novice in the field of textiles to a manager of a mill, albeit a faltering one. He was twenty-three years old.

Spencer's parents had much to do with his early success. James Lee Love was the consummate Victorian father. His letters to Spencer brimmed with advice regarding the young man's character, his filial obligations, and his future. When Spencer was deciding which business to pursue, his father dismissed department stores, motor trucks, and airplanes. Instead, he pushed cotton: it was steady and rewarding for those with energy, character, and ability. Until the older man's death, father and son carried on a voluminous correspondence, mostly concerning business matters, always filled with advice from James Lee. Spencer's father was a thoughtful man, well-informed about political affairs and business theories, but his advice often had little bearing on the realities of the textile industry. James Lee Love had grand ideas and dreamed of living well, but the professor, like his brother Robert, was a poor businessman. Often in debt, he repeatedly asked Spencer to "do his duty" by him. For the most part, Spencer treated his father with great forbearance and respect.[7]

Spencer also corresponded regularly with his older sister, Cornelia Spencer Love, and with his mother. The female members of the Love family frequently tempered James Lee's advice. Cornelia was sympathetic toward her father's frustrated ambitions; Julia was acerbic. In one letter to her son, Julia railed against her husband and the whole Love family, saying they were "never *decided* about anything—shrink from committing themselves and consequently have little enthusiasm—are not red blooded in fact." Julia Love was a strong-willed woman who instilled in her son personal ambition and, one suspects, the decisiveness and single-mindedness he demonstrated in his business life. Disappointed by James Lee's lack of success, Julia invested in her son all of her frustrated aspirations. When Spencer returned from the Great War, promoted from lieutenant to major and recommended for a Distinguished Service Medal, Julia was delighted. She wrote, "You have filled your Mother's heart with something she has always craved for one of you—perhaps with an unholy ambition—that is *to be distinguished*."[8]

Spencer's family also taught him the importance of money and social standing. When he went to Gastonia, his mother hoped he could improve her dividends from the Old Mill. "I *need* the money. Later I may be dead! I want it *now*, *regularly*, so I can do a few things I want to do before I die. There never was a woman of my station worse tied up for want of money than I've been since I married." Julia never reaped the benefits of her son's success. She died in 1920, only a year after Spencer took charge of the Old Mill.[9]

Julia's words, however, appear to have lingered in her son's memory. Spencer married a cousin, Sara Elizabeth Love, in January 1922.

James Lee Love with Cornelia and Spencer, ca. 1905.
(James Spencer Love Papers, Southern Historical Collection,
University of North Carolina at Chapel Hill)

Shortly after the wedding, hard times hit the mill, and Spencer feared he would fail Elizabeth as his father had failed his mother. Love confided to his diary that he "would never have married if I had anticipated these troubles and conditions coming so bad and so soon." What Spencer Love meant by bad times was relative. Business improved slightly by the following year, enough so that he could buy Elizabeth a platinum bracelet for their first wedding anniversary and trade in his Cadillac for a new one. Spencer and Elizabeth's time in Gastonia revolved around his work at the mill and a social life of dances and tennis at the country club, evenings playing cards with friends or going to the movies, and occasional trips to New York, Philadelphia, and Boston.[10]

Love was a reflective young man, and he recorded in his diary his ambivalence toward wealth. On the one hand, he desired it. He wanted to be a good provider for his family, and his definition of "good" was expansive: diamond jewelry for Elizabeth, a new Cadillac nearly every year, regular gifts to his sister, and support to his father. But he also suspected that his many comforts and advantages "may not be too good for me." Even as he yearned for wealth and status, he also wished to be "of some use in the world in a Christian way." Love pursued his objectives relentlessly and succeeded spectacularly. He provided handsomely for his family and in later years gave generously to charity. His growing power and prestige brought him seats on government and industry councils and propelled him onto the boards of universities and his church—positions he filled responsibly. Power, prestige, and wealth were the tangible measures of Love's success, but it was the day-to-day challenge of business that drove him.[11]

Between 1919 and 1923 the Old Mill taxed Love's skills. Starting as a novice in the textile industry's chaotic period of postwar readjustment, he had to struggle to make the business profitable. One morning in 1922 he sat with his head in his hands and later confided to his diary that "each succeeding week sees me more and more depressed as I realize we are losing money faster than ever and outlook is blacker than ever for profitable margins." Although business improved by the end of the year, Love decided that drastic action was necessary. The Old Mill was primarily a spinning operation with a small weaving department whose cloth production had pulled the firm through the lean years. Love now resolved to switch his resources to full-scale weaving. Gastonia, chiefly a spinning center, had few experienced weavers, so Love decided to move.[12]

Burlington appealed to Love because it offered a plentiful supply
of skilled weavers. And the city's businessmen were eager to attract
him. After negotiations with the chamber of commerce, Love decided
to build his new mill in the Alamance County town. He and his father
contributed $50,000 worth of machinery from the Old Mill and
$200,000 from the sale of its real estate, while Burlington citizens
subscribed to $200,000 worth of stock in the new Burlington Mills
Company. The company's first board of directors was dominated by
prominent local businessmen; Love, his father, and Daniel Rhyne
were the only members of the board not from Alamance County. The
Pioneer Plant was constructed quickly. The company announced in
January 1924 that a contract would be let for a 60,000-square-foot
building, two warehouses, and seventy mill houses. In October workers were spinning the first yarn; by 1925 Burlington Mills employed
200 people, working a day shift from 7:00 A.M. to 6:00 P.M. and a night
shift from 6:00 P.M. to 5:30 A.M.[13]

The move to Burlington did not immediately solve Love's problems. Like other Alamance County factories, the Pioneer Plant first
produced cotton products: dress goods, stiffening for women's hats,
and material for railroad signal flags. Love found he had no better
luck marketing these products than did his rivals. For a time he even
considered getting out of the textile business altogether. But, unable
to afford such a drastic move, he decided instead to experiment with a
relatively new synthetic yarn, rayon—or as it was then more commonly
called, "artificial silk."[14]

Rayon had arrived in the South in 1925, when the Bemberg company of Barmen, Germany, a manufacturer of high-quality rayon yarn
by an exclusive stretch spinning process, began pouring the thick
concrete floors of its first U.S. subsidiary in Elizabethton. Three
years later, Germany's leading producer of rayon yarn, the Glanzstoff company of Elberfeld, opened a branch nearby. The post–World
War I fashion revolution, combined with protective tariffs, spurred the
American rayon industry's spectacular growth. As one industry publi-
cist put it, "With long skirts, cotton stockings were quite in order; but
with short skirts, nothing would do except sheer, smooth stockings.
. . . It was on the trim legs of post-war flappers, it has been said, that
rayon first stepped out into big business." Dominated by a handful of
large European companies, rayon spinning mills clustered along the
Appalachian mountain chain. By World War II more than 70 percent

of American rayon production took place in the southern states, with half of the national total in Virginia and Tennessee alone.[15]

Love was one of the first mill men to investigate the possibilities of rayon yarn. The earliest fruits of his experimentation were bedspreads, spreads that have become part of the legend surrounding the origins of Burlington Mills. According to workers, the yarn was "sorry" and terrible to weave. The original looms were not wide enough to produce the bedspreads in one piece, so the spreads were cut and sewn with a seam running down the middle. Although the coverlets were stiff, shiny, and awkward, they became immensely popular. Not only did Burlington Mills survive; the introduction of rayon and the production of artificial silk bedspreads even inaugurated a period of expansion. As the company grew, so did the folklore surrounding it. Frequent additions to the plant and conversions to the most modern machinery gave rise to the story that the mill always had one wall made of wood, ready to be knocked out for enlargement. Workers like Versa Haithcock, who started with Burlington Mills in 1928, added to the legend. Watching the installation of new twisters, Haithcock remarked to a fellow worker that the machines would be difficult to move. When the man replied that they were permanent, Haithcock rejoined, "You don't know Burlington Mill; if they took a notion to move one over here, they'd move it, if they had to dig a hole down in the ground, dig a tunnel, and come out on the outside."[16]

The legends of Burlington's expansion were based in fact. In 1926 Love organized a new company, Holt, Love and Holt. The firm built a weave shed close to the Pioneer Plant and began producing "wide textile novelties," as its bedspreads were called. That same year Love built Alamance Novelty Mills nearby and began manufacturing upholstery goods, draperies, and spreads. He quickly ironed the wrinkles out of rayon production. Wide Jacquard looms eliminated the need to sew the coverlets down the middle, and silk looms proved more effective than traditional cotton looms. In 1928 Love constructed the North Carolina Silk Mills and Piedmont Weavers to manufacture rayon dress goods. Love himself managed all of the new mills, which were located in the Piedmont Heights area. He had no attachment to cotton, and remarked a decade later to a colleague, "We would have been far better off if we could have started in 1927 with a clean slate instead of being burdened with the old cotton mill to carry through." With the introduction of new machinery and improvements in rayon yarn, he transformed initially unattractive bedspreads into an eminently marketable product. By the early 1930s Burlington Mills offered more than ten patterns, including the Tree of Life, the Rose of Sharon, and the "basket number," all dubbed by the *Journal of Commerce* "an outstanding success."[17]

The bedspreads were not the only element in Love's prosperity. He also led the industry in instituting new marketing techniques. Love broke with custom and engaged his own selling agent in New York in 1929, thus eliminating the intermediary commission houses and establishing direct contact between Burlington and its customers. Between 1926 and 1928 sales increased from $1 million to $5 million, and the weekly payroll of Burlington Mills rose from $2,000 to $5,500. The administrative skills Love learned in the army and the values he absorbed from his parents had borne fruit and would shape his management style in the years to come. Decades later, when an interviewer asked Love what drove him, he responded, "The challenge of competition, the desire to keep your organization on top, the personal satisfaction of accomplishment, the desire to improve yourself."[18]

Most of the workers on the Burlington Mills payroll lived in the Piedmont Heights village next to the mill complex. When Lottie Adams arrived there in 1927, she thought she had come to "the end of the world." The village, like the mill that spawned it, had been built in the middle of a cornfield on the outskirts of town, close to the route of the Southern Railway. Seventy mill houses lined streets of red mud, and a small business district and a few boarding houses marked the village's borders. Each gable- or hip-roofed house had three to five rooms, indoor plumbing, a porch, and a garden plot. A cottage rented for a dollar a week, and the mill initially paid for electricity. But Love did nothing to make the village attractive. There were no street lights, no trees, no flowers, shrubs, or grass—only "mud, mud, mud." Love considered older forms of paternalistic control and mill-sponsored welfare work expensive and ineffectual, so he did not build a company store, a school, a church, or a community building. Residents of Piedmont Heights would create their village life with relatively little interference from J. Spencer Love.[19]

Piedmont Heights was marked by the restlessness that had long characterized mill communities. Only thirteen of the seventy families living in the village in 1927 had been in Burlington in 1924. Even the success of rayon, which guaranteed the life of Burlington Mills, did not at first encourage workers to take up permanent residence. By 1929 the village population had again changed almost completely; only thirteen families remained from 1927, and only two of them were from the original 1924 group. Some mobility was undoubtedly due to millhands' habitual search for a better job. Versa Haithcock, for example, felt no particular dislike for the Pioneer Plant or Piedmont Heights; he just thought, "the job over yonder was better than the one I had." But like many other southern textile workers in the 1920s, those who spent only a short time in the Piedmont Heights mill village did so because there was no steady work there. The mill's early years were erratic. Cotton goods did not sell; the mill ran irregularly; and workers no doubt left in search of more constant employment.[20]

Many of the people who came to Piedmont Heights were experienced millhands who had left the farm years before. They still had ties to rural communities and returned often to visit relatives, but the country was no longer home. Piedmont Heights residents blended persistent rural customs with a growing involvement in town life. Villagers kept gardens, maintained a community hog pen, and drove wagons as well as automobiles over the muddy village streets. But Piedmont Heights was not an isolated rural community. Although the mill and village complex was built in a cornfield, it stood on the outskirts of a town of several thousand people, and mill workers went into Burlington to shop, see a show, or visit the doctor.

Young people who had grown up in mill communities were especially drawn to the delights of more urban pursuits. Their social life expanded beyond the confines of prayer meetings and neighborhood parties to encompass movies and public dances. The more daring ventured to roadhouses and poolrooms. Versa Haithcock, for instance, was born in Graham, the county seat of Alamance County, where both his parents had worked in the mill. In 1920 the family moved to Carrboro, where Versa got his first mill job on the day after his fourteenth birthday. He worked at the Carrboro mill for two years and then took to the road, hiring on at other North Carolina mills in Haw River, Thomasville, High Point, Fayetteville, and Roxboro, as well as a mill in Danville, before ending up in Burlington. He stayed in Burlington a year and then traveled for two more years before returning to settle in Piedmont Heights. Until he married, he lived in boardinghouses and spent his evenings in poolrooms.[21]

Mill communities had always embraced both the rough and the

respectable, and in the narrow confines of a village there was sometimes conflict between the two. Men ready to use fists, knives, and
guns to settle a quarrel stood against those whose weapons were
words and prayer. Gatherings that began with social drinking sometimes ended up in drunken brawls, sending intoxicated men tumbling
into the streets. In the 1920s several circumstances conspired to make
the rough life stand in starker contrast to the respectable. Prohibition added a patina of vice to the whiskey making and selling that
had supplemented southerners' income for decades. Automobiles
brought bootleggers and liquor into the village and furnished a private
place for drinking, carousing, and "messing around." Finally, and
perhaps most distressing, young women seemed to be deserting the
ranks of the respectable to join the rowdy.

In the late 1920s residents nicknamed Piedmont Heights "Little
Chicago"; they considered it a place "rough as pig iron," where you
could "buy a drink anywhere you wanted." In their imaginations the
village seemed to combine the qualities of a western boomtown and
the Chicago of Prohibition years—filled with bootleg whiskey and
violence. The extraordinarily high turnover of villagers aggravated the
situation. Love's aloofness also meant that villagers had no arbiter of
last resort when their self-policing efforts failed. Until "respectable"
families asserted their own way of life, the village was dominated by
the rowdy activities of men. Like Versa Haithcock, many of them were
young and single, and they plunged eagerly into the street life of Little
Chicago.[22]

Gambling and fighting accompanied village drinking and bootlegging. While the rough life permeated the village streets, there were
two places in particular where men congregated to drink and play: the
poolroom and the community hog pen. Inside the poolroom stood
three tables: one for pool, one for poker, and one for craps. A man
stationed in a nearby car gave a signal if the sheriff came by. Then,
cards and dice slid into pockets and everyone snatched up a cue. At
the hog pen, men adjourned with whiskey and hymnals to serenade
the swine. Dewey McBride once asked a long-suffering wife, whose
husband drank on and off the job, where the Fourth of July celebration was to be held. She replied, "Down there at Carter's god-damned
hog pen, I reckon. There's where everything else happens around
here."[23]

Drinking provoked many of the fights that seemed endemic to the
village, fights that might not have happened or lasted long except that

the participants were too drunk to realize how badly they hurt each other. Versa Haithcock, who believed that Piedmont Heights was "the roughest place, when I come back there in 1928, I've ever seen," was at the cafe one night when two deputy sheriffs, Mr. Ireland and Mr. Pickard, arrived. It was a winter night when snow was blowing and sleet was on the ground. "There was a fellow [Mr. Macon], I think he sold a drink now and then. Well, I won't say that. I'll say he had a pint in his belt. Macon was standing there, leaning up against the barber-shop door. Well, Ireland didn't have no business doing what he done no way, and the way he done it. 'Boy, what you got in your pocket?' [he asked.] Macon said, 'Nothing.' 'Come here, let me see.' [Macon] walked around the corner of the barbershop. Ireland walked around the corner of the barbershop after him. Well, then Macon started to run. Ireland started running after him. Macon slipped on the ice and fell down, and that pint of liquor fell out and went sliding along the ice. Ireland grabbed him by the arm and Macon got up, and when he got up he had that pint of liquor in his hand, and he just come over there and got Ireland right over the eye, and just busted his head wide open. The blood just poured. But you know, [Pickard] got his gun out and brought him on back to the barbershop. Mr. Ireland was standing there and he said, 'Hold this boy here 'til I go in here and see if I can wash a little of this blood off my head and get it stopped.' Well, a bunch of 'em standing there, you know how a bunch are like that. They kept looking at Macon, saying, 'Run! Run!' Well, there wasn't no fence around [the mill] then, and Macon just standing there, and Pickard was just standing there with his hand on his arm—I don't believe he had a hold on him. Somebody opened the cafe door and Macon just pushed Mr. Pickard like that, and it was slick anyway, and he fell in the door. And Macon started running down through the mill yard. Mr. Pickard jumps up and hollers, 'Halt! Halt!' and grabs out a gun. And he just shot two or three times straight up, and Macon just kept going. I never have seen him since."[24]

The high drama of that evening was not often repeated, but well into the 1930s public drunkenness and fighting plagued the mill village. Lottie Adams peered fearfully from her window to see men staggering to and from the sawdust pile where they hid their liquor; her mother was reluctant to let her go out, even in the company of her fiancé. For years Gladys McBride watched painfully as her husband, Dewey, drank up the family cash. He had seldom drunk before they moved to Piedmont Heights, and she blamed the crowd who worked at the mill for his behavior. Indeed, Gladys often felt she would "rather have died than see the weekend come—that was the bunch at Burlington Mills."[25]

New forms of communication added to the ferment. It seemed to many workers that the world had somehow shifted under their feet after World War I. Movies, radio, and the automobile transformed American life, penetrating the smallest Piedmont mill village and the deepest Appalachian hollow. Nearly everyone went to the movies. From the first inch-square peep show viewers in the 1890s, motion pictures had captivated working-class audiences. Families scraped together nickels and dimes to "go to the show" in the hastily erected theaters of America's working-class neighborhoods. Movies became especially entrancing after the introduction of sound in 1926. There were more than 22,000 movie theaters in the United States by 1931, with seating for more than 11 million people. Radio was even more popular. By 1930, 40 percent of American families had radios, and many more listened to sets owned by friends and relatives. NBC and CBS broadcast symphonies, operas, dance music, jazz, baseball games, and presidential addresses, feeding programs to 150 stations in 1931. Automobiles, too, broadened horizons. In 1900 there had been only 8,000 cars in America; by 1931 there were almost 26 million. Of course, car owners were not evenly distributed. Farmers and residents of small communities had high rates of ownership, but less than one out of every three working-class families was likely to buy a car.[26]

Alamance County shared in national trends. Burlington shops carried the decade's new fashions, and the styles in the Sears catalog were only about three months behind what was available in New York department stores. In the late 1910s the county began to prepare itself for the influx of automobiles, getting its first macadamized road just before World War I and street lights in Burlington in 1921. When *The Third Alarm*, a film about firemen, played at the Rose Theater in 1923, the newspaper advertisement for the show exclaimed, "Dad—don't say it! It can't be true!" and referred to the "heart-rending scene" in which the firehorses were replaced by firetrucks. The paper also noted that by 1920 it had been "a foregone conclusion that it was only a matter of a short while before the business of livery stable proprietors would be reduced to the sale of work animals, and that the blacksmith would . . . be compelled to close up his shop." The Burlington Police Department bought its first patrol car in 1926, and by

1927 the Buick Company estimated that it sold half a million dollars' worth of automobiles in Alamance and adjacent Caswell County. At the close of the decade there were twelve automobile dealers in Alamance County alone.[27]

The automobile was irresistible. It allowed people greater choice in where to live and work; it permitted distant friends and relatives to visit more often; and it gave people fun and excitement they had never before experienced. One evening in 1929, a Burlington woman, who was "too hilarious and had too many drinks," was dumped unceremoniously from an automobile by her male companion. The police picked her up and put her in the city jail. Later, as she walked from the cell block to the courtroom, she ran her fingers through "her glossy marcel" and wondered how she got where she was. She speculated to the judge, who fined her five dollars and court costs, that her companion had ditched her because he feared that as they drove through the business district, she might "scream out of sheer joy."[28]

Changing attitudes toward sexuality accompanied the new forms of entertainment and transportation. Automobiles allowed young people to move their courting out of the parlor and away from the watchful eyes of their elders. Earlier in the century movies and suggestive dances had been considered the exclusive province of the urban working class. But by the 1920s dances such as the grizzly bear, lovers' two-step, and "shaking the shimmy" had been toned down and accepted by middle-class Americans, who paid dancing instructors to teach them the latest ragtime steps. Popular magazines, particularly between 1923 and 1927, asserted that love, not marriage, was enough reason for sexual relations. Movies, such as the 1926 film, *Dancing Mothers*, challenged the sexual double standard, and the sharp line between good and bad women blurred as women adopted a more provocative public style. What once might have been considered immoral came to be seen as merely frivolous or irresponsible.[29]

Indeed, to many mill workers like Dewey McBride it seemed that young women were the vanguard of change. McBride recalled that prior to World War I, when an unmarried woman arrived in a mill village, she found herself in a double bind. The first thing the boss man did was find out if she would go out with him. If she would, she kept her job; "if she wouldn't, she kept going." But if the family with whom she was boarding found out how she was keeping her position, they forced her to leave. After the war Dewey felt people "didn't give a darn" as long as the woman paid her rent. America's "new women" wore short sheathlike dresses, sheer silk stockings, and shiny waved hair. They smoked cigarettes. They drank liquor. They drove cars. And they danced. The glittery world of the 1920s, with its talking movies, shimmy dancing, and gleaming automobiles, made surprising inroads into southern mill villages, where cotton print dresses and denim overalls had once been the uniforms. Although some women continued to be fearful observers of village revels, others joined in lively parties and drove to roadhouses where they drank bootleg whiskey, flirted, and danced. And like young women in Elizabethton and elsewhere, Burlington flappers saved their money to buy the clothes and shoes that enabled them to "dress up fit to kill."[30]

A 1935 study revealed how enthusiastically mill workers embraced the pleasures introduced in the 1920s. Sociologist Frances Hampton interviewed 122 textile workers in Leaksville, Spray, and Draper—a mill complex thirty miles northwest of Burlington. Her study showed how much times had changed since the days James Pharis remembered, when the only thing to do in summertime was to go to the mineral spring. "The road would get thick with people going to the spring, trying to spend a bigger part of their Sundays with nothing to do but just drink water and talk." Now, on soft summer evenings, millhands moved inside to listen to the radio or walked to the theater to see a movie. Eighty-seven of Hampton's 122 informants had radios in their homes, and, with the exception of some housewives who listened while they worked, most people gave broadcasts their undivided attention. Stringband music and jazz were their favorite programs. Although half of those interviewed owned Victrolas, most considered them "out-of-date" compared to a radio. One family found the radio so alluring that they sold their piano in order to purchase one.[31]

Workers also read the popular literature that advertised new routes to romance and adventure. Several drugstores operated lending libraries of about 200 books, mostly westerns, romances, and detective novels. Hampton found that textile workers were fond of magazines such as *True Stories, Western Stories, True Romance, Detective Stories,* and *Movie Magazine.* But men and women continued to enjoy traditional pastimes as well. They read the Bible and religious papers, gathered for prayer meetings—which for some were "the only entertainment we have"—and went hunting, fishing, blackberrying, and visiting.[32]

Mill workers also had surprisingly broad access to automobiles.

About half of Hampton's informants either owned a car or had use of one, and half of those regularly took weekend trips; one-third went riding for the sheer pleasure of it. Workers pinched pennies to buy an automobile. Mary Thompson credited her father's purchase of a car to her mother's frugal housekeeping. For Mary, automobile outings were not only fun but one of the few times her entire family could be together. "If my father wasn't working at all on Sunday, we'd always go up in the mountains or somewhere and take a picnic dinner, all the whole family. It was a carful."[33]

Because of their higher wages, hosiery workers, more than other millhands, could enjoy the consumerism and cultural diversity of the 1920s and 1930s. By 1931 there were thirty-two hosiery mills in Burlington; the only other North Carolina community to approach that number was High Point, with sixteen plants. The demand for form-fitting, or full-fashioned, hose brought unprecedented income to hosiery workers, whose real earnings rose almost 35 percent between 1923 and 1929. Even during the Depression, hosiery mills continued to run steadily, forming an oasis of prosperity in the sluggish textile industry. When Dr. Carroll Lupton drove north from New Orleans to North Carolina in the midst of the Great Depression, he was struck by the signs of a flourishing economy in Burlington. "The full-fashioned hosiery business was in full swing. The younger people—I mean people under forty years old, most of 'em—were working in those hosiery mills. And you see the little young ladies walking around with pretty little muskrat jackets on. Beautiful. And they were buying new Fords and Plymouths and Oldsmobiles, and it was real prosperity. Those people was the only people I saw, from New Orleans up this way, who had regular work."[34]

Hosiery work was better paying, physically easier, and cleaner than nearly any job in a cotton mill. The machinery was not as dangerous and the air was not laden with dust. When people left a hosiery mill at the end of their shift, they did not walk down the street covered with the lint that branded others as mill workers. But hosiery jobs were not easy to get, as Frank Webster, a footer in Burlington's Tower Hosiery Mill, explained. "At that time, a hosiery job, you almost had to live a lifetime to get one because people made good money on those machines. They tried to stick with it. For a newcomer to work his way in, somebody almost had to croak out or die before you'd get a machine. In other words, you'd have to wait for your time to come and sometimes that was lengthy."[35]

Any job in hosiery was desirable, but full-fashioned work was the real prize. The machinery that produced ladies' seamed hose was far more complicated and demanding than the simple equipment that turned out socks. Full-fashioned hosiery workers commanded the highest wages in the textile industry, and young people avidly sought the well-paying jobs that would enable them to enjoy a higher standard of living than their parents. Roy Auton remembered that once he got work in a hosiery mill, he "traded cars and got married and bought furniture for two rooms and was paying cash for my groceries and rent." Hosiery workers could also spend more money on entertainment than other millhands, who had to plan carefully the fate of every dollar. James Ross's novel, *They Don't Dance Much*, set in a thinly disguised Burlington, captured the spirit with which some hosiery workers enjoyed their newfound prosperity. Much of the action takes place in a roadhouse outside the city limits where cotton and hosiery mill workers gathered to drink, dance, and gamble: "The freest spenders out there that night were the folks that worked in the hosiery mill in Corinth. In the main they were young fellows, because only a young man can see well enough to run a knitting machine. I guess they averaged making forty dollars a week, or about as much as a cotton-mill hand made in a month. Most of them could count on their eyes giving out on them about the time they got to be thirty years old, and it looked like they would be saving against that day. But none of them ever saved any. They all kept good cars, and most of them managed to find a gold-digging girl."[36]

The appeal of hosiery lay not only in bigger paychecks but also in the prestige associated with the job. One mother told of her daughter's trudging from one hosiery firm to another in search of work. She herself had "tried to get her to go in the mill with me so I could learn her up. She said, no indeed, she didn't intend ever to work in a cotton mill. She was goin' to get herself a job in a full-fashioned hosiery mill." Hosiery managers claimed that their industry attracted the best workers. As in cotton, the most-skilled, highest paying jobs were reserved for men, but women's work in hosiery was also well paid. School-teachers left classrooms to enter the mills, drawn by the prospect of earning more by knitting than by teaching, and the mills could "take the best kids out of high school." A hosiery worker was "king bee."[37]

While the new management techniques of the 1920s were stripping weavers and other cotton mill workers of their skills, full-fashioned hosiery was replete with skilled jobs. Knitters and fixers performed the most complex tasks. A full-fashioned knitting machine weighed several tons, measured forty to forty-two feet in length, and had thousands of moving parts. A knitter's job was so desirable that men often worked up to six months without pay to gain a position. It took years to progress from a mere "needle-pusher" to a "real fixer," who could tear down a machine and put it back together again. Because of their ability to manipulate these machines, highly skilled fixers could express their creativity by designing the patterns of socks and stockings. One fixer adapted his machine to pattern socks with a design of Roy Rogers and Trigger, and during the presidential campaign of 1928 another set up the pattern so that the names "Hoover" and "Al Smith" ran across the sock. As late as 1938 the Bureau of Labor Statistics estimated that 64 percent of employees in hosiery were skilled, 23 percent semiskilled, and only 13 percent unskilled.[38]

As cotton mill workers desperately hunted jobs during the Depression, hosiery workers were hunted by the expanding industry. One evening Roy Auton walked out the gate of a hosiery mill in Newton, North Carolina, and stopped to light a cigarette. The mill superintendent, standing in his office, watching a union man at the gate, saw him give Auton a flyer. The next day Roy was fired. When the superintendent refused to tell him why, Auton "just took off east and went to Burlington—that was the hosiery center of the South—and found a place where they was just opening up a mill and putting in new machinery. They'd pay me a day's wages if I was coming home for the weekend, to see if I could bring any more back with me. So I'd stop up at the mill, and I got one or two to go, and then the superintendent told the watchman not to let me in. So I just stopped at the gate, and he'd say, 'I can't let you in.' I'd say, 'Well, I don't need but two or three this time. I'll catch them when they come out.' So I took right close to forty hands away from him by him treating me like he did."[39]

Although consumer goods came more readily to hosiery workers, millhands of every stripe—cotton, rayon, and silk—did their best to enjoy the new forms of entertainment, fashion, and transportation. Yet incorporating novel pleasures into an older way of life did not come easily. Burlington, like other communities, remained an arena of competing values. Not everyone accepted the newfangled ways described in national magazines. When, on a ten-dollar bet, Nannie Pharis bobbed her hair and came home looking like a flapper, her son refused to speak to her. Herman Truitt, who graduated from high school in

1928, remembered that his class had to be satisfied with a banquet at the Alamance Hotel; a dance was out of the question because the authorities "didn't allow us to belly rub sponsored by the school." Stella Carden remembered driving more than a hundred miles with her boyfriend one weekend to visit friends and go dancing. But the couple spent the evening on the side of the ballroom because neither one of them had danced before.[40]

Novel diversions did not immediately conquer older forms of entertainment. While vaudeville and minstrel shows were on the decline nationally, they still had great drawing power in the South. The Mack Theater in Burlington regularly hosted vaudeville productions throughout the 1920s, shows like Don Davis's Dancing Dollies and the Land of Laughter Company, which featured comedians in blackface, harmony singers, and a crystal ball reader—all for a mere twenty cents. Workers could also take in a movie at the Rose Theater, such as *The Town That Forgot God*, with the special added attraction of the Galvin Duo steel guitar pickers. Throughout the 1920s Hollywood vied with minstrel shows and local stringband and gospel programs for audience dimes and loyalty. In one week in February 1927 Rudolph Valentino in *The Son of the Sheik* played opposite a fifty-character minstrel show at the Municipal Theater. In 1929 films like Buster Keaton's *Spite Marriage*, Mary Pickford's *Coquette*, and Clara Bow's *Dangerous Curves* ran in town at the same time that the East Burlington Presbyterian Church had an ice cream supper with stringband music and two congregations hosted a special gospel evening with Mr. and Mrs. George Dibble. Mr. Dibble, who had performed with Billy Sunday, was billed as the "Caruso of Gospel Singing"; Mrs. Dibble spoke the gospel.[41]

If anything outside the mill dictated workers' times of recreation, it was radio programming. In 1930 workers in Gastonia petitioned for a change in hours. They wanted to start work fifteen minutes earlier so they could get home before 6:00 P.M., when "Amos 'n' Andy" came on the radio. The mill agreed. Ralph Latta, who lived in Piedmont Heights, also scheduled his time around "Amos 'n' Andy." He used to leave his brother's house to walk to his girlfriend's just as the show came on. "If it was summertime, or a lot of times in wintertime, because people played their radios pretty loud, I could listen to that all the way. They said that the world was nearer at a standstill during that thirty minutes than any other thirty minutes during the twenty-four hours."[42]

*The Hagenbeck and Wallace Show, which frequently performed in Burlington
during the 1920s. The man on stage in a suit and tie is Jack Dempsey.*
(Courtesy of Robert Horne, Burlington, N.C.)

Workers were not only loyal to their favorite shows; increasingly
they supplied the content of local broadcasts. In the early 1920s
companies such as Columbia, Okeh, Paramount, and Victor sought to
boost record sales in the South by recording southern music. Led by
Fiddlin' John Carson of Atlanta, guitarists, fiddlers, and banjo pickers
who once played only for house parties and square dances began
performing on local radio stations and making records in Charlotte,
Atlanta, and New York.[43]

Carson, the mill worker who composed "Little Mary Phagan," was
a renowned Georgia fiddler and singer. Like other stringband musicians, he gained his reputation playing in fiddlers' contests and taking
his music on the road, where he passed the hat and sold song sheets to
earn gas money. When WSB, the first radio station in the South, began
broadcasting in Atlanta in 1922, Fiddlin' John became a regular per-
former. The following year he made the first recording of southern
stringband music for Okeh Records. The head of the company was
not impressed, but the initial issue of 500 records sold out at one
Atlanta fiddlers' convention.[44]

Commercial radio sponsors soon recognized the drawing power of
stringband musicians. By 1934 Crazy Water Crystals featured more

than a hundred Carolina musicians on its programs broadcast over Charlotte's WBT. The radio and recordings advertised musicians' talents and helped them to book paying performances. After his radio and record debut, Fiddlin' John put together a band, the Virginia Reelers, and toured Tennessee, Kentucky, Virginia, West Virginia, Illinois, and the Carolinas.[45]

Many of these musicians were mill workers who made little money from their playing but laid the foundation of broadcast country music for others to build upon. Charlie Poole was perhaps the Piedmont's most famous mill musician. Born to mill parents in Randolph County, North Carolina, in 1892, he received an early introduction to the stringband tradition as well as factory labor. By the time he was eight or nine years old, Poole had taken his first mill job and had begun to master the five-string banjo. Music came to govern his life. He married in 1912 and tried to settle down as a responsible husband and steady worker, but the lure of the road and the desire to take his music to new audiences proved too strong. Poole was in Canada when his son was born and in jail for drunkenness when his wife and child moved to Danville; soon afterward, he and his wife were divorced. Over the next thirteen years he came to epitomize the hard-drinking "rambling man" of musical tradition—the type of man who breathed spirit into the rough life and bred heartache in mill mothers trying to husband their families' resources. Drinking and brawling, he picked his banjo through the mill villages of the Southeast and the coal camps of West Virginia and Pennsylvania, occasionally returning to Spray, where his sister lived, to work in the mill and earn a few dollars before heading out again. Poole and two other Spray musicians, his brother-in-law Posey Rorer and Norman Woodlief, christened themselves the "North Carolina Ramblers" and in 1925 left for New York to try their hand at making records. They met with almost immediate success. The Ramblers' first recording for Columbia Records sold more than 100,000 copies at a time when 5,000 was considered a good seller and 20,000 an unqualified hit.[46]

The biggest market for the Ramblers' music was back home. Poole, unlike Fiddlin' John Carson, did not write his own songs. He drew on a repertoire of traditional stringband music, augmented by Tin Pan Alley tunes and songs he learned from the vaudeville shows that played in mill towns. Southern advertisers relied on Poole's local origins and his unique sound to sell his records. Dozens of stringbands began to copy Poole's style of blending old and new; some

*The Swingbillies, one of the Piedmont's many stringbands, at radio station WPTF
in Raleigh, North Carolina, ca. 1936.*
(Courtesy of Harvey Ellington, Oxford, N.C., and Della Coulter, Folklife Section,
North Carolina Arts Council)

even posed as the Ramblers in hopes of cashing in on the band's
popularity.[47]

Charlie Poole's music was part of a blossoming regional culture that
spread over the Piedmont's airwaves and highways. The radio and the
phonograph put millhands across the region in touch with each other,
allowing those who missed the traveling musicians' performances to
hear and enjoy the same music. On Saturday nights workers listened
to the Grand Ole Opry and danced to the tunes of local celebrities
playing in the studios of Charlotte's WBT and Atlanta's WSB. In a sense,
millhands carried on a conversation through their favorite songs,
talking not so much about the factory as about the stuff of daily life—
family and friends, romance, and personal tragedy. Songs like "Wreck
on the Highway" and "Little Mary Phagan" drew on local events and
personal experiences. Their lyrics and sentiments struck chords of
recognition among fellow workers, who eagerly tuned in to hear the

musicians they had once supported in their own communities. Eventually homogenized and commercialized as "the Nashville sound," country music in the 1920s and 1930s bolstered a sense of unique, regionwide identity.

When Dr. Carroll Lupton finished his medical internship in New Orleans and began looking for a practice, he was drawn to Burlington. Familiar with the area because his father was a Methodist minister in nearby Hillsborough, Lupton was attracted by the town's prosperity and its proximity to his family. Despite his middle-class background, Lupton became a respected friend to many villagers. He sympathized with the ends to which poverty pushed some people, and he accepted human frailties. But when he first came to Piedmont Heights, it seemed "a pretty rough place" to him. "All the streets were dirt and mud, and the people lived in the old, little mill houses. They were dreary looking. They were not painted. It was dangerous for a stranger to go in that area at night. They'd cut his automobile tires, or throw rocks at him, or beat him up. I knew one man who was making whiskey on his kitchen stove. I knew another man who was selling whiskey, had a little four-year-old boy that would crawl up underneath the house, which is built very low to the ground, a grown man couldn't crawl under it. And they'd hide his whiskey back in the chimneys, and when a customer would come, he'd send his little four-year-old boy in to get it." Lupton also knew that even though Burlington Mills was providing work, a textile job was not much of a living. To him, those men selling whiskey were "just truly up against it economically, and trying to feed their families the best they could."[48]

Lupton treated mill workers for malaria, pellagra, diphtheria, and venereal disease. But he "never fussed at them because they had a venereal disease, because the good Lord, I guess He put those urges in us." As Lupton came to know everyone on the hill, he learned "which woman was fiddling around with which of her neighbors. I knew which one of the women that her husband was fiddling around with. And it'd happen sometimes that one of them would pick up a venereal infection, and I knew exactly where she got it from. Then the mate came in with it, and I knew that he'd caught it from his wife, but he wasn't sure because I knew some of the other ladies he's fooling with." While Lupton, as the village doctor, may have known of these liaisons, workers did not flaunt their behavior. Men might drink and fight publicly, but illicit sex and women's drinking were still matters to be concealed from most eyes. Lupton once commented to his father on the events that took place behind closed doors. "You're a minister and I'm a doctor, but you just don't have any idea what goes on. You go in, and this lady meets you at the door with a smile on her face, and invites you in, and children and husband all come in, and ask you to have a prayer with them. But a doctor knows of four nights before that, there's a big drunken party and trading wives and husbands. And somebody got hurt, and he had to go out there. He knows what's going on. When they see the preacher coming, they run up the front room, get the Bible and dust all the dust off it, and straighten the place up, and grab the old whiskey bottles off and hide 'em back in somewhere. And we walk in, it's all setting out on the tables."[49]

The rough life that charged Piedmont Heights streets often spilled over into the complex of Burlington Mills plants. Until the company built fences around its factories, whiskey was brought to the doors and sold to workers, who drank on the job with impunity. Even as late as the 1920s and early 1930s, when jobs were no longer plentiful and the penalty for drinking could be a long spell of unemployment, some workers challenged the rules. Fighting in the mill brought immediate dismissal, but workers continued to wrangle with each other and with boss men. Mildred Edmonds remembered that in the Pioneer Plant men would "just get mad and fight." One day, she was working in the weave room and heard something go "clammety!" "I looked down and the blood was coming down the floor. Right above me laid a man, and another man had an iron pipe and knocked him in the head. It was rough, honey."[50]

Violence in the mills sometimes stemmed from differences of opinion between millhands and boss men. Burlington Mills employed the prototype of a rigid, authoritarian boss in the person of "Old Man-Slave Driver" Jim Copland. Born in Lee County, Alabama, in about 1874 and raised on a farm, James Copland, Sr., began his long career in the textile industry as a weaver with the Swift Manufacturing Company in Columbus, Georgia, where he was promoted to overseer. The course of his life traced out a map of the textile South. He served as a weave room overseer at the Judson Mills in Greenville, South Carolina, and at the Dan River Mills in Schoolfield, Virginia. In 1927, when he was fifty-three years old, he came to Burlington, where the rayon industry was burgeoning, and he ended his life there, having climbed from overseer to superintendent to mill owner. Copland had little formal education, but he knew machinery intimately. As he

moved north from Alabama into the heart of the Piedmont, he gathered experience and a troop of workers who followed him from mill to
mill. They did so not because they liked him particularly but because
he managed to go where jobs were available, and he hired friends,
family, and workers who had been loyal to him.[51]

Icy Norman was among those who owed their jobs to Jim Copland.
Icy's father, David, was a man who traveled to and from cotton mills,
so Icy spent her childhood shuttling between a farm in Wilkes County,
North Carolina, and the village of Schoolfield, Virginia, where her
father worked in the mill for Jim Copland. In the late 1920s, when
David Norman grew too sick to work, the family returned to the farm,
where Copland was a regular visitor. Icy's father died in 1928; her
mother sold the farm and took Icy and her brothers, Dewey and
Barney, to a nearby mill.

As it turned out, the mill ran only one week out of three, and Mrs.
Norman decided they could not stay there and make a living. "We got
in my daddy's old T-model. The whole two weeks that the mill stood
there, we was on the road hunting jobs. We went everywhere. Back
then the Depression was starting. Mills was closing down. You just
couldn't get a job. Every freight train that you seen pass was loaded
down with people going from town to town, hoboing." After driving
through much of the Piedmont, the Normans finally arrived in Burlington, at one of Spencer Love's mills. "It was a little old wooden mill,
two rooms, and they had everything in it. And so we drove up, and
Dewey and Barney got out. You know, anybody could go in, any time
day or night that they wanted to. There was a little old bitty machine
shop. I can just see that little old shop now. They didn't have but two
hands a-working. So Barney asked that man, 'Can you tell us how to
find Mr. Copland?' [Copland] come out and was just tickled to death.
And he told Mama, 'Well, I promised the last time I seen Mr. Norman—I take it he's gone?' And Mama says, 'Yes.' And he says, 'I
promised Mr. Norman that if you ever needed any help and I could
give you-all a job, that I wanted you to come to me. I reckon that's why
you-all have come, ain't you?' And Mama says, 'Yes, we've been
everywhere hunting a job.' And he says, 'Well, you don't have to hunt
no farther. You've got a job. We're tearing the cotton out and putting in
all rayon.' "[52]

Copland had come to Burlington Mills in 1927 to supervise the
conversion from cotton to rayon. He oversaw that change, as well as
the conversion from silk to rayon in many other Alamance mills. In the

early 1930s he left Burlington Mills and worked simultaneously as superintendent of the Plaid Mill and general manager of two other mills in the county. His energy appeared limitless. Icy Norman recalled that at one point in the early years of the Pioneer Plant, when there was still a lot of drinking in the factory, Copland would work all day and then patrol the mill every two hours at night.[53]

In Icy Norman's eyes, Copland was "just like a daddy." She had known him since her childhood, and he was kind to her. But she also knew he had another side: "He was hateful. Now, if he liked you, he liked you. That's the kind of man he was. He was a regular old tyrant if you made him mad." Other workers remembered Copland as a "ball of fire," who would "just pitch a fit" when something went wrong in the mill, or as a man who would "give you a whupping and then he'd laugh at you." Icy never felt Copland's wrath, but Hester Taylor did. Hester, too, had known Copland in Schoolfield. She was an audacious, devil-may-care girl, who had little respect for rules and regulations. One day while she was weaving, Copland came by and fingered her cloth, remarking that it would make a pretty dress. That night she sneaked a piece of it home and made herself one. The next morning, bold as brass, she walked up to Copland and asked him how he liked her outfit. He responded, "You ought to be killed."[54]

Copland was adept at pushing workers to maximum production. Most millhands referred to him as "Old Man" Copland, but some called him "Slave Driver." Copland was himself a driven man, and he expected everyone to work as hard as he did. Betty Davidson recalled the day Copland came through the mill and noticed that she had a pickwheel missing. " 'Betty, you see that pickwheel's missing?' And he caught ahold of my arm and he didn't realize how big his hands was, and left the print of all of his fingers on my arm. He didn't aim to hurt me, he just did it." Betty's husband, Lloyd, passed on a story he had heard from his father, who had also worked for Jim Copland in Schoolfield. "This incident happened one winter when it was real bad. This man in the spring of the year, he told Mr. Copland, 'See the sunshine? I'm going to get out there and make me a crop.' And so he left the mill and went out. That coming winter come a big snow, and so this man was working, and Mr. Copland come up to him and said, 'See the big snow outdoors? Now you get out there in it.' That was his way of getting even."[55]

Many workers appreciated Copland's ability to run a mill and keep machines in order so they could make production, but few seemed to like or respect him as a person. Generally, mill workers respected supervisors who had learned their trade from the bottom up; such boss men commanded loyalty because they honored the roots of their knowledge and the workers who shared it. But Copland seldom demonstrated that regard for his hands, and in return they did not esteem him. When he identified himself as a "working man," it left a bad taste in workers' mouths. Ralph Latta had worked for Copland in one of the Piedmont Heights mills and found him "overbearing." Many years later he witnessed that same attitude outside the mill. "I was in a store in Burlington once, went in there to get an overcoat. It was about Christmastime and it was one of the nicer stores in Burlington. I was the only customer in there. There was four clerks standing back there talking. And I decided I'd just wait there. I walked in a little ways—see how long I'd stand there before someone come to wait on me. Well, I stood there and stood there, and directly Old Man Jim come in. And they like to run over the top of me getting to Mr. Copland. 'What can I do for you? What can I do for you?' He was a great big man. 'Well, I need a hat.' Well, they took down one. He said, 'How much is it?' 'Ten dollars.' He said, 'Hell, man, I can't pay that for that. Put it back. I'm a working man.' I just turned around and went on up the street and bought the coat from somewhere else."[56]

Jim Copland served Spencer Love well. Copland's tenure bridged the years between Burlington Mills's faltering start and its assertive expansion. In the 1930s Burlington Mills abandoned the intensely personal style of supervision employed by Copland. But during the company's infancy, his combination of technical expertise, rough-and-tumble discipline, and personal connections to workers proved invaluable. Although he seemed to operate most often in a hat-stomping mode, a gentler side emerged when he dealt with workers like Icy Norman.

Icy began work on September 20, 1929, "so green" that she did not know she would get paid only after she had learned her job. As she recalled, Mr. Copland took her over to Dewey McBride. " 'I want you to fix a place for this little girl. She's going to learn how to wind. Give her two spools of thread and show her how to tie the weaver's knot.' If I had knowed I had to work through all that rigamarole learning to tie that knot, my mama could have showed me—you see, Mama was a weaver. I sat on that little old box all day long tying that old weaver's knot. I thought, I'll never make it. Jim Copland and Old Man Smith come by and sat down there. Jim says, 'How's my little girl doing?' I says, 'Mr. Copland, I ain't doing. I can't tie that knot.' And he sat there and watched me. The more they watched me the scared-er I got.

"When I started home, Dewey McBride gave me two spools of thread. He says, 'You take this home, and you practice tonight.' And I said, 'Well, I'll take it, but I'll never tie that knot. Why can't you just tie a knot like this?' He says, 'You can't do that, Icy. It's got to be a weaver's knot. It can't be no chickenhead knot.' Well, I went home and I set down there and started after supper. I told Mama, 'Mama, I've had to do this all day long. I can't tie it.' Well, Mama showed me how to tie it. She could shut her eyes and tie them just as fast. You're supposed to tie a weaver's knot on that middle finger and the thumb, and hold it with this [the index] finger. I couldn't do that.

"Next day, on the old box I sat. The more I studied about that thing, the more I hated that. Oh, I hated that mill. Ooh, how I hated it! And I thought, 'Well, if this is all they got for me to do, I don't want it.' I went home and I was crying. Mama says, 'What are you crying about?' I says, 'Because I can't tie that old knot.' And she says, 'I've told you how to tie it, and I've showed you how to tie it. That's the only way you can tie a weaver's knot.' I said, 'Mama, there's a way that I can tie that knot and it's a weaver's knot, and it's all the same thing. I don't care what they say.' And I just cried and cried.

"One day on that box I was doing my best to do like the boss man told me, and that thing would slide out every time. So all at once something come to me just like it spoke: Tie it on your forefinger. I put it on there, and I'd tie them things as fast as you could wink an eye. And there come Jim Copland and Old Man Smith. And I thought, 'Lord, I better not let them see me do that.' Jim Copland says, 'Well, how's my little girl doing? You can tie that knot now, can't you?' I says, 'If you'll let me tie it the way I want to tie it.' He said, 'What do you mean? It has got to be absolutely a weaver's knot. Let me see what you're talking about.' I'd put that thing down there and I'd just tie them and tie them, and he looked at that knot, and he said, 'Do it slow.' I got so I could do it just as fast. And I did."[57]

Although Icy finally conquered the weaver's knot, she continued to hate the mill. She was afraid of ruining the yarn, afraid she could not do her job, afraid she would not make any money to help the family. "I'd go home and I'd cry all night long. I was getting paid for what little I done. That wasn't much. I think I made a quarter one day, and one day I made fifteen cents." The young girl sitting on a box, crying, attracted the attention of Spencer Love, who regularly came through the mill. Love often stopped to talk with workers in the early years of the mill, creating a favorable impression on them. He developed a special relationship with Icy, and decades later she remembered the first time he sat down by her. "I didn't know who he was. I didn't know that he owned that mill—him and his daddy. He was good-looking. He was young then. He says, 'You look like you been crying.' I sat down and I says, 'You know, I hate this place.' And I started crying. He put his arm around my neck. He says, 'Honey, don't cry. You'll catch on to it.'" One day, Love and his father came through the mill and called Icy over. She had just found out who the two men were. She went over to them and said, "'Are you-all Mr. Loves? Lord, mercy! Here I've been talking to your boy, telling him all my troubles and a-crying. Telling him how bad I hated my job. And he owned the mill. I apologize. But I do hate it.' Him and his daddy sat there and talked with me. Every time they'd come through the mill they'd sit down there. If they hadn't encouraged me like they did, and Mr. Copland, I wouldn't have stayed in that mill."[58]

With the help of two sisters who worked next to her, Icy became a proficient winder. Each day she ran a little more yarn, though she still refused to look at the production board. Once she mastered the task and began drawing ten dollars a week, she was well satisfied and came to love her work. She eventually contrasted herself to those workers who watched the clock and waited for Friday. "I took an interest in my job. I'd study to see which would be the best [way to do things] and which I thought would be best for the company. I tried to keep my job up."[59]

Icy stuck with her job because she felt an obligation to contribute to her family's welfare and to do right by Jim Copland, who had given her work in memory of her father. The loyalty she gave to her family later came to encompass Love and Burlington Mills. Perhaps it was because of the personal encouragement she had received in those first trying days; perhaps it was a measure of her own character. But when others left the mill during slack times, she stayed on. At one point, roles were reversed and she was the one encouraging Love. "I know work was getting so bad, Spence Love come down there and he look like he was so down and out. I said, 'Mr. Love, you look like you're mighty low this morning.' He says, 'I am. I'm just on rock bottom. I don't know which way to do for the best; I'm going to have to close the place down.' I says, 'Well, there's always a brighter day a-coming. My mama told me that when I come here and I told you how bad I hated this place. But I really love to work here now. I'll stick with you through thick and thin. If you sink, I'll go down with you.' I laughed and he got to laughing. He says, 'You just beat all I've ever seen.' "[60]

Business did improve for Love, mainly because of his own management. In 1929 he responded to a query directed to mill executives by the editor of the *Southern Textile Bulletin*, who asked, "What's the matter with the cotton manufacturing industry?" Love's reply not only identified the problems but proposed solutions as well. He argued that the industry was top-heavy with concerns that had made exorbitant profits during the war but lacked the knowledge and efficiency to be successful during normal times. Until such mills were eliminated, he foresaw very close margins in the industry. He pointed to the need for new methods of cost accounting to adjust for the obsolescence of machinery and for the mixing of rayon and other fibers with cotton, which made manufacturing more complex. And he identified the need to pay closer attention to selling and distribution policies.[61]

Love's actions demonstrated his determination to carry out his own recommendations. By 1930 the demand for rayon dress goods was more than his existing mills could handle, so Love took advantage of the Depression to expand. But instead of building new mills in the Piedmont Heights complex, he ventured outside Burlington and began buying closed or failing mills across the Piedmont, essentially for their buildings. The mills were stripped of their old machinery and reequipped with Jacquard and dobby looms for weaving rayon. One commentator on the industry, W. H. Rose, recognized the audacity and savvy of Love's approach. "It requires freedom from hampering tradition and considerable courage to scrap machinery that is still capable of doing its work, and the leaders in the weaving industry today are those who have met these requirements." Rose noted, too, that scrapping the machinery prevented it from being used by the competition to produce lower-quality, cheaper fabrics.[62]

Love also made innovations in personnel management. Over the years he moved away from boss men like Jim Copland and became one of the first textile men to professionalize shop floor supervision. Love did not believe that overseers had to be "steeped in technology with a textile engineering degree" or to have worked their way up through the ranks in order to be good managers. If they knew business, they could pick up textiles—much as he had. One observer summed up Love's policy concerning supervisors: "He recruited . . . from the graduate business schools, tossed them more responsibility than most could handle soon after they arrived, culled out those who faltered, and rapidly promoted the rest."[63]

Attention to current fashion, professionalized management, and a dedication to modern equipment fueled the growth of Burlington Mills. By 1934 the company was the largest weaver of rayon in the nation. When Love announced plans to reopen a mill in High Point, he was greeted with "expressions of gratification from all walks of the city's life. Businessmen were especially pleased and those workers who were thrown out of work when the Stehli plant closed were jubilant." At the end of 1936—only twelve years from the day the first yarn was spun under Burlington's name—Burlington Mills had twenty-two plants operating in nine communities. The next year Love consolidated his units into the Burlington Mills Corporation and listed its stock on the New York Stock Exchange.[64]

Love's goals for the company were flexible, but not even he anticipated the rapid expansion that occurred during the 1930s. He thought the company was "near the saturation point of what we can economically handle" in 1931, and he likened the growth of the previous few years to the rise of other giant corporations: "If we continued to expand in the future with the same rapidity as we have in the past year or two we would be as big as the Standard Oil Company before a great many years."[65] The thought spurred him on, and when opportunities for expansion arose, he seized them.

In his quest for profits, Love insisted on a free hand with labor. Like most textile executives, he was adamantly opposed to unions. But the tactics he employed to defeat them were in some ways as rationalized as his other management policies. He tried to keep his wage scale just above the competition's, simultaneously providing an incentive for workers to choose Burlington and deflating one motive for unionizing. He also carefully screened potential employees. He had men in the mills who kept their ears open for gossip and complaints in order to anticipate and head off trouble. And he installed fences around his mills and issued photo identification cards, which workers had to show to security guards in order to enter the plant.[66]

After the initial expansion of Burlington Mills in the 1920s, Love never again concentrated mills as he had in the Piedmont Heights area. Rather, he scattered them throughout the Piedmont, with the advantage that "labor [was] obtainable and [could] reside with a minimum of social and industrial problems." An industry publication described this policy of decentralization as designed to allow "both plants and employees . . . fully [to] enjoy the benefits of small town and rural surroundings." Another observer interpreted the policy as a "strategic defense against labor activity."[67]

Burlington civic leaders disapproved of Love's policy of dispersing mills, for they believed that the city had not received a full reward for the opportunities it had provided him. In 1935, when Love tried unsuccessfully to get some street improvements near one of his mills in downtown Burlington, his father reminded him of why the city might be reluctant to act. Burlington citizens had put up $200,000 in stock subscriptions for the first mill in the 1920s, and many stockholders had waited "weary years" for any return. Many more had not been able to hold out and had sold their stock at a loss before the company became successful. The largest mill area, Piedmont Heights, was outside the city limits and paid no taxes. Moreover, Love had moved his company's headquarters to Greensboro in 1935. James Lee Love continued, "Your sound and sensible policy of scattering your mills in other sections and of moving your offices and the residences of your officers elsewhere,—all these are matters that the Burlington people look at very differently from your own views."[68]

Burlington workers also took a jaundiced view of the practices Love initiated to increase production and profits. Although Love was not a pioneer in introducing scientific management to the textile industry, he may have been the first to embrace it wholeheartedly and exploit it thoroughly. He polished his management style in the 1930s, and by 1938–39, when Burlington Mills acquired the nearby Plaid Mill, workers were in for a shock. Harry Rogers described the changes since the days when the young Spencer Love put his arm around a weeping Icy Norman. "When Burlington Industries came in, textiles began to change a lot. They were strictly for Burlington Mills. A human being just didn't mean too much to them. The machinery did. They changed their attitude, I reckon. They kept close count of all the figures. 'How much production did you get? How was the quality?' That's all they were interested in. They tried to put across that they were interested in the human side of it, but I don't think they were." Overseers as well as machine operators felt the weight of Love's policies. James Pharis, who came to the Plaid Mill from another Burlington Mills plant, recalled that "it'd get pretty pinky" sometimes. "The way Burlington Mills handled things back in them days was, a big methods-and-standards man would come down out of Greensboro and we'd have a meeting. Well, they'd have a plan. In that plan was getting more work out of somebody for the same money. If you didn't do it, then the question would be 'Why couldn't you sell them on it?' That was the only thing that ever worried me at the Plaid Mill. Trying to sell the people and make them happy, and, you know, that's one hell of a job."[69]

Pharis was fairly successful selling the stretch-out. He always anticipated a "flap about it," but none ever came. Elsewhere, though, workers did protest. Ralph Latta grew up in Orange County, just east of Alamance, and spent his life working in textile mills. One day, while Latta was working in Piedmont Heights, a time study man came down from Greensboro. "He had a big piece of paper and he drawed off on there that out of eight hours it'd take you so long to do this, so long to do that, so long to do something else, so long to go to the restroom, so long to eat. After he did that, somebody said, 'You draw a picture of an airplane on that piece of paper and make it fly off, then we'll take it. Until you do, we don't.' You can figure things out like that on paper, but they just don't pan out."[70]

For Love, however, the new technology and management techniques did pan out. His rationalized approach to business, combined with the knowledge and drive of men like Jim Copland, transformed the textile industry. But the process was lengthy and onerous. The rough life, which disrupted the mill and disturbed the Piedmont Heights mill village, endured for more than a decade. It persisted in part because people liked it. Beneath the tone of censure with which workers later related the story of Little Chicago and the Pioneer Plant, there was also a sense of pride and an appreciation for the vitality of life there. Workers, especially men, discounted the argument that alcohol impeded their abilities. Dewey McBride related a perhaps apocryphal story in which some boss men removed the shuttles from a Crompton-Knowles loom in order to examine the machine and then could not get them back in. For three days and three nights, the bosses worked over the loom. Finally, a weaver and loom fixer who had been demoted because he was always drunk offered to fix it. Irritably the boss replied, "You crippled devil, if you don't get out of the way, I'll take you to the door and throw you out." But when they finally let the man work on the loom, he had it running in an hour. Even those who suffered saw the good side of the rough life. As Gladys McBride put it, "That was a crooked mill, but people worked and they enjoyed it."[71]

While Love and Copland struggled to impose their will inside the mill, other forces were at work in the village. In 1924 some residents of the new mill village sought to recreate an institution that had previously given them a sense of stability and belonging. For these men and women, solace was not found in a bottle, and fellowship did not abide in songfests at the hog pen. Instead, they spent their time, energy, and meager savings organizing a church. In June, some forty Baptists in Piedmont Heights formed a congregation and began meeting in various homes and at Glen Hope Elementary School, but hard times at Burlington Mills between 1924 and 1926 broke up the congregation. Some members left in search of steadier work, and those who remained trekked into town for services at the First Baptist Church. By 1927 the only formal religious group that remained in Piedmont Heights was a Sunday school class.

Several members of the class had belonged to the Pomona Baptist Church in Greensboro before moving to Burlington to work in the Pioneer Plant. On September 13, 1927, a Sunday school class from Pomona visited the Piedmont Heights group, and the two classes held a joint meeting. At the close of the meeting, the group prepared to leave, lamenting the fact that Piedmont Heights had no preacher. One member, Grace Pyrtle, reminded them that among their visitors was a young Sunday school teacher, George Washington Swinney, who had recently experienced a call to the ministry. The group invited him to speak. Swinney later told Grace Pyrtle's son-in-law, Ralph Latta, that he "could have went through the floor." But instead, he rose and delivered an extemporaneous sermon, "Prepare to Meet Thy God." That day, "Preacher" Swinney launched his career. Swinney impressed the Sunday school class, and they invited him to preach regularly. Soon his sermons had attracted a devout following, and in June 1928, the congregation of the Glen Hope Church, named after the school in which it met, called Swinney as its pastor. Four months later the congregation elected a six-member committee to find a lot on which to build a church.[72]

George Washington Swinney was thirty years old when he delivered his first sermon in Piedmont Heights. Born in the Blue Ridge Mountains of Floyd County, Virginia, in 1897, the son of farmers Samuel and Mary Young Swinney, he soon followed the well-worn path into the cotton mills of the Piedmont. When George was about ten, his father died; Mary Swinney, like many turn-of-the-century widows, left the farm and took her six children to the mills. They traveled first

Preacher George Washington Swinney, ca. 1945.
(Courtesy of the Glen Hope Baptist Church, Burlington, N.C.)

to Schoolfield, where, with three years of education behind him, George began working as a doffer. He never returned to school. In 1908 the family moved across the state line to Draper, North Carolina, and George found work in the spinning room of a blanket mill. The Swinneys packed up once more in 1920 and went to Greensboro, where George worked again as a doffer in the Pomona Cotton Mill. The next year he met and married Etta Gay Dalton.

Etta Gay's background was similar to George's in many respects. She, too, was born to poor mountain farmers in Floyd County, in 1903, and received little formal education and no religious training. Etta Gay lost both of her parents at an early age. Her siblings were split up, and she was taken in by a wealthy family to work as a servant. Of her childhood Etta Gay remembered that she "never did know anything but work. Housework, mostly. They had cows to care for. You had to get out and milk cows when the snow was above your knees. I just filled the place of a servant." Etta Gay left when she felt threatened by her guardian. "He wasn't married at that time and I could sense he was gonna ruin my life. I knew nothing at all about the Bible. You know, the Bible says, a virtuous woman, her price is far above rubies. But that was in my heart. I didn't want to go that way. So I left home. I didn't know where I'd go, where I'd wind up. I must have been about fifteen." After a brief stay with another family in Virginia, she traced one of her sisters to Greensboro and joined her there. Through her brother-in-law, Etta Gay got a job spooling at the Pomona Cotton Mill, where she met George Swinney.[73]

The Swinneys raised six children, including a son who followed his father into the ministry. Etta Gay worked until her first child was born and then retired from public work to devote herself to raising her children and, later, to supporting her husband's calling. She played a crucial role in Swinney's ministerial career. "The secret of [Swinney's] success was his wife," Ralph Latta believed. "There's not a better woman ever lived than that woman. She didn't go with him in revival meetings. She said her place was at home with the kids praying for the Preacher. That was her calling." According to Latta's wife, Helen, "Her prayer life is the thing that's made Mrs. Swinney what she is. She's a praying woman."[74]

At the time of their marriage, neither George nor Etta Gay had any religious inclinations or any sign that George would be a minister. In fact, members of the congregation who knew Swinney in those early years in Pomona remembered him as a man who liked a drink and a good time. He was a promising ballplayer; he hunted and fished and loved to play practical jokes. Although his "rough" reputation might have been exaggerated later to accentuate the extent of his conversion, Robert Latta, who grew up in the mill village and later became a minister himself, laughingly recalled, "I never heard him say much about his life before he became a Christian, but I can imagine. He was the type of person that whatever he went at he would have gone at it all the way. And if he were living a life that was not Christian, I can imagine he went all the way there, too."[75]

In May 1923 an itinerant preacher who called himself Reverend King raised a revival tent near the Swinneys' home and changed the course of their lives. The Swinneys attended the revival to hear King, who could not read and had someone else pronounce the text from the Bible before he expounded upon it. The revival had an immediate effect on George. "We went to the tent meeting and he was saved," Etta Gay recalled. "Oh, I don't know whether the first or second night. He was converted. He said it felt like two big hands just got down under his arms and lifted him up." Etta Gay's conversion took longer, but both Swinneys began attending the Pomona Baptist Church, and they were soon baptized in Rock Creek. George took an active role in the church, working as a janitor, usher, and Sunday school teacher.[76]

Swinney felt a call to the ministry in 1927, and soon afterward the Glen Hope Church provided him with an opportunity to answer. Rather than filling him with joy, however, the offer of the new pastorate caused Swinney to wrestle with self-doubt. The minister of Burlington's First Baptist Church, the Reverend Martin Buck, who had encouraged the initial formation of the Glen Hope congregation, disapproved of Swinney's selection because he lacked education. Swinney feared that Buck might be right. Anxiety over the enormous task of starting a new church and doubt about his own abilities pressed upon him. One night he gave in to his discouragement and called upon a friend and fellow minister, John Cox, for help. Cox found him in the middle of a broom sage field, crying. They prayed together in the moonlight, and Cox buttressed Swinney's flagging spirit.

"Did God call you to that work, George?"
"Yes."
"Well, you're going, if I have to whip you."[77]

Swinney accepted the pastorate, but until 1930 he and his family lived in Greensboro because the Glen Hope congregation could not afford to provide a salary or a parsonage. Swinney took the bus to downtown Burlington each Sunday and walked five miles out to the village in time for services, accompanied by Etta Gay when they had enough money for a babysitter. Finally, in February 1930, Burlington Mills donated the use of a mill house for the family, and the Swinneys moved to the village. The congregation began paying the preacher twenty-five dollars a week.

From the outset, Swinney established a personal rapport with church and community members. The title by which they addressed him indicated the nature of his role in Piedmont Heights. Mildred Overman, long-time educational director at Glen Hope, explained, "Some people call their pastor 'Reverend.' Some call their pastor 'Doctor.' Some address him as 'Mister.' But we know our pastor as 'Preacher' Swinney." The title "Preacher" signified a familiarity not conveyed by "Doctor" or "Reverend" and acknowledged the aspect of his ministry most valued by Swinney's congregation—his preaching. Swinney was not a learned man who delivered exegeses of the Scriptures from his pulpit. Although he worked constantly on his reading and understanding of the Bible, his knowledge of the Scriptures was "wide rather than deep." Self-conscious about his lack of schooling, he often apologized for his grammar when he knew that better-educated people were present at a service. But his "murder of the King's English" did not affect his message. Ralph Latta remembered one evening at a prayer meeting when Swinney was reading from the Bible. "This fellow was reading on a little ahead of him. He got to a word he couldn't pronounce and he thought, 'I'll just wait right there till the Preacher gets there and see what that word is, how to pronounce it.' When Preacher got to that word he said, 'How true that is' and just missed that word and went right on to the next one. And that has been a saying up there ever since, 'How true that is.' "[78]

Swinney was not only a minister but also a friend and companion to many villagers. He would often walk into the Latta home, go to the refrigerator, grab a Coke, and sit down and visit. With his conversion he had renounced baseball and drinking, but he still loved to hunt and fish and play practical jokes. Through these pastimes he formed strong friendships with many of the village men, and recreation proved an asset to his ministry in surprising ways. Ralph Latta recalled the first time his brother met Preacher Swinney, one night on a successful fox hunt. At the end of the hunt, his brother said, "Well, if you can preach like you can hunt, I'm gonna hear you." He listened, converted, and joined the church.[79]

Fishing was also an important theme of Swinney's ministry. "I Go A-Fishing," the title drawn from St. Peter, was one of Swinney's best-loved sermons. In it he compared people to different kinds of fish—old catfish, for instance, who were nothing but mouth. Although the sermon "wasn't expository preaching, it really got people's attention." Dr. Lupton, a good friend of the Preacher, told a parablelike story about one of Swinney's fishing trips that illustrated the relationship Swinney enjoyed with the village men, a relationship of equality rooted in their common backgrounds. "Two barbers named Coley, they were brothers, and Preacher Swinney had been out on a city lake, fishing. Story was that they came by his house and said, 'Let's go fishing, Preacher!' 'Well, I can't do that,' he says, 'I've got my good clothes on; I've got to hold prayer meeting at seven or seven-thirty.' 'Oh, we'll have you back in plenty of time for that! And don't worry, you just ride in the boat and talk to us and you can hold a fishin' rod, too.' One of the boys hooked a tremendous big fish. It was a bass, weighed about ten pounds. Everybody's excited, and they got the fish in the boat, and the old fish started flopping and jumping. And it looked, [for] all the world, [like] it was going to jump right back out of the boat, and get back in the water. The Preacher, without even thinking, just fell right down on top of that fish, and wrapped around with it, and they subdued it until they got it quieted down so it couldn't get away. Then they were coming in, and they brought it by just to show me. The Preacher said, 'Well, I've got to go preach.' I looked at him, I says, 'Look at yourself.' He had fish scales and slime and mud off the bottom of that boat, completely covered up with it. He had to make a mad dash to get a little clean clothes on to go to church. That's the type of people they were."[80]

Such bonds between the Preacher and Piedmont Heights villagers lay at the heart of Swinney's ministry. He had no more, and in many cases less, education than most mill workers. He understood firsthand their working conditions, their family life, and the pleasures and perils of their amusements. He renounced the aspects of that world that he considered sinful, and he embraced the rest. In his preaching and ministering he urged his congregation to follow his path, to wrestle with sin and subdue it.

The Reverend Clarence Vaughn, Swinney's son-in-law, assistant pastor, and successor, described Swinney as an "exhorter" rather than a teacher, a preacher who could lift the people with his sermons. The Reverend Robert Latta elaborated. "An 'exhorter' tries to get you to act on what you already know. [Swinney] was not a teacher in the sense that he would bring out things in the Scriptures that you had never seen before, but he could take a story in the Bible that you had read a thousand times and he could make it live. He could tell a story and just make you feel that you were there and make you *feel* the truth that you already knew, and make you want to act upon it." According to Latta, Swinney was always "conscious of God's presence." To those who heard Preacher Swinney, that awareness acted as a direct transmitter of God's word. In Sarah Andrews's view, "He was not a preacher from education, he preached from what God told him."[81]

In the heyday of the Glen Hope Church, "there were people coming forward at just about any invitation" to be converted. Mrs. Andrews had been baptized once by Swinney but "never had no real change" until one Sunday in church when "Preacher Swinney preached on being borned again. I never gave being borned again much of a thought, but I know I'd read it in the Bible a lot. I just thought it was changing your mind, that you knowed you was going to do the right thing about everything. I was baptized and dipped, but I still weren't satisfied. One day Preacher Swinney was a-preaching and he said people might think there wasn't nothing to it, but said if you pray through until you hit the rock, the fire will fly. And that just got on me, and something did happen."[82]

To Preacher Swinney the rough life was a challenge to his call, and he took as his primary task the redemption of Little Chicago. In this he used three tools: example, prayer, and shame. The impact of the Swinneys' mere presence in the village is impossible to calculate. Dr. Lupton believed that "Preacher Swinney changed their whole way of thinking about morals and religious values, and values in life." He inspired his followers to pull their community together. By the mid-1930s Piedmont Heights was "a completely changed vicinity. It was hard to drive through the church area on Sunday morning, the cars parked around there so much. Everybody was going."[83]

It was not only from the pulpit that Swinney worked his will on the villagers. He also confronted people directly, although privately. Whatever his method of persuasion, "some of the people who had been bootlegging, they either reformed real quickly or moved out." A village that strangers had once feared to enter was transformed into a community where a person could drive around and "feel just as safe as if I was in my mother's arms."[84]

The peer pressure of Christians was a powerful force. And it was not only Swinney who evangelized; so did newly inspired converts. Reformed villagers admonished their rowdy neighbors. On his rounds, Dr. Lupton often encountered meetings between sinners and the saved. "'Now you ought not to sell this whiskey 'round here like this,'" the saved would say, "'You should become a Christian and go to church, and give up this ungodly life, and ask for forgiveness.' Well, everytime [the sinner] would turn around, he'd run into somebody working on him, and inviting him to prayer meeting, and places like that. He had either to submit or get out." William Robertson, one of the original employees of the Pioneer Plant, who claimed that he donated the first fifteen cents to the Glen Hope Church, saw the transformation of the mill village as a joint crusade by Swinney and other Christians. For him, the problem was "a bunch of sinners that haven't been saved yet, that was all. But we got 'em. We tamed 'em. That fifteen cents started 'em off. . . . We got out of Chicago."[85]

Preacher Swinney was not completely successful in creating a uniform code of behavior in the village. Not everyone reformed or joined the church. While some men tempered their behavior without becoming churchgoers, others ignored Swinney and Glen Hope and continued to act as they had always done. Prayer seemed to take a backseat to fear in at least one reformation. Helen McBride went to church every Sunday morning to ask Preacher Swinney to pray for her father, who went drinking every Saturday night. But Dewey did not stop drinking or start going to church until he suffered two heart attacks.[86]

Still other villagers had their own religious traditions, and, while appreciating Swinney's labor to make the village a safer place to live, they were also somewhat disturbed by the extent of his power. Mattie Shoemaker and her sister Mildred Edmonds were Catholics who thought Swinney was a fine man, but they questioned the utter devotion so many people had to him. As Mildred said, "Some people thought to hang onto his coattails and get pulled right into heaven." As Catholics, the Shoemaker sisters were outside the Baptist church-based community, and they looked upon events from a different perspective. They remembered coming home from a drive in the country with their mother and getting out of the car to hear a cacophony of screaming and shouting. They ran into the house, sure that murder was being committed, and peeked out the window only to see an exuberant prayer meeting going on next door.[87]

Cottage prayer meetings were among the most effective methods of fostering the village's budding Christian community. By the mid-1930s, instead of the discordant noises of fighting and drinking, the sounds of prayer filled the evening air. Men sometimes attended these gatherings, but they were the special province of women. The meetings offered a place where, under the protection of a loving faith, women could open their hearts to each other as well as to God. Lottie Adams had fond memories of the evenings when her husband walked down to the store to visit with other men while the women congregated on her porch. The women would "just sit and laugh and talk and have a fellowship and have a good time. And a lot of times when we was in here, we'd just have a regular prayer meeting. Get talking about the Lord, you know. Several old ladies would come in and love to talk about the Lord. And read the Bible. Some of 'em would pray. We used to have a lovely time."[88]

At such meetings villagers prayed about their work, their families, their health, and their souls. Members presented community problems to God and to each other for solution. At times of crisis, such as the Depression or the 1934 General Textile Strike, they met more frequently. In hard times the faithful shared food as well as spiritual nourishment. Prayer meetings bolstered individuals' faith while at the same time strengthening the human ties between community members, who often provided the help that villagers asked of God.[89]

The process of forging a godly refuge in Little Chicago was not accomplished overnight. But through Swinney's influence, many Piedmont Heights villagers accepted Christ and changed their personal behavior. Members of the congregation formed a communal bond based on loyalty to Swinney and to the church they had created together, as well as to their shared spiritual beliefs. The redemption of their community was not a miracle, but the fruit of much work and mutual adjustment.

As the transformation of Piedmont Heights villagers into God-loving, Devil-fearing Christians unfolded, its effects carried over into the mill. Indeed, the histories of the two institutions were closely entwined. The first brick building housing the Glen Hope Church, completed in 1931, sat on a lot donated by Burlington Mills, and the front door of the church faced the front door of the Pioneer Plant across the street. A photograph taken in the 1940s, showing Preacher

Swinney and the congregation gathered on the front steps of the church, has several strands of barbed wire in the foreground. The church and mill were so close that in order to frame the entire congregation, the photographer had to stand behind the mill fence, giving the impression that the mill's barbed wire enclosed the congregation.

Spencer Love observed Swinney's work in the village for nearly three years before he donated the use of a mill house and a lot for the church. He was a careful, canny businessman who made considered investments, and the Glen Hope Church was one of them. Once he decided to support Swinney's work, he did so wholeheartedly. Love allowed church members to go through the mill soliciting pledges of a day's wages for the church's building fund, and later to sell sandwiches and drinks from a dope cart, with the proceeds to go to the church. Burlington Mills also paid the church's electric bill for many years. The company donated the parsonage, and in 1949, when fire destroyed the church, it helped Glen Hope to rebuild. Villagers commonly believed that if the church needed anything, all Swinney had to do was call on Love. As the Reverend Clarence Vaughn discovered, looking back through the minutes of a deacons' meeting, church members were more inclined to put their faith in Spencer Love than in God's love. During a discussion of the church's lack of funds, Swinney suggested they pray about the matter, but the deacons suggested that he go talk to Spencer Love.[90]

Supporting the Glen Hope Church was a wise move on Love's part. As Dr. Lupton observed, "The mill management saw the value of improvement in the attitude and well-being of their employees. In other words, Monday morning'd come along, instead of a whole bunch of them hanging [about]—they'd been out on wild parties over the weekend, and drunk, and some of them'd be in jail—they were there at work. The absenteeism dropped. To the management, that church was a great investment." Clarence Vaughn concurred. He believed that Swinney had taken "vile women and drunkards" and made them into good Christians. As a matter of course, they became better workers.[91]

The kind of relationship that existed between the Glen Hope Church and Burlington Mills had a long tradition in the textile South. Liston Pope, who studied churches and mills in Gastonia in the 1920s, concluded, "The cultural context in which executives and ministers alike live and work bluntly decrees that making good tire fabrics and good Christians are correlative processes, and the direc-

Glen Hope Baptist Church during the 1940s. The fence in the foreground surrounded the Pioneer Plant of Burlington Mills.
(Courtesy of the Glen Hope Baptist Church, Burlington, N.C.)

tors of each process have learned that cooperation is profitable for them all." In neither case was the purpose of the mill or the church in question. Swinney's main goal was to save souls; the creation of a responsible work force was a beneficial side effect. Love was a sincere Christian, but one who recognized that a population that lived by the values Swinney preached would be sober, dependable, and a boon to his business. The relationship between many mill churches and mills was symbiotic and reciprocal, but not one in which power was shared equally. The Glen Hope Church would have survived without the support of Burlington Mills, but it would not have flourished so splendidly.[92]

In making gifts to the church, Spencer Love never demanded a return obligation from Preacher Swinney. The relationship between the two was more subtle. Ralph Latta firmly believed that "Preacher Swinney wasn't on a string. He wasn't a puppet." But—and it was an important qualification—"if there come any labor troubles, he didn't take sides either way." Latta felt that Swinney's sympathies would have been "with the people," but he did not remember that Swinney ever expressed them from the pulpit or in any public forum. During the 1934 textile strike, when the Piedmont Heights plants shut down along with mills throughout the county, Swinney was the only minister to hold services every night. He ran the following notice in the newspaper: "As the mill is standing people have time to attend church, the pastor will preach each evening next week at 7:30 o'clock." At least one worker, Walt Pickard, who was deeply involved in the 1934 strike and union activities, interpreted Swinney's actions as antagonistic to the strikers. "Preacher Sweeney, of the Baptist Church on the Burlington mill hill, started three-weeks Protracted Meeting in the middle of the strike, when Protracted Meeting wasn't due at all. He did it to get people off the picket lines, and talk against the union."[93]

Pickard implied that Swinney was a mouthpiece for mill management. Undoubtedly, Swinney was grateful for the mill's support of his work, but his loyalties were more complicated. Certainly, he must have seen the strike as divisive and disruptive of the community. His response, like that of ministers observed by Pope in Gastonia, was to divert workers' attention from the strike to religion. Swinney did not intend to help the mill owners at the expense of the mill workers but to heal what he saw as a wound in the community. Like many other ministers, Swinney believed that the adoption of Christian values by individual men and women was the solution to social problems. He hoped that mill owners and managers would share those values, but his particular audience was mill workers. Avoiding the issue of power within the mills, Swinney turned to the Lord to arbitrate the strike and accepted the ultimate resolution as something beyond his control.

But the aftermath of the strike led to a crisis that Swinney refused to leave in the Lord's hands. In 1935 Burlington Mills decided to sell the Piedmont Heights mill houses. Swinney quite correctly perceived the danger to his carefully wrought community. Although the mill gave villagers the first option to buy, Swinney and his wife feared that some church members might decide to leave. As Etta Gay remembered, "When they sold the houses to individuals, we thought we were ruined."[94] Swinney once more took his rhetorical powers into the streets and persuaded members of the congregation to buy their houses from the mill and stay.

Ina Lee Wrenn and her husband had moved to Burlington from the nearby village of Glencoe and had begun working in the Pioneer Plant in 1927. Ina Lee, too, credited Swinney with the gradual change in the village. She appreciated the fact that "people began to act like people" and she no longer had to go home immediately after work and stay there to avoid public rowdiness. When the sale of the mill houses began, the Wrenns intended to build a home away from the village, but Preacher Swinney heard about their plans first. "So he came there one night and talked to my husband about it. He wanted my husband to buy this place up here. He said they were going to try to keep all the older families, the settled people, or the people that went to church here that they could. And not just get in a whole bunch of new ones again. And he prevailed with my husband."[95]

The selling off of the mill village, which at first presented the possibility of a community's demise, in the end actually strengthened the influence of the Glen Hope Church. The sale presented Swinney with the opportunity to continue his policy of culling the mill village population by encouraging respectable Christian folk to stay. The purchase of a mill house implied a commitment to the community and alleviated the problem of a chronically shifting population.[96]

At the same time that Swinney was shaping a community of people with shared values—values that often tolerated only a narrow range of behavior—he also propounded a doctrine that encouraged workers to speak for themselves, a doctrine that could be interpreted to sanction both individual and collective action. Along with salvation through faith, baptism by immersion, and separation of church and state, Baptist theology espoused the independence of each congregation and the freedom of individual and collective worship. Baptists valued democracy, as the Reverend Robert Latta attested. "In Baptist churches people feel free to complain. Baptist churches are supposed to be a democracy, you know, one of the last bastions of democracy we have, and they just feel like they've got a right to complain. One of the things that Baptists have always held dear, that although the minister occupied a place of prominence, that he is really no different from them. No more important. God may speak to them just as much as He may speak to the minister. When it comes to making a decision, the person in the pew has just as much authority as anybody else to cast his vote as to which way he wants to go, so far as the church is concerned."[97]

The strength of this belief carried over into the mill. Some church members found in their theology an endorsement of a political form of fellowship and a justification for joining the union—even for striking. But for others the evangelical emphasis on individual responsibility worked against trade unionism. According to his son, Ralph Latta was a case in point. "My dad worked in the mills all of his life and he never made three dollars an hour. In spite of all the bad conditions and the low wages and everything else, he was always antiunion. He didn't want somebody else coming in and trying to run things. If conditions weren't like he thought they ought to be, he didn't mind speaking up."[98]

This same independent-mindedness led Baptist churches to dismiss ministers with whom they disagreed. Swinney was an exception. But even he was not immune to the grumblings of his congregation, especially when his passion for revivals drew him away from Piedmont Heights. Swinney exhorted not only from his own pulpit but also from tents, tabernacles, and pulpits throughout the state. He was one of the first ministers to take to the airwaves, broadcasting the Lord's word over a weekly radio program. His popularity as a radio minister led to invitations to preach at revivals in Virginia, Tennessee, Georgia, and South Carolina, as well as in North Carolina. One year he spent more than forty weeks on the road, traveling with his own musicians and singers. People followed him from one meeting to the next, especially on Saturday nights. He was a vigorous, sometimes fiery, speaker with a rich resonant voice. He started out slowly and then "got airborne," preaching at a peak of intensity for ten to fifteen minutes before quickly closing and issuing an invitation to the people to respond to his message. At the end of a service he was wringing wet with sweat.[99]

Swinney had the utmost faith that God would provide the means for his words to be heard. The Latta family crisscrossed the Piedmont accompanying Swinney to hundreds of revivals. "I remember one night he was in revival," Robert Latta recalled, "and during the service a thunderstorm came up. The thunder was so loud that you could hardly hear anybody, even when they tried to have a song service before the message. So when it came time for him to bring his message, it was just all anybody could do to hear with the thunder and lightning. And I'll never forget. He stepped up to the pulpit and said, 'Let's pray.' I was close enough, I guess, I could hear. I don't remember his exact words, but he said, 'Lord, I came here tonight to do your will. This is your business. And the people can't hear me with the thunder and lightning. If you want me to preach tonight, you stop it!' The thunder stopped and you could have heard a pin drop. And he preached. You can imagine the impression that made on that church that night."[100]

Some members of the congregation felt that Swinney should not spend so much time away from his home pulpit. The deacons raised this issue at one meeting, but Swinney declared that he would offer his resignation before he would give up his travels. The deacons did not press the matter. Although the church was the joint creation of Preacher Swinney and the mill villagers, Swinney's position led him to assume a proprietary role. "He kinda felt like the church was his," Ralph Latta explained, "He knew it wasn't and if you asked him, [he'd say], 'No, it's not mine, it belongs to the people,' which was right. But he organized it; he seen it grow from nothing. And a man can't help but feel—We referred to it a lot of times, I do now, as 'Preacher Swinney's church.' But that was just a saying, nobody believed that."[101]

In most ways Swinney more than satisfied his congregation. The religion he brought to Glen Hope grew out of his rural and mill village background and met the needs of Piedmont Heights residents. Religion was a concrete affair for mill villagers. They expected their ministers to be visible symbols of their faith and objects of loyalty. Swinney was both. He preached a familiar theology in which the world was a battleground between the Lord and the Devil and souls were in mortal danger if their caretakers indulged in sin: card playing, dancing, gambling, drinking, or swimming with members of the opposite sex. Swinney had renounced those sins, and his life was a model for his congregation. Although his long absences from the pulpit were disturbing, their cause, spreading the Lord's word through revivals, was admirable.[102]

Swinney continued to preach at Glen Hope until a heart attack at the age of seventy-six forced him to retire from the pulpit. His forty-year pastorate was most unusual. Mill village Baptist churches normally had a very high turnover of ministers. Typically, ministers had more education than mill workers and came from cultural backgrounds unlike their congregation's, making it difficult for them to understand and sympathize with workers' needs. In the 1920s mill villagers across the Piedmont turned away from Baptist and Methodist churches toward emerging sects like the Church of God, Pentecostal Holiness, and Free-Will Baptist, whose preachers were often fellow mill workers. Sect churches were filled with warmth, enthusiastic preaching, and a "vigorous emotional massage," which proved more compelling to mill workers than traditional services.[103]

Preacher Swinney managed to provide that warmth and enthusiasm within the boundaries of an established Baptist church. He had none of the fear or contempt for the sects that Liston Pope found among other Baptist and Methodist ministers. Sarah Andrews, baptized and born again under Swinney's influence, frequently played the piano and attended services at a nearby Holiness Church without ever feeling that she jeopardized her relationship with her pastor. Because of his background, his personality, and his skill and passion as a revivalist, Swinney combined both the stability of a traditional denomination and the fervor of the sects. Together, he and the villagers of Piedmont Heights built an institution that fulfilled their spiritual desires and became the polestar of the community.[104]

Swinney and his congregation fought hard for the godly life. By the mid-1930s they believed they had created an oasis of morality and righteousness in a world that had "turned upside down." But theirs was only one response to changing times. While members of Glen Hope Church battled ungodly behavior in their village, other activists seethed at the sins of mill owners who disregarded their obligations and stretched workers' endurance for a pitiful wage. When the New Deal created a political opening, these men and women acted on their anger and their dreams, drawing from a common heritage the moral authority for a stinging rebuke. In the conflict that followed, even Piedmont Heights was not immune.[105]

A Multitude of Sins

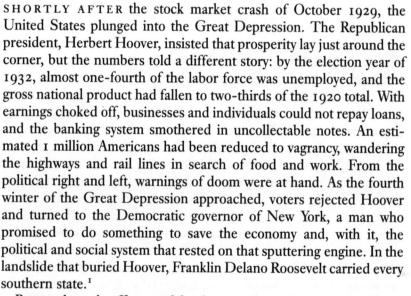

SHORTLY AFTER the stock market crash of October 1929, the United States plunged into the Great Depression. The Republican president, Herbert Hoover, insisted that prosperity lay just around the corner, but the numbers told a different story: by the election year of 1932, almost one-fourth of the labor force was unemployed, and the gross national product had fallen to two-thirds of the 1920 total. With earnings choked off, businesses and individuals could not repay loans, and the banking system smothered in uncollectable notes. An estimated 1 million Americans had been reduced to vagrancy, wandering the highways and rail lines in search of food and work. From the political right and left, warnings of doom were at hand. As the fourth winter of the Great Depression approached, voters rejected Hoover and turned to the Democratic governor of New York, a man who promised to do something to save the economy and, with it, the political and social system that rested on that sputtering engine. In the landslide that buried Hoover, Franklin Delano Roosevelt carried every southern state.[1]

Roosevelt took office on March 4, 1933, and moved swiftly to counter economic catastrophe. But the rapid-fire legislation that closed banks and set an agricultural revolution in motion did little for industry. Only the threat of a labor-backed bill that tackled unemployment by cutting the workweek to thirty hours prodded Roosevelt into action. On June 16, 1933—the ninety-ninth of the famous Hundred Days—the president signed the National Industrial Recovery Act (NIRA) into law.[2]

The NIRA, which lifted antitrust regulations and endorsed trade associations, drew on the legacy of World War I. It also reflected the political clout of the Cotton Textile Institute. Despite support from the owners of larger and better-established southern mills, the CTI had been unable to discipline small mills fighting for their piece of the economic pie. This minority of "nonconformers" ran night shifts and ignored the CTI's campaign for output restriction and price stabilization. By 1933 the CTI's leadership was ready to buttress voluntarism with government control. Backed by the CTI and other trade associations, the NIRA created a new federal agency, the National Recovery Administration (NRA). Under NRA direction, employers were allowed to draw up "codes of fair competition" designed to increase profits by controlling production, hours, and wages. At the same time, the NIRA's business architects accepted a provision pushed through by prolabor New Dealers such as Senator Robert F. Wagner of New York. Reviving the principles laid down by the National War Labor Board, Section 7(a) of the NIRA asserted the right of employees "to organize and bargain collectively through representatives of their own choosing."[3]

The CTI, headed by George A. Sloan, an energetic, hard-driving Vanderbilt Law School graduate and former army officer, moved at once to draw up the first of the NRA codes. The Textile Code incorporated Section 7(a) and provided for a minimum wage of twelve dollars per week (thirteen dollars for northern workers), a forty-hour week, and the prohibition of child labor. The CTI, in effect, became the Code Authority, with responsibility for enforcing the code, an extraordinary move by which private industry grasped public regulatory power. The United Textile Workers of America, representing less than 3 percent of the country's textile workers at the time, had virtually no say in the negotiations and no representation on the Code Authority. The only effective critic of these maneuvers was Senator James F. Byrnes of South Carolina, who insisted on a special committee to study the stretch-out and mediate related disputes. As a perceptive southern mill worker put it a few months later, "the mill men formulated . . . the textile code . . . themselves." Widely praised as a "remarkable . . . patriotic thing," the Textile Code—and the NRA—served the declared interests of industry.[4]

This outcome, however, was by no means obvious at the time. The NIRA was a patchwork of conflicting ideas. Its major premise was that scarcity could produce recovery: by restricting output, owners would drive up profits; the benefits would trickle down to workers, providing employment and insuring industrial peace. But the NIRA also contained the seeds of a federal labor policy, for Section 7(a) implied a connection between independent unions and collective bargaining on the one hand and better pay, purchasing power, and recovery on the other. General Hugh S. Johnson, the blustery head of the NRA, saw strikes as "acts of aggression that sabotaged the drive for recovery." Roosevelt himself was a "patron" of labor, more concerned with protective legislation than with helping workers to help themselves through unions. Yet Roosevelt did give Section 7(a) his tacit support, and no president before or since has so successfully conveyed the impression that ordinary people could confide in him personally and directly and that he had their interests at heart.[5]

The president launched the NRA's "great cooperative campaign" in a blaze of publicity. He used his fireside chats to rally popular opinion, urging radio listeners to write letters signifying their support. He compared the agency's emblem, a blue eagle with spread wings, to the bright badges worn by soldiers "in the gloom of night . . . to be sure comrades do not fire on comrades. On that principle, those who cooperate in this program must know each other at a glance." In the spirit of World War I's Liberty Bond drive, Hugh Johnson organized parades and deployed speakers. He called on housewives to boycott businesses that failed to display the Blue Eagle: "It is women in the homes—and not soldiers in uniform—who will this time save our country."[6]

In this oratory of patriotism and reform, southern workers heard a message directed to them. "I want you to know that I am for you in this most wonderful undertaking," Henry Coyle of Gaffney, South Carolina, wrote to Roosevelt. "I believe it will be a National Faith Recovery Administration. I am a long ways from you in distance yet my faith is in you my heart with you and I am for you sink or swim." In hundreds of similar letters, Coyle's fellow workers voiced a sense of civic responsibility, a willingness to take the law of the land at face value and grasp the possibility for self-empowerment it contained. To southern millhands, recovery legislation seemed to place the government's imprimatur on ideals of equity and cooperation. It ensured owners a fair return on investment but denied them, in the words of the Brandon Mill strikers of 1929, "the moral right to take advantage of the employes in order to pile up profits." Section 7(a) supplemented the eroding props of workers' independence with the possibility of formal workers' associations. Everyone, from the lowliest sweeper to the most skilled loom fixer, could sign on as "members of the NRA," joining a fervent campaign to put the industry, and the nation, back on their feet.[7] In all this, the New Deal resonated with the past even as it spoke

The Blue Eagle, symbol of the National Recovery Administration.

to present needs. But the NIRA also promised something altogether new: the intervention of the federal government as a lever against local elites and guarantor of workers' rights.

Hopes ran high throughout the spring and summer of 1933. Even before the Textile Code went into effect, its adoption touched off a speculative boom in the industry. Anticipating cost increases, which would result from the code itself as well as from a new processing tax on raw cotton authorized by the Agricultural Adjustment Act, manufacturers increased production, and buyers scooped up their inventories at a rapid clip. In June the Blue Eagle appeared in mill office windows all across the Piedmont, signaling compliance with the Textile Code. Prices, employment, and sales all climbed, and the industry enjoyed its most profitable year since 1928.[8]

By fall, however, recovery gave way to a season of discontent. It was one thing for trade associations to endorse the principle of self-regulation, but quite another for hard-pressed mills to sustain the short-term losses that lower production and higher labor costs might bring. And manufacturers had no intention of joining a "great cooperative movement" with organized labor or conceding an inch of authority on the factory floor. As demand dropped, a "bitter wail" went up against the cotton processing tax, mill men returned to the competitive strategies of the 1920s, and workers across the Piedmont began complaining about "Code chiselers" who defied the spirit and the letter of the NIRA.[9]

Addressing themselves to the president or to Hugh Johnson, men and women with little formal education labored to explain in writing "facts from my very heart," scratching their feelings on cheap ruled pads. They had read about the code or heard the news on the radio and felt duty-bound to tell the proper authorities how the Blue Eagle was faring in their locale. They began in a tone of familiarity and confidence: "You ask us over the Radio to write to you if we see where the N.R.A. do not help us Textile workers." "Just a few lines in regards to some conditions existing in [two] cotton mills of the Piedmont section of South Carolina." "It is one o'clock in the morning, I could not sleep for thinking of writing you and explaining how we are treated." Next came descriptions of the complex grievances that arose out of daily practices on the shop floor and accounts of the myriad ways in which owners circumvented "this wonderful law." Some writers stuck to detailed eyewitness reports. But as the Depression hit bottom in the winter of 1933–34, cotton mill people, "speaking for the human lives around me," searched for words adequate to convey ever-intensifying pain.[10]

The significance of this extraordinary correspondence between ordinary people and their government can scarcely be exaggerated. In the privacy of their homes, workers who lacked access to education and power—and thus the means of affecting public debate—spoke with candor about the most intimate details of their working lives. They did so with a cloud of fear and a knowledge of economic vulnerability hovering over every word. Southern millhands inhabited a world in which letter writing was a political act of enormous courage, and in case after case they closed with a plea for anonymity: it would cost them their jobs, and more, if mill officials knew what they had done. A woman with a "sick husband and children to support" tried to put her letter directly on a train because "the Washington mail is [being] watched here." Jessie Belk, who had just lost her job, wrote on behalf of the spinners and doffers of a Charlotte mill. "Please dont call my name," she pled twice in the course of an angry letter. "If you do they will fire my husband. . . . and we would finish starving to death." Even a foreman was not immune. "Please keep my name secret," wrote H. A. Lloyd, "or my job, such as it is, will not be worth five cents to me."[11]

Above all, these men and women spoke out against bosses who were trying to outproduce their competitors by "stretch[ing] out the stretch-out system." Nothing had made workers more "glad and Proud" than the eight-hour law. Henry Coyle, for one, had been ecstatic. "Honorable Mr Roosevelt. *Our President of the United States of America*," he wrote. "I want you to know that it is a great pleasure to me to see my people . . . who use to work from ten to twelve hours a day for such little pay. Now Working eight hours a day and walking around with a smile on their faces and a friendly howdy-do." But those smiles had vanished as men and women in every part of the mill found themselves doing as much work in eight hours as they had once done in twelve.[12]

The most notorious example of industry rationalization in the 1920s had been the multiple-loom system. It had targeted the more highly paid workers, many of whom were adult men, and under the Textile Code their situation continued to deteriorate. "We are being worked so hard until we just can not stand the strain," wrote "the oppressed weavers" of the Fulton Bag and Cotton Mill in Atlanta. "Our wages are practially the same as when we were only operating half the number of looms we are now forced to operate if we hold our jobs. . . . It is Nattrely Killing poor cotton mill folks."[13]

In some ways the stretch-out of 1933 seemed but a continuation of established trends. Writing to "the greatest women in the world"— Eleanor Roosevelt and Secretary of Labor Frances Perkins—a young girl in Conestee, South Carolina, traced her family's spiraling fortunes to the late 1920s, summing up the experiences of a people in an account of her own special woes. Her father had died on Christmas Eve, 1928, "leaving my mother with 15 . . . small children I am 16 years old now at the age of six years old I had TB of the hip bone [extrapulmonary tuberculosis] I was at hayes hospital clinton S C I stayed one year in [plaster of Paris] and i went from there to Shriners hospital there I had and opration on my hip 3 three times so I am cripled for Life ... i am unedeucatied not able to do no labor work.... my mother was runing 22 Looms making from 19 to 22 dollars per week ... then in 1931 1932 they streched out and put her on 40 Looms her average wages was 11 and 12 dollars per week then they streched out to 50 and 60 Loom and She countent make production they turned her off would not Let her work there. She was with us Little children for the mercy of the world to feed."[14]

Still, code chiseling went beyond anything southern millhands had known before. Automation and formal attempts at scientific management had been limited for the most part to larger, more prosperous mills. As long as they could pay low piecework rates, small undercapitalized firms had often kept less productive employees on the payroll. Children, older people, mothers bearing the burden of a double workday—such workers might not produce as much as young adults, but they were valued as a reserve of cheap labor. Minimum wage standards changed all that. Spurred by rising labor costs, mills of all kinds climbed aboard the rationalization bandwagon, culling out weaker workers and tightening the workday by methods that seemed cold-blooded and crude.

Textiles had always been a "young people's industry." With no savings, pensions, or Social Security to fall back on, millhands worked as long as they possibly could. But earnings peaked at age thirty, then declined. When production quotas doubled, older workers were often the first to go. A sixty-year-old sweeper, an employee of twenty-six years, found his workload doubled. The "Pore old man all most gave out and the Boss weaver told him if he could not do the Job he Did not want him." A spooler with a sick husband and five children to support was laid off when she couldn't make production. "You will have to get some of that production off the hands," she wrote to the NRA, "so the older and Middle race can work to Make a living as well as the younger race." P. M. Mooney from Columbia, South Carolina, summed it up: "The time is near at hand when there will be no old people in the mill villages because of the Stretch-out-System."[15]

If the assault on the weave room had symbolized the reorganization of work in the 1920s, the spinners' plight told the story of 1933. Most spinners were women; their wages hovered near the bottom of the scale; and they stood to benefit most from the minimum wage. For that very reason, the stretch-out hit hardest at them. In mill after mill, officials pegged the twelve-dollar weekly wage to production quotas that only the fastest workers could meet. "The mill man ar laying off all the hand that cant make 12$ on the Job So thay can work the best hand at 12$." "Last nite thay cut of women with little children and they sed it was Pitiful to here them crying and beggin on account of thir children." "Would you let the people in the Pacific Mills starve to death?" asked a nineteen-year-old spinner. "That's exactly what is going to happen if something is[n't] done about it. They are being cut off in big droves."[16]

Those who did manage to hold on to their jobs found work "unbearable." "One of the boss men told my sister if they did go on eight hours and pay $12.00 a week that they would sure put out some hard work for it," wrote one spinner. Driven "faster and faster and then FASTER," women left the mills dog-tired. "When i came out of the mill down here last Friday evening I had worked so hard till I felt like I was nearer dead than I was liveing I wondered if I would ever get home seem to me like that every step would be the last one I couldn't even walk straight I had worked so hard till I just staggered like a drunk man and I wasn't the only girl that come out of the mill in that condition." Outsiders confirmed women's complaints. The stretch-out is "eating the very heart out of these workers," cried a salesman who came "in very intimate personal contact with hundreds and thousands" of cotton mill folk. Some likened the mills to "slave driven [sweat] shops." Others swore, "They are killing the women."[17]

Mill folk treasured the sociability, dignity, and autonomy they had carved from the hard rock of factory labor, and nothing more vividly reveals their sense of loss than the metaphors of slavery and emancipation that laced their letters to Roosevelt. Throughout American history the notion of "wage slavery" had symbolized the threat that capitalism posed to the republican principles of independence and control over the fruits of one's own labor. Slaves, for their part, had seen themselves as God's chosen people, destined for deliverance like the Children of Israel. Mill workers drew on both traditions, combining the language of republicanism with Old Testament images to describe the blow they had sustained.

"Men and women are being killed inch by inch by this terrible system," wrote one man. "During the last few years men have been carried away from their work dead or unconscious. I ask you to read of the cruelty of Pharoah to the Israelites to get a comparison. Although the Israelites worked in fresh air while the mill people are shut in and have to breathe the same air over and over again. . . . For God's sake and humanity's sake deliver these people from a hell on earth." A letter from North Charlotte took up the theme. "We are just like the Children of Israel were while They were under bondage. only They were driven with sticks and clubs. and we are forced with athority." And a Greenville, South Carolina, worker contrasted present realities with the dream of liberty nourished by the Great War. "The stretch out system is worse than Roman slavery. If our government had surrendered their arms to the Kaiser of Germany in 1918 our textile people would have been better off."[18]

No wonder the stretch-out was so bitterly contested, for at its heart lay the issue of labor control. "Unfair workloads" were prohibited by the Textile Code; but mill owners remained the arbiters of fairness, and they were determined to keep it that way. When the UTW and other critics urged the NRA to set standard workloads for the entire industry, Joseph E. Sirrine, a textile engineer from Greenville, spoke most authoritatively in the industry's defense. In a pamphlet written for the CTI in 1934, he portrayed the stretch-out as a simple, and inevitable, matter of managerial and technological progress. Sirrine rested his argument on a comparison with the automobile industry, in which Henry Ford had pioneered high wages and the moving assembly line as an effective means of extracting high levels of productivity with a minimum of personal supervison. In an automobile plant the speed of the assembly line determined the amount of time a worker could allot to each task. In textiles, production depended on many variables—the quality of the yarn, the humidity of the atmosphere, the condition of the machines, the will and ability of the operative. Under such conditions there were two routes to labor discipline: piece rates and hard-driving supervision on the one hand (overseers who "could look mean and 'cuss' big") or automation and scientific management on the other. In either case, only the individual mill owner could decide, from day to day, how many machines each worker could comfortably tend. According to Sirrine, concerns about the stretch-out were misplaced: excessive machine loads would result in inferior cloth; no "right-thinking employer" could afford to "impose an undue burden on his workers. . . . [Each employer must] be in a position to work out his problems in his own way." Neither government regulations nor workers' desires could be permitted to dilute this most essential aspect of management's authority.[19]

While employees described conditions so bad "it is filling the Hospitials with almost complete invalids" and driving people "into insanity," industry spokesmen maintained, as they had throughout the 1920s, that the stretch-out was "a Blessing When Properly Applied."[20] Ignoring the notion that overproduction was one of the major ills the Textile Code was supposed to cure, they argued that the installation of new, more efficient machines and a further subdivision of tasks would eliminate the need for old-style authoritarianism and increase productivity, while increased productivity would translate into higher wages for everyone. Such arguments rang increasingly hollow as evidence mounted that automation and production quotas were being used as a bludgeon to drive the defenseless—or the rebellious—out of the mills, thus adding to unemployment and eroding the market for consumer goods. Even the *Southern Textile Bulletin* admitted that there were instances of abuse. What workers passionately reported, subsequent events confirmed: individual mill men, acting in their own self-interest, nullified the benefits of shortened hours both for workers and for themselves as a group. By the fall of 1933 production once more outran demand, warehouses bulged with unsold goods, and textile workers by the thousands joined the ragged ranks of the unemployed.

In contrast to the provision for "fair" machine loads—where the industry's commitment to new forms of labor discipline was at stake—the Textile Code's wage guidelines appear to have been generally observed. The impact was negligible in the North, where most workers already earned at least thirteen dollars a week. But in the South, where even in the 1920s textile wages hovered 25 percent below those paid in other parts of the country, a twelve-dollar wage base made a difference. The hourly earnings of southern women workers doubled between July 1933 and August 1934, while men's rose by 70 percent. Between 1933, just before the Textile Code went into effect, and the winter of 1934, the North-South wage differential fell from 39 to 18 percent.[21]

Yet income rivaled the stretch-out as a source of workers' discontent. For one thing, even twelve dollars a week (or $624 a year) was hardly a living wage. At that rate, the millhand lucky enough to work full time would have earned considerably less than the amount one scholar calculated as the minimum budget necessary to keep "the wolf of starvation" from a family's door. For another, the millhand who worked full time was rare indeed.[22]

The length of the workweek in textiles had always been erratic and arbitrary, and the problem had intensified in the 1920s. In order to keep extra workers around, managers routinely sent full-time employees home for a day or two a week, while spare hands took over their machines. When business was slow or warehouses were overstocked, mills shifted to "short time," then operated around the clock when orders came in. The Textile Code institutionalized such practices, allowing the Code Authority to set industrywide production schedules, and thus manipulate hours and wages, without labor's consent. In December 1933 and again in May 1934 the Code Authority responded to the problem of swollen stocks by mandating a 25 percent cut in machine hours. Many mills simply shut down every fourth week, slicing wages accordingly.

In earlier times mill workers had adjusted to such fluctuations by leaving for another mill or falling back on traditional ways of making-do. Now—with little choice, but with new leverage—they appealed to the NRA. "These mills are carrying out a program of curtailing operations which is putting thousands of workers on the verge of destitution," wrote a foreman at the Cramerton Mills in Gaston County. "Very few of them are getting to work as much as forty hours a week, and thousands of them are getting to work only eight hours a week." Evidence of low weekly earnings poured in from across the South. A woman from Belmont, North Carolina, enclosed a pay stub totaling $4.20. Her question was simple: How can we live on that?[23]

The problem, as government investigators saw it, was that workers "misunderstood" the code and assumed that it promised twelve dollars a week no matter how many hours they worked, when in fact the mandated minimum was thirty cents an hour, which would add up to twelve dollars only for a full forty-hour week. There was misunderstanding, to be sure, but the problem ran deeper than that. In the excitement surrounding the formulation of the Textile Code, not even UTW leaders had realized the extent of discretionary power retained by the industry. Mill folk knew that curtailments were eating away the minimum wage, and they could trace quite accurately how it all began. "I'll tell you from experience," a woman from Belmont explained. "Work [used to be] easy but the boss men kept getting more and more [overbearing] each day. . . . As the years flew by and the depression came on, curtailment began. wages were cut in half. and more work put on the workers."[24] At issue was the owners' right to such unilateral power. If management could dictate nationwide curtailments, and thus erase wage gains, what happened to the "great cooperative movement" in which workers thought they were engaged? What happened to the New Deal's promise of a fair return for willing labor?

Short time—that is, weeks of less than forty hours' work—was the key, but it was not the only threat to workers' hopes for a living wage. Some renegade mills simply ignored the law, paying less than the minimum even for full-time work.[25] Such practices may have been the exception rather than the rule, but word traveled fast through textile communities, and these mills symbolized for workers the impunity with which owners could disregard the law. More commonly, managers continued the old trick of manipulating job classifications to their own advantage. Men and women found themselves reclassified into categories such as learner, cleaner, or outside worker that were exempt from the minimum wage. Experienced hands suffered the indignity of being classified as "learners" and paid little or nothing at all.[26]

Taken together, short time, production curtailments, and job reclassifications undermined the minimum wage just as the stretch-out spoiled the eight-hour day. This was the way workers summed up the motive, the method, and the crime: The mill men want to pay "the people the very least they can get by with"; they "are doing all they can to get Back on Long hours and a starvation wage"; they "seem to pick every tecnical point possible to defeat The Code of fair Competition and to hold labor down." By August 1934 only 37 percent of the men and 16 percent of the women in southern mills had realized the promise of a twelve-dollar week.[27]

Minimum wage rates did have one major effect: they practically obliterated customary differences between the highest- and lowest-paid occupations in the mill. Investigating charges that the minimum had become the maximum, the U.S. Bureau of Labor Statistics emphasized three points. The first was that in many jobs—particularly those held by women—twelve dollars was, in fact, the most that anyone could earn. The second was that wage scales had indeed flattened, although differentials had not disappeared. The third was that this flattening had occurred because unskilled workers were making more, not because skilled workers were making less.[28]

To many workers, this last point flew in the face of experience. It did not take into account job reclassifications. Nor did it speak to the disappointment of experienced weavers whose paychecks shrank when they worked forty hours at the same hourly wage they had previously drawn for a fifty-hour week. At issue, too, were arbitrary definitions of "skill." Men and women throughout the mill took pride in good work, in giving "perfect satisfaction." They rejected a one-dimensional equation between speed and skill and insisted that experience should count for something; wage levels that ignored long years of hard work and small moves up the job ladder posed a threat to social identity. Fifteen twisters complained that "the hands has ben treated [awful] durty. . . . They . . . just pay us hands that is learnt the same wages [as] the hands that are learning . . . and clame it is all [unskilled] labor." Mill officials say it doesn't take "skill labor to operate machinery in the mills. . . . [If] from 5 to 20 years is not considered skilled work I would like to know what would be a skilled worker in the cotton mills."[29]

To make matters worse, even when wages did go up, hikes in the cost of living undermined the gain. Regional wage differentials had been sanctioned by the Textile Code on the grounds that southern workers enjoyed a lower cost of living than their counterparts in the North. Questionable on its face, that argument lost force when the cost of goods purchased by textile workers rose more steeply in the South than in the North. Some workers blamed the situation on owners who tried to offset wage increases by charging for water and electricity and upping the rent on company houses. Although probably not widespread, such practices were maddening because they violated customary rights and underscored the shoddiness of mill housing. "Since the N.R.A. Law was passed our wages were raised," conceded one woman. "But since then we have to pay house rent light bill encluding water which we dont have in the house . . . our water comes from pumps in the street." Another man rejected out of hand the argument that in-kind contributions made up for low wages: "We all pay for our Watter and Lights and house Rent and coal and Wood thay Dont Give us Nothing But hard Work." The problem, in any case, was broader; costs rose across the board. In 1933, for instance, the North Carolina General Assembly passed a 3 percent sales tax—despite arguments that such a tax imposed an unfair burden on workers and that it would decrease demand and deepen the depression. Earning so little to begin with, some southern millhands had taken home delightfully fatter paychecks when the code went into effect. No wonder they protested when curtailments caused their real income to plunge by 25 percent, leaving them virtually no better off than when the NRA experiment began.[30]

Dips in real income registered quickly on workers who "live right up to every penny we make," and their grasp of the situation was subtle and clear. One woman pointed out the injustice of a regressive sales tax and the absurdity of the notion that North Carolina workers were faring well in a low-cost-of-living state. "What is 12 dollar per week for a family at the price everything is selling at & 3 cent sale tax on every dollar to save the big realestate man & the rich property owners." A seventeen-year-old girl was urged by her co-workers to ask the NRA to eliminate the wage differential. "We are citizens of the United States & we should receive as much for our services as paid elsewhere. Though we are Southeren people it takes just as much to live on as it does anywhere. . . . Though lot of stuff is raised down here that doesnt prove that we can live for nothing. . . . We just cant raise clothes which we need as much as food even if we do raise a very few vegetables in summer we cant in winter. So just imagine you are one of us for about thirty minutes just a poor cotton Textile worker . . . how would you feel if it were you[?]"[31]

A letter to the *Charlotte Observer* made a valiant effort to show an indifferent or hostile public exactly what had happened to the standard of living under the NIRA.

I am a textile worker. Since the early age of twelve I've shuffled up and down the hot, noisy, smelly alleys of a cotton mill, working in practically every department. I know my associates, better I believe, than the average outsider. And because of this I'm in position to write about them in my own humble way.

That many of my assertions will be denied or disbelieved is, of course, to be expected. Consequently I shall confine myself in statements which are capable of substantiation.

So I'll turn back the pages, and we will see what was going on before the NRA was ever born. . . .

My weekly earnings [as a speeder] averaged $11.50. I was supporting, (or trying) a family of five. Here's how I spent my hard earned $11.50.

Grocery bill. . .$7.00
Clothes. . .Nothing

Rent. . .Free
Fuel. . .$1.00
Doctor. . .Nothing
Dentist. . .Nothing
School books (for the year). . . $2.15
Church. . .10 cents
Insurance. . .$1.25
Luxuries. . .Nothing
Total. . .$11.50

Under the code I'm paid $12.00 weekly (the minimum) as a skilled workman. My family hasn't decreased. And thank God it hasn't increased. Here's my new budget.

Grocery bill (at increased prices under NRA). . .$8.40
Clothes. . .Nothing
Rent. . .$1.50
Fuel. . .$1.00
Doctor. . .Nothing
Dentist. . .Nothing
School books. . .Nothing
Church. . .Nothing
Insurance. . .$1.10
Luxuries . . .Nothing
[Total . . . $12.00]

If there's a statistician or budget fiend that can show me how to cut my budget so I can do better, his efforts will be appreciated.[32]

Textile trade associations had eagerly embraced wage-and-hour legislation, and industry leaders continued to support those provisions of the Textile Code despite the mounting evidence that many mills were circumventing the law. Not so, Section 7(a), which had been tacked on to the recovery program by New Deal friends of labor. To its advocates, Section 7(a) embodied the principles of worker self-organization, election of representatives without interference from management, and majority-rule collective bargaining. To industrialists, the clause was a bothersome concession, palatable only because of its vagueness and lack of enforcement procedures and because it could, in any case, be interpreted to sanction company unions. Vacillating between the two positions was the Roosevelt administration, unclear about what Section 7(a) meant or how it could be implemented but hopeful that the NIRA would guarantee industrial peace rather than ignite labor conflict.[33]

To millions of American workers, by contrast, the law's meaning seemed plain: just as the NIRA sanctioned employers' associations, so it endorsed and protected employees' organizations. That interpretation was reinforced by labor insurgents who would eventually break with the AFL to form the Congress of Industrial Organizations. Astute, aggressive organizers such as John L. Lewis of the United Mine Workers issued a compelling summons: "The President wants you to join the union." And mine workers throughout the southern mountains answered his call. The UTW, on the other hand, failed to grasp the opportunities presented by the NIRA. It launched no Piedmont organizing campaign. Agents did not throng to the southern field. Yet within less than a month after passage of the act, union locals had reportedly sprung to life in 75 percent of South Carolina's mills. From an estimated 40,000 in September 1933, UTW membership leaped to 270,000 by August 1934. To the shock of labor leaders, government officials, and businessmen alike, southern workers began "organizing Just as fast as we can."[34]

At the outset, local unionists viewed themselves less as management's adversaries than as willing partners in a grand patriotic enterprise. Some formed completely independent workers' organizations, such as the "American Workers Protective Association," which wrote its own constitution "built on the principles of the National Recovery Act" and endeavored "to bring forth normal conditions in our section as set forth in this Act." Here and there, loom fixers organized along craft lines. But most southern millhands tried to "band together and stand for there right[s]" as locals of the UTW. "We want to organize and support the NRa do our part and stand by our president," explained UTW members demanding an end to layoffs at South Carolina's giant Pelzer plant. "To increase buying power the wheels of industry must turn."[35]

Management gave its habitual response: appeals to company loyalty, threats to shut down the mill, aspersions against the UTW, and wholesale firings and lockouts of union members. At a Shelby, North Carolina, mill, overseers took UTW members aside and showed them articles in the *Southern Textile Bulletin* proving that the "Union was RUSSIAN REDS" and that only "dam fools would join." Undaunted, the local's president went to the mill office to ask for a 25 percent raise.

The answer: "You are not going to get any 25% raise; [we will] shut down and order the hands to move." A South Carolina worker reported that a card room overseer had driven a union speaker away from the mill and announced "that he hope the time would come when people would have to get on their Knees and Beg him for Bread." The night boss in the weave room of a South Carolina mill led a small posse of second hands in an attack on a union member. First they took him to the mill's stair tower and told him, "If you are here at daylight you will be strung up." When the man refused to leave, they held a gun to his head and dragged him from the mill.[36]

Much of this wrangling took place between boss men and workers on the factory floor. But when the situation became serious, mill presidents and treasurers joined the fray. In October 1933 workers at Stonecutter Mills in Spindale, North Carolina, organized a UTW local. Stonecutter president, Kenneth Simpson (K. S.) Tanner, son of Bobo Tanner, the pioneer textile entrepreneur, responded with the time-honored tactic of the yellow-dog contract. By January 24, 1934, he was claiming that three-fourths of his employees had signed a pledge not to join the union but to "take up their business direct and individually" with him. Unionists disputed the numbers and swore that those who signed had been coerced. Overseers had called "girls into a vacant room and bluffed them into signing the petition . . . without reading it under threat of loosing their job." Meanwhile, the weavers were told that the the mill would shut down if the majority "did not sign up."[37]

Tanner also took the ideological offensive, circulating a "Heart to Heart Talk" meant to counter the growth of union-mindedness at his mill. His appeal rested on an ironic contrast: the bad old days of his father's generation versus the progress of his own.

Thirty-five years ago, mill people had no water or lights in their homes. They trudged through muddy streets to the mill, where they worked eleven to twelve hours a day. . . . A "good" superintendent or overseer was one who could look mean and "cuss" big.

But as the years went by great improvements were made. As the textile industry grew, mill companies began to consider the welfare of employees. Tremendous sums have been spent for recreation and education. . . . There are Y.M.C.A.'s, community buildings, night schools, kindergartens, domestic science classes, swimming pools, parks, playgrounds, textile bands, baseball, gardens and flowers. . . . Superintendents and overseers must now be kind and considerate. No cursing. . . . There is a fine spirit of brotherly love manifest between employer and employee. Each needs the other and must work together for mutual good.

Into this idyll, Tanner continued, a new threat had come. Labor unions, which had ruined hundreds of mills "up North" were now coming "down South," smuggled in by a false interpretation of the NIRA. "If we turn against our employers, can we blame them if they withdraw support from our churches, schools, baseball teams, and all the things that have meant so much to us? Can we blame them if they charge us regular prices for coal, and ask the same rent as such houses usually rent for? . . . We can kill every kind feeling of brotherly love. Instead of friendship and sympathy in time of trouble we can have cold, calculating indifference. . . . And we can ruin and close down our mills and throw thousands out of employment to become objects of charity. *Let us count the cost before we go too far.*"[38]

When neither brotherly love nor veiled threats prevailed, Tanner, and others like him, simply fired union members, a tactic usually justified by the image of union organizers as "outside agitators" who brandished false promises and fattened on union dues. Necessity, however, gave this practice a new twist. Now it was the federal government, represented by an enormously popular president, that seemed to be stirring up the hornet's nest of unionization, while many locals were self-organized and UTW organizers were actually few and far between. Besides, by almost any interpretation, Section 7(a) frowned upon firings for union membership alone. For both these reasons, subterfuges had to be found. In most cases the excuse was inferior work, an accusation that was hard to bear and virtually impossible to disprove.

Laura McGhee had worked for thirty-five years at the famous Graniteville Mills in South Carolina. And for thirty-five years she had, as she put it, "kept up my job and given perfect satisfaction." Indeed, her "work was the best work that any worker could do." She had never joined a union, for reasons that to her seemed the essence of common sense. "There was no union whatever in Graniteville S. C. before the National Industrial Recovery Act was made law as the Employers would not allow it . . . they would discharge anyone who joined a Union, but after the Law was passed and put in effect, we thought that we would be protected by the Federal Government [and] that no Employer could discharge any worker because they joined a Union of their own choosing." On June 19, 1933, just three days after Roosevelt signed the NIRA, McGhee paid her dues and proudly became a "Full Member" of a new UTW local. She held "small group meetings" in her house and entertained UTW representatives when they came to town. On August 8 the second hand got orders to fire her on the grounds that she "couldn't keep up [her] work." If her work had not been satisfactory, she concluded, they would have fired her long before. They "discharged me for Joining the Union."[39]

Long and faithful employment was no defense. A loom fixer who had worked at the Pacolet Mill in South Carolina since he was nine years old took a deep interest in the union and lost his job on that account. Also fired for union activity were "life livers" at Graniteville Mills. "I was born here," wrote one stalwart, "and most of the union folks are old citizen of this place."[40]

With such experiences behind them, southern unionists began to see organization not as a means of cooperation but as preparation for a fight. The president of a Forest City local—who was "one hudred per cent union and will be till [Gabriel] blows the last trumped"—called on Roosevelt to intervene before "WE HAVE TO CALL OUR UNION MEMBERS TO ARMS AGINST THIS FORKED TAIL EVIAL." "Since the People are getting tired of being Knocked [around] and treated like dogs they are going to be a bad times down here," warned an anonymous employee at the Dunean Mill in Greenville. "If we cant get work [we'll] make them shut the mill down if it takes fighting to do it. . . . if aint something done at once is going to be war."[41]

As predicted, a wave of wildcat strikes like those of 1929 rolled across the country. Forced to respond to this unexpected turn of events, on August 5, 1933, Roosevelt created the National Labor Board (NLB) to settle disputes. The NLB, though it lacked legal clout, began hammering out enduring principles of labor law. Unfortunately for millhands, the NLB had no authority over industries whose codes already provided for labor boards. Textile firms fell under the jurisdiction of the Cotton Textile National Industrial Relations Board, which had emerged haphazardly out of a committee to study the stretch-out. Overwhelmed by the sheer volume of code violation complaints, NRA director Hugh Johnson had transformed the study committee into an all-purpose labor board headed by Robert W. Bruere of New York, an economist, editor, and arbitrator. The Bruere Board, as it came to be known, appointed state boards representing management, labor, and the public. These boards, in turn, set up committees in each mill to adjust differences between managers and workers. In practice, this rickety administrative structure proved totally inadequate to its task. Few state boards ever materialized; mill committees, where they appeared at all, functioned under management's thumb; and the Bruere Board followed the incredible procedure of forwarding complaints to the Code Authority—headed by George Sloan and synonymous with the CTI.[42]

Through the fall and winter of 1933–34, southern workers combined attempts at self-organization with good-faith appeals to the Bruere Board. South Carolina's Horse Creek Valley, one of the South's oldest textile centers, a union stronghold in the nineteenth century, and a center of UTW strength during World War I, was a case in point. Naomi Duke had worked at the Bath Mill for eighteen years, "did the work alright, had no kick on it," until she and her relatives joined the UTW. "And from that time on the Union people have been fired until there are more than 100 families out of work." Mills throughout the valley "all display the Eagle. *We Do Our Part*, and we go ask for work they say they do not need help, and every day people come here and go right to work. Some come as far as 100 miles and we are left to starve."[43]

Soon, workers at Bath, Graniteville, and other Horse Creek Valley mills went out on strike "to make the mills live up to the code." The state appeals board apparently persuaded the companies to put strikers back to work, but this seeming victory turned quickly into a de facto lockout. "The Mill Company's are still fighting us," reported Mrs. J. W. Hallman. "They claim we quit our jobs and if we get back we will either take any job we can get or drop our Union and beg back our job. But my honest belief is that we can't put over the president's new deal the N.R.A. and go back and beg." Critical to the union's ability to hold out were New Deal federal relief programs for the unemployed that forbade discrimination against strikers. But as with other New Deal efforts, local control effectively countered national policy. How, Mrs. Hallman asked, can we fight to "win our rights" when the president of Graniteville Mills is chairman of the county relief committee? "The relief workers get their orders from him. . . . They think they will be able to . . . starve us out [and] force us to do there bidding And there wont be any thing to the N.R.A. in the south." Evictions and blacklisting followed. "They happen to have our name where ever we go. they no you are from the vally." As the conflict dragged on, Horse Creek Valley legislators introduced a bill prohibiting evictions "during the depression and emergency." The bill failed, but it indicated both the extent of the crisis and the efforts of mill workers to make themselves heard in public, political debate.[44]

Until the Great Depression, political letter writing was a male, and mostly urban, upper-class affair. The 1920s, however, set the stage for change. Radio broadcasts gauged listeners' interests by urging them to write to their local stations. In the early 1930s news programs gained prominence, informing a vast audience about national and international events, and listeners transferred the habit of letter writing to the radio news. The Depression lent special urgency to federal policies, and Franklin Roosevelt's mastery of the radio put him in touch with a grass-roots constituency in a way no president had been before. Roosevelt repeatedly urged people to write to him. And they did, in unprecedented numbers. Especially striking was the upsurge of political writing among groups that had seldom written before: farmers, laborers, southerners, and women.[45]

Nothing in the experience of mill village women encouraged political participation. They could not vote until the 1920s, and enfranchisement meant little to poor folk living in one-party states and unincorporated towns. Yet women were avid radio listeners and enthusiastic fans. Franklin Roosevelt was a master of the medium; gathering to hear his intimate fireside chats, women who had never seen themselves as political actors felt empowered to voice their opinions, confide in the president, and "join the NRA."

Verbal expressiveness lay at the heart of the "porch culture" through which women pieced together a neighborly, kin-oriented community life. Whether gossiping with friends or gathering in cottage prayer meetings, women put a premium on empathy and collaborative self-expression. By contrast, men congregated at the store and the pool hall; they played, fought, and made music together, communicating more through gesture and action than through words. In formal settings male oratory usually prevailed. But letters, written in private, drew on the female art of conversation; through vivid images and personal detail, they appealed to imagination; their goal was to persuade powerful men to walk for a moment in mill workers' shoes. Letters, of course, differ from speech; they are shaped for an audience and by stylistic convention. But in this case spontaneity and urgency narrowed the difference; the oral culture that flourished in the private domain carried over into women's efforts to put "facts from my very heart" into written form.[46]

This urgency grew in part out of women's roles as mothers, their responsibilities as mobilizers of family resources and nurturers of human life. But it also reflected their sense of themselves as *providers*, as participants in a culture of wage-earning work. To them, as to their menfolk, the iconography of the Blue Eagle evoked notions of political and industrial democracy. They may have been "poor widow women" or mothers worried on behalf of their children, but they were also protagonists in economic struggle, not supporting characters confined to the home. Some apologized for their boldness or their poor education; some spoke of special vulnerabilities. Yet by and large their letters stressed courage rather than weakness. These women believed they had a right and a duty to protest against "the condition of things here at our mills," and they expected their protests to be heeded by the leaders of their land.[47]

This double consciousness—this sense of self as both nurturer and wage earner—was rooted in the material realities of cotton mill life. From the outset, women had played an important role in the family wage economy. As the number of adult men in the textile work force rose, the proportion of women fell, but with the decline of child labor in the 1920s, the burden of wage earning that was lifted from the shoulders of young children came to rest on their mothers instead. Particularly striking was the increase of married women in the work force during the Great Depression, despite the widespread belief that scarce jobs should be reserved for men. In 1930 almost half of North Carolina's female textile workers were married; by 1940 that proportion had risen to nearly 72 percent. The age of the female labor force shifted upward as well. Whereas in 1930 around 36 percent of the state's women textile workers were between the ages of twenty-five and forty-four, by 1940 that figure stood close to 64 percent. The family labor system, which had characterized the industry from its earliest years, changed when children left the mill, but it did not disappear. As long as mill work paid "Just a niff to Keep Sole and Body to gather," families could survive only by pooling the wages of everyone over the legal working age of sixteen.[48]

A spooler who prided herself on being "a good hand with five years of experience back of me," had married a weaver and quit work when her babies came. Her husband died, and she went back to the mill.

"They gave me a trial only to lay me off because I could not get production under the code. I ask you what is to become of me and my little ones and others who are unemployed. . . . Are we to live on charity the remainder of our days? Are we to be given a chance to earn our bread? . . . We want justice. I appeal to you one and all in the name of God and for the sake of ragged and hungry children, what are you going to do about it?" For this woman the boundaries between "mother" and "worker" were permeable indeed. Pride in work coexisted with responsibility for children. She might have treasured a husband who earned enough to spare her the burden of a double working day, but she also valued the security of knowing that she was "a good hand." Deprived of a husband's support, she demanded not charity but justice and "a chance to earn our bread."[49]

Widowhood was only one of many twists of fate that could make a woman the chief breadwinner in a family—and then plunge families into frightening poverty. "[T]hey are ten (10) of us in family," wrote a woman from Lancaster, South Carolina. "My husban is not a able man to doe much work. . . . They was four (4) of us working an when the 8 Eight hour law came in they turned us all off. . . . I am in dibt an no job an am all most out of doores have not Bed Clothes to Keep us warm through the Cold Weather. . . . [W]e are Bair of clothes an Bair footed."[50]

Neither a working husband nor a two-parent income guaranteed security, as both men and women well knew. Jessie Belk had been spinning "ever since I was eleven years old and am now. . . the mother of 10 children." She had a "good working husband does not drink gambl or run around & spend what he makes." Still, he earned only thirteen dollars a week; worse, he had been out sick for two weeks when a stretch-out cost Belk her job. Reduced to a single paycheck when she was already in the hole, she used every cent she had to "pay for the babys milk. . . . My Kids are all naked for clothe and we dont hardly have bread to eat." Jessie Belk, too, hoped for intervention from the NRA so she "could work and help make bread for my babys." Preoccupied with a woman's responsibility for "bread making"—in all its dimensions—she traced even her most personal troubles to broader economic roots. "This city," she wrote, "dont try to help the mill People they just have to grub it out the best way they can." It was poverty that had ruined her husband's stomach. Who wouldn't be sick, she asked, if they had to "eat fat Back and grease three times a day"?[51]

Women were outraged when they found their wage-earning roles belittled and their jobs suddenly taken away. Della Turner was angry enough to report her treatment to a local magistrate. "Sent out" because "she couldnt run 10 sides," she went "back To The Mill the next night and Told The Boss she was a Widow Woman and had one child and No Means of [making] a living except by her work. The over Sear Told her to give her child away and get her a man to Take Care of her."[52]

The Depression breathed new life into the maxim that "a woman's place was in the home." According to a Gallup Poll conducted in 1936, 82 percent of Americans believed that employers should not hire married women.[53] Yet despite the intense competition for jobs in the textile industry and the fact that women benefited more from minimum wage legislation than did men, few millhands assumed that once a woman married she had a "man to take care of her" and should "go home."

There were those, like J. F. Chapman of Greenville, who suggested that Roosevelt "Pass a Law to cut all of these married Women off that has a husband Working." But in almost every case they were advocating an equal distribution of resources, not the exclusion of women from textile jobs. A weaver named M. J. James explained. "A man that has his wife at work in the mill, if they are both receiving $12 or $13 each they can live very well, and a man that has no help can not meet his expenses." As a consequence, "some of them are making good money others are from hand to mouth nearly Starving." Single women had special problems, since they earned less than men and were excluded from company-owned houses. Mary Howell wrote that "my father is dead and my mother cant take care of her self. . . . they layed me off because I wasnt living in they company houses. . . . and I couldnt live there by my self. . . . I think it would be better if they would let some of those married wemon stay at the house. and give some of those single people more of the work. that havnt got any husbands to work for us. nor havnt any homes." Most common of all were complaints aimed at lower level supervisors who took advantage of their power to consolidate their own families' positions in the mill. "As soon as the 8 hrs & $12 a week come in effect," a South Carolina man wrote, the section hands "laid others off & put their wives to work."[54]

In the 1930s, then, no less than before, millhands saw the family as the basic wage-earning unit. But that unit was now subject to new forms of stress and strain. When jobs had been plentiful, the family labor system could sometimes work to the employee's advantage; an overseer might "walk lightly" with an individual, lest a whole family take off for another mill.[55] With jobs scarce and hungry farmers waiting at the mill gate, the balance of power tipped the other way.

J. R. Livingston worked at a silk mill where they "dock the weaver for every defect whether the weaver is responsible or not. . . . I want my wife to quit. and she wants to quit. but we fear they will discharge me if she does. . . . They display the Blue Eagle. and in my opinion a firm who work a person for the verry meager wadge they pay every where at this time. and take part of that wadge away from them. knowing at the time they could not do so if Jobs were more planty full I say a firm or man who will do that is a disgrace to the Blue Eagle and should not be alowed to display same."[56]

The experiences of Mrs. B. M. Miller and Mrs. Viola Tate indicated that the Livingstons had reason to be afraid. Mrs. Miller worked at the Chadwick-Hoskins Mill in Charlotte. "They added so much to my job I simply couldnt keep it up. They kept adding on until I had three jobs. It was more than I could do so I had to quit. I thought I would get me a cow and stay at home with my children." Mrs. Miller's overseer saw her resignation as a protest against the stretch-out and fired her husband in retaliation. "I offered to go back on the job running it the best I could to keep from moving as we were in no shape to move but it was useless. They told us to get out. . . . Cold weather comming on and our children without food or clothes is just more than we [can] bear. Understand I am not asking for charity what we do want is work."[57]

Mrs. Tate was a weaver and her husband was a smash hand at the Pilot Mills in Raleigh, North Carolina. "They doubled up on him so much that the work began make him [nervous] and began to loose weight and his doctor advised him to change Job's so he has been asking thim for two months to give him a set of Looms." Finally, Mr. Tate could take no more; he "put in his notice" and told the overseer he "was giving up the smash Job." The following Monday morning, the overseer asked Mrs. Tate where her husband was. When she told him that Mr. Tate had "left to find work," he said, "You can go to." That evening he fired her son and son-in-law as well. I have been working here for twenty years, Mrs. Tate concluded, always gave "good work made perfect cloth and turned off good production never lose no time and now I have been . . . thrown out of a Job Through no fault of mine."[58]

In job consciousness, family orientation, and readiness to grasp the opportunities for protest offered by the NRA, there was much that men and women shared. But gender still had its impact on mill workers' lives. Unlike codes in other industries, the Textile Code did not institutionalize sex discrimination by sanctioning separate pay scales for men and women. Then again, as the Women's Bureau of the U.S. Department of Labor explained, the minimum wage it prescribed was "so low as to allow for a differential without providing a specific female exception." Despite the flattening of wage scales, women continued to earn less than men. Female letter writers did not point out this inequity; nor did they question a division of labor that gave them the major responsibility for cooking, cleaning, and child care even at a time when both women and men were being "worked to death."[59] But women's expectations of the NRA went beyond the letter of the law, and they used the forum it created to voice their concerns in their own special ways.

Some, like Syble Brown, the sixteen-year-old girl who suffered from "TB of the hip bone," wrote to Eleanor Roosevelt and Frances Perkins, assuming a bond of womanhood between themselves and the "greatest women" of the land. For a year, Mrs. R. S. Duckworth hesitated to say what was on her mind, wishing she had the "education to write our kind President and tell him of some of the hard ships we poor mothers of the textile communities are having." Finally, she decided to write to Mrs. Roosevelt instead. The result was an eloquent description of how a woman who had never done public work viewed her place in society and felt the Depression's sting. Until 1931, her husband made a good living, "but since then we have had a hard time trying to even feed and clothe our family. . . . our children haven't sufficient clothes to go to school and haven't all their books. I can't buy milk for them any more, and two of them need medical attention bad. I haven't been to church in nearly 3 years because I couldn't get decent clothes and part of the time my children had to stay out of Sunday School because of no clothes to wear. . . . We poor people of the labor class had great hopes when the N.R.A. was organized . . . but our hopes *have gone*, for we haven't been benefited because the mill owners haven't carried it out as the pres. meant it to be."[60]

Among women's unique concerns was the sexual dimension of economic power. Section hands threw their weight around by "cursing the ladies. I've heard them curse women in there and talk to them like dogs," Eula McGill recalled. "I heard language that I'd never heard in my life when I went in that mill; I'd never heard no such terms and profanity and vulgarity and just downright what people'd call gutter talk." During union organizing drives, women found "vulgar notes" on their machines, left there by antiunion workers with the tacit consent of management.[61]

There were also reports of sexual harassment of a more serious kind, which pointed a finger at unscrupulous boss men, not at workers on either side of the union divide. These letters seldom came from fathers or from the victims themselves. Instead, mothers intervened in their daughters' defense. In doing so, they portrayed male aggression as a many-sided threat. At stake was a young girl's integrity, a family's livelihood, and a parent's authority in the home.

A Charlotte widow found her family hounded from mill to mill. "I have four daughters who have to work in the Cotton Textile Mills an because they try to up hold their pride and will not go out with the Boss men these Boss men lays them off or fines them now this was the case at the Calvin Mills here because one of the Boss men ensulted one of the Girls and she reported it to the Supt and the Supt. discharged all four. . . . They got them a nother job here in Charlotte at the Highland Park Manf. Co. and all of the time they was working there the overseer was after one of them . . . to slip off from me at night & meet him and because she would not give him dates . . . he discharged all of them at this mill. so I am writing you to see if there is not some one that can put a stop to this practis in the Mills so as it will be a decent place for decent people to work in."[62]

Mrs. Ethel Reid worked at the Chadwick-Hoskins Mill for twenty-four years and raised two daughters in the mill village. On several occasions, a second hand, a "married man with a family," tried to date her nineteen-year-old daughter, Annie. "The first time he tried to get her to meet him in the Tower and went there and motioned for her to come and she refused. Her being a cleaner she would have to go to him for supplies and he asked her to kiss him and give him some sugar. He also asked her for a date in my home after she refused to meet him at other places. When she refused all this [he gave another woman her job]. I went to the overseer . . . and asked him why they taken her job away from her. . . . Now his reply was this—Because I wanted to and it is non of your d— business."[63]

Such protests against sexual harassment were a measure of the expansive vision of workers' rights touched off by the NIRA. In reality, of course, the Textile Code offered women no such protections. Even the issue of workloads—the most ubiquitous of workers' grievances—had been acknowledged merely as an afterthought. Only in regard to hours, wages, and child labor were the code's dictates specific and clear. Yet here too, as we have seen, workers invested the Blue Eagle with a power and meaning that transcended the intentions of those who wrote the law.

The problems of mill children, for instance, were barely touched by the formal abolition of child labor. When industry representatives announced their willingness to include a child labor amendment in the code, they were "greeted by ringing cheers" and praised for their generosity. In fact, the employers had conceded little, for the Depression had already dealt the final blow to a declining institution. Conspicuously absent were any comments on this much-heralded reform from mill workers themselves. This silence can be attributed in part to the fact that parents as well as children continued to assume young people's contributions to family survival. And many letters to the NRA were written by adolescents who were supporting aged or disabled parents or speaking in their illiterate parents' behalf. At the same time, millhands coveted the chance for their children to go to school and complained because the NIRA did little to remove the economic barriers that held the youngsters back. A fifteen-year-old girl reported that her father had been laid off when he joined a loom fixers organization. "Dady has just been two hundred and fifty miles and couldent get a Job and . . . he has now walked his shoes off his feet. . . . I have five little sisters and one little brother I trully hope that If the blue eagle is true that my dady might have a Job here so we five girls might stay on in school." A woman who was denied work because she could not "hold down 81 looms" also worried about educating her five children. Both the worries she felt and the solution she proposed were widely shared. "If they would take [off] the stretch system," she argued, "they could give lots of Jobs to others & every body could have a chance to . . . get clothes and book . . . and send our children to school."[64]

Black millhands also tried to invoke the promise of the NRA. The Textile Code at first exempted from its provisions the cleaning and "outside" jobs to which most blacks were relegated and then, by amendment, fixed the wage scale for those jobs at 75 percent of that provided for other workers. Despite such exclusion, black mill workers, like white women and children, saw themselves as hard-working

"Citizens" who deserved a "fair deal," and they did their best to take advantage of the New Deal's protection.[65]

A fireman who was among the best-paid black workers in his mill spoke up for his friends. "Mr. Johnson 10 coloreds men ask me to tell you how hard they work . . . for nothing you might as well say." Worst of all was the situation of the scrubbers, who labored for six dollars a week. "They scrubb up dirt and grease and also tobacco spat of the floor. . . . These Scubber Keep down disease in this cotton mill. Trying their very best to keep the mill Clean. . . . I think these Scrubber oughted to get 30 cent an hours or more. because they earn it." Another group of black workers refused to take their employer's word about the code and wrote to Hugh Johnson at NRA headquarters instead. "You said the N.R.A. are soppose to help Every body But the Employers are unfair to the Colord workers of Belmont N.C." A black man named George Washington Conor summed it up: "They aint give the Colard help any chanch at all."[66]

White "sweepers" were covered by the Textile Code; black "scrubbers" were not. The narrow line between the two could create tensions among workers and invite employer abuse. Mrs. Dora Adams, for instance, protested that in her mill "the sweepers have been marked up as scrubbers and down with the Negros and Just being paid eight dollars a week." A man at Honea Path, South Carolina, spelled out the problem as he saw it. "The sweepers in the southern cotton mills are all white men, a lot of them with families to support." Yet the mills are being "allowed to chisel the sweepers" by classifying them as scrubbers. "These scrubbers are colored women that use water and chemicals to clean the floor. My work is sweeping up the waste that falls from the machinary, putting the waste in containers, carried to the waste house bailed up and sold to waste mills. . . . You can see very plainly that my job does not fit in with scrubbers."[67]

Given the surrounding social realities, such thinking comes as no surprise. But the complexities that lay beneath the surface of white workers' comments invite a closer look. Notable first of all is the relative absence of racial obsessions in millhands' appeals to the NRA, an absence that may testify to the success of segregation or to the ability of economic preoccupations to crowd out other concerns. White workers who did acknowledge their black compatriots were often clinging to the tiny advantages race could afford, doing so in terms that differed little from those of skilled workers angry at being reduced to the level of the unskilled. Almost as common—and less expected—were writers who took for granted patterns of experience that crossed the color line.

One example, remarkable for its ideological slant but not for its casual mixture of compassion and thoughtless racial slurs, came from an elderly sweeper named Clarence J. Swink. Writing to Hugh Johnson, Swink described the practices by which Cannon Mills denied its workers the minimum wage. "Rastus however in this instance as ever is geting the worst of it. . . . The colored yard hands, four in number recieve 18 cts per hour while the white hands recieve 25 cts per hour for the same work altho some of the blacks are stronger and work better. . . . Just now there is an actual curtailment of the running time of the mill owing it is claimed to a 'lack of orders' but which I suspect is only a resumption of the old scheme to curtail operation in order to prevent the workers from getting enoungh money to make them feel in the least indipendent, for according to the southern code of ethics 'the nigger and the poor white must be kept poor in order for industry to thrive as a result of their labor.' "[68]

Clarence Swink was not the only white worker who included blacks in the community of cotton mill folk. Percy Kite worked "on the Mill yard With a Negro that has been truck driver for several years. And we two do all the . . . heavy straining work by our selves. . . . They say we are not in the code and that they can work us for what they please." Fritz Howell filed a department-by-department report on code violations at a Bessemer City mill, including the fact that outside workers, mostly black men, were working "50 to 60 hours per week, 5 to 10 c per hour." And a "minister of the gospell [who] had started a Little mission tabernille" for mill workers in Greenville ended his plea to the NRA with some alarming news: "Poor Colored People [are] Starving to death here."[69]

Eula McGill remembered how her supervisor laughed when he heard she was helping to organize a UTW local at the Selma Manufacturing Company in Birmingham, Alabama. " 'Hey,' " he said, " 'you going to get Rosa into the union?' And I said, 'Yes, if she'll join.' (She was one of the black women that worked there—and they made less than we did). He said, 'You going to call her sister?' I said, 'Sure I'm going to call her sister. I work with her, don't I?' And he just went on."[70]

None of these comments and experiences suggest a hidden world of interracial solidarity in the textile mills. But they do caution against easy generalizations about the function and importance of white work-ers' racial attitudes. The letters also suggest the human understand-ings that crosscut even an industry notorious for racial exclusion.[71]

Whether they were men or women, weavers who found their wages cut to the minimum or spinners who could barely keep up their sides, most who wrote to the NRA spoke not just for themselves but for "the textile people . . . my own class of people . . . that are being oppressed so much." And they made clear where they placed the blame: on "low down Boss-men," "cut throat textile operators," "extortionate hoggish mill officials," or, more generally, "the blood thirsty rich."[72]

Mill owners could, with justification, attribute curtailments to stag-nant or declining markets and argue that the stretch-out offered their only means of cutting labor costs and upping profits and stockholders' dividends. Yet a Federal Trade Commission survey indicated that during most of the NIRA period (until the summer of 1934), southern mills enjoyed rates of return ranging from 6.42 to 12.44 percent. These were impressive profits for a "sick industry" in the midst of the Great Depression. New England mills suffered by comparison, and the industry's migration southward peaked in 1935, leaving ghost towns in the Northeast where textile mills had thrived. To be sure, growth had slowed and the narrowing of the regional wage differential posed a real challenge to southern mills, which owed their spec-tacular success to cheap labor. But fears of economic disaster were highly exaggerated. In fact, bankruptcies of smaller, less efficient mills were more than offset by the flow of New England capital into the region, and firms such as Burlington Mills that pressed their advantage through diversification and investment in labor-saving ma-chinery emerged from the Depression relatively unscathed. A Win-ston-Salem millhand's comment was not far off the mark: "These textile Industrial has Made Money ever Since I have new of textile Mills and they are still making Big Money."[73]

In any case, to millhands the question went beyond whether higher wages would cut into profit margins and stockholders' dividends. Coming, as it did, on the heels of a decade in which heightened expectations had clashed with management strategies that violated the unspoken terms of mill village life, the Depression threw age-old inequities into sharp relief. In the past, mill folk had tolerated what they could not change, concentrating on their own family and commu-nity affairs. But accommodation did not necessarily imply assent. Now these "poor working class . . . people" believed they had a friend in the White House, their opinions had been solicited, and rights and privileges had been extended to them that could shift the balance of power in the mills.[74] They responded by voicing feelings long held but ordinarily repressed. Meshing the ethos of the mill village with the vocabulary of protest that emerged as the national climate of opinion shifted to the left, southern workers spoke out against injustices taken for granted in less troubled times. In doing so, they pushed at the boundaries of political debate. How should wealth be distributed? What was an adequate "standard of living"? Should the state regulate business for the common good? What role should workers play in shaping the economic and political institutions that so decisively shaped their lives?

Mill officials "claim they are not making money," wrote one Gastonia worker whose letter was published in the *Charlotte Observer*. "Well if they are not making money, I ask you, how can they afford to build these fine mansions to live in? How can every member of the family own his or her own car? . . . How can they afford to take trips to foreign countries? How can they afford to send their children to college and obtain the best education? When the poor mill worker can't make enough money to buy milk for his under-nourished children and can't buy books to send them to school . . . and the mothers must watch the flour sack like a hawk watching a chicken to get hold of them to make little under-garments for her children."[75]

How could such conditions be changed? A widow from Tucapau, South Carolina, had a modest suggestion. "They could cut down the pay on some of the supers and overseers and president and give to [the] help." An outside observer seconded her opinion. J. Vernon Phillips, a salesman for a large oil company, believed he was well placed "between the common worker and the Capitalist" to tell Roosevelt "the real truth." "On paper the mills have complied with the Code they signed. Actually, they have evaded it in every way their scheming brains could devise. . . . They have won much sympathy from the minority stockholders . . . people who have not received any dividends on their monies invested for several years—by telling them that dividends are not paid because of the high wages paid the common worker, whereas if one will but investigate their books he will invariably find that the *real* reason . . . is that the majority stockholders have robbed the treasury thru HIGH—yes most outrageous salaries and bonuses."[76]

Vernon Phillips had a point. The earnings of mill officials were shrouded in secrecy. Mill men commonly published no financial statements, strangled government and university efforts to investigate the industry, and gave their own stockholders the sketchiest of reports. Often one man served as president or secretary-treasurer of nine or ten mills, collecting a salary from each corporation in the "chain." Whether they presided over such chains or headed larger, integrated corporations, many mill officials weathered the Depression without undue distress. In 1937, when a mill worker might take home $624 a year at best, the president of Cannon Mills earned $50,000. Three years later Spencer Love reported a salary of $91,939, a sum that almost doubled when government contracts brought renewed prosperity to the industry during World War II.[77]

Religion, as we have seen, could help reconcile people to a new industrial order. At the same time, evangelicals inhabited a sacred world in which God's judgment fell with awful finality on rich and poor alike. Women were the mainstay of the southern church, and they in particular spoke truth to power in religious terms. Some measured their employers against New Testament ideals of justice and mercy. Others evoked the Old Testament in pitiless condemnations, certain that an angry God was on their side.[78]

A woman from Belmont apologized for her "poor education," then drew a dramatic contrast between the "big mill men" and the workers. "Just suppose you were a spinner," she urged government officials, with "the oil whizzing about your face," the closed windows, the suffocating heat, the measly paycheck carried home at the end of the week. Now, "picture Mr Sloan [head of the CTI], sitting down in a big nice cool dining room. and eating the finest of food. picture him and his big mill men sitting in their offices. with window wide open and electric fans turning picture them with their big salary. while the working man . . . strains every nerve in his body. and only make 30 cents an hour. God has been merciful with you . . . men. He has spared your lives you have obtained education, and hold high offices in life. will you help a working man as your Master has helped you. will you be merciful with us. in the time of trouble For the Book of All Books says (Blessed are the merciful, for they must obtain mercy) Don't be led by false reports on our wages and the stretch out system. But try your best to give us justice. And I'm sure that your reward will be great in Heaven."[79]

The letters that Mrs. Sadie Harris of Greenwood, South Carolina, wrote to her local paper crackled with Old Testament indignation. "I am sorry the mills are so depressed for money. The officials always have a poor mouth, their pockets well filled and stomachs filled with the luxuries of life. Poor little fellows, we cannot afford to weep over them. . . . They are only ordinary men with great salaries and feel their importance, but they are no more in God's sight or as much as the poor man or woman, who is so depressed and toiling all day in the mills, almost as severe as the penitentiary. . . . God says it is better to give than to receive. Wait until judgment day comes. . . . It will be a sad day for the . . . people who have trampled God's poor in the ground. . . . You cannot get around the Almighty. Money cannot buy our Heavenly Father. Money can buy all kinds of lies, and every kind of traitor in this world, but [Judgment Day] will tell the world who is who. . . . The world will see then who is chosen for God's children." While the mill owners languish in "everlasting torment," our "dearly beloved President & the first Lady of the land" will be blessed for their "goodness of heart in cooperating with the working class [and] rewarded at judgement day, with the brightest crowns."[80]

How common was such resentment against the "great salaries" of "ordinary men"? A federal labor official investigating complaints against the Durham Cotton Manufacturing Company thought it was widespread indeed. He found the complainant, Mr. Willoughby, to be "very earnest and above the average in intelligence, but the ideas which he has in mind differ very little from those of a great many others who are interested in improving conditions in the textile industry. Mr. Willoughby suggests that hours be shortened, and work load decreased so that more workers can be employed. To enable management to take care of increased labor costs, in the event this is done, he feels that salaries of officers should be reduced and unnecessary office help eliminated."[81]

Once the salaries of mill officials were reduced, to what might the "working man" aspire? On this point, opinion coalesced around modest desires. "Every man and woman who gives . . . an honest day's work should receive sufficient pay to afford daily sustenance under healthful surroundings, with a small excess to lay aside for emergencies," one man explained. In sum, "The laborer is worthy of his hire." The New Deal had promised a living wage—or so it seemed. This, at least, southern mill workers claimed as their due. And if hard times required sacrifices, they should be shared equally, not piled on the bent backs of the poor.[82]

But money was not the only issue. At stake were fundamental ethical values, as well as the nation's fate. "The bosses . . . haven't any feeling for any human being they only look at life in the terms of dollars and cents. . . . and the dried up people who have worked for them a great many yrs stand out and witness against them," wrote Haynes Willoughby about his long struggle with the management of the Durham Cotton Manufacturing Company. In the context of an economic catastrophe, men who piled up "fat profet" were a threat to society, enemies of the common good.[83]

No one had consulted mill workers about industrial policy, but they had their own theories, which they were quick to share. Frank B. Sexton offered "to make a little speech to the Senate . . . I want to say there is no way out in my [opinion] except a federal law to control hours and wages. Why because the mill can cut wages thereby cut the cost of manufacturing and then become an unfair competitor and force the others to cut to get any business and you know labor is left the burden to carry." A Laurens, South Carolina, man argued that the nation would "never pull out of this depression until the vast number of unemployed are put to work and start a buying power. There never has been such a thing as overproduction. The answer to that question is underconsumption. The government has people on direct relief rolls that have actually been run off of jobs in cotton mills on account of this damnable stretch out system."[84]

Working-class people saw themselves as champions of civic virtue, the one hope for salvaging the American dream. "The Laboring People here are trying to uphold our President and also the code. We believe in it—We talk it—And we would so love to live it," wrote Mrs. B. M. Miller from Charlotte. "Dear demacrate Friend," wrote a man in Bessemer City, "I am trying to Provide By the code . . . but our country is not. Our overseer . . . dont wont us to no any thing about the NRA code . . . but I am going to provide by it Even if I do loss my Job."[85]

Piedmont millhands viewed Roosevelt as a "God sent man," an emancipator who could turn patterns of domination upside down. This was not just a matter of hero worship; southern workers, like their counterparts across the country, were convinced that Roosevelt shared their attitudes and values. They welcomed the revolution they thought he might bring and were ready to follow him in any progressive direction.[86] Never had the mill owners' credibility sunk so low; never had workers dared to voice such discontent. The result was a movement in search of a leader. Workers organized unions, tangled with overseers, and coupled appeals for help with promises of political support. But no one knew better than they the imposing advantages of corporate power. If millhands were to help bring a New Deal to the mill towns, they would need resolute outside intervention.

Big business "fought and opposed your election," a North Charlotte worker told Roosevelt. "They are crippling the New Deal, retarding prosperity, and how they would like to see you put out of commission. . . . This country has been entirely too lopsided for some time and just ready to topple over when you took over the reins and if you don't watch them close they are liable to upset us yet. . . . Remember your promise to . . . give America back to the American people." To Haynes Willoughby, "The bosses is a bunch of rascals and I only see two ways to handle them and one of them is to encourage the workers to organize and force them crooks to do the right thing or else let the Government pass a law that will force them to do the right thing. . . . The quicker the government learns the boss class can not be trusted and builds a wall of protection around it the better it will be for all."[87]

Two letters from Shelby, a hotbed of union organizing in North Carolina, struck similar themes. "You sure will haft to watch the dirty mfg of the south as they will give there help a dirty deal if you dont show them your power to deal with such," Livingston V. Hinson urged. "If you dont pin down on this dirty Bunch down hear in n.c. this industral act will be a failure & this is what the mfg wants so as they can do as they have in the past. Pay a starveation wage." Observed W. H. Crisp: "The Bigest trouble i find [is that no one] who has violated any of these N.R.A. codes has Bin punished for violating them . . . so you see the mfg Supt & Bosses dont seam to care what you say & do. they are goin head long & contrary to your wishes & seam to want to tear up & destroy you & your plans & i think you should give all such mills a severe punishment."[88]

This question of enforcement—indeed, of "severe punishment"— was foremost in many people's minds. "The laws of our country are strictly enforced against the highwaymen, kidnappers and other classes of robbers," wrote the president of a UTW local at Rockingham, North Carolina. "This being the case why should'nt the law be enforced against Mill Owners[?]" An angry Winston-Salem man insisted that the manufacturers "never have wanted the working class of People to have anything and they aint going to let him have anything Either if they can get out of it. . . . But Now Mr Roosevelt you have the

... Power to Make these textile Industrials do and you can Make them do if you will. ... they Have Been Rocked in a cradle So long until they think they still have got to Be Rocket. ... I think that you can stop there cradle from Bein Rocket. I say let them Suffer Just as they have let us Suffer." A "little woman" in South Carolina conjured an unforgettable image as she warned the president of what he was up against and told him what he had to do. "Oh how they all love Hoover. ... These old slimy serpants crowling spiting their Poison fighting your Program and the Government dont let them fool you with their slimy tongue. ... President Roosevelt ... use that big stick."[89]

Clarence Swink viewed the situation from a unique vantage point. He was only a sweeper, but he owed his job at Cannon Mills to the fact that he was "a relative of one of the large stock holders of this company. ... But this fact does not prevent me from sympathising with those who are kept in penury throuth the manipulations of an organization which has always seemed to make the subjegation of labor a special study. ... The Blue Eagle has learned to cover a multitude of sins since he alighted in the Piedemont area. The Textile Code [is] shrunken and stretched to accommodate the demands of selfishness and greed. The traditional principals of intrigue, coersion and intimidation of labor upon which this industry has prospered and builded mighty fortunes in the past are still as aggressive, and persistent as ever. ... I believe the only efficient and pemanent cure will be derived by taking over of all industry under acutal government ownership and operation with the elimination of individual interest and profit. Such a course would be backed by the enthusiastic support of one hundred Million loyal Americans who see in such a course the only hope for preservation of the ideals of human liberty. ... Government ownership ... is the only solution. Let us have it General Johnson, Let us have it."[90]

This outpouring of faith, anger, and fear was shunted through a bureaucratic maze. Complaints wound their way through local mill committees and state appeals boards until they reached the Bruere Board, which sent them to the industry-dominated Code Authority. Investigators then contacted the complainant's employer. If the mill denied wrongdoing, the case was closed. Between August 8, 1933, and August 8, 1934, the board received 3,920 complaints. It authorized ninety-six investigations and resolved only one wage-and-hour dispute in a worker's favor. It found no evidence of a stretch-out or of firings for union activity. It completely ignored the National Labor Board's philosophy of majority rule, arguing instead that owners were obligated to bargain only when a union local represented *every* worker in a mill, and it held no representation elections. In short, the Bruere Board made no attempt to put teeth into Section 7(a).[91]

The shortcomings of such industry self-policing were not lost on the people who worked in the mills. "If Mr. Sloan thinks that mill workers in S[outh] C[arolina] are satisfied with their wages," advised one worker, "he ought to investigate among the workers and not among the mill officials and office force." A weaver at Charlotte's Chadwick-Hoskins Mill objected to the practice of appointing "big mill men" to the textile boards. "They are not going to turn in . . . any kind of report which would . . . mean that they would have to pay out more money from their own pockets. The thing . . . to do, is to appoint some good, Honest, Hard working man, say one from each mill community, so he . . . could get the true fact of this stretch-out system."[92]

Given the many methods by which managers could "positively control . . . the actions and expressions of speech of their help," how could "the true fact" be known? The suggestions were various and shrewd. Send "goverment men to go secretly among the mills." "Go to the homes of the workers & . . . find out houw the poor people are having to live." A man who had always wanted to be a detective offered his services. "I Know if I had the chanch I could Bring some things to the light." From the tiny village of Glencoe, A. W. Litton sent his promise to step forward, whatever the cost. "If Mr green finds out that i rote you this he will fire me and run me off this [place] but if you cant find out that Mr. W G. Green is [violating] the N.R.A. law in every way call for me and i will show what is going on here."[93]

The state appeals process was so biased and ineffectual that UTW officials were hard pressed to persuade southern workers to use it at all. The North Carolina board, for instance, was headed by an economics professor named Theodore S. Johnson who had allegedly been "hand-picked" by *Southern Textile Bulletin* editor David Clark. Paul Christopher, a weaver who led the unionization effort at the Cleveland Cloth Mill in Shelby and went on to work for the UTW, spearheaded an unsuccessful "dump Johnson" campaign. But as Christopher well knew, the problem went beyond individuals. As he put it, "No matter what personnel composes such State agencies, it is almost a sure bet that the pressure of the manufacturers will alter their

... judgement," while small-town mill owners had the "power, money and influence" to "bulldose every citizen" who came to the workers' defense. Public sentiment, in any case, usually reinforced corporate influence. A Belmont man got the runaround—what he called "the ha! ha!"—everywhere he turned. "It is impossible for me to get justice around here . . . when the press, the [pulpit,] and many others here are unfriendly to labor they only say our complants are imaginary." A millhand who had lived in Burlington all his life reported "the dirty work [Burlington Mills] is pulling off behind the back of the Great Blue Eagle." I have "done my part," he concluded, but to no avail. There were exceptions, to be sure. In Rocky Mount, Thomas J. Pearsall, a young lawyer who would later become an influential member of the state legislature, headed an NRA advisory committee that reported "flagrant violations of the textile code" and pled for authority to conduct its own investigations and remove Blue Eagles where violations were found.[94] But such vigorous local efforts made little headway in a larger context of antipathy or neglect. Ignoring the Bruere Board's labyrinthine procedures, southern workers appealed directly to Hugh Johnson or the president, prayed to God, and put their faith in the NRA.

Frustration reached the boiling point when these efforts failed to bring results. Mrs. B. M. Miller of the Chadwick-Hoskins Mill began her correspondence with federal officials on a calm, altruistic note. "I just feel it my duty to notify you" of the stretch-out at the Hoskins plant. "Please investigate . . . for I am sure you can have it straigtend out." When the stretch-out continued, she quit her job. In retaliation, her husband was fired. By December 1933 Mrs. Miller had joined the UTW and was helping the Charlotte Central Labor Union gather and file workers' complaints. Notified—for the third time—that her own grievances had still not reached "the right Board," she wrote in exasperation to Secretary of Labor Frances Perkins. "Now if there is a right board I, as well as all the Laboring people of Charlotte would like to know where it is. . . . We have just lots of good citizens in Textile Plants, but we cant come out of bondage alone. We must have help. We must have some one to breake the shackles. We need action now. If we don't get it, it will lead to strikes. WHO WILL BE TO BLAME? NOT THE LABORING PEOPLE. BUT THE PEOPLE WHO HAS POWER TO HELP US NOW."[95]

For North Carolina unionists, events at K. S. Tanner's Stonecutter Mills in Spindale proved the final straw. When management began firing union members and raising production quotas, millhands filed numerous complaints. Tanner denied the accusations, and the state appeals board dismissed all seventy-seven grievances. On February 12, 1934, 250 of the plant's 400 workers walked out. Women and children blocked the railroad tracks to prevent trains from unloading coal and cotton. Strikers and nonstrikers traded threats, curses, and insults as unionists mounted picket lines at the mill. So serious was the situation that the appeals board, for once, intervened, asking Tanner to conduct an election to determine whether the workers wanted UTW representation. In response, Tanner sponsored a contest that pitted the UTW against a company union. Workers marked their ballots in front of management poll watchers; Tanner counted the votes and announced that his hand-picked ticket had won.

Theodore Johnson, chairman of the appeals board, dismissed the UTW's call for a fair election, and unionists shut down the mill once more. When Tanner tried unsuccessfuly to reopen the plant with 100 armed men deputized by the local sheriff, Johnson issued an edict giving management a clean bill of health and ordering strikers back to work. Unionists returned, only to find that nine of their leaders had been fired. At wit's end, they laid their troubles before the Bruere Board, which upheld Johnson's "fair and impartial" handling of the situation.[96]

The NRA's performance in this dispute, together with its response to a similar imbroglio at Shelby's Cleveland Cloth Mill, a firm owned by former governor O. Max Gardner, destroyed every scrap of hope that cooperation with the state board could improve conditions in North Carolina. Paul Christopher and other unionists from Shelby and Spindale persuaded the state federation of labor to submit no further grievances. Spindale union leader Yates Kindrick warned Bruere that "a general strike is inevitable unless relief is given."[97]

On May 22, 1934, the Code Authority ignored the suffering already caused by short time, unemployment, and rising living costs and again attacked the problem of overproduction with a 25 percent cut in machine hours. The UTW threatened a strike but backed down in exchange for a labor representative on the Bruere Board and allowed the cutback to take effect. At that point, southern workers took matters into their own hands. Beginning on July 14, in the northern Alabama community of Guntersville, wildcat strikes rolled across the state, pulling 20,000 workers out of the mills. Strikers demanded a twelve-dollar minimum wage for a thirty-hour week, abolition of the stretch-out, reinstatement of workers fired for union activity, and union recognition. Two days after the Alabama walkout, North Carolina unionists threatened a similar strike. Rushing once again to catch up with the rank and file, UTW officials called for a special convention in New York City on August 14. Southern unionists showed up in force, proud of their battle scars and eager for a fight. On the first day of the convention, southerners presented more than fifty resolutions calling for a general strike. On the second day, union officials adopted the goals Alabama unionists had set. On the fourth day, more than a dozen southern workers took to the podium. W. N. Adcock from Huntsville, Alabama, testified with bandages on his head: "I have been wounded in the head and shot in the leg, but I am ready to die for the union." The response was overwhelming. With only ten dissenting votes, the delegates approved a walkout to begin at midnight on September 1.[98]

Cushioned by overstocked warehouses, certain of their advantage, and contemptuous of the UTW, employers settled in for a short siege. The CTI refused to meet with UTW representatives, much less to negotiate. *Southern Textile Bullletin* editor David Clark urged Alabama mill men to see the strike as a golden opportunity. Sooner or later, he wrote, "the status of the racketeers must be settled, and this is probably a good time." Alabama mill men responded with a lockout. They simply closed shop and adopted a policy of wait and see.[99]

Union vice-president Francis Gorman took on the formidable task of organizing walkouts at hundreds of mills scattered across a vast region from Maine to Georgia. In 1929 Norman Thomas had accused the UTW of using "horse and buggy tactics in an automobile age." But Gorman took his cue from the rising generation of millhands. He went on the radio, gaining hours of air time at no expense. He encouraged "flying squadrons" of cars and trucks to speed through the countryside—and they did, closing mills so rapidly that "tabulators almost lost check." Since North and South Carolina refused to observe Labor Day, the Carolinians who failed to report to work on Monday, September 3, were the first to follow Alabama workers in signaling the depth of rank-and-file support. On Tuesday, they were joined by workers in every textile center in the nation; by September 15, press reports claimed the strikers stood 400,000 strong. The General Strike had rapidly become the largest single labor conflict in American history.[100]

Workers' response to the strike call took everyone by surprise. For

*Francis Gorman (left), vice-president of the United Textile Workers, and George
Sloan (right), head of the Cotton Textile Institute, using the radio to air their
differences during the General Strike of 1934.*

(Courtesy of the National Archives and Records Service)

the moment at least, complacency disappeared, washed away in a tide
of shock and fear. A relief worker in Erwin, North Carolina, hoped
that she would never again "have such a horrible sensation as that
which came over me when I first saw the picket line." When a flying
squadron arrived at a hosiery mill in Catawba County, the owner "had
a pistol in his hand, and he said he'd kill the first s.o.b. that took over
the switch." If any more "flying mobs . . . come to this town," he
threatened, "we will call on the state for flying squadrons of armed
militia to run them off the roads." Other manufacturers also combined
armed self-defense with calls for military intervention. On September
3, Paul Christopher led a flying squadron that closed twenty-seven
mills in the Shelby area. But when he and some 2,000 unionists
arrived at K. S. Tanner's Stonecutter Mills, they found themselves
facing machine guns and a private police force with "strict orders to
shoot." From Gaston County, a hub of strike activity in 1934 as it had
been five years earlier, came an urgent petition signed by twenty-two
mill owners. Once again mill workers were parading through the
streets of Gastonia, but this time "spontaneous celebration" had given
way to the specter of class war. "Several times daily hundreds of men,
women and children parade through town yelling, screaming, threatening and intimidating citizens of the town, stating that they intend
confiscating automobiles and other personal property as their needs
demand. . . . Our situation is desperate, much more desperate than
we can express in words. Law and order no longer exists, except for
the surrender of personal and property rights by a majority of the
substantial citizenship and unless something is done within the next
twenty-four hours no authority can be held responsible for results."
To panicked townsmen, the strike represented "the gravest emergency which has confronted our people since Reconstruction Days."[101]

Governor Ibra Blackwood of South Carolina mobilized the National Guard the moment the strike began; Governor J. C. B. Ehringhaus of North Carolina held out for two days as telegrams and
telephone calls came in; Governor Eugene Talmadge of Georgia, who
had built his reputation as a champion of the common man, delayed
action until September 15—three days after winning a landslide primary election. Whatever the route, the result was the same. By September 7, 14,000 National Guardsmen were on duty in the Carolinas.
Within a week after that, Talmadge had ordered the largest peacetime
mobilization of troops in Georgia's history, declared martial law in the
mill villages, and incarcerated 126 pickets in a barbed wire "concen-

Union members marching down the main street of Gastonia, North Carolina, during the 1934 General Strike.
(Courtesy of AP/Wide World Photos)

tration camp" near the spot where Germans had been interned during World War I.[102]

Talmadge's actions were particularly disheartening because they were so unexpected. Mill worker J. M. Zimmerman had believed the governor's assurance that the strikers "had a friend in the Governor's chair. . . . I supported you. . . . I spent my own money and used my own car to help elect you to your office and for my trouble and expense you had my daughter and myself . . . penned up like cows, not because we had committed any crime or any violence but because you wished to keep us in slavery. My daughter and I helped to close several mills. . . . We did not go to make trouble, we went to help the workers close the mills until the owners . . . decided to give us better [working] conditions and cut out the Damable Stretch-out System but you want us to work for just as little as can be paid. . . . It seems to me that your plans are to herd the men and weomen that are trying to better their condition up in a . . . Detention Camp and let someone else who is almost ready to starve take their jobs at starvation wages. . . . sending out guards, tends to create violence. . . . and such tactics as you are useing will eventually bring about a Revolution. I am not an educated expert," Zimmerman concluded, but "you are useing dam poor judgment."[103]

Jonathan Worth Daniels, editor of the Raleigh *News and Observer*, was among the few "outside the ranks of the strikers themselves" who actively opposed the use of military force. Daniels privately believed that "there is a concerted effort in the State and the South to break down labor in this strike and that the . . . liberties of the people are really jeopardized. . . . [T]here is a war on to the death to crush labor back to the point where it was before any New Deal . . . began." In public the young editor did his best to trim and hedge "without failing to take a vigorous position." Even so, he found himself completely out of step with the "propertied people of the State"; a barrage of criticism greeted his calls for "reason and reasonableness" on all sides.[104]

On one point Daniels and his critics would have agreed. Not least among the issues raised by the strike was the meaning of "liberty" in a society marked by staggering disparities of wealth and reeling under an economic crisis that brought those inequalities into sharp focus. The Gaston County mill owners who likened the strike to "Reconstruction Days" were unusual in their straightforward defense of property rights. Once Governor Ehringhaus announced that he would not send the National Guard to communities where workers had "voluntarily" joined the strike, most of those who begged for military protection did so not in their own behalf but for the sake of loyal employees who were being denied the "right to work." In some cases, men who had adamantly opposed the principle of representation through majority rule suddenly reversed themselves, polled their workers, and declared that even though their mill was "highly unionized," a majority opposed the strike. Strikers disputed these numbers or argued that they proved only the employers' ability to frighten, manipulate, and coerce. As one Roanoke Rapids woman put it, the mill men got the "troops to guard the mills . . . on a schemed lie."[105]

K. S. Tanner spoke for the manufacturers in this war of words. He thanked Governor Ehringhaus "for my Company and for the working people with whom I am associated here for the protection which you have given to the constitutional right of every man to work if he pleases without interference or molestation. Had this right not been maintained I shudder to think of the social and economic future of our state. I wish that you might have been in Spindale to see the contrast

National Guardsmen rounding up strikers in Newman, Georgia, and preparing to load them on trucks bound for an internment camp outside Atlanta, 1934.
(Courtesy of AP/Wide World Photos)

registered in the faces of the working people. On Wednesday there was fear and a sense of hopelessness that mob violence had so effectively brought chaos to the community, but this morning when I watched the people come to work they were eager and happy and confident, for everyone felt that law and order are still in force, and that liberty is not lost."[106]

Needless to say, strikers saw things differently. When they spoke of the right to work, they envisioned a world in which jobs were plentiful, work was bearable, and everyone took home a fair day's pay. They, too, called for law enforcement, but the mill owners were the culprits they had in mind. Workers' appeals spoke of employees forced to join company unions to keep their jobs, of "exconvicts and bootleggers" acting as special deputies, of North Carolina citizens who "have had their rights forcibly interfered with," and of union officials "thrown in jail without justifiable cause." "If you have any degree or sense of justice," Richard Roy Lawrence, president of the North Carolina State Federation of Labor, wrote to Governor Ehringhaus, "I implore you to put a stop to this damnable outrage immediately."[107]

At first, not even the arrival of soldiers, heavily armed and instructed to "shoot to kill," dampened rebellious spirits. Young women in particular gave the strike a special flair. They were "conspicuous by [their] vehemence" on the picket line. They led marches, holding aloft the American flag. A young " 'squadronette' who wore a blue dress, gold earrings, and smoked steadily" explained female tactics at Cannon Mills. "The town's full of deputies, sawed-off shotguns and soldiers with rifles. If we get them out over there, we will have to kid them and make them ashamed to work while everybody else is striking." Jonathan Daniels caught the flavor of the times: "Those cars and lines of cars were something new and strange, wicked and terrifying. Or so manufacturers thought. But I remember particularly the young women taunting the soldiers and the high laughter. Like war, the people love it. . . . It was good to be young then, good to go in tumultuous crowd and shout at the fence of the Old Man's House, good to climb into Fords and rush across counties to join other familiar-unfamiliar young people in clamoring at the mesh wire of mill gates."[108]

Of course, "high laughter" could go only so far in such an explosive situation. Inevitably, there was violence at those mesh wire gates. Soldiers, deputies, and vigilantes inflicted most of the damage. "The troops and national guards have been called out on us and the officers seem to be using the poor half starved strikers for a target," wrote "a Wife and Mother and a Textile Worker" in Belmont. "They have been shot down, like shooting at a rabbit."[109] Where strikers clashed with strike breakers, employers portrayed themselves as peacekeepers, barely able to hold back loyal—but armed and angry—workers. Unionists, on the other hand, believed they spoke for everyone, the brave and the timid alike, while owners stopped at nothing to stir up strife.

In an incident at Orr Cotton Mills in Anderson, South Carolina, night shift employees beat strikers with picker sticks—weavers' tools that Mack Duncan described as "a big old wooden stick about half the size of a ball bat." The *Textile Bulletin* dubbed this an "employees revolt" against "force and coercion" by the union. Union loyalists saw it as a clash between "boys who acted a gentleman and stuck to their

Dancing pickets outside the Clark Thread Mill in Austell, Georgia, 1934.
(Courtesy of the Archives of Labor and Urban Affairs, Wayne State University)

word" and members of a company-created "Picker stick club"—made up of people who didn't have "sense enough to stick together."[110]

Geddes Dodson at the Dunean Mill in Greenville and Lacy Wright at the Cone family's White Oak plant in Greensboro remembered similar incidents. "They brought big boxes of new picker sticks up there and put them in the weave room," Dodson recalled. "And they told us, 'Now if them flying squads goes to sticking their head in them windows, start cracking heads, and the company'll stand behind you.'" While employees armed themselves, the National Guard lined up outside the mill. "Whenever they thought the flying squad was going to break the National Guard's line, the captain says, 'Anybody crosses the line, shoot him down.' That's what kept them out."[111]

Dodson did as he was told, but Wright reacted differently. Instructed by his overseer to "go out the door and get you a picker stick," Wright replied, "In place of going out of that side of the building and getting me a picker stick, I'm going back on this side and find me a hole. I'm going out of here." What, at that moment, was on Lacy's mind? "I'll tell you what I thought, at that time. I didn't say much about it, because I couldn't afford to. I [thought] if them people were that interested in getting them a better situation where they worked, that they were willing to get out and go somewheres to try to shut somebody else down, even if they had to fight about it, that they must have something that we didn't already have. That's exactly what my thoughts was."[112]

Two women in Seneca, South Carolina, reported another version of this divide-and-conquer strategy. A majority of the workers had voted to join the General Strike. But the overseers soon persuaded 109 workers to sign cards promising to have nothing to do with the union. "That left us 338 in the union that are faithful and are sticking to-geather. . . . 109 can't run [the] mill so they take those cards to the country people to come in here & take our jobs." The mayor asked the governor to send in troops "to protect mill & people. But they are for the [nonunion] of course. If not why are they guarding the [nonunion] from homes to Mill. Right there is where Gov. Blackwood has handed us a dirty deal. For when we struck we struck for all. not for union only. The cards that have been dilivered among the people to signe is to signe your life away at Lonsdale Mill. It says not to associate with union members and do just as bos'es requirs them to do. . . . Then the Flying squardens went from mill to mill. So the Shirff began to debitise boys without a doubt has never had a gun in their hands before. Thats why so many people is killed to day. They are just shot to see fall."[113]

The bloodiest battle occurred at the Chiquola Mill in Honea Path, where the work force was divided "about half and half" for and against the union. Mack Duncan, looking back from a vantage point of forty years, remembered the moment well. "My daddy was a nonunion man. They tried to get him to join the union and he talked against it. Well, we worked three days like that. Then we went in on a Thursday morning. We couldn't even get to the plant. They'd called in some flying squadrons. They had the mill surrounded—five or six thick from the front to the back. And a lot of the strikers had sticks and clubs in their hands. So the company and the town authorized just about anybody that could carry a gun to be deputized. And they deputized some young, to me they were boys. And they would let them through, and they would go up in the mill windows. And you could see guns sticking out the mill windows. And they began passing out picker

Striking workers fresh from a confrontation with police outside the Trion Cotton Mill in Trion, Georgia, 1934. A deputy sheriff and a union loyalist were killed in the clash. After the fight the pickets re-formed their lines and closed the mill.
(Courtesy of the Archives of Labor and Urban Affairs, Wayne State University)

sticks. Some of them would bring a bundle. And they began passing the bundles out the window. I was in the mill office helping another fellow. We didn't have enough picker sticks to go round. So we were in there cutting off broom handles to give people to use as clubs. I would have left if my dad hadn't been there. He was a loom fixer at that time, and he had a gun; they'd deputized him. The strikers didn't like that when they saw those bundles coming out. So they converged on that window and they began fighting with their clubs through the window. Well, there was Mr. Marcel Shaw. We called him Buck Shaw. He was a striker. He ran up to the window, and there was a Mr. Commings who was a nonunion man. He was taking the picker sticks out the window. Getting them and taking them out. So Mr. Shaw hit him on the head. Well, somebody else hit Mr. Shaw. And they busted his head. Then all of a sudden you heard shooting. For about five minutes it was just a din.

"The people that had the guns were nonunion people. Nobody ever saw a striker with a gun. It was a regular riot, was what it was. And some of the people were shot down through their bodies. A fellow [named] Cox, he'd been an operator of the elevator in the mill. And he'd had a little run-in with a cloth doffer. The operator was a union man, and he had an ice pick. But the cloth doffer was nonunion, and he had a gun. And he shot the union man two or three times. I got sick myself from seeing so much blood, and I almost fainted. But I went to him. He got shot in the head. He was lying in a puddle of his own blood. I didn't see how anybody could bleed that much. And his eyes looked like they had set back in his head like he was dying. I didn't think I'd ever see him alive again. And when it was over there was a lot of people hurt lying on the ground. They'd been shot and beat. And seven people were killed. And some of the others were crippled for life."[114]

Duncan's story, like Vesta Finley's memory of "broken fellowship" in the churches of Marion during the 1929 strike, shows how efforts at change could rip the fabric of village life, heightening a "little run-in" into a brawl that left people dead or crippled for life. That such schisms existed is not in doubt. But what was the nature of those divisions? Who joined the "Picker stick club"? Who remained "loyal" to the company, who "faithful" to the union? Who was so callous as to shoot "to see fall"? What conjunction of people and events swept one village into the union camp, while leaving another torn apart and others untouched by the storm?

Of one thing we can be sure. The 1934 General Strike of the textile industry cannot be understood as a single event, comparable to citywide general strikes or to strikes by national unions against integrated industries. The depth of union support, and the violence of repression, differed from community to community and state to state over a large and varied region. At the same time, the tribulations imposed by the social relations of labor cut through the industry, from the tiniest rural mill to the most imposing corporation. And textile folk throughout the South shared a distinctive culture. In short, broad-brushed generalizations must await fine-grained local studies. And yet we can speculate, underlining diversity and suggesting the lines along which communities might divide.

A brief look at two North Carolina communities—Durham and Burlington—should illustrate how much the General Strike differed from place to place. In Durham the strike was "100 percent effective" and enjoyed considerable outside support. A base had been laid by a flurry of union organizing during World War I, followed by underground skirmishes throughout the 1920s. The UTW's dynamic Alfred

Hoffmann appeared on the scene in 1927, set up the Piedmont Organizing Council, and helped pump energy into the union cause. Kemp
P. Lewis, successor to William A. Erwin at the flagship Erwin Mills,
and William F. Carr, textile manufacturer and mayor of the city, led an
effective opposition that included spies, blacklists, and the like. But
the balance shifted with passage of the NIRA. Under the umbrella of
Section 7(a), the UTW organized the Bull City Local, which included
seven separate locals in Durham mill villages. A Durham organizer
named Albert Beck helped push through the General Strike resolution at the UTW's August 14, 1934, convention, and mass meetings
of local textile workers endorsed the UTW's demands. On Saturday,
September 1, some 2,500 workers rallying at the Carolina Theatre
adopted "On to Victory" as their slogan. They listened to speeches
that combined patriotism (the strike was aimed at the employers and
implied no "disloyalty against the government and what it has been
trying to do for us") with threats to strikebreakers ("that's a good way
not to grow old") and promises of interracial class solidarity ("the
colored of the city are . . . backing us"). On Sunday, placards appeared
all over the city: "No more boards and no more juggling around—no
more tricks and no more waiting while government boards give us the
run-around. . . . The hour for final action is at hand." On Monday,
Durham mill owners observed Labor Day—for the first time ever—
and promised to open the gates as usual on Tuesday morning. But
when the mill whistles blew, "Durham proved itself the best fortified
strike center in the Carolinas. . . . Approximately 5,200 textile workers
. . . remained in their homes or formed impregnable picket lines that
paralyzed" the mills.[115]

The Durham strike was a marvel of self-organization. World War I
veterans patrolled the picket lines. Committees of young women,
supervised by older ones, made up the "strike sick committee" and the
"commissary committee." Additional groups took in new members
and planned entertainment "to see that strikers will be jolly during the
strike period." Local businesses, including department stores, bak-
eries, beauty shops, jewelry stores, and cafes, took out a full-page
prounion advertisement in the *Durham Sun* and supplied food, credit,
and tents to the strikers. Tobacco workers' locals, black and white,
pledged their support.[116] No National Guardsmen paced the city's
streets. Kemp Lewis, head of Erwin Mills, was denied entrance to his
office by his own employees; it rankled, but he didn't call the police for
fear of stirring up "bitter antagonisms." Durham, as he told his stock-

holders, was "permeated with a union sentiment." Only when the strike officially ended three weeks later did Durham mill folk return to work, and they did so with a victory parade announcing "We Killed the Stretch-out."[117]

Such announcements of victory were, to put it mildly, premature. Yet, in Durham, false optimism revealed a deeper truth. Although the stretch-out continued, the breadth of support for the strike protected Durham workers from the wholesale firings that would purge unionists from other mills. By World War II, Durham could be counted among the best-organized communities in the Carolinas.

Burlington presented a different pattern: flying squadrons, walk-outs, and bursts of class antagonism subsided quickly, scarring individuals but leaving little historical trace. On Wednesday, September 5, a caravan of cars and trucks swooped down on the Piedmont Heights area, then dashed through Alamance County, leaving dozens of silent mills in its track. In most cases, mill officials gave orders to "stop off" the machines as soon as the flying squadron appeared. But this was a temporary retreat. By the next morning two companies of National Guardsmen armed with automatic rifles and machine guns were scattered throughout the county, protecting mills against further attack and breaking up picket lines so that nonstriking hands could trickle in to work.[118]

Gracie Pickard and her brother Walt were among the most active agitators, and Gracie in particular was a thorn in the guardsmen's side. At one point, the soldiers forced her into a truck and drove her around town—a mock kidnapping meant to humiliate Gracie and send a message to other women about the dangers of the street. Gracie, however, refused to be intimidated. According to Walt, when the soldiers released her, "my sister stood proud, knowing it was for the union." Later, while demonstrating at the Plaid Mill, Gracie was arrested by a sheriff who "just watched to get his hands on her. He didn't like her."[119]

An exchange between Gracie Pickard and Mattie and Mildred Shoemaker hints at how notions of respectability, prior allegiances, and other intangibles of background and temperament could put workers on opposite sides. The Shoemaker sisters, who were among a half dozen or so women who continued to work in the winding room at the Pioneer Plant, traded angry words with Gracie at the factory gate. That evening, the sheriff, a friend of the Shoemakers' father, came to the house to tell them, " 'You know that thing'—that's what he called her, 'that thing'—he didn't call her a lady. I don't know whether she was a lady. She could have been. But he called her 'that thing.' 'You know that thing that talked to you this morning. Well, she sure is on the inside looking out. She's down at the county jail.' "[120]

On one side of this cultural cleavage stood those like Gracie Pickard whose expanding notions of citizenship, liberty, and justice led them to defy armed guards and march through the streets carrying an American flag to indicate "the patriotic spirit of the champions of the strike cause." On the other were the Shoemakers and their friends, caught in a web of social relations that included the sheriff and lower-level supervisors, to whom the strikers seemed a "tacky-looking bunch." In the middle stood what seems in Burlington to have been a cautious majority, sympathetic toward the strikers but skeptical about the strike. Jesse Brooks had helped organize a union local at the Plaid Mill, but he advised against the walkout. "You've not got money in your treasury, and some of these other unions ain't going to back you up." Lloyd Davidson stayed out of work until "we'd seen that we was just losing time and it wasn't going to amount to anything really, we wasn't going to get anything out of it. Your chances are real slim on something like that because as a rule most of the people working are week to week, or payday to payday. You can't stay out very long. The company can stand it a lot longer than you can, and so they break you down."[121]

Yet, even in Burlington, differences among workers paled beside sharper antagonisms. On September 14 a large crowd of workers clashed with National Guardsmen at the Plaid Mill. Several strikers, including Gracie Pickard, suffered slight bayonet wounds, and others were clubbed. At three o'clock the next morning, two men stopped a Ford roadster by the gate and hurled a bundle of dynamite over the fence. About $100 worth of glass windows were broken, but no other damage occurred. The next morning packages of dynamite were found in other mills.[122]

The "Burlington Dynamite Case" became a cause célèbre, with students and faculty at the University of North Carolina rallying to the defense of the eight textile workers accused of conspiracy and other crimes, while Spencer Love and other mill owners hired private detectives to aid the prosecution. The evidence was flimsy and riddled with contradictions, but the trial ended with stiff sentences for all concerned.[123]

Spencer Love's reactions are instructive, in part because they were widely shared. The call for a general strike was, in his opinion, "nothing but a racket. The Union membership is nothing like what it is alleged to be [and] in fact only involves a small percentage of our section. However, if a general strike is called I feel pretty sure that it would spread aided and abetted by hoodlums and dissatisfied workers in spots and by what you might call mob psychology." Spencer left for his country retreat during the early days of the strike, resigned to the fact that the troops could do more to open the mills than he. But he was back by September 7, watching the situation and occasionally reporting his observations to his sister Cornelia in nearby Chapel Hill, who shared his dismissal of workers' complaints. She wrote to him after a radio broadcast by the UTW's Francis Gorman, "I could so cheerfully poison Gorman, the ignorant boor. . . . His reply to Sloan's statement that the stretch-out was practically extinct was to the effect that Sloan had never sweated himself sick and fainting over horrible machinery, dragged home his exhausted and worn-out body, etc., etc." Spencer was particularly outraged by Socialist leader Norman Thomas, who stopped in Burlington to deliver a speech to a thousand people gathered in the city park on Main Street. "Thomas gave a speech in Burlington today," he wrote to Cornelia, "and was just as vitriolic as one man could possibly be and aimed at only one thing which was stirring people up to rebellion and sedition against the status quo. . . . My personal feeling is that such people ought to be in jail as they simply go around the country fomenting trouble." Spencer's feelings about Secretary of Labor Frances Perkins were slightly more charitable. "All of the manufacturers consider Miss Perkins at the bottom of the trouble in the country today," he told Cornelia, "but I am inclined to think that she is simply a thoroughly impractical idealist who lets agitators and organizers make a cat's paw of her." Spencer kept detectives employed long after the court case had ended, amassing a file on what he came to call the "three cornered fight between the communists, socialists and union organizers."[124]

A personal tragedy in the Love family revealed just how deep was the schism between mill men and their workers, even in a town where unionism never took root. In April 1935 Love's fourteen-month-old son Phillip died in his crib. The child had been put to bed at 2:00 P.M. for a nap, and when the maid returned at 5:00 P.M. he was dead. According to the autopsy, the cause of death was interstitial streptococcus pneumonia. The doctor explained that the disease attacked rapidly and that the death rate in afflicted children was more than 75 percent. Love had the autopsy performed in Greensboro and requested further pathology tests from Duke Hospital in Durham. Attached to the autopsy was a note explaining that Mr. Love had requested further tests because he "suspects some evidence of foul play due to some labor disturbance at his mill."[125]

To describe differences between communities is one thing. To understand the patterns of choice and behavior within a single mill village is quite another. Strike activists were drawn from the post–World War I generation that had grown up in the mills. But who were their opponents? Who feared or opposed the union from the start, crossed the picket lines, wielded a picker stick, or fired a gun? The evidence, though scanty, points toward two main sources of company support. One consisted of lower-ranking supervisors and their kin. Charges of favoritism, of "Boss men [who] are runig the Mills with thire on people," were high on the list of mill workers' complaints. In the small, homogeneous world of the mill village, such personal alliances could easily mushroom into political conflict. When push came to shove in the General Strike, it is not hard to imagine where the families of second hands and foremen came down. The second group of company supporters is more elusive, but just as significant: the newcomers who, as the Seneca women put it, "come in here & take our jobs."[126]

In the 1930s, as in the 1880s when the South's industrial revolution began, changes in the countryside set the stage for events in the mill. The agricultural depression of the 1920s had already inflated the labor supply. Now, New Deal farm policies encouraged crop reductions, displacing countless tenants and sharecroppers as landlords idled land and used government subsidies and low-interest loans to buy machinery. The Agricultural Adjustment Act amounted to an "American enclosure movement," driving another wave of southerners from the land.[127]

When the Textile Code mandated a forty-hour week, small mills accustomed to running one long shift switched to two eight-hour shifts, hiring many more workers than could be housed on the mill hill. The factories were flooded with spare hands hanging on to the hope of steady work and farmers with one foot still in the countryside. No longer was the village synonymous with the mill. In mill workers' letters, the resulting tensions were a constant theme. Usually the writers accused "selfesh farmers" of taking away their jobs. Less often, but with sharp insight, they shifted the blame to employers who used surplus labor to keep the union out.[128]

By the 1930s many cotton mill people had traveled far from their rural roots. Textile work was their "only means of livelihood"; they had no other way "to get bread." Farmers, by contrast, seemed blessed with options. "The farmers here in the Southland have about four months leisure time and they take their flivers and some of them drive many miles taking their families to the mills to work," said one worker. "After the Contery People has made ther winters Rashins they ort not to come in and take the Poblic work. . . . There is more comes to work in cars then lives on the hill and we are the ones Pays the Rent and suffers," wrote another.[129]

These images of well-to-do farmers battening off part-time work in the mills said more about millhands' anxieties than about farmers' lives. But they do attest to an important Depression era phenomenon: the rising number of part-time workers who lived outside the mill village, and thus beyond the reach of its historical memory and social ties—and of its new-found militancy. "Farmers are brought in from the country to replace those that are dissatisfied with the work," explained a man from Spray. "Thay won't complain." "They give the farmers the work in steed of folks in the Village and if we speak to one another thay Will Lay Both of us off."[130]

In this, as in much else, mill folk looked to national leaders to set things right. "It seems to me as though we have not had a fair deal," argued Leona Jones. "The President has helped the farmer by giving them Federal Aid so that they can make a crop and now the Mill Executives have allowed them to come here and take our jobs and then tell us to go some where else and get a job. Now the farmers don't have to depend on working in the mill for a living. They have a place to live and plenty to eat and it seems to me the best solution of the problem would be to send the farmers back to the farm so that we can have our jobs then we can buy farm products from them and all of us have a living."[131]

Workers, then, were divided into at least three camps: the "large families and special friends [of] the overseers and superintendents," the "green hands," and the "union hands." Such categories, of course, cannot account for the intangibles of individual motivation. But they do set the boundaries of an explosive mix: tight-knit communities that included desperate newcomers and fierce loyalists of opposite persuasions. Into this situation came local officials, who transformed hundreds of townspeople, farmers, and nonunion workers into deputy sheriffs, in effect putting a large and untrained private police force at the disposal of frightened employers. The result was inevitable. The wonder is that more violence did not ensue.[132]

We must also remember that the UTW could offer no material support. Its treasury was practically empty; fewer than ten paid organizers covered the entire South. By contrast, the power and authority of the manufacturers loomed large for all to see. The same needs—for food, clothing, coal for a fire with "winter coming on"—that sent some workers to the picket line inevitably propelled others into fighting for their jobs. At Honea Path, Mack Duncan recalled, "One of the men made the statement that he'd rather get killed there at the mill trying to get work to keep his family going than he would starve to death at home and see his family starve to death."[133]

Even those who had readily cast their lot with the strikers found hunger forcing them onto the sidelines or back to work. Hoyle McCorkle's experience in Charlotte must have been duplicated thousands of times. "I went out there every night on the picket line, and the streets would be lined up. They'd hurl insults at one another. A few would go in, and some wouldn't go in. They'd call them that did go in scabs. [The union] told us they'd feed us. But they didn't. So Mama and Daddy sat down one night and said, 'We've got to go back to work. We're running out of food.' So they went back to work."[134]

Eula McGill, whose career as a union activist began in Birmingham in 1934, traced the strike's rise and fall at the Selma Manufacturing Company. Birmingham, unlike most textile centers, was a diversified industrial town with a history of unionism. McGill's mother had taken her to union rallies and Labor Day celebrations during World War I; her father was a steelworker who secretly held a union card; her sister had joined a hosiery union. In 1934 Eula was working as a spinner at the Selma Manufacturing Company but living with her family outside the mill village. Despite her union sympathies, when her co-workers began organizing a UTW local she was among the last to know. "For a long time, they didn't want me to know it. They were afraid of me because I lived in another part of town. They told me later they were afraid to approach me because they didn't know how I felt." By September the Selma local had signed up a majority of the workers, and when the strike call came, "hell, everybody come out, nonunion as well as union. We shut it down tighter than a door nail. We were in the mining area—the mines were organized by that time. We had the support of the miners; we had the support of the building trades."[135]

Yet even in this relatively favorable environment, McGill's local had a hard time. "There were one or two paid organizers in the state, and they couldn't supervise. It was just bigger than they could handle. They weren't prepared to handle something that big. We were just more or less left pretty well to fend for ourselves the best we could. We didn't have no strike benefits. I had no income. I had no way even to get out to the picket line—I had no carfare, so I had to go home and stay for most of the duration of the strike in order to have some place to live and eat." Some of McGill's compatriots, less committed to begin with, ended up helping the company recruit strikebreakers from Georgia—for bounties of $100, or so it was said. By the time the UTW called the strike off, "most of our men had kind of chickened out on us," McGill recalled. "And most of us that were sticking were the women." Why did the men "chicken out"? "I just don't understand that, unless they thought we were going to lose—which we did. A hundred dollars was a lot of money in them days."[136]

To be sure, there were long-term, rank-and-file workers who, from the outset, simply feared and distrusted the union or sided with the company. To Perry Hicks in Marion, union leaders like Sam Finley, Lawrence Hogan, and Dan Elliott seemed "bossy and overbearing." Their assertiveness cut against the grain of mill village culture. Unionists, wrote one woman, "just grumble and keep up a disturbance among good people That are willing to work." They are "dangerous & stubborn . . . and ask for more [than the] mill official can give." Besides, some people felt that the mill owner "was their benefactor." "They were what you call 'loyal workers,'" Sam Finley recalled. "They thought the company'd think more of them. In the long run, they didn't."[137]

Bessie Buchanan, who had arrived at Erwin Mills in Durham when she was just a little girl, never joined a union or went to a union meeting. But the labor conflicts of the 1930s and 1940s left a mark that came out in her dreams. "It was just before World War II, and I dreamed that the Germans had built a wire fence around the whole world, and everybody was in that wire fence. And I was out hollering, 'The Germans are coming! The Germans are coming!' And they got me. And they carried me up in an old barn and put a white uniform on me. And they was going to shave my head. They'd shave your hair off, and then they'd throw you over in [a] lion pit, if you didn't come over and do what they wanted you to do and join the union.

"Then I says, 'Why are you all doing this to me? I never joined a union in my life, and I never had no part of it.' And one of the girls says, 'Could you prove that?' And she opened a door and said, 'You see that road out there? There's a gang of men with these knives going this way, swords going that way, and if you can walk down that line and not get killed, I'll let you out of here.' Well, I didn't know how in the world I'd do it, but I prayed and I prayed. And said, 'Lord, go with me.' And I went down that line, and I was not harmed. And when I got out, I was the only person out."[138]

Buchanan's "vision" had multiple meanings. It came to her in the midst of a long, drawn-out strike, at a time when she had a boarder who was a strong union supporter. Bessie Buchanan dreaded conflict and respected W. A. Erwin, the "daddy" of Erwin Mills. Yet in her dream, it is not easy to tell whom she feared more—the unionists "hollering nasty things" to people who crossed the picket line or the owner-judges demanding that she prove her lifelong loyalty.[139]

All in all, the stories we heard—in interviews and in letters to the NRA—caution against too readily ascribing workers' behavior to company loyalty or antiunion conviction. A variety of pragmatic motives also impelled men and women to brave cries of "scab" and slip in to work, succumb to threats or bribes, or lie low and wait the conflict out. Speaking eloquently for those whose silence did not imply consent was a Greenville woman who signed her letter "Just a laborer begging for justice." "I like thousands of others did not strike with the union, because we knew we would loose our jobs like thousands of others have done before us. Even though we might have had faith in the union we simply could'nt offord to quit because we live right up to every penny we make. . . . It is true that every textile worker in the south would walk out of the Mill to day if they were not afraid of starvation. I dont *believe* that God intended people to suffer as we have suffered. . . . The life of the average textile worker is a Tragic thing." Why, then, did some workers cast their lot with the company? From this woman's perspective, the question is badly put. Why so many were willing to risk so much seems more to the point.[140]

By the third week of the General Strike, mills throughout the country were slowly resuming production, and UTW organizers admitted that "force and hunger" were driving strikers back to work. Roosevelt deflected union pressure to intervene, instead appointing a special mediation board headed by John G. Winant. The Winant Board, however, quickly shifted from mediation to study, as the CTI made it clear that, as far as the industry was concerned, there would be no negotiation. On September 17 the Winant Board presented its findings: the Bruere Board should be replaced by a neutral body, the Federal Trade Commission should decide whether the industry could afford higher wages, and a special committee should investigate stretch-out complaints. On September 21 President Roosevelt announced the Winant Board's conclusions and added his personal plea to its request that the UTW call off the strike and that employers take back striking workers. The next day, the UTW complied. The General Strike officially ended on September 22, twenty-two days after it began.[141]

The reckless assertion by UTW vice-president Francis Gorman that this was among "the most amazing victories ever recorded in the annals of the A.F. of L." has taken its place as one of the tawdriest claims in American labor history.[142] But this is judgment in retrospect. After all, an investigative committee had lent legitimacy to workers' complaints; a new Textile Labor Relations Board had promised genuine investigations in place of industry self-policing, and the president himself had declared that strikers could return to their jobs without penalty or prejudice. Only gradually would the truth emerge: there was no machinery for preventing a wholesale purge of strikers and unionists from the mills. The UTW was in shambles. And within a year, the Supreme Court would declare the NIRA unconstitutional, bringing the New Deal program for industrial recovery to an abrupt end.

Through the fall and into winter, letters from southern mill workers indicated not a quick fading away of local unions but efforts to hold out despite overwhelming odds. Workers at two mills owned by J. C. Self in Greenwood had seen union organizing as "our only hope for future protection & justice, in the textile industry. So the people here seized this opportunity wholeheartedly. . . . Then the general strike was ordered. We of course, stood loyal to our obligations. . . . Thinking [there] would be, no discrimination on the employees." Self responded with a ten-week lockout. When the mill finally reopened, members of a company-sponsored "Community Boosters Club" received free coal and first choice of jobs. Those who refused to join were fired. The remaining union families were threatened with eviction. Still, not everyone gave in. "It looks like the owner of this mill is doing every thing he can to tare our union up," Mrs. Ruby Brown told Roosevelt, "but I feel like you will help us in some way where we can hole our people to-geather for our rights. . . . You know who put you where you are to-day the good old American people did. . . . the people are begain to wonder what you are going to do stay with us or turn your back on us."[143]

Adding her testimony was the indomitable Sadie Harris. Publicly, in her letters to the editor of the *Greenwood Tribune*, she was, as the expression went, all "fire and tow." "You tell a lie when you say we didn't win," she informed a procompany writer who signed himself "Et Cetera." "These two mills are closed, yes, (why?). . . . It is done to try and disorganize the union. . . . To be sure you hold your job [but] you are no more in God's sight than we unionists are, and not so much, for we are His people, and you belong to Satan's army. . . . We want you to know . . . [w]e will fight the bitter fight for the restoration of our jobs. . . . I am 61 years of age," she concluded, "a little woman in height, but I'll face a giant, if necessary; don't let that fool you." Privately, however, even Sadie Harris acknowledged desperation. "I could write many pages," she told Franklin Roosevelt, "of poverty, children barefooted, no wearing apparall & many young babies without a fire. . . . if not given immediate assistance . . . the undertakers will be kept busy. . . . there will be many little mounds made in the cemeteries." As for herself, "I am getting very helpless & will have to apply to Greenwood Co. officials to get in the County home, for my children are unable to keep me."[144]

From across the Piedmont came similar stories of employers "break[ing] up our union," of workers forced to "submit." In communities such as Durham employers adamantly denied charges of discrimination. Yet unionists who returned to their jobs found themselves laid off one by one. In Gastonia, where the General Strike had verged on class warfare, the aftermath was more of the same. Writing to Roosevelt, Mrs. Ruby Mitchell, a "union woman" who served on the negotiating committee at the Loray Mill, explained. "[W]e tried to . . . return to our jobs. . . . we were met & turned back before we got to the Mill by 100 bad Men as they are Called, that was appoineted by the Mill officials to keep us out — Those 100 men had knifes — Black jakes — Clubs, & other deadly weapons." The committee went to talk to the manager. "He said —— Before he would work the union help he would Close the Mill down — That he was Not Compelled to work them — that you might run the U.S. But He was going to Run the Loray Mill as [he saw] fit. . . . The Loray Mill Co. has given the union member Movenng orders. [We are going] to be throwed out in the streets to the mercy of the world!"[145]

Eviction was the employers' ultimate weapon, for nothing produced more terror than the prospect of being out on the road with "no where to go" and "cold weather . . . coming on." A striker in Roanoke Rapids reported that families that had been "fired and run out of the mill houses" were living in hog pens and cow sheds. B. E. Brookshire from Williamston, South Carolina, lost his job when he was elected president of his union local. After the General Strike his son and daughter were discharged as well. "Then they Forced me out of the house i was Living in i had no other place to go. . . . i have tried over 300 cotton mills for work and they will not hire me because I belong to the union. . . . There is Starvation ahead if i don't get work at *once*. . . . Please for God's Sake help me get work."[146]

Evidence of blacklisting came from many quarters. A superintendent at Cowpens, South Carolina, wrote, "If you Will arrange to have some one with the Proper authority to come here and walk into the office Unexpectdly you can get . . . a list of names of those who were on strike [which] has 'No' Written by each name which means they are Never to be re-employed. . . . I would gladly go with a person and show where these records are as they are not kept in the filling cabinet [but] in the presidents office." Despite the certainty that "coming into the open in this way . . . Will Mean that I will never get another Job in the Mills," this man offered to travel to Washington "for one way expense" to tell what he knew. Shortly after the strike James Pharis was working as a supervisor in a plant owned by Burlington Mills at Reidsville, North Carolina. He matter-of-factly recalled an incident described by dozens of workers and denied by as many mill owners. While Pharis was hiring people for a new third shift, a fellow came up to him and said, " 'Mr. Pharis, I don't know whether you know it or not, but that fellow over there, he's the leader of that flying squadron.' I just caught it in time. I told that fellow, 'We got all we can use tonight. We got all we can use. We can't use you. I'll let you know if we see where we can use you.' And I come that nigh to putting him to work."[147]

Quickly in some places, more gradually in others, resolution faded into anger and despair. "Unless there is something done in the next week or so. there will be war. in the united States," warned Ruby

Brown. Mrs. Mason of Roanoke Rapids was not a union member, but her husband, a World War I veteran, "a good Clean Charratar a good husband as far as he Could," was "*1000* pir cent." Now he and hundreds of others were facing "the Winter snows with out clothes and (Xmas) With out a penny." "Please read Carfully and think (deep)," Mrs. Mason told the "President of U.S.A." "Something must be done because ... 4000 people That stood faithful and dutfuly Through out This awful Strike ... are getting Blood thirsty here. [They] has Blood in there eyes." Isaac Randall also saw violence ahead. "Labor cannot tolerate this kind of treatment forever; there must be something done, or ... Pleading fingers will be turned into threating claws."[148]

The General Strike, whatever else it may have been, was a moment in history that laid bare longings and antagonisms ordinarily silenced, distorted, or repressed. Cotton mill people in the 1930s may not have subscribed to an abstract, universalistic notion of class solidarity. If nothing else, deep racial divisions militated against such perceptions. But mill folk did see themselves as a people apart, exploited by men with interests opposed to their own and denied opportunities for progress that had seemed within their grasp. Their militancy sprang in part from a defense of traditional values and in part from a desire to exert control over their changing place in a new, more expansive world—and it must be understood on its own terms and in its own historical moment. The 10,000 mourners who converged on the funeral of the strikers killed at Honea Path, the hundreds of young men and women who climbed into Fords and clamored at the mesh wire of mill gates, the workers in Durham who firmly denied executives access to the mills—these people broke through the restraints imposed by economic defenselessness and dropped the mask of resignation to make a mark on their times.[149]

We can only speculate about what might have happened had the General Strike occurred later, after the Wagner National Labor Relations Act had strengthened workers' right to organize and labor insurgents had formed the CIO. The strike itself might have ended as it did, but with less devastating effects. As it was, working-class leaders—those who had seized the opportunities for political participation and collective action offered by the New Deal—were purged from the mills, while those who stayed suffered a debilitating erosion of faith and will.

The secretary of Local 2265 in Kannapolis, writing to Francis

Gorman, described those feelings well. "Our local is gone and it dont seem there is any use to try now as they have lost faith in the union. We have had so many promises and nothing done I myself am almost ready to give up. . . . What is wrong[?] have the whole works sold out[?] . . . We as a poor hungry people cannot live with[out] something to eat and something to wear and to keep us warm How do you people in Washington think we can go on living on air and promises What we need is help and if you cannot get that for us then say so and we will not depend on promises any longer. . . . it looks like Cannon Mills are running the whole thing We want to know if they run the whole country it looks like it. . . . Please . . . do something that we may be able to still have faith in our Government."[150]

Millhands learned from their history, and in 1934 the lesson for many was a deep distrust of government and trade unions alike. Above all, the General Strike drove home the cost of challenging the established order. Better the familiar securities of job and home than "air and promises," followed by exile, suffering, and defeat.[151]

Southern workers did not abandon efforts to gain a voice in mill affairs. Their disillusionment with the NRA and their abortive strike helped spur passage of the Wagner Act in 1935 and the Fair Labor Standards Act in 1938. Heartened by the restructuring of labor law, the CIO launched a southern organizing drive; by the end of World War II textile unionism had established a beachhead in the region. Still, labor's victories in other major industries bypassed the textile South. Southern legislators, unhindered by working-class bargaining power, led a postwar attack on labor's legislative gains. The unorganized South remained a mecca for runaway shops and, as migration out of the region accelerated with World War II, a constant source of cheap labor.[152]

Within this environment, textile manufacturers intensified the strategies they had developed in the 1920s and 1930s. The combined effects of worker resistance and New Deal legislation made it impossible to push wages down. But neither the unions nor the federal government went beyond this issue to the deeper questions of mechanization and labor control. The result, by the 1970s, was a wholesale replacement of people by machines.[153]

To this long-term commitment to technological change, mill men added the destruction of the communities they had founded and tried so hard to subdue. This process had begun under the NRA, with the employment of increasing numbers of workers who lived "off the hill." The General Strike itself may have forwarded this trend by setting neighbor against neighbor and leaving wounds that were hard to mend.

An "old widow woman" at the Lonsdale Mill in South Carolina complained, "Part of the union folks have signed a 'yellow dog' Card, and turned against us & are talking and treating the union people so we can't hardly bear it. . . . We Can't even walk through one of the 'scabs' yard because we are Union members. . . . They wont go to Church with us, they Claim the union is not fit to associate with. . . . One of our best members in the union & Baptist Church here was asked Not [to sing in the choir] any more because he was a member of the Union. Our children Can't go to Sunday School or school either without being jeered at. All because we are trying to do what is right & for the best."[154]

Mack Duncan remembered that Honea Path "became a divided place" after the strike. "The people that belonged to the union didn't have anything to do with the people that were nonunion, and vice versa. And some of the people that had been real good neighbors never spoke to each other. Some of them even left the community. Pulled up and left. I went along with what my dad had to say. And he was loyal to the company. But after the incident happened, I was in school, and I'd read. And personally I believe the union is what's put America where it is today—people sticking together. Because industry never done anything until the union took over. They've got to keep good relations with the people now. My feeling then was antiunion because my dad was. But if I'd have been an adult and thinking for myself, I would have joined the union."[155]

Hoyle McCorkle in Charlotte had spent every night on the picket line until his family ran out of food and had to go back to work. "They called us scabs," he remembered. Four or five years later the label still stuck. One day Hoyle's older sister was playing in the yard with a neighbor's daughter. " 'Betty McCorkle,' " the girl's mother said. " 'You get away from here. You're nothing but scab.' And my sisters are pretty defiant anyway. She said, 'Old lady, look, my mama and daddy was the scabs and went back to work. I didn't have nothing to do with that.' "[156]

The mill owners, too, felt the sting of alienation. David Clark's response was a mean-spirited campaign aimed at discrediting the New Deal and whipping workers into line. By contrast, Kemp Lewis, president of Erwin Mills, looked back on the strike with "great sadness. . . . Our feeling is that our Company has done as much for the people working for it as any cotton mill company in the entire South," he wrote. "This being the case, you can easily understand . . . the terrific disappointment it was to us to have a majority of them follow a strange leader, who came to preach all sorts of wild doctrines and who filled them full of poison and hatred." Disappointment aside, Lewis was determined to "forget it all and look to the future," pushing ahead with new machinery, increased workloads, and the elimination of unnecessary workers. To Marjorie Potwin, a long-time social worker in the mills, the sad thing was that the "good mills"—the mills that had invested heavily in welfare policies—had lost the most, because they had the most to lose. "Socially-minded" mill owners might wonder, "What matters? Where the appreciation, and the loyalty? . . . Why not save one's self the trouble and the money?"[157]

Company towns had given southern mill owners unique and formidable powers. But the mill village system was never a foolproof instrument of labor control. That fact was driven home in the labor upheavals of the 1920s and 1930s, even as automobiles, a labor surplus, and New Deal legislation undermined the system's economic rationale. The Fair Labor Standards Act diminished the South's competitive advantage, while New Deal agricultural policy pushed more farmers off the land, permanently ending the necessity of providing housing in order to attract a scarce labor supply. Burlington Mills began selling its villages in the wake of the General Strike, and other firms followed suit. With the aid of improvements in highway transportation, which they helped promote, southern mill owners gradually dismantled their villages and hired workers from the surrounding countryside or relocated to rural industrial parks.[158]

The retired workers we talked to welcomed rising wages and the diminution of company control, but they remembered the unraveling of social relations as a personal loss. Work was severed from community life. People "didn't visit like they once did," and neighbors seemed distant and aloof. "People misses a lot by not having community," said Mary Thompson. "I believe it made you more secure or something. But now you're scattered. You work maybe one place, then work way over yonder, and you don't get close to nobody."[159]

Some manufacturers saw the dispersion of people and the collapse of community in a more favorable light. A North Carolina textile promoter explained. "[Our] goal was to have one industrial employee from every farm family in [the county]. We stressed that continually until I think it got to the point that people believed it, and the employment practices of the mills we brought here confirmed it. They found that by scattering their labor they were never available in large enough numbers to attract the union. When you get a lot of people living in one community, living in one mill village, they're naturally objects of concern—and, of course, exploitation—by labor unions. But scattering these people out all over the county turned out to be a very healthy concept."[160]

George Dyer, looking back on a lifetime in the mills of Charlotte, remembered much that was pleasant and good. But when he searched for words to sum up his views and bring his story to an end, this is what he said: "The corporations take advantage of people. They can do it because they can. That's the reason they do it, they can and they get away with it. It say, 'Justice for All,' and it ain't justice for all. It's justice for some, but it ain't for all. You say you're all equal—you ain't. We're divided. Our country right now is divided. The man's got money, he can get what he wants, the man ain't got it can't do nothing. The man's got money, got power. That's about all I have to say."[161]

ICY NORMAN and Lacy Wright supported the 1934 General Textile Strike quietly. Icy refused to cross the picket line at Burlington Mills. Lacy refused a boss man's order to take up picker sticks against a flying squadron. Years later, Icy and Lacy left textile work feeling betrayed, yet each found a way to turn pain into dignity.

In the 1940s Lacy joined a long and bitter fight for a union contract at the Cone family's White Oak plant in Greensboro. He served as a steward and later as president of his union local, until declining health cut short his leadership activities. "I noticed when I was young that the [cotton] dust bothered me," he recalled. "But, of course, I didn't realize what it could do. Over the years, I began to notice my energy was being sapped; normal work made me short-winded." Poor eyesight and deafness were also legacies of his years in the mill. In 1966, at the age of sixty-one, Lacy quit because he "just couldn't breathe anymore." After almost half a century of service in the Cone family's mills, he was rewarded with a pension of fourteen dollars a month. Wright's illness was misdiagnosed until 1975, when a physician recognized that he suffered from byssinosis, or brown lung.

Wright turned that diagnosis into a challenge to protect others. He helped organize fellow cotton mill workers into the Carolina Brown Lung Association (CBLA) and presided over its Greensboro chapter. "I don't need anyone to tell me I can't breathe. There's nothing that I can do about that now. I only want to spend the time I have left helping other people. Our Lord and Savior told us we are our brothers' keepers, and some way, all my life, I have never been able to get away from that."

Lacy found support for his convictions among a group of young activists fresh from a campaign in the coal fields of Harlan County, Kentucky. These men and women had witnessed firsthand the suffering caused by black lung and learned the value of raising occupational health issues as an organizing strategy. In 1975 they extended their work to the textile industry by establishing screening clinics for brown lung in five Piedmont communities. As retired workers confronted their common condition, they rekindled old friendships and overcame isolation. Out of the clinics emerged permanent organizations dedi-

Lacy Wright, 1976. Photograph by Georgia Springer and Sally Court.
(Courtesy of Southern Exposure*)*

cated to winning compensation and lobbying for cleaner mills. By 1981 the CBLA claimed 7,000 members and a staff of more than 40 lawyers and organizers.

The Brown Lung Association focused national attention on the devastating effects of breathing cotton dust and pressured the U.S. Department of Labor's Occupational Safety and Health Administration (OSHA) to improve air quality standards in the mills. Disabled workers, many breathing only with the help of portable oxygen tanks, packed OSHA hearings, where they testified to the human costs of mill air clouded with lint, management slow to acknowledge brown lung, and doctors who attributed their wheezing and coughing to something other than cotton dust. Worried by the impact of such scenes, one textile industry trade journal wondered whether federal regulators would "be as big a bane to the industry as were the flying squads of union organizers in the 1930s." The year 1984 marked a victory for the movement. Joining forces with the Amalgamated Clothing and Textile Workers Union, the CBLA helped convince OSHA to implement a new cotton dust standard in the mills.

This victory, however, coincided with the group's decline. When the political climate shifted to the right in the 1980s, the CBLA's funding sources dried up virtually overnight. Success, on the one hand, and internal problems, on the other, further sapped the group's vitality. By 1987 the Carolina Brown Lung Association was "a shell of what it used to be. But it still struggled to survive."[1]

During the forty-seven years that Icy Norman worked at Burlington Mills, the company underwent enormous change. After the defeat of the 1934 strike, it could pursue unchecked the diversification and technological innovation begun in the 1920s. The company inaugurated overseas operations in the 1940s and during the next decade added cotton, woolen, and worsted textiles to the synthetics that had become its trademark. To reflect this growth, Burlington Mills changed its name to Burlington Industries in 1955. Spencer Love, who served as both chairman of the board and president, died of a heart attack in 1962, but his policy of staying on the cutting edge of technological innovation persisted. During the 1970s Burlington Industries spent millions of dollars on modern equipment that allowed the corporation to cut its labor force drastically and institute another stretch-out.

By the time Icy Norman retired in 1976, Burlington Industries was the world's largest textile firm. She had worked for it longer than any other employee, keeping her promise to stay with Spencer Love and the company through good times and bad. "I did everything they ever asked me to do." Nonetheless, the company forced Icy to retire shortly after her sixty-fifth birthday and six months before fulfilling the conditions of a new profit-sharing plan. "I begged them to let me work on but they wouldn't. I could have got that big profit sharing they all get now." Supervisors pleaded her case, but corporate policy was immutable.

Icy felt that her loyalty had been betrayed. "I feel like I was part in making the Burlington Industries because I come there and stayed with them. I went with them through thick and thin. I give the best part of my life to the Burlington Industries. It kind of hurt me to think that as long as I stayed there and as faithful as I worked, that I didn't get none of that profit. I felt like I was part of the Burlington Mill. Because Burlington Mill was nothing but a two-room plant when I went there."

On the day of her retirement, Icy had her hair fixed at Burlington Industries' expense. Her boss then drove her to Greensboro, where she toured the corporate headquarters and dined with a group of executives. "I went up to that main office. They carried me all over that thing. I met everybody. Each floor had a different carpet, different design, different furniture. I went clean up to the top. You know what they had in the top? They had the prettiest white rug. It was a beautiful thing. Beautiful furniture. Everything was white." Company officials feted and photographed her and praised her loyalty to Burlington Industries, but they refused to budge on the profit-sharing question.

Icy did not let corporate policy tarnish either her relationship with fellow workers or the satisfaction she garnered from work well done. She looked back on her life at Burlington Industries with joy and only a touch of melancholy. "I said I didn't have no family. But in the other sense of the word, I've got a big family, because I try to go in fellowship and do for other people. If they need something, I try to help them. If I can do them a favor, I'm there to do it. Of course, some people may think that ain't no joy in doing that. But it is. You just come right down to it, you get more joy out of doing some little something than anything in the world. You know, money can't buy happiness. Money can't buy joy. That's why I said I enjoyed working on my job. I got a pleasure out of it, and it made me happy to do my job. When I come out of that mill, I know that I done the very best I could. Somewhere along the way I felt a peaceable mind.

Icy Norman holding a picture of her mother, 1984. Photograph by Mary Murphy.

"We had good years, we had bad years. I reckon that goes through life. Like I said, everybody up there felt like just one family. We['d] just laugh and joke. We'd play. We'd all work together and tried to pull together. When I left the Burlington Mill, I left my family. They all felt like my brothers and sisters. I worked with some of them so long. I was the oldest one in the Pioneer Plant, the oldest hand they had. When those others come along, I got acquainted with them, I growed to love them. And I growed to fellowship with them. It was just like leaving one of my family. I couldn't help but cry. I said all the time I wasn't going to cry. When I went out and started home, I did cry, but they didn't notice."[2]

N O T E S

ABBREVIATIONS

ATM   *American Textile Manufacturer*
JSL Papers   James Spencer Love Papers. Southern Historical Collection, University of North Carolina at Chapel Hill
NRA Records Records of the National Recovery Administration. Record Group 9. Records of the Cotton Textile National Industrial Relations Board and the Textile National Industrial Relations Board. Entries 398, 401, and 402. National Archives, Washington, D.C. Unless otherwise noted, all materials are filed alphabetically by mill name.
STB   *Southern Textile Bulletin*
SWTE   *Southern and Western Textile Excelsior*
TM   *Textile Manufacturer*
TB   *Textile Bulletin*
TE   *Textile Excelsior*
TW   *The Textile Worker*

PREFACE

1. Hall, "An Oral History of Industrialization," and "Oral History Program Enriches Prospects for Researchers." The best introduction to oral history is Paul Thompson, *Voice of the Past*.

2. For these statistics and a similar profile of the entire Piedmont industrialization project, see Abernathy, Hudson, and Blackman, "Collective Profile of Interviewees."

3. For interwar intellectual life, see Singal, *War Within*. For these early oral history projects, see Rawick, *The American Slave*; Federal Writers' Project, *These Are Our Lives*; and Terrill and Hirsch, *Such As Us*.

4. For the problem of authority in historical evidence, see Frisch, "Oral History, Documentary, and the Mystification of Power," and Foucault, *Power/Knowledge*, pp. 78–92.

5. Rosa Holland interview, pp. 30–31. On silence in oral sources, see Passerini, "Italian Working Class Culture Between the Wars." Two projects are in progress that should radically expand our understanding of this little-studied event: a dissertation-in-progress by Janet Irons at Duke University and a Research Consortium for the Southwide Strike of 1934 directed by Vera Rony at the State University of New York at Stony Brook.

6. Tannenbaum, "The South Buries Its Anglo-Saxons," pp. 205, 210–11.

7. For changing attitudes toward industrialization, see Carlton, *Mill and Town*, pp. 129–70, and Shapiro, *Appalachia on Our Mind*, pp. 162-85. Quotation is from Tannenbaum, "The South Buries Its Anglo-Saxons," p. 206.

8. Broadus Mitchell, *Rise of Cotton Mills*; Cash, *Mind of the South*, esp. p. 204; Herring, *Welfare Work*; Rhyne, *Some Southern Cotton Mill Workers*; Pope, *Millhands and Preachers*; and Morland, *Millways of Kent*. The quotation is from Nichols, "Does the Mill Village Foster Any Social Types?" Melton McLaurin's *Paternalism and Protest*, which argued against the image of southern millhands as a "docile, submissive labor force," was a partial exception. The 1980s promise a fresh view, for the study of southern textiles is becoming a minor cottage industry. See, for instance, Beatty, "Textile Labor in the North Carolina Piedmont," and "Edwin Holt Family"; De-Natale, "Traditional Culture and Community"; Flamming, "Work, Family, and Community"; Frederickson, "Place to Speak Our Minds"; Hodges, *New Deal Labor Policy*; Janiewski, *Sisterhood Denied*; Newman, "Work and Community Life"; Quinney, "Childhood in a Southern Mill Village"; and Selby, "Industrial Growth and Worker Protest," and " 'Better to Starve in the Shade.' " Black workers began entering the textile industry in large numbers only in the 1960s. For their experiences, see Byerly, *Hard Times Cotton Mill Girls*, and Frederickson, "Four Decades of Change."

CHAPTER ONE

1. John Wesley Snipes interview, September 20, 1976, pp. 3–5. An excellent introduction to the relationship between agriculture and industrialization is Hahn and Prude, *Countryside in the Age of Capitalist Transformation*. The best discussion of antebellum backcountry society is Hahn, *Roots of Southern Populism*, pp. 15–85. See also Genovese, "Yeoman Farmers." Studies of North Carolina Piedmont counties that set an antebellum context include Kenzer, "Portrait of a Southern Community," and Durrill, "Producing Poverty." Guion Griffiths Johnson, *Antebellum North Carolina*, discusses regional and class differences. For a first-person account, see John Brevard Alexander, *Reminiscences*, pp. 151–76.

2. On the necessity of interdependence in a subsistence-based agricultural society, see Robert A. Gross, "Culture and Cultivation," pp. 45–47. Of course, it was impossible to achieve self-sufficiency, as pointed out in Breen, "Empire of Goods." On how two antebellum farm families in North Carolina balanced production and consumption, see Watson, *An Independent People*, pp. 20–23, and Menius, "James Bennitt," pp. 319–22. For a useful discussion of various definitions of community, see Bender, *Community and Social Change*, pp. 3–11. On the producer ideology and antebellum fence laws, see Hahn, "Common Right and Commonwealth," pp. 58–65, and McDonald and McWhiney, "From Self-Sufficiency to Peonage," pp. 1105–6.

3. Information on North Carolina is drawn from Lefler and Newsome, *North Carolina*, pp. 366, 380, 392–93. On South Carolina, see Carlton, *Mill and Town*, p. 14, and Ford, "Rednecks and Merchants," pp. 298–99.

4. Durrill, "Producing Poverty," p. 764; Genovese, "Yeoman Farmers"; and Watson, "Conflict and Collaboration," p. 296. See also Watson, *Jacksonian Politics.*

5. A good introduction to the abundant literature on changes in the postbellum agricultural economy is Woodman, "Sequel to Slavery." On the crop lien, see Woodward, *Origins of the New South*, pp. 180–84, and Hahn, *Roots of Southern Populism*, pp. 176–86.

6. On wartime devastation, see Woodward, *Origins of the New South*, pp. 177–78; Lefler and Newsome, *North Carolina*, p. 477; and McDonald and McWhiney, "From Self-Sufficiency to Peonage," p. 1115. On antebellum strategies, see Hahn, *Roots of Southern Populism*, pp. 47–48, and Menius, "James Bennitt," p. 316. On postbellum credit locking farmers into cash-crop production, see Hahn, *Roots of Southern Populism*, pp. 170–203, and Gavin Wright, *Political Economy of the Cotton South*, pp. 158–84.

7. Durrill, "Producing Poverty," looks at the consequences of fence laws and higher taxes in Union County, North Carolina. See also Hahn, *Roots of Southern Populism*, pp. 239–68, and McDonald and McWhiney, "From Self-Sufficiency to Peonage."

8. Lefler and Newsome, *North Carolina*, p. 521, for crop figures. On tenancy, see Williams and Wakefield, "Farm Tenancy in North Carolina," esp. pp. 22–23.

9. Hahn, *Roots of Southern Populism*, pp. 137–203; Durrill, "Producing Poverty"; Lefler and Newsome, *North Carolina*, p. 524; and Janiewski, "From Field to Factory," pp. 12–14.

10. Fred Yoder interview, pp. 6–7.

11. North Carolina Bureau of Labor Statistics, *Annual Report . . . 1887*, pp. 72, 101, 96, 91.

12. Quoted in Hahn, " 'Unmaking' of the Southern Yeomanry," p. 195.

13. For overviews of the Alliance, see McMath, *Populist Vanguard*, and Goodwyn, *Democratic Promise*, pp. 3–274. On women's participation, see Jeffrey, "Women in the Southern Farmers' Alliance," pp. 75–91, and Lu Ann Jones, " 'The Task That Is Ours,' " pp. 22–47.

14. *Progressive Farmer*, May 10, 1892, and Fred Yoder interview, pp. 7–8. On Populism and its aftermath, see Goodwyn, *Democratic Promise*, pp. 275–556; Woodward, *Origins of the New South*, pp. 235–90, 321–49; and Kousser, *Shaping of Southern Politics.*

15. Eller, *Miners, Millhands, and Mountaineers*, pp. xix–xx, 3–38.

16. Gavin Wright, *Old South, New South*, pp. 55–57, 110–22, and Woodward, *Origins of the New South*, pp. 406–8.

17. Fite, *Cotton Fields No More*, pp. 102–19. For testimony and images of southern farmers gathered during the Depression, see Federal Writers' Project, *These Are Our Lives*; Terrill and Hirsch, *Such As Us*; and Hagood, *Mothers of the South.*

18. Hagood, *Mothers of the South*, p. 34, and George and Tessie Dyer interview, p. 4. For comparisons of different tenure classes, see Taylor and Zimmerman, "North Carolina Farmers," and Anderson, "Farm Family Living."

19. Dickey and Branson, "How Farm Tenants Live," pp. 20–23.

20. Farmers quoted in Robinson, *Living Hard*, pp. 120, 107–8, 130–31. On the mobility of farm labor, see Gavin Wright, *Old South, New South*, pp. 65–66. A lyrical firsthand account of tenant farming is Rosengarten, *All God's Dangers*.

21. Quotation from Dickey and Branson, "How Farm Tenants Live," p. 23.

22. John Wesley Snipes interview, September 20, 1976, pp. 7–8 and passim; Vesta and Sam Finley interview, p. 2; and Alice Grogan Hardin interview, p. 4. A good description of turn-of-the-century rural life can be found in Nathans, *Quest for Progress*, pp. 5–10. On accommodation to a market economy, see Lu Ann Jones, " 'The Task That Is Ours,' " and Hahn, *Roots of Southern Populism*, p. 201. In *Breaking the Land*, Daniel explores the blend of continuity and change in the postbellum South. For a comparison to mid-nineteenth-century New England, see Robert A. Gross, "Culture and Cultivation."

23. John Wesley Snipes interview, September 20, 1976, p. 15, and anonymous interview. On planting and butchering by signs, see Vinnie Partin interview, August 9, 1974, pp. 22–24, and Lula Johnson Lacock interview, p. 9. An excellent discussion of folk farming and medical beliefs can be found in DeNatale, "Traditional Culture and Community," pp. 36–39, 70–79.

24. Daniel, "Crossroads of Change," p. 432.

25. Lee A. Workman interview, pp. 83–84, and George and Tessie Dyer interview, p. 6. On cutting and selling railroad crossties, see John Wesley Snipes interview, September 20, 1976, pp. 30–31, and Chester Copeland interview, p. 14. On working for the railroad, see Frank Gilbert interview, pp. 1, 16.

26. Anonymous interview. See also Glenn E. and Gladys Hollar interview, pp. 1–9, and George and Tessie Dyer interview, pp. 2, 6. For a descriptive overview of southern farm women's work, see Lu Ann Jones, " 'The Task That Is Ours,' " pp. 5–21.

27. Glenn E. and Gladys Hollar interview, pp. 27–28, and anonymous interview. Other interviews that discuss women as farmers include Junie Aaron interview, pp. 1–2; Eunice Austin interview, p. 1; and Dolly Moser interview, untranscribed. On taking in washing and agricultural wage labor, see Stella Carden interview, p. 5, and Letha Ann Sloan Osteen interview, p. 13. On boarders, see Reid A. Maynard interview, p. 36.

28. John Wesley Snipes interview, September 20, 1976, p. 17, and Vesta and Sam Finley interview, p. 4. For general discussions, see Hagood, *Mothers of the South*, esp. pp. 108–27, and U.S. Department of Labor, Children's Bureau, *Rural Children*.

29. Vesta and Sam Finley interview, p. 5; anonymous interview; and Betty and Lloyd Davidson interview, pp. 1, 19–20.

30. Kathryn Killian and Blanche Bolick interview, pp. 2–3, and Frank Webster interview, p. 13.

31. Edward and Mary Harrington interview, pp. 17–18, 26. For general discussions of southern farm women and field work, see Janiewski, "From Field to Factory," pp. 7–62, and Hagood, *Mothers of the South*, pp. 77–91.

32. Eunice Austin interview, pp. 1–3. See also Kathryn Killian and Blanche Bolick interview, pp. 3–4.

33. Robinson, *Living Hard*, pp. 132, 134. Although we need more precise studies of how farm women's work changed, much evidence suggests that their participation in field work increased or took on a new urgency under cash-crop farming. See Hagood, *Mothers of the South*, pp. 77–91; Hahn, *Roots of Southern Populism*, p. 201; and Lu Ann Jones, " 'The Task That Is Ours.' "

34. Ila Rice interview, untranscribed, and Hattie Suggs interview, untranscribed.

35. Myrtle Gentry interview, p. 9, and George and Tessie Dyer interview, pp. 4–5.

36. Janiewski, "From Field to Factory," pp. 7–62, and Eula and Vernon Durham interview, pp. 36–37. Faragher, *Women and Men on the Overland Trail*, p. 181, makes a similar argument about commercial agriculture's effect on male-female relations in the nineteenth-century Midwest.

37. James and Nannie Pharis interview, pp. 20–22; anonymous interview; and Edward and Mary Harrington interview, p. 25.

38. Glenn E. and Gladys Hollar interview, pp. 1–7, and Dolly Moser interview, untranscribed. Moser, age ninety-three when interviewed, said that one reason she declined offers of remarriage was worry about how a stepfather would treat her children. She concluded her recollections: "I've had it pretty tough. I don't know how I've lived this long."

39. Anderson, "Farm Family Living," p. 36.

40. Frank Webster interview, p. 32, and Icy Norman interview, p. 14. A study of black and white owner, renter, and sharecropper families in three North Carolina counties found an average of seventy-six visits with neighbors a year. See Taylor and Zimmerman, "North Carolina Farmers," p. 85.

41. Asa Spaulding interview, pp. 8–9, 15–16, and Paul and Pauline Griffith interview, p. 10.

42. Dickey and Branson, "How Farm Tenants Live," pp. 31–32.

43. Anonymous interview.

44. Jesse L. Brooks interview, p. 33; Lillie Morris Price interview, p. 9; and Asa Spaulding interview, pp. 13–14.

45. John Wesley Snipes interview, September 20, 1976, pp. 11, 24; John Wesley Snipes interview, November 20, 1976, p. 4; and Icy Norman interview, pp. 19, 27.

46. Alice Grogan Hardin interview, p. 1, and Roy Ham interview, pp. 29–30.

47. Claude C. Thomas interview, p. 3. On courting in the countryside, see John Wesley Snipes interview, September 20, 1976, p. 12; Icy Norman interview, pp. 16–17; and Harvey Ellington and Sam Pridgen interview, pp. 22–24.

48. Durham *Tobacco Plant* quoted in Webb, *Jule Carr*, p. 94. On merchants' role in mill building, see Carlton, *Mill and Town*, pp. 49–59; Broadus Mitchell, *Rise of Cotton Mills*, pp. 256–57; and Freeze, "Master Mill Man," pp. 9–32. For discussions of the "New South" movement, see Woodward, *Origins of the New South*, pp. 131–54, and Gaston, *New South Creed*.

49. Broadus Mitchell, *Rise of Cotton Mills*, pp. 106–7; Carlton, *Mill and Town*, pp. 40–81; Woodward, *Origins of the New South*, pp. 131–35; Pope, *Millhands and Preachers*, pp. 13–20; Lefler and Newsome, *North Carolina*, pp. 503–19; and Collins, "Cotton Textile Industry," p. 385. The quotation is from Nathans, *Quest for Progress*, p. 29.

50. On railroad growth in North and South Carolina respectively, see Lefler and Newsome, *North Carolina*, pp. 517–18, and Carlton, *Mill and Town*, pp. 21–23.

51. Lefler and Newsome, *North Carolina*, pp. 512–13; Woodward, *Origins of the New South*, p. 137; and Carlton, *Mill and Town*, pp. 13–26.

52. Broadus Mitchell, *Rise of Cotton Mills*, pp. 9–76; Carlton, *Mill and Town*, p. 40; Lefler and Newsome, *North Carolina*, p. 397; Griffin and Standard, "Cotton Textile Industry, Part II"; and Griffin, "North Carolina Textile Industry," pp. 34–40.

53. Murphy, "Burlington, North Carolina," and Ashe and Weeks, *Biographical History of North Carolina*, pp. 181–89. The quotation is from Caldwell Ragan interview, pp. 6–7.

54. Lefler and Newsome, *North Carolina*, p. 508; Broadus Mitchell, *Rise of Cotton Mills*, pp. 77–159, 232–76; Carlton, *Mill and Town*, pp. 40–81; and Collins, "Cotton Textile Industry," pp. 358–92.

55. Woodward, *Origins of the New South*, pp. 113, 150–51; Carlton, *Mill and Town*, p. 67; Broadus Mitchell, *Rise of Cotton Mills*, pp. 106–7, 144–47; and "Record of Notable Achievement," pp. 311–26.

56. Gerald W. Johnson, *Southern Industrialist*, pp. 10–35, esp. pp. 13, 24, 82.

57. Ibid., pp. 44–84, esp. pp. 36, 48.

58. Kuhn, "Durham, North Carolina"; Rand, " 'I Had to Like It,' " pp. 1–10; Ashe, *Biographical History of North Carolina*, pp. 114–21; and James R. Young, *Textile Leaders of the South*, pp. 61, 747.

59. Webb, *Jule Carr*, pp. 12, 35, 64.

60. Ibid., pp. 80–82.

61. Ibid., pp. 104–11.

62. Ibid., pp. 232, 176–89; Carr quoted on pp. 232, 188.

63. Biographical sketches of the Cones can be found in Ashe and Weeks, *Biographical History of North Carolina*, pp. 109–21, and Powell, *Dictionary of North Carolina Biography*, pp. 412–13. The quotations are from the Ben and Ceasar Cone interview, pp. 1, 9.

64. Broadus Mitchell, *Rise of Cotton Mills*, pp. 106–7; Carlton, *Mill and Town*, pp. 40–81; and Woodward, *Origins of the New South*, pp. 131–35. For purposes of comparison, see E. P. Thompson, "Time, Work-Discipline, and Industrial Capitalism."

65. Janiewski, "From Field to Factory," pp. 57–60.

66. DeNatale, "Traditional Culture and Community," pp. 17–19.

67. Janiewski, "From Field to Factory," pp. 60–62, and Freeze, "Piedmont Cotton Mill Families."

68. Flossie Moore Durham interview, pp. 1–4.

69. Albert Sanders interview, pp. 1–6.

70. Holland Thompson, *From Cotton Field to Cotton Mill*, p. 71; " 'Wage Earners in the Cotton Textile Industry,' Report of the U.S. Commission of Labor," *STB*, September 7, 1911, pp. 4, 17; McHugh, "Family Labor System," p. 19; and James and Nannie Pharis interview, p. 28.

71. McHugh, "Family Labor System," p. 19; " 'Wage Earners in the Cotton Textile Industry,' " pp. 4, 17; Carlton, *Mill and Town*, p. 114; John F. Schneck, "Who is Neighbor to this Family?," *TM*, July 16, 1914, p. 7; Jessie Lee Carter interview, pp. 1–6; and J. M. Robinette interview, pp. 1–4.

72. Martin Lowe interview, pp. 5–6, 23.

73. Grover Hardin interview, pp. 2–3.

74. Paul and Pauline Griffith interview, pp. 11–13.

75. Ernest Hickum interview, pp. 1–6; song quoted in Whisnant, *All That Is Native and Fine*, p. 7. Another example of an older man who returned to farming after a "flurry with the mills" can be found in Letha Ann Sloan Osteen interview, pp. 2, 13–15.

76. James and Dovie Gambrell interview, untranscribed.

77. Betty and Lloyd Davidson interview, pp. 1–2; Emma Whitesell interview, pp. 1–3; and Kathryn Killian and Blanche Bolick interview, pp. 16–19.

78. Lee A. Workman interview, pp. 5–8.

79. Mack Duncan interview, p. 55.

80. Claude C. Thomas interview, pp. 4–7.

81. Alice Grogan Hardin interview, pp. 1–9.

82. John Wesley Snipes interview, September 20, 1976, pp. 25–26, 32, and John Wesley Snipes interview, November 20, 1976, pp. 11–17.

83. Mrs. Howard K. (Josephine) Glenn interview, pp. 2–4.

84. Eva B. Hopkins interview, pp. 33–34.

85. Edward and Mary Harrington interview, pp. 14–15, 26.

86. Ila Rice interview, untranscribed, and anonymous interview.

CHAPTER TWO

1. Forrest Lacock interview, pp. 19–20. On the importance of learning in the early development of the textile industry, see Prude, "Early New England Textile Mills," p. 3, and Gavin Wright, *Old South, New South*, pp. 131–32.

2. "Southern Cotton Spinners' Association," *SWTE*, May 12, 1900, p. 7.

3. A variety of interpretations of England's Industrial Revolution are forwarded in Ashton, *Industrial Revolution*; Landes, *Unbound Prometheus*; Mantoux, *Industrial Revolution*; Marx, *Capital*; and Polanyi, *Great Transformation*. A more recent overview is

Floud and McCloskey, *Economic History of Britain*. Recent articles that review the literature are F. Stuart Jones, "New Economic History," and P. K. O'Brien, "Typology for the Study of European Industrialization."

4. The development of the textile industry in the United States is discussed in Jeremy, *Transatlantic Industrial Revolution*; Kulik, "Beginnings of the Industrial Revolution in America"; Prude, *Coming of Industrial Order*; Tucker, *Samuel Slater*; Wallace, *Rockdale*; and Ware, *Early New England Cotton Manufacture*. The development of the ring frame and the Northrop loom are discussed in Chen, "Differences in Costs and Productivity," pp. 554–56; Copeland, *Cotton Manufacturing Industry*, pp. 54–111; Feller, "Draper Loom," pp. 320–42, and "Technological Change"; Galenson, *Migration of Cotton Textile Industry*, pp. 39–46; and Wallace, *Rockdale*, pp. 124–47.

5. New England's textile machinery industry is covered in Knowlton, *Pepperell's Progress*; Gibb, *Saco-Lowell Shops*; and Navin, *Whitin Machine Works*. Not every mill could afford new machinery. Many began operations with used frames and looms bought from northern firms. Better-capitalized firms, however, took advantage of available technology. A discussion of the equipment in early southern mills is contained in Blicksilver, *Cotton Manufacturing in the Southeast*, pp. 24–27, and Massachusetts Bureau of Statistics of Labor, *Cotton Manufactures*, p. 43. The social implications of industrialization remain a controversial subject among historians. Marx, *Capital*, offered the most detailed critique of the consequences of technology in a capitalist economy. The liberal-whig position in best expressed in Rostow, *Stages of Economic Growth*, and Landes, *Unbound Prometheus*. Beginning in the 1960s, a new generation of radical political economists and historians extended the contributions of Marx. See Braverman, *Labor and Monopoly Capital*; Edwards, *Contested Terrain*; Gordon, Edwards, and Reich, *Segmented Work, Divided Workers*; Marglin, "What Do Bosses Do?"; Montgomery, *Workers' Control*; and Noble, *America by Design*, and *Forces of Production*. A recent critique of Marglin is Landes, "What Do Bosses Really Do?"

6. North Carolina Department of Agriculture, *North Carolina and Its Resources*, p. 91; Carlton, *Mill and Town*, pp. 45, 54; and Robert Sidney Smith, *Mill on the Dan*, pp. 7–10. An exhaustive study of waterpower and steam power is contained in Hunter, *History of Industrial Power*.

7. U.S. Department of the Interior, Census Office, *Water-Power of the United States*, p. 726.

8. Quoted in Hammond, "Cotton Industry of This Century," p. 252. For similar observations see Robert Sydney Smith, *Mill on the Dan*, p. 21; "Cost of Mill Power," *STB*, October 12, 1910, p. 8; and Advertisement, *STB*, April 28, 1921, p. 13.

9. Blicksilver, *Cotton Manufacturing in the Southeast*, pp. 16–17, and Carlton, *Mill and Town*, p. 46.

10. Institute for Research in Social Science, "Survey of Catawba Valley," pp. 92–96.

11. Quoted in Glass, "Arista Cotton Mill," p. 3.

12. Glass, "Southern Mill Hills"; Bresler, "Industrial Vernacular Architecture"; Coolidge, *Mill and Mansion*, pp. 73–93; and Bishir, "Building the Myth."

13. The following discussion of the production process is drawn from Copeland, *Cotton Manufacturing Industry*, pp. 54–111.

14. Anonymous interview.

15. Carl and Mary Thompson interview, pp. 3–5, 32.

16. Gavin Wright, *Old South, New South*, pp. 133–35. See also Carlson, "Labor Supply," pp. 65–72; Copeland, *Cotton Manufacturing Industry*, pp. 86–87; Doane, "Regional Cost Differentials"; Kohn, *Cotton Mills of South Carolina*, p. 48; and Uttley, *Cotton Spinning and Manufacturing*, pp. 68–69. For a discussion of the advantages of Northrop looms, see Chen, "Differences in Costs and Productivity," p. 556. An interesting reminiscence of the early years is George M. Wright, "Then and Now," *STB*, March 5, 1931, p. 34a.

17. Beatty, "Lowells of the South"; Blicksilver, *Cotton Manufacturing in the Southeast*, pp. 10–12; Galenson, *Migration of Cotton Textile Industry*, p. 165; Massachusetts Bureau of Statistics of Labor, *Cotton Manufactures*, p. 54; Uttley, *Cotton Spinning and Manufacturing*, pp. 58–59; and T. M. Young, *American Cotton Industry*, p. 90.

18. The paternalistic boardinghouse system, where Yankee farm girls worked a few years before marriage, seemed to offer a New World solution to the permanent poverty that marked working-class life in England's "dark satanic mills." But a constant stream of inventions and new manufacturing methods—all designed to speed up production and lower labor costs—undermined the Lowell experiment. Working conditions deteriorated and the Yankee mill girls left the factories, to be replaced by poorer Irish families. Child labor increased, and men joined women at the machines. See Dublin, *Women at Work*; Prude, *Coming of Industrial Order*; and Tucker, *Samuel Slater*.

19. Kohn, *Cotton Mills of South Carolina*, p. 23.

20. For a discussion of the family labor system in the South, see McHugh, "Family Labor System," and Gavin Wright, *Old South, New South*, pp. 138–46.

21. Chester Copeland interview, pp. 15–16.

22. Forrest Lacock interview, p. 19, and Perry Hicks interview, p. 6. Accommodation to industrial life in New Hampshire mills is discussed in Hareven, *Family Time and Industrial Time*, pp. 120–53.

23. McHugh, "Family Labor System," p. 22, and Davidson, *Child Labor Legislation*, pp. 275–78.

24. Janiewski, *Sisterhood Denied*, pp. 55–65; McHugh, "Family Labor System," pp. 16–73; U.S. Congress, Senate, *Woman and Child Wage-Earners*, 1:525; and Naomi Trammell interview, p. 5.

25. Saxonhouse and Wright, "Two Forms of Cheap Labor," and Terrill, "Eager Hands," pp. 84–99. The quotation is from Gregg, "Essays on Domestic Industry," p. 229.

26. McKelway, "Child Wages in the Cotton Mills," pp. 15–16. General discussions of child labor reform are included in Davidson, *Child Labor Legislation*; Trattner, *Crusade for the Children*; and Stephen B. Wood, *Constitutional Politics in the Progressive*

Era. On North Carolina, see Gilmore, " 'Any Values Their Puny Arms Can Win' "; on South Carolina, see Carlton, *Mill and Town*, pp. 176–77, 203.

27. North Carolina Bureau of Labor and Printing, *Annual Report . . . 1901*, p. 208, and McKelway, "Child Wages in the Cotton Mills," p. 8.

28. Davidson, *Child Labor Legislation*, pp. 12–13, and Inabinet and Inabinet, *Old Mill Stream*, p. 22.

29. Recent studies of Hine's photographs are Curtis and Mallach, *Photography and Reform*, and Kemp, *Lewis Hine*.

30. Clark's role in the battle against child labor is discussed extensively in Stephen B. Wood, *Constitutional Politics in the Progressive Era*. On Clark's background, see Powell, *Dictionary of North Carolina Biography*, pp. 372–73.

31. McHugh, "Family Labor System," p. 65, and Davidson, *Child Labor Legislation*, p. 273. See Rand, " 'I Had to Like It,' " p. 37, for an example of the Erwin Mills in Durham using child labor as late as 1928.

32. Ada Mae Wilson interview, p. 7, and Jessie Lee Carter interview, p. 18.

33. Emma Williams interview, August 21, 1974, pp. 35, 38.

34. Ethel Faucette interview, p. 20, and Geddes E. Dodson interview, pp. 3–4.

35. Uttley, *Cotton Spinning and Manufacturing*, p. 57; Davidson, *Child Labor Legislation*, p. 12; and U.S. Congress, Senate, *Woman and Child Wage-Earners*, 1:190.

36. Allie Smith interview, p. 2.

37. Jessie Lee Carter interview, p. 3.

38. Inabinet and Inabinet, *Old Mill Stream*, p. 11; Lacy Wright interview, p. 2; and Grover Hardin interview, p. 11. See also Eva B. Hopkins interview, p. 2.

39. Ila Dodson interview, pp. 9–10.

40. Alice Evitt interview, pp. 1, 30, and Curtis Enlow interview, pp. 1–2.

41. George and Mamie Shue interview, p. 44, and Davidson, *Child Labor Legislation*, p. 277.

42. Anonymous interview; Edna Y. Hargett interview, p. 3; and Inabinet and Inabinet, *Old Mill Stream*, p. 7.

43. James and Nannie Pharis interview, p. 27, and Carl and Mary Thompson interview, p. 26.

44. Naomi Trammel interview, pp. 4–5, 9–10.

45. Paul Cline interview, p. 1, and Kohn, *Cotton Mills of South Carolina*, p. 46.

46. Carlton, *Mill and Town*, pp. 114–15; Williamson, *Crucible of Race*, pp. 429–44; Lebsock, *Free Women of Petersburg*, pp. 172–75; McLaurin, *Paternalism and Protest*, p. 135; Allen Heath Stokes, Jr., "Black and White Labor"; and Gavin Wright, *Old South, New South*, pp. 177–86.

47. Quoted in Frederickson, "Four Decades of Change," p. 29. According to Frederickson, 10 percent of South Carolina textile workers were black in 1920. After World War I blacks took on tasks that were more varied and required more skill than their classification as menial laborers would indicate.

48. Inabinet and Inabinet, *Old Mill Stream*, p. 21; Robert Sidney Smith, *Mill on the*

Dan, pp. 163–64; Byerly, *Hard Times Cotton Mill Girls*, p. 35; and Jessie Lee Carter interview, pp. 36–37. See also Holland Thompson, *From Cotton Field to Cotton Mill*, p. 120, and Thomas, "Fort Mill," p. 112.

49. Quoted in Beatty, "Textile Labor in the North Carolina Piedmont," p. 495. In 1880 over 57 percent of all mill workers were female. Women outnumbered men in every age group, but the discrepancy was greatest among those between the ages of sixteen and twenty-four. See Gavin Wright, *Old South, New South*, pp. 139, 144.

50. Mack Duncan interview, pp. 50–51, and anonymous interview.

51. McHugh, "Family Labor System," pp. 55–73; Gavin Wright, *Old South, New South*, p. 145; and Saxonhouse and Wright, "Two Forms of Cheap Labor," pp. 17–21.

52. Janiewski, *Sisterhood Denied*, p. 115.

53. Paul and Pauline Griffith interview, p. 53, and Mack Duncan interview, pp. 33–34.

54. Eula and Vernon Durham interview, pp. 11–12.

55. Byerly, *Hard Times Cotton Mill Girls*, p. 76. Women began to assume some low-level managerial positions in the 1930s after scientific management created the need for more precise record keeping. In 1935 the *STB* identified Mrs. Edna Reed of Nashville, Tennessee, as the only known female spinning overseer in the South. See *STB*, November 7, 1935, p. 14.

56. Gavin Wright, "Cheap Labor and Southern Textiles, 1880–1930," p. 609. For New England textile workers, see Hareven, *Family Time and Industrial Time*, pp. 259–86.

57. For similar attitudes among French textile workers, see Reddy, *Rise of Market Culture*, p. 136. For New England workers, see Hareven, *Family Time and Industrial Time*, pp. 69–84.

58. Paul Cline interview, p. 1.

59. Baxter Holman interview, untranscribed.

60. Baxter J. Merritt interview, pp. 6–7.

61. Geddes E. Dodson interview, pp. 6–7, 28–29.

62. Martin Lowe interview, p. 14.

63. Carl and Mary Thompson interview, pp. 24–26, 31–34.

64. Ibid., pp. 2–3, 29–31.

65. Roy Lee and Mary Ruth Auton interview, pp. 49, 51; Hoyle and Mamie McCorkle interview, p. 12; and Icy Norman interview, pp. 1–2, 15, 51.

66. Alice Copeland interview, p. 10.

67. John Wesley Snipes interview, August 22, 1979, untranscribed.

68. Gordon Sims interview, p. 10.

69. Quoted in Escott, *Many Excellent People*, p. 228. See also Holland Thompson, *From Cotton Field to Cotton Mill*, pp. 133–35, and Carlton, *Mill and Town*, pp. 175, 252. In 1909, 84 percent of North Carolina millhands worked sixty or more hours per week. See Phillip J. Wood, *Southern Capitalism*, p. 44.

70. Chen, "Differences in Costs and Productivity," p. 534.

71. Flossie Moore Durham interview, p. 11, and Alice Evitt interview, pp. 1, 29. See also Kohn, *Cotton Mills of South Carolina*, p. 44. The practice of pegging children's wages to the number of machines they tended made good economic sense to owners. Mills could not fill spinning jobs with experienced workers, so rather than assuming the costs of learning or having machines stand idle, they gave children "little" jobs and paid them only for what they could do. These modified piece rates also provided an incentive for children to master their jobs quickly; the more machines they tended, the higher their earnings rose. See Chen, "Differences in Costs and Productivity," p. 537.

72. Martin Lowe interview, pp. 7, 11; Gavin Wright, "Cheap Labor and Southern Textiles, 1880–1930," p. 608; and Kohn, *Cotton Mills of South Carolina*, p. 44.

73. Paul and Pauline Griffith interview, p. 39.

74. MacDonald, *Southern Mill Hills*, p. 148. See also Rhyne, *Some Southern Cotton Mill Workers*, pp. 164–74.

75. Broadus Mitchell, *Rise of Cotton Mills*, p. 2. See also Galenson, *Migration of Cotton Textile Industry*, pp. 174–76, and Stephen Jay Kennedy, *Profits and Losses in Textiles*, p. 252.

76. Frank Durham interview, pp. 17–18, and U.S. Public Health Service, "Affections of the Respiratory Tract," pp. 43–62.

77. Grover Hardin interview, pp. 18–19, 23.

78. Carl and Mary Thompson interview, p. 52.

79. Ibid., p. 61.

80. Edna Y. Hargett interview, p. 47, and Mack Duncan interview, p. 31.

81. Naomi Trammell interview, pp. 15–16.

82. Alice Evitt interview, p. 39; Mozelle Riddle interview, pp. 18–19; and Eva B. Hopkins interview, p. 14.

83. Alice Evitt interview, pp. 36, 44. See also, "An Ill Wind," and Byerly, *Hard Times Cotton Mill Girls*, pp. 85–86.

84. Mack Duncan interview, p. 33, and James and Nannie Pharis interview, pp. 4–5. See also Dewey Helms interview, p. 8, and J. C. Edwards, "Yesteryear Experiences," *Textile Industries*, July 1948, pp. 143–44.

85. Betty and Lloyd Davidson interview, p. 54.

86. Grover Hardin interview, p. 12.

87. Paul and Pauline Griffith interview, p. 62.

88. Mozelle Riddle interview, pp. 19–20; Curtis Enlow interview, p. 4; Frank Durham interview, p. 18; Viola Pitts interview, untranscribed; and Willie Mae Honnecutt interview, untranscribed.

89. Myrtle Gentry interview, p. 7; Willie Mae Honnecutt interview, untranscribed; and Edna Y. Hargett interview, pp. 48–49.

90. Mattie Shoemaker and Mildred Shoemaker Edmonds interview, March 23, 1979, pp. 29–31.

91. Anonymous interview. Such stoppages could be a mixed blessing. Some mills

required "make up time" if machines had been idle for part of the day, and workers had to stay late. See *STB*, March 5, 1931, p. 34a.

92. U.S. Congress, Senate, *Woman and Child Wage-Earners*, 1:270–71; Ralph Austin interview, p. 2; and Murphy Yomen Sigmon interview, pp. 10–11.

93. Ethel Faucette interview, pp. 24–25.

94. Eula and Vernon Durham interview, pp. 58–59.

95. Paul Cline interview, p. 17.

96. Eva B. Hopkins interview, p. 15.

97. Frank Durham interview, pp. 60–61.

98. Edna Y. Hargett interview, pp. 47–48.

99. Cash, *Mind of the South*, p. 217. This discussion of relations between management and workers draws on the insights of Edwards, *Contested Terrain*. Also of value are Brecher and Work Relations Group, "Uncovering Hidden History"; Chandler, *Visible Hand*, pp. 50–78; Cressey and MacInnes, "Voting for Ford"; Gordon, Edwards, and Reich, *Segmented Work, Divided Workers*, pp. 48–99; and Montgomery, *Workers' Control*, pp. 9–37.

100. Everett Padgett interview, p. 8.

101. Inabinet and Inabinet, *Old Mill Stream*, p. 11.

102. Pascal S. Boyd, "Then and Now," *STB*, March 5, 1931, p. 34a.

103. Harry Rogers interview, July 21, 1977, pp. 11–12; Gilman, *Human Relations*, p. 142; and Potwin, *Cotton Mill People of the Piedmont*, p. 150.

104. *STB*, November 2, 1911, p. 7, and Potwin, *Cotton Mill People of the Piedmont*, pp. 143–44.

105. Potwin, *Cotton Mill People of the Piedmont*, pp. 143–44, and Eula and Vernon Durham interview, p. 15.

106. James Pharis interview, July 24, 1977, p. 41, and Icy Norman interview, p. 40.

107. Eva B. Hopkins interview, pp. 2–3, and Paul Cline interview, pp. 20–21.

108. *STB*, November 2, 1911, p. 7, and Frank Durham interview, p. 45.

109. Paul Cline interview, p. 21, and Letha Ann Sloan Osteen interview, p. 21.

110. Grover Hardin interview, p. 16. Having children under the control of their parents was not always the most effective way of ensuring hard, steady work. In the 1910s some mills began giving children a bonus for perfect attendance. Rather than including the bonus in the regular pay envelope, which usually went to the parents, manufacturers gave the money directly to the children. See North Carolina Cotton Manufacturers' Association, *Proceedings of the Eleventh Annual Convention*, pp. 20–21.

111. Flossie Moore Durham interview, pp. 22–23, and Frank Durham interview, pp. 46–47.

112. Eva B. Hopkins interview, p. 26, and Mattie Shoemaker and Mildred Shoemaker Edmonds interview, March 23, 1979, p. 23.

113. Gilman, *Human Relations*, pp. 146–47, and Mack Duncan interview, p. 60.

114. Eula and Vernon Durham interview, p. 10, and U.S. Congress, Senate, *Woman and Child Wage-Earners*, 1:608.

115. Harry Rogers interview, July 21, 1977, p. 12.

116. Mattie Shoemaker and Mildred Shoemaker Edmonds interview, March 23, 1979, pp. 28–29.

117. Gilman, *Human Relations*, pp. 142–43, and Betty and Lloyd Davidson interview, p. 57.

118. Geddes E. Dodson interview, pp. 4–5.

119. Lacy Wright interview, pp. 26–31. See also McHugh, "Family Labor System," p. 28; MacDonald, *Southern Mill Hills*, p. 44; and Massachusetts Bureau of Statistics of Labor, *Cotton Manufacturers*, pp. 67–68.

120. Two accounts of the Knights' southern campaign are McLaurin, *Knights of Labor in the South*, and *Paternalism and Protest*, pp. 68–119. For a broader study of the Knights of Labor, see Leon Fink, *Workingmen's Democracy*.

121. McLaurin, *Paternalism and Protest*, pp. 86–89.

122. Ibid., pp. 120–77.

123. North Carolina Bureau of Labor and Printing, *Annual Report . . . 1901*, pp. 420, 424.

124. Ibid., pp. 415–16.

125. Ibid., pp. 416, 399.

126. Ibid., p. 423.

127. Ibid., p. 420, and *Alamance Gleaner*, October 11, 1900, p. 2.

128. The following discussion of the Haw River conflict is drawn from Dowd, "Strikes and Lockouts," p. 138; Raleigh *News and Observer*, October 5, 1900, p. 1, October 6, 1900, p. 1, October 10, 1900, p. 2, October 18, 1900, p. 3, October 19, 1900, pp. 1–2, October 20, 1900, pp. 1–2, October 25, 1900, p. 2, October 31, 1900, p. 4, November 21, 1900, p. 1, and November 30, 1900, p. 2; and *Alamance Gleaner*, October 11, 1900, p. 2, October 18, 1900, p. 3, November 1, 1900, p. 3, November 15, 1900, p. 3, November 22, 1900, p. 3, November 29, 1900, p. 3, and December 6, 1900, p. 2. For further discussion of the strike, see McLaurin, *Paternalism and Protest*, pp. 156–61, and Nathans, *Quest for Progress*, pp. 36–37.

129. Raleigh *News and Observer*, October 18, 1900, p. 1, and October 10, 1900, p. 2; and North Carolina Bureau of Labor and Printing, *Annual Report . . . 1901*, p. 416.

130. *Alamance Gleaner*, November 1, 1900, p. 3.

131. On disfranchisement and the larger political context in which the Haw River strike occurred, see Escott, *Many Excellent People*, pp. 252–62; Goodwyn, *Democratic Promise*; Kousser, *Shaping of Southern Politics*; and Schwartz, *Radical Protest and Social Structure*, pp. 281–87. South Carolina disfranchised blacks through a constitutional convention in 1895, but the state's Democratic leaders had less success in restricting white, working-class political participation. See Kousser, *Shaping Southern Politics*, pp. 145–52, and Carlton, *Mill and Town*, pp. 215–72.

132. *Alamance Gleaner*, November 22, 1900, p. 3, and November 29, 1900, p. 3; T. M. Young, *American Cotton Industry*, p. 83; and Blanshard, *Labor in Southern Cotton Mills*, p. 48.

133. Mrs. Howard K. (Josephine) Glenn interview, pp. 7, 20; Alice Grogan Hardin interview, p. 12; and George and Tessie Dyer interview, p. 37.

134. Edna Y. Hargett interview, p. 57.

135. North Carolina Bureau of Labor and Printing, *Annual Report . . . 1902*, p. 182; Paul Cline interview, p. 15; and Rodgers, "American Industrial Worker," pp. 663, 671. For more on the turn-of-the-century building boom and labor turnover, see Holland Thompson, *From Cotton Field to Cotton Mill*, p. 71; U.S. Congress, Senate, *Woman and Child Wage-Earners*, 1:126–27; *STB*, September 7, 1911, pp. 4, 17; Gilman, *Human Relations*, p. 130; McHugh, "Family Labor System," p. 19; and Carlton, *Mill and Town*, pp. 152–53.

136. *ATM*, August 13, 1908, p. 14, and Kohn, *Cotton Mills of South Carolina*, p. 60.

137. North Carolina Bureau of Labor and Printing, *Annual Report . . . 1907*, p. 250; Zelma Murray interview, pp. 5–6; and Alice Hardin interview, p. 13.

138. Alice Evitt interview, p. 32.

139. Parker, "South Carolina Cotton Mill," p. 332; Blaine H. Wofford interview, untranscribed; and "The Help Question From the Superintendent's Point of View," *SWTE*, August 4, 1906, p. 13.

140. *TM*, May 18, 1911, p. 7, and *Gastonia News*, reprinted in *SWTE*, July 29, 1905, p. 7.

141. *Manufacturers' Record*, April 13, 1907, p. 6; Kohn, *Cotton Mills of South Carolina*, p. 200; and *SWTE*, August 18, 1906, p. 3.

142. Carlton, *Mill and Town*, p. 142, and "The Mill Help Question Discussed by Mill Men," *SWTE*, April 20, 1907, p. 17.

143. Alice Evitt interview, pp. 30–31, and *ATM*, August 13, 1908, p. 14.

144. *SWTE*, August 4, 1906, p. 13, and May 26, 1906, p. 10.

145. Alice Evitt interview, p. 31, and "Shooting Affairs at Dallas, N.C.," *STB*, July 4, 1912, p. 18. For similar incidences, see Massachusetts Bureau of Statistics of Labor, *Cotton Manufactures*, p. 55.

146. *SWTE*, April 20, 1907, p. 4, and *STB*, January 28, 1915, p. 3.

147. *ATM*, October 29, 1908, p. 5.

CHAPTER THREE

1. U.S. Congress, Senate, *Woman and Child Wage-Earners*, 1:520, 523. The coal mining communities of Appalachia have defined the popular image of the company town, yet even at the height of the coal boom in the mid-1920s they housed no more than 79 percent of all miners in West Virginia and 64 percent of those in eastern Kentucky and southwest Virginia. This compared with figures of 51 percent in the bituminous coal fields of Pennsylvania and 12 percent in the steel towns of the Northeast and Midwest. See Eller, *Miners, Millhands, and Mountaineers*, p. 162, and

U.S. Department of Labor, Bureau of Labor Statistics, *Housing by Employers*, pp. 57, 161.

2. U.S. Congress, Senate, *Woman and Child Wage-Earners*, 1:530, 538.

3. Myrtle Stanley interview, p. 5, and Potwin, *Cotton Mill People of the Piedmont*, p. 42. Gutman, "Work, Culture, and Society," and Tilly and Scott, *Women, Work, and Family*, are models for studying patterns of change and continuity in industrializing societies. For a comparative perspective on New England textile communities, see Hareven, *Family Time and Industrial Time*; Prude, *Coming of Industrial Order*; and Tucker, *Samuel Slater*. Recent community studies in the Piedmont are DeNatale, "Traditional Culture and Community," and Flamming, "Work, Family, and Community."

4. Chester Copeland interview, p. 5.

5. Glass, "Southern Mill Hills," and "Glencoe Cotton Mills," pp. 2, 5, and Glassie, *Material Folk Culture*, pp. 64–124. See also Bresler, "Industrial Vernacular Architecture," and U.S. Congress, Senate, *Woman and Child Wage-Earners*, 1:529–30.

6. Clay, "Daniel Augustus Tompkins," pp. 1–165; Winston, *Builder of the New South*, pp. 3–229; Tompkins, *Cotton Mill, Commercial Features*, pp. 116–21; and Glass, "Southern Mill Hills," pp. 143–45. In 1916, 73 percent of southern mill houses had either three or four rooms and 97 percent were of frame construction. See U.S. Department of Labor, Bureau of Labor Statistics, *Housing by Employers*, pp. 44–45.

7. Glass, "Southern Mill Hills," pp. 145–47; Draper, "Southern Textile Village Planning"; and Holland Thompson, *From Cotton Field to Cotton Mill*, p. 180. A number of Draper's plans are available in the North Carolina Collection, University of North Carolina at Chapel Hill.

8. William Gregg, *Graniteville Report, 1854*, quoted in Hammond, "Cotton Industry of This Century," p. 137, and Tompkins, *Cotton Mill, Commercial Features*, pp. 34–35.

9. Tompkins, *Cotton Mill, Commercial Features*, p. 117.

10. Perry Hicks interview, p. 4; U.S. Congress, Senate, *Woman and Child Wage-Earners*, 1:531, 534; Benjamin H. Smith, "Southern Cotton Mill Community," p. 26; and U.S. Department of Labor, Bureau of Labor Statistics, *Housing by Employers*, p. 144.

11. U.S. Congress, Senate, *Woman and Child Wage-Earners*, 1:526, 530, 534; Mack Duncan interview, pp. 27–28; Sam Finley interview, p. 4; U.S. Department of Labor, Bureau of Labor Statistics, *Housing by Employers*, pp. 151–52; Ralph Austin interview, field notes; and Harvey Ellington and Sam Pridgen interview, p. 88.

12. U.S. Department of Labor, Bureau of Labor Statistics, *Housing by Employers*, p. 12; U.S. Congress, Senate, *Woman and Child Wage-Earners*, 1:537.

13. Quoted in Carlton, *Mill and Town*, p. 245; see pp. 215–72 for a perceptive discussion of Blease's political career. The best comparison of politics in North and South Carolina is Key, *Southern Politics*, pp. 131–35, 211–15.

14. Key, *Southern Politics*, p. 145; Carlton, *Mill and Town*, p. 270; and Garraty, *Dictionary of American Biography: Supplement Seven*, pp. 398–99. There is no

authoritative biography of Johnston, but the *Dictionary* entry provides a useful guide to major sources.

15. Key, *Southern Politics*, p. 211. On the formation of North Carolina's Democratic elite, see Gail Williams O'Brien, *Legal Fraternity*, esp. pp. 141–42.

16. Beatty, "Textile Labor in the North Carolina Piedmont," p. 489, and Everett Padgett interview, pp. 6–8.

17. Henderson Monroe Fowler Books, entries for July 16, 1878, December 11 and 16, 1879, January 22, March, and May 11 and 18, 1880, Southern Historical Collection, University of North Carolina at Chapel Hill. For a more detailed account of this star-crossed romance, see Escott, *Many Excellent People*, p. 209.

18. Verna Stackhouse interview, pp. 24–26.

19. John Wesley Snipes interview, November 20, 1976, p. 29; Paul and Louise Jones interview, untranscribed; and Louise Jones interview, September 20, 1976, p. 16. For other accounts of surveillance by mill owners, see Rand, " 'I Had to Like It,' " pp. 66–72, and Freeze, "Master Mill Man," pp. 59–82. For the argument that such personal involvement seldom translated into benevolent paternalism, see Beatty, "Textile Labor in the North Carolina Piedmont."

20. Carl and Mary Thompson interview, p. 46, and Newman, "Work and Community Life," p. 212. On village policemen, see also Albert Sanders interview, p. 19.

21. Potwin, *Cotton Mill People of the Piedmont*, p. 105; Carl and Mary Thompson interview, p. 46; Paul Cline interview, p. 13; and Blaine H. Wofford interview, untranscribed.

22. Roy Eubanks interview, untranscribed; Herring, *Welfare Work*, p. 99; and Carl and Mary Thompson interview, p. 46.

23. Mack Duncan interview, p. 40. See also Carlton, *Mill and Town*, pp. 103–6; Pope, *Millhands and Preachers*, pp. 143–61; and Herring, *Welfare Work*, pp. 86–105.

24. Raleigh *News and Observer*, November 3, 1929, quoted in Pope, *Millhands and Preachers*, p. 150, and Mack Duncan interview, p. 41.

25. Luther Riley interview, p. 2.

26. MacDonald, *Southern Mill Hills*, pp. 149–50; DeNatale, "Traditional Culture and Community," pp. 32–34; Quinney, "Childhood in a Southern Mill Village," pp. 184–85; and Pope, *Millhands and Preachers*, pp. 70–95.

27. Blaine H. Wofford interview, untranscribed; U.S. Congress, Senate, *Woman and Child Wage-Earners*, 1:520, 522, 525, and 16:28. The only figures available for northern mill workers are from Fall River, Massachusetts, where no company housing was provided. Monthly expenditures there for housing were virtually the same as those for southern mill families living in private rental property. See U.S. Congress, Senate, *Woman and Child Wage-Earners*, 16:181.

28. U.S. Congress, Senate, *Woman and Child Wage-Earners*, 1:520–21, and Bessie Buchanan interview, July 1977, p. 19. Federal investigators reported that for most southern mill families it was "out of the question for one member . . . to have a room

to himself and almost as much so to have a bed alone." Northern millhands' easier access to privately owned rental housing made the problem of overcrowding much less severe for them. See U.S. Congress, Senate, *Woman and Child Wage-Earners*, 16:29, 181. For discussions of middle-class domestic architecture and its emphasis on the separation of public and private space, see Clark, *American Family Home*, pp. 42–46, and Gwendolyn Wright, *Building the Dream*, pp. 96–113.

29. John Harrison Cook, *Mill Schools of North Carolina*, pp. 1–13, and Carlton, *Mill and Town*, pp. 94–103.

30. John Harrison Cook, *Mill Schools of North Carolina*, pp. 9, 41, and U.S. Congress, Senate, *Woman and Child Wage-Earners*, 1:571.

31. John Harrison Cook, *Mill Schools of North Carolina*, p. 31, and George and Mamie Shue interview, p. 1. In 1925, 59 percent of mill schools in North Carolina provided no more than seven years of instruction. See John Harrison Cook, *Mill Schools of North Carolina*, pp. 4–5.

32. John Harrison Cook, *Mill Schools of North Carolina*, pp. 37–38, and Rhyne, *Some Southern Cotton Mill Workers*, pp. 76–77. See also Hutton, "Social Participation," p. 27.

33. "Demand for Labor," *SWTE*, April 14, 1906, p. 10; Tompkins, *Cotton Mill, Commercial Features*, p. 35; and U.S. Congress, Senate, *Woman and Child Wage-Earners*, 1:600, 605–6. See also McLaurin, *Paternalism and Protest*, pp. 36–37.

34. U.S. Congress, Senate, *Woman and Child Wage-Earners*, 1:601, and North Carolina Bureau of Labor Statistics, *Annual Report . . . 1887*, p. 152.

35. U.S. Congress, Senate, *Woman and Child Wage-Earners*, 1:601; Paul and Don Faucette interview, p. 35; and Alice Evitt interview, pp. 5–6.

36. U.S. Congress, Senate, *Woman and Child Wage-Earners*, 1:599, 606; Herring, *Welfare Work*, pp. 187–95; and George and Mamie Shue interview, p. 32.

37. The ranking of Piedmont mills is from Nelson, *Managers and Workers*, p. 116. For a discussion of the origins of industrial welfare work, see Brandes, *American Welfare Capitalism*; Brody, *Workers in Industrial America*, pp. 48–81; and Weinstein, *Corporate Ideal in the Liberal State*, pp. 3–39. The only systematic survey of welfare activities in Piedmont mills is Herring, *Welfare Work*, but it covers only North Carolina firms. Information on South Carolina mills can be found in Kohn, *Cotton Mills of South Carolina*; Ellis, "Model Factory Town"; Ely, "American Industrial Experiment"; and Few, "Constructive Philanthropy." Although sometimes included in descriptions of welfare capitalism, the provision of schools, churches, and low-cost housing should not be considered "welfare work," since manufacturers provided such facilities from the outset as a means of attracting workers and treated their cost as part of the expense of doing business. See U.S. Congress, Senate, *Woman and Child Wage-Earners*, 1:596. Useful studies of welfare work in other industries include U.S. Department of Labor, Bureau of Labor Statistics, *Employers' Welfare Work*, and *Welfare Work for Employees*; Gwendolyn Wright, *Building the Dream*, pp. 177–92; Ozanne, *Century of Labor-Management Relations*; Meyer, *Five Dollar Day*; and Zahavi, "Negotiated Loyalty." See

also Hareven, *Family Time and Industrial Time*, pp. 38–68, for an account of welfare work at a large New England textile firm.

38. O. W. Douglas, "Industrial Recreation and Welfare," *STB*, September 26, 1918, p. 4; Lena Rivers Smyth, "Welfare Work Accomplishing Results," *STB*, November 2, 1916, p. 3; W. J. Lauck, "Future Labor Supply of Southern Mills," *TM*, May 18, 1911, p. 7; George V. S. Michaels, "Safeguarding Textile Employees," *STB*, April 20, 1911, p. 5; and E. S. Draper, "Community Work in Southern Mill Villages," *STB*, May 8, 1919, p. 31.

39. Lena Rivers Smyth, "Welfare Work Accomplishing Results," *STB*, November 2, 1916, p. 3; Carlton, *Mill and Town*, pp. 129–214.

40. E. J. Watson, "South's Labor Conditions," *ATM*, June 25, 1908, p. 15; J. M. Davis, "Development of Welfare Work," *TM*, February 24, 1910, p. 3; Gertrude Beeks, "Conditions Surrounding the Cotton Mills of the South," *SWTE*, July 21, 1906, p. 5; and Thomas F. Parker, "The South Carolina Mill Village—A Manufacturer's View," *TM*, December 15, 1910, p. 3.

41. "Social Effect of the Mills," *TM*, January 27, 1910, p. 3; William Nelson, "Southern Cotton Mill Operatives," *STB*, July 29, 1915, p. 4; "Welfare Work," *SWTE*, January 20, 1906, p. 10; W. R. Lynch, "Welfare Work in North Carolina Mills," *STB*, February 1, 1917, p. 3; and A. S. Winslow, "Mill Life in the South," *TM*, February 24, 1910, p. 4. The "Health and Happiness" issues were published on December 20, 1917, December 25, 1919, and November 22, 1923.

42. A mill president, as quoted by Gertrude Beeks, "In Southern Cotton Mills," *SWTE*, August 11, 1906, p. 18, and North Carolina Bureau of Labor and Printing, *Annual Report . . . 1905*, p. 252. See also U.S. Congress, Senate, *Woman and Child Wage-Earners*, 1:127.

43. Bernard M. Cone, "Some Phases of Welfare Work," *STB*, July 4, 1912, p. 4.

44. National Civic Federation, *Examples of Welfare Work*, p. 8; Thomas F. Parker, "The South Carolina Mill Village—A Manufacturer's View," *TM*, December 15, 1910, p. 3; and Icy Norman interview, p. 7. For examples of mothers' clubs and baby contests, see the *STB*'s "Health and Happiness" issues cited in n. 41 above.

45. Thomas F. Parker, "The South Carolina Mill Village—A Manufacturer's View," *TM*, December 15, 1910, p. 3; Hoyle and Mamie McCorkle interview, p. 16; and L. W. Clark, "The Efficiency of Mill Workers," *STB*, September 28, 1911, p. 4. For more on domestic science classes, bands, and baseball teams, see Herring, *Welfare Work*, pp. 106–18, 129–31, 135–46, and the *STB*'s "Health and Happiness" issues cited in n. 41 above.

46. E. H. T. Foster, "The Y.M.C.A. in the Textile Industry," *STB*, November 26, 1914, p. 4; Charles R. Towson, "Welfare Work," *STB*, April 6, 1916, p. 4; and L. W. Clark, "The Efficiency of Mill Workers," *STB*, September 28, 1911, p. 4.

47. A. S. Winslow, "Mill Life in the South," *TM*, February 24, 1910, p. 4; L. W. Clark, "The Efficiency of Mill Workers," *STB*, September 28, 1911, p. 4; C. E. House, "Does the Playground Pay?," *STB*, August 31, 1916, pp. 4–5; and Thomas F.

Parker, "The South Carolina Cotton Mill," *TM*, November 4, 1909, p. 3.

48. Kohn, *Cotton Mills of South Carolina*, p. 22; George V. S. Michaels, "Safeguarding Textile Employees," *STB*, April 20, 1911, p. 5; Charles Lee, "The Promotion of Savings Among Operatives," *STB*, September 28, 1911, p. 5; and Gertrude Beeks, "In Southern Cotton Mills," *SWTE*, August 11, 1906, p. 18.

49. "Demand for Labor," *SWTE*, April 14, 1906, p. 10; David Clark, "Effect of Welfare Work on Industrial Unrest," *STB*, July 22, 1915, p. 5; Mack Duncan interview, pp. 90, 94; and Charlotte *Labor Herald*, August 17, 1923, p. 4. See also Albert Sanders interview, pp. 24-26.

50. Roy Lee and Mary Ruth Auton interview, p. 41; Thomas F. Parker, "The South Carolina Mill Village—A Manufacturer's View," *TM*, December 15, 1910, p. 3; Simon, "Class, Community, and Conflict," p. 54; W. R. Lynch, "Evolution of Welfare Work in Southern Mill Communities," *STB*, July 8, 1915, p. 3; MacDonald, *Southern Mill Hills*, p. 150; and Herring, *Welfare Work*, pp. 115, 123–24, 126, 133. See also George and Mamie Shue interview, p. 30. Similar responses to welfare projects among shoe workers are discussed in Zahavi, "Negotiated Loyalty." For an example of a welfare worker's attitudes toward millhands and of her difficulties in organizing uplift projects, see [Clara E. Kenyon] to Gertrude Beeks, n.d., and "An Account of the Work of the Trained Nurse, Miss Clara E. Kenyon," n.d., Box 80, National Civic Federation Papers, Manuscript Department, New York Public Library, New York, New York.

51. DeNatale, "Traditional Culture and Community," pp. 55–56. On the mill village as a segregated community and the mill worker as a "social type," see Nichols, "Does the Mill Village Foster Any Social Types?," and Vance, *Human Geography of the South*, p. 293.

52. Grover Hardin interview, p. 35, and Ethel Faucette interview, p. 35. See also Newman, "Work and Community Life," p. 207.

53. Byerly, *Hard Times Cotton Mill Girls*, p. 176. On changes in the age of marriage, see McHugh, "Family Labor System," pp. 30–32, and Potwin, *Cotton Mill People of the Piedmont*, p. 32.

54. James and Nannie Pharis interview, p. 8, and Eula and Vernon Durham interview, p. 41.

55. Frank Durham interview, p. 37, and Carl and Mary Thompson interview, pp. 13–14.

56. Naomi Trammel interview, p. 18, and Eula and Vernon Durham interview, pp. 42, 50–51.

57. Eula and Vernon Durham interview, pp. 45, 49; Myrtle Gentry interview, p. 19; and Kathryn Killian and Blanche Bolick interview, p. 14.

58. Ralph Austin interview, p. 24.

59. George and Mamie Shue interview, pp. 19–21.

60. Edna Y. Hargett interview, p. 25. On middle-class courtship and honeymoons, see Rothman, *Hands and Hearts*, esp. pp. 280–82.

61. Rhyne, *Some Southern Cotton Mill Workers*, p. 107; Carrie Gerringer interview,

p. 19; and Letha Ann Sloan Osteen interview, p. 10. For more on workers' mobility, see U.S. Congress, Senate, *Woman and Child Wage-Earners*, 1:126–28. Hutton, "Social Participation," offers an excellent discussion of the stabilizing core of semipermanent residents. See esp. pp. 12, 43, 56.

62. Arthur W. Page, "The Cotton Mills and the People," *SWTE*, June 8, 1907, p. 3, and Lacy Wright interview, pp. 21–22. See also Hutton, "Social Participation," p. 65.

63. Louise Jones interview, September 20, 1976, p. 19, and Carl and Mary Thompson interview, pp. 30–31. Federal investigators reported that in 1907, 26 percent of southern textile families kept an average of two boarders. See U.S. Congress, Senate, *Woman and Child Wage-Earners*, 1:546–47.

64. Ethel Faucette interview, pp. 42–45.

65. Icy Norman interview, pp. 14–15, and Edward and Mary Harrington interview, pp. 20–21.

66. Hoyle and Mamie McCorkle interview, pp. 1, 3, 5.

67. Curtis Enlow interview, p. 16, and Edna Y. Hargett interview, p. 5. For accounts of children's chores, see Carl and Mary Thompson interview, pp. 7, 65; George and Mamie Shue interview, pp. 11–12; and Christine McCallum interview, p. 8.

68. Ethel Faucette interview, p. 15; Louise Jones interview, September 20, 1976, p. 42; Edna Y. Hargett interview, p. 6; Carl and Mary Thompson interview, pp. 11–12; and Jessie Lee Carter interview, p. 10.

69. Herman Truitt interview, p. 43; Emma Whitesell interview, p. 38; Grover Hardin interview, p. 7; and Eula and Vernon Durham interview, p. 31.

70. Inabinet and Inabinet, *Old Mill Stream*, p. 34, and James and Nannie Pharis interview, p. 53.

71. Eula and Vernon Durham interview, pp. 31–33.

72. Herman Truitt interview, pp. 40–41. For examples of typical mill family diets, see U.S. Congress, Senate, *Woman and Child Wage-Earners*, 16:37–129.

73. Goldberger, Wheeler, and Sydenstricker, "Pellagra Incidence," p. 1653, and "Study of the Relation of Diet to Pellagra Incidence"; and U.S. Public Health Service, *Study of Endemic Pellagra*, pp. 18, 70–71. The best historical account of these federal pellagra studies is Etheridge, *Butterfly Caste*. Slightly more than 9 percent of households had one or more definite cases of pellagra. Another 7 percent had "suspicious" cases that were almost certainly pellagra but did not meet all of the investigators' clinical criteria. After age fifty—a time when children were likely to be grown and out on their own—the incidence of pellagra among women declined sharply. Women fifty and older suffered only 2 percent of all cases.

74. U.S. Public Health Service, *Study of Endemic Pellagra*, pp. 20–37, and Goldberger, Wheeler, and Sydenstricker, "Study of the Relation of Diet to Pellagra Incidence." An examination of mill workers' household budgets conducted in 1907–8 revealed that hunger and malnutrition haunted many families besides those stricken with pellagra. Researchers concluded that 20 percent of villagers lived "in the direst poverty. They are underfed, or underclothed, or they have not enough fire to keep them warm." Another 51 percent were "living in poverty of one degree or another."

Some are barely above the starvation line; others have enough for food and clothing and a few of the other things considered as necessities in the fair standard of living, yet they feel the pinch of poverty somewhere" (U.S. Congress, Senate, *Woman and Child Wage-Earners*, 16:170).

75. Page, *Southern Cotton Mills and Labor*, p. 24; Paul and Don Faucette interview, pp. 29, 32; and Charles Foster interview, p. 14. See also Ralph Austin interview, pp. 10–12. The quotation from Page was originally rendered in dialect.

76. Sally Fowler interview, untranscribed; Carl and Mary Thompson interview, pp. 47–49; and Edna Y. Hargett interview, pp. 23–24. See also Quinney, "Childhood in a Southern Mill Village," pp. 174, 178, 184, 187–88. Most studies of the textile industry overlook these forms of interdependence and emphasize the importance of paternalism and dependency. Particularly significant in this regard are Broadus Mitchell, *Rise of Cotton Mills*; Tannenbaum, "South Buries Its Anglo-Saxons"; and Boyte, "Textile Industry." An equally influential, if contradictory, theme is that of mill workers' "individualism." See, especially, Cash, *Mind of the South*, pp. 32–46, 249–50, 365, 397.

77. Paul and Don Faucette interview, pp. 26, 28–30.

78. Potwin, *Cotton Mill People of the Piedmont*, p. 17. See also Quinney, "Childhood in a Southern Mill Village," p. 174.

79. Grover Hardin interview, p. 10.

80. James and Nannie Pharis interview, pp. 28–29.

81. U.S. Congress, Senate, *Woman and Child Wage-Earners*, 1:453; North Carolina Bureau of Labor and Printing, *Annual Report . . . 1906*, p. 129, and *Annual Report . . . 1901*, p. 160; North Carolina Bureau of Labor Statistics, *Annual Report . . . 1896*, p. 199; and Holland Thompson, *From Cotton Field to Cotton Mill*, pp. 234–36. See also North Carolina Bureau of Labor Statistics, *Annual Report . . . 1896*, pp. 198–99, and North Carolina Bureau of Labor and Printing, *Annual Report . . . 1902*, p. 280. In 1907 only 3 percent of all mill fathers were "noncontributing by reason of idleness." On average, those men were over forty-nine years old—too old to find steady, first-time jobs in the mills. See U.S. Congress, Senate, *Woman and Child Wage-Earners*, 1:455–56.

82. Icy Norman interview, p. 7.

83. Mareda Cobb and Carrie Yelton interview, p. 25, and Carrie Gerringer interview, pp. 20–21. On the changing composition of the work force and the sexual division of household labor, see U.S. Congress, Senate, *Woman and Child Wage-Earners*, 1:424; U.S. Department of Labor, Women's Bureau, *Lost Time and Labor Turnover*, p. 36; and MacDonald, *Southern Mill Hills*, p. 53.

84. Mack Duncan interview, pp. 47–49.

85. Carrie Gerringer interview, pp. 21–22; Myrtle Cleveland interview, p. 4; Hoyle and Mamie McCorkle interview, p. 8; and Gertrude Shuping interview, untranscribed.

86. Lewis Durham interview, pp. 60–61, and Edna Y. Hargett interview, p. 17.

87. Edna Y. Hargett interview, pp. 21–22, and Esther Jenks interview, pp. 40–41.

See also, U.S. Department of Labor, Women's Bureau, *Lost Time and Labor Turnover*, pp. 32–33.

88. Baxter Holman interview, untranscribed; Byerly, *Hard Times Cotton Mill Girls*, pp. 98–99; and Carl and Mary Thompson interview, pp. 18–19. See also Mack Duncan interview, p. 74; Mary Padgett interview, p. 7; Stella Carden interview, pp. 22–24; and Simon, "Class, Community, and Conflict," pp. 15–16.

89. Byerly, *Hard Times Cotton Mill Girls*, p. 99.

90. U.S. Department of Labor, Women's Bureau, *Lost Time and Labor Turnover*, pp. 15, 67, 84, 158, 164, and Sydenstricker, Wheeler, and Goldberger, "Disabling Sickness," p. 2048. The statistics on time lost due to personal illness excluded time away from work because of pregnancy and the complications of childbirth.

91. Fannie Marcom interview, untranscribed; Carrie Gerringer interview, p. 15; and Byerly, *Hard Times Cotton Mill Girls*, pp. 79–81. See also Nell Sigmon interview, p. 43, and Quinney, "Childhood in a Southern Mill Village," pp. 174–75.

92. Louise Jones interview, October 31, 1978, untranscribed; Mack Duncan interview, pp. 48; and Fannie Marcom interview, untranscribed. On abortions, see Nell Sigmon interview, p. 44, and Mareda Cobb and Carrie Yelton interview, p. 53.

93. Kathryn Killian and Blanche Bolick interview, field notes; Carrie Gerringer interview, pp. 22–23; Gertrude Shuping interview, untranscribed; Maxie Oakley interview, untranscribed; and Louise Jones interview, October 13, 1976, pp. 2–3. See also Nell Sigmon interview, p. 43.

94. Edna Y. Hargett interview, p. 11.

95. Ibid., p. 5, and Carl and Mary Thompson interview, p. 7.

96. Roy Lee and Mary Ruth Auton interview, p. 42, and James and Nannie Pharis interview, p. 53. See Ralph Austin interview, pp. 13–14, for a description of a similar game called "Peggy."

97. Harry Rogers interview, February 2, 1979, pp. 5–6; Lora and Edward Wright interview, p. 7; Carl and Mary Thompson interview, p. 7; and Ralph Austin interview, p. 1.

98. Charles Foster interview, pp. 19–20.

99. U.S. Congress, Senate, *Woman and Child Wage-Earners*, 1:436–37; Mack Duncan interview, p. 42; and Carrie Gerringer interview, p. 3.

100. Walter Vaughn interview, untranscribed. For a similar pattern of parent-child relationships among Polish immigrants, see Bodnar, Simon, and Weber, *Lives of Their Own*, p. 93.

101. Edna Y. Hargett interview, p. 64, and Eva B. Hopkins interview, pp. 11, 35–36. See also Carl and Mary Thompson interview, p. 15.

102. Ila Dodson interview, p. 23; Emma Williams, quoted in Quinney, "Childhood in a Southern Mill Village," p. 176; and anonymous interview. For a comparative perspective, see Rubin, *Worlds of Pain*, p. 37. Rubin observes that middle-class fathers are also often remembered as distant members of the family, but their detachment usually results from a preoccupation with professional and work life rather than emotional withdrawal.

103. Herman Truitt interview, p. 16, and Charles Foster interview, p. 12.

104. Lewis Durham interview, p. 39; James and Nannie Pharis interview, p. 19; and George and Mamie Shue interview, p. 32.

105. Anonymous interview. Compare Rubin, *Worlds of Pain*, pp. 34–37.

106. Ibid.

107. Harvey Ellington and Sam Pridgen interview, pp. 97–98.

108. Anonymous interview.

109. Carl and Mary Thompson interview, pp. 10–11.

110. Charles Foster interview, p. 13. See also DeNatale, "Traditional Culture and Community," pp. 87–90, and Ralph Austin interview, p. 9.

111. Mozelle Riddle interview, pp. 27–28; Edna Y. Hargett interview, pp. 29–30; Hoyle and Mamie McCorkle interview, p. 7; and Vinnie Partin interview, July 3, 1975, pp. 13–14.

112. James and Nannie Pharis interview, pp. 7–8. See also Quinney, "Childhood in a Southern Mill Village," pp. 178–80.

113. Frances Latta interview, p. 11, and Edna Y. Hargett interview, pp. 23, 24, 28.

114. Edna Y. Hargett interview, p. 28, and James and Nannie Pharis interview, p. 43.

115. Paul and Don Faucette interview, pp. 28–29, and Hoyle and Mamie McCorkle interview, p. 5. Hutton, "Social Participation," offers a detailed description of visiting patterns in a single village; see esp. pp. 47–60. For a comparative perspective, see Ellen Ross, "Survival Networks," pp. 10–11, and Ulrich, *Good Wives*, pp. 51–67.

116. James and Nannie Pharis interview, p. 8, and Edna Y. Hargett interview, pp. 20–21. See also Hutton, "Social Participation," pp. 19, 48–49.

117. Paul and Don Faucette interview, p. 28; Vernon Saunders interview, p. 11; and Alice Evitt interview, p. 8. For further discussion of the use of family networks for the purposes of discipline and control, see DeNatale, "Traditional Culture and Community," pp. 62–70; Newman, "Work and Community Life," pp. 204–25; and U.S. Congress, Senate, *Woman and Child Wage-Earners*, 1:589–90. Ross, " 'Not the Sort that Would Sit on the Doorstep,' " offers an excellent comparative perspective.

118. Flossie Moore Durham interview, p. 13, and Paul and Pauline Griffith interview, pp. 12–13.

119. John Wesley Snipes interview, August 22, 1979, untranscribed. For a comparative perspective on women's concerns, see Taylor, *Eve and the New Jerusalem*, pp. 272–73.

120. Lewis Durham interview, p. 11, and Louise Jones interview, September 20, 1976, p. 58.

121. Carrie Gerringer interview, p. 25.

122. Dr. Carroll Lupton interview, pp. 21–24.

123. Roy Lee and Mary Ruth Auton interview, p. 43; Paul and Don Faucette interview, p. 3; and Harvey Ellington and Sam Pridgen interview, pp. 10–11, 18–19, 35–36.

124. Quoted in North Carolina Arts Council, Folklife Section, *Charlotte Country Music Story*, p. 11.

125. Paul and Pauline Griffith interview, p. 20; Ruth Williams interview, untranscribed; and Mozelle Riddle interview, p. 30.

126. Carl and Mary Thompson interview, p. 40.

127. James and Nannie Pharis interview, p. 48.

128. George and Mamie Shue interview, pp. 17–18.

129. Ralph Simmons interview, p. 11, and Ethel Faucette interview, p. 58.

130. Lora and Edward Wright interview, p. 37.

131. George and Tessie Dyer interview, p. 5.

132. Alice Evitt interview, p. 16.

133. George and Tessie Dyer interview, p. 6. See also Quinney, "Childhood in a Southern Mill Village," pp. 184–86. For comparative perspectives on the social meanings of evangelical religion, see Paul E. Johnson, *Shopkeeper's Millennium*; Mathews, *Religion in the Old South*; and E. P. Thompson, *Making of the English Working Class*, pp. 350–400.

134. Pope, *Millhands and Preachers*, pp. 126–40.

135. Ibid., pp. 147–48, and Herring, *Welfare Work*, pp. 100–101.

136. Eva B. Hopkins interview, p. 27, and George and Mamie Shue interview, pp. 3–4.

CHAPTER FOUR

1. "Southern Labor Outlook," *STB*, May 23, 1918, p. 6, and "The Labor Situation," *STB*, May 16, 1918, p. 12.

2. "Going Wild," *STB*, September 26, 1918, p. 12, and "The Labor Situation," *STB*, May 16, 1918, p. 12.

3. "Going Wild," *STB*, September 26, 1918, p. 12. The companies most strapped for labor reduced their hours from sixty to fifty-six, and a handful went as low as forty-eight. Mill men reasoned that they could produce more goods by running fewer hours with a full complement of help rather than observing the standard workweek and allowing machines to stand idle.

4. "The Labor Situation," *STB*, May 16, 1918, p. 12, and "Going Wild," *STB*, September 26, 1918, p. 12.

5. "Attempting Discord," *STB*, February 6, 1919, p. 18, and Lenoir Chambers, "A Disinterested View of Strike Situation," *STB*, August 18, 1921, p. 5.

6. Conner, *National War Labor Board*, pp. vii, 108.

7. George Sinclair Mitchell, *Textile Unionism*, pp. 39–40; Frederick B. Gordon, "Mill Workers and the War," *STB*, November 21, 1918, pp. 4, 6, 12, 28; and Conner, *National War Labor Board*, p. 129.

8. Tindall, *Emergence of the New South*, p. 49; Gerstle, "Politics of Patriotism," p. 85;

Rosenzweig, *Eight Hours for What We Will*, pp. 171–228; and Corbin, *Life, Work, and Rebellion*, pp. 176–90.

9. "Revolt of the Rank and File." For background on the UTW and the AFL, see Brooks, "United Textile Workers of America"; Lahne, *Cotton Mill Worker*, pp. 189–215; Green, *World of the Worker*, pp. 100–132; and Brody, *Workers in Industrial America*, pp. 41–44.

10. George Sinclair Mitchell, *Textile Unionism*, pp. 42–46, and "President's Column," *TW* 6 (March 1919): 465–68.

11. George Sinclair Mitchell, *Textile Unionism*, pp. 46–49; *Charlotte Observer*, February 26, 1919, p. 4, and March 4, 1919, p. 5.

12. Editorial reprinted in the *Concord Times*, April 17, 1919, p. 3, and George and Mamie Shue interview, p. 34.

13. *Charlotte Observer*, May 28, 1919, p. 2; *Charlotte News*, May 28, 1919, p. 2; and George and Mamie Shue interview, p. 34.

14. Powell, *Dictionary of North Carolina Biography*, pp. 149–51; Horton, "Political Career of Thomas Walter Bickett"; and Raleigh *News and Observer*, September 15, 1919, pp. 1–2.

15. *Charlotte Observer*, May 31, 1919, p. 2, and June 2, 1919, p. 2, and George Sinclair Mitchell, *Textile Unionism*, p. 47.

16. "A New Era," *STB*, June 5, 1919, p. 14, and Raleigh *News and Observer*, September 15, 1919, p. 1.

17. *Charlotte Observer*, June 1, 1919, p. 2, and June 6, 1919, p. 16, and *Charlotte News*, June 4, 1919, p. 2, and June 6, 1919, p. 2.

18. George Sinclair Mitchell, *Textile Unionism*, p. 47, and "Address of James Barrett," *TW* 9 (February 1922): 518.

19. E. L. Chapman to the *Charlotte Observer*, June 13, 1921, p. 6; Charlotte *Labor Herald*, March 21, 1924, p. 7; George Sinclair Mitchell, *Textile Unionism*, pp. 51–52; and *Charlotte Observer*, June 2, 1921, p. 1.

20. Lenoir Chambers, "A Disinterested View of Strike Situation," *STB*, August 18, 1921, p. 6, and Gerald W. Johnson, "The Cotton Strike," p. 647.

21. *Charlotte Observer*, June 9, 1921, p. 6.

22. Ibid., June 13, 1921, p. 6.

23. "Following Strange Men," *STB*, June 23, 1921, p. 18, and Mrs. Ellington to David Clark, "President's Column," *TW* 9 (August 1921): 225.

24. "Address of James F. Barrett," *TW* 9 (February 1922): 516–17. See also Charlotte *Labor Herald*, August 31, 1923, p. 11.

25. Charlotte *Labor Herald*, March 21, 1924, p. 1. See also Mary Kelleher to the editor, *TW* 11 (June 1923): 148–49.

26. Charlotte *Labor Herald*, April 5, 1924, p. 4.

27. Mrs. Ellington to David Clark, "President's Column," *TW* 9 (August 1921): 226.

28. *Charlotte Observer*, June 2, 1921, p. 13, and July 21, 1921, p. 4; Lenoir Cham-

bers, "A Disinterested View of Strike Situation," *STB*, August 18, 1921, pp. 5, 8; and *Charlotte Observer*, July 25, 1921, p. 1.

29. *Concord Times*, August 11, 1921, p. 1; *Charlotte Observer*, August 14, 1921, p. 8; Gerald W. Johnson, "The Cotton Strike," p. 647; *Charlotte Observer*, August 16, 1921, p. 1, and August 15, 1921, p. 1; and Lenoir Chambers, "The Strike Situation," reprinted from the *Greensboro Daily News* in the *Concord Times*, August 18, 1921, p. 7. On Morrison's early political career, see Abrams, "Progressive-Conservative Duel," p. 426, and Magruder, "Administration of Governor Cameron Morrison," pp. 28–33.

30. Gerald W. Johnson, "The Cotton Strike," p. 647; Charlotte *Labor Herald*, August 31, 1923, p. 11; George Sinclair Mitchell, *Textile Unionism*, p. 58; Edgar Smith, in *TW* 9 (March 1922): 588–89; and Gavin Wright, *Old South, New South*, pp. 137, 149–53.

31. Murchison, *King Cotton Is Sick*, pp. 92-93; Michl, *Textile Industries*, pp. 105–10; and Steven Jay Kennedy, *Profits and Losses*, pp. 122–26.

32. Tindall, *Emergence of the New South*, p. 121, and Murchison, *King Cotton Is Sick*, pp. 71–107.

33. Lahne, *Cotton Mill Worker*, pp. 203–14, and Edmonds, *Why Cotton Mills Have Been Moving South*, p. 40. Workers at the mammoth Amoskeag Manufacturing Company in Manchester, New Hampshire, did not share fully in the victory. There, management forced a return to longer hours. See Hareven, *Family Time and Industrial Time*, pp. 287–339.

34. Steven Jay Kennedy, *Profits and Losses*, p. 29, and Tindall, *Emergence of the New South*, pp. 76–78.

35. Marley, "Southern Textile Epoch," p. 19, and James R. Young, *Textile Leaders of the South*, pp. 87, 757. For other examples, see "Passing of Another Generation," *STB*, September 27, 1923, pp. 8, 29.

36. Gilman, *Human Relations*, p. 94, and Gavin Wright, *Old South, New South*, pp. 150–55.

37. John Wesley Snipes interview, November 20, 1976, p. 30.

38. Herring, *Welfare Work*, p. 122; Smith and Nyman, *Technology and Labor*, p. 53; and Gavin Wright, *Old South, New South*, p. 150. In 1923 the average annual turnover rate remained high at 190 percent. See U.S. Department of Labor, Women's Bureau, *Lost Time and Labor Turnover*, p. 109.

39. *TW* 12 (June 1924): 146.

40. Gavin Wright, *Old South, New South*, pp. 210–11, and Murchison, *King Cotton Is Sick*, p. 147.

41. H. D. Martin, "Preventable Losses in Textile Mills," *STB*, April 20, 1922, p. 1, and "Preventing Leaks in Mill Operations," *STB*, July 28, 1927, pp. 7, 34.

42. Charlotte *Labor Herald*, April 4, 1924, p.3, and July 25, 1924, p. 5.

43. "Organization of Working Forces," *STB*, March 22, 1923, p. 5, and "Proposal for the Labor Reorganization of the No. 1 Weaving Department in Loray Mills of the Manville-Jenckes Company, Gastonia, N.C.," February 1928, p. 1, Barnes Textile

Reports, Museum of American Textile History, North Andover, Massachusetts.

44. H. D. Martin, "Advantages of New Equipment," *STB*, May 1, 1924, p. 7, and B. A. Peterson, "Advantages of Automatic Spoolers and High Speed Warpers," *STB*, July 17, 1924, pp. 11–13. The following discussion of technological and managerial innovation draws on the insights of Edwards, *Contested Terrain*; Gordon, Edwards, and Reich, *Segmented Work, Divided Workers*; and Noble, *America by Design*, and *Forces of Production*.

45. Advertisement, *STB*, February 19, 1925, p. 38, and B. A. Peterson, "Advantages of Automatic Spoolers and High Speed Warpers," *STB*, July 17, 1924, pp. 11–13.

46. Lora and Edward Wright interview, pp. 18, 20–21, and B. A. Peterson, "Advantages of Automatic Spoolers and High Speed Warpers," *STB*, July 17, 1924, p. 11. See also Stern, "Mechanical Changes in the Cotton-Textile Industry," p. 319. J. B. Harris, a superintendent from Greenwood, South Carolina, reported that after his mill installed automatic spoolers and warpers in 1926, they needed "only one-half as many operatives." See *STB*, November 7, 1929, p. 20.

47. Advertisements, *STB*, November 27, 1924, pp. 3–8; "Cone Group of Mills Carry Out Large Rehabilitation Program and Increase Capacity," *Textile World*, February 4, 1928, pp. 397, 400, 403; W. S. Lee, "Electricity: The Power Behind the South," *SWTE*, May 19, 1906, p. 15; and Robert Sidney Smith, *Mill on the Dan*, p. 178. See also advertisement, *STB*, April 28, 1921, p. 13, and W. T. Jenkins, "Electrification of Laurens Cotton Mills," *Textile World*, February 5, 1927, pp. 383, 385. For discussions of the changes brought about by the use of individual electric motors, see "Electric Power in the Textile Industry," *STB*, August 12, 1915, pp. 4–5; Sidney B. Paine, "Electricity and the Textile Industry," *STB*, April 26, 1928, pp. 12, 32; and H. W. Redding, "Twenty Years' Development in Electrical Equipment," *STB*, March 5, 1931, pp. 34, 46.

48. W. S. Lee, "Electricity: The Power Behind the South," *SWTE*, May 19, 1906, p. 15. On pick counters, see advertisements, *STB*, August 2, 1928, p. 16, July 11, 1929, p. 28, June 11, 1931, p. 17, and December 26, 1928, p. 18; Oscar E. Elsas, "Piece Rate Wage System in Cotton Mills," *STB*, April 29, 1915, p. 3; and "Root Loom Counters," *STB*, July 24, 1924, pp. 20–22.

49. "Textile Engineering and What it Means to the Textile Industry," p. 1, Barnes Textile Reports, Museum of American Textile History, North Andover, Massachusetts, and Frederick W. Taylor, quoted in Montgomery, *Workers' Control*, p. 115.

50. Letter from P. M. Mooney, July 14, 1933, Olympia Cotton Mills, NRA Records 398.

51. Sam Finley interview, pp. 1–3; U.S. Department of Labor, Bureau of Labor Statistics, *Labor in Cotton-Goods Manufacturing*, pp. 34, 36; and Painter, "Southern Labor Revolt," p. 17.

52. Smith and Nyman, *Technology and Labor*, p. 18.

53. Geddes E. Dodson interview, pp. 31–32, and Mack Duncan interview, pp. 37–38.

54. R. D. Burgess to Frances Perkins, October 4, 1934, Laurens Mill, NRA Records 402. For further discussion of the multiple-loom system, see Elliott Dunlap Smith, "Lessons of the Stretch Out: A Preliminary Report of a Study of Some Human Problems in the Management of Technological Change," *Mechanical Engineering* 56 (1934): 73–80; Albert Palmer, "Costs of Manufacturing and the Multiple System of Loom Operation: Weaver and His Work Present Large Opportunities for Savings," *Textile World*, February 2, 1929, pp. 183–84, 287; and J. M. Barnes, "The Labor Extension System," *STB*, July 5, 1928, pp. 7, 35.

55. Bernard Cone, "What a Manufacturer Says," in Tippett, *When Southern Labor Stirs*, pp. 314–15.

56. "Proposal for the Labor Reorganization of the No. 1 Weaving Department in Loray Mills of the Manville-Jenckes Company, Gastonia, N.C.," February, 1928, p. 4, Barnes Textile Reports, Museum of American Textile History, North Andover, Massachusetts, and Sam Finley interview, pp. 10–11. On time-and-motion studies, see Smith and Nyman, *Technology and Labor*, pp. 82–91, and Rehn, *Scientific Management*, pp. 109–12.

57. Barnes Textile Service to F. L. Jenckes, May 21, 1928, pp. 1–2; "Preliminary Survey of the Spinning Department at Loray Mill and High Shoals Mill, Manville-Jenckes Company, Gastonia, N.C.," July 1927, p. 2; "Preliminary Proposal for the Reorganization of the Spinning Department Labor in the Loray Mill, Manville-Jenckes Company, Gastonia, N.C.," April 1928, pp. 2, 19, Barnes Textile Reports, Museum of American Textile History, North Andover, Massachusetts; and Pope, *Millhands and Preachers*, p. 230. Most scholars have followed Liston Pope in arguing that the labor troubles at Loray sprang partly from the fact that Johnstone imposed efficiency measures arbitrarily, "without benefit of time studies [or] carefully established job standards." The Barnes reports reveal that Johnstone's actions were, in fact, well planned. See Pope, *Millhands and Preachers*, pp. 229–30.

58. W. O. Conley to Franklin D. Roosevelt, September 13, 1934, complaints of workers, individuals, NRA Records 401; Ada Mae Wilson interview, p. 3; Mack Duncan interview, p. 35; and Lowe, "Effect of Technological Advances," p. 9.

59. Sam Finley interview, p. 6; James Pharis interview, pp. 7–8, 11; and Holland Thompson, "Southern Textile Situation," pp. 117–18. Beginning in July 1928, the *Southern Textile Bulletin* printed numerous articles on the question of "why the experienced man at the age of 40 years is being turned down for younger men" in promotions to overseer. See, for example, "Can You Tell Him?," *STB*, July 26, 1928, p. 16.

60. W. M. McLaurine, "Modern Methods Demand Modern Men," *STB*, April 2, 1931, p. 14; and Elliott Dunlap Smith, "Lessons of the Stretch Out: A Preliminary Report of a Study of Some Human Problems in the Management of Technological Change," *Mechanical Engineering* 56 (1934): 79–80.

61. Lora and Edward Wright interview, pp. 4–5; "Superintendents and Overseers Doing Fine Work," *STB*, December 14, 1933, p. 14; Grover Hardin interview, pp. 17–18; and Sam Finley interview, p. 6.

62. Naomi Trammel interview, pp. 34–35.

63. Mrs. Howard K. (Josephine) Glenn interview, p. 10; Lloyd and Betty Davidson interview, pp. 35–36; and Edna Y. Hargett interview, p. 64.

64. Herring, "12 Cents, the Troops and the Union," pp. 199–200, and Frankel, "Southern Textile Women," p. 49.

65. The best overviews of this strike wave are Tippett, *When Southern Labor Stirs*; Bernstein, *Lean Years*, pp. 1–43; Tindall, *Emergence of the New South*, pp. 339–53; and Painter, "Southern Labor Revolt." The following account of the Elizabethton strike is drawn from Hall, "Disorderly Women." See also Hodges, "Challenge to the New South," pp. 343–57.

66. Bessie Edens interview, p. 1; George F. Dugger, Sr., interview, p. 25; *Knoxville News Sentinel*, May 19, 1929; East Tennessee District Supreme Court, *American Bemberg Corp. v. George Miller, et al.*

67. Honard Ward interview, untranscribed.

68. *Knoxville News Sentinel*, May 19 and May 27, 1929; Robert (Bob) and Barbara Moreland interview, untranscribed; and Flossie Cole Grindstaff interview, untranscribed.

69. Tindall, *Emergence of the New South*, pp. 349–50, and Painter, "Southern Labor Revolt," pp. 31–34.

70. Caldwell Ragan interview, p. 41; Tindall, *Emergence of the New South*, p. 75; Pope, *Millhands and Preachers*, pp. 233–34; and Ratchford, "Toward Preliminary Social Analysis," p. 361.

71. Tindall, *Emergence of the New South*, pp. 344–45, and Haessly, " 'Mill Mother's Lament': The Intellectual Left," pp. 7, 13–14, 25–26, 28–29.

72. Vesta and Sam Finley interview, pp. 18–20, 42, and Sam Finley interview, p. 11.

73. Vesta and Sam Finley interview, pp. 14, 43.

74. Perry Hicks interview, pp. 2, 17–18; Tippett, *When Southern Labor Stirs*, p. 128; and *Charlotte Observer*, August 29, 1929, p. 3.

75. *Asheville Advocate*, September 20, 1929, p. 1, and Sam Finley interview, pp. 8, 16, 18.

76. Sam Finley interview, p. 12; Vesta and Sam Finley interview, pp. 21–22; and Lillie Morris Price interview, pp. 34, 40–41, 54–55.

77. Bernstein, *Lean Years*, pp. 36–37, and Selby, "Industrial Growth and Worker Protest," pp. 113–20.

78. Bernstein, *Lean Years*, pp. 205–6; Montgomery, *Workers' Control*, p. 160; Green, *World of the Worker*, pp. 104, 123, 127; and "Labor's Interest in Industrial Waste Elimination," *TW* 15 (May 1927): 36. For one of the most important of the New England strikes, see Hareven, *Family Time and Industrial Time*, pp. 287–354.

79. Gerstle, "Politics of Patriotism," and Alfred Hoffmann to A. J. Muste, July 17, 1928, American Federation of Teachers Papers, Archives of Labor History and Urban Affairs, Wayne State University, Detroit, Michigan. Thanks to Dolores Janiewski for sharing this letter with us.

80. Robert (Bob) Cole interview, pp. 6–7; Vesta and Sam Finley interview, pp. 18–19; and Alfred Hoffmann, "The Mountaineer in Industry," pp. 2–7.

81. These relatively successful, self-initiated strikes have received little scholarly attention. See George Sinclair Mitchell, *Textile Unionism*, p. 79, and *Greenville News*, March 27, April 4, 11, and 17, May 6, 17, 19, and 24, and June 1, 4, 14, and 21, 1929.

82. Selby, "Industrial Growth and Worker Protest," pp. 111–13, 150, 160.

83. Governor O. Max Gardner presents an instructive example of the depth of employer opposition to unionization. Gardner responded to the labor disturbances of the 1920s by calling for higher wages; in the 1930s he became a New Dealer. Yet even Gardner remained a staunch foe of unionization, both at his own Cleveland Cloth Mill and in his role as a leader of the Cotton Textile Institute. He was also one of the main architects of the consolidation of North Carolina industrialists' political power in the 1930s. See Morrison, *Governor O. Max Gardner*, pp. 136–38, 144–45, 179–80. For the UTW's attitude toward its female constituency, see Janiewski, *Sisterhood Denied*, pp. 154–55 and Brooks, "United Textile Workers of America," pp. 77–79.

84. *Knoxville News Sentinel*, May 5, 1929, and *The Nation*, October 2, 1929, p. 340.

85. Bernstein, *Lean Years*, pp. 33–40, and Robert Sidney Smith, *Mill on the Dan*, pp. 294–324.

86. Perry Hicks interview, p. 17; Sam Finley interview, p. 21; Haessly, "'Mill Mother's Lament': The Intellectual Left," pp. 4, 14, 20–26; Larkin, "Ella May's Songs," and "Story of Ella May"; Vorse, "Gastonia," p. 705; and Wiley, "Songs of the Gastonia Textile Strike," pp. 90–91.

87. *Greenville News*, May 7, 12, 14, and 21, and June 14 and 18, 1929; Vesta and Sam Finley interview, pp. 12–13; and Sam Finley interview, pp. 16–17.

88. Frankel, "Southern Textile Women," p. 49; *Knoxville News Sentinel*, March 14, 1929; *Greenville News*, April 4, 1929; and "The Reds at Gastonia," *STB*, April 11, 1929, p. 27. See also *Greenville News*, April 17, 1929.

89. Perry Hicks interview, p. 21, and Vesta and Sam Finley interview, pp. 56–57.

90. Sam Finley interview, p. 15; Department of Research and Education, Federal Council of the Churches of Christ in America, "The Strikes at Marion, North Carolina," pp. 10–11; and Tippett, *When Southern Labor Stirs*, pp. 120–21, 124–25.

91. Pope, *Millhands and Preachers*, p. 258; Howie, "New South in the North Carolina Foothills"; and Sam Finley interview, p. 4.

92. Ada Mae Wilson interview, pp. 25–26.

93. Hoyle and Mamie McCorkle interview, pp. 5–7, and Sam Finley interview, p. 10. See also Tindall, *Emergence of the New South*, pp. 339–40.

94. Hoyle and Mamie McCorkle interview, p. 7.

95. Byerly, *Hard Times Cotton Mill Girls*, pp. 114–15.

96. Janiewski, *Sisterhood Denied*, p. 138; Gavin Wright, "Cheap Labor and Southern Textiles, 1880–1930," p. 611; Esther Gillis interview, untranscribed; and Stella Carden interview, pp. 21–22.

97. George and Mamie Shue interview, pp. 32–33.

98. John Wesley Snipes interview, November 20, 1976, pp. 37–38; Edna Y. Hargett interview, p. 11; and Gilman, *Human Relations*, p. 164.

99. Alice Evitt interview, pp. 48–50.

100. Vesta and Sam Finley interview, pp. 8, 16–17. For insights into the experience of this post–World War I generation, see Howie, "New South in the North Carolina Foothills," and Herring, "Metamorphosis of the Docile Worker," pp. 3–10, and "Industrial Relations," pp. 124–31.

101. Lillie Morris Price interview, pp. 37–38.

102. The best source for Wiggins's life is Haessly, " 'Mill Mother's Lament': Ella May." For such "maternal consciousness" in female militancy, see Kaplan, "Female Consciousness and Collective Action," pp. 545–66.

103. Larkin, "Ella May's Songs," p. 383.

104. Ibid., p. 383; Haessly, " 'Mill Mother's Lament': Ella May," pp. 4–5, 9–11, and " 'Mill Mother's Lament': The Intellectual Left," pp. 17–18.

105. Wiggins, *Fiddlin' Georgia Crazy*, pp. 23–34, and Dinnerstein, *Leo Frank Case*, pp. 10–13, 17–19, 33, 139–40.

106. Wiggins, *Fiddlin' Georgia Crazy*, pp. 35–36.

107. For gender differences in storytelling styles, see Baldwin, "Women's Roles in Family Storytelling."

108. *Elizabethton Star*, March 13, 1929, and *Knoxville News Sentinel*, March 15 and May 16, 1929.

109. East Tennessee District Supreme Court, *American Bemberg Corp. v. George Miller, et al.*

110. *Knoxville News Sentinel*, May 17, 1929.

111. Ibid.; East Tennessee District Supreme Court, *American Bemberg Corp. v. George Miller, et al.*

112. Carter County (Tenn.) Chancery Court, *American Bemberg Corp. v. George Miller, et al.*; Tennessee State Court of Appeals, *American Glanzstoff Corp. v. George Miller, et al.*

113. For the role of such "disorderly women" in other contexts, see Davis, *Society and Culture in Early Modern France*, pp. 124–51, and Ulrich, *Good Wives*, pp. 191–97.

114. For this cultural dynamic in the mountains, see Whisnant, *All That Is Native and Fine*, p. 48.

115. Vesta and Sam Finley interview, pp. 17–18; *Greensboro Daily News*, August 25, 1935, p. 4b; and Huff, "Conference of Southern Workers," p. 29.

116. Herring, "Industrial Relations," p. 128; Bessie Edens interview, p. 50; and Tindall, *Emergence of the New South*, p. 353.

117. Sylvia Jenkins Cook, *From Tobacco Road to Route 66*, pp. 85–86; Herring, "Cycles of Cotton Mill Criticism," pp. 113–25; *Greenville News*, April 5, 1929; "Time for Clear Thinking," *STB*, April 11, 1929, p. 26; and "Governor Gardner Discusses Industrial Problems," *STB*, October 10, 1926, pp. 9-11.

118. Gavin Wright, *Old South, New South*, pp. 207–13.

119. Nichols, "Does the Mill Village Foster Any Social Types?," pp. 350–57.

120. Mrs. B. M. Miller to Hugh Johnson, July 23, 1933, Chadwick-Hoskins Co., NRA Records 398, and Huff, "Conference of Southern Workers," p. 4.

CHAPTER FIVE

1. Tindall, *Emergence of the New South*, p. 76, and McGregor, *Hosiery Manufacturing Industry in North Carolina*, pp. 4–7.

2. Reid A. Maynard interview, p. 61.

3. On the history of the Love family in Gaston County, see James Lee Love, "Memorandum to Edward A. Addiss, Subject: Origin Textile Mills: Builders, 10 March 1937," JSL Papers. Grier Love's professed ambition was to see a cotton mill built for every distillery destroyed. Other Gaston County manufacturers shared his goal. Liston Pope found that the decline of the liquor interests and the rise of cotton mills in Gaston was interpreted as a "moral revolution." Between 1891 and 1900 Love's goal was more than attained: seventeen new mills were built, and the number of distilleries dropped from about forty to sixteen. See *History of North Carolina*, pp. 194–95, and Pope, *Millhands and Preachers*, p. 28.

4. Reminiscence of James Spencer Love, February 24, 1919, JSL Papers.

5. James Spencer Love to Julia Spencer Love, January 2, 1919, JSL Papers.

6. Filene, *Him/Her/Self*, pp. 100–101, 130.

7. James Lee Love to James Spencer Love, February 16, 1919, JSL Papers. For a discussion of the relationship between Victorian fathers and sons, see Filene, "Between a Rock and a Soft Place," and "The 'Secret Desire' of Lincoln Steffans."

8. Julia Spencer Love to James Spencer Love, April 30, 1919, and February 7, 1919, JSL Papers. Julia Spencer Love was the daughter of another strong-willed woman, Cornelia Phillips Spencer, who, in 1895, became the first woman to receive an honorary degree of LL.D. from the University of North Carolina. For a biographical sketch of Cornelia Phillips Spencer, see Alderman and Harris, *Library of Southern Literature*, pp. 5049–52.

9. Julia Spencer Love to James Spencer Love, April 30, 1919, JSL Papers.

10. Diary of James Spencer Love, March 28, 1922, and January 25 and June 29, 1923, JSL Papers.

11. Ibid., January 1, 1922.

12. Ibid., December 14, 1921, and March 27 and 28, 1922.

13. *Burlington: A Review*, pp. 1, 3; *Commerce and Finance*, January 2, 1924; untitled clipping, January 28, 1925, in Clipping Files, Burlington Industries, Public Relations Department, Greensboro, North Carolina.

14. Diary of James Spencer Love, February 11, 1925, JSL Papers.

15. Markham, *Competition in the Rayon Industry*, pp. 1–38, 97, 186, 193, 209; Leeming, *Rayon*, pp. 1–82; and Holly, "Elizabethton, Tennessee," pp. 123, 127–28, 133.

16. *Burlington: A Review*, p. 3; *Burlington Times-News*, November 30, 1980, p. 5a; and Versa Haithcock interview, untranscribed.

17. James Spencer Love to Edward A. Addiss, April 5, 1937, JSL Papers, and *Journal of Commerce*, January 3, 1933, in Clipping Files, Burlington Industries, Public Relations Department, Greensboro, North Carolina.

18. On the expansion of Burlington Mills, see *Burlington: A Review*, p. 3. See also *Bur-Mil Review* (October–November 1953); *STB*, September 16, 1926; *Greensboro Daily News*, June 2, 1929; and *Journal of Commerce*, January 3, 1933, all in Clipping Files, Burlington Industries, Public Relations Department, Greensboro, North Carolina. For the interview with Love, see "Sketch of James Spencer Love," *American Fabrics* (Summer 1953), p. 89, in Clipping Files, Burlington Industries, Public Relations Department, Greensboro, North Carolina.

19. Lottie Adams interview, untranscribed.

20. Miller, *Burlington, Graham, and Haw River, 1924–25*, and *Burlington, Graham and Haw River, 1927–28*, and *Miller's Official Burlington, Graham and Haw River, 1929–30*. City directory listings are often incomplete, yet even if the number of families who remained in Piedmont Heights was underrepresented, the figures still indicate a high degree of mobility. Versa Haithcock interview, untranscribed.

21. Versa Haithcock interview, untranscribed.

22. Mattie Shoemaker and Mildred Shoemaker Edmonds interview, March 23, 1979, p. 17, and Versa Haithcock interview, untranscribed. The settlement of Piedmont Heights followed a pattern similar to that discussed in studies of boomtowns. The literature on boomtowns deals primarily with the American West. See, for example, Dykstra, *Cattle Towns*; Duane A. Smith, *Rocky Mountain Mining Camps*; and Olien and Olien, *Oil Booms*. For studies of contemporary boomtowns, see Moen et al., *Women and the Social Costs of Economic Development*; Davenport and Davenport, *Boom Towns and Human Services*; and Freudenburg, "People in the Impact Zone."

23. Versa Haithcock interview, untranscribed, and Dewey and Gladys McBride interview, untranscribed.

24. Versa Haithcock interview, untranscribed, and Ralph Latta interview, p. 22.

25. Lottie Adams interview, untranscribed, and Dewey and Gladys McBride interview, untranscribed.

26. President's Research Committee on Social Trends, *Recent Social Trends*, pp. 940–42, 946, and Stricker, "Affluence for Whom?," pp. 30–32. For a history of working-class attitudes toward movies, see Sklar, *Movie-Made America*.

27. Yellis, "Prosperity's Child," p. 51; Whitaker, Cook, and White, *Centennial History of Alamance*, pp. 232, 236; *Burlington Daily News*, January 22, 1923, p. 4; *Burlington Daily Times-News*, Centennial Edition, May 9, 1949; *Burlington Daily News*, March 1, 1927, p. 1; and *Miller's Official Burlington, Graham, and Haw River, 1929–30*.

28. *Burlington Daily News*, July 24, 1929, p. 1. For a discussion of the impact of the automobile on family and community life, see Lynd and Lynd, *Middletown*, pp. 251–63.

29. Peiss, *Cheap Amusements*, pp. 100–104, 187; President's Research Committee

on Social Trends, *Recent Social Trends*, pp. 417–19; Fass, *The Damned and the Beautiful*, p. 307; May, *Great Expectations*, p. 87; and Fishbein, " 'Dancing Mothers,' " p. 243.

30. Dewey and Gladys McBride interview, untranscribed, and Myers, "Field Notes, Textile Strike in the South," p. 5. For purposes of comparison, see Ewen, *Immigrant Women*, pp. 25–26, 197–202, and Peiss, *Cheap Amusements*, pp. 63–67.

31. Hampton, "New Leisure," and James Pharis interview, p. 7. Hampton's sample of 122 workers included members of ninety families. For purposes of analysis she divided her sample by age and gender: the oldest group, age 40 and over, consisted of 23 men and 14 women; the age group in the middle, 26 to 39 years old, had 27 men and 28 women; and the youngest group, 16 through 25 years of age, had only 3 men and 27 women. On the popularity of the radio, see Hampton, "New Leisure," pp. 60–63.

32. Hampton, "New Leisure," p. 49.

33. Ibid., p. 64, and Carl and Mary Thompson interview, pp. 10–11.

34. *Davison's Textile Blue Book, July 1930–July 1931*, pp. 680–82, 686–88; Stricker, "Affluence for Whom?," p. 14; and Dr. Carroll Lupton interview, p. 2.

35. Frank Webster interview, p. 3.

36. Roy Lee and Mary Ruth Auton interview, p. 2, and James Ross, *They Don't Dance Much*, p. 67. Ross wrote in another edition of his book that he had aimed merely "to show it the way it was" (New York: Popular Library, 1976, frontispiece). His description of hosiery workers' wages, youth, and eyesight were accurate. See Federal Writers' Project, *These Are Our Lives*, pp. 177–79, and interviews with Joseph Crutchfield, Reid A. Maynard, Ernest Chapman, and Roy Lee and Mary Ruth Auton.

37. Federal Writers' Project, *These Are Our Lives*, p. 155; Reid A. Maynard interview, p. 69; and Ernest Chapman interview, p. 17.

38. Ivey Heavnor interview, unrecorded; Collins, "Twenty-four to a Dozen," pp. 28–29; and de Haan, *Full-Fashioned Hosiery Industry*, pp. 106–7. For a description of fixers' and knitters' skills, see also Joseph Crutchfield interview.

39. Roy Lee and Mary Ruth Auton interview, pp. 2–3.

40. James and Nannie Pharis interview, p. 10; Herman Truitt interview, p. 45; and Stella Carden interview, p. 15.

41. *Burlington Daily News*, January 23, 1923, p. 4, February 10, 1923, p. 4, February 2, 1927, p. 3, February 5, 1927, p. 4, June 6, 1929, p. 3, August 3, 1929, p. 2, July 12, 1929, p. 4, and September 24, 1929, p. 1.

42. "Getting Home for Amos 'n Andy," *STB*, May 29, 1930, p. 19, and Ralph Latta interview, pp. 18–19.

43. Wiggins, *Fiddlin' Georgia Crazy*, pp. 74–75.

44. Ibid., pp. 64–65, 69–70, 73–76.

45. Coulter, "The Piedmont Tradition," pp. 7–11, and Wiggins, *Fiddlin' Georgia Crazy*, pp. 80–81.

46. Rorrer, *Rambling Blues*, pp. 13, 17, 23, 29, 31.

47. Ibid., p. 41.

48. Dr. Carroll Lupton interview, pp. 2–3.

49. Ibid., pp. 13, 18–19.

50. Mattie Shoemaker and Mildred Shoemaker Edmonds interview, March 23, 1979, p. 17. On drinking in the mill, see Icy Norman interview, p. 51, and *Burlington Times-News*, 1972, in Clipping Files, Burlington Industries, Public Relations Department, Greensboro, North Carolina. For references to fighting in mills, see Versa Haithcock interview, untranscribed; Ralph Latta interview, pp. 44–45; Stella Carden interview, p. 21; William and Margaret Robertson interview, untranscribed; Dewey and Gladys McBride interview, untranscribed; *SWTE*, November 6, 1906, p. 14; "Supt. Yow Assaulted," *STB*, February 1, 1923, p. 21; "Severely Slashed," *STB*, February 3, 1916, p. 13; and "Overseer Shoots Operative," *STB*, March 21, 1912, p. 16.

51. *Builders of Alamance*, p. 16; *Burlington Daily Times-News*, Centennial Edition, May 9, 1949; Betty and Lloyd Davidson interview, p. 5; and Alice Copeland interview, pp. 3–4.

52. Icy Norman interview, pp. 29–31.

53. Ibid., p. 53.

54. Ibid., p. 39; Versa Haithcock interview, untranscribed; William and Margaret Robertson interview, untranscribed; and Hester Taylor interview, untranscribed.

55. Betty and Lloyd Davidson interview, pp. 24, 23.

56. Ralph Latta interview, pp. 8, 40. Copland used his accumulated knowledge of the textile industry to start his own company after he retired. According to local legend, he at first "just traveled, did what he wanted to do and said he got through with that stuff in a year's time." Then, in the early 1940s, he called together his children, pooled their money, and started Copeland Fabrics in Hopedale. Copland had become an expert on rayon technology and had developed a loom improvement called the leno motion attachment, which allowed the production of high quality, low cost rayon marquisettes. Thanks to that invention, his mill operated at 162 picks per minute during its first month of production, while most established firms were operating at 132 picks per minute. Copeland Fabrics produced the same amount of material as other mills with 22 percent fewer looms and with fewer weavers each operating a greater number of machines. See Ralph Latta interview, p. 39, and *Burlington Daily Times-News*, Centennial Edition, May 9, 1949.

57. Icy Norman interview, pp. 36–39.

58. Ibid., pp. 43–44, 47.

59. Ibid., pp. 51–52.

60. Ibid., pp. 53–54.

61. "What's Wrong with the Textile Industry," *STB*, January 31, 1929, pp. 25–26.

62. Rose, "Rayon Weaving in the South," p. 64, clipping in Scrapbook, JSL Papers. The expansion of Burlington Mills during the Depression is also discussed in Phillip J. Wood, *Southern Capitalism*, pp. 169–71.

63. "A Man, a Fiber, a Textile Empire," *Textile World*, June 1973, p. 83.

64. *Burlington: A Review*, p. 4; *High Point Enterprise*, September 30, 1935; *Textile*

World, June 1973; and *Textile Age*, 1954, all in Clipping Files, Burlington Industries, Public Relations Department, Greensboro, North Carolina.

65. James Spencer Love to Cornelia Spencer Love, May 20, 1931, JSL Papers.

66. Gillespie, "J. Spencer Love—Industrial Genius," unreferenced clipping, in Clipping Files, Burlington Industries, Public Relations Department, Greensboro, North Carolina; Icy Norman interview, p. 52; and James Spencer Love to James Lee Love, October 9, 1933, James Spencer Love to Cornelia Spencer Love, January 25 and 29, 1935, and Cornelia Spencer Love to James Spencer Love, January 30 and February 4, 1935, JSL Papers.

67. Rose, "Rayon Weaving in the South," p. 66; "How Rayon Grew up in the South," *American Wool and Cotton Reporter*, December 14, 1950, p. 55; and *Burlington Daily Times-News*, Golden Jubilee edition, 1937, clippings, Scrapbook, JSL Papers.

68. James Lee Love to James Spencer Love, May 16, 1935, JSL Papers.

69. Harry Rogers interview, July 21, 1977, pp. 16–17, and James Pharis interview, p. 33. See also Jesse L. Brooks interview, pp. 13–14.

70. Ralph Latta interview, p. 37.

71. Dewey and Gladys McBride interview, untranscribed.

72. On the institutional history of the Glen Hope Baptist Church, see the *Glen Hope Baptist Church Directory*, 1980, and various scrapbooks and clippings in the Glen Hope Church office. See also the interviews of Ralph Latta, the Reverend Robert Latta, the Reverend Clarence Vaughn, Dr. Carroll Lupton, Icy Norman, Lottie Adams, Mildred Overman, Ina Lee Wrenn, and Etta Gay Dalton Swinney.

73. Etta Gay Dalton Swinney interview, untranscribed.

74. Ralph Latta interview, pp. 29–31.

75. Rev. Robert Latta interview, pp. 7–8.

76. "This Is Your Life," untranscribed tape recording, and Etta Gay Dalton Swinney interview, untranscribed.

77. "This Is Your Life."

78. Ibid., and Ralph Latta interview, p. 35. In his study of Gastonia, Liston Pope noted that the term "Doctor" was used frequently in "uptown" churches—predominantly Presbyterian, Episcopalian, Lutheran, and Methodist—by congregations that regarded their ministers as "very scholarly." He also noted that these men infrequently felt called to a ministry in a mill church. See Pope, *Millhands and Preachers*, p. 95.

79. Ralph Latta interview, pp. 28–29.

80. Rev. Robert Latta interview, p. 6, and Dr. Carroll Lupton interview, pp. 7–8.

81. Rev. Clarence Vaughn interview, unrecorded; Rev. Robert Latta interview, pp. 3, 2; and anonymous interview. On southern evangelical religion see Mathews, *Religion in the Old South*, and Bruce, *They All Sang Hallelujah*.

82. Rev. Robert Latta interview, p. 14, and anonymous interview.

83. Dr. Carroll Lupton interview, pp. 4–5.

84. Ibid., pp. 4, 19–20.

85. Ibid., pp. 14–15, and William and Margaret Robertson interview, untranscribed.

86. Dewey and Gladys McBride interview, untranscribed.

87. Mattie Shoemaker and Mildred Shoemaker Edmonds interview, Summer 1979, unrecorded.

88. Lottie Adams interview, untranscribed.

89. Pope noted that mill villagers tended to approach their religion as a solution to concrete problems. "It 'works' and 'changes things,'" was the attitude he found in Gastonia. Villagers in Piedmont Heights seemed to share that belief. See Pope, *Millhands and Preachers*, p. 86.

90. Ralph Latta interview, pp. 4–5, 7–8; *Burlington Daily News*, clipping, n.d., Glen Hope Church files; and Rev. Clarence Vaughn interview, unrecorded.

91. Dr. Carroll Lupton interview, p. 15, and Rev. Clarence Vaughn interview, unrecorded.

92. Pope, *Millhands and Preachers*, p. 325.

93. Ralph Latta interview, pp. 7, 36; *Burlington Daily Times-News*, September 15, 1934, p. 7; and Pickard, *Burlington Dynamite Plot*, pp. 8–9.

94. Etta Gay Dalton Swinney interview, untranscribed. Spencer Love was the first southern mill man to sell off his mill village. On the sale of the Piedmont Heights houses, see *Burlington: A Review*, p. 3.

95. Ina Lee Wrenn interview, untranscribed.

96. Liston Pope discovered in Gastonia that an unstable village population was one of the chief problems faced by mill churches. The First Baptist Church in Gastonia, an "uptown" church, received 1,116 new members in the ten years between 1928 and 1938; and a Baptist mill church in the thirteen years between 1925 and 1938 accepted 2,330 new members. But both churches started and ended with congregations of roughly the same size. See Pope, *Millhands and Preachers*, p. 85.

97. Armstrong and Armstrong, *Baptists of America*, p. 257, and Rev. Robert Latta interview, p. 30.

98. Rev. Robert Latta interview, p. 31.

99. Ibid., p. 3.

100. Ibid., pp. 13–14.

101. Ralph Latta interview, p. 60.

102. Pope, *Millhands and Preachers*, pp. 114, 88.

103. Pope found that the average length of a pastorate in mill churches in Gaston County was 75 percent of that in rural churches and 71 percent of that in uptown churches. See Pope, *Millhands and Preachers*, pp. 89–90, 113.

104. Anonymous interview.

105. Dewey and Gladys McBride interview, untranscribed.

CHAPTER SIX

1. Schlesinger, *Coming of the New Deal*, pp. 1–23; Graham, "Years of Crisis"; and Jensen, *America in Time*, pp. 157–61.

2. For early New Deal industrial policy, see Bernstein, *Turbulent Years*, pp. 23–36, 172–85; Leuchtenburg, *Franklin Roosevelt*, pp. 55–58, 64–70; and Hodges, *New Deal Labor Policy*.

3. Leuchtenburg, "New Deal and the Analogue of War"; Galambos, *Competition and Cooperation*, pp. 126, 158–60, 174; and Bernstein, *Turbulent Years*, pp. 27–31.

4. Galambos, *Competition and Cooperation*, pp. 109–10, 134, 204, 209–26; Clarence J. Swink to Hugh S. Johnson, November 6, 1933, Cannon Mills, NRA Records 398; and Hodges, *New Deal Labor Policy*, pp. 49, 51, 53.

5. Hodges, *New Deal Labor Policy*, pp. 44, 58, 63; Bernstein, *Turbulent Years*, p. 172; Leuchtenburg, "New Deal and the Analogue of War," p. 131, and *Franklin Roosevelt*, p. 108; and McElvaine, *Down and Out*, pp. 5–6.

6. Sussmann, *Dear FDR*, p. 63, and Leuchtenburg, "New Deal and the Analogue of War," pp. 120–21.

7. Henry Grady Coyle to Franklin Delano Roosevelt (hereafter FDR), September 4, 1933, Limestone Mill, NRA Records 398; *Greenville News*, May 10, 1929; and Employees of Randolph Mills to Hugh Johnson, February 27, 1934, Randolph Mills, NRA Records 398. See also Essie Crawford to the National Recovery Administration, August 30, 1933, Woodside Mills, NRA Records 398.

8. Hodges, *New Deal Labor Policy*, p. 56.

9. Ibid., p. 57.

10. Letter to FDR, October 19, 1934, general correspondence, unsigned, NRA Records 401; Ralph B. Bower to Hugh S. Johnson, February 26, 1934, American Cotton Mills; D. H. Powers to Hugh S. Johnson, September 6, 1933, Gaffney Mfg. Co.; Mrs. J. W. Hallman to Eleanor Roosevelt, January 29, 1934, Graniteville Mfg. Co.; L. J. Hollifield to Mr. Forbush, September 10, 1933, Ella Mills, NRA Records 398; and letter to FDR, October 19, 1934, Greenville, general correspondence, unsigned, NRA Records 401.

11. Fachia Hamilton to FDR, September 1933, Iceman Mill; Jessie Belk to Hugh S. Johnson, July 24, 1933, Louise Mill; and H. A. Lloyd to Hugh S. Johnson, November 24, 1933, Cramerton Mills, NRA Records 398.

12. Mrs. N. M. Caldwell to Hugh S. Johnson, July 27 [1933], Hoskins Chadwick Co., and Henry Grady Coyle to FDR, September 4, 1933, Limestone Mill, NRA Records 398. See also Ralph B. Bower to Hugh S. Johnson, February 26, 1934, American Cotton Mills, NRA Records 398.

13. Letter to FDR, March 21, 1934, Fulton Bag and Cotton Mills No. 2, NRA Records 398, and Mrs. Luther Gregory to FDR, September 14, 1934, Lockhart Mill, NRA Records 402.

14. Syble Brown to Eleanor Roosevelt, August 2, 1934, Conestee Mill, NRA Records 398.

15. Lahne, *Cotton Mill Worker*, p. 124; James Bramlette to L. R. Gilbert, August 24, 1933, Riverside Mills; letter from Mrs. Rosa Lamb, April 25, 1934, Faytex Mills; and letter from P. M. Mooney, July 14, 1933, Olympia Cotton Mills, NRA Records 398.

16. R. W. Russell to FDR, July 25, 1933, Brown Mill; P. W. Hutchins to Hugh S. Johnson, October 31, 1933, Clinchfield Textile Cotton Mills; and Miss Veannah Timmons to FDR, July 19, 1933, Pacific Mills, NRA Records 398.

17. Mrs. J. G. Hutchison to FDR, December 5, 1933, Highland Park Mill no. 3; Belle Seymoure to FDR, August 1, 1933, Lancaster Cotton Mills, Chester Plant no. 1, NRA Records 398; J. Vernon Phillips to FDR, September 13, 1934, Phillips Engineering Co., NRA Records 402; S. J. Ginyss to Hugh S. Johnson, January 4, 1934, Cannon Mills Plant no. 6; and J. S. Binns to FDR, September 3, 1934, Springsteen Cotton Mill, NRA Records 398. See also Lottie Gardner to FDR, March 21, 1934, Tucapau Mills, NRA Records 398.

18. Letter from P. M. Mooney, July 14, 1933, Olympia Cotton Mills, NRA Records 398; Mrs. M. G. Hunter and family to FDR, October 1, 1934, miscellaneous, NRA Records 402; and letter to Hugh S. Johnson, January 15, 1934, Dunean Mill, enclosing article entitled "The Stretch-Out Evil," NRA Records 398.

19. Joseph E. Sirrine, "The Truth About 'Stretch-Out,'" *STB*, December 13, 1934, pp. 3–4, 27, and Hodges, *New Deal Labor Policy*, pp. 66–67. Quotations are from K. S. Tanner, "A Heart to Heart Talk," January 24, 1934, Stonecutter Mills Co., NRA Records 398, and Joseph E. Sirrine, "The Truth About 'Stretch-Out,'" *STB*, December 13, 1934, p. 27.

20. Annie L. West to FDR, September 18, 1934, Saxon Mills, NRA Records 402, and "Mill Engineer Says Stretch-Out a Blessing When Properly Applied," *STB*, January 25, 1934, p. 12.

21. Hodges, *New Deal Labor Policy*, pp. 13, 57, and Hinrichs, "Wage Rates," p. 617.

22. Quoted in Hodges, *New Deal Labor Policy*, p. 32.

23. H. A. Lloyd to Hugh S. Johnson, November 24, 1933, Cramerton Mills, and Mrs. S. A. B. to FDR, October 21, 1933, Acme Spinning Co., NRA Records 398.

24. Letter to John G. Winant, Marion Smith, and Raymond Ingersoll, September 7, 1934, general correspondence, unsigned, NRA Records 401.

25. For examples, see Miss Inez Broome to Hugh S. Johnson, October 25, 1933, Aragon-Baldwin Mill, and letter from Ada Fisher, November 16, 1933, Lincolnton Cotton Mill, NRA Records 398.

26. For examples, see Mrs. J. H. Morrow to Hugh S. Johnson, December 6, 1933, Dover Mill; E. W. Hilley to FDR, December 21, 1933, Appleton Mill; and Miss Veannah Timmons to FDR, July 19, 1933, Pacific Mills, NRA Records 398.

27. Letter to dear friend, August 1, 1933, Acme Spinning Co.; Vernon L. Hinson to Hugh S. Johnson, August 21, 1933, Eton Mfg. Co.; W. G. W. to FDR, September 8, 1933, Pelzer Mills, NRA Records 398; and Hinrichs, "Wage Rates," p. 622.

28. Hinrichs, "Wage Rates," p. 614.

29. Laura McGhee affidavit, August 10, 1933, Graniteville Mfg. Co.; letter to dear friend, August 1, 1933, Acme Spinning Co.; and M. J. James to Francis Gorman, March 24, 1934, Alice Cotton Mill, NRA Records 398.

30. Miss Wretha Smith to Hugh S. Johnson, April 25, 1934, Waverly Mills, NRA

Records 398; Mr. O. O. Tisdale to FDR, September 23, 1934, closed cases, miscellaneous, NRA Records 402; Lefler and Newsome, *North Carolina*, pp. 612–13; Phillip J. Wood, *Southern Capitalism*, pp. 130–31; Hinrichs, "Wage Rates," pp. 623–25; and U.S. Department of Labor, Women's Bureau, *Employed Women*, p. 16.

31. Letter to FDR, October 19, 1934, general correspondence, unsigned, NRA Records 401; Mrs. J. C. Hutchison to Hugh S. Johnson, July 12, 1934, Highland Park Mill no. 3; and Miss Wretha Smith to Hugh S. Johnson, April 25, 1934, Waverly Mills, NRA Records 398.

32. Undated newspaper clipping, letter to the editor, *Charlotte Observer*, A. F. Brigmon, Bennettsville, S.C., clipped to Mrs. R. S. Duckworth to Eleanor Roosevelt, September 16, 1934, Mooresville Cotton Mill, NRA Records 398.

33. Brody, *Workers in Industrial America*, p. 126, and James A. Gross, *Making of the National Labor Relations Board*, pp. 10–11, 14–15.

34. Tindall, *Emergence of the New South*, p. 505; Hodges, *New Deal Labor Policy*, pp. 60–61; and letter to FDR, April 23, 1934, Watts Mill, NRA Records 398.

35. J. Dooley to Hugh S. Johnson, August 9, 1933, Holt-Williamson Manufacturing Co.; Miss Margaret Nyers to Hugh S. Johnson, October 19, 1933, Oneida Cotton Mill; D. H. Powers to Hugh S. Johnson, September 6, 1933, Gaffney Mfg. Co.; and W. G. W. to FDR, September 8, 1933, Pelzer Mills, NRA Records 398.

36. Affidavit, November 18, 1933, Shelby Cotton Mill; letter to Board of Codes, March 12, 1934, Republic Mills; and affidavit from B. W. Pitman, August 28, 1934, Brandon Mills, NRA Records 398.

37. Prior, "From Community to National Unionism," pp. 69–70, and "Facts of Spindale Dispute," February 13, 1934, Stonecutter Mills, NRA Records 398.

38. K. S. Tanner, "A Heart to Heart Talk," January 24, 1934, Stonecutter Mills, NRA Records 398.

39. Laura McGhee affidavit, August 10, 1933, Graniteville Mfg. Co., NRA Records 398.

40. Earnest Mabry to FDR, January 22, 1934, Pacolet Mills, and Mrs. J. W. Hallman to Eleanor Roosevelt, January 29, 1934, Graniteville Mfg. Co., NRA Records 398.

41. S. D. Abernathy to FDR, April 4, 1934, Florence Mills, and letter to FDR, October 23, 1933, Dunean Mill, NRA Records 398.

42. James A. Gross, *Making of the National Labor Relations Board*, pp. 15, 17; Hodges, *New Deal Labor Policy*, pp. 62–72, 92; and Bernstein, *Turbulent Years*, pp. 172–73, 302–4.

43. Miss Naomi Duke to Miss Perkins, August 10, 1933, Bath Mill, NRA Records 398. See "No More to Fool," *STB*, October 9, 1930, p.14, for memory of the 1900 conflict.

44. L. Coleman to FDR, May 1, 1934, Graniteville Mills; Mrs. J. W. Hallman to Eleanor Roosevelt, January 29, 1934, Graniteville Mfg. Co.; Mrs. Lorena Queen to Hugh S. Johnson, October 29, 1933, Lockhart Mills, NRA Records 398; and "Labor Asks Law to Prevent Mill Village Evictions," *STB*, March 1, 1934, p. 31.

45. Sussmann, *Dear FDR*, pp. 13–14, 65, 72, 112, 135, 139–47.

46. For gender differences in communication styles, see Faragher, *Women and Men on the Overland Trail*, pp. 128–33, and Jordan and Kalčik, *Women's Folklore, Women's Culture*, pp. ix–xiv. For the exclusion of women from public political discourse, see Alexander, "Women, Class and Sexual Differences," pp. 136, 145–46.

47. Letter to dear friend, August 1, 1933, Acme Spinning Co., NRA Records 398.

48. Janiewski, "From Field to Factory," p. 121, and Mrs. L. C. Galloway to FDR, July 25, 1933, Glenwood Cotton Mills, NRA Records 398.

49. An Unemployed Widow, "Fallacies in the Code," letter to the editor, *Greenville News*, n.d., Conestee Mill, NRA Records 398.

50. Mrs. Maxie Cassidy to FDR, November 20, 1933, Lancaster Cotton Mill, NRA Records 398. See also letter from Mrs. Rosa Lamb, April 25, 1934, Faytex Mills, NRA Records 398.

51. Jessie Belk to Hugh S. Johnson, July 24, 1933, Louise Mill, NRA Records 398.

52. Letter from R. L. Holsenback, September 29, 1933, Langley Mill, NRA Records 398. See also Mrs. G. C. Hudson to FDR, October 11, 1933, Mathews Mill, NRA Records 398.

53. Milkman, *Gender at Work*, p. 28.

54. J. F. Chapman to FDR, August 24, 1933, Poe Mill; M. J. James to Francis Gorman, March 24, 1934, Alice Cotton Mill; Mary Howell to L. R. Gilbert, August 24, 1933, Efird Mfg. Co.; and S. H. Twitty to Hugh S. Johnson, May 7, 1934, Hermitage Cotton Mill, NRA Records 398.

55. Blaine H. Wofford interview, untranscribed.

56. Letter from J. R. Livingston, January 17, 1934, Angle Silk Mill, NRA Records 402.

57. Mrs. B. M. Miller to Hugh S. Johnson, October 12, 1933, Chadwick-Hoskins Mill, NRA Records 398.

58. Mrs. Viola Tate to Hugh S. Johnson, March 1, 1934, Pilot Cotton Mills Co., NRA Records 398.

59. U.S. Department of Labor, Women's Bureau, *Women in the Economy*, p. 94, and *Employed Women*, pp. 16–19, and letter to Hugh S. Johnson, May 15, 1934, American Cotton Mills, NRA Records 398.

60. Syble Brown to Eleanor Roosevelt, August 2, 1934, Conestee Mill, and Mrs. R. S. Duckworth to Eleanor Roosevelt, September 16, 1934, Mooresville Cotton Mill, NRA Records 398.

61. Eula McGill interview, p. 33, and History of Spindale Local 1993, July 28, 1934, Stonecutter Mills, NRA Records 398.

62. Mrs. Mary Steele to FDR, April 30, 1934, Highland Park Mill no. 3, NRA Records 398.

63. Letter from Mrs. Ethel Reid, December 10, 1933, Chadwick-Hoskins Co., Mill no. 1, NRA Records 398. See also Mrs. Ethel Reid to L. R. Gilbert, February 1, 1934, Chadwick-Hoskins Co., Mill no. 1, NRA Records 398.

64. Hodges, *New Deal Labor Policy*, p. 51; Gavin Wright, *Old South, New South*, p.

152; Miss Margaret Nyers to Hugh S. Johnson, October 19, 1933, Oneida Cotton Mill; and letter to Benjamin Geer, August 11, 1933, Eureka Lancaster Mill, NRA Records 398.

65. U.S. Department of Labor, Women's Bureau, *Employed Women*, p. 72, and letter from "Citizens," September 28, 1933, Erlanger Cotton Mill, NRA Records 398.

66. Moses Bradley to Hugh S. Johnson, August 10, 1933, Hartsville Cotton Mill; letter to Hugh S. Johnson, October 6, 1933, Linford Mill; and George Washington Conor to FDR, July [2], 1933, Mooresville Cotton Mill, NRA Records 398.

67. Letter from Mrs. Dora Adams, August 1, 1933, Newry Mill, and L. B. Killey to Hugh S. Johnson, April 19, 1934, Chiquola Mfg. Co., NRA Records 398.

68. Clarence J. Swink to Hugh S. Johnson, August 12, 1933, Cannon Mills, NRA Records 398.

69. Percy Kite to Hugh S. Johnson, April 3, 1934, Fountain Cotton Mill Co.; Fritz Howell to Robert Bruere, March 10, 1934, American Cotton Mills, NRA Records 398; and Rev. J. T. Chapman to FDR, October 25, 1934, Woodside Cotton Mills, NRA Records 402.

70. Eula McGill interview, pp. 41, 49.

71. For the class-specific functions of racialist ideology, see Fields, "Ideology and Race in American History," esp. pp. 155–60.

72. W. G. M., "Blondie on the Spot?," letter to the editor, *Greenville News*, August 2, 1934, Conestee Mill; Mrs. Mary Steele to FDR, April 30, 1934, Highland Park Mill no. 3; James Bramlette to L. R. Gilbert, August 24, 1933, Riverside Mills, NRA Records 398; J. M. Zimmerman to Mr. Eugene Talmadge, January 14, 1935, mill unknown, miscellaneous, NRA Records 402; and Mrs. J. G. Hutchison to FDR, December 5, 1933, Highland Park Mill, NRA Records 398. See also Mrs. Sadie Harris to FDR, October 17, 1934, Mathews Mill, NRA Records 402.

73. John W. Kennedy, "General Strike in the Textile Industry," pp. 102–4, and F. T. Thompson to FDR, February 24, 1935, miscellaneous cases closed, NRA Records 402.

74. Mrs. Sadie Harris, "The Mill Labor Situation," letter to the editor, *Greenwood Tribune*, n.d., Conestee Mill, NRA Records 398.

75. Undated newspaper clipping, letter to the editor, *Charlotte Observer*, clipped to Mrs. R. S. Duckworth to Eleanor Roosevelt, September 16, 1934, Mooresville Cotton Mill, NRA Records 398.

76. Lottie Gardner to FDR, March 21, 1934, Tucapau Mill, NRA Records 398, and J. Vernon Phillips to FDR, September 13, 1934, Phillips Engineering Co., NRA Records 402.

77. Ratchford, "Toward Preliminary Social Analysis," pp. 365–66; U.S. Congress, House, *To Regulate the Textile Industry*, p. 114; Phillip J. Wood, *Southern Capitalism*, p. 78; and "Bosses' Pay Is Way Up," *PM*, April 13, 1942, clipping, Scrapbook, p. 84, vol. 21-S, JSL Papers.

78. For a suggestive study of working-class women and religion, see Valenze, *Prophetic Sons and Daughters*.

79. Letter to John G. Winant, Marion Smith, and Raymond Ingersoll, September 7, 1934, general correspondence, unsigned, NRA Records 401.

80. Mrs. Sadie Harris, "The Mill Labor Situation," letter to the editor, *Greenwood Tribune*, n.d., Conestee Mill, NRA Records 398; Sadie Harris, letter to the editor, *Greenwood Tribune*, n.d., clipped to letter from W. S. Johnson, October 20, 1934, Mathews Mill; and Mrs. Sadie Harris to FDR, October 17, 1934, Mathews Mill, NRA Records 402.

81. W. R. Taliaferro, Jr., to Textile Labor Relations Board, January 16, 1937, Durham Cotton Mfg. Co., NRA Records 402.

82. J. Vernon Phillips to FDR, September 13, 1934, Phillips Engineering Co., NRA Records 402.

83. Haynes Willoughby to FDR, January 10, 1937, Durham Cotton Mfg. Co., NRA Records 402.

84. Frank B. Sexton to FDR, March 22, 1937, B. C. and C. W. Mayo Knitting Mill, NRA Records 402, and letter to FDR, April 23, 1934, Watts Mill, enclosing undated newspaper clipping, letter to the editor, Laurens, S.C., August 2, 1934.

85. Mrs. B. M. Miller to Frances Perkins, December 13, 1933, Chadwick-Hoskins Co., and Fritz Howell to Robert Bruere, March 10, 1934, American Cotton Mills, NRA Records 398.

86. Henry Grady Coyle to FDR, September 4, 1933, Limestone Mill, NRA Records 398, and McElvaine, *Down and Out*, pp. 14–16.

87. P. C. Burkholder to FDR, September 14, 1934, miscellaneous, and Haynes Willoughby to FDR, January 10, 1937, Durham Cotton Mfg. Co., NRA Records 402.

88. Livingston V. Hinson to Hugh S. Johnson, July 30, 1933, Cleveland Cloth Mills, NRA Records 398, and W. H. Crisp to FDR, October 22, 1934, Dilling Mills of Kings Mountain, NRA Records 402.

89. Geo. D. Byrd to FDR, November 15, 1934, miscellaneous cases closed; F. T. Thompson to FDR, February 24, 1935, miscellaneous cases closed, NRA Records 402; and letter to FDR, April 12, 1934, Watts Mill, NRA Records 398.

90. Clarence J. Swink to Hugh S. Johnson, August 12, 1933, Cannon Mills, and Clarence J. Swink to Hugh S. Johnson, November 6, 1933, Cannon Mills, NRA Records 398.

91. Hodges, *New Deal Labor Policy*, p. 392; Bernstein, *Turbulent Years*, pp. 303–4; and "Text of Winant Report As Given to President," *STB*, September 27, 1934, pp. 6–7.

92. M. J. James to Francis Gorman, March 24, 1934, Alice Cotton Mill, NRA Records 398; letter to John G. Winant, Marion Smith, and Raymond Ingersoll, September 7, 1934, general correspondence, unsigned, NRA Records 401; and Frank Snipes to FDR, August 4, 1933, Chadwick-Hoskins Co., NRA Records 398.

93. J. R. Livingston to Frances Perkins, February 3, 1935, mill unknown, NRA Records 402; W. H. Fowler to Hugh S. Johnson, July 26, 1933, Appalache Mill; C. G. Clark to L. R. Gilbert, n.d., Cannon Mills; A. W. Litton to Hugh S. Johnson,

August 20, 1934, Glencoe Cotton Mill, NRA Records 398. See also G. W. Thomas to Hugh S. Johnson, March 22, 1934, Union Buffalo Mills, NRA Records 398; Mr. O. O. Tisdale to FDR, September 23, 1934, closed cases, miscellaneous, NRA Records 402; and letter from R. H. Greene, November 30, 1933, Lancaster Cotton Mills, Chester Plant no. 1, NRA Records 398.

94. Prior, "From Community to National Unionism," p. 75; Paul R. Christopher to Francis Gorman, November 27, 1934, Gastonia Thread Yarn Mills, NRA Records 402; Gary Fink, *Biographical Dictionary of American Labor Leaders*, pp. 59–60; Garrison, "Paul Revere Christopher"; letter from E. N. Wallace, December 12, 1933, Eagle Yarn Mills; E. H. Waddell to FDR, October 12, 1933, Burlington Mills, NRA Records 398; Geo. D. Byrd to FDR, November 15, 1934, miscellaneous cases closed, NRA Records 402; and Thomas J. Pearsall to Hugh S. Johnson, August 11, 1933, Saxon Mills, NRA Records 398.

95. Mrs. B. M. Miller to Hugh S. Johnson, July 23, 1933, Chadwick-Hoskins Co., and Mrs. B. M. Miller to Frances Perkins, December 13, 1933, Chadwick-Hoskins Co., NRA Records 398.

96. Prior, "From Community to National Unionism," pp. 69–77.

97. Quoted in ibid., p. 76.

98. Ibid., p. 82, and Hodges, *New Deal Labor Policy*, pp. 96, 98–99.

99. Hodges, *New Deal Labor Policy*, pp. 97–98.

100. *The Nation*, October 2, 1929, p. 340; John W. Kennedy, "General Strike," pp. 51–61; and Bernstein, *Turbulent Years*, pp. 308–9.

101. Mrs. William N. Tillinghast to Miss Anne W. Tillinghast, September 5, 1934, Tillinghast Family Papers, Manuscripts Department, Perkins Library, Duke University, Durham, North Carolina; Roy Lee and Mary Ruth Auton interview, pp. 7–11; H. M. Yount, reply to survey conducted by governor's office, September 19, 1934, Newton Glove Company, Newton, N.C., box 114, Adjutant General's Department Papers, North Carolina Division of Archives and History, Raleigh, North Carolina; Garrison, "Paul Revere Christopher," pp. 34–35; Ratchford, "Toward Preliminary Social Analysis," p. 361; Petition to Governor J. C. B. Ehringhaus, September 5, 1934, box 103, and Benjamin B. Gossett to Governor Ehringhaus, September 14, 1934, box 104, J. C. B. Ehringhaus Governor's Papers, 1933–37, North Carolina Division of Archives and History, Raleigh, North Carolina.

102. Hodges, *New Deal Labor Policy*, p. 107; Allen, "Eugene Talmadge and the Great Textile Strike," p. 237; and *New York Times*, September 20, 1934, p. 3.

103. J. M. Zimmerman to Eugene Talmadge, January 14, 1935, mill unknown, miscellaneous, NRA Records 402.

104. Jonathan Daniels to Josephus Daniels, September 20 [1934], Jonathan Daniels Papers, Southern Historical Collection, University of North Carolina at Chapel Hill.

105. Groves Thread Company to Governor J. C. B. Ehringhaus, September 5, 1934, and petition to Governor Ehringhaus, September 5, 1934, box 103, J. C. B.

Ehringhaus Governor's Papers, 1933–37, North Carolina Division of Archives and History, Raleigh, North Carolina; and Mrs. C. W. Polk to FDR, September 12, 1934, Rosemary Mfg. Co., NRA Records 402.

106. K. S. Tanner to Governor J. C. B. Ehringhaus, September 7, 1934, box 104, J. C. B. Ehringhaus Governor's Papers, 1933–37, North Carolina Division of Archives and History, Raleigh, North Carolina. See also Sulon B. Stedman to Governor J. C. B. Ehringhaus, September 10, 1934, box 104, J. C. B. Ehringhaus Governor's Papers, 1933–37, North Carolina Division of Archives and History, Raleigh, North Carolina.

107. R. R. Lawrence to Governor J. C. B. Ehringhaus, September 7, 1934, box 103, J. C. B. Ehringhaus Governor's Papers, 1933–37, North Carolina Division of Archives and History, Raleigh, North Carolina, and Garrison, "Paul Revere Christopher," pp. 23–24.

108. *Columbia State*, September 7, 1934, and Raleigh *News and Observer*, September 11, 1934, Harriet L. Herring clipping file, North Carolina Collection, University of North Carolina at Chapel Hill, and Daniels, *Southerner Discovers the South*, p. 26. See also Raleigh *News and Observer*, September 11, 1934, Harriet L. Herring clipping file, North Carolina Collection, University of North Carolina at Chapel Hill.

109. Letter to John G. Winant, Marion Smith, and Raymond Ingersoll, September 7, 1934, general correspondence, unsigned, NRA Records 401.

110. Mack Duncan interview, p. 15; *STB*, June 28, 1934, p. 10; letter to FDR, July 23, 1934, Orr Cotton Mill; and Sanford Cleveland affidavit, June 23, 1934, Orr Cotton Mill, NRA Records 398.

111. Geddes E. Dodson interview, pp. 24–25.

112. Lacy Wright interview, pp. 15–17.

113. Mrs. Irene Ramsey and Mrs. Rosie Nimmons to FDR, September 16, 1934, Lonsdale Mill, NRA Records 402.

114. Mack Duncan interview, pp. 13–18.

115. Janiewski, *Sisterhood Denied*, pp. 153–57; *Raleigh Times*, September 3, 1934; Durham *Sunday Herald-Sun*, August 19, August 25, and September 2, 1934; *Durham Sun*, September 1, 1934; and Durham *Morning Herald*, September 5, 1934, Harriet L. Herring clipping file, North Carolina Collection, University of North Carolina at Chapel Hill. For studies of two other communities where the strike enjoyed wide support, see Martin, "Southern Labor Relations in Transition," and Flamming, "Mill Village."

116. Raleigh *News and Observer*, August 25, 1934, and Durham *Morning Herald*, September 1, 1934, Harriet L. Herring clipping file, North Carolina Collection, University of North Carolina at Chapel Hill. See also Luther Riley interview, p. 9.

117. Quotations from Janiewski, *Sisterhood Denied*, p. 160. See also letter from Sollie Hancock, September 4, 1934, Durham Cotton Mfg. Co., NRA Records 402.

118. Edward and Mary Harrington interview, p. 11, and *Burlington Daily Times-*

News, September 6, 1934, p. 1, September 7, 1934, p. 10, September 8, 1934, pp. 6, 10, September 10, 1934, pp. 1, 8, and September 12, 1934, p. 1.

119. Pickard, *Burlington Dynamite Plot*, p. 7, and Mattie Shoemaker and Mildred Shoemaker Edmonds interview, March 23, 1979, pp. 8–9.

120. Mattie Shoemaker and Mildred Shoemaker Edmonds interview, March 23, 1979, pp. 8–9.

121. *Burlington Daily Times-News*, September 12, 1934, p. 10; Sallie Johnson and Rena Capes interview, untranscribed; Jesse L. Brooks interview, p. 21; and Betty and Lloyd Davidson interview, p. 42.

122. *Burlington Daily Times-News*, September 14, 1934, pp. 6, 8, and Exhibit B, Resume of Situation—By Areas, United Textile Workers Strike, 1934, p. 2, [January 19, 1935], Adjutant General's Department Papers, North Carolina Division of Archives and History, Raleigh, North Carolina.

123. Couch, "Case of the 'Burlington Dynamiters,'" unidentified clipping, Clipping File, North Carolina Collection, University of North Carolina at Chapel Hill; James Spencer Love to Cornelia Spencer Love, January 25, 1935, and Cornelia Spencer Love to James Spencer Love, January 30 and February 4, 1935, JSL Papers.

124. James Spencer Love to Cornelia Spencer Love, August 29, September 7, 18, 28, 1934, and January 29, 1935, and Cornelia Spencer Love to James Spencer Love, September 6, 1934, JSL Papers.

125. Wiley D. Forbus, M.D., to James Spencer Love, April 30, 1935, and autopsy report, May 1, 1935, JSL Papers.

126. Mrs. Clio Marthus to Hugh S. Johnson, November 24, 1933, Industrial Cotton Mill, NRA Records 398, and Mrs. Irene Ramsey and Mrs. Rosie Nimmons to FDR, September 16, 1934, Lonsdale Mill, NRA Records 402.

127. Gunnar Myrdal, quoted in Gavin Wright, *Old South, New South*, p. 238. For these developments, see Daniel, *Breaking the Land*, pp. 91–133, 155–84.

128. Edward N. Akin, "Mr. Donald's Help," and Eugene and Carl Lindsey to Hugh S. Johnson, August 2, 1933, Courteney Mfg. Co., NRA Records 398.

129. B. R. Payseur to Robert Bruere, April 3, 1934, Kings Mountain Mfg. Co., NRA Records 398, and Mrs. Mary Thomas to FDR, January 19, 1934, China Grove Mills, NRA Records 398.

130. C. W. Land to Hugh S. Johnson, July 4, 1933, Draper Mills, and H. E. Abernathy to FDR, August 2, 1933, Acworth Cotton Mill, NRA Records 398. For this increase in the number of farmers working part-time in the mills and the presence of large numbers of "spare hands," see Phillip J. Wood, *Southern Capitalism*, p. 70, and Lowitt and Beasley, *One Third of a Nation*, pp. 175–76.

131. Leona Jones to Dr. B. M. Squires, October 30, 1934, Pacific Mills, NRA Records 402.

132. *New York Times*, September 8, 1934, p. 2.

133. Mack Duncan interview, p. 19.

134. Hoyle and Mamie McCorkle interview, pp. 27–28.

135. Eula McGill interview, pp. 18–22, 43–44, 49–51.

136. Ibid., pp. 51–54.

137. Perry Hicks interview, p. 19; Mrs. W. G. Anthony to FDR and Eleanor Roosevelt, April 25, 1936, Alma Mills, NRA Records 402; Mack Duncan interview, p. 21; and Sam Finley interview, p. 15.

138. Bessie Buchanan interview, June, 1977, pp. 33–34.

139. Ibid., p. 14.

140. Letter to FDR, October 19, 1934, general correspondence, unsigned, NRA Records 401.

141. Hodges, *New Deal Labor Policy*, pp. 112–15.

142. Quoted in ibid., p. 117.

143. Mrs. J. G. Minor to FDR, November 5, 1934, Greenwood Cotton Mill; W. S. Johnson to FDR, October 20, 1934, Mathews Mill; and Mrs. Ruby Brown to FDR, December 3, 1934, Mathews Mill, NRA Records 402.

144. Undated newspaper clipping, Mrs. Sadie Harris, South Greenwood, S.C., letter to the editor, *Greenwood Tribune*, clipped to letter from W. S. Johnson, October 20, 1934, Mathews Mill, and Mrs. Sadie Harris to FDR, October 17, 1934, Mathews Mill, NRA Records 402. See also "Resolutions of the Greenwood Mill Community Booster's Club," February 26, 1935, Greenwood Cotton Mill, NRA Records 402.

145. Mrs. Kenneth Sims to FDR, November 20, 1934, Worth Spinning Company, NRA Records 402; Janiewski, *Sisterhood Denied*, pp. 160–61; E.O. Steinbach to Mr. Edward C. McDonald, December 4, 1934, Durham Cotton Mfg. Co.; and Mrs. Ruby Mitchell to FDR, October 5, 1934, Loray Mill, NRA Records 402.

146. Milan Owens to FDR, October 10, 1934, Ware Shoals Manufacturing Company; W. A. Davis to FDR, November 8, 1934, Mathews Cotton Mill; Mrs. C. W. Polk to FDR, September 12, 1934, Rosemary Mfg. Co.; and B. E. Brookshire to FDR, November 25, 1935, Laurens Cotton Mills, NRA Records 402.

147. D. G. Floyd to FDR, January 8, 1935, Cowpens Mfg. Co., NRA Records 402, and James Pharis interview, p. 25.

148. Mrs. Ruby Brown to FDR, December 3, 1934, Mathews Mill; Mrs. Mason to FDR, January 28, 1935, Rosemary Mfg. Co.; Mrs. Mason to Judge W. P. Stacy, November 23, 1934, Rosemary Mfg. Co.; and Isaac H. Randall to FDR, February 18, 1935, miscellaneous, NRA Records 402.

149. Helpful to our thinking was Lears, "Concept of Cultural Hegemony."

150. G. W. McElroy to Francis Gorman, November 1, 1934, Cannon Cotton Mills, NRA Records 402.

151. For a similar point about the repeated setbacks of nineteenth-century democratic movements, see Escott, *Many Excellent People*, pp. 263–66.

152. The NIRA was struck down by the Supreme Court in 1935. Congress replaced it with legislation sponsored by Senator Robert F. Wagner of New York. For two perspectives on how Wagner's initiatives combined with working-class pressures

to strengthen New Deal labor policies, see Skocpol, "Political Response to Capitalist Crisis," pp. 178–81, and Hays, "New Deal: After Fifty Years," pp. 3–10. For the consolidation of industrialists' power in one state and the postwar consequences, see Phillip J. Wood, *Southern Capitalism*, pp. 149–99. Other critical views of post–World War II economic developments include Bartley, "Era of the New Deal," and Cobb, *Selling of the South*.

153. Gavin Wright, *Old South, New South*, pp. 216–26, 236–38, and Chip Hughes, "New Twist for Textiles."

154. Mrs. Mary Alice Ellenburgh to FDR, September 1934, Lonsdale Mill, NRA Records 402.

155. Mack Duncan interview, pp. 18–19.

156. Hoyle and Mamie McCorkle interview, p. 27.

157. Kemp P. Lewis to Anne Wetmore Tillinghast, December 18, 1934, Tillinghast Family Papers, Manuscripts Department, Perkins Library, Duke University, Durham, North Carolina; Janiewski, *Sisterhood Denied*, p. 161; and Marjorie Potwin, "Speaking of Discrimination," *STB*, March 7, 1935, pp. 5, 20.

158. Herring, *Passing of the Mill Village*, pp. 8–23, 128–31; Triplette, "One-Industry Towns," pp. 72–137, 225–34; Pope, *Millhands and Preachers*, pp. 191–95; and Morrison, *Governor O. Max Gardner*, pp. 181–82.

159. Carl and Mary Thompson interview, pp. 47–48. See also Glass, "Southern Mill Hills."

160. J. Raymond Shute interview, pp. 56–57. See also Ceasar Cone to Harriet Herring, "Long Range Program for Modernization of Cone Mills' Greensboro Villages," March 1, 1950, Harriet Laura Herring Papers, Southern Historical Collection, University of North Carolina at Chapel Hill.

161. George and Tessie Dyer interview, pp. 51–52.

EPILOGUE

1. Lacy Wright interview; Finger, "Textile Men," pp. 54–65; Conway, *Rise, Gonna Rise*, pp. 58–75; Hughes, "A New Twist for Textiles"; and Judkins, "Occupational Health and the Developing Class Consciousness," and *We Offer Ourselves as Evidence*.

2. *Burlington: A Review*, pp. 5–12; Phillip J. Wood, *Southern Capitalism*, pp. 169–71, 196–97; and Icy Norman interview, pp. 15, 54–55, 61–64.

BIBLIOGRAPHY

INTERVIEWS

Unless otherwise indicated, all interview tapes and transcripts are located in the Southern Historical Collection, Wilson Library, University of North Carolina at Chapel Hill.

Aaron, Junie. Interview by Jacquelyn Hall, Conover, N.C., December 12, 1979.

Adams, Lottie. Interview by Mary Murphy, Burlington, N.C., March 23, 1979.

Austin, Eunice. Interview by Jacquelyn Hall, Newton, N.C., July 2, 1980.

Austin, Ralph. Interview by James Leloudis, Charlotte, N.C., June 14, 1979.

Auton, Roy Lee and Mary Ruth. Interview by Jacquelyn Hall, Maiden, N.C., February 28, 1980.

Brooks, Jesse L. Interview by Cliff Kuhn, Burlington, N.C., July 20, 1977.

Buchanan, Bessie. Interview by Lanier Rand, Durham, N.C., June 1977. Interview by Lanier Rand, Durham, N.C., July, 1977.

Carden, Stella. Interview by Mary Murphy, Burlington, N.C., April 25, 1979.

Carter, Jessie Lee. Interview by Allen Tullos, Greenville, S.C., May 5, 1980.

Chapman, Ernest. Interview by Mary Murphy, Burlington, N.C., June 4, 1979.

Cleveland, Myrtle. Interview by Allen Tullos, Greenville, S.C., October 22, 1979.

Cline, Paul. Interview by Allen Tullos, Greenville, S.C., November 3, 1979.

Cobb, Mareda, and Carrie Yelton. Interview by Patty Dilley and Jacquelyn Hall, Hickory, N.C., June 16 and 18, 1979.

Cole, Robert. Interview by Jacquelyn Hall, Elizabethton, Tenn., July 10, 1981.

Cone, Ben and Ceasar. Interview by E. P. Douglass, Greensboro, N.C., July 28, 1981.

Copeland, Alice. Interview by Cliff Kuhn, Burlington, N.C., June 29, 1977.

Copeland, Chester. Interview by Ray Moretz, Teer Community, Orange County, N.C., November 16, 1982.

Crutchfield, Joseph. Interview by Allen Tullos, Burlington, N.C., June 26 and November 5, 1979.

Davidson, Betty and Lloyd. Interview by Allen Tullos, Burlington, N.C., February 2 and 15, 1979.

Dodson, Geddes E. Interview by Allen Tullos, Greenville, S.C., May 26, 1980.

Dodson, Ila H. Interview by Allen Tullos, Greenville, S.C., May 23, 1980.

Dugger, George F., Sr. Interview by Jacquelyn Hall, Elizabethton, Tenn., August 9, 1979.

Duncan, Mack. Interview by Allen Tullos, Greenville, S.C., June 7 and August 30, 1979.

Durham, Eula and Vernon. Interview by James Leloudis, Bynum, N.C., November 29, 1978.

Durham, Flossie Moore. Interview by Mary Frederickson and Brent Glass, Bynum, N.C., September 2, 1976.

Durham, Frank. Interview by Douglas DeNatale, Bynum, N.C., September 10 and 17, 1979.

Durham, Lewis. Interview by Brent Glass, Bynum, N.C., August 15, 1976.

Dyer, George and Tessie. Interview by Lu Ann Jones, Charlotte, N.C., March 5, 1980.

Edens, Bessie. Interview by Mary Frederickson, Elizabethton, Tenn., August 14, 1975.

Ellington, Harvey, and Sam Pridgen. Interview by Allen Tullos, Oxford, N.C., March 1 and April 5, 1979.

Enlow, Curtis. Interview by Allen Tullos, Greenville, S.C., November 9, 1979.

Eubanks, Roy. Interview by Vann Vogel, Bynum, N.C., October 29 and December 7, 1978.

Evitt, Alice. Interview by James Leloudis, Charlotte, N.C., July 18, 1979.

Faucette, Ethel. Interview by Allen Tullos, Burlington, N.C., November 16, 1978, and January 4, 1979.

Faucette, Paul and Don. Interview by Allen Tullos, Burlington, N.C., January 7, 1979.

Finley, Sam. Interview by Sam Howie, Marion, N.C., September 11, 1976. Appalachian Oral History Project, Appalachian State University, Boone, N.C.

Finley, Vesta and Sam. Interview by Mary Frederickson and Marion Roydhouse, Marion, N.C., July 22, 1975.

Foster, Charles. Interview by Brent Glass, Swepsonville, N.C., March 4, 1976.

Fowler, Sally. Interview by Douglas DeNatale, Bynum, N.C., August 29, 1979.

Gambrell, James and Dovie. Interview by Allen Tullos, Greenville, S.C., May 4, 1980.

Gentry, Myrtle. Interview by Allen Tullos, Greenville, S.C., October 22, 1979.

Gerringer, Carrie. Interview by Douglas DeNatale, Bynum, N.C., August 11, 1979.

Gilbert, Frank. Interview by Patty Dilley, Conover, N.C., Summer 1977.

Gillis, Esther. Interview by Robert Korstad and James Leloudis, High Point, N.C., Fall 1984.

Glenn, Mrs. Howard K. (Josephine). Interview by Cliff Kuhn, Burlington, N.C., June 27, 1977.

Griffith, Paul and Pauline. Interview by Allen Tullos, Greenville, S.C., March 24, 1980.

Grindstaff, Flossie Cole. Interview by Jacquelyn Hall, Elizabethton, Tenn., July 11, 1981.

Haithcock, Versa. Interview by Mary Murphy, Burlington, N.C., April 4, 1979.

Ham, Roy. Interview No. 1 by Patty Dilley, Newton, N.C., Summer 1977.

Hardin, Alice Grogan. Interview by Allen Tullos, Greenville, S.C., May 2, 1980.

Hardin, Grover. Interview by Allen Tullos, Greenville, S.C., March 25, 1980.

Hargett, Edna Y. Interview by James Leloudis, Charlotte, N.C., July 19, 1979.

Harrington, Edward and Mary. Interview by Mary Murphy, Burlington, N.C., February 28, 1979.

Heavnor, Ivey. Unrecorded interview by Mary Murphy and Patty Dilley, Catawba County, N.C., July 23, 1979.

Helms, Dewey. Interview by Sam Howie, Marion, N.C., January 10, 1976. Appalachian Oral History Project, Appalachian State University, Boone, N.C.

Hicks, Perry. Interview by Sam Howie, Marion, N.C., December 31, 1975. Appalachian Oral History Project, Appalachian State University, Boone, N.C.

Hickum, Ernest. Interview by Allen Tullos, Greenville, S.C., March 27, 1980.

Holland, Rosa. Interview by Mary Frederickson and Marion Roydhouse, Marion, N.C., July 22, 1975.

Hollar, Glenn E. and Gladys. Interview by Jacquelyn Hall, Conover, N.C., February 26 and 28, 1980.

Holman, Baxter. Interview by Robert Korstad, Winston-Salem, N.C., June 11, 1984.

Honnecutt, Willie Mae. Interview by Allen Tullos, Charlotte, N.C., January 31, 1980.

Hopkins, Eva B. Interview by Lu Ann Jones, Charlotte, N.C., March 5, 1980.

Jenks, Esther. Interview by Dolores Janiewski, Durham, N.C., April 26, 1977.

Johnson, Sallie, and Rena Capes. Interview by Mary Murphy, Burlington, N.C., March 20, 1979.

Jones, Louise. Interview by Mary Frederickson, Bynum, N.C., September 20, 1976. Interview by Mary Frederickson, Bynum, N.C., October 13, 1976. Interview by Margaret Lee, Bynum, N.C., October 31, 1978.

Jones, Paul and Louise. Interview by Douglas DeNatale, Bynum, N.C., October 23, 1979.

Killian, Kathryn, and Blanche Bolick. Interview by Jacquelyn Hall, Newton, N.C., December 12, 1979.

Lacock, Forrest. Interview by Brent Glass and Lee Southerland, Carrboro, N.C., February 6, 1975.

Lacock, Lula Johnson. Interview by Brent Glass and Lee Southerland, Carrboro, N.C., February 6, 1975.

Latta, Frances. Interview by Valerie Quinney, Carrboro, N.C., July 8, 1975.

Latta, Ralph. Interview by Mary Murphy, Mebane, N.C., May 7, 1984.

Latta, Rev. Robert. Interview by Mary Murphy, Monroe, N.C., April 17, 1984.

Lowe, Martin. Interview by Allen Tullos, Greenville, S.C., October 19 and 21, 1979.

Lupton, Dr. Carroll. Interview by Mary Murphy, Greensboro, N.C., May 18, 1979.

McBride, Dewey and Gladys. Interview by Mary Murphy, Burlington, N.C., May 16, 1979.

McCallum, Christine. Interview by Valerie Quinney, Carrboro, N.C., July 9, 1975.

McCorkle, Hoyle and Mamie. Interview by James Leloudis, Charlotte, N.C., July 11, 1979.

McGill, Eula. Interview by Jacquelyn Hall, Atlanta, Ga., February 1976.

Marcom, Fannie. Interview by Mary Murphy, Durham, N.C., July 17, 1979.

Maynard, Reid A. Interview by Allen Tullos, Burlington, N.C., February 6 and 13 and April 3, 1979.

Merritt, Baxter J. Interview by Allen Tullos, Charlotte, N.C., February 1, 1980.

Moreland, Robert (Bob) and Barbara. Interview by Jacquelyn Hall, Elizabethton, Tenn., July 11, 1981.

Moser, Dolly. Interview by Jacquelyn Hall, Hickory, N.C., December 13, 1979.

Murray, Zelma. Interview by Brent Glass, Glencoe, N.C., March 4, 1976.

Norman, Icy. Interview by Mary Murphy, Burlington, N.C., April 6 and 30, 1979.

Oakley, Maxie. Interview by Mary Murphy, Durham, N.C., July 12, 1979.

Osteen, Letha Ann Sloan. Interview by Allen Tullos, Greenville, S.C., June 8, 1979.

Overman, Mildred. Interview by Allen Tullos, Burlington, N.C., April 17, 1979.

Padgett, Everett. Interview by Allen Tullos, Greenville, S.C., May 28, 1980.

Padgett, Mary. Interview by Allen Tullos, Greenville, S.C., May 28, 1980.

Partin, Vinnie. Interview by Valerie Quinney, Carrboro, N.C., August 9, 1974. Interview by Valerie Quinney and Joan Sherman, Carrboro, N.C., July 3, 1975.

Pharis, James. Interview by Cliff Kuhn, Burlington, N.C., July 24, 1977.

Pharis, James and Nannie. Interview by Allen Tullos, Burlington, N.C., December 5, 1978, and January 8 and 30, 1979.

Pitts, Viola. Interview by Lu Ann Jones, Charlotte, N.C., April 21, 1980.

Price, Lillie Morris. Interview by Mary Frederickson and Marion Roydhouse, Asheville, N.C., July 22, 1975.

Ragan, Caldwell. Interview by Robert A. Ragan, Gastonia, N.C., April 3, 1976.

Rice, Ila. Interview by Patty Dilley and Jacquelyn Hall, Hickory, N.C., June 15, 1979.

Riddle, Mozelle. Interview by Douglas DeNatale, Bynum, N.C., November 1 and 13, 1978.

Riley, Luther. Interview by Lanier Rand, Durham, N.C., July, 1977.

Robertson, William and Margaret. Interview by Allen Tullos, Burlington, N.C., March 27, 1979.

Robinette, J. M. Interview by Cliff Kuhn, Burlington, N.C., July 1977.

Rogers, Harry. Interview by Cliff Kuhn, Burlington, N.C., July 21, 1977. Interview by Allen Tullos, Burlington, N.C., February 2, 1979.

Sanders, Albert N. Interview by Allen Tullos, Greenville, S.C., May 30, 1980.

Saunders, Vernon. Interview by Allen Tullos, Durham, N.C., May 24, 1979.

Shoemaker, Mattie, and Mildred Shoemaker Edmonds. Interview by Mary Murphy, Burlington, N.C., March 23, 1979. Unrecorded interview by Mary Murphy, Burlington, N.C., Summer 1979.

Shue, George and Mamie. Interview by James Leloudis, Charlotte, N.C., June 20, 1979.

Shuping, Gertrude. Interview by Lu Ann Jones, Charlotte, N.C., February 29 and March 6, 1980.

Shute, J. Raymond. Interview by Wayne Durrill, Monroe, N.C., June 25, 1982.

Sigmon, Murphy Yomen. Interview by Patty Dilley, Hildebran, N.C., July 27, 1979.

Sigmon, Nell. Interview by Jacquelyn Hall, Newton, N.C., December 13, 1979.

Simmons, Ralph. Interview No. 1 by Patty Dilley, Conover, N.C., Summer 1977.

Sims, Gordon. Interview by Hugh Brinton, Carrboro, N.C., June 26, 1974.

Smith, Allie. Interview by Valerie Quinney, Carrboro, N.C., March 19 and 21, 1974.

Snipes, John Wesley. Interview by Brent Glass, Bynum, N.C., September 20, 1976. Interview by Brent Glass, Bynum, N.C., November 20, 1976. Interview by Douglas DeNatale, Bynum, N.C., August 22, 1979.

Spaulding, Asa. Interview by Walter B. Weare, Durham, N.C., April 13, 1979.

Stackhouse, Verna. Interview by Cliff Kuhn, Burlington, N.C., July 19, 1977.

Stanley, Myrtle. Interview by Hugh Brinton and Valerie Quinney, Carrboro, N.C., May 13, 1974.

Suggs, Hattie. Interview by Jacquelyn Hall, Pauls Valley, Okla., Summer 1980.

Swinney, Etta Gay Dalton. Interview by Mary Murphy, Burlington, N.C., April 25, 1979

Taylor, Hester. Interview by Mary Murphy, Burlington, N.C., April 25, 1979.

Thomas, Claude C. Interview by Lu Ann Jones, Charlotte, N.C., April 18, 1980.

Thompson, Carl and Mary. Interview by James Leloudis, Charlotte, N.C., July 19, 1979.

Trammel, Naomi. Interview by Allen Tullos, Greenville, S.C., March 25, 1980.

Truitt, Herman. Interview by Allen Tullos, Burlington, N.C., December 15, 1978, and January 19 and 31, 1979.

Vaughn, Rev. Clarence. Unrecorded interview by Mary Murphy, Burlington, N.C., August 1, 1983.

Vaughn, Walter. Interview by Allen Tullos, Greenville, S.C., May 3, 1980.

Ward, Honard. Interview by Jacquelyn Hall, Elizabethton, Tenn., n.d.

Webster, Frank. Interview by Allen Tullos, Burlington, N.C., January 30, 1979.

Whitesell, Emma. Interview by Cliff Kuhn, Burlington, N.C., July 27, 1977.

Williams, Emma. Interview by Valerie Quinney, Carrboro, N.C., August 21, 1974. Interview by Ray Moretz, Carrboro, N.C., November 1, 1982.

Williams, Ruth. Interview by Douglas DeNatale, Bynum, N.C., August 23, 1979.

Wilson, Ada Mae. Interview by Allen Tullos, Charlotte, N.C., February 1, 1980.

Wofford, Blaine H. Interview by Allen Tullos, Charlotte, N.C., February 1, 1980.

Workman, Lee A. Interview by Patty Dilley, Brookford, N.C., June 1977.

Wrenn, Ina Lee. Interview by Allen Tullos, Burlington, N.C., March 10, 1975.

Wright, Lacy. Interview by Bill Finger and Chip Hughes, Greensboro, N.C., March 10, 1975.

Wright, Lora and Edward. Interview by Allen Tullos, Greenville, S.C., June 7 and November 11, 1979.

Yoder, Dr. Fred. Interview by Brent Glass, Chapel Hill, N.C., September 20, 1975.

MANUSCRIPTS

Burlington, North Carolina
  Glen Hope Baptist Church
    Scrapbooks and Clipping File
Chapel Hill, North Carolina
  North Carolina Collection, University of North Carolina
    Clipping File
    Harriet L. Herring Clipping File
  Southern Historical Collection, University of North Carolina
    Jonathan Worth Daniels Papers
    Henderson Monroe Fowler Books
    Harriet Laura Herring Papers
    James Spencer Love Papers
Detroit, Michigan
  Archives of Labor History and Urban Affairs, Wayne State University
    American Federation of Teachers Papers
Durham, North Carolina
  Manuscripts Department, Perkins Library, Duke University
    Tillinghast Family Papers
Greensboro, North Carolina
  Burlington Industries, Public Relations Department
    Clipping Files
New York, New York
  Manuscripts Department, New York Public Library
    National Civic Federation Papers
North Andover, Massachusetts
  Museum of American Textile History
    Barnes Textile Reports
Raleigh, North Carolina
  North Carolina Division of Archives and History
    Adjutant General's Department Papers
    J. C. B. Ehringhaus Governor's Papers, 1933–37
Washington, D.C.
  National Archives
    Records of the National Recovery Administration, Record Group 9, Records
    of the Cotton Textile National Industrial Relations Board and the Textile
    National Industrial Relations Board. Entries 398, 401, and 402.

GOVERNMENT DOCUMENTS

Massachusetts

Massachusetts Bureau of Statistics of Labor. *Cotton Manufactures in Massachusetts and the Southern States: Part II of the Annual Report for 1905.* Boston: Wright and Porter Printing Company, 1905.

North Carolina

Anderson, W. A. "Farm Family Living Among White Owner and Tenant Operators in Wake County, 1926." North Carolina Agricultural Experiment Station, Bulletin No. 269. September 1929.

North Carolina Bureau of Labor and Printing. *Fifteenth Annual Report . . . 1901.* Raleigh: Edwards and Broughton and E.M. Uzzell, 1902.

————. *Sixteenth Annual Report . . . 1902.* Raleigh: Edwards and Broughton, 1903.

————. *Nineteenth Annual Report . . . 1905.* Raleigh: E. M. Uzzell and Co., 1905.

————. *Twentieth Annual Report . . . 1906.* Raleigh: E. M. Uzzell and Co., 1906.

————. *Twenty-First Annual Report . . . 1907.* Raleigh: E. M. Uzzell and Co., 1908.

North Carolina Bureau of Labor Statistics. *First Annual Report . . . 1887.* Raleigh: Josephus Daniels, 1887.

————. *Tenth Annual Report . . . 1896.* Winston: M. I. and J. C. Stewart, 1897.

North Carolina Department of Agriculture. *North Carolina and Its Resources.* Winston: M. I. and J. C. Stewart, 1896.

Taylor, Carl C., and C. C. Zimmerman. "Economic and Social Conditions of North Carolina Farmers." [Raleigh: State Board of Agriculture, 1923.]

Williams, Robin M., and Olaf Wakefield. "Farm Tenancy in North Carolina, 1880–1935." North Carolina Agricultural Experiment Station. Agricultural Experiment Research Station Information Series No. 1. September 1937.

Tennessee

Chancery Court, Carter County. *American Bemberg Corp. v. George Miller, et al.* Minute books Q and R, Chancery Court Minutes, July 22, 1929. Carter County Courthouse, Elizabethton.

East Tennessee District Supreme Court. *American Bemberg Corp. v. George Miller, et al.* Tennessee Supreme Court Records, January 29, 1930, record of evidence, typescript, box 660, Tennessee Supreme Court Records. Tennessee State Library and Archives, Nashville.

————. *American Glanzstoff Corp. v. George Miller, et al.* C/A 1, September 5, 1930. Tennessee Supreme Court and Court of Appeals Office, Knoxville.

United States

U.S. Congress. House. *To Regulate the Textile Industry: Hearings before the Subcommittee of the Committee on Labor on H.R. 238.* Part 3. 75th Cong., 1st sess. Washington, D.C.: Government Printing Office, 1937.

U.S. Congress. Senate. *Report on the Condition of Woman and Child Wage-Earners in the United States.* Vol. 1, *Cotton Textile Industry.* Senate Document No. 645, 61st Cong., 2d sess. Washington, D.C.: Government Printing Office, 1910.

_____. *Report on the Condition of Woman and Child Wage-Earners in the United States.* Vol. 16, *Family Budgets of Typical Cotton-Mill Workers.* Senate Document No. 645, 61st Cong., 2d sess. Washington, D.C.: Government Printing Office, 1911.

U.S. Department of Commerce. Bureau of the Census. *Fifteenth Census of the United States, 1930.* Vol. 3, pt. 2, *Population.* Washington, D.C.: Government Printing Office, 1932.

U.S. Department of Labor. Bureau of Labor Statistics. *Employers' Welfare Work.* By Elizabeth Lewis Otey. Bulletin No. 123. Washington, D.C.: Government Printing Office, 1913.

_____. *Housing by Employers in the United States.* By Leifur Mangusson. Bulletin No. 269. Washington, D.C.: Government Printing Office, 1920.

_____. *Wages and Hours of Labor in Cotton-Goods Manufacturing, 1910–1928.* Bulletin No. 492. Washington, D.C.: Government Printing Office, 1929.

_____. *Welfare Work for Employees in Industrial Establishments in the United States.* Bulletin No. 250. Washington, D.C.: Government Printing Office, 1919.

U.S. Department of Labor. Children's Bureau. *Rural Children in Selected Counties of North Carolina.* By Frances Sage Bradley and Margaretta A. Williamson. Rural Child Welfare Series No. 2. Bulletin No. 33. Washington, D.C.: Government Printing Office, 1918.

U.S. Department of Labor. Women's Bureau. *Employed Women Under N.R.A. Codes.* By Mary Elizabeth Pidgeon. Bulletin No. 130. Washington, D.C.: Government Printing Office, 1935.

_____. *Lost Time and Labor Turnover in Cotton Mills: Study of Cause and Extent.* Bulletin No. 52. Washington, D.C.: Government Printing Office, 1926.

_____. *Women in the Economy of the United States of America: A Summary Report.* By Mary Elizabeth Pidgeon. Bulletin No. 155. Washington, D.C.: Government Printing Office, 1937.

U.S. Department of the Interior. Census Office. *Tenth Census of the United States, 1880.* Vol. 16, *Water-Power of the United States.* Washington: Government Printing Office, 1885.

U.S. Public Health Service. *A Review of the Literature Relating to Affections of the Respiratory Tract in Individuals Exposed to Cotton Dust.* By B. H. Caminita, William F. Baum, Paul A. Neal, and R. Schneiter. Public Health Bulletin No. 297. Washington, D.C.: Government Printing Office, 1947.

_____. *A Study of Endemic Pellagra in Some Cotton-Mill Villages of South Carolina.* By

Joseph Goldberger, G. A. Wheeler, Edgar Sydenstricker, and Wilford I. King. Hygenic Laboratory Bulletin No. 153. Washington, D.C.: Government Printing Office, 1929.

NEWSPAPERS

Alamance Gleaner
Asheville Advocate
Burlington: A Review (Special Golden Anniversary Issue, 1973)
Burlington Daily News
Burlington Daily Times-News
Burlington Times-News
Charlotte News
Charlotte Observer
Columbia *State*
Concord Times
Durham *Morning Herald*
Durham Sun
Durham *Sunday Herald-Sun*
Greensboro Daily News
Greenville News
Knoxville News Sentinel
Marion Progress
New York Times
Progressive Farmer
Raleigh *News and Observer*
Raleigh Times

TRADE AND UNION JOURNALS

American Textile Manufacturer
American Wool and Cotton Reporter
Charlotte *Labor Herald*
Commerce and Finance
Journal of Commerce
Manufacturers' Record
Mechanical Engineering
Southern and Western Textile Excelsior
Southern Textile Bulletin
Textile Bulletin
Textile Excelsior

Textile Industries
Textile Manufacturer
The Textile Worker
Textile World

DIRECTORIES

Clark's Directory of Southern Textile Mills, January 1, 1929. Charlotte: Clark Publishing Co., 1929.

Davison's Textile Blue Book, July 1929–July 1930. New York: Davison Publishing Co., 1929.

Davison's Textile Blue Book, July 1930–July 1931. New York: Davison Publishing Co., 1930.

Glen Hope Baptist Church Directory. 1980.

Miller, Ernest H., comp. *Burlington, Graham and Haw River, N.C. City Directory, 1924–25*. Vol. 3. Asheville: The Miller Press, 1924.

———. *Burlington, Graham and Haw River, N.C. City Directory, 1927–28*. Vol. 4. Asheville: The Miller Press, 1927.

———. *Miller's Official Burlington, Graham and Haw River, N.C. City Directory, 1929–30*. Vol. 5. Asheville: The Miller Press, 1929.

BOOKS

Alderman, Edwin Anderson, and Joel Chandler Harris, eds. *Library of Southern Literature*. Atlanta: Martin and Hoyt Co., [1909–13].

Alexander, John Brevard. *Reminiscences of the Past Sixty Years*. Charlotte: Ray Printing Co., 1908.

Armstrong, O. K., and Marjorie Armstrong. *The Baptists of America*. Garden City, N.Y.: Doubleday, 1979.

Ashe, Samuel A., ed. *Biographical History of North Carolina: From Colonial Times to the Present*. Vol. 3. Greensboro: Charles L. Van Noppen, 1906.

Ashe, Samuel A., and Stephen B. Weeks, eds. *Biographical History of North Carolina: From Colonial Times to the Present*. Vol. 7. Greensboro: Charles L. Van Noppen, 1908.

Ashe, Samuel A., Stephen B. Weeks, and Charles L. Van Noppen, eds. *Biographical History of North Carolina: From Colonial Times to the Present*. Vol. 8. Greensboro: Charles L. Van Noppen, 1917.

Ashton, Thomas Southcliffe. *The Industrial Revolution, 1760–1830*. London: Oxford University Press, 1948.

Bender, Thomas. *Community and Social Change in America*. Clarke A. Sanford-

Armand G. Erpf Lecture Series on Local Government and Community Life. New Brunswick: Rutgers University Press, 1978.

Bernstein, Irving. *The Lean Years: A History of the American Worker, 1920–1933*. Baltimore: Penguin Books, 1966.

———. *Turbulent Years: A History of the American Worker, 1933–1941*. Boston: Houghton Mifflin, 1970.

Blanshard, Paul. *Labor in Southern Cotton Mills*. New York: New Republic, 1927.

Blauner, Robert. *Alienation and Freedom: The Factory Worker and His Industry*. Chicago: University of Chicago Press, 1964.

Blicksilver, Jack. *Cotton Manufacturing in the Southeast: An Historical Analysis*. Atlanta: Bureau of Business and Economic Research, School of Business Administration, Georgia State College of Business Administration, 1959.

Bodnar, John E., Roger Simon, and Michael P. Weber. *Lives of Their Own: Blacks, Italians, and Poles in Pittsburgh, 1900–1960*. Urbana: University of Illinois Press, 1982.

Brandes, Stuart D. *American Welfare Capitalism, 1880–1940*. Chicago: University of Chicago Press, 1976.

Braverman, Harry. *Labor and Monopoly Capital: The Degradation of Work in the Twentieth Century*. New York: Monthly Review Press, 1974.

Brody, David. *Workers in Industrial America: Essays on the Twentieth-Century Struggle*. New York: Oxford University Press, 1980.

Bruce, Dickson D., Jr. *And They All Sang Hallelujah: Plain-Folk Camp-Meeting Religion, 1800–1845*. Knoxville: University of Tennessee Press, 1974.

Builders of Alamance. Burlington, N.C.: Burlington Chamber of Commerce, 1951.

Byerly, Victoria. *Hard Times Cotton Mill Girls: Personal Histories of Womanhood and Poverty in the South*. Ithaca: ILR Press, 1986.

Carlton, David L. *Mill and Town in South Carolina, 1880–1920*. Baton Rouge: Louisiana State University Press, 1982.

Cash, W. J. *The Mind of the South*. New York: Alfred A. Knopf, 1941.

Chandler, Alfred D., Jr. *The Visible Hand: The Management Revolution in American Business*. Cambridge: Harvard University Press, 1977.

Clark, Clifford Edward, Jr. *The American Family Home, 1800–1960*. Chapel Hill: University of North Carolina Press, 1986.

Cobb, James C. *The Selling of the South: The Southern Crusade for Industrial Development, 1936–1980*. Baton Rouge: Louisiana State University Press, 1982.

Conner, Valerie Jean. *The National War Labor Board: Stability, Social Justice, and the Voluntary State in World War I*. Chapel Hill: University of North Carolina Press, 1983.

Conway, Mimi. *Rise, Gonna Rise: A Portrait of Southern Textile Workers*, Garden City, N.Y.: Doubleday, 1979.

Cook, John Harrison. *A Study of the Mill Schools of North Carolina*. New York: Teachers College, Columbia University, 1925.

Cook, Sylvia Jenkins. *From Tobacco Road to Route 66: The Southern Poor White in Fiction*. Chapel Hill: University of North Carolina Press, 1976.

Coolidge, John. *Mill and Mansion, A Study of Architecture and Society in Lowell, Massachusetts, 1820–1865*. New York: Columbia University Press, 1942.

Copeland, Melvin Thomas. *The Cotton Manufacturing Industry of the United States*. Cambridge: Harvard University, 1912.

Corbin, David. *Life, Work, and Rebellion in the Coal Fields: The Southern West Virginia Miners, 1880–1922*. Urbana: University of Illinois Press, 1981.

Curtis, Verna Posever, and Stanley Mallach. *Photography and Reform: Lewis Hine and the National Child Labor Committee*. Milwaukee: Milwaukee Art Museum, 1984.

Daniel, Pete. *Breaking the Land: The Transformation of Cotton, Tobacco, and Rice Cultures since 1880*. Urbana: University of Illinois Press, 1985.

Daniels, Jonathan. *A Southerner Discovers the South*. New York: Macmillan, 1938.

Davenport, Judith A., and Joseph Davenport III, eds. *Boom Towns and Human Services*. Laramie: University of Wyoming, Department of Social Work, 1979.

Davidson, Elizabeth H. *Child Labor Legislation in the Southern Textile States*. Chapel Hill: University of North Carolina Press, 1939.

Davis, Natalie Zemon. *Society and Culture in Early Modern France: Eight Essays*. Stanford: Stanford University Press, 1975.

Dinnerstein, Leonard. *The Leo Frank Case*. New York: Columbia University Press, 1968.

Dublin, Thomas. *Women at Work: The Transformation of Work and Community in Lowell, Massachusetts, 1826–1860*. New York: Columbia University Press, 1979.

Dykstra, Robert R. *The Cattle Towns*. New York: Atheneum, 1976.

Edmonds, Richard Woods. *Cotton Mill Labor Conditions in the South and New England*. Baltimore: Manufacturers' Record Publishing Co., 1925.

Edwards, Richard C. *Contested Terrain: The Transformation of the Workplace in the Twentieth Century*. New York: Basic Books, 1979.

Eller, Ronald D. *Miners, Millhands, and Mountaineers: Industrialization of the Appalachian South*. Knoxville: University of Tennessee Press, 1982.

Escott, Paul D. *Many Excellent People: Power and Privilege in North Carolina, 1850–1900*. Chapel Hill: University of North Carolina Press, 1985.

Etheridge, Elizabeth W. *The Butterfly Caste: A Social History of Pellagra in the South*. Westport, Conn.: Greenwood Publishing Co., 1972.

Ewen, Elizabeth. *Immigrant Women in the Land of Dollars: Life and Culture on the Lower East Side, 1890–1925*. New York: Monthly Review Press, 1985.

Faragher, John Mack. *Women and Men on the Overland Trail*. New Haven: Yale University Press, 1982.

Fass, Paula S. *The Damned and the Beautiful: American Youth in the 1920s*. New York: Oxford University Press, 1977.

Federal Writers' Project. *These Are Our Lives: As Told by the People and Written by Members of the Federal Writers' Project of the Works Progress Administration in North*

Carolina, Tennessee, and Georgia. Chapel Hill: University of North Carolina Press, 1939. Reprint. New York: W. W. Norton and Co., 1975.

Filene, Peter G. *Him/Her/Self: Sex Roles in Modern America*. 2d ed. Baltimore: The Johns Hopkins University Press, 1986.

Fink, Gary, ed. *Biographical Dictionary of American Labor Leaders*. Westport, Conn.: Greenwood Press, 1974.

Fink, Leon. *Workingmen's Democracy: The Knights of Labor and American Politics*. Urbana: University of Illinois Press, 1983.

Fite, Gilbert C. *Cotton Fields No More: Southern Agriculture, 1865–1980*. Lexington: University Press of Kentucky, 1984.

Floud, Roderick, and Donald N. McCloskey. *The Economic History of Britain since 1700*. 2 vols. Cambridge: Cambridge University Press, 1981.

Foucault, Michel. *Power/Knowledge: Selected Interviews and Other Writings, 1972–1977*. Edited and translated by Colin Gordon. New York: Pantheon Books, 1980.

Galambos, Louis. *Competition and Cooperation: The Emergence of a National Trade Association*. Baltimore: The Johns Hopkins University Press, 1966.

Galenson, Alice. *The Migration of the Cotton Textile Industry from New England to the South, 1880–1930*. New York: Garland Publishing, Inc., 1985.

Garraty, John A., ed. *Dictionary of American Biography: Supplement Seven, 1961–1965*. New York: Charles Scribner's Sons, 1981.

Gaston, Paul M. *The New South Creed: A Study in Southern Mythmaking*. New York: Alfred A. Knopf, 1970.

Gibb, George Sweet. *The Saco-Lowell Shops: Textile Machinery Building in New England, 1813–1949*. Cambridge: Harvard University Press, 1950.

Gilman, Glenn. *Human Relations in the Industrial Southeast: A Study of the Textile Industry*. Chapel Hill: University of North Carolina Press, 1956.

Glassie, Henry. *Pattern in the Material Folk Culture of the Eastern United States*. Philadelphia: University of Pennsylvania Press, 1971.

Glickman, Rose L. *Russian Factory Women: Workplace and Society, 1880–1914*. Berkeley and Los Angeles: University of California Press, 1984.

Goodwyn, Lawrence. *Democratic Promise: The Populist Moment in America*. New York: Oxford University Press, 1976.

Gordon, David M., Richard Edwards, and Michael Reich. *Segmented Work, Divided Workers: The Historical Transformation of Labor in the United States*. New York: Cambridge University Press, 1982.

Green, James R. *The World of the Worker: Labor in Twentieth-Century America*. New York: Hill and Wang, 1980.

Gross, James A. *The Making of the National Labor Relations Board: A Study in Economics, Politics, and the Law*. Vol. 1, *1933–1937*. Albany: State University of New York Press, 1974.

Haan, Johannis Dirk de. *The Full-Fashioned Hosiery Industry in the U.S.A.* The Hague: Mouton, 1957.

Hagood, Margaret Jarman. *Mothers of the South: Portraiture of the White Tenant Farm Woman.* Chapel Hill: University of North Carolina Press, 1939. Reprint. New York: W. W. Norton and Co., 1977.

Hahn, Steven. *The Roots of Southern Populism: Yeoman Farmers and the Transformation of the Georgia Upcountry, 1850–1890.* New York: Oxford University Press, 1983.

Hahn, Steven, and Jonathan Prude, eds. *The Countryside in the Age of Capitalist Transformation: Essays in the Social History of Rural America.* Chapel Hill: University of North Carolina Press, 1985.

Hareven, Tamara K. *Family Time and Industrial Time: The Relationship Between the Family and Work in a New England Industrial Community.* New York: Cambridge University Press, 1982.

Herring, Harriet L. *Passing of the Mill Village: Revolution in a Southern Institution.* Chapel Hill: University of North Carolina Press, 1949.

————. *Welfare Work in Mill Villages: The Story of Extra-Mill Activities in North Carolina.* Chapel Hill: University of North Carolina Press, 1929.

————. *Worker and Public in the Southern Textile Problem.* Greensboro: The Industrial Seminar for Ministers, 1930.

History of North Carolina. Vol. 5, *North Carolina Biography.* Chicago and New York: Lewis Publishing Co., 1919.

Hodges, James A. *New Deal Labor Policy and the Southern Cotton Textile Industry, 1933–1941.* Knoxville: University of Tennessee Press, 1986.

Hunter, Louis C. *A History of Industrial Power in the United States, 1780–1930.* 2 vols. Charlottesville: University Press of Virginia, 1979.

Inabinet, Judi G., and Charles R. Inabinet. *The Old Mill Stream.* Vol. 2. Rock Hill, S.C.: The London Printery, 1976.

Janiewski, Dolores E. *Sisterhood Denied: Race, Gender, and Class in a New South Community.* Philadelphia: Temple University Press, 1985.

Jensen, Malcolm C. *America in Time: America's History Year by Year Through Text and Pictures.* Boston: Houghton Mifflin, 1977.

Jeremy, David John. *Transatlantic Industrial Revolution: The Diffusion of Textile Technologies Between Britain and America, 1790–1830s.* Cambridge: MIT Press, 1981.

Johnson, Gerald W. *The Making of a Southern Industrialist: A Biographical Sketch of Simpson Bobo Tanner.* Chapel Hill: University of North Carolina Press, 1952.

Johnson, Guion Griffiths. *Antebellum North Carolina: A Social History.* Chapel Hill: University of North Carolina Press, 1937.

Johnson, Paul E. *A Shopkeeper's Millennium: Society and Revivals in Rochester, New York, 1815–1837.* New York: Hill and Wang, 1978.

Jordan, Rosan A., and Susan J. Kalčik, eds. *Women's Folklore, Women's Culture.* Philadelphia: University of Pennsylvania Press, 1985.

Judkins, Bennett M. *We Offer Ourselves as Evidence: Toward Workers' Control of Occupational Health.* Westport, Conn.: Greenwood Press, 1986.

Kemp, John R. *Lewis Hine: Photographs of Child Labor in the New South.* Jackson: University Press of Mississippi, 1986.

Kennedy, Stephen Jay. *Profits and Losses in Textiles: Cotton Textile Financing Since the War.* New York: Harper and Brothers, 1936.

Key, V. O. *Southern Politics in State and Nation.* New York: Alfred A. Knopf, 1949.

Knowlton, Evelyn. *Pepperell's Progress: History of a Cotton Textile Company, 1844–1945.* Cambridge: Harvard University Press, 1948.

Kohn, August. *The Cotton Mills of South Carolina.* Columbia: South Carolina Department of Agriculture, Commerce and Immigration, 1907.

Kousser, J. Morgan. *The Shaping of Southern Politics: Suffrage Restriction and the Establishment of the One-Party South, 1880–1910.* New Haven: Yale University Press, 1974.

Lahne, Herbert J. *The Cotton Mill Worker.* New York: Farrar and Rinehart, 1944.

Lander, Ernest McPherson, Jr. *The Textile Industry in Antebellum South Carolina.* Baton Rouge: Louisiana State University Press, 1969.

Landes, David S. *The Unbound Prometheus: Technological Change and Industrial Development in Western Europe from 1750 to the Present.* Cambridge: Cambridge University Press, 1969.

Lebsock, Suzanne. *The Free Women of Petersburg: Status and Culture in a Southern Town, 1784–1860.* New York: W. W. Norton and Co., 1984.

Leeming, Joseph. *Rayon: The First Man-Made Fiber.* Brooklyn: Chemical Publishing Co., 1950.

Lefler, Hugh Talmage, and Albert Ray Newsome. *North Carolina: The History of a Southern State.* 3d ed. Chapel Hill: University of North Carolina Press, 1973.

Leuchtenburg, William E. *Franklin Roosevelt and the New Deal, 1932–1940.* New York: Harper and Row, 1963.

Lowitt, Richard, and Maurine Beasley, eds. *One Third of a Nation: Lorena Hickok Reports on the Great Depression.* Urbana: University of Illinois Press, 1981.

Lynd, Robert S., and Helen Merrell Lynd. *Middletown: A Study in Contemporary American Culture.* New York: Harcourt, Brace and Co., 1929.

MacDonald, Lois. *Southern Mill Hills: A Study of Social and Economic Forces in Certain Textile Mill Villages.* New York: Alexander L. Hillman, 1928.

McElvaine, Robert S. *Down and Out in the Great Depression: Letters From the "Forgotten Man."* Chapel Hill: University of North Carolina Press, 1983.

McGregor, Clarence H. *The Hosiery Manufacturing Industry in North Carolina and Its Marketing Problems.* Chapel Hill: Graduate School of Business Administration, Research Paper Series, 1965.

McLaurin, Melton Alonza. *The Knights of Labor in the South.* Westport, Conn.: Greenwood Press, 1978.

———. *Paternalism and Protest: Southern Cotton Mill Workers and Organized Labor, 1875–1905.* Westport, Conn.: Greenwood Publishing Corp., 1971.

McMath, Robert C., Jr. *Populist Vanguard: A History of the Southern Farmers' Alliance.* Chapel Hill: University of North Carolina Press, 1975.

Mantoux, Paul. *The Industrial Revolution in the Eighteenth Century.* New York: Harper and Row, 1961.

Markham, Jesse W. *Competition in the Rayon Industry*. Cambridge: Harvard University Press, 1952.

Marshall, F. Ray. *Labor in the South*. Cambridge: Harvard University Press, 1967.

Marx, Karl. *Capital: A Critical Analysis of Capitalist Production*. 3 vols. Moscow: Progress Publishers, 1954.

Mathews, Donald G. *Religion in the Old South*. Chicago: University of Chicago Press, 1977.

May, Elaine Tyler. *Great Expectations: Marriage and Divorce in Post-Victorian America*. Chicago: University of Chicago Press, 1980.

Meyer, Stephen, III. *The Five Dollar Day: Labor, Management, and Social Control in the Ford Motor Company, 1908–1921*. Albany: State University of New York Press, 1981.

Michl, H. E. *The Textile Industries: An Economic Analysis*. Washington, D.C.: The Textile Foundation, 1938.

Milkman, Ruth. *Gender at Work: The Dynamics of Job Segregation by Sex During World War II*. Urbana: University of Illinois Press, 1987.

Mitchell, Broadus. *The Rise of Cotton Mills in the South*. Baltimore: The Johns Hopkins University Press, 1921.

———. *William Gregg: Factory Master of the Old South*. Chapel Hill: University of North Carolina Press, 1928.

Mitchell, George Sinclair. *Textile Unionism and the South*. Chapel Hill: University of North Carolina Press, 1931.

Moen, Elizabeth, Elise Boulding, Jane Lillydahl, and Risa Palm. *Women and the Social Costs of Economic Development: Two Colorado Case Studies*. Boulder, Colo.: Westview Press, 1981.

Montgomery, David. *Workers' Control in America: Studies in the History of Work, Technology, and Labor Struggles*. New York: Cambridge University Press, 1979.

Morland, John Kenneth. *Millways of Kent*. Chapel Hill: University of North Carolina Press, 1958.

Morrison, Joseph L. *Governor O. Max Gardner: A Power in North Carolina and New Deal Washington*. Chapel Hill: University of North Carolina Press, 1971.

Murchison, Claudius T. *King Cotton Is Sick*. Chapel Hill: University of North Carolina Press, 1930.

Nathans, Sydney. *The Quest for Progress: The Way We Lived in North Carolina, 1870–1920*. Chapel Hill: University of North Carolina Press for the North Carolina Department of Cultural Resources, 1983.

National Civic Federation. *Examples of Welfare Work in the Cotton Industry: Conditions and Progress, New England and the South*. New York: National Civic Federation, 1910.

Navin, Thomas R. *The Whitin Machine Works since 1831: A Textile Machinery Company in an Industrial Village*. Cambridge: Harvard University Press, 1950.

Nelson, Daniel. *Managers and Workers: Origins of the New Factory System in the United States, 1880–1920*. Madison: University of Wisconsin Press, 1975.

Noble, David F. *America by Design: Science, Technology, and the Rise of Corporate Capitalism*. New York: Alfred A. Knopf, 1977.

―――. *Forces of Production: A Social History of Industrial Automation*. New York: Alfred A. Knopf, 1984.

North Carolina Arts Council. Folklife Section. *The Charlotte Country Music Story*. Raleigh: North Carolina Arts Council, Folklife Section, 1985.

North Carolina Cotton Manufacturers' Association. *Proceedings of the Eleventh Annual Convention, Asheville, N.C., June 8 and 9, 1917*. Charlotte: The Observer Printing House, 1917.

O'Brien, Gail Williams. *The Legal Fraternity and the Making of a New South Community, 1848–1882*. Athens: University of Georgia Press, 1986.

Olien, Roger M., and Diana Davids Olien. *Oil Booms: Social Change in Five Texas Towns*. Lincoln: University of Nebraska Press, 1982.

Ozanne, Robert. *A Century of Labor-Management Relations at McCormick and International Harvester*. Madison: University of Wisconsin Press, 1967.

Page, Myra. *Southern Cotton Mills and Labor*. New York: Workers Library Publishers, 1929.

Peiss, Kathy Lee. *Cheap Amusements: Working Women and Leisure in Turn-of-the-Century New York*. Philadelphia: Temple University Press, 1986.

Pickard, Walt. *Burlington Dynamite Plot*. New York: International Labor Defense, n.d.

Polanyi, Karl. *The Great Transformation*. New York: Farrar and Rinehart, 1944.

Pope, Liston. *Millhands and Preachers: A Study of Gastonia*. New Haven: Yale University Press, 1942.

Potwin, Marjorie A. *Cotton Mill People of the Piedmont: A Study in Social Change*. New York: Columbia University Press, 1927.

Powell, William S., ed. *Dictionary of North Carolina Biography*. Vol. 1, *A–C*. Chapel Hill: University of North Carolina Press, 1979.

President's Research Committee on Social Trends. *Recent Social Trends in the United States: Report of the President's Research Committee on Social Trends*. New York: McGraw-Hill Book Co., 1933.

Prude, Jonathan. *The Coming of Industrial Order: Town and Factory Life in Rural Massachusetts, 1810–1860*. New York: Cambridge University Press, 1983.

Rawick, George P., ed. *The American Slave: A Composite Autobiography*. Vol. 1, *From Sundown to Sunup: The Making of the Black Community*. Westport, Conn.: Greenwood Publishing Co., 1972.

Reddy, William M. *The Rise of Market Culture: The Textile Trade and French Society, 1750–1900*. New York: Cambridge University Press, 1984.

Rehn, Henry Joseph. *Scientific Management and the Cotton Textile Industry*. Chicago: private ed., distributed by the University of Chicago Libraries, 1934.

Rhyne, Jennings J. *Some Southern Cotton Mill Workers and Their Villages*. Chapel Hill: University of North Carolina Press, 1930.

Robinson, John L., ed. *Living Hard: Southern Americans in the Great Depression*.

Washington, D.C.: University Press of America, 1981.

Rorrer, Kinney. *Rambling Blues: The Life and Songs of Charlie Poole*. London: Old Time Music, 1982.

Rosengarten, Theodore. *All God's Dangers: The Life of Nate Shaw*. New York: Avon Books, 1975.

Rosenzweig, Roy. *Eight Hours for What We Will: Workers and Leisure in an Industrial City, 1870–1920*. New York: Cambridge University Press, 1983.

Ross, James. *They Don't Dance Much*. Boston: Houghton Mifflin, 1940. Reprint. Carbondale: Southern Illinois University Press, 1975.

Rostow, W. W. *The Stages of Economic Growth: A Non-Communist Manifesto*. Cambridge: Cambridge University Press, 1960.

Rothman, Ellen K. *Hands and Hearts: A History of Courtship in America*. New York: Basic Books, 1984.

Rubin, Lillian Breslow. *Worlds of Pain: Life in the Working-Class Family*. New York: Basic Books, 1976.

Schlesinger, Arthur M., Jr. *The Coming of the New Deal*. Boston: Houghton Mifflin, 1958.

Schwartz, Michael. *Radical Protest and Social Structure: The Southern Farmers' Alliance and Cotton Tenancy, 1880–1890*. New York: Academic Press, 1976.

Shapiro, Henry D. *Appalachia on Our Mind: The Southern Mountains and Mountaineers in the American Consciousness, 1870–1920*. Chapel Hill: University of North Carolina Press, 1978.

Singal, Daniel Joseph. *The War Within: From Victorian to Modernist Thought in the South, 1919–1945*. Chapel Hill: University of North Carolina Press, 1982.

Sklar, Robert. *Movie-Made America: A Social History of American Movies*. New York: Random House, 1975.

Smith, Duane A. *Rocky Mountain Mining Camps: The Urban Frontier*. Bloomington: Indiana University Press, 1967.

Smith, Elliott Dunlap, in collaboration with Richard Carter Nyman. *Technology and Labor: A Study of the Human Problems of Labor Saving*. New Haven: published for the Institute of Human Relations by Yale University Press, 1939.

Smith, Robert Sidney. *Mill on the Dan: A History of Dan River Mills, 1882–1950*. Durham: Duke University Press, 1960.

Stansell, Christine. *City of Women: Sex and Class in New York, 1789–1860*. New York: Alfred A. Knopf, 1986.

Stokes, Durward T. *Company Shops: The Town Built by a Railroad*. Winston-Salem: John F. Blair, 1981.

Sussman, Leila A. *Dear FDR: A Study of Political Letter-Writing*. Totowa, N.J.: Bedminster Press, 1963.

Taylor, Barbara. *Eve and the New Jerusalem: Socialism and Feminism in the Nineteenth Century*. New York: Pantheon Books, 1983.

Terrill, Tom E., and Jerrold Hirsch, eds. *Such As Us: Southern Voices of the Thirties*. Chapel Hill: University of North Carolina Press, 1978.

Thompson, E. P. *The Making of the English Working Class*. New York: Vintage Books, 1966.

Thompson, Holland. *From the Cotton Field to the Cotton Mill: A Study of the Industrial Transition in North Carolina*. New York: The Macmillan Co., 1906.

Thompson, Paul. *The Voice of the Past: Oral History*. New York: Oxford University Press, 1978.

Tilly, Louise A., and Joan W. Scott. *Women, Work, and Family*. New York: Holt, Rinehart and Winston, 1978.

Tindall, George Brown. *The Emergence of the New South, 1913–1945*. A History of the South, vol. 10. Baton Rouge: Louisiana State University Press, 1967.

Tippett, Tom. *When Southern Labor Stirs*. New York: Jonathan Cape and Harrison Smith, 1931.

Tomlins, Christopher L. *The State and the Unions: Labor Relations, Law, and the Organized Labor Movement in America, 1880–1960*. New York: Cambridge University Press, 1985.

Tompkins, D. A. *Cotton Mill, Commercial Features: A Text-Book for the Use of Textile Schools and Investors*. Charlotte: published by the author, 1899.

Trattner, Walter I. *Crusade for the Children: A History of the National Child Labor Committee and Child Labor Reform in America*. Chicago: Quadrangle Books, 1970.

Tucker, Barbara M. *Samuel Slater and the Origins of the American Textile Industry, 1790–1860*. Ithaca: Cornell University Press, 1984.

Ulrich, Laurel Thatcher. *Good Wives: Image and Reality in the Lives of Women in Northern New England, 1650–1750*. New York: Oxford University Press, 1983.

Uttley, T. W. *Cotton Spinning and Manufacturing in the United States of America*. Manchester, Eng.: Victoria University of Manchester Press, 1905.

Valenze, Deborah M. *Prophetic Sons and Daughters: Female Preaching and Popular Religion in Industrial England*. Princeton: Princeton University Press, 1985.

Vance, Rupert B. *Human Geography of the South: A Study in Regional Resources and Human Adequacy*. Chapel Hill: University of North Carolina Press, 1932.

Wallace, Anthony F. C. *Rockdale: The Growth of an American Village in the Early Industrial Revolution*. New York: W. W. Norton and Co., 1972.

Ware, Caroline F. *The Early New England Cotton Manufacture: A Study in Industrial Beginnings*. Boston: Houghton Mifflin, 1931.

Watson, Harry L. *An Independent People: The Way We Lived in North Carolina, 1770–1820*. Chapel Hill: University of North Carolina Press for the North Carolina Department of Cultural Resources, 1983.

———. *Jacksonian Politics and Community Conflict: The Emergence of the Second American Party System in Cumberland County, North Carolina*. Baton Rouge: Louisiana State University Press, 1981.

Webb, Mena. *Jule Carr: General without an Army*. Chapel Hill: University of North Carolina Press, 1987.

Weinstein, James. *The Corporate Ideal in the Liberal State, 1900–1918*. Boston: Beacon Press, 1968.

Whisnant, David E. *All That Is Native and Fine: The Politics of Culture in an American Region*. Chapel Hill: University of North Carolina Press, 1983.

Whitaker, Walter, in collaboration with Staley A. Cook and Howard A. White. *Centennial History of Alamance County, 1849–1949*. Burlington, N.C.: Burlington Chamber of Commerce, 1949.

Wiggins, Gene. *Fiddlin' Georgia Crazy: Fiddlin' John Carson, His Real World, and the World of His Songs*. Urbana: University of Illinois Press, 1987.

Williamson, Joel. *The Crucible of Race: Black-White Relations in the American South Since Emancipation*. New York: Oxford University Press, 1984.

Winston, George Tayloe. *A Builder of the New South, Being the Story of the Life Work of Daniel Augustus Tompkins*. Garden City, N.Y.: Doubleday, Page and Co., 1920.

Wood, Phillip J. *Southern Capitalism: The Political Economy of North Carolina, 1880–1980*. Durham: Duke University Press, 1986.

Wood, Stephen B. *Constitutional Politics in the Progressive Era: Child Labor and the Law*. Chicago: University of Chicago Press, 1968.

Woodward, C. Vann. *Origins of the New South, 1877–1913*. A History of the South, vol. 9. Baton Rouge: Louisiana State University Press, 1951.

―――. *Thinking Back: The Perils of Writing History*. Baton Rouge: Louisiana State University Press, 1986.

Wright, Gavin. *Old South, New South: Revolutions in the Southern Economy Since the Civil War*. New York: Basic Books, 1986.

―――. *The Political Economy of the Cotton South: Households, Markets and Wealth in the Nineteenth Century*. New York: W. W. Norton and Co., 1978.

Wright, Gwendolyn. *Building the Dream: A Social History of Housing in America*. New York: Pantheon Books, 1981.

Young, James R., ed. *Textile Leaders of the South*. Anderson, S.C.: James R. Young, 1963.

Young, T. M. *The American Cotton Industry*. New York: Charles Scribner's Sons, 1902.

ARTICLES

Abrams, Douglas Carl. "A Progressive-Conservative Duel: The 1920 Democratic Gubernatorial Primaries in North Carolina." *North Carolina Historical Review* 55 (October 1978): 421–43.

Alexander, Sally. "Women, Class and Sexual Differences in the 1830s and 1840s: Some Reflections on the Writing of Feminist History." *History Workshop* 17 (Spring 1984): 125–49.

Allen, John E. "Eugene Talmadge and the Great Textile Strike in Georgia, September 1934." In *Essays in Southern Labor History: Selected Papers, Southern Labor History Conference, 1976*, edited by Gary Fink and Merl E. Reed, pp. 224–43. Westport, Conn: Greenwood Press, 1977.

Baldwin, Karen. "'Woof!' A Word on Women's Roles in Family Storytelling." In *Women's Folklore, Women's Culture*, edited by Rosan A. Jordan and Susan J. Kalčik, pp. 149–62. Philadelphia: University of Pennsylvania Press, 1985.

Bartley, Numan V. "The Era of the New Deal as a Turning Point in Southern History." In *The New Deal and the South*, edited by James C. Cobb and Michael V. Namorato, pp. 135–46. Jackson: University Press of Mississippi, 1984.

Beatty, Bess. "The Edwin Holt Family: Nineteenth-Century Capitalists in North Carolina." *North Carolina Historical Review* 63 (October 1986): 511–35.

――――. "Lowells of the South: Northern Influence on the Nineteenth-Century North Carolina Textile Industry." *Journal of Southern History* 53 (February 1987): 37–62.

――――. "Textile Labor in the North Carolina Piedmont: Mill Owner Images and Mill Worker Response, 1830–1900." *Labor History* 25 (Fall 1984): 485–503.

Boyte, Harry. "The Textile Industry: Keel of Southern Industrialization." *Radical America* 6 (March–April 1972): 4–49.

Brecher, Jeremy, and the Work Relations Group. "Uncovering the Hidden History of the American Workplace." *Review of Radical Political Economics* 10 (Winter 1978): 1–23.

Breen, T. H. "An Empire of Goods: The Anglicization of Colonial America, 1690–1776." *Journal of British Studies* 25 (October 1986): 467–99.

Carlson, Leonard A. "Labor Supply, the Acquisition of Skills, and the Location of Southern Textile Mills, 1880–1900." *Journal of Economic History* 41 (March 1981): 65–73.

Chen, Chen-Han. "Regional Differences in Costs and Productivity in the American Cotton Manufacturing Industry, 1880–1910." *Quarterly Journal of Economics* 55 (August 1941): 533–66.

Collins, Herbert. "The Idea of a Cotton Textile Industry in the South, 1870–1900." *North Carolina Historical Review* 34 (July 1957): 358–92.

Coulter, Della. "The Piedmont Tradition." In *Charlotte Country Music Story*, pp. 7–11. Raleigh: North Carolina Arts Council, Folklife Section, 1985.

Cressey, Peter, and John MacInnes. "Voting for Ford: Industrial Democracy and the Control of Labor." *Capital and Class* 11 (Summer 1980): 5–33.

Daniel, Pete. "The Crossroads of Change: Cotton, Tobacco, and Rice Cultures in the Twentieth-Century South." *Journal of Southern History* 50 (August 1984): 429–56.

Department of Research and Education, Federal Council of the Churches of Christ in America. "The Strikes at Marion, North Carolina." *Information Service* 8 (December 28, 1929): 1–15.

Dickey, J. A., and E. C. Branson. "How Farm Tenants Live: A Social-Economic Survey in Chatham County, N.C." *University of North Carolina Extension Bulletin* 2 (November 16, 1922): 1–47.

Doane, David P. "Regional Cost Differentials and Textile Location: A Statistical Analysis." *Explorations in Economic History* 9 (Fall 1971): 3–34.

Dowd, Jerome. "Strikes and Lockouts in North Carolina." *Gunton's Magazine* 20 (February 1901): 136–41.

Draper, E. S. "Southern Textile Village Planning." *Landscape Architect* 18 (October 1927): 1–28.

Durrill, Wayne K. "Producing Poverty: Local Government and Economic Development in a New South County, 1874–1884." *Journal of American History* 71 (March 1985): 764–81.

Ellis, Leonora Beck. "A Model Factory Town." *Forum* 32 (September 1901): 60–65.

Ely, Richard T. "An American Industrial Experiment." *Harper's Magazine* 105 (June 1902): 39–45.

Feller, Irwin. "The Diffusion and Location of Technological Change in the American Cotton-Textile Industry, 1890–1970." *Technology and Culture* 15 (October 1974): 569–93.

———. "The Draper Loom in New England Textiles, 1894–1914: The Study of the Diffusion of an Innovation." *Journal of Economic History* 26 (September 1966): 320–47.

Few, William P. "The Constructive Philanthropy of a Southern Cotton Mill." *South Atlantic Quarterly* 8 (January 1909): 82–90.

Fields, Barbara J. "Ideology and Race in American History." In *Region, Race, and Reconstruction: Essays in Honor of C. Vann Woodward*, edited by J. Morgan Kousser and James M. McPherson., pp. 143–77. New York: Oxford University Press, 1982.

Filene, Peter G. "Between a Rock and a Soft Place: A Century of American Manhood." *South Atlantic Quarterly* 84 (Autumn 1985): 339–55.

———. "The 'Secret Desire' of Lincoln Steffans." *Harvard Magazine* 88 (September–October 1985): 72A–72H.

Finger, Bill. "Textile Men: Looms, Loans, and Lockouts." *Southern Exposure* 3 (Winter 1976): 54–65.

Fishbein, Leslie. " 'Dancing Mothers' (1926): Flappers, Mothers, Freud, and Freedom." *Women's Studies* 12 (March 1986): 241–50.

Ford, Lacy K. "Rednecks and Merchants: Economic Development and Social Tensions in the South Carolina Upcountry, 1865–1900." *Journal of American History* 71 (September 1984): 294–318.

Frankel, Linda. "Southern Textile Women: Generations of Survival and Struggle." In *My Troubles Are Going to Have Trouble with Me: Everyday Trials and Triumphs of Women Workers*, edited by Karen Brodkin Sacks and Dorothy Remy, pp. 39–60. New Brunswick: Rutgers University Press, 1984.

Frederickson, Mary. "Four Decades of Change: Black Workers in Southern Textiles, 1941–1981." *Radical America* 16 (November–December 1982): 27–44.

Frisch, Michael. "Oral History, Documentary, and the Mystification of Power: A Case Study Critique of Public Methodology." *International Journal of Oral History* 6 (June 1985): 118–25.

Genovese, Eugene D. "Yeoman Farmers in a Slaveholders' Democracy." In *Fruits of Merchant Capital: Slavery and Bourgeois Property in the Rise and Expansion of Capitalism*, edited by Eugene D. Genovese and Elizabeth Fox-Genovese, pp. 249–64. New York: Oxford University Press, 1983.

Gerstle, Gary. "The Politics of Patriotism: Americanization and the Formation of the CIO." *Dissent* 33 (Winter 1986): 84–92.

Glass, Brent. "Southern Mill Hills: Design in a 'Public' Place." In *Carolina Dwelling: Towards Preservation of Place, In Celebration of the North Carolina Vernacular Landscape*, edited by Doug Swaim, pp. 138–49. Raleigh: School of Design, North Carolina State University, 1978.

Goldberger, Joseph, G. A. Wheeler, and Edgar Sydenstricker. "Pellagra Incidence in Relation to Sex, Age, Season, Occupation, and 'Disabling Sickness' in Seven Cotton-Mill Villages of South Carolina During 1916." *Public Health Reports* 35 (July 9, 1920): 1650–61.

_____. "A Study of the Relation of Diet to Pellagra Incidence in Seven Textile-Mill Communities of South Carolina in 1916." *Public Health Reports* 35 (March 19, 1920): 648–713.

Gorn, Elliott J. "'Gouge and Bite, Pull Hair and Scratch': The Social Significance of Fighting in the Southern Backcountry." *American Historical Review* 90 (February 1985): 18–43.

Graham, Otis L., Jr. "Years of Crisis: America in Depression and War, 1933–1945." In *The Unfinished Century: America Since 1900*, edited by William E. Leuchtenburg, pp. 357–459. Boston: Little, Brown and Co., 1973.

Gregg, William. "Essays on Domestic Industry, Or An Inquiry into the Expediency of Establishing Cotton Manufactures in South Carolina." Reprinted in D. A. Tompkins, *Cotton Mill, Commercial Features: A Text-Book for the Use of Textile Schools and Investors*, pp. 203–40. Charlotte: published by the author, 1899.

Griffin, Richard W. "Reconstruction of the North Carolina Textile Industry, 1865–1885." *North Carolina Historical Review* 41 (January 1964): 34–53.

Griffin, Richard W., and Diffie W. Standard. "The Cotton Textile Industry in Ante-Bellum North Carolina, Part I: Origin and Growth to 1830." *North Carolina Historical Review* 34 (January 1957): 15–35.

_____. "The Cotton Textile Industry in Ante-Bellum North Carolina, Part II: An Era of Boom and Consolidation, 1830–1860." *North Carolina Historical Review* 34 (April 1957): 131–64.

Gross, Robert A. "Culture and Cultivation: Agriculture and Society in Thoreau's Concord." *Journal of American History* 69 (June 1982): 42–61.

Gutman, Herbert G. "Work, Culture, and Society in Industrializing America, 1815–1919." *American Historical Review* 78 (June 1973): 531–88.

Hahn, Steven. "Common Right and Commonwealth: The Stock-Law Struggle and the Roots of Southern Populism." In *Region, Race, and Reconstruction: Essays in Honor of C. Vann Woodward*, edited by J. Morgan Kousser and James M. McPherson, pp. 51–88. New York: Oxford University Press, 1982.

————. "The 'Unmaking' of the Southern Yeomanry: The Transformation of the Georgia Upcountry, 1860–1890." In *The Countryside in the Age of Capitalist Transformation: Essays in the Social History of Rural America*, edited by Steven Hahn and Jonathan Prude, pp. 179–203. Chapel Hill: University of North Carolina Press, 1985.

Hall, Jacquelyn Dowd. "Disorderly Women: Gender and Labor Militancy in the Appalachian South." *Journal of American History* 73 (September 1986): 354–82.

————. "An Oral History of Industrialization: Learning by Listening." *Institute for Research in Social Science Newsletter* 66 (April 1981): 5–9.

————. "Oral History Program Enriches Prospects for Researchers." *Institute for Research in Social Science Newsletter* 61 (November 1976): 6–10.

Herring, Harriet L. "Cycles of Cotton Mill Criticism." *South Atlantic Quarterly* 28 (April 1929): 113–25.

————. "Industrial Relations in the South and the NIRA." *Social Forces* 12 (October 1933): 124–31.

————. "The Metamorphosis of the Docile Worker." In *Worker and Public in the Southern Textile Problem*, pp. 3–10. Greensboro: The Industrial Seminar for Ministers, 1930.

————. "The South Goes to the Bindery." *Social Forces* 9 (March 1931): 428–31.

————. "12 Cents, the Troops and the Union." *The Survey* 59 (November 15, 1927): 199–202.

Hinrichs, A. F. "Wage Rates and Weekly Earnings in the Cotton-Textile Industry. 1933–34." *Monthly Labor Review* 40 (January–June 1935): 612–25.

Hoffmann, Alfred. "The Mountaineer in Industry." *Mountain Life and Work* 5 (January 1930): 2–7.

Hodges, James A. "Challenge to the New South: The Great Textile Strike in Elizabethton, Tennessee, 1929." *Tennessee Historical Quarterly* 23 (December 1964): 343–57.

Huff, Tess. "A Conference of Southern Workers." *Labor Age* 21 (August 1932): 4–5, 29.

Hughes, Chip. "A New Twist for Textiles." In *Working Lives: The Southern Exposure History of Labor in the South*, edited by Marc S. Miller, pp. 338–51. New York: Pantheon Books, 1980.

"An Ill Wind." In *I Am a Woman Worker: A Scrapbook of Autobiographies*, edited by Andria Taylor Hourwich and Gladys L. Palmer, p. 51. New York: Affiliated Schools for Workers, 1936.

Jeffrey, Julie Roy. "Women in the Southern Farmers' Alliance: A Reconsideration of the Role and Status of Women in the Late Nineteenth-Century South." *Feminist Studies* 3 (Fall 1975): 72–91.

Jenkins, W. T. "Electrification of Laurens Cotton Mills." *Textile World* 3 (February 5, 1927): 383–85.

Johnson, Gerald W. "The Cotton Strike." *The Survey* 46 (September 1, 1921): 646–47.

Jones, F. Stuart. "The New Economic History and the Industrial Revolution." *South African Journal of Economics* 52 (June 1984): 113–32.

Judkins, Bennett M. "Occupational Health and the Developing Class Consciousness of Southern Textile Workers: The Case of the Brown Lung Association." *Maryland Historian* 13 (Spring–Summer 1982): 55–71.

Kaplan, Temma. "Female Consciousness and Collective Action: The Case of Barcelona, 1910–1918." *Signs* 7 (Spring 1982): 545–66.

Landes, David S. "What Do Bosses Really Do?" *Journal of Economic History* 46 (September 1986): 585–624.

Larkin, Margaret. "Ella May's Songs." *The Nation* 129 (October 9, 1929): 382–83.

————. "The Story of Ella May." *New Masses* 5 (November 1929): 3–4.

Lears, T. J. Jackson. "The Concept of Cultural Hegemony: Problems and Possibilities." *American Historical Review* 90 (June 1985): 567–93.

Leuchtenburg, William E. "The New Deal and the Analogue of War." *Change and Continuity in Twentieth-Century America*, edited by John Braeman, Robert H. Bremner, and Everett Walters, pp. 81–143. Columbus: Ohio State University Press, 1964.

McDonald, Forrest and Grady McWhiney. "The South From Self-Sufficiency to Peonage: An Interpretation." *American Historical Review* 85 (December 1980): 1095–1118.

McKelway, A. J. "Child Wages in the Cotton Mills: Our Modern Feudalism." *Child Labor Bulletin* 2 (May 1913): 7–16.

Marglin, Stephen A. "What Do Bosses Do? The Origins and Functions of Hierarchy in Capitalist Production." *The Review of Radical Political Economics* 6 (Summer 1974): 33–60.

Marley, Harold P. "A Southern Textile Epoch." *The Survey* 65 (October 1, 1930): 17–20, 55, 58.

Martin, Charles H. "Southern Labor Relations in Transition: Gadsden, Alabama, 1930–1943." *Journal of Southern History* 47 (November 1981): 545–68.

Menius, Arthur C., III. "James Bennitt: Portrait of an Antebellum Yeoman." *North Carolina Historical Review* 58 (Autumn 1981): 305–26.

Newman, Dale. "Work and Community Life in a Southern Textile Town." *Labor History* 19 (Spring 1978): 204–25.

Nichols, Jeannette Paddock. "Does the Mill Village Foster Any Social Types?" *Social Forces* 2 (March 1924): 350–57.

O'Brien, P. K. "Do We Have a Typology for the Study of European Industrialization in the XIXth Century?" *Journal of European Economic History* 15 (Fall 1986): 291–333.

Parker, Thomas F. "The South Carolina Cotton Mill—A Manufacturer's View." *South Atlantic Quarterly* 8 (October, 1909): 328–37.

Passerini, Luisa. "Italian Working Class Culture Between the Wars: Consensus to Fascism and Work Ideology." *International Journal of Oral History* 1 (February 1980): 4–27.

Prude, Jonathan. "The Social System of Early New England Textile Mills: A Case Study, 1812–40." In *Working-Class America: Essays on Labor, Community, and American Society*, edited by Michael H. Frisch and Daniel J. Walkowitz, pp. 1–36. Urbana: University of Illinois Press, 1983.

Quinney, Valerie. "Childhood in a Southern Mill Village." *International Journal of Oral History* 3 (November 1982): 167–92.

Ratchford, Benjamin Ulysses. "Toward Preliminary Social Analysis: II. Economic Aspects of the Gastonia Situation." *Social Forces* 8 (March 1930): 359–67.

"A Record of Notable Achievement in the Textile World." *Skyland Magazine* 1 (December 1913): 311–26.

"The Revolt of the Rank and File." *The Nation* 109 (October 25, 1919): 540.

Rodgers, Daniel T. "Tradition, Modernity, and the American Industrial Worker: Reflections and Critique." *Journal of Interdisciplinary History* 7 (Spring 1977): 655–81.

Ross, Ellen. " 'Not the Sort that Would Sit on the Doorstep': Respectability in Pre–World War I London Neighborhoods." *International Labor and Working Class History* (Spring 1985): 39–59.

――――. "Survival Networks: Women's Neighbourhood Sharing in London Before World War I." *History Workshop* 15 (Spring 1983): 4–27.

Saxonhouse, Gary, and Gavin Wright. "Two Forms of Cheap Labor in Textile History." In *Technique, Spirit and Form in the Making of Modern Economies: Essays in Honor of William N. Parker*, edited by Gary Saxonhouse and Gavin Wright, pp. 3–31. Research in Economic History, Supplement 3. Greenwich, Conn.: JAI Press, 1984.

Selby, John G. " 'Better to Starve in the Shade than in the Factory': Labor Protest in High Point, North Carolina, in the Early 1930s." *North Carolina Historical Review* 65 (January 1987):43–64.

Skocpol, Theda. "Political Response to Capitalist Crisis: Neo-Marxist Theories of the State and the Case of the New Deal." *Politics and Society* 10 (1980): 155–201.

Stern, Boris. "Mechanical Changes in the Cotton-Textile Industry, 1910 to 1936." *Monthly Labor Review* 45 (August 1937): 316–43.

Stricker, Frank. "Affluence for Whom?—Another Look at Prosperity and the Working Classes in the 1920s." *Labor History* 24 (Winter 1983): 5–33.

Sydenstricker, Edgar, G. A. Wheeler, and Joseph Goldberger. "Disabling Sickness Among the Population of Seven Cotton Mill Villages of South Carolina in Relation to Family Income." *Public Health Reports* 33 (November 22, 1918): 2038–51.

Tannenbaum, Frank. "The South Buries Its Anglo-Saxons." *Century* 106 (June 1923): 205–15.

Terrill, Tom E. "Eager Hands: Labor for Southern Textiles, 1850–1860." *Journal of Economic History* 36 (March 1976): 84–101.

Thompson, E. P. "Time, Work-Discipline, and Industrial Capitalism." *Past and Present* 38 (December 1967): 56–97.

Thompson, Holland. "The Southern Textile Situation." *South Atlantic Quarterly* 29 (April 1930): 113–25.

Vorse, Mary Heaton. "Gastonia." *Harpers* 159 (November 1929): 700–710.

Watson, Harry L. "Conflict and Collaboration: Yeomen, Slaveholders, and Politics in the Antebellum South." *Social History* 10 (October 1985): 273–98.

Wiley, Stephen R. "Songs of the Gastonia Textile Strike of 1929: Models of and for Southern Working-Class Woman's Militancy." *North Carolina Folklore Journal* 30 (Fall–Winter 1982): 87–98.

Woodman, Harold D. "Sequel to Slavery: The New History Views the Postbellum South." *Journal of Southern History* 43 (November 1977): 523–54.

Wright, Gavin. "Cheap Labor and Southern Textiles before 1880." *Journal of Economic History* 39 (September 1979): 655–80.

————. "Cheap Labor and Southern Textiles, 1880–1930." *Quarterly Journal of Economics* 96 (November 1981): 605–29.

Yellis, Kenneth A. "Prosperity's Child: Some Thoughts on the Flapper." *American Quarterly* 21 (Spring 1969): 44–64.

Zahavi, Gerald. "Negotiated Loyalty: Welfare Capitalism and the Shoeworkers of Endicott Johnson, 1920–1940." *Journal of American History* 70 (December 1983): 602–20.

DISSERTATIONS, THESES, AND UNPUBLISHED PAPERS

Abernathy, Cathy, Lynn Hudson, and Alisa Blackman. "Collective Profile of Interviewees." Research report, Southern Oral History Program, University of North Carolina at Chapel Hill, 1981 and 1986.

Akin, Edward N. " 'Mr. Donald's Help': Donald Comer, Avondale's Birmingham Operatives, and the United Textile Workers, 1933–34." Paper presented at the annual meeting of the Southern Historical Association, 1980.

Bishir, Catherine W. "Building the Myth: Architecture, History, and the Colonial Revival in the South." Paper presented at the annual meeting of the Organization of American Historians, 1987.

Bresler, Helen. "Industrial Vernacular Architecture: The Mill Villages of Glencoe and Bynum." Seminar paper, University of North Carolina at Chapel Hill, 1979.

Brooks, Robert R. R. "The United Textile Workers of America." Ph.D. dissertation, Yale University, 1935.

Clay, Howard Bunyan. "Daniel Augustus Tompkins: An American Bourbon." Ph.D. dissertation, University of North Carolina at Chapel Hill, 1951.

Collins, Camilla A. "Twenty-four to a Dozen: Occupational Folklore in a Hosiery Mill." Ph.D. dissertation, Indiana University, 1978.

DeNatale, Douglas. "Traditional Culture and Community in a Piedmont Textile

Mill Village." M.A. thesis, University of North Carolina at Chapel Hill, 1980.

Flamming, Doug. "Mill Village: Rural Culture and Cotton Mill Workers in Dalton, Georgia, 1880–1940." Paper presented at the annual meeting of the Southern Historical Association, 1986.

————. "Work, Family, and Community in the Crown Cotton Mills of Dalton, Georgia, 1880–1940." Ph.D. dissertation, Vanderbilt University, in progress.

Frederickson, Mary. "A Place to Speak Our Minds: The Southern Summer School for Women Workers." Ph.D. dissertation, University of North Carolina at Chapel Hill, 1981.

Freeze, Gary Richard. "Agricultural Origins of Piedmont Cotton Mill Families, 1880–1900: The Case of the Forest Hill Community, Concord, North Carolina." Seminar paper, University of North Carolina at Chapel Hill, 1981.

————. "Master Mill Man: John Milton Odell and Industrial Development in Concord, North Carolina, 1877–1907." M.A. thesis, University of North Carolina at Chapel Hill, 1980.

Freudenburg, William. "People in the Impact Zone: The Human and Social Consequences of Energy Boomtown Growth in Four Western Colorado Communities." Ph.D. dissertation, Yale University, 1979.

Garrison, Joseph Yates. "Paul Revere Christopher: Southern Labor Leader, 1910–1974." Ph.D. dissertation, Georgia State University, 1976.

Gilmore, Glenda E. " 'Any Values Which Their Puny Arms Can Win': The Crusade for North Carolina's Mill Children." Seminar paper, University of North Carolina at Charlotte, 1985.

Haessly, Lynn. " 'Mill Mother's Lament': Ella May, Working Women's Militancy, and the 1929 Gaston County Textile Strikes." Seminar paper, University of North Carolina at Chapel Hill, 1984.

————. " 'Mill Mother's Lament': The Intellectual Left's Reshaping of the 1929 Gaston County Textile Strikes and Songs." Seminar paper, University of North Carolina at Chapel Hill, 1984.

Hammond, Seth. "The Cotton Industry of This Century." Ph.D. dissertation, Harvard University, 1941.

Hampton, Frances. "New Leisure: How Is It Spent? A Study of What 122 Textile Workers of Leaksville, Spray and Draper are Doing with the New Leisure Created by the N.R.A. as Applied to Certain Types of Activities." M.A. thesis, University of North Carolina, 1935.

Hays, Samuel P. "The New Deal: After Fifty Years." Paper presented at the Woodrow Wilson International Center for Scholars, Washington, D.C., 1985.

Holly, John F. "Elizabethton, Tennessee: A Case of Southern Industrialization." Ph.D. dissertation, Clark University, 1949.

Horton, Sandra Sue. "The Political Career of Thomas Walter Bickett." M.A. thesis, University of North Carolina at Chapel Hill, 1965.

Howie, Sam. "The New South in the North Carolina Foothills: A Study of the

Early Industrial Experience in McDowell County." M.A. thesis, Appalachian State University, 1978.

Hutton, Sybil V. Wilson. "Social Participation of Married Women in a South Carolina Mill Village." M.A. thesis, University of Kentucky, 1948.

Institute for Research in Social Science. "A Survey of the Catawba Valley: A Study Made by the Institute for Research in Social Science for the Tennessee Valley Authority." Typescript, University of North Carolina at Chapel Hill, 1935.

Janiewski, Dolores E. "From Field to Factory: Race, Class, Sex, and the Woman Worker in Durham, 1880–1940." Ph.D. dissertation, Duke University, 1979.

Jones, Lu Ann. " 'The Task That Is Ours': White North Carolina Farm Women and Agrarian Reform, 1886–1914." M.A. thesis, University of North Carolina at Chapel Hill, 1983.

Kennedy, John W. "The General Strike in the Textile Industry, September, 1934." M.A. thesis, Duke University, 1947.

Kenzer, Robert Charles. "Portrait of a Southern Community, 1849–1881: Family, Kinship, and Neighborhood in Orange County, North Carolina." Ph.D. dissertation, Harvard University, 1982.

Kuhn, Cliff. "Durham, North Carolina." Working Paper, Southern Oral History Program, University of North Carolina at Chapel Hill, 1980.

Kulik, Gary. "The Beginnings of the Industrial Revolution in America: Pawtucket, Rhode Island, 1672–1829." Ph.D. dissertation, Brown University, 1980.

Lowe, Joan. "Effect of Technological Advances on the West Durham Textile Community." Seminar paper, Duke University, 1979.

McHugh, Cathy Louise. "The Family Labor System in the Southern Cotton Textile Industry, 1880–1915." Ph.D. dissertation, Stanford University, 1981.

Magruder, Nathaniel Fuqua. "The Administration of Governor Cameron Morrison of North Carolina, 1921–1925." Ph.D. dissertation, University of North Carolina at Chapel Hill, 1968.

Moretz, Ray. "From Farm to Mill: Carrboro, 1900–1954." Seminar paper, University of North Carolina at Chapel Hill, 1982.

Murphy, Mary. "Burlington, North Carolina." Working paper, Southern Oral History Program, University of North Carolina at Chapel Hill, 1980.

Myers, James. "Field Notes: Textile Strikes in South." Typescript, North Carolina Collection, University of North Carolina at Chapel Hill, 1929.

Painter, David S. "The Southern Labor Revolt of 1929." Seminar paper, University of North Carolina at Chapel Hill, 1974.

Prior, John P. "From Community to National Unionism: North Carolina Textile Labor Organizations, July 1932–September 1934." M.A. thesis, University of North Carolina at Chapel Hill, 1972.

Rand, H. Lanier. " 'I Had to Like It': A Study of a Durham Textile Community." Honors essay, University of North Carolina at Chapel Hill, 1977.

Selby, John G. "Industrial Growth and Worker Protest in a New South City: High

Point, North Carolina, 1859–1959." Ph.D. dissertation, Duke University, 1984.

Simon, Bryant. "Class, Community, and Conflict: The Cone Mills of Greensboro, N.C., 1895–1930." Seminar paper, Yale University, 1986.

Smith, Benjamin H. "The Social Significance of the Southern Cotton Mill Community." M.A. thesis, Emory University, 1925.

Stokes, Allen Heath, Jr. "Black and White Labor and the Development of the Southern Textile Industry, 1880–1920." Ph.D. dissertation, University of South Carolina, 1977.

Thomas, Nancy Biggs. "Fort Mill: Transition from a Farming to a Textile Community, 1880–1920." M.S. thesis, Winthrop College, 1984.

Triplette, Ralph R., Jr. "One-Industry Towns: Their Location, Development, and Economic Character." Ph.D. dissertation, University of North Carolina at Chapel Hill, 1974.

MISCELLANEOUS

Glass, Brent. "Glencoe Cotton Mills." Historic American Engineering Record of the Heritage Conservation and Recreation Service, HAER NC-6. Library of Congress, Washington, D.C.

———. "Salem Manufacturing Company: Arista Cotton Mill." Historic American Engineering Record of the Heritage Conservation and Recreation Service, HAER NC-3. Library of Congress, Washington, D.C.

Swinney, George Washington. "This Is Your Life." Untranscribed tape recording of a ceremony held on Swinney's fortieth anniversary as pastor of the Glen Hope Baptist Church, Burlington North Carolina, September 10, 1967. Copy held by the Southern Oral History Program, University of North Carolina at Chapel Hill.